Family Therapy
CONCEPTS AND METHODS

Family Therapy
CONCEPTS AND METHODS

ELEVENTH EDITION

Michael P. Nichols
College of William and Mary

with Sean D. Davis
Alliant International University

PEARSON

Boston Columbus Indianapolis New York San Francisco Hoboken
Amsterdam Cape Town Dubai London Madrid Milan Munich Paris Montréal Toronto
Delhi Mexico City São Paulo Sydney Hong Kong Seoul Singapore Taipei Tokyo

VP and Editorial Director: Jeffery W. Johnston
Executive Editor: Julie Peters
Program Manager: Megan Moffo
Editorial Assistant: Pamela DiBerardino
Executive Product Marketing Manager: Christopher Barry
Executive Field Marketing Manager: Krista Clark
Team Lead Project Management: Bryan Pirrmann
Team Lead Program Management: Laura Weaver
Procurement Specialist: Deidra Skahill
Art Director: Diane Lorenzo

Art Director Cover: Diane Lorenzo
Cover Art: Miriamrb/Fotolia
Media Project Manager: Michael Goncalves
Editorial Production and Composition Services: Lumina Datamatics, Inc.
Full-Service Project Manager: Saraswathi Muralidhar
Printer/Binder: Edwards Brothers Malloy
Cover Printer: Phoenix Color/Hagerstown
Text Font: Times LT Pro 10/12 pts

Many of the designations by manufacturers and sellers to distinguish their products are claimed as trademarks. Where those designations appear in this book, and the publisher was aware of a trademark claim, the designations have been printed in initial caps or all caps.

Between the time website information is gathered and then published, it is not unusual for some sites to have closed. Also, the transcription of URLs can result in typographical errors. The publisher would appreciate notification where these errors occur so that they may be corrected in subsequent editions.

Library of Congress Cataloging-in-Publication Data
Nichols, Michael P., author.
  Family therapy : concepts and methods / Michael P. Nichols, College of William and Mary with Sean D. Davis, Alliant International University. — Eleventh edition.
    pages cm
  Includes bibliographical references and index.
  ISBN 978-0-13-382660-9 — ISBN 0-13-382660-0 1. Family psychotherapy. I. Davis, Sean D., author. II. Title.
  RC488.5.N53 2016
  616.89'156—dc23
                                                                    2015032118

10 9 8 7 6 5 4 3 2 1

                                                           Student Edition
                                                    ISBN 10: 0-13-382660-0
                                                ISBN 13: 978-0-13-382660-9

                                                                      eText
                                                    ISBN 10: 0-13-382681-3
                                                ISBN 13: 978-0-13-382681-4

                                                                    Package
                                                    ISBN 10: 0-13-430074-2
                                                ISBN 13: 978-0-13-430074-0

PEARSON

CONTENTS

7   Experiential Family Therapy   131

8   Psychoanalytic Family Therapy   149

THE STAGES OF THE FAMILY LIFE CYCLE

Family Life-Cycle Stage	Emotional Process of Transition: Key Principles	Second-Order Changes in Family Status Required to Proceed Developmentally
Leaving home: single young adults	Accepting emotional and financial responsibility for self	a. Differentiation of self in relation to family of origin b. Development of intimate peer relationships c. Establishment of self in respect to work and financial independence
The joining of families through marriage: the new couple	Commitment to new system	a. Formation of marital system b. Realignment of relationships with extended families and friends to include spouse
Families with young children	Accepting new members into the system	a. Adjusting marital system to make space for children b. Joining in childrearing, financial and household tasks c. Realignment of relationships with extended family to include parenting and grandparenting roles
Families with adolescents	Increasing flexibility of family boundaries to permit children's independence and grandparents' frailties	a. Shifting of parent–child relationships to permit adolescent to move into and out of system b. Refocus on midlife marital and career issues c. Beginning shift toward caring for older generation
Launching children and moving on	Accepting a multitude of exits from and entries into the family system	a. Renegotiation of marital system as a dyad b. Development of adult-to-adult relationships c. Realignment of relationships to include in-laws and grandchildren d. Dealing with disabilities and death of parents (grandparents)
Families in later life	Accepting the shifting generational roles	a. Maintaining own and/or couple functioning and interests in face of physiological decline: exploration of new familial and social role options b. Support for more central role of middle generation c. Making room in the system for the wisdom and experience of the elderly, supporting the older generation without overfunctioning for them d. Dealing with loss of spouse, siblings, and other peers and preparation for death

MAJOR EVENTS IN THE HISTORY OF FAMILY THERAPY

	Social and Political Context	Development of Family Therapy
1945	F.D.R. dies, Truman becomes president World War II ends in Europe (May 8) and the Pacific (August 14)	Bertalanffy presents general systems theory
1946	Juan Perón elected president of Argentina	Bowen at Menninger Clinic Whitaker at Emory Macy Conference Bateson at Harvard
1947	India partitioned into India and Pakistan	
1948	Truman reelected U.S. president State of Israel established	Whitaker begins conferences on schizophrenia
1949	Communist People's Republic of China established	Bowlby: "The Study and Reduction of Group Tensions in the Family"
1950	North Korea invades South Korea	Bateson begins work at Palo Alto V.A.
1951	Julius and Ethel Rosenberg sentenced to death for espionage Sen. Estes Kefauver leads Senate probe into organized crime	Ruesch & Bateson: *Communication: The Social Matrix of Society* Bowen initiates residential treatment of mothers and children Lidz at Yale
1952	Eisenhower elected U.S. president	Bateson receives Rockefeller grant to study communication in Palo Alto Wynne at NIMH
1953	Joseph Stalin dies Korean armistice signed	Whitaker & Malone: *The Roots of Psychotherapy*
1954	Supreme Court rules school segregation unconstitutional	Bateson project research on schizophrenic communication Bowen at NIMH
1955	Rosa Parks refuses to move to the back of the bus; Martin Luther King, Jr., leads boycott in Montgomery, Alabama	Whitaker in private practice, Atlanta, Georgia. Satir begins teaching family dynamics in Chicago
1956	Nasser elected president of Egypt Soviet troops crush anti-Communist rebellion in Hungary	Bateson, Jackson, Haley, & Weakland: "Toward a Theory of Schizophrenia" Bowen at Georgetown

(continued)

	Social and Political Context	Development of Family Therapy
1957	Russians launch *Sputnik I* Eisenhower sends troops to Little Rock, Arkansas, to protect school integration	Jackson: "The Question of Family Homeostasis" Ackerman opens the Family Mental Health Clinic of Jewish Family Services in New York Boszormenyi-Nagy opens Family Therapy Department at EPPI in Philadelphia
1958	European Common Market established	Ackerman: *The Psychodynamics of Family Life*
1959	Castro becomes premier of Cuba Charles de Gaulle becomes French president	MRI founded by Don Jackson
1960	Kennedy elected U.S. president	Family Institute founded by Nathan Ackerman (renamed the Ackerman Institute in 1971) Minuchin and colleagues begin doing family therapy at Wiltwyck
1961	Berlin Wall erected Bay of Pigs invasion	Bell: *Family Group Therapy* Family Process founded by Ackerman and Jackson
1962	Cuban Missile Crisis	Bateson's Palo Alto project ends Haley at MRI
1963	Kennedy assassinated	Haley: *Strategies of Psychotherapy*
1964	Johnson elected U.S. president Nobel Peace Prize awarded to Martin Luther King, Jr.	Satir: *Conjoint Family Therapy* Norbert Wiener dies (b. 1894)
1965	Passage of Medicare Malcolm X assassinated	Minuchin becomes director of Philadelphia Child Guidance Clinic Whitaker at University of Wisconsin
1966	Red Guards demonstrate in China Indira Gandhi becomes prime minister of India	Brief Therapy Center at MRI begun under directorship of Richard Fisch Ackerman: *Treating the Troubled Family*
1967	Six-Day War between Israel and Arab states Urban riots in Cleveland, Newark, and Detroit	Watzlawick, Beavin, & Jackson: *Pragmatics of Human Communication* Dicks: *Marital Tensions*
1968	Nixon elected U.S. president Robert Kennedy and Martin Luther King, Jr., assassinated	Don Jackson dies (b. 1920) Satir at Esalen
1969	Widespread demonstrations against war in Vietnam	Bandura: *Principles of Behavior Modification* Wolpe: *The Practice of Behavior Therapy*
1970	Student protests against Vietnam War result in killing of four students at Kent State	Masters & Johnson: *Human Sexual Inadequacy* Laing & Esterson: *Sanity, Madness and the Family*
1971	Twenty-Sixth Amendment grants right to vote to 18-year-olds	Nathan Ackerman dies (b. 1908)
1972	Nixon reelected U.S. president	Bateson: *Steps to an Ecology of Mind* Wynne at University of Rochester
1973	Supreme Court rules that states may not prohibit abortion Energy crisis created by oil shortages	Center for Family Learning founded by Phil Guerin Boszormenyi-Nagy & Spark: *Invisible Loyalties*
1974	Nixon resigns Gerald Ford becomes 39th president	Minuchin: *Families and Family Therapy* Watzlawick, Weakland, & Fisch: *Change*

	Social and Political Context	Development of Family Therapy
1975	Vietnam War ends	Mahler, Pine, & Bergman: *The Psychological Birth of the Human Infant* Stuart: "Behavioral Remedies for Marital Ills"
1976	Carter elected U.S. president	Haley: *Problem-Solving Therapy* Haley to Washington, D.C.
1977	President Carter pardons most Vietnam War draft evaders	Family Institute of Westchester founded by Betty Carter American Family Therapy Academy (AFTA) established
1978	Camp David Accords between Egypt and Israel U.S. and People's Republic of China establish diplomatic relations	Hare-Mustin: "A Feminist Approach to Family Therapy" Selvini Palazzoli et al.: *Paradox and Counterparadox*
1979	England's Margaret Thatcher becomes West's first woman prime minister Iranian militants seize U.S. Embassy in Tehran and hold hostages	Founding of Brief Therapy Center in Milwaukee Bateson: *Mind and Nature*
1980	Reagan elected U.S. president U.S. boycotts summer Olympic Games in Moscow	Haley: *Leaving Home* Milton Erickson dies (b. 1901) Gregory Bateson dies (b. 1904)
1981	Sandra Day O'Connor becomes first woman justice of Supreme Court Egyptian president Sadat assassinated	Hoffman: *The Foundations of Family Therapy* Madanes: *Strategic Family Therapy* Minuchin & Fishman: *Family Therapy Techniques*
1982	Equal Rights Amendment fails ratification Falklands war	Gilligan: *In a Different Voice* Fisch, Weakland, & Segal: *Tactics of Change* *The Family Therapy Networker* founded by Richard Simon
1983	U.S. invades Grenada Terrorist bombing of Marine headquarters in Beirut	Doherty & Baird: *Family Therapy and Family Medicine* Keeney: *Aesthetics of Change*
1984	Reagan reelected U.S. president U.S.S.R. boycotts summer Olympic Games in Los Angeles	Watzlawick: *The Invented Reality* Madanes: *Behind the One-Way Mirror*
1985	Gorbachev becomes leader of U.S.S.R.	de Shazer: *Keys to Solution in Brief Therapy* Gergen: "The Social Constructionist Movement in Modern Psychology"
1986	Space shuttle *Challenger* explodes	Anderson et al.: *Schizophrenia and the Family* Selvini Palazzoli: "Towards a General Model of Psychotic Family Games"
1987	Congress investigates the Iran–Contra affair	Tom Andersen: "The Reflecting Team" Guerin et al.: *The Evaluation and Treatment of Marital Conflict* Scharff & Scharff: *Object Relations Family Therapy*
1988	*George H. W. Bush elected U.S. president*	Kerr & Bowen: *Family Evaluation* Virginia Satir dies (b. 1916)

(continued)

	Social and Political Context	Development of Family Therapy
1989	The Berlin Wall comes down	Boyd-Franklin: *Black Families in Therapy*
1990	Iraq invades Kuwait	Murray Bowen dies (b. 1913) White & Epston: *Narrative Means to Therapeutic Ends*
1991	Persian Gulf War against Iraq	Harold Goolishian dies (b. 1924)
1992	Clinton elected U.S. president	Family Institute of New Jersey founded by Monica McGoldrick
1993	Ethnic cleansing in Bosnia Los Angeles police officers convicted in Rodney King beating	Israel Zwerling dies (b. 1917) Minuchin & Nichols: *Family Healing*
1994	Republicans win majority in Congress Nelson Mandela elected president of South Africa	David and Jill Scharf leave Washington School of Psychiatry to begin the International Institute of Object Relations Therapy
1995	Oklahoma City federal building bombed	Carl Whitaker dies (b. 1912) John Weakland dies (b. 1919) Salvador Minuchin retires Family Studies Inc. renamed The Minuchin Center
1996	Clinton reelected U.S. president	Edwin Friedman dies (b. 1932) Eron & Lund: *Narrative Solutions in Brief Therapy* Freedman & Combs: *Narrative Therapy*
1997	Princess Diana dies in auto accident Hong Kong reverts to China	Michael Goldstein dies (b. 1930)
1998	President Clinton impeached by House of Representatives	Minuchin, Colapinto, & Minuchin: *Working with Families of the Poor*
1999	President Clinton acquitted in impeachment trial	Neil Jacobson dies (b. 1949) John Elderkin Bell dies (b. 1913) Mara Selvini Palazzoli dies (b. 1916)
2000	George W. Bush elected U.S. president	Millennium Conference, Toronto, Canada
2001	September 11 terrorist attacks	James Framo dies (b. 1922)
2002	Sex abuse scandal in Catholic Church Corporate corruption at Enron	Lipchik: *Beyond Techniques in Solution-Focused Therapy*
2003	U.S. invades Iraq	Greenan & Tunnell: *Couple Therapy with Gay Men*
2004	George W. Bush reelected U.S. president	Gianfranco Cecchin dies (b. 1932)
2005	Hurricane Katrina devastates New Orleans	Steve de Shazer dies (b. 1940)
2006	Democrats regain control of U.S. House and Senate	Minuchin, Nichols, & Lee: *Assessing Families and Couples*
2007	Shootings at Virginia Tech	Jay Haley dies (b. 1923) Lyman Wynne dies (b. 1923) Insoo Kim Berg dies (b. 1934) Albert Ellis dies (b. 1913) Thomas Fogarty dies (b. 1927)
2008	Barack Obama elected U.S. president	Michael White dies (b. 1949)

	Social and Political Context	Development of Family Therapy
2009	Worldwide economic recession	Sprenkle, Davis, & Lebow: *Common Factors in Couple and Family Therapy*
2010	Earthquake in Haiti	LaSala: *Coming Out, Coming Home* Dattilio: *Cognitive-Behavioral Therapy with Couples and Families*
2011	Earthquake and tsunami in Japan	Cose: *The End of Anger*
2012	Mass shootings in Newton CT Barack Obama reelected U.S. president	Betty Carter dies (b. 1929)
2013	Death of Nelson Mandela Affordable Healthcare Act	Alan Gurman dies (b. 1945)
2014	Ebola epidemic in West Africa	Donald Bloch dies (b. 1923)

FOREWORD

In this volume, Mike Nichols tells the story of family therapy—and tells it very well. It's hard to imagine a more readable and informative guide to the field.

Born in the late 1950s, family therapy seemed to spring fully formed out of the heads of a group of seminal thinkers. Over six decades later, both theory and practice show the uncertainties and doubts that define maturity. But in the beginning—as the story-tellers say—there was Gregory Bateson on the West Coast, a tall, clean-shaven, angular intellectual, who saw families as systems, carriers of ideas. On the East Coast was Nathan Ackerman, short, bearded, portly, the quintessential charismatic healer, who saw families as collections of individuals struggling to balance feelings, irrationalities, and desires. Bateson and Ackerman complemented each other perfectly, the Don Quixote and Sancho Panza of the family systems revolution.

For all the diversity of the 1960s that saw the new clinical practice called *family therapy* take a variety of names—systemic, strategic, structural, Bowenian, experiential—there was also a remarkable solidarity in the shared beliefs that defined the field.

As family therapy succeeded and expanded, it was extended to encompass different client populations, with specific interventions for various special groups—clients with drug addictions, hospitalized psychiatric patients, the welfare population, violent families, and so on. All posed their own complexities. Practitioners responded to this expanded family therapy with an array of new approaches, some of which even questioned the fundamental allegiance to systems thinking.

The challenges to systems theory (the official science of the time) took two forms. One was purely theoretical: a challenge to the assumption that systemic thinking was a universal framework, applicable to the functioning of all human collectives. A major broadside came from feminists who questioned the absence of concepts of gender and power in systems thinking and pointed to the distorting consequences of gender-less theory when focusing on family violence. The other challenge concerned the connection between theory and practice: a challenge to the imposition of systems theory as the basis for therapeutic practice. The very techniques that once defined the field were called into question. Inevitably, the field began to re-open for examination of its old taboos: the individual, intrapsychic life, emotions, biology, the past, and the particular place of the family in culture and society.

As is always characteristic of an official science, the field tried to preserve established concepts while a pragmatic attention to specific cases was demanding new and specific responses. As a result, today we have an official family therapy that claims direct descendance from Bateson and a multitude of excellent practitioners doing sensitive and effective work that is frequently quite different from what systems theory prescribes.

I see the therapeutic process as an encounter between distinct interpersonal cultures. Real respect for clients and their integrity can allow therapists to be other than fearfully cautious, can encourage them to be direct and authentic—respectful and compassionate—but also at times honest and challenging.

This conception of the therapist as an active knower—of himself or herself *and* of the different family members—is very different from the neutral therapist of the constructivists. But, of course, these two prototypes are entirely too simplified. Most practitioners fall somewhere between these two poles of neutrality and decisiveness.

The choice between action and interventionism, on the one hand, and meaning and conversation, on the other, is but one of the questions the field is grappling with today; there are many others. Are the norms of human behavior universal, or are they culturally constructed products of political and ideological constraint? How do we become experts? How do we know what we know? Can we influence people? Can we not influence them? How do we know that we are not simply agents of social control? How do we know that we are accomplishing anything at all?

These questions and the rich history and contemporary practice of family therapy are explored in *Family Therapy: Concepts and Methods*. It is a thorough and thoughtful, fair and balanced guide to the ideas and techniques that make family therapy such an exciting enterprise. Dr. Nichols has managed to be comprehensive without becoming tedious. Perhaps the secret is the engaging style of his writing, or perhaps it is how he avoids getting lost in abstraction while keeping a clear focus on clinical practice. In any case, this superb book has long set the standard of excellence as the best introduction and guide to the practice of family therapy.

Salvador Minuchin, M.D.

Boca Raton, Florida

PREFACE

One thing that sometimes gets lost in academic discussions of family therapy is the feeling of accomplishment that comes from sitting down with an unhappy family and being able to help them. Beginning therapists are understandably anxious and not sure they'll know how to proceed. ("How do you get *all* of them to come in?") Veterans often speak in abstractions. They have opinions and discuss big issues—postmodernism, managed care, second-order cybernetics. While it's tempting to use this space to say Important Things, I prefer to be a little more personal. Treating troubled families has given me the greatest satisfaction imaginable, and I hope that the same is or will be true for you.

New to This Edition

In this eleventh edition of *Family Therapy: Concepts and Methods*, I've tried to describe the full scope of family therapy—its rich history, the classic schools, the latest developments—but with increasing emphasis on clinical practice. There are a lot of changes in this edition:

◆ New Digital Enhancements in the Pearson eText

- **Videos:** Links to video clips of therapists have been embedded for students to view throughout the chapters of the Pearson eText. Students are prompted to reflect on and analyze the videos via an accompanying question.
- **Chapter Quizzes:** At the end of each chapter Summary, students will find two self-assessments marked by a checkmark icon. In the Pearson eText, they click on the icon and the quiz appears. The first one prompts them to test their knowledge of chapter concepts by taking a multiple-choice quiz.

The second quiz icon prompts them to apply their knowledge of chapter concepts by responding to open-ended questions by typing their response and submitting it for immediate feedback. These self-assessments can reinforce understanding of key chapter concepts and support application of newly learned content.

◆ Content Changes in the New Edition

- ◆ New section on the impact of the Affordable Care Act
- ◆ Recommendations for establishing a fee-for-service private practice
- ◆ Revised and expanded section on attachment theory
- ◆ Questions to ask when doing a genogram
- ◆ More specific interventions from the MRI approach
- ◆ Detailed guidelines for making a structural family therapy assessment
- ◆ New section with guidelines on using family sculpting
- ◆ More specific techniques used in object relations family therapy
- ◆ Expanded section on spirituality and religion
- ◆ Expanded and updated section on families and technology
- ◆ Guidelines for therapeutic letter writing
- ◆ New research chapter including a discussion of why research has failed to influence practice and suggestions for bridging the research-practice gap
- ◆ New case studies

Instructor Supplements

An instructor's manual, test bank, and PowerPoint slides are available to accompany this text. They can be downloaded at www.pearsonhighered.com/educator.

Acknowledgments

Albert Einstein once said, "If you want to learn about physics, pay attention to what physicists do, not what they say they do." When you read about therapy, it can be hard to see past the jargon and political packaging to the essential ideas and practices. So in preparing this edition, I've traveled widely to visit and observe actual sessions of the leading practitioners. I've also invited several master therapists to share some of their best case studies with you. The result is a more pragmatic, clinical focus. I hope you like it.

So many people have contributed to my development as a family therapist and to the writing of this book that it is impossible to thank them all. But I would like to single out a few. To the people who taught me family therapy—Lyman Wynne, Murray Bowen, and Salvador Minuchin—thank you. Some of the people who went out of their way to help me prepare this eleventh edition were Yvonne Dolan, Jerome Price, Deborah Luepnitz, William Madsen, Frank Dattilio, Vicki Dickerson, Douglas Breunlin, and Salvador Minuchin. And I owe a huge debt of gratitude to Sean Davis for his extensive and thoughtful contributions to this edition. Sean has the rare combination of academic smarts and clinical sophistication that makes his perspective so valuable. To paraphrase John, Paul, George, and Ringo, I get by with *a lot* of help from my friends—and I thank them one and all. I am especially grateful to Julie Peters at Pearson for making a hard job easier.

Finally, I would like to thank my postgraduate instructors in family life: my wife, Melody, and my children, Sandy and Paul. In the brief span of forty-five years, Melody has seen me grow from a shy young man, totally ignorant of how to be a husband and father, to a shy middle-aged man, still bewildered and still trying. My children never cease to amaze me. If in my wildest dreams I had imagined children to love and be proud of, I wouldn't even have come close to children as fine as Sandy and Paul.

M. P. N.

THE FOUNDATIONS OF FAMILY THERAPY

Leaving Home

There wasn't much information on the intake sheet. Just a name, Holly Roberts, the fact that she was a senior in college, and her presenting complaint: "trouble making decisions."

The first thing Holly said when she sat down was, "I'm not sure I need to be here. You probably have a lot of people who need help more than I do." Then she started to cry.

It was springtime. The tulips were up, the trees were turning leafy green, and purple clumps of lilacs perfumed the air. Life and all its possibilities stretched out before her, but Holly was naggingly, unaccountably depressed.

The decision Holly was having trouble making was what to do after graduation. The more she tried to figure it out, the less able she was to concentrate. She started sleeping late, missing classes. Finally, her roommate talked her into going to the counseling center. "I wouldn't have come," Holly said. "I can take care of my own problems."

I was into cathartic therapy back then. Most people have stories to tell and tears to shed. Some of the stories, I suspected, were dramatized to elicit sympathy. We seem to give ourselves permission to cry only with some very acceptable excuse. Of all the human emotions we're ashamed of, feeling sorry for yourself tops the list.

I didn't know what was behind Holly's depression, but I was sure I could help. I felt comfortable with depression. Ever since my senior year in high school when my friend Alex died, I'd been a little depressed myself.

♦ ♦ ♦

After Alex died, the rest of the summer was a dark blur. I cried a lot. And I got mad whenever anybody suggested that life goes on. Alex's minister said that his death wasn't really a tragedy because now "Alex was with God in heaven." I wanted to scream, but I numbed myself instead. In the fall, I went off to college, and, even though it seemed disloyal to Alex, life did go on. I still cried from time to time, but with the tears came a painful discovery. Not all of my grief was for Alex. Yes, I loved him. Yes, I missed him. But his death provided me the justification to cry about the everyday sorrows of my own life. Maybe grief is always like that. At the time, though, it struck me as a betrayal. I was using Alex's death to feel sorry for myself.

◆ ◆ ◆

What, I wondered, was making Holly so sad? In fact, Holly didn't have a dramatic story. Her feelings weren't focused. After those first moments in my office, she rarely cried. When she did, it was more an involuntary tearing up than a sobbing release. She talked about the future and not knowing what she wanted to do with her life. She talked about not having a boyfriend, but she didn't say much about her family. If the truth be told, I wasn't much interested. Back then, I thought home was a place you left in order to grow up.

Holly was hurting and needed someone to lean on, but something made her hold back, as though she didn't quite trust me. It was frustrating. I wanted to help.

A month went by, and Holly's depression got worse. I started seeing her twice a week, but we weren't getting anywhere. One Friday afternoon, Holly was feeling so despondent that I didn't think she should go back to her dorm alone. I asked her instead to lie down on the couch in my office and, with her permission, I called her parents.

Mrs. Roberts answered the phone. I told her that I thought she and her husband should come to Rochester and meet with me and Holly to discuss the advisability of Holly taking a medical leave of absence. Unsure as I was of my authority back then, I steeled myself for an argument. Mrs. Roberts surprised me by agreeing to come at once.

The first thing that struck me about Holly's parents was the disparity in their ages. Mrs. Roberts looked like a slightly older version of Holly; she couldn't have been much over thirty-five. Her husband looked sixty. It turned out that he was Holly's stepfather. They had married when Holly was sixteen.

Looking back, I don't remember much that was said in that first meeting. Both parents were worried about Holly. "We'll do whatever you think best," Mrs. Roberts said. Holly's stepfather, Mr. Morgan, said they could arrange for a good psychiatrist "to help Holly over this crisis." But, Holly didn't want to go home, and she said so with more energy than I'd heard from her in a long time. That was on Saturday. I said that there was no need to rush into a decision, so we arranged to meet again on Monday.

When Holly and her parents sat down in my office on Monday morning, it was obvious that something had happened. Mrs. Roberts's eyes were red from crying. Holly glared at her and looked away. Mr. Morgan turned to me. "We've been fighting all weekend. Holly heaps abuse on me, and when I try to respond, Lena takes her side. That's the way it's been since day one of this marriage."

The story that emerged was one of those sad histories of jealousy and resentment that turn ordinary love into bitter, injured feelings and, all too often, tear families apart. Lena Roberts was thirty-four when she met Tom Morgan. He was a robust fifty-six. The second obvious difference between them was money. He was a stockbroker who'd retired to run a horse farm. She was waitressing to support herself and her daughter. It was a second marriage for both of them.

Lena thought Tom could be the missing father figure in Holly's life. Unfortunately, Lena couldn't accept all the rules Tom wanted to enforce, and so he became the wicked stepfather. He made the mistake of trying to take over and, when the predictable arguments ensued, Lena sided with her daughter. There were tears and midnight shouting matches. Twice Holly ran away for a few days. This triangle nearly proved the marriage's undoing, but things calmed down after Holly left for college.

Holly expected to leave home and not look back. She would make new friends. She would study hard and choose a career. She would never depend on a man to support her. Unfortunately, she left home with unfinished business. She hated Tom for the way he treated her mother. He was always demanding to know where her mother was going, who she was going with, and when she would be back. If she was the least bit late, there would be a scene. Why did her mother put up with it?

Blaming her stepfather was simple and satisfying. But another set of feelings, harder to face, was eating at Holly. She hated her mother for marrying Tom and for letting him be so mean to her. What had her mother seen in him? Had she sold out for a big house and a fancy car? Holly didn't have answers to these questions; she didn't even allow them into full awareness. Unfortunately, repression doesn't work like putting something away in a closet and forgetting about it. It takes a lot of energy to keep unwelcome emotions at bay.

Holly found excuses not to go home during college. It didn't even feel like home anymore. She buried herself in her studies. But rage and bitterness gnawed at her until, in her senior year, facing an uncertain future, knowing only that she couldn't go home again, she gave in to hopelessness. No wonder she was depressed.

I found the whole story sad. Not knowing about family dynamics and never having lived in a stepfamily, I wondered why they couldn't just try to get along. Why did they have so little sympathy for each other? Why couldn't Holly accept her mother's right to find love a second time around? Why couldn't Tom respect the priority of his wife's relationship with her daughter? And why couldn't Lena listen to her daughter's adolescent anger without getting so defensive?

That session with Holly and her parents was my first lesson in family therapy. Family members in therapy talk not about actual events but about reconstructed memories that resemble the original experiences only in certain ways. Holly's memories resembled her mother's memories very little, and her stepfather's not at all. In the gaps between their truths, there was little room for reason and no desire to pursue it.

Although that meeting may not have been terribly productive, it did put Holly's unhappiness in perspective. No longer did I think of her as a tragic young woman all alone in the world. She was that, of course, but she was also a daughter torn between running away from a home she no longer felt part of and being afraid to leave her mother alone with a man she didn't trust. I think that's when I became a family therapist.

To say that I didn't know much about families, much less about how to help them, would be an understatement. But family therapy isn't just a new set of techniques; it's a whole new approach to understanding human behavior—as fundamentally shaped by its social context.

The Myth of the Hero

Ours is a culture that celebrates the uniqueness of the individual and the search for an autonomous self. Holly's story could be told as a coming-of-age drama: a young person's struggle to break away from childhood and provincialism, to take hold of adulthood and promise and the future. If she fails, we're tempted to look inside the young adult, the failed hero.

While the unbounded individualism of the hero may once have been encouraged more for men than women, as a cultural ideal it casts its shadow on us all. Even if Holly cared about connection as well much as autonomy, she may be judged by the prevailing image of accomplishment.

We were raised on the myth of the hero: the Lone Ranger, Robin Hood, Wonder Woman. When we got older, we searched for real-life heroes: Eleanor Roosevelt, Martin Luther King Jr., Nelson Mandela. These men and women stood for something. If only we could be a little more like these larger-than-life individuals who seemed to rise above their circumstances.

Only later did we realize that the circumstances we wanted to rise above were part of the human condition—our inescapable connection to our families. The romantic image of the hero is based on the illusion that authentic selfhood can be achieved as an autonomous individual. We do many things alone, including some of our most heroic acts, but we are defined and sustained by a network of human relationships. Our need to worship heroes is partly a need to rise above littleness and self-doubt, but it is perhaps equally a product of imagining a life unfettered by all those pesky relationships that somehow never quite go the way we want them to.

When we do think about families, it's often in negative terms—as burdens holding us back or as destructive elements in the lives of our patients. What catches our attention are differences and discord. The harmonies of family life—loyalty, tolerance, solace, and support—often slide by unnoticed, part of the taken-for-granted background of life. If we would be heroes, then we must have villains.

These days there's a lot of talk about dysfunctional families. Unfortunately, much of this amounts to little more than parent bashing. People suffer because of what their parents did: their mother's career, their father's unreasonable expectations—these are the causes of their unhappiness. Perhaps this is an advance on stewing in guilt and shame, but it's a long way from understanding what really goes on in families.

One reason for blaming family sorrows on the personal failings of parents is that it's hard for the average person to see past individual personalities to the structural patterns that make them a family—a system of interconnected lives governed by strict but unspoken rules.

People feel controlled and helpless not because they are victims of parental folly and deceit but because they don't understand the forces that tie husbands and wives and parents and children together. Plagued by anxiety and depression, or merely troubled and uncertain, some people turn to psychotherapy for help. In the process, they turn away from the irritants that propel them into therapy. Chief among these are unhappy relationships—with friends and lovers, and with our families. Our disorders are private ailments. When we retreat to the safety of a synthetic relationship, the last thing we want is to take our families with us. Is it any wonder, then, that when Freud ventured to explore the dark forces of the mind, he locked the family outside the consulting room?

Psychotherapeutic Sanctuary

Psychotherapy was once a private enterprise. The consulting room was a place of healing, yes, but it was equally a sanctuary, a refuge from a troubled and troubling world.

Buffeted about in love and work, unable to find solace elsewhere, adults came to therapy to find satisfaction and meaning. Parents, worried about their children's behavior, sent them for guidance and direction. In many ways, psychotherapy displaced the family's role in solving the problems of everyday life.

Freud excluded the family from psychoanalysis to help patients feel safe to explore the full range of their thoughts and feelings.

It's possible to look back on the days before family therapy and see those who insisted on segregating patients from their families as exponents of a fossilized view of mental disorder, according to which psychiatric maladies are firmly embedded inside the heads of individuals. Considering that clinicians didn't begin treating families together until the mid-1950s, it's tempting to ask, "What took them so long?" In fact, there were good reasons for conducting therapy in private.

The two most influential approaches to psychotherapy in the twentieth century, Freud's psychoanalysis and Rogers's client-centered therapy, were both predicated on the assumption that psychological problems arise from unhealthy interactions with others and can best be alleviated in a private relationship between therapist and patient.

Freud's discoveries indicted the family, first as a breeding ground of childhood seduction and later as the agent of cultural repression. If people grew up a little bit neurotic—afraid of their own natural instincts—who should we blame but their parents?

Given that neurotic conflicts were spawned in the family, it seemed natural to assume that the best way to undo the family's influence was to isolate relatives from treatment, to bar their contaminating influence from the psychoanalytic operating room. Because psychoanalysis focused on the patient's memories and fantasies, the family's presence would only obscure the subjective truth of the past. Freud wasn't interested in the living family; he was interested in the family-as-remembered.

World History Archive/Newscom

Freud excluded the family from psychoanalysis to help patients feel safe to explore the full range of their thoughts and feelings.

By conducting treatment in private, Freud safeguarded patients' trust in the sanctity of the therapeutic relationship and thus maximized the likelihood that they would repeat, in relation to the analyst, the understandings and misunderstandings of childhood.

◆ ◆ ◆

Carl Rogers also believed that psychological problems stemmed from destructive family relations. Each of us, Rogers said, is born with an innate tendency toward *self-actualization*. Left to our own devices, we tend to follow our own best interests. Unhappily, said Rogers, our instinct for actualization gets subverted by our craving for approval. We learn to do what we think others want, even though it may not be what's best for us.

Gradually, this conflict between self-fulfillment and need for approval leads to denial of our authentic selves—and even the feelings that signal them. We swallow our anger, stifle our exuberance, and bury our lives under a mountain of expectations.

The therapy Rogers developed was designed to help patients uncover their real feelings. The Rogerian therapist listens sympathetically, offering compassion and understanding. In the presence of such an accepting listener, patients gradually get in touch with their own inner promptings.

Like the psychoanalyst, the client-centered therapist maintains absolute privacy in the therapeutic relationship to avoid any possibility that patients' feelings might be subverted to win approval. Only an objective outsider could be counted on to provide the unconditional acceptance to help patients rediscover their real selves. That's why family members had no place in the process of client-centered therapy.

Family versus Individual Therapy

As you can see, there were valid reasons for conducting psychotherapy in private. Although a strong claim can be made for individual psychotherapy, equally strong claims can be made for family therapy.

Individual psychotherapy and family therapy each offer an approach to treatment and a way of understanding human behavior. Both have their virtues. Individual therapy provides the concentrated focus to help people face their fears and learn to become more fully themselves. Individual therapists have always recognized the importance of family life in shaping personality, but they have assumed that these influences are internalized and that intrapsychic dynamics become the dominant forces controlling behavior. Treatment can and should, therefore, be directed at the person and his or her personal makeup. Family therapists, on the other hand, believe that the dominant forces in our lives are located externally, in the family. Therapy, in this framework, is directed at changing the organization of the family. When family organization is transformed, the life of every family member is altered accordingly.

This last point—that changing a family changes the lives of its members—is important enough to elaborate. Family therapy isn't predicated merely on changing the individual patient in context. Family therapy exerts change on the entire family; therefore, improvement can be lasting because each family member is changed and continues to exert synchronous change on other family members.

Almost any human difficulty can be treated with either individual or family therapy, but certain problems are especially suited to a family approach, among them problems with children (who must, regardless of what happens in therapy, return home to their parents), complaints about a marriage or other intimate relationship, family feuds, and symptoms that develop in an individual at the time of a major family transition.

If problems that arise around family transitions make a therapist think first about the role of the family, individual therapy may be especially useful when people identify something about themselves that they've tried in vain to change while their social environment remains stable. Thus, if a woman gets depressed during her first year at college, a therapist might wonder if her sadness is related to leaving home and leaving her parents alone with each other. But if the same woman were to become depressed in her thirties, during a long period of stability in her life, we might wonder if there was something about her approach to life that wasn't working for her. Examining her life in private—away from troubled relationships—doesn't, however, mean that she should believe she can fulfill herself in isolation from other people.

The view of persons as separate entities, with families acting on them, is consistent with the way we experience ourselves. We recognize the influence of others—especially as obligation and constraint—but it's hard to see that we are embedded in a network of relationships, that we are part of something larger than ourselves.

Thinking in Lines, Thinking in Circles

Mental illness has traditionally been explained in linear terms—medical or psychological. Both paradigms treat emotional distress as a symptom of internal dysfunction with historical causes.

Linear explanations take the form of *A* causes *B*. This works fine for some things. If you're driving along and your car suddenly sputters to a stop, go ahead and look for a simple explanation. Maybe you're out of gas. If so, there's a simple solution. Human problems are usually a bit more complicated.

Individual therapists think in terms of *linear causality* when they explore what happened to make individuals behave the way they do. If a young woman has low self-esteem, perhaps it's because her mother constantly criticizes her. Family therapists prefer to think in terms of *circular causality* and consider people's mutual influence on each other. Thus, the young woman's moping around the house might be a response to her mother's fault-finding—and the mother's finding fault might be a response to the young woman's moping around the house. The more the mother criticizes, the more the young woman withdraws, *and* the more the young woman withdraws, the more the mother criticizes.

The term *circular causality* calls attention to the cycles of interaction in relationships. But in fact the term is somewhat of a misnomer, because the focus is not on causality—how something got started—but on the ongoing transactions that sustain it. In some cases, maybe something in the past did trigger an unhappy pattern of interaction. But the past is over; therapists can only

work with what's going on in the present. Although the mother in the earlier example may only have started reproaching her daughter when she started avoiding social activities, her continuing attempts to motivate the girl with criticism may only serve to perpetuate a circular pattern of withdrawal-and-criticism.

When things go wrong in relationships, most of us are generous in giving credit to other people. Because we look at the world from inside our own skins, it's easy to see other people's contributions to our mutual problems. Blaming is only natural. The illusion of unilateral influence tempts therapists too, especially when they hear only one side of a story. But once we understand that reciprocity is the governing principle of relationships, we can begin to get past thinking in terms of villains and victims.

Suppose that a father complains about his teenage son's behavior.

Father: It's my son. He's rude and defiant.

Therapist: Who taught him that?

Instead of accepting the father's perspective that he's a victim of his son's villainy, the therapist's question invites him to look for patterns of mutual influence. The point isn't to shift blame from one person to another but to get away from blame altogether. As long as he sees the problem as his son's doing, the father has little choice but to hope the boy will change. (Waiting for other people to change is like planning your future around winning the lottery.) Learning to think in circles rather than lines empowers us to look at the half of the equation we can control.

The Power of Family Therapy

The power of family therapy derives from bringing parents and children together to transform their interactions. Instead of isolating individuals from the emotional origins of their conflict, problems are addressed at their source.

What keeps people stuck is their inability to see their own participation in the problems that plague them. With eyes fixed firmly on what recalcitrant others are doing, it's hard for most people to see the patterns that bind them together. The family therapist's job is to give them a wake-up call. When a husband complains that his wife nags, and the therapist asks how he contributes to her doing that, the therapist is challenging the husband to see the hyphenated him-and-her of their interactions.

♦ ♦ ♦

When Bob and Shirley came for help with marital problems, her complaint was that he never shared his feelings; his was that she always criticized him. This is a classic trading of complaints that keeps couples stuck as long as they fail to see the reciprocal pattern in which each partner provokes in the other precisely the behavior he or she can't stand. So the therapist said to Bob, "If you were a frog, what would you be like if Shirley changed you into a prince?" When Bob countered that he doesn't talk with her because she's so critical, it seemed to the couple like the same old argument—but the therapist saw this as the beginning of change—Bob starting to speak up. One way to create an opening for change in rigid families is to support the blamed person and help bring him back into the fray.

When Shirley criticized Bob for complaining, he tried to retreat, but the therapist said, "No, continue. You're still a frog."

Bob tried to shift responsibility back to Shirley. "Doesn't she have to kiss me first?"

"No," the therapist said. "In real life, you have to earn that."

♦ ♦ ♦

In the opening of *Anna Karenina*, Tolstoy wrote: "All happy families resemble one another; each unhappy family is unhappy in its own way." Every unhappy family may be unhappy in its own way, but everyone stumbles over the same familiar challenges of family life. It's no secret what those challenges are—learning to live together, dealing with difficult relatives, chasing after children, coping with adolescence, and so on. What not everyone realizes, however, is that a relatively small number of systems dynamics, once understood, illuminate those challenges and enable families to move successfully through the predictable dilemmas of life. Like all healers, family therapists sometimes deal with bizarre and baffling cases, but much of their work is with ordinary human beings learning life's painful lessons. Their stories, and the stories of the men and women of family therapy who have undertaken to help them, are the inspiration for this book.

CHAPTER 1

THE EVOLUTION OF FAMILY THERAPY

A Revolutionary Shift in Perspective

In this chapter, we explore the antecedents and early years of family therapy. There are two compelling stories here: one of personalities, one of ideas. The first story revolves around the pioneers—visionary iconoclasts who broke the mold of seeing life and its troubles as a function of individuals and their personalities. Make no mistake: The shift from an individual to a systemic perspective was a revolutionary one, providing those who grasped it with a powerful tool for understanding and resolving human problems.

The second story in the evolution of family therapy is one of ideas. The restless curiosity of the first family therapists led them to ingenious new ways of conceptualizing the joys and sorrows of family life.

As you read this history, stay open to surprises. Be ready to reexamine easy assumptions—including the assumption that family therapy began as a benevolent effort to support the institution of the family. The truth is, therapists first encountered families as adversaries.

LEARNING OUTCOMES

- ♦ Describe the circumstances that led to the birth of family therapy.
- ♦ List the founders of family therapy and where they practiced.
- ♦ List the first family therapy theories and when they were popular.
- ♦ Describe early family therapy theoretical concepts.

The Undeclared War

Although we came to think of asylums as places of cruelty and detention, they were originally built to rescue the insane from being locked away in family attics. Accordingly, except for purposes of footing the bill, hospital psychiatrists kept families at arm's length. In the 1950s, however, two puzzling developments forced therapists to recognize the family's power to alter the course of treatment.

Therapists began to notice that often when a patient got better, someone else in the family got worse, almost as though the family *needed* a symptomatic member. As in the game of hide-and-seek, it didn't seem to matter who "It" was as long as someone played the part. In one case, Don Jackson (1954) was treating a woman for depression. When she began to improve, her husband complained that she was getting worse. When she continued to improve, the husband lost his job. Eventually, when the woman was completely well, the husband killed himself. Apparently this man's stability was predicated on having a sick wife.

Another strange story of shifting disturbance was that patients often improved in the hospital only to get worse when they went home.

CASE STUDY

In a bizarre case of Oedipus revisited, Salvador Minuchin treated a young man hospitalized for trying to scratch out his eyes. The man functioned normally in Bellevue but returned to self-mutilation each time he went home. He could be sane, it seemed, only in an insane world.

It turned out that the young man was extremely close to his mother, a bond that grew even tighter during the seven years of his father's mysterious absence. The father was a compulsive gambler who disappeared shortly after being declared legally incompetent. The rumor was that the Mafia had kidnapped him. When, just as mysteriously, the father returned, his son began his bizarre attempts at self-mutilation. Perhaps he wanted to blind himself so as not to see his obsession with his mother and hatred of his father.

But this family was neither ancient nor Greek, and Minuchin was more pragmatist than poet. So he challenged the father to protect his son by beginning to deal directly with his wife, and then he challenged the man's demeaning attitude toward her, which had driven her to seek her son's protection. The therapy was a challenge to the family's structure and, in Bellevue, working with the psychiatric staff to ease the young man back into the family, into the lion's den.

Minuchin confronted the father, saying, "As a father of a child in danger, what you're doing isn't enough."

"What should I do?" asked the man.

"I don't know," Minuchin replied. "Ask your son." Then, for the first time in years, father and son began talking. Just as they were about to run out of things to say, Dr. Minuchin commented to the parents: "In a strange way, he's telling you that he prefers to be treated like a child. When he was in the hospital he was twenty-three. Now that he's returned home again, he's six."

What this case dramatizes is how parents use their children as a buffer to protect them from intimacy. To the would-be Oedipus, Minuchin said, "You're scratching your eyes for your mother, so that she'll have something to worry about. You're a good boy. Good children sacrifice themselves for their parents."

Families are made of strange glue—they stretch but never let go. Few blamed the family for outright malevolence, yet there was an invidious undercurrent to these observations. The official story of family therapy is one of respect for the family, but maybe none of us ever quite gets over the adolescent idea that families are the enemy of freedom.

◆ Small Group Dynamics

Those who first sought to understand and treat families found a ready parallel in small groups. **Group dynamics** were applicable to family therapy because group life is a complex blend of individual personalities and properties of the group.

In 1920, the pioneering social psychologist William McDougall published *The Group Mind*, in which he described how a group's continuity depends on boundaries for differentiation of function and on customs and habits to make relationships predictable. A more scientific approach to group dynamics was developed in the 1940s by Kurt Lewin, whose *field theory* (Lewin, 1951) guided a generation of researchers. Drawing on the Gestalt school of perception, Lewin developed the notion that a group is more than the sum of its parts. The transcendent property of groups has obvious relevance to family therapists, who must work not only with individuals but also with family systems—and their famous resistance to change.

Analyzing what he called *quasi-stationary social equilibrium*, Lewin pointed out that changing group behavior requires "unfreezing." Only after something shakes up a group's beliefs will its members be prepared to change. In individual therapy this process is initiated by the unhappy experiences that lead people to seek help. When someone decides to meet with a therapist, that person has already begun to unfreeze old habits. When families come for treatment, it's a different story.

Richard T. Nowitz/Corbis

The first people to practice family therapy turned to group therapy for a model.

Family members may not be sufficiently unsettled by one member's problems to consider changing their ways. Furthermore, family members bring their own reference group with them, with all its traditions and habits. Consequently, more effort is required to unfreeze, or shake up, families before real change can take place. The need for unfreezing foreshadowed early family therapists' concern about disrupting family homeostasis, a notion that dominated family therapy for decades.

Wilfred Bion was another student of group functioning who emphasized the group as a whole, with its own dynamics and structure. According to Bion (1948), most groups become diverted from their primary tasks by engaging in patterns of *fight–flight, dependency*, and *pairing*. Bion's basic assumptions are easily extrapolated to family therapy: Some families skirt around hot issues like a cat circling a snake. Others use therapy to bicker endlessly, never really contemplating compromise, much less change.

Dependency masquerades as therapy when families allow therapists to subvert their autonomy in the name of problem solving. Pairing is seen in families when one parent colludes with the children to undermine the other parent.

The **process/content** distinction in group dynamics had a major impact on family treatment. Experienced therapists learn to attend as much to *how* people talk as to the content of their discussions. For example, a mother might tell her daughter that she shouldn't play with Barbie dolls because she shouldn't aspire to an image of bubble-headed beauty. The *content* of the mother's message is, "Respect yourself as a person." But if the mother expresses her point of view by disparaging the daughter's wishes, then the *process* of her message is, "Your feelings don't count."

Unfortunately, the content of some discussions is so compelling that therapists get sidetracked from the process. Suppose that a therapist invites a teenager to talk with his mother about wanting to drop out of school. The boy mumbles something about school being stupid, and his mother responds with a lecture about the importance of education. A therapist who gets drawn in to support the mother's position may be making a mistake. In terms of content, the mother might be right: A high school diploma can come in handy. But maybe it's more important at that moment to help the boy learn to speak up for himself—and for his mother to learn to listen.

Role theory, explored in the literatures of psychoanalysis and group dynamics, had important applications to the study of families. The expectations that roles carry bring regularity to complex social situations.

Roles tend to be stereotyped in most groups, and so there are characteristic behavior patterns of group members. Virginia Satir (1972) described family roles such as "the placator" and "the disagreeable one" in her book *Peoplemaking*. If you think about it, you may have played a fairly predictable role in your family. Perhaps you were "the good child," "the moody one," or "the rebel." The trouble is, such roles can be hard to put aside.

One thing that makes role theory so useful in understanding families is that roles tend to be complementary. Say, for example, that a woman is a little more anxious to spend time with her boyfriend than he is. Maybe, left to his own devices, he'd call twice a week. But if she calls three times a week, he may never get around to picking up the phone. If their relationship lasts, she may always be the pursuer and he the distancer. Or take the case of two parents, both of whom want their children to behave themselves at the dinner table. The father has a slightly shorter fuse—he tells them to quiet down five seconds after they start getting rowdy, whereas his wife would wait half a minute. If he always speaks up, she may never get a chance. Eventually these parents may become polarized into complementary roles of strictness and leniency. What makes such reciprocity resistant to change is that the roles reinforce each other.

It was a short step from observing patients' reactions to other members of a group—some of whom might act like siblings or parents—to observing interactions in real families. Given the wealth of techniques for exploring interpersonal relationships developed by group therapists, it was natural for some family therapists to apply a group treatment model to families. What is a family, after all, but a group of individuals?

From a technical viewpoint, group and family therapies are similar: Both are complex and dynamic, more like everyday life than individual therapy. In groups and families, patients must react to a number of people, not just a therapist, and therapeutic use of this interaction is the definitive mechanism of change in both contexts.

On closer examination, however, it turns out that the differences between families and groups are so significant that the group therapy model has only limited applicability to family treatment. Family members have a long history and, more importantly, a future together. Revealing yourself to strangers is a lot safer than exposing yourself to members of your own family. There's no taking back revelations that might better have remained private—the affair, long since over, or the admission that a woman cares more about her career than about her husband. Continuity, commitment, and shared distortions all make family therapy very different from group therapy.

Therapy groups are designed to provide an atmosphere of warmth and support. This feeling of safety among sympathetic strangers cannot be part of family therapy, because instead of separating treatment from a stressful environment, the stressful environment is brought into the consulting room. Furthermore, in group therapy, patients can have equal power and status, whereas democratic equality isn't appropriate in families. Someone has to be in charge. Furthermore, the official patient in a family is likely to feel isolated and stigmatized. After all, he or she is "the problem." The sense of protection in being part of a compassionate group of strangers, who won't have to be faced across the dinner table, doesn't exist in family therapy.

◆ The Child Guidance Movement

It was Freud who introduced the idea that psychological disorders were the result of unsolved problems of childhood. Alfred Adler was the first of Freud's followers to pursue the implication that treating the growing child might be the most effective way to prevent adult neuroses. To that end, Adler organized child guidance clinics in Vienna, where not only children but also families and teachers were counseled. Adler offered support and encouragement to help alleviate children's feelings of inferiority, so they could work out a healthy lifestyle, achieving confidence and success through social usefulness.

Although child guidance clinics remained few in number until after World War II, they now exist in every city in the United States, providing treatment of childhood problems and the complex forces contributing to them. Gradually, child guidance workers concluded that the real problem wasn't a child's symptoms, but rather the tensions in families that were the source of those symptoms. At first there was a tendency to blame the parents, especially the mother.

The chief cause of children's problems, according to David Levy (1943), was *maternal overprotectiveness*. Mothers who had themselves been deprived of love became overprotective of their children. Some were domineering, others overindulgent. Children of domineering mothers were submissive at home but had difficulty making friends; children with over indulgent mothers were disobedient at home but well behaved at school.

During this period, Frieda Fromm-Reichmann (1948) coined one of the most damning phrases in the history of psychiatry, the **schizophrenogenic mother**. These domineering, aggressive, and rejecting women, especially when married to passive men, were thought to provide the pathological parenting that produced schizophrenia.

The tendency to blame parents, especially mothers, for problems in the family was an evolutionary misdirection that continues to haunt the field. Nevertheless, by paying attention to what went on between parents and children, Levy and Fromm-Reichmann helped pave the way for family therapy.

John Bowlby's work at the Tavistock Clinic exemplified the transition to a family approach. Bowlby (1949) was treating a teenager and making slow progress. Feeling frustrated, he decided to see the boy and his parents together. During the first half of a two-hour session, the child and parents took turns complaining about each other. During the second half of the session, Bowlby interpreted what he thought each of their contributions to the problem were. Eventually, by working together, all three members of the family developed sympathy for each other's point of view.

Although he was intrigued by this conjoint interview, Bowlby remained wedded to the one-to-one format. Family meetings might be a useful catalyst, but only as a supplement to the *real* treatment, individual psychotherapy.

What Bowlby tried as an experiment, Nathan Ackerman saw to fruition—family therapy as the primary form of treatment. Once he saw the need to understand the family in order to diagnose problems, Ackerman soon took the next step—family treatment. Before we get to that, however, let us examine comparable developments in marriage counseling and research on schizophrenia that led to the birth of family therapy.

◆ Marriage Counseling

For many years there was no apparent need for a separate profession of marriage counselors. People with marital problems talked with their doctors, clergy, lawyers, and teachers. The first centers for marriage counseling were established in the 1930s. Paul Popenoe opened the American Institute of Family Relations in Los Angeles, and Abraham and Hannah Stone opened a similar clinic in New York. A third center was the Marriage Council of Philadelphia, begun in 1932 by Emily Hartshorne Mudd (Broderick & Schrader, 1981).

At the same time these developments were taking place, a parallel trend among some psychoanalysts led to conjoint marital therapy. Although most analysts followed Freud's prohibition against contact with a patient's family, a few broke the rules and experimented with therapy for married partners.

In 1948, Bela Mittleman of the New York Psychoanalytic Institute published the first account of concurrent marital therapy in the United States. Mittleman suggested that husbands and wives could be treated by the same analyst, and that by seeing both it was possible to reexamine their irrational perceptions of each other (Mittleman, 1948). This was a revolutionary notion: that the reality of interpersonal relationships might be at least as important as their intrapsychic representations.

Meanwhile in Great Britain, where **object relations** were the central concern of psychoanalysts, Henry Dicks and his associates at the Tavistock Clinic established a Family Psychiatric Unit. Here couples referred by the divorce courts were helped to reconcile their differences (Dicks, 1964). Subsequently, Michael and Enid Balint affiliated their Family Discussion Bureau with the Tavistock Clinic, adding that clinic's prestige to their marital casework and indirectly to the field of marriage counseling.

In 1956, Mittleman wrote a more extensive description of marital disorders and their treatment. He described a number of complementary marital patterns, including aggressive/submissive and detached/demanding. These odd matches are made, according to Mittleman, because courting couples see each other's personalities through the eyes of their illusions: She sees his detachment as strength; he sees her dependency as adoration.

At about this time Don Jackson and Jay Haley were exploring marital therapy within the framework of communications analysis. As their ideas gained prominence, the field of marital therapy was absorbed into the larger family therapy movement.

Many writers don't distinguish between marital and family therapy. Therapy for couples, according to this way of thinking, is just family therapy applied to a particular subsystem. We tend to agree with this perspective, and therefore you will find our description of various approaches to couples and their problems embedded in discussions of the models considered in this book. There is, however, a case to be made for considering couples therapy a distinct enterprise (Gurman, 2008, 2011).

Historically, many of the influential approaches to couples therapy came before their family therapy counterparts. Among these were cognitive-behavioral marital therapy, object-relations marital therapy, and emotionally-focused couples therapy.

Beyond the question of which came first, couples therapy differs from family therapy in allowing a more in-depth focus on the experience of individuals. Sessions with whole families tend to be noisy affairs. While it's possible in this context to talk with family members about their hopes and fears, it isn't possible to spend much time exploring the psychology of any one individual—much less two. Therapy with couples, on the other hand, permits greater focus on both dyadic exchanges and the underlying experience of intimate partners.

Research on Family Dynamics and the Etiology of Schizophrenia

Families with schizophrenic members proved to be a fertile area for research because their pathological patterns of interaction were so magnified. The fact that family therapy emerged from research on schizophrenia led to the hope that family therapy might be the way to cure this baffling form of madness.

◆ Gregory Bateson—Palo Alto

One of the groups with the strongest claim to originating family therapy was Gregory Bateson's schizophrenia project in Palo Alto, California. The Palo Alto project began in the fall of 1952 when Bateson received a grant to study the nature of communication. All communications, Bateson (1951) contended, have two different levels—*report* and *command*. Every message has a stated content, for instance, "Wash your hands; it's time for dinner," but in addition, the message carries how it is to be taken. In this case, the second message is that the speaker is in charge. This second message—**metacommunication**—is covert and often unnoticed. If a wife scolds her husband for running the dishwasher when it's only half full, and he says OK but turns around and does the same thing two days later, she may be annoyed that he didn't listen to her. She means the message. But maybe he didn't like the metamessage. Maybe he doesn't like her telling him what to do as though she were his mother.

 Watch this video on Gregory Bateson, one of the most influential early family therapy pioneers. What do you think was his greatest contribution?

www.youtube.com/watch?v=AqiHJG2wtPI&index=2&list=PLT10BSjdk4VOrdigJrT8KQaWFvZ2mGKPh

Bateson was joined in 1953 by Jay Haley and John Weakland. In 1954 Bateson received a grant to study schizophrenic communication. Shortly thereafter the group was joined by Don Jackson, a brilliant psychiatrist who served as clinical consultant.

Bateson and his colleagues hypothesized that family stability is achieved by feedback that regulates the behavior of the family and its members. Whenever a family system is threatened—that is, disturbed—it endeavors to maintain stability, or **homeostasis**. Thus, apparently puzzling behavior might become understandable if it were seen as a homeostatic mechanism. For example, if whenever two parents argue, one of the children exhibits symptomatic behavior, the symptoms may be a way to stop the fighting by uniting the parents in concern. Thus, symptomatic behavior can serve the cybernetic function of preserving a family's equilibrium.

In 1956 Bateson and his colleagues published their famous report "Toward a Theory of Schizophrenia," in which they introduced the concept of the **double bind**. Patients weren't crazy in some meaningless way; they were an extension of a crazy family environment. Consider someone in an important relationship in which escape isn't feasible and response is necessary. If he or she receives two related but contradictory messages on different levels but finds it difficult to recognize or comment on the inconsistency (Bateson, Jackson, Haley, & Weakland, 1956), that person is in a double bind.

Because this concept is often misused as a synonym for paradox or simply contradiction, it's worth reviewing each feature of the double bind as the authors listed them:

1. Two or more persons in an important relationship
2. Repeated experience
3. A primary negative injunction, such as "Don't do X or I will punish you"
4. A second injunction at a more abstract level conflicting with the first, also enforced by punishment or perceived threat
5. A tertiary negative injunction prohibiting escape and demanding a response. Without this restriction the victim won't feel bound
6. Finally, the complete set of ingredients is no longer necessary once the victim is conditioned to

perceive the world in terms of double binds; any part of the sequence becomes sufficient to trigger panic or rage

Most examples of double binds in the literature are inadequate because they don't include all the critical features. Robin Skynner (1976), for instance, cited: "Boys must stand up for themselves and not be sissies"; but "Don't be rough . . . don't be rude to your mother." Confusing? Yes. Conflict? Maybe. But these messages don't constitute a double bind; they're merely contradictory. Faced with two such statements, a child is free to obey either one, alternate, or even complain about the contradiction. This and similar examples neglect the specification that the two messages are conveyed on different levels.

A better example is given in the original article. A young man recovering in the hospital from a schizophrenic episode was visited by his mother. When he put his arm around her, she stiffened. But when he withdrew, she asked, "Don't you love me anymore?" He blushed, and she said, "Dear, you must not be so easily embarrassed and afraid of your feelings." Following this exchange, the patient assaulted an aide and had to be put in seclusion.

Another example of a double bind would be a teacher who urges his students to participate in class but gets impatient if one of them actually interrupts with a question or comment. Then a baffling thing happens. For some strange reason that scientists have yet to decipher, students tend not to speak up in classes where their comments are disparaged. When the professor finally gets around to asking for questions and no one responds, he gets angry. ("Students are so passive!") If any of the students has the temerity to comment on the professor's lack of receptivity, he may get even angrier. Thus, the students will be punished for accurately perceiving that the teacher really wants only his own ideas to be heard and admired. (This example is, of course, purely hypothetical.)

We're all caught in occasional double binds, but a schizophrenic has to deal with them continually—and the effect is maddening. Unable to comment on the dilemma, the schizophrenic responds defensively, perhaps by being concrete and literal, perhaps by speaking in metaphors. Eventually the schizophrenic may come to assume that behind every statement lies a concealed meaning.

The discovery that schizophrenic symptoms made sense in the context of some families may have been a scientific advance, but it also had moral and political overtones. Not only did these investigators see themselves as avenging knights bent on rescuing **identified patients** by slaying family dragons, but they were also crusaders in a holy war against the psychiatric establishment. Outnumbered and surrounded by hostile critics, the champions of family therapy challenged the assumption that schizophrenia was a biological disease. Psychological healers everywhere cheered. Unfortunately, they were wrong.

The observation that schizophrenic behavior seems to *fit* in some families doesn't mean that families *cause* schizophrenia. In logic, this kind of inference is called "Jumping to Conclusions." Sadly, families of schizophrenic members suffered for years under the assumption that they were to blame for the tragedy of their children's psychoses.

◆ Theodore Lidz—Yale

Theodore Lidz refuted the notion that maternal rejection was the distinguishing feature of schizophrenic families. Frequently the more destructive parent is the father (Lidz, Cornelison, Fleck, & Terry, 1957a). After describing some of the pathological characteristics of fathers in schizophrenic families, Lidz turned his attention to the marital relationship. What he found was an absence of *role reciprocity*. In a successful relationship, it's not enough to fulfill your own role—that is, to be an effective person; it's also important to balance your role with your partner's—that is, to be an effective pair.

In focusing on the failure to arrive at cooperative roles, Lidz identified two types of marital discord (Lidz, Cornelison, Fleck, & Terry, 1957b). In the first, **marital schism**, husbands and wives undermine each other and compete openly for their children's affection. These marriages are combat zones. The second pattern, **marital skew**, involves serious character flaws in one partner who dominates the other. Thus one parent becomes passive and dependent while the other appears to be a strong parent figure, but is in fact a pathological bully. In all these families,

unhappy children are torn by conflicting loyalties and weighed down with the pressure to balance their parents' precarious marriages.

◆ Lyman Wynne—National Institute of Mental Health

Lyman Wynne's studies of schizophrenic families began in 1954 when he started seeing the parents of hospitalized patients in twice-weekly sessions. What struck Wynne about these families was the strangely unreal qualities of their emotions, which he called *pseudomutuality* and *pseudohostility*, and the nature of the boundaries around them—*rubber fences*—apparently flexible but actually impervious to outside influence (especially from therapists).

Pseudomutuality (Wynne, Ryckoff, Day, & Hirsch, 1958) is a facade of harmony. Pseudomutual families are so committed to togetherness that there's no room for separate identities. The surface unity of pseudomutual families obscures the fact that they can't tolerate deeper, more honest relationships, or independence.

Pseudohostility is a different guise for a similar collusion to stifle autonomy (Wynne, 1961). Although apparently acrimonious, it signals only a superficial split. Pseudohostility is more like the bickering of situation-comedy families than real animosity. Like pseudomutuality, it undermines intimacy and masks deeper conflict, and like pseudomutuality, pseudohostility distorts communication and impairs rational thinking.

Courtesy of S. H. McDaniel, University of Rochester Medical Center

Lyman Wynne's studies linked communication deviance in families to thought disorder in schizophrenic patients.

The **rubber fence** is an invisible barrier that stretches to permit limited extrafamilial contact, such as going to school, but springs back if that involvement goes too far. The family's rigid structure is thus protected by its isolation. Instead of having its eccentricities modified in contact with the larger society, the schizophrenic family becomes a sick little society unto itself.

Wynne linked the new concept of *communication deviance* to the older notion of *thought disorder*. He saw communication as the vehicle for transmitting thought disorder, the defining feature of schizophrenia. Communication deviance is a more interactional concept, and more readily observable. By 1978 Wynne had studied over 600 families and gathered incontrovertible evidence that disordered communication is a distinguishing characteristic of families with young adult schizophrenics.

◆ Role Theorists

The founders of family therapy gained momentum for their fledgling discipline by concentrating on communication. Doing so may have been expedient, but focusing exclusively on this one aspect of family life neglected individual intersubjectivity as well as broader social influences.

Role theorists, like John Spiegel, described how individuals were differentiated into social roles within family systems. This important fact was obscured by simplistic versions of systems theory, in which individuals were treated like interchangeable parts. As early as 1954, Spiegel pointed out that the system in therapy includes the therapist as well as the family (an idea reintroduced later as **second-order cybernetics**). He also made a valuable distinction between "interactions" and "transactions." Billiard balls *interact*—they collide but remain essentially unchanged. People *transact*—they come together in ways that not only alter each other's course but also bring about internal changes.

R. D. Laing's analysis of family dynamics was more polemical than scholarly, but his observations helped popularize the family's role in psychopathology. Laing (1965) borrowed Karl Marx's concept of **mystification** (class exploitation) and applied it to the "politics of families." Mystification means distorting someone's experience by denying or relabeling it. An example of this is a parent telling a child who's feeling sad, "You must be tired" (*Go to bed and leave me alone*).

Mystification distorts feelings and, more ominously, reality. When parents mystify a child's experience, the child's existence becomes inauthentic. Because their feelings aren't accepted, these children project a *false self*. In mild instances, this produces a lack of authenticity, but when the real self/false self split is carried to extremes, the result is madness (Laing, 1960).

From Research to Treatment: The Pioneers of Family Therapy

We have seen how family therapy was anticipated by developments in hospital psychiatry, group dynamics, interpersonal psychiatry, the child guidance movement, marriage counseling, and research on schizophrenia. But who actually started family therapy? Although there are rival claims to this honor, the distinction should probably be shared by John Elderkin Bell, Don Jackson, Nathan Ackerman, and Murray Bowen. In addition to these founders of family therapy, Jay Haley, Virginia Satir, Carl Whitaker, Lyman Wynne, Ivan Boszormenyi-Nagy, and Salvador Minuchin were also significant pioneers.

◆ John Bell

John Elderkin Bell, a psychologist at Clark University in Worcester, Massachusetts, who began treating families in 1951, occupies a unique position in the history of family therapy. He may have been the first family therapist, but he is mentioned only tangentially in two of the most important historical accounts of the movement (Guerin, 1976; Kaslow, 1980). The reason for this is that although he began seeing families in the 1950s, he didn't publish his ideas until a decade later. Moreover, unlike the other parents of family therapy, he had few offspring. He didn't establish a clinic, develop a training program, or train well-known students.

Bell's approach (Bell, 1961, 1962) was taken directly from group therapy. *Family group therapy* relied primarily on stimulating open discussion to help families solve their problems.

Bell believed that family groups go through predictable phases, as do groups of strangers. In his early work (Bell, 1961), he carefully structured treatment in a series of stages. First was a *child-centered phase*, in which children were encouraged to express their wishes and concerns. In the *parent-centered stage*, parents typically complained about their children's behavior. During this phase, Bell was careful to soften the harshest parental criticisms in order to focus on problem solving. In the final, or *family-centered*, stage, the therapist equalized support for the entire family while they continued to improve their communication and work out solutions to their problems. The following vignette illustrates Bell's (1975) style of intervening:

> After remaining silent for a few sessions, one father came in with a great tirade against his son, daughter, and wife. I noticed how each individual in his own way, within a few minutes, was withdrawing from the conference. Then I said, "Now I think we should hear what Jim has to say about this, and Nancy should have her say, and perhaps we should also hear what your wife feels about it." (p. 136)

◆ ◆ ◆

Three specialized applications of group methods to family treatment were *multiple family group therapy, multiple impact therapy*, and *network therapy*.

Peter Laqueur developed **multiple family group therapy** in 1950 at Creedmoor State Hospital in New York (Laqueur, 1966, 1976). Multiple family group therapy involved four to six families seen together for weekly sessions of ninety minutes. Laqueur and his cotherapists conducted family groups like traditional therapy groups with the addition of encounter-group and psychodrama techniques. Although multiple family therapy lost its most creative force with Peter Laqueur's untimely death, it is still occasionally used in hospital settings, both inpatient (McFarlane, 1982) and outpatient (Gritzer & Okum, 1983).

Robert MacGregor and his colleagues at the University of Texas Medical Branch in Galveston developed **multiple impact therapy** as a way to maximize their impact on families who came from all over Texas (MacGregor, 1967, 1972). Team members met with various combinations of family members and then assembled in a group to make recommendations. Although multiple impact therapy is no longer practiced, its intense but infrequent meetings prefigured later developments in experiential therapy (Chapter 7) and the Milan model (Chapter 5).

Network therapy was developed by Ross Speck and Carolyn Attneave for assisting families in crisis by assembling their entire social network—family, friends, neighbors—in gatherings of as many as fifty people. Teams of therapists were used, and the emphasis was on breaking destructive patterns of relationship and mobilizing support for new options (Ruevini, 1975; Speck & Attneave, 1973).

◆ Palo Alto

The Bateson group stumbled onto family therapy more or less by accident. Once they began to interview schizophrenic families in 1954, hoping to decipher their strange patterns of communication, project members found themselves drawn into helping roles by the pain of these unhappy people (Jackson & Weakland, 1961). Although Bateson was the scientific leader of the group, Don Jackson and Jay Haley were most influential in developing family treatment.

Jackson rejected the psychodynamic concepts he'd been taught and focused instead on the dynamics of interchange between persons. Analysis of communication was his primary instrument.

Jackson's concept of **family homeostasis**—families as units that resist change—was to become the defining metaphor of family therapy's early years. In hindsight, we can say that the focus on homeostasis overestimated the conservative properties of families. At the time, however, the recognition that families resist change was enormously productive for understanding what keeps patients from improving.

In *Schizophrenic Symptoms and Family Interaction* (Jackson & Weakland, 1959), Jackson illustrated how patients' symptoms preserve stability in their families. In one case, a young woman diagnosed as catatonic schizophrenic had as her most prominent symptom a profound indecisiveness. When she did act decisively, her parents fell apart. Her mother became helpless and her father became impotent. In one family meeting, her parents failed to notice when the patient made a simple decision. Only after listening to a taped replay of the session *three times* did the parents finally hear their daughter's statement. This woman's indecision was neither crazy nor senseless; rather, it protected her parents from facing their own conflicts. This is one of the earliest published examples of how even psychotic symptoms can be meaningful in the family context. This article also contains the shrewd observation that children's symptoms are often an exaggerated version of their parents' problems.

Another construct important to Jackson's thinking was the distinction between *complementary* and *symmetrical* relationships. (Like so many of the seminal ideas of family therapy, this one was first articulated by Bateson.) **Complementary relationships** are those in which partners are different in ways that fit together, like pieces of a jigsaw puzzle: If one is logical, the other is emotional; if one is weak, the other is strong. **Symmetrical relationships** are based on similarity. Marriages between two people who both have careers and share housekeeping chores are symmetrical. (Incidentally, if you actually find a couple who shares responsibilities equally, you'll know you're not in Kansas, Dorothy!)

Jackson's (1965) **family rules** hypothesis was based on the observation that within any committed unit (dyad, triad, or larger group), there are redundant behavior patterns. Rules (as students of philosophy learn when studying determinism) can describe regularity, rather than regulation. A corollary of the rules hypothesis is that family members use only a fraction of the full range of behavior available to them. This seemingly innocent fact is what makes family therapy so useful.

Jackson's therapeutic strategies were based on the premise that psychiatric problems resulted from the way people behave with each other. In order to distinguish functional interactions from those that were dysfunctional (*problem maintaining*), he observed when problems occurred and in what context, who was present, and how people responded to the problem. Given the assumption that symptoms are homeostatic mechanisms, Jackson would wonder out loud how a family might be worse off if the problem got solved. An individual might want to get better, but the family may need someone to play the sick role. Even positive change can be a threat to the defensive order of things.

A father's drinking, for example, might keep him from making demands on his wife or disciplining his children. Unfortunately, some family therapists jumped from the observation that symptoms may serve a purpose to the assumption that some families *need* a sick member, which, in turn, led to a view of parents victimizing **scapegoated** children. Despite the fancy language, this was part of the time-honored tradition of blaming parents for the failings of their children. If a six-year-old misbehaves around the house, perhaps we should look to his parents. But a husband's drinking isn't necessarily his wife's fault; and it certainly wasn't fair to imply that parents were responsible for the schizophrenic symptoms of their children.

◆ ◆ ◆

Don Jackson described problematic patterns of communication in ways that are still useful.

Courtesy of Don Jackson

The great discovery of the Bateson group was that there's no such thing as a simple communication; every message is qualified by a different message on another level. In *Strategies of Psychotherapy*, Jay Haley (1963) explored how covert messages are used in the struggle for control that characterizes many relationships. Symptoms, he argued, represent an incongruence between levels of communication. The symptomatic person does something, such as touching a doorknob six times before turning it, while at the same time denying that he's *really* doing it. He can't help it; it's his illness. Meanwhile, the person's symptoms—over which he has no control—have consequences. A person who has a compulsion of such proportions can hardly be expected to hold down a job, can he?

Since symptomatic behavior wasn't reasonable, Haley didn't try to reason with patients to help them. Instead, therapy became a strategic game of cat and mouse.

Haley (1963) defined therapy as a directive form of treatment and acknowledged his debt to Milton Erickson, with whom he studied hypnosis. In what he called *brief therapy*, Haley zeroed in on the context and possible function of a patient's symptoms. His first moves were designed to gain control of the therapeutic relationship. Haley cited Erickson's device of advising patients that in the first interview there will be things they may be willing to say and other things they'll want to withhold, and that these, of course, should be withheld. Here, of course, the therapist is directing patients to do precisely what they would do anyway and thus subtly gaining the upper hand.

The decisive techniques in brief therapy were *directives*. As Haley put it, it isn't enough to explain problems to patients; what counts is getting them to *do* something about them.

One of Haley's patients was a freelance photographer who compulsively made silly blunders that ruined every picture. Eventually he became so preoccupied with avoiding mistakes that he was too nervous to take pictures at all. Haley instructed the man to go out and take three pictures, making one deliberate error in each. The paradox here is that you can't accidentally make a mistake if you are doing so deliberately.

In another case, Haley told an insomniac that if he woke up in the middle of the night he should get out of bed and wax the kitchen floor. Instant cure! The cybernetic principle here: People will do anything to get out of housework.

Another member of the Palo Alto group who played a leading role in family therapy's first decade was Virginia Satir, one of the great charismatic healers. Known more for her clinical artistry than for theoretical contributions, Satir's impact was most vivid to those lucky enough to see her in action. Like her confreres, Satir was interested in communication, but she added an emotional dimension that helped counterbalance what was otherwise a relatively cool and calculated approach.

Satir saw troubled family members as trapped in narrow roles, such as *victim, placator, defiant one*, or *rescuer*, that limited options and sapped self-esteem. Her concern with freeing family members from the grip of such life-constricting roles was consistent with her major focus, which was always on the individual. Thus, Satir was a humanizing force in the early days of family therapy, when others were so enamored of the systems metaphor that they neglected the emotional life of families.

Satir was justly famous for her ability to turn negatives into positives. In one case, cited by Lynn Hoffman (1981), Satir interviewed the family of a local minister, whose teenage son had gotten two of his classmates pregnant. On one side of the room sat the boy's parents and siblings. The boy sat in the opposite corner with his head down. Satir introduced herself and said to the boy, "Well, your father has told me a lot about the situation on the phone, and I just want to say before we begin that we know one thing for sure: We know you have good seed." The boy looked up in amazement as Satir turned to the boy's mother and asked brightly, "Could you start by telling us your perception?"

◆ Murray Bowen

Like many of the founders of family therapy, Murray Bowen was a psychiatrist who specialized in schizophrenia. Unlike others, however, he emphasized theory, and to this day Bowen's theory is the most fertile system of ideas in family therapy.

Bowen began his clinical work at the Menninger Clinic in 1946, where he studied mothers and their schizophrenic children. His major interest at the time was mother–child symbiosis, which led to his concept of **differentiation of self** (autonomy and levelheadedness). From Menninger, Bowen moved to NIMH, where he developed a program to hospitalize whole families with schizophrenic members. This project expanded the focus on mother–child symbiosis to include the role of fathers and led to the concept of *triangles* (diverting conflict between two people by involving a third).

Beginning in 1955, when Bowen started bringing family members together to discuss their problems, he was struck by their **emotional reactivity**. Feelings overwhelmed reason. Bowen felt families' tendency to pull him into the center of this **undifferentiated family ego mass**, and he had to make a concerted effort to remain objective (Bowen, 1961). The ability to remain neutral and focus on the process, rather than content, of family discussions is what distinguishes a therapist from a participant in a family's drama.

To control the level of emotion, Bowen encouraged family members to talk to him, not to each other. He found that it was easier for family members to avoid becoming reactive when they spoke to the therapist instead of to each other.

Bowen discovered that therapists weren't immune to being sucked into family conflicts. This awareness led to his greatest insight: Whenever two people are struggling with conflict they can't resolve, there is an automatic tendency to involve a third party. In fact, as Bowen came to believe, a **triangle** is the smallest stable unit of relationship.

A husband who can't stand his wife's habitual lateness but is afraid to say so may start complaining to his children. His complaining may let off steam, but the very process of complaining to a third party makes him less likely to address the problem at its source. We all complain about other people from time to time, but what Bowen realized was that this triangling process is destructive when it becomes a regular feature of a relationship.

Another thing Bowen discovered about triangles is that they spread out. In the following case, a family became entangled in a whole labyrinth of triangles.

CASE STUDY

One Sunday morning "Mrs. McNeil," who was anxious to get the family to church on time, yelled at her nine-year-old son to hurry up. When he told her to "quit bitching," she slapped him. At that point her fourteen-year-old daughter, Megan, grabbed her, and the two of them started wrestling. Then Megan ran next door to her friend's house. When the friend's parents noticed that she had a cut lip and Megan told them what had happened, they called the police.

One thing led to another, and by the time the family came to therapy, the following triangles were in place: Mrs. McNeil, who'd been ordered out of the house by the family court judge, was allied with her lawyer against the judge; she also had an individual therapist who joined her in thinking she was being harassed by the child-protective workers. The nine-year-old was still mad at his mother, and his father supported him in blaming her for flying off the handle. Mr. McNeil, who was a recovering alcoholic, formed an alliance with his sponsor, who felt that Mr. McNeil was on his way to a breakdown unless his wife started being more supportive. Meanwhile Megan had formed a triangle with the neighbors, who thought her parents shouldn't be allowed to have children. In short, everyone had an advocate—everyone, that is, except the family unit.

In 1966 an emotional crisis in Bowen's family led to a personal voyage of discovery that turned out to be as significant for Bowen's theory as Freud's self-analysis was for psychoanalysis.

As an adult, Bowen, the oldest of five children from a tightly knit rural family, kept his distance from his parents and the rest of his extended family. Like many of us, he mistook avoidance for emancipation. But as he later realized, unfinished emotional business stays with us, making us vulnerable to repeat conflicts we never worked out with our families.

Bowen's most important achievement was detriangling himself from his parents, who'd been accustomed to complaining to him about each other. Most of us are flattered to receive such confidences, but Bowen came to recognize this triangulation for what it was. When his mother complained about his father, he told his father: "Your wife told me a story about you; I wonder why she told me instead of you." Naturally, his father mentioned this to his mother, and, naturally, she was not pleased.

Although his efforts generated the kind of emotional upheaval that comes of breaking family rules, Bowen's maneuver was effective in keeping his parents from trying to get him to take sides—and made it harder for them to avoid discussing things between themselves. Repeating what someone says to you about someone else is one way to stop triangling in its tracks.

Through his efforts in his own family Bowen discovered that *differentiation of self* is best accomplished by developing personal relationships with as many members of the family as possible. If visiting is difficult, letters and phone calls can help reestablish relationships, particularly if they're personal and intimate. Differentiating one's self from the family is completed when these relationships are maintained without becoming emotionally reactive or taking part in triangles.

◆ Nathan Ackerman

Nathan Ackerman was a child psychiatrist whose pioneering work with families remained faithful to his psychoanalytic roots. Although his interest in intrapsychic conflict may have seemed less innovative than the Palo Alto group's communications theory, he had a keen sense of the overall organization of families. Families, Ackerman said, may give the appearance of unity, but underneath they are split into competing factions. This you may recognize as similar to the psychoanalytic model of individuals, who, despite apparent unity of personality, are actually minds in conflict, driven by warring drives and defenses.

Ackerman joined the staff at the Menninger Clinic and in 1937 became chief psychiatrist of the Child Guidance Clinic. At first he followed the child guidance model of having a psychiatrist treat the child and a social worker see the mother. But by the mid-1940s, he began to experiment with having the same therapist see both. Unlike Bowlby, Ackerman did more than use these conjoint sessions as a temporary expedient; instead, he began to see the family as the basic unit of treatment.

In 1955 Ackerman organized the first session on family diagnosis at a meeting of the American Orthopsychiatric Association. At that meeting, Jackson, Bowen, Wynne, and Ackerman learned about each other's work and joined in a sense of common purpose. Two years later Ackerman opened the Family Mental Health Clinic of Jewish Family Services in New York City and began teaching at Columbia University. In 1960 he founded the Family Institute, which was renamed the Ackerman Institute following his death in 1971.

Although other family therapists downplayed the psychology of individuals, Ackerman was as concerned with what goes on inside people as with what goes on between them. He never lost sight of feelings, hopes, and desires. In fact, Ackerman's model of the family was like the psychoanalytic model of individuals writ large; instead of conscious and unconscious issues, Ackerman talked about how families confront some issues while avoiding others, particularly those involving sex and aggression. He saw his job as bringing family secrets into the open.

To encourage families to relax their emotional restraint, Ackerman himself was unrestrained. He sided first with one member of a family and later with another. He didn't think it was necessary—or possible—to always be neutral; instead, he believed that balance was achieved in the long run by moving back and forth, giving support now to one, later to another family member. At times he was unabashedly blunt. If he thought someone was lying, he said so. To critics who suggested this directness might generate too much anxiety, Ackerman replied that people get more reassurance from honesty than from false politeness.

◆ Carl Whitaker

Even among the iconoclastic founders of family therapy, Carl Whitaker stood out as the most irreverent. His view of psychologically troubled people was that they were alienated from feeling and frozen into devitalized routines (Whitaker & Malone, 1953). Whitaker turned up the heat. His "*Psychotherapy of the Absurd*" (Whitaker, 1975) was a blend of warm support and emotional goading, designed to loosen people up and help them get in touch with their experience in a deeper, more personal way.

Given his inventive approach to individual therapy, it wasn't surprising that Whitaker became one of the first to experiment with family treatment. In 1943 he and John Warkentin, working in Oak Ridge, Tennessee, began to include spouses and eventually children in treatment. Whitaker also pioneered the use of cotherapy, in the belief that a supportive partner helped free therapists to react without fear of countertransference.

Whitaker never seemed to have an obvious strategy, nor did he use predictable techniques, preferring, as he said, to let his unconscious run the therapy (Whitaker, 1976). Although his work seemed totally spontaneous, even outrageous at times, there was a consistent theme. All of his interventions promoted flexibility. He didn't so much push families to change in a particular direction as he challenged them to open up—to become more fully themselves and more fully together.

In 1946 Whitaker became chairman of the department of psychiatry at Emory University, where he continued to experiment with family treatment with a special interest in schizophrenics and their families. During this period Whitaker organized a series of forums that eventually led to the first major convention of the family therapy movement. Beginning in 1946 Whitaker and his colleagues began twice-yearly conferences during which they observed and discussed each other's work with families. The group found these sessions enormously helpful, and mutual observation, using one-way vision screens, became one of the hallmarks of family therapy.

Whitaker resigned from Emory in 1955 and entered private practice, where he and his partners at the Atlanta Psychiatric Clinic developed an *experiential* form of psychotherapy, using a number of provocative techniques in the treatment of families, individuals, groups, and couples (Whitaker, 1958).

During the late 1970s Whitaker seemed to mellow and added a greater understanding of family dynamics to his shoot-from-the-hip interventions. In the process, the former wild man of family therapy became one of its elder statesmen. Whitaker's death in April 1995 left the field with a piece of its heart missing.

◆ Ivan Boszormenyi-Nagy

Ivan Boszormenyi-Nagy, who came to family therapy from psychoanalysis, was one of the seminal thinkers in the movement. In 1957 he founded the Eastern Pennsylvania Psychiatric Institute in Philadelphia, where he attracted a host of highly talented colleagues. Among these were James Framo, one of the few psychologists in the early family therapy movement, and Geraldine Spark, a social worker who collaborated with Boszormenyi-Nagy on *Invisible Loyalties* (Boszormenyi-Nagy & Spark, 1973).

Boszormenyi-Nagy went from being an analyst, prizing confidentiality, to a family therapist, dedicated to openness. One of his most important contributions was to add ethical accountability to the usual therapeutic goals and techniques. According to Boszormenyi-Nagy, neither pleasure nor expediency is a sufficient guide to human behavior. Instead, he believed that family members have to base their relationships on trust and loyalty and that they must balance the ledger of entitlement and indebtedness. He died in 2008.

◆ Salvador Minuchin

When Minuchin first burst onto the scene, it was the drama of his clinical interviews that captivated people. This compelling man with the elegant Latin accent would seduce, provoke, bully, or bewilder families into changing—as the situation required. But even Minuchin's legendary flair didn't have the same galvanizing impact as the elegant simplicity of his structural model.

Minuchin began his career as a family therapist in the early 1960s when he discovered two patterns common to troubled families: Some are *enmeshed*—chaotic and tightly interconnected; others are *disengaged*—isolated and emotionally detached. Both lack clear lines of authority. Enmeshed parents are too close to their children to exercise leadership; disengaged parents are too distant to provide effective support.

Family problems are tenacious and resistant to change because they're embedded in powerful but unseen structures. Take, for example, a mother futilely remonstrating with a willful child. The mother can scold, punish, or reward, but as long as she's enmeshed (overly involved) with the child, her efforts will lack force because she lacks authority. Moreover, because the behavior of one family member is always related to that of others, the mother will have trouble stepping back as long as her husband remains uninvolved.

Once a social system such as a family becomes structured, attempts to change the rules constitute what family therapists call *first-order change*—change within a system that itself remains invariant. For the mother in the previous example to start practicing stricter discipline would be first-order change. The enmeshed mother is caught in an illusion of alternatives. She can be strict or lenient; the result is the same because she remains trapped in a triangle. What's needed is *second-order change*—a reorganization of the system itself.

Minuchin worked out his ideas while struggling with the problems of juvenile delinquency at the Wiltwyck School for Boys in New York. Family therapy with urban slum families was a new development, and publication of his discoveries (Minuchin, Montalvo, Guerney, Rosman, & Schumer, 1967) led to his becoming the director of the Philadelphia Child Guidance Clinic in 1965. Minuchin brought Braulio Montalvo and Bernice Rosman with him, and they were joined in 1967 by Jay Haley. Together they transformed a traditional child guidance clinic into one of the great centers of the family therapy movement.

In 1981 Minuchin moved to New York and established what is now known as the Minuchin Center for the Family, where he taught family therapists from all over the world. He also continued to turn out a steady stream of the most influential books in the field. His 1974 *Families and Family Therapy* is deservedly the most popular book in the history of family therapy, and his 1993 *Family Healing* contains some of the most moving descriptions of family therapy ever written.

◆ Other Early Centers of Family Therapy

In New York, Israel Zwerling and Marilyn Mendelsohn organized the Family Studies Section at Albert Einstein College of Medicine and Bronx State Hospital. Andrew Ferber was named director in 1964, and later Philip Guerin, a protégéof Murray Bowen's, joined the section. Nathan Ackerman served as a consultant, and the group assembled an impressive array of family therapists with diverse orientations. These included Chris Beels, Betty Carter, Monica McGoldrick, Peggy Papp, and Thomas Fogarty. Philip Guerin became director of training in 1970 and shortly thereafter founded the Center for Family Learning in Westchester, where he and Thomas Fogarty developed one of the finest family therapy training programs in the nation.

As we mentioned previously, Robert MacGregor and his colleagues in Galveston, Texas developed *multiple impact therapy* (MacGregor, 1967). It was a case of necessity being the mother of invention. MacGregor's clinic served a population scattered widely over southeastern Texas, and many of his clients had to travel hundreds of miles. Therefore, to have maximum impact in a short time, MacGregor assembled a team of professionals who worked intensively with the families for two full days. Although few family therapists have used such marathon sessions, the team approach continues to be one of the hallmarks of the field.

In Boston the two most significant early contributions to family therapy were both in the experiential wing of the movement. Norman Paul developed an *operational mourning* approach designed to resolve impacted grief, and Fred and Bunny Duhl set up the Boston Family Institute, where they developed *integrative family therapy*.

In Chicago, the Family Institute of Chicago and the Institute for Juvenile Research were important centers of the early scene in family therapy. At the Family Institute, Charles and Jan Kramer developed a clinical training program, which was later affiliated with Northwestern University Medical School. The Institute for Juvenile Research also mounted a training program under the leadership of Irv Borstein, with the consultation of Carl Whitaker.

The work of Nathan Epstein and his colleagues, first formulated in the department of psychiatry at McMaster University in Hamilton, Ontario, was a problem-centered approach (Epstein, Bishop, & Baldarin, 1981). The McMaster model goes step by step—elucidating the problem, gathering data, considering alternatives for resolution, and assessing the learning process—to help families understand their own interactions and build on their newly acquired coping skills. Epstein later relocated to Brown University in Rhode Island.

Important developments in family therapy also occurred outside the United States: Robin Skynner (1976) introduced psychodynamic family therapy at the Institute of Family Therapy in London; British psychiatrist John Howells (1971) developed a system of family diagnosis as a necessary step for planning therapeutic intervention; and West German Helm

Stierlin (1972) integrated psychodynamic and systemic ideas in treating troubled adolescents. In Rome, Maurizio Andolfi worked with families early in the 1970s and established a training clinic that continues to accept clients and students today. In 1974 Andolfi also founded the Italian Society for Family Therapy; in Milan Mara Selvini Palazzoli and her colleagues founded the Institute for Family Studies in 1967.

◆ ◆ ◆

Now that you've seen how family therapy emerged in several different places at once, we hope you haven't lost sight of one thing: There is a tremendous satisfaction in seeing how people's behavior makes sense in the context of their families. Meeting with a family for the first time is like turning on a light in a dark room.

The Golden Age of Family Therapy

In their first decade, family therapists had all the bravado of new kids on the block. "Look at this!" Haley and Jackson and Bowen seemed to say when they discovered how the whole family was implicated in the symptoms of individual patients. While they were struggling for legitimacy, family clinicians emphasized their common beliefs and downplayed their differences. Troubles, they agreed, came in families. But if the watchword of the 1960s was "Look at this"—emphasizing the leap of understanding made possible by seeing whole families together—the rallying cry of the 1970s was "Look what I can do!" as the new kids flexed their muscles and carved out their own turf.

The period from 1970 to 1985 saw the flowering of the classic schools of family therapy as the pioneers established training centers and worked out the implications of their models. The leading approach to family therapy in the 1960s was the communications model developed in Palo Alto. The book of the decade was *Pragmatics of Human Communication*, the text that introduced the systemic version of family therapy. The model of the 1980s was strategic

therapy, and the books of the decade described its three most vital approaches: *Change* by Watzlawick, Weakland, and Fisch[1]; *Problem-Solving Therapy* by Jay Haley; and *Paradox and Counterparadox* by Mara Selvini Palazzoli and her Milan associates. The 1970s belonged to Salvador Minuchin. His *Families and Family Therapy* and the simple yet compelling model of *structural family therapy* it described dominated the decade.

Structural theory seemed to offer just what family therapists were looking for: a straightforward way of describing family organization and a set of easy-to-follow steps to treatment. In hindsight we might ask whether the impressive power of Minuchin's approach was a product of the method or the man. (The answer is, probably a little of both.) But in the 1970s the widely shared belief that structural family therapy could be easily learned drew people from all over the world to what was then the epicenter of the family therapy movement: the Philadelphia Child Guidance Clinic.

The strategic therapy that flourished in the 1980s was centered in three unique and creative groups: MRI's brief therapy group, including John Weakland, Paul Watzlawick, and Richard Fisch; Jay Haley and Cloe Madanes in Washington, DC; and Mara Selvini Palazzoli and her colleagues in Milan. But the leading influence on the decade of strategic therapy was exerted by Milton Erickson, albeit from beyond the grave.

Erickson's genius was much admired and much imitated. Family therapists came to idolize Erickson the way we as children idolized Captain Marvel. We'd come home from Saturday matinees all pumped up, get out our toy swords, put on our magic capes—and presto! *We* were superheroes. We were just kids and so we didn't bother translating our heroes' mythic powers into our own terms. Unfortunately, many of those starstruck by Erickson's legendary therapeutic tales did the same thing. Instead of grasping the principles on which they were predicated, many therapists just tried to imitate his "uncommon techniques." To be any kind of competent therapist, you must keep your psychological distance from the supreme

---

[1]Although actually published in 1974, this book and its sequel, *The Tactics of Change*, were most widely read in the 1980s.

artists—the Minuchins, the Milton Ericksons, the Michael Whites. Otherwise you end up aping the magic of their styles, rather than grasping the substance of their ideas.

Part of what made Haley's strategic directives so attractive was that they were a wonderful way to gain control over people—for their own good—without the usual frustration of trying to convince them to do the right thing. (Most people know what's good for them. The hard part is getting them to *do* it.) So, for example, in the case of a person who is bulimic, a strategic directive might be for the patient's family to set out a mess of fried chicken, french fries, cookies, and ice cream. Then, with the family watching, the patient would mash up all the food with her hands, symbolizing what goes on in her stomach. After the food was reduced to a soggy mess, she would stuff it into the toilet. Then when the toilet clogged, she would have to ask the family member she resented most to unclog it. This task would symbolize not only what the person with bulimia does to herself but also what she puts the family through (Madanes, 1981).

What the strategic camp added to Erickson's creative approach to problem solving was a simple framework for understanding how families got stuck in their problems. According to the MRI model, problems develop from mismanagement of ordinary life difficulties. The original difficulty becomes a problem when mishandling leads people to get stuck in more-of-the-same solutions. It was a perverse twist on the old adage, "If at first you don't succeed, try, try again."

The Milan group built on the ideas pioneered at MRI, especially the use of the therapeutic double bind, or what they referred to as *counterparadox*. Here's an example from *Paradox and Counterparadox* (Selvini Palazzoli, Boscolo, Cecchin, & Prata, 1978). The authors describe a counterparadoxical approach to a six-year-old boy and his family. At the end of the session, young Bruno was praised for acting crazy to protect his father. By occupying his mother's time with fights and tantrums, the boy generously allowed his father more time for work and relaxation. Bruno was encouraged to continue doing what he was already doing, lest this comfortable arrangement be disrupted.

The appeal of the strategic approach was pragmatism. Making use of the cybernetic metaphor, strategic therapists zeroed in on how family systems were regulated by negative feedback. They achieved results simply by disrupting the interactions that maintained symptoms. What eventually turned therapists off to these approaches was their gamesmanship. Their interventions were transparently manipulative. The result was like watching a clumsy magician—you could see him stacking the deck.

Meanwhile, as structural and strategic approaches rose and fell in popularity, four other models of family therapy flourished quietly. Though they never took center stage, *experiential, psychoanalytic, behavioral*, and *Bowenian* models grew and prospered. Although these schools never achieved the cachet of family therapy's latest fads, each of them produced solid clinical approaches, which will be examined at length in subsequent chapters.

Summary

For many years therapists resisted the idea of seeing patients' families in order to safeguard the privacy of the therapeutic relationship. Freudians excluded the real family to uncover the unconscious, introjected family; Rogerians kept the family away to provide unconditional positive regard; and hospital psychiatrists discouraged family visits lest they disrupt the benign milieu of the hospital.

Several converging developments in the 1950s led to a new view—namely, that the family was an organic whole. Although clinicians in hospitals and child guidance clinics prepared the way for family therapy, the most important breakthroughs were achieved in the 1950s by people who were scientists first, healers second. In Palo Alto, Gregory Bateson, Jay Haley, and Don Jackson discovered that schizophrenia made sense in the context of pathological family communication. Schizophrenics weren't crazy in some meaningless way; their behavior made sense in their families. Murray Bowen's observation of how mothers and their schizophrenic offspring go through cycles of closeness and distances was the forerunner of the *pursuer–distancer* dynamic.

These observations launched the family therapy movement, but the excitement they generated blurred the distinction between what researchers observed and what they concluded. What they observed was that the behavior of schizophrenics *fit* with their families; what they concluded was that the family was the *cause* of schizophrenia. A second conclusion was even more influential. Family dynamics—double binds, pseudomutuality, undifferentiated family ego mass—began to be seen as products of a system, rather than features of persons who share certain qualities because they live together. Thus was born a new creature, the *family system.*

Who was the first to practice family therapy? This turns out to be a difficult question. As in every field, there were visionaries who anticipated the development of family therapy. Freud, for example, treated "Little Hans" by working with his father as early as 1909. Such experiments weren't, however, sufficient to challenge the authority of individual therapy until the climate of the times was receptive. In the early 1950s family therapy was begun independently in four different places: by John Bell at Clark University, Murray Bowen at NIMH, Nathan Ackerman in New York, and Don Jackson and Jay Haley in Palo Alto.

These pioneers had distinctly different backgrounds. Not surprisingly, the approaches they developed were also quite different. This diversity still characterizes the field today. In addition to those just mentioned, others who made significant contributions to the founding of family therapy were Virginia Satir, Carl Whitaker, Ivan Boszormenyi-Nagy, and Salvador Minuchin.

What we've called family therapy's golden age—the flowering of the schools in the 1970s and 1980s—was the high-water mark of our self-confidence. Armed with Haley's or Minuchin's latest text, therapists set off with a sense of mission. What drew them to activist approaches was certainty and charisma. What soured them was hubris. To some, structural family therapy—at least as they saw it demonstrated at workshops—looked like bullying. Others saw the cleverness of the strategic approach as manipulative. Families were described as stubborn; they couldn't be reasoned with. Therapists got tired of that way of thinking.

In the early years, family therapists were animated by confidence and conviction. Today, in the wake of managed care and biological psychiatry, we're less sure of ourselves.

Although we may be less cocky, we are certainly more effective (Sexton & Datachi, 2014). While the early years were dominated by creative ideas (e.g., Haley, 1962), the field today focuses more on effective interventions (e.g., Nichols & Tafuri, 2013). Much has been learned about families and family systems. Methods have been refined (Minuchin, Reiter, & Borda, 2014). What has emerged is "a more participatory, more culturally and gender sensitive, and more collaborative set of methods that builds on a set of common factors with a stronger evidence base" (Lebow, 2014, p. 368).

In subsequent chapters we'll see how today's family therapists have managed to synthesize creative new ideas with some of the best of the earlier models. But as we explore each of the famous models in depth, we'll also see how some good ideas have been unwisely neglected.

All the complexity of the family therapy field should not obscure its basic premise: The family is the context of human problems. Like all human groups, the family has emergent properties—the whole is greater than the sum of its parts. Moreover, no matter how many and varied the explanations of these emergent properties are, they all fall into two categories: *structure* and *process.* The structure of families includes *triangles, subsystems*, and *boundaries.* Among the processes that describe family interaction—*emotional reactivity, dysfunctional communication*, and so on—the central concept is *circularity.* Rather than worrying about who started what, family therapists treat human problems as a series of moves and countermoves in repeating cycles.

Click here to apply your knowledge of chapter concepts.

Click here to test your application and analysis of the content found within this chapter.

Getting Started

◆ The Initial Telephone Call

The goal of the initial contact is to get an overview of the presenting problem and arrange for the family to come for a consultation. Listen to the caller's description of the problem and identify all members of the household as well as others who might be involved (including the referral source and other agencies). Although the initial phone call should be brief, it's important to establish a connection with the caller as a basis for engagement. Then schedule the first interview, specifying who should attend (usually everyone in the household) and the time and place.

While there are things you can say to encourage the whole family to attend, the most important consideration is attitudinal. First, understand and respect that the worried mother who wants you to treat her child individually or the unhappy husband who wants to talk to you alone has a perfectly legitimate point of view, even if it doesn't happen to coincide with your own. But if you expect to meet with the entire family, at least for an initial assessment, a matter-of-fact statement that that's how you work will get most families to agree to a consultation.

When the caller presents the problem as limited to one person, a useful way to broaden the focus is to ask how the problem is affecting other members of the family. If the caller balks at the idea of bringing in the family or says that a particular member won't attend, say that you'll need to hear from everyone, at least initially, in order to get as much information as possible. Most people accept the need to give their point of view; what they resist is the implication that they're to blame.[1]

---

[1]Not all therapists routinely meet with the whole family. Some find that they have more room to maneuver by meeting first with individuals or subgroups and then gradually involving others. Others attempt to work with the *problem-determined system*, only those people directly involved. Still others try to determine who are the "customers," those who seem most concerned. The point to remember is that family therapy is more a way of looking at things than a technique that always requires seeing the entire family together.

CHAPTER 2

BASIC TECHNIQUES OF FAMILY THERAPY

From Symptom to System

LEARNING OUTCOMES

- ◆ Discuss and demonstrate the basic skills required for the initial client contact and interview, the early and middle phases of treatment, and termination.

- ◆ Describe the basic issues for which to assess when working with families, and summarize techniques for doing so.

- ◆ Discuss the basic ethical responsibilities of family therapy.

- ◆ Describe principles guiding work with marital violence and the sexual abuse of children.

- ◆ Describe the basics of working with managed care and establishing a private practice.

The initial phone contact should be relatively brief to avoid developing an alliance with just one family member.

Finally, because most families are reluctant to sit down and face their conflicts, a reminder call before the first session helps cut down on the no-show rate.

◆ The First Interview

The goal of the first interview is to build an alliance with the family and develop a hypothesis about what's maintaining the presenting problem. It's a good idea to come up with a tentative hypothesis (in technical terms, a hunch) after the initial phone call and then test it in the first interview. (Remain open to refuting, not just confirming, your initial hypothesis.) The point isn't to jump to conclusions but to start actively thinking.

The primary objectives of a consultation are to establish rapport and gather information. Introduce yourself to the contact person and then to the other adults. Ask parents to introduce their children. Shake hands and greet everyone. Orient the family to the room (observation mirrors, videotaping, toys for children) and to the format of the session (length and purpose). Repeat briefly what the caller told you over the phone (so as not to leave others wondering), and then ask for elaboration. Once you've acknowledged that person's point of view ("So what you're saying is . . .?"), ask the other members of the family for their viewpoints.

One of the things beginning therapists worry about is that bringing in the whole family may lead to a shouting match that will escalate out of control. The

antidote to arguing is insisting that family members speak one at a time. Giving everyone a chance to talk and be heard is a good idea in every case; with emotionally reactive families, it's imperative.

Most families are anxious and uncertain about therapy. They're not sure what to expect, and they may be uncomfortable discussing their concerns in front of the whole family. And above all, most people are afraid that someone is going to blame them or expect them to change in ways they aren't prepared to. For these reasons, it's important to establish a bond of sympathy and understanding with every member of the family.

A useful question to ask each person is, "How did *you* feel about coming in?" This helps establish the therapist as someone willing to listen. If, for example, a child says "I didn't want to come" or "I think it's stupid," you can say "Thanks for being honest."

While most of the first session should be taken up with a discussion of the presenting problem, this problem-centered focus can have a disheartening effect. Spending some time exploring family members' interests and accomplishments is never wasted and sometimes dramatically changes the emotional energy of sessions. People need to be seen as more than just problems (the distant father, the rebellious teenager); they need to be seen as three-dimensional human beings.

Bringing in the whole family means including young children. The presence of the children allows you to see how their parents relate to them. Are the parents able to get the children to play quietly in the corner if you ask them to? Do they overmanage minor squabbles between siblings? Do both parents interact with the children or only the mother? Children of about five and under should be provided with toys. The inhibited child who is fearful of the family's disapproval will sit quietly on a chair and may be afraid to play. The aggressive child will attack the toys and play violent games. The anxious child will flit around the room, unable to settle on any one thing. The enmeshed child will frequently interrupt the parents' conversation with the therapist.

In gathering information, some therapists find it useful to take a family history, and many use **genograms** to diagram the extended family network (see Chapter 4). Others believe that whatever history is important will emerge in the natural course of events; they prefer to concentrate on the family's presenting complaint and the circumstances surrounding it.

Family therapists develop hypotheses about how family members might be involved in the presenting problem by asking what they've done to try to solve it and by watching how they interact. Ideas are as important as actions, so it's useful to notice unhelpful explanations of problems as well as unproductive interactions.

Two kinds of information that are particularly important are solutions that don't work and transitions in the life cycle. If whatever a family has been doing to resolve their difficulties hasn't worked, it may be that those attempts are part of the problem. A typical example is overinvolved parents trying to help a shy child make friends by coaxing and criticizing him. Sometimes family members will say they've "tried everything." Their mistake is inconsistency. They give up too quickly.

Despite the natural tendency to focus on problems and what causes them, it is a family's strengths, not their weaknesses, that are most important in successful therapy. Therefore, the therapist should search for resilience (Walsh, 1998). What have these people done well? How have they handled problems successfully in the past? Even the most discouraged families have been successful at times, but those positive episodes may be obscured by the frustration they feel over their current difficulties.

Although it isn't always apparent (especially to them), most families seek treatment because they have failed to adjust to changing circumstances. If a couple develops problems within a few months after a baby's birth, it may be because they haven't shifted effectively from being a unit of two to a unit of three. A young mother may be depressed because she doesn't have enough support. A young father may be jealous of the attention his wife lavishes on the baby.

Although the strain of having a new baby may seem obvious, it's amazing how often depressed young mothers are treated as though there were something wrong with them—"unresolved dependency needs," "inability to cope," or perhaps a Prozac deficiency. The same is true when families develop problems around the time a child starts school, enters

Monkey Business Images/Corbis

The challenge of first interviews is to develop an alliance without accepting at face value the family's description of one person as the problem.

adolescence, or reaches some other developmental milestone. The transitional demands on the family are obvious, *if* you think about them.

Young therapists may have no experience with some of the challenges their clients are facing. This underscores the need to remain curious and respectful of families' predicaments rather than jumping to conclusions. For example, a young therapist couldn't understand why so many clients with young children rarely went out together as a couple. He assumed that they were avoiding being alone together. Later, with small children of his own, he began to wonder how those couples got out at all!

Family therapists explore the process of family interaction by asking questions about how family members relate to each other and by inviting them to discuss their problems with one another in the session. The first strategy, asking *process* or *circular* questions, is favored by Bowenians, and the second, by structural therapists. In either case, the question is, What's keeping the family stuck?

Once a therapist has met with a family, explored the problem that brings them to treatment, made an effort to understand the family's context, and formulated a hypothesis about what needs to be done to resolve the problem, he or she should make a recommendation to the family. This might include consulting another professional (a learning disability expert, a physician, a lawyer) or even suggesting that the family doesn't need—or doesn't seem ready for—treatment. Most often, however, the recommendation will be for further meetings. Although many therapists try to make recommendations at the end of the first interview, doing so may be hasty. If it takes two or three sessions to form a bond with the family, understand their situation, and assess the feasibility of working with them, then take two or three sessions.

If you think you can help the family with their problems, offer them a *treatment contract*. Acknowledge why they came in, say that it was a good idea, and say that you think you can help. Then establish a meeting time, the frequency and length of sessions, who will attend, the presence of observers or use of videotape, the fee, and how insurance will be handled. Remember that resistance doesn't magically disappear after the first (or fourteenth) session. Stress the importance of keeping appointments, the need for

everyone to attend, and your willingness to hear concerns about you or the therapy. Finally, don't forget to emphasize the family's goals and the strengths they have to meet them.

First Session Checklist

1. Make contact with each member of the family, and acknowledge his or her point of view about the problem and feelings about coming to therapy.

2. Establish leadership by controlling the structure and pace of the interview.

3. Develop a working alliance with the family by balancing warmth and professionalism.

4. Compliment clients on positive actions and family strengths.

5. Maintain empathy with individuals and respect for the family's way of doing things.

6. Focus on specific problems and attempted solutions.

7. Develop hypotheses about unhelpful interactions around the presenting problem. Be curious about why these have persisted. Also notice helpful interactions that can support the family in moving forward.

8. Don't overlook the possible involvement of family members, friends, or helpers who aren't present.

9. Offer a treatment contract that acknowledges the family's goals and specifies the therapist's framework for structuring treatment.

10. Invite questions.

◆ The Early Phase of Treatment

The early phase of treatment is devoted to refining the initial hypothesis into a formulation about what's maintaining the problem and beginning to work on resolving it. Now the strategy shifts from building alliances to challenging actions and assumptions. Most therapists are able to figure out what needs to change; what sets good therapists apart is their willingness to push for those changes.

"Pushing for change" may suggest a confrontational style. But what's required to bring about change isn't any particular way of working; rather, it is a relentless commitment to helping make things better. This commitment is evident in Michael White's dogged questioning of problem-saturated stories, Phil Guerin's calm insistence that family members stop blaming each other and start looking at themselves, and Virginia Goldner's determined insistence that violent men take responsibility for their behavior.

No matter what techniques a therapist uses to push for change, it's important to maintain a therapeutic alliance. Although the term *therapeutic alliance* may sound like jargon, there's nothing abstract about it. It means listening to and acknowledging the client's point of view. It is this empathic understanding that makes family members feel respected—and makes them open to accepting challenges.

Regardless of what model they follow, effective therapists are persistent in their pursuit of change. This doesn't just mean perseverance. It means being willing to intervene, at times energetically. Some therapists prefer to avoid confrontation and find it more effective to use gentle questions or persistent encouragement. Regardless of whether they work directly (and at times use confrontation) or indirectly (and avoid it), good therapists are finishers. Strategies vary, but what sets the best therapists apart is their commitment to doing what it takes to see families through to successful resolution of their problems.

Effective family therapy addresses interpersonal conflict, and the first step in doing so is to bring it into the consulting room and locate it between family members. Often this isn't a problem. Couples in conflict or parents arguing with their children usually speak right up about their disagreements. If a family only came because someone sent them (the court, the school, the Department of Protective Services), begin by addressing the family's problem with these agencies. How must the family change to resolve their conflict with these authorities?

When one person is presented as the problem, a therapist challenges linearity by asking how others are involved (or affected). What role did others play in creating (or managing) the problem? How have they responded to it?

For example, a parent might say, "The problem is Malik. He's disobedient." The therapist might ask, "How does he get away with that?" or "How do you respond when he's disobedient?" A less confrontational therapist might ask, "How does his disobedience affect you?"

In response to a family member who says "It's me, I'm depressed," a therapist might ask "Who in the family is contributing to your depression?" The response "No one" would prompt the question, "Then who's helping you with it?"

Challenges can be blunt or gentle, depending on the therapist's style and assessment of the family. The point, incidentally, isn't to switch from blaming one person (a disobedient child, say) to another (a parent who doesn't discipline effectively) but to broaden the problem to an interactional one—to see the problem as shared and co-maintained. Maybe mother is too lenient with Malik because she finds father too strict. Moreover, she may be overinvested in the boy because of emotional distance in the marriage.

The best way to challenge unhelpful interactions is to point out patterns that seem to be keeping people stuck. A useful formula is "The more you do X, the more he does Y—and the more you do Y, the more she does X." (For X and Y, try substituting *nag* and *withdraw* or *control* and *rebel*.) Incidentally, when you point out what people are doing that isn't working, it's a mistake to then tell them what they *should* be doing. Once you shift from pointing out something to giving advice, the client's attention shifts from their own behavior to you and your advice.[2] Consider this exchange:

Therapist: When you ignore your wife's complaints, she feels hurt and angry. You may have trouble accepting the anger, but she doesn't feel supported.

Client: What should I do?

Therapist: I don't know. Ask your wife.

Even though family therapists sometimes challenge assumptions or actions, they continue to listen to people's feelings. Listening is a silent activity, rare in our time, even among therapists. Family members seldom listen to each other for long without becoming

---

[2]Being anxious to change people is one of the two greatest handicaps for a therapist. (The other is the need to be liked.) Being attached to what *should be* distracts a therapist from figuring out what *is*—and it communicates a pressure that does the same thing to clients.

defensive. Unfortunately, therapists don't always listen, either—especially when they're eager to offer advice. But remember that people aren't likely to reconsider their assumptions until they've been heard and understood.

Homework can be used to test flexibility (simply seeing if it's carried out measures willingness to change), to make family members more aware of their role in problems (telling people just to notice something, without trying to change it, is often instructive), and to suggest new ways of relating. Typical homework assignments include suggesting that overinvolved parents hire a babysitter and go out together, having argumentative partners take turns talking about their feelings and listening to one another without saying anything (but noticing tendencies to become reactive), and having dependent family members practice spending time alone (or with someone outside the family) and doing more things for themselves. Homework assignments that are likely to generate conflict, such as negotiating house rules with teenagers, should be avoided. Difficult discussions should be saved for when the therapist can act as referee.

Early Phase Checklist

1. Identify major conflicts, and bring them into the consulting room.

2. Develop a hypothesis and refine it into a formulation about what the family is doing to perpetuate (or fail to resolve) the presenting problem. A formulation should consider process and structure, family rules, triangles, and boundaries.

3. Keep the focus on primary problems and the interpersonal conditions supporting them. But do not neglect to support constructive interactions.

4. Assign homework that addresses problems and the underlying structure and dynamics perpetuating them.

5. Challenge family members to see their own roles in the problems that trouble them.

6. Push for change, both during the session and between sessions at home.

7. Make use of supervision to test the validity of formulations and effectiveness of interventions.

◆ The Middle Phase of Treatment

When therapy is anything other than brief and problem focused, much of the middle phase is devoted to helping family members deal more constructively with each other in sessions. If a therapist is too active in this process—filtering all conversation through himself or herself—family members won't learn to deal with each other.

For this reason, in the middle phase the therapist should take a less active role and encourage family members to interact more with each other. As they do so, the therapist can step back and observe. When dialogue bogs down, the therapist can either point out what went wrong or simply encourage family members to keep talking—but with less interruption and criticism.

When family members address their conflicts directly, they tend to become reactive. Anxiety is the enemy of listening. Some therapists (e.g., Bowenians) attempt to control anxiety by having family members talk only to them. Others prefer to let family members deal with their own anxiety by helping them learn to talk with each other less defensively (by saying how they feel and acknowledging what others say). However, even therapists who work primarily with family dialogue need to interrupt when anxiety escalates and conversations become destructive.

Thus, in the middle phase of treatment, the therapist takes a less directive role and encourages family members to begin to rely on their own resources. The level of anxiety is regulated by alternating between having family members talk with each other or with the therapist. In either case the therapist encourages family members to get beyond trading blame to talking about what they feel and what they want—and to learn to see their own part in unproductive interactions.

What enables therapists to push for change without provoking resistance is an empathic bond with clients. We mentioned the working alliance in our discussion of the opening session, but it's such an important subject that we would like to re-emphasize it. Although there is no formula for developing good relationships with clients, four attitudes are important in maintaining a therapeutic alliance: calmness, curiosity, empathy, and respect.

Calmness on the part of the therapist is an essential antidote to the anxiety that keeps families from seeing their dilemmas in a broader perspective. Two things that enable a therapist to remain calm arc: (1) not taking responsibility for solving a family's problems, and (2) knowing where to look for the constraints that are keeping them from doing so. Letting go of the illusion that anyone but the clients can solve their problems allows a therapist to concentrate on the job at hand, which is helping clients *in the session* discover something new and useful. Calmness conveys confidence that problems, however difficult, can be solved.

Curiosity implies that the therapist doesn't know all the answers. The curious therapist says, in effect, "I don't fully understand, but I'd like to."

Empathy and respect have been reduced to clichés, but since we think both are essential, let us be clear about what we mean. People resist efforts to change them by therapists they feel don't understand them. That makes it difficult for therapists to get anywhere if they can't put themselves in their clients' shoes and get a sense of what the world looks like to them. Some therapists are all too ready to say "I understand" when they don't. You can't fake empathy.

Instead of telling an overprotective mother that you understand her worrying, be honest enough to ask, "How did you learn to be a worrier?" or say, "I've never been a single mom. Tell me what it is that scares you."

Finally, respect. What passes for respect in therapists isn't always sincere. Being respectful doesn't mean treating people with kid gloves, nor does it mean accepting their version of events as the only possible way to look at the situation. Respect means treating clients as equals, not patronizing them or deferring to them out of fear of making them angry. Respecting people means believing in their capacity for change.

Middle Phase Checklist

1. Use intensity to challenge family members, ingenuity to get around resistance, and empathy to reduce defensiveness.

2. Avoid being so directive that the family doesn't learn to improve their own ways of relating to each other.

3. Foster individual responsibility and mutual understanding.

4. Make certain that efforts to improve relationships are having a positive effect on the presenting complaint.

5. When meeting with subgroups, don't lose sight of the whole family picture, and don't neglect any individuals or relationships—especially those contentious ones that are so tempting to avoid.

6. Does the therapist take too active a role in choosing what to talk about? Have the therapist and family developed a social relationship that has become more important than addressing conflicts? Has the therapist assumed a regular role in the family (an empathic listener to the spouses or a parent figure to the children), substituting for a missing function in the family? When therapists find themselves drawn to taking an active response to family members' needs, they should ask themselves who in the family should be taking that role, and then encourage that person to do so.

◆ Termination

Termination comes for brief therapists as soon as the presenting problem is resolved. For psychoanalysts, therapy may continue for years. For most therapists, termination comes somewhere between these two extremes and has to do with a family feeling that they've achieved what they came for and the therapist's sense that treatment has reached a point of diminishing returns.

In individual therapy, where the relationship to the therapist is often the primary vehicle of change, termination focuses on reviewing the relationship and saying good-bye. In family therapy, the focus is more on what the family has been doing. Termination is therefore a good time to review what they've accomplished.

It can be helpful to ask clients to anticipate upcoming challenges: "How will you know when things are heading backward, and what will you do?" Families can be reminded that their present harmony can't be maintained indefinitely and that people have a tendency to overreact to the first sign of relapse, which can trigger a vicious cycle. To paraphrase Zorba the Greek, life *is* trouble. To be alive is to confront difficulties. The test is how you handle them.

Finally, although in the business of therapy no news is usually good news, it might be a good idea to check in with clients a few weeks after termination to see how they're doing. This can be done with a letter, e-mail, phone call, or brief follow-up session. A therapeutic relationship is of necessity somewhat artificial or at least constrained. But there's no reason to make it less than human—or to forget about families once you've terminated with them.

◆ Termination Checklist

1. Has the presenting problem improved?
2. Is the family satisfied that they have achieved what they came for, or are they interested in continuing to learn about themselves and improve their relationships?
3. Does the family understand what they were doing that wasn't working and how to avoid similar problems in the future?
4. Do minor recurrences of problems reflect the lack of resolution of some underlying dynamic or merely that the family has to readjust to function without the therapist?
5. Have family members developed and improved relationships outside the immediate family context as well as within it?

> ▶ Watch this video of a termination session with a woman in therapy who was attempting to stop using drugs so she could get her son back. What does the therapist do to help the client understand her progress?

Family Assessment

The reason we're reviewing assessment after the guidelines for treatment is that assessment is a complex subject, deserving more consideration than it usually gets.

◆ The Presenting Problem

Every first session presents the fundamental challenge of being a therapist: A group of unhappy strangers walks in and hands you their most difficult problem—and expects you to solve it.

> "My fifteen-year-old is failing tenth grade. What should I do?"
> "We never talk anymore. What's happened to our marriage?"
> "It's me. I'm depressed. Can you help me?"

There are land mines in these opening presentations: "What should we do?" "What's wrong with Johnny?" These people have been asking themselves these questions for some time, maybe years. And they usually have fixed ideas about what the answers are, even if they don't always agree. Furthermore, they have typically evolved strategies to deal with their problems, which they insist on repeating even if they haven't worked. In this, they are like a car stuck in the mud with wheels spinning, sinking deeper and deeper into the mire.

The stress of life's troubles makes for anxiety, and anxiety makes for inflexible thinking. And so families who come for therapy tend to hold tenaciously to their assumptions: "He (or she) is hyperactive, depressed, bipolar, insensitive, selfish, rebellious," or some other negative attribute that resides inside the complicated machinery of the stubborn human psyche. Even when the complaint is phrased in the form of "*We* don't communicate," there's usually an assumption of where the responsibility lies—and that somewhere is usually elsewhere.

Exploring the presenting symptom is the first step in helping families move from a sense of helplessness to an awareness of how by working together they can overcome their problems. It may seem obvious that the first consideration should be the presenting complaint. Nevertheless, it's worth emphasizing that inquiry into the presenting problem should be detailed and empathic. The minute some therapists hear that a family's problem is, say, misbehavior or poor communication, they're ready to jump into action. They know how to deal with misbehaving children and communication problems. But before therapists get started, they should realize that they're *not* dealing with misbehaving children or communication problems: rather, they're dealing with a unique instance of one of these difficulties.

In exploring the presenting complaint, the goal for a systemic therapist is to question the family's settled certainty about who has the problem and why. Therefore, the first challenge for a family therapist is to move families from *linear* ("It's Johnny") and *medical model* thinking ("He's hyperactive") to an *interactional* perspective. To initiate this shift, a therapist begins by asking about the presenting problem. But these inquiries are aimed not merely at getting details about the condition-as-described but to open up the family's entrenched beliefs about what is the problem and who has it.

Helpful questions convey respect for family members' feelings but skepticism about accepting the identified patient as the only problem in the family. Helpful questions continue to explore and open things up. Helpful questions invite new ways of seeing the problem, or the family generally. Unhelpful questions accept things as they are described and concentrate only on the identified patient. To be effective in this first stage, a therapist's attitude should be, "I don't fully understand, but I'm interested. I'm curious about the particular way you organize your life." A therapist who is too eager ingratiate himself or herself by saying, "Oh, yes, I understand," closes off exploration.

The next thing to explore is the family's attempts to deal with the problem: What have they tried? What's been helpful? What hasn't worked? Has anyone other than those present been involved in trying to help (or hinder) with these difficulties? This exploration makes room to discover how family members may be responding in ways that perpetuate the presenting problem. This isn't a matter of shifting blame—say, from a misbehaving child to an indulgent parent.[3] Nor do we mean to suggest that family problems are typically caused by how people treat the identified patient.

In fact, what family therapists call *circular causality* is a misnomer. The shift from linear to circular thinking not only expands the focus from individuals to patterns of interaction but also moves away from cause-and-effect explanations. Instead of

joining families in a logical but unproductive search for who started what, circular thinking suggests that problems are sustained by an ongoing series of actions and reactions. Who started it? It doesn't matter.

◆ Understanding the Referral Route

It's important for therapists to understand who referred their clients and why. What are their expectations? What expectations have they communicated to the family? It's important to know whether a family's participation is voluntary or coerced, whether all or only some of them recognize the need for treatment, and whether other agencies will be involved with the case.

When therapists make a family referral, they often have a particular agenda in mind.

CASE STUDY

A college student's counselor referred him and his family for treatment. The young man had uncovered a repressed memory of sexual abuse and assumed that it must have been his father. The family therapist was somehow supposed to mediate between the young man, who couldn't imagine who else might have been responsible for this vaguely remembered incident, and his parents, who vehemently denied that any such thing had ever happened.

Did the counselor expect confrontation, confession, and atonement? Some sort of negotiated agreement? What about the boy himself? It's best to find out.

It's also important to find out if clients have been in treatment elsewhere. If so, what happened? What did they learn about themselves or their family? What expectations or concerns did the previous therapy generate? It's even more important to find out if anyone in the family is currently in treatment. Few things are more likely to cause a stalemate than two therapists pulling in different directions.

◆ Identifying the Systemic Context

Regardless of who a therapist elects to work with, it's imperative to have a clear understanding of the interpersonal context of the problem. Who is in the

---

[3]It's always worth remembering that even actions that perpetuate problems usually have benign intentions. Most people are doing the best they can.

family? Are there important figures in the life of the problem who aren't present? Perhaps a live-in boyfriend? A grandmother who lives next door? Are other agencies involved? What is their input? Does the family see them as helpful?

Remember that family therapy is an approach to people in context. The most relevant context may be the immediate family, but families don't exist in a vacuum. It may be important to meet with the teachers and counselors of a child who's having trouble at school. There are even times when the family isn't the most important context. Sometimes, for example, a college student's depression has more to do with what's going on in the classroom or dormitory than with what's happening back home.

◆ Stage of the Life Cycle

Most families come to treatment not because there's something inherently wrong with them but because they've gotten stuck in a life-cycle transition (see Chapter 3). Sometimes this will be apparent. Parents may complain, for example, that they don't know what's gotten into Janey. She used to be such a good girl; but now that she's fourteen, she's become sullen and argumentative. (One reason parenting remains an amateur sport is that just when you think you've got the hang of it, the kids get a little older and throw you a whole new set of curves.) Adolescence is that stage in the **family life cycle** when young parents have to grow up and relax their grip on their children.

Sometimes it isn't obvious that a family is having trouble adjusting to a new stage in the life cycle. Couples who marry after living together for years may not anticipate how matrimony stirs up unconscious expectations about what it means to be a family. More than one couple has been surprised to discover a sharp falling off in their sex life after tying the knot. At other times, significant life-cycle changes occur in the grandparents' generation, and you won't always learn of these influences unless you ask.

Always consider life-cycle issues in formulating a case. One of the best questions a therapist can ask is, Why now?

◆ Family Structure

The simplest systemic context for a problem is an interaction between two parties. She nags and he withdraws. Parental control provokes adolescent rebellion, and vice versa. But sometimes a dyadic perspective doesn't take in the whole picture.

Family problems become entrenched because they're embedded in powerful but unseen structures. Regardless of what approach a therapist takes, it's wise to understand something about a family's **structure**. What are the **subsystems** and the nature of the **boundaries** between them? What is the status of the boundary around the couple or family? What **triangles** are present? Are individuals and subsystems protected by boundaries that allow them to operate without undue interference—but with access to support?

In enmeshed families, parents may intrude into sibling conflicts so regularly that brothers and sisters never learn to settle their own differences. In disengaged families, parents may not only refrain from interrupting sibling quarrels but also fail to offer sympathy and support for a child who feels bad about a sibling's treatment.

Here, too, there is a temporal dimension. If a wife goes back to work after years of staying home with the children, the parental subsystem is challenged to shift from a complementary to a symmetrical form. Whether or not family members complain directly about these strains, they're likely to be relevant.

◆ Communication

Although some couples come to therapy saying they have "communication problems" (usually meaning that one person won't do what the other one wants), working on communication has become a cliché in family therapy. Because communication is the vehicle of relationship, all therapists deal with it.

Although conflict doesn't magically disappear when family members start to listen to each other, it's unlikely that conflicts will get solved *before* people start to listen to each other (Nichols, 2009). If, after a session or two (and the therapist's encouragement), family members still seem unwilling to listen to each other, talk therapy will be an uphill battle.

Family members who learn to listen to each other with understanding often discover that they don't need to change each other (Jacobson & Christensen, 1996). Many problems can be solved, but the problem of living with other people who don't always see things the way you do isn't one of them.

Drug and Alcohol Abuse

The most common mistake novice therapists make regarding substance abuse is to overlook it. Substance abuse is especially common with people who are depressed or anxious. It's also associated with violence, abuse, and accidents. Although it may not be necessary to ask every client about drug and alcohol consumption, it's critical to inquire carefully if there's any suspicion that this may be a problem. Don't be too polite. Ask straightforward and specific questions.

Questions that may help to uncover problem drinking (Kitchens, 1994) include the following:

- Do you feel you are a normal drinker?
- How many drinks a day do you have?
- How often do you have six or more drinks?
- Have you ever awakened after a bout of drinking and been unable to remember part of the day or evening before?
- Does anyone in your family worry or complain about your drinking?
- Can you stop easily after one or two drinks? Do you?
- Has drinking ever created problems between you and your partner?
- Have you ever gotten into trouble at work because of your drinking?
- Do you ever drink before noon?

These same questions can be asked about substances other than alcohol. If a member of a family who's seeking couples or family therapy seems to be abusing drugs or alcohol, think twice about assuming that talk therapy will be the answer to the family's problems.

Domestic Violence and Sexual Abuse

If there is any hint of domestic violence or sexual abuse, a therapist should look into it. The process of questioning can start with the family present, but when there is any suggestion of abuse, it may be wise to meet with family members separately to allow them to talk more openly.

Most states require professionals to report any suspicion of child abuse. Reporting suspected child abuse can jeopardize a therapeutic alliance, but sometimes therapy needs to take second place to safety. Any clinician who considers not reporting suspected child abuse should consider the possible consequences of making a mistake.

Perpetrators and victims of childhood sexual maltreatment don't usually volunteer this information. Detection is up to the clinician, who may have to rely on indirect clues. Further exploration may be indicated if a child shows any of the following symptoms: sleep disturbance, encopresis or enuresis, abdominal pain, an exaggerated startle response, appetite disturbance, sudden unexplained changes in behavior, overly sexualized behavior, regressive behavior, suicidal thoughts, or running away (Edwards & Gil, 1986; Campbell, Cook, LaFleur, & Keenan, 2010).

Extramarital Affairs

The discovery of an affair is a crisis that will strike many couples some time in their relationship. Infidelity is common, but it's still a crisis, and it can destroy a marriage.

Extramarital involvements that don't involve sexual intimacy, although less obvious, can sabotage treatment if one or both partners regularly turn to third parties to deal with issues that should be worked out together. (One clue that an outside relationship is part of a triangle is that it isn't talked about.) Would-be helpful third parties may include family members, friends, and therapists.

CASE STUDY

A couple once came to therapy complaining that the intimacy had gone out of their relationship. It wasn't so much a matter of conflict; they just never seemed to spend any time together. After a few weeks of slow progress, the wife mentioned that she'd been seeing an individual therapist. When the couple's therapist asked why, she replied that she needed someone to talk to. When he asked why she hadn't told him, she said, "You didn't ask."

◆ Gender

Gender inequalities contribute to family problems in a variety of ways. A wife's dissatisfaction may have deeper roots than the family's current problems. A husband's reluctance to become more involved in the family may be as much a product of cultural programming as a flaw in his character.

Every therapist must work out individually how to avoid the extremes of naively ignoring gender inequality or imposing his or her personal point of view on clients. One way to strike a balance is to raise questions but allow clients to find their own answers. You can raise moral questions without being moralistic. It is, however, not reasonable to assume that both partners enter marriage with equal power or that complementarity is the only dynamic operating in their relationship.

Conflict over gender expectations, whether discussed openly or not, is especially common given the enormous shifts in cultural expectations in recent decades. Is it still considered a woman's duty to follow her husband's career, moving whenever necessary for his advancement? Is it still true that women should be strong, self-supporting, and the primary (which often turns out to be a euphemism for *only*) caregivers for infants and young children?

Regardless of the therapist's values, do the gender roles established in a couple seem to work for them? Or do unresolved differences, conflicts, or confusions appear to be sources of stress? Perhaps the single most useful question to ask about gender equality is, "How does each partner experience the fairness of give-and-take in their relationship?"

It's not uncommon for differences in gender socialization to contribute to conflict in couples (Patterson, Williams, Grauf-Grounds, & Chamow, 1998), as the following example illustrates.

CASE STUDY

Kevin complained that Courtney was always checking up on him, which made him feel that she didn't trust him. Courtney insisted that she only asked about what Kevin was doing in order to be part of his life. She expected the same interest in her life from him. She wasn't checking up on him; she just wanted them to share things.

When Courtney asked Kevin too many questions, he got angry and withdrew, which made her feel shut out. Happy not to be interrogated any further, Kevin didn't notice how hurt and angry Courtney was until finally she exploded in tearful recrimination. Kevin felt helpless in the face of Courtney's crying, and so he did his best to placate her. When he reassured her that he loved her and promised to tell her more about what was going on in his life, she calmed down and peace was restored. Until the next time.

For couples like Courtney and Kevin, gender socialization contributes to a pursuer–distancer dynamic. Men are typically socialized to value independence and to resist anything they see as an effort to control them. Thus, Kevin interpreted Courtney's questions about his activities as attempts to restrict his freedom. Courtney, on the other hand, was socialized to value caring and connection. Naturally, she wanted to know what was going on in Kevin's life. She couldn't understand why he got so defensive about her wanting them to check in with each other.

While it's a mistake to ignore gender socialization in favor of family dynamics, it's also a mistake to assume that gender socialization isn't influenced by family dynamics. In the previous example, the enmeshed family that Courtney grew up in reinforced the notion that family members should share everything and that independent activities were a sign of disloyalty. Kevin's reluctance to tell his wife everything he was doing was partly a residue of his coming from a family with two bossy and controlling parents.

◆ Culture

In assessing families for treatment, therapists should consider the unique subculture of the family (McGoldrick, Pearce, & Giordano, 2005) as well as how unquestioned assumptions from the larger culture may affect a family's problems (Doherty, 1991).

In working with minority families, it may be more important for therapists to develop *cultural sensitivity* than to actually share the same background as their clients. Families may come to trust a therapist who has taken the time to learn about their particular culture as much as one who happens to be of the same race or nationality.

One way to develop cultural sensitivity is to make connections after working hours. For example, a white therapist could attend an African American church service in the community where his or her clients live, go to a Latino dance, or visit an Asian community center. Doing these things won't make you an expert, but it may demonstrate to client families that you care enough to respect their ways. It's also important to take a *one-down position* in regard to cultural and ethnic diversity—that is, to ask your clients to teach you about their experience and traditions, rather than assume the role of expert.

The challenge for a practitioner is twofold: learning to respect diversity and developing sensitivity to some of the issues faced by members of other cultures and ethnic groups. Numerous books are available describing the characteristics and values of various ethnic groups, many of which are listed in the section on multiculturalism in Chapter 10. In addition to these academic books, novels such as *The Kite Runner*, *Beloved*, *Song of Solomon*, *How the Garcia Girls Lost their Accent*, *The Mambo Kings Play Songs of Love*, *The Scent of Green Papaya*, *The Brief Wondrous Life of Oscar Wao*, and *The Joy Luck Club* often bring other cultures more vividly to life.

In working with clients from other cultures, it's more important to be respectful of differences and to be curious about other ways of doing things than to attempt to become an expert on ethnicity. Yet while it's important to respect other people's differences, it can be a problem to accept uncritically statements to the effect that "We do these (counterproductive) things because of our culture." Unfortunately, it's difficult for a therapist from another culture to assess the validity of such claims. Perhaps the best advice is to be curious. Stay open-minded, but ask questions.

The Ethical Dimension

Most therapists are aware of the ethical responsibilities of their profession:

♦ Therapy should be for the client's benefit, not to work out unresolved issues for the therapist.

♦ Clients are entitled to confidentiality, and so limits on privacy imposed by requirements to report to probation officers, parents, or managed care companies should be made clear from the outset.

♦ Therapists should avoid exploiting the trust of their clients and students and therefore must make every effort to avoid dual relationships.

♦ Professionals are obligated to provide the best possible treatment; if they aren't qualified by training or experience to meet the needs of a particular client, they should refer the case to someone who is.

Whenever there is any question or doubt regarding ethical issues, it's a good idea to consult with a colleague or supervisor.

> Watch this video of a beginning therapist experiencing a clash in values with her client. What do you learn from the supervisor about navigating ethical dilemmas?

Although most therapists are aware of their own responsibilities, many think less than they might about the ethical dimensions of their clients' behavior. This is an area where there are no hard-and-fast rules. However, a complete and conscientious assessment of every family should include some consideration of family members' entitlements and obligations. What obligations of loyalty do members of a family have? Are invisible loyalties constraining their behavior? (Boszormenyi-Nagy & Spark, 1973) If so, are these loyalties just and equitable? What is the nature of the partners' commitment to each other? Are these commitments clear and balanced? What obligations do family members have with regard to fidelity and trustworthiness? Are these obligations being met?

A good place to start in understanding the ethical responsibilities of clinical practice is with the guidelines of your profession. The Ethics Code of the American Psychological Association (APA), for example, outlines principles such as these:

♦ Psychologists offer services only within the areas of their competence based on their education, training, supervision, and professional experience.

♦ When understanding age, gender, race, ethnicity, culture, national origin, religion, sexual orientation, disability, language, or socioeconomic status is essential for the effective delivery of services, psychologists will have or seek out training and supervision in these areas or make the appropriate referrals.

♦ When psychologists become aware of personal problems that might interfere with their professional duties, they take appropriate measures, such as obtaining professional assistance and determining whether they should limit, suspend, or terminate their work-related duties.

The Code of Ethics for the National Association of Social Workers (NASW) mandates the following:

♦ Social workers should not engage in dual relationships with clients or former clients.

♦ Social workers should not solicit private information from clients unless it is essential to providing services.

♦ Social workers should not disclose confidential information to third-party payers unless clients have authorized such disclosure.

♦ Social workers should terminate services to clients when such services are no longer required.

The American Counseling Association (ACA, 2014) covers many of the same issues as the APA and NASW, yet it provides further mandates related to social media, such as:

♦ Counselors are not allowed to maintain a relationship with current clients through social media.

♦ Counselors must wait five years after the last clinical contact to have a sexual or romantic relationship with a former client or a family member of a client. This applies to both in-person and electronic interactions or relationships.

While some of these principles may seem obvious, they provide fairly strict guidelines within which practitioners should operate. When it comes to working with couples and families, however, complications arise that create a host of unique ethical dilemmas.

When, for example, should a family therapist share with parents information learned in sessions with a child? If a twelve-year-old starts drinking, should the therapist tell her parents?

Recently, professional codes of conduct have added guidelines to address issues involved in treating couples and families. For example, the APA specifies that when a psychologist provides services to several people who have a relationship (such as spouses or parents and children), he or she must clarify at the outset which individuals are clients and what relationship he or she will have with each person. In addition, if it becomes apparent that a psychologist may be called on to perform potentially conflicting roles (such as family therapist and then witness for one party in divorce proceedings), he or she must attempt to clarify and modify those rules or withdraw from them appropriately.

Similarly, the NASW states that when social workers provide services to couples or family members, they should clarify with all parties the nature of their professional obligations to the various individuals receiving services. And when social workers provide counseling to families, they should seek agreement among the parties concerning each individual's right to confidentiality.

The American Association for Marriage and Family Therapy (AAMFT, 2001) publishes its own code of ethics, which covers many of the same points as the codes of the APA and NASW. The AAMFT does, however, directly address complications with respect to confidentiality when a therapist sees more than one person in a family. Without a written waiver, a family therapist should not disclose information received from any family member, presumably not even to other family members.

Still, as with many things, it may be easier to expound ethical principles in the classroom than to apply them in the crucible of clinical practice. Consider the following:

It's clear that therapists must protect their clients' right to confidentiality. But what if a woman reveals she's having an extramarital affair and isn't sure whether to end it? When she goes on to say that her marriage has been stale for years, the therapist recommends a course of couples therapy to see if the marriage can be improved. The woman agrees. But when the therapist then suggests that she either break off the affair or tell her husband about it, the woman adamantly refuses. What should the therapist do?

Can a therapist offer effective couples treatment while one of the partners is carrying on an extramarital relationship? How much pressure should a therapist exert on a client to do something he or she doesn't want to do? How much pressure should a therapist apply to urge a family member to reveal a secret that might have dangerous consequences? When does a therapist have the right to discontinue treatment of a client who wants to continue, because the client refuses to accept the therapist's recommendation?

One way to resolve ambiguous ethical dilemmas is to use your own best judgment. In the case of the woman who wanted to work on her marriage but wasn't willing to end her affair or inform her husband, a therapist might decline to offer therapy under circumstances that would make it unlikely to be effective. In that case, the therapist would be obligated to refer the client to another therapist.

Subprinciple 1.10 of the AAMFT's Code of Ethical Principles (2011) states that "Marriage and family therapists respectfully assist persons in obtaining appropriate therapeutic services if the therapist is unable or unwilling to provide professional help. And Subprinciple 1.11 states that "Marriage and family therapists do not abandon or neglect clients in treatment without making reasonable arrangements for the continuation of such treatment."

Given the same set of circumstances, another therapist might decide that even though the woman refuses to end her affair, treating the couple might make it possible for the woman to break off the affair later or to talk to her husband about it. In this scenario, the therapist would be bound by the principle of confidentiality not to reveal what the woman discussed in private.

While the outlines of ethical professional conduct are clear, the pressures on practitioners are often powerful and subtle. When dealing with clients who are having affairs or considering divorce—or marriage, for that matter—therapists may be influenced by their own unconscious attitudes as well as clients' projections. What would you assume, for example, about a therapist whose depressed, married clients all tended to get divorced after their individual therapy? What might you speculate about the level of satisfaction in that therapist's own marriage?

The risk involved in trusting your own judgment in ambiguous ethical situations lies in imposing your own values on what should be a professional decision. The principles of sound ethical practice are broader and may be stricter than our own private morality and good intentions. When in doubt, we recommend that clinicians ask themselves two questions: First, what would happen if the client or important others found out about your actions? Thus, for example, strategically telling two siblings in separate conversations that each is the only one mature enough to end the fighting between them violates the "what if" principle, because it's entirely possible that one or both might brag to the other about what the therapist said. (Trust me!)

The second question to ask in ethical decision making is, Can you talk to someone you respect about what you're doing or considering? If you're afraid to discuss with a colleague that you are treating two married couples in which the wife of one is having an affair with the husband of the other or that you're considering lending a client money, you may be guilty of the arrogance of assuming that you are above the rules that govern your profession. Feeling compelled to keep something secret suggests that it may be wrong. The road to hell is paved with the assumption that this situation is special, that this client is special, or that you are special.

The following red flags signal potentially unethical practices:

- *Specialness*—Something about this situation is special; the ordinary rules don't apply.
- *Attraction*—Intense attraction of any kind, not only romantic but also being impressed with the status of the client.
- *Alterations in the therapeutic frame*—Longer or more frequent sessions, excessive self-disclosure, being unable to say no to the client, and other

things that signal a potential violation of professional boundaries.

♦ *Violating clinical norms*—Not referring someone in a troubled marriage for couples therapy, accepting personal counseling from a supervisor, and so on.

♦ *Professional isolation*—Not being willing to discuss your decisions with professional colleagues.

♦ ♦ ♦

The Marriage and Family Therapy License

In 1964, California created the marriage and family therapy license, and in 2009 Montana became the fiftieth state to offer an MFT license. This milestone added to the legitimacy of the profession and opened doors for inclusion in federal programs such as Substance Abuse and Mental Health Services and the Veterans Administration. Today MFT is one of the fastest growing mental health disciples, inclusion in more federal programs is pending, and managed care panels are increasingly accepting MFTs.

What does it take to obtain an MFT license? Though requirements vary by state, plan on competing a master's degree that prepares you to work with couples and families and includes approximately 500 hours of practicum experience, followed by one or two years of post-degree supervised clinical experience, and a state licensing exam. Education and experience requirements vary from state to state and reciprocity is rarely granted; therefore, you must take the licensing exam in whatever state in which you plan to practice.

The MFT license is similar to licensed professional counselors (LPCs) and licensed clinical social workers (LCSWs) in that a master's degree is the terminal degree and in most states job opportunities and responsibilities are similar. Working systemically with couples and families is the main thing that sets the MFT apart from other master's level licenses. The MFT license differs most from a license in psychology. Licensure in psychology requires a doctoral degree and extensive training in research and diagnostic testing. Historically, doctoral-level psychologists have been paid more and have had a wider range of job opportunities. The recent downturn in the economy has changed this somewhat, and many agencies are now replacing psychology positions with lower-paying master's level clinicians. It's unclear whether this trend will continue, but at present licensed MFTs have very good prospects in the job market.

Family Therapy with Specific Presenting Problems

Once, most family therapists assumed that their approach could be applied to almost any problem. Today, it has become increasingly common to develop specific techniques for particular populations and problems.

The following are samples of special treatment approaches for two frequently encountered clinical problems: marital violence and sexual abuse of children. While we hope these suggestions will provide some ideas for dealing with these difficult situations, remember that responsible therapists recognize the limits of their expertise and refer cases they aren't equipped to handle to more experienced practitioners.

Marital Violence

The question of how to treat marital violence polarizes the field like no other. The prevailing paradigm is to separate couples, referring the offender to an anger management program and treating his partner in a battered women's group (Edleson & Tolman, 1992; Gondolf, 1995). Traditional couples therapy is seen as dangerous because placing a violent man and his abused partner in close quarters and inviting them to address contentious issues puts the woman in danger and provides the offender with a platform for self-justification (Bograd, 1984, 1992; Avis, 1992; Hansen, 1993). Treating the partners together implies that they share responsibility for the violence and confers a sense of legitimacy on a relationship that may be malignant.

The argument for seeing violent couples together is that violence is the outcome of mutual provocation—an escalation, albeit unacceptable, of the emotionally destructive behavior that characterizes many relationships (Goldner, 1992; Minuchin & Nichols, 1993). When couples are treated together, violent partners can learn to recognize the emotional triggers that set them off and take responsibility for controlling their actions. Their mates can learn to recognize the same danger signals and take responsibility for ensuring their own safety.

Because few systemic therapists advocate treating couples together when the violence has gone beyond pushing and shoving, some of the debate between advocates of a systemic versus an offender-and-victim model is between apples and oranges. Michael Johnson (1995) argues that there are two types of partner violence in families. The first type is *patriarchal terrorism*, which is part of a pattern in which violence is used to exercise control over a partner. Patriarchal terrorism is frequent and severe and tends to escalate over time. The second pattern is *common couple violence* and doesn't involve a pattern of power and control. This violence erupts as a response to a particular conflict, is more likely to be mutual, occurs infrequently, and tends not to escalate. Nevertheless, many feminist thinkers remain opposed to couples therapy when any form of violence is present (Bograd, 1984; Avis, 1992; Hansen, 1993).

In the absence of empirical evidence showing gender-specific group treatment to be safer or more effective than couples therapy (Brown & O'Leary, 1995; Feldman & Ridley, 1995; Smith, Rosen, McColum, & Thomsen, 2004), clinicians remain split into two camps when it comes to the treatment of marital violence. Rather than choose between attempting to resolve the relationship issues that lead to violence or concentrating on providing safety and protection for the victims of violence, it's possible to combine elements of both approaches—not, however, by doing traditional couples therapy.[4]

In working with violent couples, there must be no compromise on the issue of safety. A therapist doesn't have to choose between maintaining therapeutic neutrality (and focusing on relationship issues) and advocating on behalf of the victim (and focusing on safety). It's possible to pursue both agendas. Relationship issues can be construed as mutual, but the perpetrator must be held responsible for the crime of violence. As Pamela Anderson said when her husband

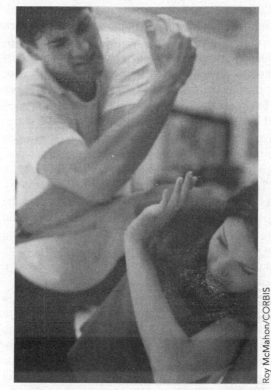

Roy McMahon/CORBIS

In cases of domestic violence, couples therapy may be inadvisable unless the man's violence is infrequent, not physically injurious, not psychologically intimidating, and not fear-producing for his partner.

Tommy Lee was arrested for domestic battery, "It takes two people to start an argument, but it only takes one to break the other one's nose."

In the initial consultation with a couple in which there is a suspicion of violence, it's useful to meet with the partners together and then separately. Seeing the couple together permits you to see them in action, while speaking with the partners privately allows you to inquire whether either of them has left out information about the level of violence or other forms of intimidation to which she has been subjected.[5]

Violent partners and battered mates trigger strong reactions in anyone who tries to help them. When such couples seek therapy, they are often polarized

---

[4]The following guidelines draw heavily from the work of Virginia Goldner and Gillian Walker, codirectors of the Gender and Violence Project at the Ackerman Institute.

[5]Domestic violence is committed by women as well as men, but to avoid having to keep writing "he or she" we will refer to violent partners as "he" and battered mates as "she."

between love and hate, blaming and feeling ashamed, wanting to escape and remaining obsessed with each other. Thus, it's not surprising that professional helpers tend to react in extremes: siding with one against the other, refusing ever to take sides, exaggerating or minimizing danger, treating the partners like children or like monsters—in other words, splitting into good and bad, just like the dynamics of the couples themselves. In order to form an alliance with both partners, it's important to convey respect for them as persons, even if you can't condone all of their actions.

To assess the level of violence, it's important to ask direct questions: "How often do conflicts between the two of you end in some kind of violence?" "When did this happen most recently?" "What's the worst thing that's ever happened?" It's important to find out if any incidents have resulted in injuries, if weapons have been used, and if one the woman is currently afraid.

In addition to assessing the level of violence, a therapist must also evaluate the partners' ability to work constructively in therapy. Is the man willing to accept responsibility for his behavior? Is he argumentative or defensive toward his partner? Toward the therapist? Is the woman willing to take responsibility for her own protection, making her physical safety the first priority? Is the couple able to talk together and take turns, or are they so emotionally reactive that the therapist must constantly interrupt to control them?

If a therapist decides to treat the couple together, it's essential to establish zero tolerance for violence. One way of doing this is to make therapy contingent on no further episodes of physical aggression. Virginia Goldner and Gillian Walker define the first couple of sessions as a consultation to determine whether it's possible to create a "therapeutic safety zone," where issues can be confronted without putting the woman in harm's way. They use these initial sessions to focus on the risk of violence and the question of safety, while reserving the right to terminate the consultation and propose other treatment alternatives if they feel the case is too volatile for couples therapy (Goldner, 1998).

With most couples it's useful to encourage dialogue as a way of exploring how the partners communicate. But violent couples tend to be emotionally reactive, and when that's the case, it's better to have them take turns talking to the therapist. The therapist should do everything possible to slow them down and make them think.

One of the best antidotes to emotionality is to ask for specific, concrete details. A good place to start is with the most recent violent incident. Ask each partner for a detailed, moment-to-moment description of what happened. Be alert for linguistic evasions (Scott & Straus, 2007). A violent man may describe his actions as the result of his partner's "provocation" or of "built-up pressures." Thus, it's not he who hits his wife; it's the pressures that are the culprit. A more subtle form of evasion is for the violent partner to describe the problem as his impulsivity. When arguments escalate, he starts to "lose it." In this formulation the man's impulsive actions are not a choice he makes but an unavoidable consequence of emotions welling up inside of him.

To this kind of evasion a therapist might respond "When you say you start to 'lose it' let's think about what you mean. What happened inside of you at that moment that you felt justified in breaking your promise never to hit her again?" The therapeutic task is to hold the man accountable for his violence, while also trying to understand him in complex and sympathetic terms. This double agenda is in contrast to either shaming the man, which will only exacerbate his rage, or trying to understand the couple's dynamics without also holding the man responsible for his actions.

Once both partners have begun to take responsibility for their actions—he for choosing to control his violent impulses, she for taking steps to ensure her safety—it becomes possible to explore the relationship issues that lead to escalating emotional reactivity (Holtzworth-Munroe, Meehan, Rehman, & Marshall, 2002). This does not, however, mean that at a certain point a violent couple can be treated just like any other couple. Exploring the interactional processes that both partners participate in should never be allowed to imply that both are equally *responsible* for acts of violence.

When the couple is ready to explore relationship issues, it should be possible to encourage dialogue, so that the therapist and couple can understand what transpires when they try to talk with each other. This brings the relationship into the consulting room. It's one thing to tell a man that he should leave before he gets too angry. It's another thing to actually observe the beginnings of emotional escalation and ask him if he's aware that he's started to get upset and interrupt his partner. It then becomes possible to say, "*This is the moment when you should leave.*" At this same point his partner can be asked if she has begun to feel the first signs of tension and fear.

Taking time-out is an almost universally employed strategy in marital violence programs. Recognizing the cues of escalating anger (racing heart, growing agitation, standing up, pacing) and removing oneself from the situation before violence occurs is encouraged as a way to head off destructive actions that the partners will later regret. Saying "I'm feeling angry (or scared), and I'm going to take a time-out" helps distinguish this safety device from simply refusing to talk. Each person must be responsible for his or her own time-outs. Telling the other person to take a time-out is not allowed, nor is trying to stop the other from leaving.

Although eliminating the escalating aggressive interactions must be the first priority, couples should also learn more constructive methods of addressing their differences. Here, there is a paradox: Violent partners must learn to control their behavior, but it is counterproductive to stifle their resentments and complaints. In fact, it is precisely this kind of suppression that leads to the emotional buildups that result in violent explosions. Moreover, a person who resorts to violence with his or her partner is usually a weak man—weak in the sense of not knowing how to articulate his feelings in a way that his partner can hear. Thus, in helping couples learn to negotiate their differences, it is essential to ensure that both partners learn to speak up and to listen to each other.

◆ Sexual Abuse of Children

When treating a family in which a child has been sexually abused, the primary goals are first to ensure that the abuse does not recur and second to reduce the long-term effects of the trauma (Trepper & Barrett, 1989). As with marital violence, treatment

of sexual abuse tends to fall into one of two categories: (1) a *child-protective approach*, which can undermine the integrity of the family, or (2) a *family systems approach*, which can fail to protect the child. We recommend supporting the family while at the same time protecting the child. When these goals seem incompatible—for example, when a father has raped his daughter—protecting the child should take precedence.

Assessment of sexual abuse is often complicated by conflicting stories about what happened (Herman, 1992; Campbell, Cook, LaFleur, & Keenan, 2010). A father may say that touching his daughter's labia was accidental, whereas the daughter may report that this has happened more than once and that she experiences it as abusive. A grandfather may claim that his caressing of his grandson is perfectly innocent, while the district attorney may file charges of indecent assault. A child-protective worker may believe that a mother is tacitly supporting her husband's abuse of her child, while a family therapist may see a mother who is doing her best to save her marriage. Such discrepancies are best resolved by social and legal agencies.

The first priority is restricting unsupervised access to children for the offender. Next a careful assessment should be made to uncover other possible incidents of abuse or patterns of inappropriate sexual expression (Furniss, 1991). The offender must take responsibility for his behavior and receive appropriate treatment for his actions (which may include legal punishment). Often these measures will have already been taken by a child-protective agency before a family is referred for therapy.

One of the goals of therapy should be to establish a support system to break through the isolation that facilitates sexual abuse and inhibits disclosure. For this reason many programs favor a multimodal approach that includes individual, group, and family sessions (Bentovim, Elton, Hildebrand, Tranter, & Vizard, 1988; Trepper & Barrett, 1989; Ramchandani & Jones, 2003). Family sessions should be geared toward increasing support for the victimized child, which may entail strengthening the parental unit.

When a child is the victim of sexual abuse, social control agents may have to step in to protect the child, which can involve taking over what might be considered parental responsibilities. In the long run, however, it is the family who will be responsible for the child. Therefore, supporting the parents in developing appropriate ways of carrying out their responsibilities, rather than taking over for them, is usually in the best interests of the child.

In cases where a father or stepfather is sent to jail for sexual crimes against his children, part of a therapist's job is to help the family draw a boundary that excludes the offender. The same is true if the children are taken out of the home and sent to live with relatives or foster parents. Subsequently, however, if reunion is planned, therapy involves gradually reopening this boundary through visits and phone calls, which gives the family and therapist the opportunity to work together to improve the family's functioning.

One of the keys to helping resolve the trauma of abuse is to give the child a safe forum to explore his or her complex and often ambivalent feelings about what happened. In addition to feeling violated and angry, the child may feel guilty about getting an adult in trouble. Often a child will secretly blame the other parent, usually the mother, for not preventing the abuse. And finally, the child may fear that his or her mother's dependence on the abuser might result in his return, leaving the child again vulnerable to abuse.

A combination of individual and conjoint sessions helps make it safe to talk about feelings. Meeting first with the nonoffending parent (or parents) allows the mother (or parents) to describe what happened and to express feelings about the abuse without having to edit what she says because the child is present.[6] Among the mother's complex feelings will surely be rage and a sense of betrayal. But a part of her may still love the abuser and miss him if he's been sentenced. She may also feel guilty for not having protected her child. It's important to make it safe for her to share all of these feelings.

When first meeting with a mother and abused daughter, it's reassuring to say that although they will probably eventually want to talk about the abuse, it's up to them to choose where to start. It's also helpful to give parents and children the choice of how much to talk about the abuse and whether to do so first in an individual session or conjointly. If children choose to discuss their feelings privately, they should be reassured that it's up to them to decide what they later want to share with their parents.

When meeting with abused children, it's helpful to explain that the more they talk about what happened, the less troubling their feelings are likely to be. However, it's essential to let them decide when and how much to open up. Abused children need to recover a sense of control over their lives (Sheinberg, True, & Fraenkel, 1994).

When family members talk about their feelings, it's wise to keep in mind that feelings don't come in either/or categories. One way to help make it safe for them to talk about complex and even contradictory emotions is to use the metaphor of parts of the self (Schwartz, 1995). Thus, an abused child might be asked, "Does part of you think your mother should have figured out what was happening?" Likewise, a mother might be asked, "Does part of you miss him?"

One problem with meeting privately with a child is that doing so creates secrets. At the end of a private session, it's helpful to ask the child what she wants to share with her family and how she wants to do it. Some children ask the therapist to take the lead in opening up some of what they want their mothers to understand but find it hard to talk about. Finally, although it's important to help children voice any thoughts they may have about feeling guilty for what happened, after exploring these feelings, abused children need to hear over and over that what happened was not their fault.

Working with Managed Care

Rarely has a profession undergone such upheaval as mental health providers experienced with the advent of **managed care**. Practitioners used to making decisions based on their own clinical judgment were now told by the managed care industry which patients they could see, which treatments to apply, what they can charge, and how many sessions they could offer. Professionals taught to maintain confidentiality in their dealings with patients found themselves negotiating with anonymous strangers over the telephone.

[6]For the sake of simplicity, the following discussion will assume the common instance of a stepfather as abuser and a mother and her abused daughter as clients.

Now several decades into its existence, the managed care industry is coming to terms with two important facts. First, while their mandate is still to contain costs, their ultimate responsibility is to see that patients receive effective treatment. Second, despite what once seemed to be a built-in adversarial relationship with practitioners, industry case managers are discovering something that clinicians should also come to terms with: that both sides profit when they begin to work in partnership.

The key to succeeding in a managed care environment is to get over the sense that the case manager is your enemy. Actually, for those who learn to collaborate effectively with managed care, case managers can be the best source of referrals.

Learning to work with managed care should begin as early as planning one's education. Most managed care companies accept licensed practitioners from all major mental health disciplines, though some will only accept certain degrees on their preferred provider lists. So, just as it's prudent to take state licensing requirements into account when planning a postgraduate education, it's also wise to consider the requirements of the major managed care companies. Moreover, because most companies require at least three years of post-degree experience, it's a good idea to begin your career in a supervised agency. Working in a public agency almost invariably includes regular internal and external oversight and the opportunity not only to refine clinical practices but also to document them in effective ways.

In areas with a high concentration of mental health providers, it may be necessary to market your skills in order to be selected as a managed care provider. Case managers are always looking for practitioners who can make their jobs easier. Showing willingness to accept crisis referrals and work with difficult cases (e.g., people with borderline personality disorder, chronic and multiproblem clients), being accessible, and having specialized expertise help make therapists attractive to managed care companies.

Once you have the opportunity to become a provider, remember to work *with* case managers, not against them. Managed care companies maintain databases that include information such as the average number of sessions a professional provides to each client. Outliers who use a significantly greater number of sessions per client are warned and referrals often decrease. Treatment plans that include clear, measurable objectives are probably the most helpful but most often poorly executed component of clinical documentation. Paperwork can be frustrating, but keep in mind that case managers have feelings, too—and they have memories.

Case managers appreciate getting succinct and informative reports. When challenged, some therapists fall back on justifying their requests by saying, "It's my clinical opinion." Being asked to justify their conclusions makes some practitioners angry. They feel they are doing their best for their patients, and they're not used to having someone looking over their shoulder. Get used to it. If you use sound clinical judgment, you should be able to provide reasons for your recommendations.

If you can't reach agreement with a case manager, don't lose your temper. If you can't be friendly, don't be hostile. Follow the grievance procedure. Do the required paperwork, and submit it on time. Write concise, well-defined treatment plans. Return phone calls promptly.

Being successful in the current health care climate means developing a results-oriented mindset. If you're trained in solution-focused therapy, by all means say so, but don't try to pass yourself off as something you're not. Calling yourself "eclectic" is more likely to sound fuzzy than flexible. Your goal is to establish a reputation for working within established time limits—and getting results.

On March 23, 2010, President Obama signed the Affordable Care Act, often referred to as Obamacare. The goal of the Affordable Care Act is to enhance the quality of health care by lowering costs, increasing provider accountability, and making health insurance available to everybody in the United States. The feasibility of these goals and the mechanisms for achieving them have been bitterly divisive political issues, and as a result Affordable Care Act has changed considerably since it was signed into law. It is unclear how the new law will affect mental health delivery, but it will likely make mental health services available to a much wider group of patients. The bill's primary impact—that people can no longer be denied health insurance or charged more based on a pre-existing mental illness—will mean that an increased number of patients will have the means to seek mental health care. If you work in a hospital or agency that serves a low-income population, it is anticipated that you will treat more people with severe problems than in the past due to their increased access to health care (Rasmussen, 2013). How the Affordable Care Act will affect private practice is still unclear.

◆ Fee-for-Service Private Practice

Managed care radically changed the face of private practice. While prior to the advent of managed care most therapists were willing to sign insurance forms to allow their patients to be reimbursed, many were unwilling to accept the increased documentation and lower reimbursement rates under managed care. These constraints drove many therapists out of private practice and into agency work. Some practitioners, however, continued their private practices but now insisted that their patients pay 100% of their fees out of pocket.

Although many well-established therapists continue to thrive in fee-for-service practices, it has become difficult (nearly impossible in some markets) to begin a private practice and attract cash-paying clients. The Affordable Care Act is expected to further erode the pool of fee-for-service clients, because many previously uninsured people will now have insurance and therefore be eligible to be treated by therapists accepting managed care. Furthermore, the Affordable Care Act stipulates that people with a Flexible Spending Account (which allows enrollees to set aside pretax money to pay for uncovered medical expenses such as therapy) are only allowed to allocate $2500 per year, which could affect the length of time people remain in treatment. Nevertheless, given that the Affordable Care Act is changing rapidly as it rolls out, it is difficult to anticipate how, if at all, it will affect those wishing to establish a private practice.

Despite these uncertainties, there will always be some people in every community who are willing to pay out of pocket for high quality, and truly confidential, mental health services. The challenge for someone wanting to establish a private practice is to learn how to position oneself in the marketplace to attract these clients. While doing so requires business savvy that you don't typically learn in graduate school, establishing and maintaining a fee-for-service practice is nevertheless possible in most metropolitan areas and can be very rewarding.

Your reputation is your most valuable asset for building a fee-for-service practice. Do all you can to establish and maintain a solid reputation, because once it is established your practice will be essentially self-perpetuating. A good reputation starts with your training and skills. The best investment you can make in your career is some form of advanced training after you obtain your graduate degree. Attendance at a training institute or taking a year-long externship will go a long way to helping you master your craft. A series of workshops can stimulate and enhance the skills of experienced practitioners, but it cannot substitute for a protracted immersion in the approach of your choice. Developing a specialty and providing training in that specialty can also help cement your reputation.

Attending networking meetings with other therapists is also helpful. Networking sessions can be a great place to meet a private practice mentor who can help show you the ropes in your local marketplace. Most communities have a core of successful private practitioners, and many are willing to help mentor someone who seems to have something to offer. Approach these mentors with an attitude of "how can I help you," rather than "how can you help me." Offer to assist with marketing, practice management, and so on in exchange for advice and counsel, instead of simply asking them to help you. Many states allow pre-licensed therapists to work under the supervision of a therapist in private practice, which is ideal because once you are licensed you will have developed your own caseload.

Marketing is also important to spreading your reputation and establishing a successful private practice. If you have a specialty, be sure to network with related professionals. If you work with couples struggling with infertility, be sure to take the local infertility doctors to lunch and bring their office staff coffee. Same with divorce lawyers if you work with divorce-related issues; churches, if you focus your practice on a particular religious tradition, and so forth. Offering to give lectures or workshops at local schools or other service organizations in, say parenting, or communication skills is other useful way to attract clients.

Building and maintaining an attractive website is vitally important in today's market. Once you have built a website (it's inexpensive and relatively easy to create one yourself), search for relevant key words (e.g., "couples therapy," "anxiety," or whatever is relevant to your practice) and make sure you're promoting your website on the first page of the search results.

A successful private practice requires management of income and expenses. An ideal office is one that allows you to keep overhead low while still projecting competence. Check the fees of local therapists to determine what you should charge for your services. Pricing your services too high, particularly if you are new to the market, will take longer to build your practice. Many clinicians start in the middle, and move up over time.

In most markets if a therapist stays clinically up to date, builds a strong reputation, markets effectively, keeps overhead low, is priced right, and can be patient, he or she can establish a successful private practice.

social class; working with managed care—there's a lot to learn, isn't there? Yes, and it takes time. But there are some things you can't learn, at least not from books.

Personal qualities, such as sincere concern for other people and dedication to making a difference, are also important. Techniques may be the tools, but human qualities are what distinguish the best therapists. You can't be an effective therapist without learning how to intervene, but without compassion and respect for people and their way of doing things, therapy will remain a technical operation, not a creative human endeavor.

Click here to apply your knowledge of chapter concepts.

Summary

Getting a whole family to come in; developing a systemic hypothesis, pushing for change; knowing when to terminate; being sensitive to ethnicity, gender, and

Click here to test your application and analysis of the content found within this chapter.

CHAPTER 3

THE FUNDAMENTAL CONCEPTS OF FAMILY THERAPY

A Whole New Way of Thinking about Human Behavior

LEARNING OUTCOMES

◆ Describe the main tenets of cybernetics.
◆ Describe the main tenets of systems theory.
◆ Describe the main tenets of social constructionism.
◆ Describe the main tenets of attachment theory.
◆ Describe contemporary working concepts of family therapy.

Prior to the advent of family therapy, the individual was regarded as the locus of psychological problems and the target for treatment. If a mother called to complain that her fifteen-year-old son was depressed, a clinician would meet with the boy to find out what was wrong. A Rogerian might look for low self-esteem, a Freudian for repressed anger, and a behaviorist for a lack of reinforcing activities. But all would assume that the forces shaping the boy's mood were located within him and that therapy, therefore, required only the presence of the patient and a therapist.

Family therapy changed all that. Today, if a mother were to seek help for a depressed teenager, most therapists would meet with the boy and his parents together. If a fifteen-year-old is depressed, it's not unreasonable to assume that something might be going on in his family. Perhaps the boy's parents don't get along and he's worried that they might get divorced. Maybe he's having a hard time living up to the expectations created by a successful older sister.

Suppose you are the therapist. You meet with the boy and his family and discover that he's not worried about his parents or jealous of his sister. In fact, everything "is fine" at home. He's just depressed. Now what?

That *now-what* feeling is a common experience when you start seeing families. Even when there is something obviously wrong—the boy is worried about his parents, or everybody is shouting and no one is listening—it's often hard to know where to start. You could start by trying to solve the family's problems for them. But then you wouldn't be helping them deal with *why* they're having problems.

To address what's making it hard for a family to cope with their problems, you have to know where to look. For that, you need some way of understanding what makes families tick. You need a theory.

When they first began to observe families discussing their problems, therapists could see immediately that everyone was involved. In the clamor of noisy quarrels, however, it's hard to see beyond personalities—the sullen adolescent, the controlling mother, the distant father—to notice the patterns that connect them. Instead of concentrating on individuals and their personalities, family therapists consider how problems may be, at least in part, a product of the relationships surrounding them. How to understand those relationships is the subject of this chapter.

Cybernetics

The first and perhaps most influential model of how families operate was **cybernetics**, the study of feedback mechanisms in self-regulating systems. What a family shares with other cybernetic systems is a tendency to maintain stability by using information about its performance.

At the core of cybernetics is the **feedback loop**, the process by which a system gets the information necessary to maintain a steady course. This feedback includes information about the system's performance and the relationship among the system's parts.

If you see behavior that persists over time, there is likely a mechanism maintaining that behavior. That mechanism operates through a feedback loop. A consistent behavior pattern is the first hint of the existence of a feedback loop. Feedback loops can be negative or positive. This distinction refers to the effect they have on homeostasis, not whether they are beneficial. **Negative feedback** indicates that a system is straying off the mark and that corrections are needed to get it back on course. It signals the system to restore the status quo. Thus, negative feedback is not such a negative thing. Its error-correcting information gives order and self-control to automatic machines, to the body and the brain, and to people in their daily lives. **Positive feedback** reinforces the direction a system is taking.

A familiar example of negative feedback occurs in a home heating system. When the temperature drops below a certain point, the thermostat triggers the furnace to heat the house back to the pre-established range. It is this self-correcting feedback loop that makes a system cybernetic, and it is the system's response to change as a signal to restore its previous state that illustrates negative feedback.

FIGURE 3.1 Circular Causality of a Feedback Loop

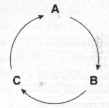

Figure 3.1 shows the basic circularity involved in a feedback loop. Each element has an effect on the next, until the last element "feeds back" the cumulative effect into the first part of the cycle. Thus A affects B, which in turn affects C, which feeds back to A, and so on.

In the example of a home heating system, A might be the room temperature, B the thermostat, and C the furnace. Figure 3.2 shows a similar cybernetic feedback loop for a couple. In this case, Jan's housecleaning efforts (output) affect how much housework gets done, which subsequently affects how much housecleaning Billie has to do, which then feeds back (input) to how much housecleaning Jan thinks still needs to be done, and so on.

FIGURE 3.2 Feedback Loop in a Couple's Housecleaning

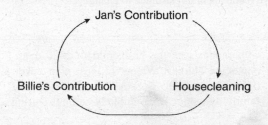

The cybernetic system turned out to be a useful metaphor for describing how families maintain stability (Jackson, 1959). Sometimes stability is a good thing, as for example, when a family continues to function as a cohesive unit despite being threatened by conflict or stress. Sometimes, however, resisting change is not such a good thing, as when a family fails to accommodate to the growth of one of its members. More about this later.

Like negative feedback, positive feedback can have desirable or undesirable consequences. If left unchecked, the reinforcing effects of positive feedback tend to compound a system's errors, leading to a **runaway** process. The hapless driver on an icy road who sends positive feedback to his automobile engine by accidentally stepping on the accelerator can spin out of control. Similarly, malignant worry, phobic avoidance, and other forms of neurotic behavior may start out with a relatively trivial concern and escalate into an out-of-control process.

Consider, for example, that a panic attack may start out as a relatively harmless instance of being out of breath, but a panicky response to breathlessness may spiral into a terrifying experience. Or, for a slightly more complex example, take the workings of the federal government. Because presidents generally surround themselves with advisers who share their viewpoint and who, because they are eager to maintain access, tend to support whatever position the president takes. This positive feedback can result in taking a bad policy and running with it—like Lyndon Johnson's escalation of the Vietnam War. Fortunately, however, the checks and balances provided by the legislative and judicial branches usually provide negative feedback to keep administrations from going too far in unwise directions. To survive and adapt to the world around them, all communication systems—including families—need a balance of negative and positive feedback. As we will see, however, early family therapists tended to overemphasize negative feedback and resistance to change.

Cybernetics was the brainchild of MIT mathematician Norbert Wiener (1948), who developed what was to become the first model of family dynamics in an unlikely setting. During

Alfred Eisenstaedt/Pix Inc./The LIFE Picture Collection/Getty Images

Norbert Wiener developed cybernetics at MIT.

World War II, Wiener was asked to design a better way to control the targeting of antiaircraft artillery (Conway & Siegelman, 2005). The German bombers blackening the skies over Europe flew at speeds over 300 miles per hour and at altitudes as high as 30,000 feet. The flight of an artillery shell to that height could take as long as twenty seconds, and firing that shot accurately—nearly two miles downrange—was no easy task. Wiener's solution was to incorporate a system of internal feedback that enabled antiaircraft guns to regulate their own operations. The signal used to control the artillery was a self-regulating *servomechanism*—the technical term for the first automated machines.

To capture the essence of the new science of control by feedback, Wiener chose the name *cybernetics*, from the Greek for "steersman." He distinguished two modes of information, discrete or continuous—digital or analog—and their diverse applications in communication, electronic computing, and automatic control systems. Moreover, he pointed out that the new technical methods of control by information feedback were, in essence, the same universal processes that nature long ago selected as its basic operating system for all living things (Wiener, 1948). He even suggested that cybernetic theory could be used to explain mental illnesses as self-reinforcing patterns of behavior—as the brain gets stuck in a biochemical rut.

Gregory Bateson learned about cybernetics from Wiener in 1942 at a series of interdisciplinary meetings called the *Macy conferences* (Heims, 1991). The dialogues between these two seminal thinkers were to have a profound impact on Bateson's application of systems theory to family therapy.

Because cybernetics emerged from the study of machines, where positive feedback loops led to destructive runaways, causing the machinery to break down, the emphasis was on negative feedback and the maintenance of *homeostasis*. A system's environment would change—the temperature would go up or down—and this change would trigger negative feedback mechanisms to bring the system back to homeostasis—the heat would go on or off. Negative feedback loops control everything from endocrine systems to ecosystems. Animal species are balanced by starvation and predators when they overpopulate and by increases in birthrates when their numbers are depleted. Blood sugar levels are balanced by increases in insulin output when they get too high and increases in appetite when they get too low.

As applied to families, cybernetics focused attention on: (1) *family rules*, which govern the range of behavior a family system can tolerate (the family's homeostatic range); (2) *negative feedback* mechanisms that families use to enforce those rules (guilt, punishment, symptoms); (3) *sequences of interaction* around a problem that characterize a system's re-action to it (feedback loops); and (4) what happens when a system's accustomed negative feedback is in-effective, triggering *positive feedback loops*.

Examples of positive feedback loops are vicious cycles, in which the actions taken only make things worse. A *self-fulfilling prophecy* is one such positive feedback loop; one's apprehensions lead to actions that precipitate the feared situation, which in turn justifies

one's fears, and so on. Another example of positive feedback is the *bandwagon effect*—the tendency of a cause to gain support simply because of its growing number of adherents. You can probably think of some fads and more than a few pop music groups that owe much of their popularity to the bandwagon effect.

As an example of a self-fulfilling prophesy, consider a young therapist who expects men to be uninvolved in family life. She believes that fathers *should* play an active role in the lives of their children, but her own experience has taught her not to expect much. Suppose she's trying to arrange for a family consultation, and the mother says that her husband won't be able to attend. How is our hypothetical therapist likely to respond? She might accept the mother's statement at face value and thus collude to ensure what she expected. Alternatively, she might challenge the mother's statement aggressively, thereby displacing her attitude toward men into her relationship with the mother—or push the mother into an oppositional stance with her husband.

Negative political campaigning is a perverse example of positive feedback escalation. One candidate smears the other, so the other smears back, and so forth, until the voters have no idea whether the candidates have any constructive ideas. The same kind of escalation leads to increasingly intrusive advertising, increasingly loud conversation at parties, longer and longer limousines, bawdier rock bands, and more and more outrageous television reality shows.

One way out of an escalating feedback loop is disarmament. Or one can simply refuse to compete. If one sibling pushes the other, the second sibling can simply refuse to push back—thereby stopping the process of escalation in its tracks. (But, don't hold your breath.)

To shift to a family example: in a family with a low threshold for the expression of anger, Marcus, the adolescent son, blows up at his parents over their insistence that he not stay out past midnight. Mother is shocked by his outburst and begins to cry. Father responds by grounding Marcus for a month. Rather than reducing Marcus's deviation—bringing his anger back within homeostatic limits—this feedback produces the opposite effect: Marcus explodes and challenges their authority. The parents respond with more crying and punishing, which further increases Marcus's anger, and so on. In this way, the intended negative feedback (crying and punishing) becomes positive feedback. It amplifies rather than diminishes Marcus's anger. The family is caught in a positive-feedback runaway, otherwise known as a vicious cycle, which escalates until Marcus runs away from home.

Later, cyberneticians like Walter Buckley and Ross Ashby recognized that positive feedback loops aren't always bad; if they don't get out of hand, they can help systems adjust to changed circumstances. Marcus's family might need to recalibrate their rules to accommodate an adolescent's increased assertiveness. The crisis that this positive feedback loop produced could lead to a reexamination of the family's rules—if the family could step out of the loop long enough to get some perspective. In so doing they would be *metacommunicating*, communicating about their ways of communicating, a process that can lead to a change in a system's rules (Bateson, 1956).

Family cyberneticians focused on the feedback loops within families, otherwise known as patterns of communication, as the fundamental source of family dysfunction. Hence the family theorists most influenced by cybernetics came to be known as the *communications school* (see Chapter 5). Faulty communication results in inaccurate feedback, so the system cannot self-correct (evaluate and change its rules) and consequently overreacts or underreacts to change.

Systems Theory

Experience teaches that what shows up as one person's behavior may be a product of relationship. The same individual may be submissive in one relationship, dominant in another. Like so many qualities we attribute to individuals, submissiveness is only half of a two-part equation. Family therapists use a host of concepts to describe how two people in a relationship contribute to what goes on between them, including *pursuer–distancer, overfunctioning–underfunctioning*, and *control-and-rebel cycles*. The advantage of such concepts is that either party can change his or her part in the pattern. But while it's relatively easy to discover themes in two-person relationships, it's more difficult to see patterns of interaction in larger groups like families. That's why family therapists found systems theory so useful.

Systems theory had its origins in the 1940s, when theoreticians began to construct models of the structure and functioning of mechanical and biological units. What these theorists discovered was that things as diverse as jet engines, amoebas, and the human brain share the attributes of a system—that is, an organized assemblage of parts forming a complex whole.

According to systems theory, the essential properties of a system arise from the relationships among its parts. These properties are lost when a system is reduced to isolated elements. The whole is greater than the sum of its parts. Thus, from a systems perspective, it would make little sense to try to understand a child's behavior by interviewing him or her without the rest of the child's family.

Although some therapists use terms like *systemic* and *systems theory* to mean little more than considering families as units, systems actually have a number of specific and interesting properties. To begin with, the shift from looking at individuals to considering the family as a system means shifting the focus to patterns of relationship.

Let's take a simple example. If a father scolds his son, his wife tells him not to be so harsh, and the boy continues to misbehave, a systemic analysis would concentrate on this sequence. For it is *sequences of interaction* that reveal how systems function. In order to focus on inputs and outputs, a systems analysis avoids asking *why* individuals do what they do.

The most radical expression of this systemic perspective was the "black box" metaphor: "The impossibility of seeing the mind 'at work' has in recent years led to the adoption of the Black Box concept from telecommunication . . . applied to the fact that electronic hardware is by now so complex that it is sometimes more expedient to disregard the internal structure of a device and concentrate on the study of its specific input–output relations. . . ." (Watzlawick, Beavin, & Jackson, 1967, p. 43) Viewing people as black boxes may seem like the ultimate expression of mechanistic thinking, but this metaphor had the advantage of simplifying the field of study by eliminating speculation about the inner workings of the mind in order to concentrate on their input and output—that is, communication and behavior.

Among the features of systems seized on by early family therapists, few were more influential than *homeostasis*, the self-regulation that keeps systems stable. Don Jackson's notion of *family homeostasis* emphasized that dysfunctional families' tendency to resist change went a long way toward explaining why, despite heroic efforts to improve, so many patients remain stuck (Jackson, 1959). Today we look back on this emphasis on homeostasis as exaggerating the conservative properties of families.

Thus, although many of the cybernetic concepts used to describe machines could be extended by analogy to human systems like the family, living systems, it turns out, cannot be adequately described by the same principles as mechanical systems.

◆ General Systems Theory

In the 1940s, an Austrian biologist, Ludwig von Bertalanffy, attempted to combine concepts from systems thinking and biology into a universal theory of living systems—from the human mind to the global ecosphere. Starting with investigations of the endocrine system, he began extrapolating to more complex social systems and developed a model that came to be called **general systems theory**.

Mark Davidson (1983), in his fascinating biography *Uncommon Sense*, summarized Bertalanffy's definition of a system as "any entity maintained by the mutual interaction of its parts, from atom to cosmos, and including such mundane examples as telephone, postal, and rapid transit systems. A Bertalanffian system can be physical like a television set, biological like a cocker spaniel, psychological like a personality, sociological like a labor union, or symbolic like a set of laws. . . . A system can be composed of smaller systems and can also be part of a larger system, just as a state or province is composed of smaller jurisdictions and also is part of a nation." (p. 26)

The last point is important. Every system is a subsystem of larger systems. But family therapists tended to forget this spreading network of influence. They treated the family as a system while largely ignoring the larger systems of community, culture, and politics in which families are embedded.

Bertalanffy used the metaphor of an organism for social groups, but an organism was an *open system*, continuously interacting with its environment. Open systems, as opposed to *closed systems* (e.g., machines), sustain themselves by exchanging resources with their environment—for example, taking in oxygen and expelling carbon dioxide.

Living organisms are active and creative. They work to sustain their organization, but they aren't motivated solely to preserve the status quo. In an open system, feedback mechanisms process information from the environment, which helps it adjust. For example, the cooling of the blood from a drop in environmental temperature stimulates centers in the brain to activate heat-producing mechanisms so that temperature is maintained at a steady level. Family therapists picked up on the concept of homeostasis, but according to Bertalanffy, an overemphasis on this conservative aspect of the organism reduced it to the level of a machine: "If [this] principle of homeostatic maintenance is taken as a rule of behavior, the so-called well-adjusted individual will be [defined as] a well-oiled robot" (quoted in Davidson, 1983, p. 104).

Unlike mechanical systems, which strive only to maintain a fixed structure, family systems also change when necessary to adapt to new circumstances. Walter Buckley (1968) coined the term **morphogenesis** to describe this plastic quality of adaptive systems.

To summarize, Bertalanffy brought up many of the issues that have shaped family therapy:

- A system as more than the sum of its parts
- Emphasis on interaction within and among systems versus reductionism
- Human systems as ecological organisms versus mechanism
- Concept of equifinality
- Homeostatic reactivity versus spontaneous activity.

Social Constructionism

Systems theory taught us to see how people's lives are shaped by their interactions with those around them. But in focusing on behavior, systems theory left something out—actually, two things: how family members' beliefs affect their actions, and how cultural forces shape those beliefs.

Constructivism

Constructivism captured the imagination of family therapists in the 1980s when studies of brain function showed that we can never really know the world as it exists out there; all we can know is our subjective experience of it. Research on neural nets (von Foerster, 1981) and the vision of frogs (Maturana & Varela, 1980) indicated that the brain doesn't process images literally, like a camera, but rather registers experience in patterns organized by the nervous system.[1] Nothing is perceived directly. Everything is filtered through the mind of the observer.

When this new perspective on knowing was reported to the family field by Paul Watzlawick (1984), the effect was a wake-up call—alerting us to the importance of cognition in family life.

Constructivism is the modern expression of a philosophical tradition that goes back as far as the eighteenth century. Immanuel Kant (1724–1804) regarded knowledge as a product of the way our imaginations are organized. The outside world doesn't simply impress itself onto the *tabula rasa* (blank slate) of our minds, as British Empiricist John Locke (1632–1704) believed. In fact, as Kant argued, our minds are anything but blank. They are active filters through which we process and interpret the world.

Constructivism found its way into psychotherapy in the *personal construct theory* of George Kelly (1955). According to Kelly, we make sense of the world by creating our own constructs of the environment. We interpret and organize events, and we make predictions that guide our actions on the basis of these constructs. You might compare this to seeing the world through a pair of eyeglasses. Because we may need to adjust constructs, therapy became a matter of revising old constructs and developing new ones—trying on different lenses to see which ones enable us to navigate the world in more satisfying ways.

The first application of constructivism in family therapy was the technique of **reframing**—relabeling behavior to shift how family members respond to it. Clients react very differently to a child seen as "hyperactive" than to one perceived as "misbehaving." Likewise, the dispirited parents of a rebellious ten-year-old will feel better about themselves if they become convinced that, rather than being "ineffective disciplinarians," they have an "oppositional child." The first diagnosis suggests that the parents should get tough but also that they probably won't succeed. The second suggests that coping with a difficult child requires strategizing. The point isn't that one description is more valid than the other, but rather that if whatever label a family applies to its problems leads to ineffective coping strategies, then perhaps a new label will alter their viewpoint and lead to a more effective response.

When constructivism took hold of family therapy in the 1980s, it triggered a fundamental shift in emphasis. Systems metaphors focused on behavior; constructivism shifted the focus to the assumptions people have about their problems. The goal of therapy changed from interrupting problematic patterns of interaction to helping clients find new perspectives on their lives.

Constructivism teaches us to look beyond behavior to the ways we interpret our experience. In a world where all truth is relative, the perspective of the therapist has no more claim to objectivity than that of the clients. Thus constructivism undermined the status of the therapist as an impartial authority with privileged knowledge of cause and cure. It's probably well to remember that even our most cherished metaphors of family life—*system, enmeshment, dirty games, triangles*, and so on—are just that: metaphors. They don't exist in some objective reality; they are constructions, some more useful than others.

In emphasizing the idiosyncratic perspective of the individual, constructivists were accused by some (e.g., Minuchin, 1991) of ignoring the social context. Once that solipsistic streak was pointed out, leading constructivists clarified their position: When they said that reality was constructed, they meant *socially* constructed.

The Social Construction of Reality

Social constructionism expanded constructivism much as family therapy expanded individual psychology. Constructivism says that we relate to the

---

[1]The eye of the frog, for example, doesn't register much but lateral movement—which may be all you really need to know if your main interest in life is catching flies with your tongue.

world on the basis of our own interpretations. **Social constructionism** points out that those interpretations are shaped by our context.

If a fourteen-year-old consistently disobeys his parents, a constructivist might point out that the boy may not think they deserve his respect. In other words, the boy's actions aren't simply a product of the parents' disciplinary efforts but also of the boy's construction of their authority. A social constructionist would add that an adolescent's attitudes about parental authority are shaped not only by what goes on in the family but also by messages transmitted from the culture at large.

At school or work, at lunch, in phone conversations, at the movies, and from television, we absorb attitudes and opinions that we carry into our families. Television, to pick one very potent influence on the average fourteen-year-old, has made today's children more sophisticated and more cynical. What communications scholar Joshua Meyrowitz (1985) said over thirty years ago in *No Sense of Place* is even more true now: today's children are exposed to the "back stage" of the adult world, to otherwise hidden doubts and conflicts, foolishness and failures of adult types they see on TV. This demystification undermines adolescent trust in traditional authority structures. It's hard to respect adult wisdom when your image of a parent is Homer Simpson.

Both constructivism and social constructionism focus on interpretation of experience as a mediator of behavior. But while constructivists emphasized the subjective mind of the individual, social constructionists place more emphasis on the intersubjective influence of language and culture (Lock & Strong, 2010). According to constructivism, people have problems not merely because of the objective conditions of their lives but also because of their interpretation of those conditions. What social constructionism adds is a recognition of how such meanings emerge in the process of talking with other people.

Therapy then becomes a process of **deconstruction**— freeing clients from the tyranny of entrenched beliefs. How this plays out in practice is illustrated in two of the most influential new versions of family therapy: the **solution-focused** model and **narrative** therapy.

Inherent in most forms of therapy is the idea that before you can solve a problem, you must figure out what's wrong. This notion seems self-evident, but it's a construction—one way of looking at things. *Solution-focused therapy* turns this assumption on its head, using a totally different construction—namely, that the best way to solve problems is to discover what people do when they're *not* having the problem.

Suppose a woman complains that her husband never talks to her. Instead of trying to figure out what's wrong, a solution-focused therapist might ask the woman if she can remember *exceptions* to this complaint. Perhaps she and her husband do have good conversations when they go for a walk or out to dinner. In that case, the therapist might simply suggest that they do more of that. We'll see how solution-focused therapy builds on the insights of constructivism in Chapter 11.

Like their solution-focused colleagues, *narrative* therapists create a shift in their clients' experience by helping them reexamine how they look at things. But whereas solution-focused therapy shifts attention from current failures to past successes in order to mobilize behavioral solutions, narrative therapy's aim is broader and more attitudinal. The decisive technique in this approach—*externalization*—involves the truly radical reconstruction of defining problems not as properties of the persons who suffer them but as alien oppressors. Thus, for example, while the parents of a boy who doesn't keep up with his homework might define him as lazy or a procrastinator, a narrative therapist would talk instead about times when "Procrastination" gets the better of him—and times when "It" doesn't.

Notice how the former construction—"The boy is a procrastinator"—is relatively deterministic, while the latter—"Procrastination sometimes gets the better of him"—frees the boy from a negative identity, and turns therapy into a struggle for liberation. We'll talk more about narrative therapy in Chapter 12.

Attachment Theory

As the field matured, family therapists showed a renewed interest in the inner life of the individuals who make up the family. Now, in addition to theories about the broad, systemic influences on family members' behavior, *attachment theory* has emerged as a leading tool for describing the deeper roots of close relationships.

Attachment theory has been especially fruitful in couples therapy (e.g., Johnson, 2002), where it helps explain how even healthy adults need to depend on each other. In the early years of family therapy, couples treatment was a therapy without a theory. With few exceptions, therapists treated couples with models designed for families (e.g., Minuchin, 1974; Haley, 1976; Bowen, 1978). The exception was behaviorists, who implied that intimacy was a product of reinforcement. Nobody talked much about love or longing. Dependency might be okay for children, but in adults, we were told, it was a sign of enmeshment.

In emotionally focused couples therapy, Susan Johnson uses attachment theory to deconstruct the familiar dynamic in which one partner criticizes and complains while the other gets defensive and withdraws. What attachment theory suggests is that the criticism and complaining are protests against disruption of the attachment bond—in other words, the nagging partner may be more insecure than angry.

The notion that how couples deal with each other reflects their attachment history can be traced to the pioneering studies of John Bowlby and Mary Ainsworth. When Bowlby graduated from Cambridge in the 1940s, it was assumed that infants became attached to their mothers as a consequence of being fed. But Konrad Lorenz (1935) showed that baby geese become attached to parents who don't feed them, and Harry Harlow (1958) found that, under stress, infant monkeys prefer the cloth-covered "mothers" that provided contact comfort to the wiremesh "mothers" that provided food. Human babies, too, become attached to people who don't feed them (Ainsworth, 1967).

In the 1940s and 1950s, a number of studies found that young children who were separated from their mothers go through a series of reactions that can be described as *protest, despair*, and finally *detachment* (e.g., Burlingham & Freud, 1944; Robertson, 1953). In attempting to understand these reactions, Bowlby (1958) concluded that the bond between infants and their parents was based on a biological drive for proximity that evolved through the process of natural selection. When danger threatens, infants who stay close to their parents are less likely to be killed by predators. Bowlby called this bond "attachment."

Attachment means seeking closeness in the face of stress. Attachment can be seen in cuddling up to mother's warm body and being cuddled in return, looking into her eyes and being looked at fondly, and holding on to her and being held. These experiences are profoundly comforting.

The child who has secure attachment experiences will develop a sense of basic security and will not be subject to morbid fears of being helpless, abandoned, and alone in the world. But the opposite is also true. Insecure attachment poisons a child's self-confidence. When threats arise, infants in secure relationships are able to direct *attachment behavior* (approaching, crying, reaching out) to their caregivers and take comfort in their reassurance (Bowlby, 1988). Infants with secure attachments are confident in the availability of their caregivers and, consequently, confident in their interactions in the world.

If a child's caregivers are generally unavailable or unresponsive to the child's needs, that child develops a sense of shame around those needs; such children doubt the validity of their needs, and feel bad for having them. They also come to believe that others cannot be depended on. They develop an *insecure attachment* (Bowlby, 1988). Insecure attachment generally falls into two categories: *anxious* and *avoidant*.

Anxiously attached children tend to have overly protective and intrusive parents. These children learn that the validity of their needs must be approved by their caregivers. As a result, over time, these children find it increasingly difficult to identify what they truly feel. Anxiously attached children cling to their caregivers; the message from the caregivers' intrusiveness is that the world is a dangerous place—you need me to manage it (Ainsworth, 1967). As an adult, anxiously attached individuals often suffer from depression and anxiety as they habitually give in to others' demands and work hard to please people. When their emotional security is threatened in adult romantic relationships, anxiously attached individuals try to restore a comfortable level of emotional closeness by frantically pulling their partner closer out of fear of losing them (Bowlby, 1973). Fear of abandonment—

"terror" might be the better term in order to convey how all consuming it is—haunts some people like nothing else.

Avoidantly attached children tend to have emotionally unavailable parents. The child will make initial attempts at seeking comfort from his or her caregiver, but when it becomes apparent that the caregiver will not respond, the child eventually gives up. A similar pattern happens with exploring—the child may start to venture out, but often gives up when faced with challenges (Ainsworth, 1967). These children learn that others will not be responsive to their needs, and in an attempt to avoid the pain of rejection, they try to cut off or otherwise not feel those unmet needs. When faced with insecurity in their intimate attachment relationships, avoidantly attached adults will often become distant and aloof in an effort to not need their partners and therefore not feel hurt by their rejection (Bowlby, 1973).

One of the things that distinguishes attachment theory is that it has been extensively studied. What is clear is that it is a stable and influential trait throughout childhood. The type of attachment shown at twelve months predicts: (1) type of attachment at eighteen months (Waters, 1978; Main & Weston, 1981); (2) frustratability, persistence, cooperativeness, and task enthusiasm at eighteen months (Main, 1977; Matas, Arend, & Sroufe, 1978); (3) social competence of preschoolers (Lieberman, 1977; Easterbrook & Lamb, 1979; Waters, Wippman, & Sroufe, 1979); and (4) self-esteem, empathy, and classroom deportment (Sroufe, 1979). The quality of relationship at one year is an excellent predictor of quality of relating up through five years, with the advantage to the securely attached infant.

What is less clearly supported by research is the proposition that styles of attachment in childhood are correlated with attachment styles in adult relationships. Nevertheless, the idea that romantic love can be conceptualized as an attachment process (Hazan & Shaver, 1987) remains a compelling if as yet unproven proposition. What the research has established is that individuals who are anxious over relationships report more relationship conflict, suggesting that some of this conflict is driven by basic insecurities over love, loss, and abandonment. Those who are anxious about their relationships often engage in coercive and distrusting ways of dealing with conflict, which are likely to bring about the very outcomes they fear most (Feeney, 1995).

Thus attachment theory offers a deeper understanding of the dynamics of familiar interactional problems. For example, a common *pursue/withdraw pattern* emerges when an anxiously attached partner pursues closeness while an avoidantly attached partner withdraws emotionally. Even though the underlying motivation for each partner is to establish emotional safety and closeness, their attachment fears of rejection lead them to act in a way that pushes their partner away, thus giving each of them less of what they long for (Johnson, 2002). Their solution has become the problem.

Being able to see behind a person's pursuing or distancing behavior to the underlying desire for connection and security can be one of a therapist's most useful insights. Interactions soften and shift when couples are helped to see and express their anxious pursuing as a fear of losing their partners, or their avoidant withdrawal as a fear of failure. A similar shift can occur between parents and children as parents are helped to understand some of their children's disruptive behavior as stemming from the child's anxiety about the parents' availability and responsiveness.

◆ ◆ ◆

After reading this chronology of how theories in family therapy have evolved, the reader may feel overwhelmed by the number of paradigm shifts in the field. It may help to point out a pattern in this apparent discontinuity. The focus of therapy has expanded toward ever-wider levels of context. This process started when therapists looked beyond individuals to their families. Suddenly, unexplainable behavior began to make sense. Early family therapists focused on behavioral interactions surrounding problems. Next it was recognized that those interactions were manifestations of a family's underlying structure, and structure became the target of change. Then family structure was seen to be a product of multigenerational processes that were governed by belief systems, and therapists aimed their interventions at those underlying beliefs.

More recently it dawned on therapists that these belief systems don't arise in a vacuum, hence the current interest in cultural influences.

Family therapists, naturalists on the human scene, discovered how behavior is shaped by transactions we don't always see. Systems concepts—feedback, circularity, and so on—helped make complex interactions predictable. In keeping with our emphasis on how ideas are actually applied in clinical practice, we will now consider the fundamental working concepts of family therapy.

The Working Concepts of Family Therapy

◆ Interpersonal Context

The fundamental premise of family therapy is that people are products of their context. Because few people are closer to us than our parents and partners, this notion can be translated into saying that a person's behavior is powerfully influenced by interactions with other family members. Thus the importance of context can be reduced to the importance of family. It can be, but it shouldn't be.

Although the family is often the most relevant context for understanding behavior, it isn't always. A depressed college student, for example, might be more unhappy about what's going on in the dormitory than about what's happening at home.

The clinical significance of context is that attempts to treat individuals by talking to them once a week may have less influence than their interactions during the remaining 167 hours of the week. Or to put this positively, often the most effective way to help people resolve their problems is to meet with them together with important others in their lives.

◆ Complementarity

Complementarity refers to the reciprocity that is the defining feature of every relationship. In any relationship one person's behavior is yoked to the other's.

Remember the symbol for yin and yang, the masculine and feminine forces in the universe?

Notice how the two parts are complementary and occupy one space. Relationships are like that. If one person changes, the relationship changes. If Tony starts doing more grocery shopping, Anne likely does less.

Family therapists should think of complementarity whenever they hear one person complaining about another. Take, for example, a husband who says that his wife nags. "She's always complaining." From the perspective of complementarity, a family therapist would assume that the wife's complaining is only half of a pattern of mutual influence. When people are perceived as nagging, it probably means that they haven't received a fair hearing for their concerns. Not being listened to by John makes Mary feel angry and unsupported. No wonder she comes across as nagging. If instead of waiting for her to complain, John starts asking her how she feels, Mary will feel like he cares about her. Or at least she's likely to feel that way. Complementarity doesn't mean that people in relationships control each other; it means that they influence each other.

A therapist can help family members get past blaming—and the powerlessness that goes with it—by pointing out the complementarity of their actions. "The more you nag, the more he ignores you. *And* the more you ignore her, the more she nags."

◆ Circular Causality

Before the advent of family therapy, explanations of psychopathology were based on linear models: medical, psychodynamic, or behavioral. Etiology was conceived in terms of prior events—disease, emotional conflict, or learning history. With the concept of *circularity*, Bateson helped change the way we think about psychopathology, from something caused by events in the past to something that is part of ongoing, circular feedback loops.

The notion of **linear causality** is based on the Newtonian model in which the universe is like a billiard table where the balls act unidirectionally on each other. Bateson believed that while linear causality is useful for describing the world of objects, it's a poor model for the world of living things, because it neglects to account for communication and mutual influence.

To illustrate this difference, Bateson (1979) used the example of a man kicking a stone. The effect of kicking a stone can be predicted by measuring the force and angle of the kick and the weight of the stone. If the man kicks a dog, on the other hand, the effect would be less predictable. The dog might respond in any number of ways—cringing, running away, biting, or trying to play—depending on the temperament of the dog and how it interpreted the kick. In response to the dog's reaction, the man might modify his behavior, and so on, so that the number of possible outcomes is unlimited.

The dog's actions (e.g., biting) loop back and affect the man's next moves (e.g., taking the Lord's name in vain), which in turn affect the dog, and so on. The original action prompts a circular sequence in which each subsequent action recursively affects the other. Linear cause and effect is lost in a circle of mutual influence.

This idea of mutual or **circular causality** is enormously useful for therapists because so many families come in looking to find the cause of their problems and determine who is responsible. Instead of joining the family in a logical but unproductive search for who started what, circular causality suggests that problems are sustained by an ongoing series of actions and reactions.

◆ Triangles

Most clients express their concerns in linear terms. It might be a four-year-old who is "unmanageable" or perhaps an ex-wife who "refuses to cooperate" about visitation rights. Even though such complaints suggest that the problem resides in a single individual, most therapists would think to look for relationship issues. "Unmanageable" four-year-olds often turn out to have parents who are ineffective disciplinarians,

and ex-wives who are "unreasonable" probably have their own sides of those stories. So a therapist, certainly a family therapist, would probably want to see the four-year-old together with her parents and to meet with both the angry father and his ex-wife.

Let's suppose that the therapist who meets with the four-year-old and her parents sees that indeed the real problem is a lack of discipline. The mother complains that the girl never does what she's told, the father nods in agreement, and the child runs around the room ignoring her mother's requests to sit still. Maybe the parents could use some advice about setting limits. Perhaps. But experience teaches that a child who misbehaves is often standing on one parent's shoulders. When children are disobedient, it usually means that their parents are in conflict about the rules or how to enforce them.

Perhaps the father is a strict disciplinarian. If so, his wife might feel that she needs to protect her daughter from her husband's harshness, and so she becomes more of a friend and ally to her child than a parent-in-charge.

Some parents are so angry with each other that their disagreements are plain to see. But many are less open. Their conflicts are painful, so they keep them private. Maybe they think that their relationship is none of the therapist's business, or perhaps the father has decided that if his wife doesn't like how he does things, "then she can damn well do them herself!" The point is this: Relationship problems often turn out to be triangular (Bowen, 1978), even though it may not always be apparent.

A less obvious example of triangular complications often occurs in the case of divorced parents who fight over visitation rights. Most divorces generate enough hurt and anger to make a certain amount of animosity inevitable. Add to that a healthy dose of parental guilt (felt and projected), and you would seem to have a formula for arguments about who gets the kids for holidays, whose turn it is to buy new sneakers, and who was late picking them up or dropping them off last weekend. Meeting with the embattled exes is likely to do little to disconfirm the assumption that the problem is between the two of them. Yet even two people who are very angry at each other will eventually find a way to work things out—unless third parties mix in.

What do you suppose happens when a divorced father complains to his girlfriend about his ex's "unreasonableness"? The same thing that usually happens when one person complains about another. The girlfriend sympathizes with him and, often as not, urges him to get tough with his ex. Meanwhile the mother is equally likely to have a friend encouraging her to become more aggressive. Thus, instead of two people left to work things out between them, one or both of them is egged on to escalate their conflict.

Do *all* relationship problems involve third parties? No, but most do.

Process/Content

Focusing on the **process** of communication (*how* people talk), rather than its **content** (*what* they talk about), may be the single most productive shift a family therapist can make. Imagine, for example, that a therapist encourages a moody freshman to talk to her parents. Imagine further that the young woman rarely expresses herself in words but rather in passive-aggressive protest and that her parents are, in contrast, all too good at putting their opinions into words. Suppose that the young woman finally begins to express her feeling that college is a waste of time, and her parents counter with an argument about the importance of staying in school. A therapist made anxious by the idea that the young woman might actually drop out of college who intervenes to support the *content* of the parents' position will miss an opportunity to support the *process* whereby the young woman learns to put her feelings into words, rather than into self-destructive actions.

Families who come for treatment are usually focused on content. A husband wants a divorce, a child refuses to go to school, a wife is depressed. The family therapist talks with the family about the content of their problems but thinks about the process by which they try to resolve them. While the family discusses what to do about the child's refusal to go to school, the therapist notices whether the parents seem to be in charge and whether they support each other. A therapist who tells the parents how to solve the problem (by making the child go to school) is working with content, not process. The child may start going to school, but the parents won't have improved their decision-making process.

Sometimes, of course, content is important. If a wife is drinking to drown her worries or a husband is molesting his stepdaughter, something needs to be done. But to the extent that therapists focus exclusively on content, they're unlikely to help families become better functioning systems.

Family Structure

Family interactions are predictable—some might say stubborn—because they are embedded in powerful but unseen structures. Dynamic patterns, like pursuer/distancer, describe the process of interaction; **structure** defines the organization within which those interactions take place. Initially, interactions shape structure; but once established, structure shapes interactions.

Families, like other groups, have many options for relating. Soon, however, interactions that were initially free to vary become regular and predictable. Once these patterns are established, family members use only a fraction of the full range of alternatives available to them (Minuchin & Nichols, 1993). Families are structured in **subsystems**—determined by generation, gender, and function—which are demarcated by interpersonal **boundaries**, invisible barriers that regulate the amount of contact with others (Minuchin, 1974).

Like the membranes of living cells, boundaries safeguard the integrity of the family and its subsystems. By spending time alone together and excluding friends and family from some of their activities, a couple establishes a boundary that protects their relationship from intrusion. Later, if they marry and have children, that boundary is preserved by making time to be alone together without the children. If, on the other hand, the couple includes their children in all of their activities, the boundary separating the generations wears thin and the couple's relationship is sacrificed to parenting. Moreover, if their parents are involved in all of their activities, children won't develop autonomy or initiative.

Psychoanalytic theory also emphasizes the need for interpersonal boundaries. Beginning with "the psychological birth of the human infant" (Mahler, Pine, & Bergman, 1975), psychoanalysts describe the progressive separation and individuation that culminates in the resolution of oedipal attachments and eventually in leaving home. But this is a one-sided emphasis on poorly defined boundaries. Psychoanalysts pay insufficient attention to the problems of emotional isolation stemming from rigid boundaries. This belief in separation as the model and measure of maturity may be an example of male psychology overgeneralized and unquestioned. The danger of people losing themselves in relationships is no more real than the danger of their isolating themselves from intimacy.

What family therapists discovered is that problems result when boundaries are either too rigid or too diffuse. Rigid boundaries permit little contact with outside systems, resulting in *disengagement*. Disengagement leaves people independent but isolated; it fosters autonomy but limits affection and nurture. Enmeshed subsystems have diffuse boundaries: They offer access to support, but at the expense of independence. Enmeshed parents are loving and attentive; however, their children tend to be dependent and may have trouble relating to people outside their family. **Enmeshed** parents respond too quickly to their children; disengaged parents respond too slowly.

Another important point about boundaries is that they are reciprocal. A mother's enmeshment with her children is related to the emotional distance between her and her husband. The less she gets from her husband, the more she needs from her children—and the more preoccupied she is with her children, the less time she has for her husband.

It should not go unnoticed that these arrangements are gendered. This doesn't make them any more right or wrong. But it should make us cautious about blaming mothers for cultural expectations that perpetuate their role as primary caretakers of children (Luepnitz, 1988). A therapist who recognizes the normative nature of the enmeshed-mother/disengaged-father syndrome but puts the burden on the mother to let go should ask himself why it doesn't occur to him to challenge the father to take hold.

◆ Family Life Cycle

When we think of the life cycle, we tend to think of individuals moving through time, mastering the challenges of one period, and then moving on to the next. The cycle of human life may be orderly, but it's not a steady, continuous process. We progress in stages with plateaus and developmental hurdles that demand change. Periods of growth and change are followed by periods of relative stability during which changes are consolidated.

The idea of a **family life cycle** adds two things to our understanding of individual development: First, families must reorganize to accommodate to the growth of their members; second, developments in any of the family's generations may have an impact on one or all of the family's members. When a son or daughter heads off to kindergarten or reaches puberty, not only must the child learn to cope with a new set of circumstances, but the whole family must readjust. Moreover, the developmental transitions that affect children aren't merely their own but their parents' as well—in some cases, even their grandparents'. The strain on a fourteen-year-old's relationship with his parents may be due as much to his father's midlife crisis or his mother's worrying about her own father's retirement as anything the boy himself is going through.

Changes in one generation complicate adjustments in another. A middle-aged father may become disenchanted with his career and decide to become more involved with his family just as his children are growing up and pulling away. His wish to get closer may frustrate their need to be on their own. Or to cite another example becoming more and more familiar, just as a man and woman begin to do more for themselves after launching their children, they may find the children back in the house (after dropping out of school, being unable to afford housing, or recovering from an early divorce) and therefore be faced with an awkward version of second parenthood.

One property that families share with other complex systems is that they don't change in a smooth, gradual process, but rather in discontinuous leaps. Falling in love and political revolutions are examples of such leaps. Having a baby is like falling in love and undergoing a revolution at the same time.

Sociologists Evelyn Duvall and Reuben Hill applied a developmental framework to families in the 1940s by dividing family life into discrete stages with tasks to be performed at each stage (Duvall, 1957; Hill & Rodgers, 1964). Family therapists Betty Carter and Monica McGoldrick (1980, 1999) enriched this

TABLE 3.1   Stages of the Family Life Cycle

Family Life-Cycle Stage	Emotional Process of Transition: Key Principles	Second-Order Changes in Family Status Required to Proceed Developmentally
Leaving home: single young adults	Accepting emotional and financial responsibility for self	a. Differentiation of self in relation to family of origin b. Development of intimate peer relationships c. Establishment of self in respect to work and financial independence
The joining of families through marriage: the new couple	Commitment to new system	a. Formation of marital system b. Realignment of relationships with extended families and friends to include spouse
Families with young children	Accepting new members into the system	a. Adjusting marital system to make space for children b. Joining in childrearing, financial and household tasks c. Realignment of relationships with extended family to include parenting and grandparenting roles
Families with adolescents	Increasing flexibility of family boundaries to permit children's independence and grandparents' frailties	a. Shifting of parent–child relationships to permit adolescent to move into and out of system b. Refocus on midlife marital and career issues c. Beginning shift toward caring for older generation
Launching children and moving on	Accepting a multitude of exits from and entries into the family system	a. Renegotiation of marital system as a dyad b. Development of adult-to-adult relationships c. Realignment of relationships to include in-laws and grandchildren d. Dealing with disabilities and death of parents (grandparents)
Families in later life	Accepting the shifting generational roles	a. Maintaining own and/or couple functioning and interests in face of physiological decline: exploration of new familial and social role options b. Support for more central role of middle generation c. Making room in the system for the wisdom and experience of the elderly, supporting the older generation without overfunctioning for them d. Dealing with loss of spouse, siblings, and other peers and preparation for death

framework by adding a *multigenerational* point of view, recognizing culturally diverse patterns and considering stages of divorce and remarriage (Table 3.1).

It's important to recognize that there is no universal version of the family life cycle. Not only do families come in a variety of forms—single-parent families, same-sexed couples, stepfamilies—but various religious, cultural, and ethnic groups may have different norms for various stages. The real value of the life-cycle concept isn't so much defining what's normal or expected at particular stages but recognizing that families often develop problems at transitions in the life cycle.

Problems develop when a family encounters a challenge—environmental or developmental—and is unable to accommodate to the changed circumstances. Thus problems are usually assumed to be a sign not of a dysfunctional family but simply of one that's failed to readjust at one of life's turning points.

◆ Family Narratives

The first family therapists looked beyond individuals to their relationships to explain how problems were perpetuated. Actions, it turned out, were embedded in interactions—and, of course, the most obvious interactions are behavioral. Double binds, problem-maintaining sequences, aversive control, triangles—these concepts all focused on behavior. But in addition to being actors in each other's lives, family members are also storytellers.

By reconstructing the events of their lives in coherent narratives, family members are able to make sense of their experience (White & Epston, 1990). Thus, it is not only actions and interactions that shape a family's life but also the stories they construct. The parents of a two-year-old who tell themselves that he's "defiant" will respond very differently than parents who tell themselves that their little one is "spunky."

Family narratives organize and make sense of experience. They emphasize certain events that reinforce the plot line and filter out events that don't fit. The parents who see their two-year-old as defiant are more likely to remember times she said no than times she said yes.

Interest in family narrative has become identified with one particular school, Michael White's narrative therapy, which emphasizes the fact that families with problems come to therapy with defeatist narratives that tend to keep them from acting effectively. But a sensitivity to the importance of personal narrative is a useful part of any therapist's work. However much a therapist may be interested in the process of interaction or the structure of family relationships, he or she must also learn to respect the influence of how family members experience events—including the therapist's input.

◆ Gender

When family therapists first applied the systems metaphor—an organization of parts plus the way they function together—they paid more attention to the organization than to the parts. Families were understood in terms of abstractions like *boundaries, triangles*, and *parental subsystems*, while family members were sometimes treated as cogs in a machine. The parts of a family system never cease being individual human beings, but the preoccupation with the way families were organized tended to obscure the personhood of the individuals who made up the family, including their psychodynamics, psychopathology, personal responsibility—and gender.

Common sense tells us that gender is a fact of life (though no one should underestimate social scientists' ability to transcend common sense). As long as society expects the primary parenting to be done by mothers, girls will shape their identities in relation to someone they expect to be like, while boys will respond to their difference as a motive for separating from their mothers. The result is what Nancy Chodorow (1978) called "the reproduction of mothering."

Traditionally, women have been raised to have more permeable psychological boundaries, to develop their identities in terms of connection, to cultivate their capacity for empathy, and to be at greater risk for losing themselves in relationships. Men, on the other hand, tend to emerge with more rigid psychological boundaries and disown their dependency needs, fear being engulfed, and often have greater difficulty empathizing with others. We all know men who are nurturing and women who are not, but these are exceptions that prove the rule.

Awareness of gender and gender inequity has long since penetrated not only family therapy but our entire culture. Translating this awareness into concrete clinical practice, however, is complicated.

There is room for disagreement between those who strive to maintain clinical neutrality and those who believe that failing to raise gender issues in treatment—money, power, child care, fairness, and so on—runs the risk of reinforcing traditional roles and social arrangements (Walters, Carter, Papp, & Silverstein, 1988). However, it is not possible to be a fair and effective therapist without being sensitive to how gender issues pervade the life of the family. A therapist who ignores gender may inadvertently show less interest in a woman's career, assume that a child's problems are primarily the mother's responsibility, have a double standard for extramarital affairs, and expect—or at least tolerate—a father's nonparticipation in the family's treatment.

If patriarchy begins at home, a gender-sensitive therapist must recognize the enduring significance of early experience and of unconscious fantasies. How children respond to their parents has significance not only for how they get along but also for the men and women they will become. When a girl speaks derisively about her "bitchy" mother, she may inadvertently be disparaging the female in herself. In addition to identification with the same-sex parent, the child's relationship with the other parent is part of what programs future experience with the opposite sex.

A gender-sensitive therapist must also avoid potential inequities in some of the basic assumptions of family therapy. The notion of *circular causality*, for example, which points to mutually reinforcing patterns of behavior, when applied to problems such as battering, incest, or alcoholism, tends to bypass questions of responsibility and makes it hard to consider influences external to the interaction, such as cultural beliefs about appropriate gender behavior. The concept of *neutrality* suggests that all parts of a system contribute equally to its problems and thus obscures differences in power and influence. The same is true of *complementarity*, which suggests that in traditional relationships between men and women, the roles are equal though different. Reconciling these contradictions is not always easy, but ignoring them isn't the answer.

◆ Culture

Among the influences shaping family behavior few are more powerful than the cultural context. A family from Puerto Rico, for example, may have very different expectations of loyalty and obligation from their adult children than, say, a white middle-class family from Minnesota. One reason for therapists to be sensitive to cultural diversity is to avoid imposing majority values and assumptions on minority groups. There are a host of excellent books and articles designed to familiarize therapists with families from a variety of backgrounds, including African American (Boyd-Franklin, 1989), Latino (Falicov, 1998), Haitian (Bibb & Casimir, 1996), Asian American (Lee, 1996), and urban poverty (Minuchin, Colapinto, & Minuchin, 2007), to mention just a few. These texts serve as guides for therapists who are about to venture into relatively unknown territory. However, the best way to develop an understanding of people from other cultures is to spend time with them.

Although they are sometimes used interchangeably, there is a difference between culture and ethnicity. **Culture** refers to common patterns of behavior and experience derived from the settings in which people live. **Ethnicity** refers to the common ancestry through which individuals have evolved shared values and customs—especially among groups that are not

Among Latino families, family loyalty is often a paramount virtue.

Monkey Business Images/Shutterstock

white Anglo-Saxon Protestants. *Culture* is the more generic term, and we have chosen it here to emphasize that cultural context is always relevant, even with a family who comes from a background similar to the therapist's.

Although cultural influences may be most obvious with families from foreign backgrounds, it is a mistake to assume that members of the same culture necessarily share values and assumptions. A young Jewish therapist might, for example, be surprised at the unsympathetic attitudes of a middle-aged Jewish couple about their children's decision to adopt an African American baby.

Appreciating the cultural context of families is complicated by the fact that most families are influenced by multiple contexts, which makes generalization difficult. For example, as noted by Nancy Boyd-Franklin (1989), middle-class African American families stand astride three cultures. There are cultural elements that may be traced to African roots, those that are part of the dominant American culture, and finally the adaptations that people of color have to make to racism in the dominant culture. Moreover, the cultural context may vary among family members. In immigrant families, for example, it's not uncommon to see conflicts between parents who retain a strong sense of ethnic identity and children who are more eager to assimilate the ways of the host country. First-generation parents may blame their children for abandoning the old ways and dishonoring the family, while the children may accuse their parents of being stuck in the past. Later, the children's children may develop a renewed appreciation for their cultural traditions.

> ▶ Watch this video of a therapist exploring a couple's ethnic heritage. What effect does their ethnicity have on the dynamics in their marriage?

The first mistake a therapist can make in working with clients from different backgrounds is to pathologize cultural differences. Although a lack of boundaries between a family and their neighbors and kin might seem problematic to a middle-class white therapist, such more inclusive family networks are not atypical for African American families.

The second mistake is to think that a therapist's job is to become an expert on the various cultures he or she works with. While it may be useful for therapists to familiarize themselves with the customs and values of the major groups in their catchment area, an attitude of respect and curiosity about other people's cultures may be more useful than imposing ethnic stereotypes or assuming an understanding of other people. It's important to acknowledge what you don't know.

The third mistake therapists make in working with families from other cultures is to accept everything assumed to be a cultural norm as functional. An effective therapist must be respectful of other people's ways of doing things without giving up the right to question what appears to be counterproductive. Although fluid boundaries may be typical among urban poor families, that doesn't mean it's inevitable for poor families to be dependent on various social services or for agency staff to presume that a family's need entitles workers to enter, unannounced and uninvited, into the family's space, physically or psychologically (Minuchin, Lee, & Simon, 1996).

Summary

We've covered a lot of ground in this chapter—from cybernetics to social constructionism, complementarity to culture. Some of these ideas may be familiar, while some may be new to you. Here's a brief summary.

Cybernetics is the study of how feedback is used to regulate mechanical systems. Applied to families, cybernetics teaches that when a family functions like a closed system the response to a problem may actually perpetuate it. To employ this concept clinically, therapists simply identify how family members have been responding to their problems and then get them to try something different.

According to *systems theory*, it's impossible to understand the behavior of individual family members without considering how the family system as a whole operates. To do so it may be necessary to look at *process* (how family members interact), and *structure* (how the family is organized).

Constructivism reintroduced cognition to family therapists. Family systems may be regulated by interpersonal interactions, but those interactions are shaped by how family members interpret each other's behavior. *Social constructionism* reminds us that families are open systems—our interpretations are shaped by assumptions we absorb from the culture.

The trajectory of these concepts broadened our focus beyond the individual to relationships, to the family as a whole, and finally to society at large. *Attachment theory* can be seen as part of an effort to restore our grounding in psychology. Attachment theory emphasizes the basic need for security in close relationships, both in childrearing and intimate partnership.

In the section on "The Working Concepts of Family Therapy," we tried to show how therapists can apply the insights of these various theories in clinical practice. Beyond the specifics, what we'd hope to get across is that families are more than a collection of individuals; they have superordinate properties that may not always be apparent. It may be obvious, for example, that there are always two parties to a relationship—and that problems, as well as solutions,

are a function of both parties. But even this reality can get lost in the heat of emotion. This is as true for therapists as for the people involved. Each of the various other working concepts offers its own particular insights into understanding family joys and sorrows.

In the following chapters, we'll see how the various schools of family therapy approach the task of understanding and treating family problems. But even as the models get specific, it's a good idea to keep in mind the general principles of family functioning explained in this chapter.

Click here to apply your knowledge of chapter concepts.

Click here to test your application and analysis of the content found within this chapter.

The pioneers of family therapy recognized that people are products of their **context**, but they limited their focus to the nuclear family. Yes, our actions are influenced by what goes on in our families. But what are the forces, past and present, that mold those influences? What makes a husband distance himself from his family? What makes a wife neglect her own development to manage her children's lives? Murray Bowen sought answers to such questions in the larger network of extended family relationships.

According to Bowen, human relationships are driven by two counterbalancing life forces: *individuality* and *togetherness*. We need companionship, and we need independence. What makes life interesting—and frustrating—is the tendency for those needs to polarize us. When one person presses for connection, the other may feel crowded and pull away. As time goes by, the pursuit of one and withdrawal of the other drives the pair through cycles of closeness and distance.

How successfully people reconcile these two polarities of human nature depends on their ability to manage emotionality, or to use Bowen's term, their *differentiation of self*. More about this later.

While no one doubts the formative influence of the family, many people imagine that once they leave home they are grown-up, independent adults, free at last of their parents' control. Some people take it as a sign of maturity to separate from their parents. Others wish they could be closer but find visits painful, and so they stay away to avoid disappointment. Once out of range of the immediate conflict, they forget and deny the discord. But our families remain with us wherever we go. As we will see, unresolved emotional reactivity to our parents is the most important unfinished business of our lives.

CHAPTER 4

BOWEN FAMILY SYSTEMS THERAPY

An Intergenerational Approach to Family Therapy

LEARNING OUTCOMES

♦ Describe the evolution of Bowen Family Systems Therapy.

♦ Describe the main tenets of Bowen Family Systems Theory.

♦ Describe healthy and unhealthy family development from a Bowen Family Systems Theory perspective.

♦ Describe the clinical goals and the conditions necessary for meeting those goals from a Bowen Family Systems Theory perspective.

♦ Discuss and demonstrate the assessment and intervention techniques of Bowen Family Systems Theory.

♦ Discuss methods for evaluating Bowen Family Systems Theory.

Sketches of Leading Figures

Murray Bowen's interest in the family began when he was a psychiatrist at the Menninger Clinic in the late 1940s. Turning his attention to the enigma of schizophrenia, Bowen was struck by the exquisite emotional sensitivity between patients and their mothers. Others called it *symbiosis*, as though it were some kind of mutation. Bowen saw it as simply an exaggeration of a natural process, a more intense version of the tendency to react emotionally that exists in all relationships.

In 1954 Bowen moved to the National Institute of Mental Health (NIMH), where he initiated a project of hospitalizing entire families containing a schizophrenic member. What he found was that the volatile bond between mothers and their emotionally disturbed offspring inevitably involved the whole family. At the heart of the problem was *anxious attachment*, a pathological form of closeness driven by anxiety. In these troubled families, people were emotional prisoners of the way the others behaved. The hallmark of these emotionally stuck-together, or *fused*, relationships was a lack of personal autonomy.

When the NIMH project ended in 1959 and Bowen moved to Georgetown University, he began working with families whose problems were less severe. What he discovered were many of the same mechanisms he had observed in psychotic families. This convinced him that all families vary along a continuum from emotional fusion to differentiation.

During his thirty-one years at Georgetown, Bowen developed a comprehensive theory of family therapy, inspired an entire generation of students, and became an internationally renowned leader of

Murray Bowen's extended family systems model is the most comprehensive theory in family therapy.

Andrea Schara/The Bowen Center for the Study of Family

the family therapy movement. He died after a long illness in October 1990.

Among the most prominent of Bowen's students are Philip Guerin and Thomas Fogarty, who joined in 1973 to form the Center for Family Learning in New Rochelle, New York. Under Guerin's leadership, the Center for Family Learning became one of the major centers of family therapy training. Guerin is a laid-back, virtuoso therapist and teacher, and two of his books, *The Evaluation and Treatment of Marital Conflict* and *Working with Relationship Triangles*, are among the most useful in all the family therapy literature.

Psychotherapy Networker

Philip Guerin's applications of Bowen theory have produced some of the most sophisticated clinical books in family therapy.

Betty Carter and Monica McGoldrick are best known for their exposition of the family life cycle (Carter & McGoldrick, 1999) and for championing feminism in family therapy. Michael Kerr was a longtime student and colleague of Bowen's and the director of training at the Georgetown Family Center. Kerr is perhaps the most faithful advocate of all Bowen's students, as his brilliant account of Bowenian theory in the book *Family Evaluation* (Kerr & Bowen, 1988) richly demonstrates. Kerr is now Director of the Bowen Theory Academy in Islesboro, Maine.

Theoretical Formulations

Family therapy's pioneers were pragmatists, more concerned with action than insight, more interested in technique than theory. Bowen was the exception. He was always more committed to systems theory as a way of thinking than as a set of interventions.

According to Bowen, we have less autonomy in our emotional lives than we like to think. Most of us are

◆ Societal Emotional Process

Bowen anticipated the contemporary concern about social influence on how families function. Kerr and Bowen (1988) cite the example of the high crime rate that results in communities with great social pressure. Bowen agreed that sexism and class and ethnic prejudice are toxic social emotional processes, but he believed that families with higher levels of differentiation were better able to resist these destructive social influences.

To the theoretical concerns of Bowenian therapists, Monica McGoldrick and Betty Carter added gender and ethnicity. These feminist Bowenians believe that ignoring gender inequalities helps perpetuate the forces that keep men and women trapped in inflexible roles. Moreover, they might point out that the previous sentence is inaccurate in implying that men and women alike are victims of gender bias. Women live with constraining social conditions *and* with men who profit from them—men who may not feel powerful with their wives and mothers but who take for granted social advantages that make it easier for men to get ahead in the world.

McGoldrick has also been a leader in calling attention to ethnic differences among families. Her book *Ethnicity and Family Therapy* (McGoldrick, Pearce, & Giordano, 1982) was a landmark in family therapy's developing awareness of this issue. Without being sensitive to how cultural values differ from one ethnic group to the next, there is a danger of therapists imposing their own ways of looking at things on families who aren't dysfunctional but simply different.

Family Dynamics

Bowen's theory is perhaps the richest in all of family therapy in terms of explaining how families work—and how they get off track. Careful readers will discover that the following principles can help us take charge of our own lives. Because, of course, blaming other people for your life's difficulties finally leads nowhere.

◆ Normal Family Functioning

Optimal development is thought to take place when family members are differentiated, anxiety is low, and partners are in good emotional contact with their own families. Most people leave home in the midst of transforming relationships with their parents from an adolescent to an adult basis. Thus the transformation is usually incomplete, and most of us, even as adults, continue to react with adolescent oversensitivity to our parents—or anyone else who pushes the same buttons.

Normally, but not optimally, people reduce contact with their parents and siblings to avoid the anxiety of dealing with them. Once out of the house and on their own, people tend to assume that they've put the old difficulties behind them. However, we all carry unfinished business in the form of unresolved sensitivities that flare up in intense relationships wherever we go. Having learned to ignore their role in family conflicts, most people are unable to prevent recurrences in new relationships.

Another heritage from the past is that the emotional attachment between intimate partners comes to resemble that which each had in their families of origin. People from undifferentiated families will continue to be undifferentiated when they form new families. Those who handled anxiety by withdrawal will tend to do the same in their marriages. Therefore, Bowen was convinced that differentiation of autonomous personalities, accomplished primarily in the family of origin, was both a description of normal development and a prescription for therapeutic progress.

Carter and McGoldrick (1999) describe the family life cycle as a process of expansion, contraction, and realignment of the relationship system to support the entry, exit, and development of family members.

In the *leaving home* stage, the primary task for young adults is to separate from their families without cutting off or fleeing to an emotional substitute. This is the time to develop an autonomous self before pairing off to form a new union.

In the *joining of families through marriage* stage, the primary task is commitment to the new couple. But this is not simply a joining of two individuals; it is a transformation of two entire systems. While problems at this stage may seem to be primarily between the partners, they often reflect a failure to separate from families of origin or cutoffs that put too much pressure on a couple. The formation of an intimate partnership requires the partners to shift their primary emotional attachment from their parents and friends to their mates. Making wedding plans, choosing a place to live, buying a car, having a baby, and selecting schools are times when this struggle may become explicit.

Families with young children must make space for the new additions, cooperate in childrearing, keep the marriage from being submerged in parenting, and realign relationships with the extended family. Young mothers and fathers must meet their children's needs for nurture and control, and they must learn to work together as a team. This is a stressful time, especially for new mothers, and it is the stage with the highest divorce rate.

> ▶ Watch this video of a Bowenian therapist interviewing a young mother about a recent loss in her family. What effect can a loss have on a young family?

The reward for parents who survive the preceding stages is to have their children turn into adolescents. *Adolescence* is a time when children no longer want to be like mommy and daddy; they want to be themselves. They struggle to become autonomous individuals and to open family boundaries—and they struggle however hard they must. Parents with satisfying lives of their own welcome (or at least tolerate) the fresh air that blows through the house at this time. Those who insist on controlling their teenagers, as though they were still little ones, may provoke escalations of the rebelliousness that's normal for this period.

In the *launching of children and moving on* stage, parents must let their children go and take hold of their own lives. This can be liberating or a time of *midlife crisis* (Nichols, 1986). Parents must not only deal with changes in their children's and their own lives but also with changes in their relationship with aging parents, who may need increasing support or at least don't want to act like parents anymore.

Families in later life must adjust to retirement, which not only means a loss of vocation but also increased proximity. With both partners home all day, the house may seem a lot smaller. Later in life families must cope with declining health, illness, and then death, the great equalizer.

One variation in the life cycle that can no longer be considered abnormal is *divorce*. With the divorce rate at 50 percent and the rate of redivorce at 61 percent (U.S. Bureau of the Census, 2014), divorce now strikes the majority of American families. The primary tasks of a divorcing couple are to end the marriage but maintain cooperation as parents. Some postdivorce families become single-parent families—consisting in the main of mothers and children—and in the vast majority of cases, staggering under the weight of financial strain. The alternative is remarriage and the formation of stepfamilies, in which, often, loneliness is swapped for conflict.

◆ Development of Behavior Disorders

Symptoms result from stress that exceeds a person's ability to manage it. The ability to handle stress is a function of differentiation: The more well-differentiated people are, the more resilient they will be and the more flexible and sustaining their relationships. In less well-differentiated people, it takes less stress to produce symptoms.

If *differentiation* were reduced to *maturity*, this formula wouldn't add much to the familiar diathesis-stress model, which says that illness develops when an individual's vulnerability is overtaxed. The difference is that differentiation isn't just a quality of individuals but also of relationships. A person's *basic* level of differentiation is largely determined by the degree of autonomy achieved in his or her family, but the *functional* level of differentiation is influenced by the quality of current relationships. Thus a somewhat immature person who manages to develop healthy relationships will be at less risk than an equally immature person who's alone or in unhealthy relationships. Symptoms develop when the level of anxiety exceeds the *system's* ability to handle it.

The most vulnerable individual (in terms of isolation and lack of differentiation) is most likely to absorb the anxiety in a system and develop symptoms. For example, a child of ten with a conduct disorder is likely to be the most triangled child in the family and thereby the one most emotionally caught up in the conflict between the parents or most affected by one of the parent's anxieties.

According to Bowen, the underlying factor in the genesis of psychological problems is *emotional fusion*, passed down from one generation to the next. The greater the fusion, the more one is programmed by primitive emotional forces, and the more vulnerable to the emotionality of others.

Emotional fusion is based on anxious attachment, which may be manifest either as dependency or isolation. Both the overly dependent and the emotionally isolated person respond to stress with emotional reactivity. The following clinical vignette illustrates how emotional fusion in the **family of origin** is transmitted.

CASE STUDY

Janet and Warren Langdon requested help for their son Martin after Mrs. Langdon found marijuana in a plastic bag at the bottom of his underwear drawer. Mr. and Mrs. Langdon didn't object when the therapist said she'd like to meet with all three of them. It turned out that the discovery of marijuana was just the latest incident in a long series of battles between Mrs. Langdon and her son. Lots of fifteen-year-olds experiment with marijuana; not all of them leave the evidence around for their mothers to find.

After meeting with the family and then talking with the boy and his parents separately, the therapist concluded that Martin did not have a serious drug problem. Of greater concern, however, were the intensity of his shouting matches with his mother and his poor social adjustment at school. What she told the family was that she was concerned not only about the marijuana but also about these other signs of unhappy adjustment and that she'd like to extend the evaluation by having a couple of meetings with Martin and his parents separately. Mr. and Mrs. Langdon agreed without enthusiasm.

After his father died, Mr. Langdon and his older sister were raised by their mother. They were all she had left, and she devoted all her energy to shaping

their lives. She was demanding and critical, and resentful of anything they wanted to do outside the family. By late adolescence, Warren could no longer tolerate his domineering mother. His sister was never able to break free; she remained single, living at home with her mother. Warren, however, was determined to become independent. Finally, in his mid-twenties, he left home and turned his back on his mother.

Janet Langdon came from a close-knit family. She and her four sisters were devoted to each other and remained best friends. After graduating from high school, Janet announced that she wanted to go to college. This was contrary to the family norm that daughters stay at home and prepare to be wives and mothers. Hence a major battle ensued between Janet and her parents; they were struggling to hold on, and she was struggling to break free. Finally she left for college, but she was ever after estranged from her parents.

Janet and Warren were immediately drawn to one another. Both were lonely and cut off from their families. After a brief, passionate courtship, they married. The honeymoon didn't last long. Never having really differentiated from his dictatorial mother, Warren was exquisitely sensitive to criticism and control. He became furious at Janet's slightest attempt to change his habits. Janet, on the other hand, sought to reestablish the closeness she'd had in her family. In order to be close, she and Warren would have to share interests and activities. But when she moved toward him, suggesting that they do something together, Warren got angry and resentful, feeling that she was impinging on his individuality. After several months of conflict, the two settled into a period of relative equilibrium. Warren put most of his energy into his work, leaving Janet to adjust to the distance between them. A year later Martin was born.

Both of them were delighted to have a baby, but what was for Warren a pleasant addition to the family was for Janet a way to fulfill a desperate need for closeness. The baby meant everything to her. While he was an infant, she was the perfect mother, loving him tenderly and caring for his every need. When Warren tried to become involved with his infant son, Janet hovered about making sure he didn't "do anything wrong." This infuriated Warren, and after a few bitter blowups he left Martin to his wife's care.

As Martin learned to walk and talk, he got into mischief, as children do. He grabbed things, refused to stay in his playpen, and fussed whenever he didn't get his way. His crying was unbearable to Janet, and she found herself unable to set limits on her precious child.

Martin grew up with a doting mother, thinking he was the center of the universe. Whenever he didn't get what he wanted, he threw a tantrum. Bad as things got, at least the family existed in a kind of equilibrium. Warren was cut off from his wife and son, but he had his work. Janet was alienated from her husband, but she had her baby.

Martin's difficulties began when he went off to school. Used to getting his own way, he found it difficult to get along with other children. His tantrums did nothing to endear him to his schoolmates or teachers. Other children avoided him, and he grew up having few friends. With teachers he acted out his father's resistance to any effort to control him. When Janet heard complaints about Martin's behavior, she sided with her son. "Those people don't know how to deal with a creative child!"

Martin grew up with a terrible pattern of adjustment to school and friends but retained his close relationship with his mother. The crisis came with adolescence. Like his father before him, Martin tried to develop independent interests outside the home. However, he was less capable of separating than his father had been, and his mother was incapable of letting go. The result was the beginning of chronic conflicts between Martin and his mother. Even as they argued and fought, they remained focused on each other. Martin spent more time battling his mother than doing anything else with his life.

Martin's history illustrates Bowen's theory of behavior disorder. Symptoms break out when the *vertical* problems of anxiety and toxic family issues intersect with the *horizontal* stresses of transition points in the life cycle. Thus Martin's greatest vulnerability came when the unresolved fusion he inherited from his mother intersected with the stress of his adolescent urge for independence.

According to Bowen, people tend to choose mates with similar levels of undifferentiation. When conflict develops, each partner will be aware of the emotional immaturity—of the other one. Each will be prepared

for change—in the other one. He will discover that her treating him like a father entails not only affectionate clinging but also tirades and temper tantrums. She will discover that he withdraws the closeness she found so attractive in courtship as soon as she makes any demands. Sadly, what turned them on to each other carries the switch that turns them off.

What follows is marital conflict, dysfunction in one of the spouses, preoccupation with one of the children, or a combination of all three. Whatever the presenting problem, however, the dynamics are similar: undifferentiation in families of origin is transmitted to marital problems, which are projected onto a symptomatic spouse or child. Thus are the problems of the past visited on the future.

Mechanisms of Change

When people ask how therapy works, they're usually interested in how therapists bring about change. That's all very well, except for one thing: therapists don't bring about change; they help clients bring about change in their own lives. Few schools of therapy appreciate this truth better than Bowen family systems therapy.

◆ Goals of Therapy

Bowenians don't try to change people, nor are they much interested in solving problems. They see therapy as an opportunity for people to learn about themselves and their relationships so that they can assume responsibility for their own problems. This is not to say, however, that therapists sit back and allow families to sort out their own conflicts. On the contrary, Bowenian therapy is a process of active inquiry, in which the therapist, guided by the most comprehensive theory in family therapy, helps family members get past blaming in order to explore their own roles in family problems.

Tracing the pattern of family problems means paying attention to *process* and *structure*. Process refers to patterns of emotional reactivity; structure, to interlocking networks of triangles.

To change a system, modification must take place in the most important triangle in the family—the one involving the marital couple. If a therapist stays in contact with the partners while remaining emotionally neutral, they can begin the process of **detriangulation** and differentiation that will profoundly affect the entire family system.

The clinical methodology tied to this formulation calls for: (1) increasing the parents' ability to manage their own anxiety, and thereby becoming better able to handle their children's behavior and (2) fortifying the couple's emotional functioning by increasing their ability to operate with less anxiety in their families of origin.

◆ Conditions for Behavior Change

Increasing the ability to distinguish between thinking and feeling, and learning to use that ability to resolve relationship problems is the guiding principle of Bowenian therapy. Lowering anxiety and increasing self-focus— the ability to see one's own role in interpersonal processes—are the primary mechanisms of change.

Understanding, not action, is the vehicle of cure. Therefore, two of the most important elements in Bowenian therapy may not be apparent to someone who thinks in terms of techniques. The atmosphere of sessions is designed to minimize emotionality. Therapists ask questions to foster self-reflection, and they direct them at individuals one at a time, rather than encourage family dialogues—which have a tendency to get overheated. Because clients aren't the only ones to respond emotionally to family dramas, Bowenian therapists strive to control their own reactivity and avoid triangulation. This is easier said than done. The keys to staying detriangled are avoiding taking sides and nudging each party toward accepting more responsibility for making things better.

Part of the process of differentiating a self is to develop a personal relationship with everyone in the **extended family**. The power of these connections may seem mysterious—particularly for people who don't think of their well-being as dependent on family ties. A little reflection reveals that increasing the number of relationships will enable an individual to spread out his or her emotional energy. Instead of concentrating one's investment in one or two family relationships, it's diffused into several.

Freud had a similar notion on an intrapsychic level. In "The Project for a Scientific Psychology," Freud described his neurological model of the mind. The immature mind has few outlets (*cathexes*) for channeling psychic energy and hence little flexibility or capacity for delay. The mature mind, on the other hand, has many channels of response, which permits greater flexibility. Bowen's notion of increasing the emotional family network is like Freud's model, writ large.

Therapy

The major techniques in Bowenian therapy include genograms, process questions, relationship experiments, detriangling, coaching, taking "I-positions," and displacement stories. Because seeing one's own role in family problems as well as how those problems are embedded in the history of the extended family are so important in Bowenian therapy, assessment is more critical in this approach than most.

◆ Assessment

Assessment begins with a history of the presenting problem. Exact dates are noted and later checked for their relationship to events in the extended family. Next comes a history of the nuclear family, including when the parents met, their courtship, their marriage, and childrearing. Particular attention is paid to where the family lived and when they moved, especially in relation to the location of the extended family. The next part of the evaluation is devoted to the history of both spouses' births, sibling positions, significant facts about their childhoods, and the functioning of their parents. All of this information is recorded on a *genogram*, covering at least three generations.

Genograms are schematic diagrams showing family members and their relationships to one another. Included are ages, dates of marriage, deaths, and geographical locations. Men are represented by squares and women by circles, with their ages inside the figures. Horizontal lines indicate marriages, with the date of the marriage written on the line; vertical lines connect parents and children (Figure 4.1).[1]

---

[1]For more detailed suggestions, see McGoldrick & Gerson, 1985.

FIGURE 4.1 Basic Symbols Used in Genograms

FIGURE 4.1 Basic Symbols Used in Genograms

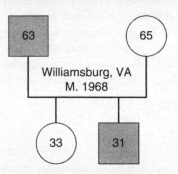

FIGURE 4.3 Genogram of Sigmund Freud's Family

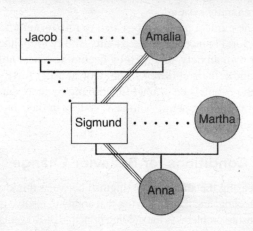

What makes a genogram more than a static portrait of a family's history is the inclusion of relationship conflicts, cutoffs, and triangles. The fact that Uncle Fred was an alcoholic or that Great Grandmother Sophie migrated from Russia is relatively meaningless without some understanding of the patterns of emotional processes passed down through the generations.

Dates of important events, such as deaths, marriages, and divorces, deserve careful study. These events send emotional shock waves throughout the family, which may open lines of communication, or these issues may get buried and family members may be progressively more cut off. Another significant piece of information on the genogram is the location of various segments of the family. Dates, relationships, and localities provide a framework to explore emotional boundaries, fusion, cutoffs, critical conflicts, amount of openness, and the number of current and potential relationships in the family.

Figure 4.2 shows symbols that can be used to describe the relationship dynamics among family members. Three parallel lines are used to indicate overly close (or fused) relationships; a zigzag line, conflict; a dotted line, emotional distance; and a broken line, estrangement (or cutoff). When these symbols are used, triangular patterns across three generations often become vividly clear—as shown in an abbreviated diagram of Sigmund Freud's family (Figure 4.3).

The history of a nuclear family begins with the courtship of the parents: What attracted them to each other? What was the early period of their relationship like? What were the problems during that period? When were the children born, and how did the parents adapt to the new additions?

Of particular interest are the stresses a family has endured and how they have adapted. This information helps to evaluate the intensity of chronic anxiety in a family and whether it is linked more to an overload of difficult life events or to a low level of adaptiveness in the family.

As Figure 4.4 shows, the bare facts of a nuclear family genogram only provide a skeleton on which to flesh out information about the Langdon family.

In gathering information about extended families, a therapist should ascertain which members of the clan are most involved with the family being assessed, for it is the nature of ongoing ties to the extended family that has a great impact on both parents and their role in the nuclear family. Of equal importance, however,

FIGURE 4.2 Genogram Symbols for Relationship Dynamics

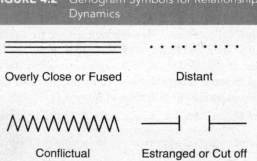

FIGURE 4.4 Langdon Family Genogram

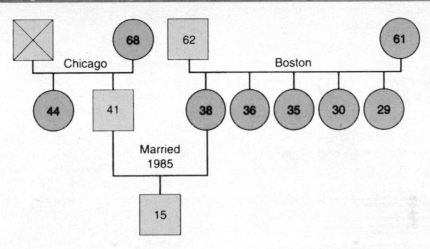

is finding out who is *not* involved, because people with whom contact has been cut off can be an even greater source of anxiety than the people with whom contact has been maintained.

 Watch this video of a therapist constructing a family genogram. Which questions would you ask when constructing a genogram?

Philip Guerin demonstrates the kinds of questions for constructing a genogram in the following vignette.

"THE INFAMOUS JERSEY SHORE"

Therapist: So, are you ready? Your attorney tells me that you're in the middle of divorce litigation and it's getting rough. Is that the main reason you came in this morning?

Patient: Yes. I'm very sad, and I wish I could make it all go away.

Therapist: How long have you been married?

Patient: We were married in '92.

Therapist: How old are you now?

Patient: 45 this past June. My birthday is June 6th.

Therapist: Where were you born?

Patient: In Mantoloking, New Jersey, as small town on the coast—the infamous Jersey Shore.

Therapist: Do you ever wish you were back there?

Patient: Only in the summer.

Therapist: How often do you go back?

Patient: Every year, at least for a few days.

Therapist: Is there anyone from your old clan still there?

Patient: My dad is still there. He's 75, been retired about five years.

Therapist: How about your mom?

Patient: She died of uterine cancer six years ago. My father tried to keep on working—he was an attorney—but his heart just wasn't in it.

Therapist: How old was your mother? How long had she been sick?

Patient: Mom was 67. She was first diagnosed 2½ years before she died.

Therapist: Tell me about that time in your life.

Patient: I can remember the phone call the day she got the news from the endometrial biopsy . . . it's like it was yesterday.

Therapist: What makes you so clear about that day?

Patient: I don't know for sure, but I think it feels like the beginning of the end of our idyllic life. . . .

Therapist: How many siblings do you have?

Patient: Three, two sisters and a brother.

Therapist: And where do you fit in that chain?

Patient: You probably could have guessed— I'm the oldest.

◆ Therapeutic Techniques

Bowenian therapists believe that understanding how family systems operate is more important than devising techniques to change them. Bowen himself spoke of technique with disdain, and he was distressed to see therapists relying on formulaic interventions.

If there were a magic bullet in Bowenian therapy— one essential technique—it would be the process question. *Process questions* are designed to explore what's going on inside people and between them: "When your boyfriend neglects you, how do you react?" "What about your wife's criticism upsets you most?" "When your daughter goes on dates, what do you worry about?" Process questions are designed to slow people down and start them thinking—not just about how others are upsetting them but about how they participate in interpersonal problems.

CASE STUDY

In interviewing a couple in which the husband was a recovering alcoholic with a history of abuse, the therapist asked, "Where are you with the thoughts about the damage you've done to your wife and kids with your alcoholism?"

When the man acknowledged responsibility for his abusive behavior and seemed genuinely remorseful, the therapist asked about his progress toward recovery, using process questions to focus on rational planning and personal responsibility. For example: "What makes that step so hard?"

"Pride."

"How does that manifest itself?"

"I get nasty."

Notice how this line of questioning explores not only the man's personal progress but also how his problems affect others in the family. Relationships take place in a systemic web of connections, but individuals are responsible for their own behavior.

Then the therapist shifted to open a discussion of the wife's role in the couple's difficulties. "So, you're getting better at taking responsibility for the drinking and the behavior connected with it? Do you think your wife appreciates what you're doing and the progress you're making?" And then a few minutes later: "Has your wife ever been able to talk to you about the things she's contributed to the relationship going sour?"

When the therapist asked the wife about her thinking, she reiterated all the annoying things her husband was doing—pressuring her to forgive him and get back together. Although he would eventually like her to consider her own role in the process, the therapist tried to empathize with her upset. "So, he's just bugging you by trying to get you to change your mind?" Then after a few minutes, the therapist tried to shift the wife to thinking more and feeling less. "Can you give me a summary of your thinking—how you came to that conclusion?" And when the wife again got angry and blamed her husband, the therapist just listened. A moment later he asked, "What do you do in the face of that abuse?"

"I get upset."

"Do you understand what it is about you that sets him off?"

"No."

"Has he ever been able to tell you?"

Notice how the therapist attempts to explore the process of the couple's relationship, asking both partners to think about what's going on between them, increase their awareness of their own contributions, and consider what they're planning to do to take responsibility to make things better.

Self-Focus

◆ Part of being a grown-up is taking responsibility for one's own emotions and the behavior those emotions drive.

- Self-focus does not release others from responsibility; it is a way for people to have more control in their own lives.
- Self-focus gives people more options for movement than a helpless victim has.
- "What percentage would you say is his (her) contribution, and what percentage is yours?"
- "What part might you be playing?"
- "What are your goals?" "What have you been doing to achieve them?" "What else?"

Philip Guerin, perhaps more than any other Bowenian, has developed clinical models that feature specific techniques for specific problems. As an example, he categorized marital conflict into four stages of severity with detailed suggestions for treating each stage (Guerin, Fay, Burden, & Kautto, 1987). In *Working with Relationship Triangles*, Guerin and his colleagues bring this same systematic approach to understanding and resolving triangles (Guerin, Fogarty, Fay, & Kautto, 1996). In early marriage, the "In-Law Triangle" is most common. Primacy of attachment and influence are the underlying issues.

In the "Wedding Gift Triangle" a young husband turns over his relationship with his mother to his wife. ("Thanks, honey.") The wife and her mother-in-law form a bond while the husband remains distant. He may like this at first but later become jealous. Guerin recommends separating the wife from overinvolvement with her mother-in-law and exploring her relationship as a wife rather than only as a mother and daughter-in-law. She might be asked to consider how her involvement in her primary parental triangle may have set her up for her present position in the in-law triangle. If there is conflict between the wife and her mother-in-law about influence over the husband, the two of them should be helped to understand what properly belongs to a son's relationship with his mother and what belongs in his relationship with his wife.

The "Loyalty Alignment Triangle" is one in which a partner and his or her parents remain overly close, with the new mate on the outside. In such cases, one or both partners never really left the family of origin. Here, most of the work should be aimed at helping the adult child work through his or her relationship with his or her parents. This doesn't mean cutting off

from them but transforming the relationship from an adolescent to an adult-to-adult basis. In the "Dominant Father-in-Law Triangle" a wife and her idealized father are united in implicit criticism of the husband. This can occur even, or especially, if the wife's father is dead. It's hard to live up to a myth.

In such cases, as with all triangles, the focus should not be on the content of the quarrels but on the triangular process underlying them. The goal is to foster an increasing primacy of the marital bond without doing damage to the relationships the partners have with their parents.

The second major technique in Bowenian therapy, after the process question, is the *relationship experiment*. Process questions are designed to help family members realize that it isn't what other people do but how they respond that perpetuates their problems. Relationship experiments are designed to help clients try something different from their usual emotionally driven responses. Some of these experiments may help resolve problems, but their primary purpose is to help clients develop the ability to resist being driven by their emotions.

CASE STUDY

The Kennedys came to therapy because sixteen-year-old David was doing badly in school. David was on the verge of flunking out of an exclusive private school partly because he was a poor student and partly because his evenings with friends included heavy drinking and marijuana smoking. His father had gotten after him to study harder and had suspended his driving privileges after he came home one school night quite drunk. Unfortunately, these efforts hadn't been very effective because David didn't respect his father, who was an alcoholic and frequently falling down drunk around the house. David's stepmother, who'd been living with them for only two years, had little ability to control him, and she knew enough not to try.

I told the parents that I wouldn't see them in family therapy because David didn't respect the father who was drunk every night and who, I added, didn't show any signs of being ready to do anything about his drinking. I did agree, however, to see David to try to help him finish the school year with passing grades.

David was able to pass the eleventh grade, and I continued to see him into the following year, not entirely comfortable in my role as substitute father figure. Although I maintained my resolve not to do therapy with a family that included a member who was actively abusing alcohol, I did meet with the family during three or four crises. The first three crises occurred when Mr. Kennedy's drinking (and, it turned out, cocaine abuse) got way out of control and his father and wife insisted that he reenter treatment.

The most prominent triangle in this case was that Mr. Kennedy's wife and father got together to pressure him to quit drinking. He had gone to rehab several times, but even the few times he'd actually finished a program, he soon returned to drinking. The only reason he ever sought help was as a result of ultimatums from his wife and father. His wife threatened to leave him, and his father threatened to cut him off from the family estate. This case would go nowhere until this triangle could be modified.

I encouraged Mr. Kennedy's wife and father to work on being less reactive while separating from each other around the issue of Mr. Kennedy's drinking. Mr. Kennedy needed to take a stand for himself, rather than comply with his wife's and his father's wishes. In fact, I wondered aloud with him if taking an honest stance with his family wouldn't mean telling them that he didn't intend to quit drinking. What he decided to tell them was that while he was willing to work on controlling his drinking and use of cocaine, he didn't intend to quit.

I encouraged Mr. Kennedy's father to back off and let the other two battle it out. Reluctantly, he agreed to do so. I then got Mrs. Kennedy to make a clear statement about how she felt about her husband's drinking but to discontinue her fruitless efforts to make him stop. I encouraged her to maintain her connection with her father-in-law but without talking about her husband all the time. Two months later, Mr. Kennedy decided to stop drinking and using cocaine.

This time he successfully completed a twenty-eight-day rehab program and entered AA and NA. Six weeks later he once again relapsed. Over the following eight months, Mr. Kennedy's drinking and cocaine abuse got much worse. Finally, after a serious altercation with a Jamaican drug dealer, Mr. Kennedy made a serious decision to get sober. This time, instead of going to the respected local rehabilitation center that his father

had recommended, he did some research on his own and decided to enter a famous drug treatment center in California. As of this writing, Mr. Kennedy has been sober for ten years.

Bowenian Therapy with Couples

The secret of couples therapy is to stay connected with both partners without letting them triangle you. Bowen would speak with each person one at a time, often beginning with the more motivated partner. He would ask questions, verify facts, and listen to people's stories. But he would frame each question to stimulate thinking rather than encourage expression of feelings. His objective was to explore the perceptions and opinions of each partner without siding emotionally with either one. It's taking sides that keeps people from learning to deal with each other.

When things are calm, feelings can be dealt with more objectively and partners can talk rationally with each other. But when feeling outruns thinking, it's best to ask questions that get couples to think more and feel less—and to talk to the therapist rather than to each other. (It's easier to hear when you aren't busy preparing to respond.) If all else fails to cool things down, Fogarty (1976b) recommends seeing spouses in separate sessions.

As partners talk, the therapist concentrates on the *process* of their interaction, not on the details under discussion. Focusing on *content* is a sign that the therapist is emotionally entangled. It may be hard to avoid being drawn in by hot topics like money, sex, and discipline of children. But a therapist's job isn't to settle disputes—it's to help couples do so. The aim is to get clients to express thoughts and opinions to the therapist in the presence of their partners. Should one break down in tears, the therapist remains calm and inquires about the thoughts that touched off the tears. If a couple begins arguing, the therapist becomes more active, calmly questioning one, then the other, focusing on their respective thoughts. Asking for detailed descriptions of events is one of the best ways to cool overheated emotion and make room for reason.

Bowenian couples therapy is designed to reduce anxiety and foster self-focus.

Metaphors of complementarity are helpful to highlight the process of interactions. Fogarty (1976b), for example, described the *pursuer–distancer* dynamic. The more one presses for communication and togetherness, the more the other distances—watches television, works late, or goes off with the children. Frequently, partners pursue and distance in different areas. Men commonly distance themselves emotionally but pursue sexually. The trick, according to Fogarty, is "Never pursue a distancer." Instead, help pursuers explore their own inner emptiness. "What's in your life besides the other person?"

To underscore the need for objectivity, Bowen spoke of the therapist as a "coach" or "consultant." He didn't mean to imply indifference but rather to emphasize the neutrality required to avoid triangulation. In traditional terms this is known as *managing countertransference*. Just as analysts are analyzed themselves so they can recognize **countertransference**, Bowen considered differentiating a self in one's own family the best way to avoid being emotionally triangled by clients.

To help partners define differentiated identities, it's useful for a therapist to take "I-positions" (Guerin, 1971)—that is, to make nonreactive observations and statements of opinion. The more a therapist takes an autonomous position in relation to a family, the easier it is for family members to define themselves to each other. Gradually, family members learn to calmly state their own beliefs and to act on them without attacking others or becoming overly upset by their responses.

After sufficient harmony had been won with progress toward self-differentiation, Bowen taught couples how emotional systems operate and encouraged them to explore those webs of relationship in their own families (Bowen, 1971).

For example, a woman locked into the role of emotional pursuer might be asked to describe her relationship with her father and then compare it with her current relationships. If lessening her preoccupation with her husband and children seems advisable, the therapist might encourage her to connect with the most emotionally distant member of her family, often her father. The idea wouldn't be to shift her attachment from one set of relationships to another but to help her understand that the intensity of her need was due in part to unfinished business.

Michael Kerr (1971) suggests that when relationship problems in the nuclear family are being discussed, therapists should occasionally ask questions about similar patterns in the family of origin. If family members see that they are repeating earlier patterns, they are more likely to recognize their own emotional reactivity. Recently, this author saw a couple unable to decide what to do with their mentally ill teenage daughter. Although the daughter was virtually uncontrollable, her mother found it difficult to consider hospitalization. When asked what her own mother would have done, without hesitating she replied that her long-suffering mother would have been too guilt-ridden even to consider placement—"no matter how much she and the rest of the family might suffer." Little more needed to be said.

Bowenian Therapy with Individuals

Bowen's success at differentiating from his own family convinced him that a single highly motivated individual can be the fulcrum for changing an entire family system (Anonymous, 1972). The goal of working with individuals is the same as with larger units: developing person-to-person relationships, seeing family members as people rather than emotionally charged images, learning to recognize triangles, and, finally, detriangling oneself (Bowen, 1974).

The process of change is begun by learning more about the larger family—who made up the family, where they lived, what they did, and what they were like. Sometimes a "good relationship" turns out to be one in which tension is managed by distancing: infrequent contact, superficial conversation, and gossiping about other family members. Therefore, it's useful to ask for descriptions rather than conclusions—not, "Do you have a good relationship with your parents?" but, "Where do your parents live? How often do you see them? What do you and your mother talk about when you're alone together? Do you ever go out to lunch, just you and your dad?"

Gathering information about the family is an excellent vehicle for the second step toward differentiation, establishing person-to-person relationships with as many family members as possible. This means getting in touch and speaking personally with them, not about other people or impersonal topics. If this sounds easy, try it. Few of us can spend more than a few minutes talking personally with certain family members without getting anxious. When this happens, we're tempted to withdraw, or triangle in another person. Gradually extending the time of personal conversation improves the relationship and helps differentiate a self.

Ultimately, differentiating yourself requires ceasing to participate in interpersonal triangles. The goal is to relate to people without gossiping or taking sides and without counterattacking or defending yourself.

Triangles can be identified by asking who or what people go to when they distance from someone with whom they have been close. One sign of a triangle is its repetitive pattern. The dynamic of a triangle is predictable because it's reactive and automatic.

Suppose that every time you talk to your mother she starts complaining about your father. Maybe it feels good to be confided in. Maybe you have fantasies about rescuing your parents—or at least your mother. In fact, the triangling is destructive to all three relationships: you and dad, dad and mom, and, yes, you and mom. In triangles, one pair is close and two are distant (Figure 4.5). Sympathizing with mom alienates dad. It also makes it less likely that she'll work out her complaints with him.

Once you recognize a triangle for what it is, you can stop participating in it. The idea is to do something to get the other two people to work out their own relationship. The most direct approach is simply to suggest that they do so. In the example just given, you might suggest that your mother discuss her concerns with your father, *and* refuse to listen to more complaints. Less direct but more powerful is to tell dad that his wife has been complaining about him, and you don't know why she doesn't tell him about it. She'll be annoyed but not forever. A more devious ploy is to overagree with mom's complaints.

FIGURE 4.5 Cross-Generational Triangle

When she says he's messy, you say he's a complete slob; when she says he's not very thoughtful, you say he's an ogre. Pretty soon she'll begin to defend him. Maybe she'll decide to work out her complaints with him, or maybe she won't. Either way you'll have removed yourself from the triangle.

Once you look for them, you'll find triangles everywhere. Common examples include griping with colleagues about the boss, telling someone that your partner doesn't understand you, undercutting your spouse with the kids, and watching television to avoid talking to your family. Breaking free of triangles may not be easy, but the rewards are great. The payoff comes not only from enriching those relationships but also from enhancing your ability to relate to anyone—friends, colleagues, clients, and your spouse and children. Furthermore, if you can remain in emotional contact but change the part you play in your family—and maintain the change despite pressures to change back—the family will have to accommodate to your change.

Useful guidelines to help families avoid falling back into unproductive but familiar patterns have been enumerated by Carter and Orfanidis (1976), Guerin and Fogarty (1972), and Herz (1991). You can also read about how to work on family tensions by resolving your own emotional sensitivities in two marvelous books by Harriet Lerner: *The Dance of Anger* (Lerner, 1985) and *The Dance of Intimacy* (Lerner, 1989).

Evaluating Therapy Theory and Results

What makes Bowen's theory so useful is that it explains the emotional forces that regulate how we relate to other people. The single greatest impediment to understanding one another is our tendency to become emotionally reactive. Like all things about relationships, emotionality is a two-way street: Some people express themselves with such emotionalism that others react to that pressure rather than hearing what the person is trying to say. Bowenian theory locates the origin of this reactivity in the lack of differentiation of self and explains how to reduce emotionalism and move toward self-control—by cultivating relationships widely in the family and learning to listen without becoming defensive or untrue to one's own beliefs.

In Bowenian theory, *anxiety* is the underlying explanation (for why people are dependent or avoidant and why they become emotionally reactive), reminiscent of Freudian conflict theory (which explains all symptoms as the result of conflicts about sex and aggression). The second pivotal concept in the Bowenian system is *differentiation*. Since differentiation is roughly synonymous with *maturity*, students might ask, To what extent is the proposition that more differentiated people function better a circular argument? In respect to the Bowenian tradition of asking questions rather than imposing opinions, we'll let this stand as an open question for your consideration.

A possible shortcoming of the Bowenian approach is that in concentrating on individuals and their extended family relationships, it may neglect the power of working directly with the nuclear family. In many cases the most expedient way to resolve family problems is to bring everyone in the household together and encourage them to face each other and address their conflicts. These discussions become may heated and contentious, but a skilled therapist can help family members realize what they're doing and guide them toward understanding.

There are times when families are so belligerent that their dialogues must be interrupted to help individuals get beyond defensiveness to the hurt feelings underneath. At such times, it's useful, perhaps imperative, to block family members from arguing with each other. But an approach, such as Bowen's, that encourages therapists to always speak to individual family members one at a time underutilizes the power of working with families in action.

Phil Guerin and Tom Fogarty have made notable contributions, not only in promulgating Bowenian theory but also in refining techniques of therapy. Both are master therapists. Betty Carter and Monica McGoldrick have made more of a contribution in studying how families work: the family life cycle, ethnic diversity, and the pervasive role of gender inequality. Because they are students of the family as well as therapists, some of their interventions have a decidedly educational flavor. In working with stepfamilies, for example, Betty Carter takes the stance of an expert and teaches the stepparent not to try to assume an equal position with the biological parent. Stepparents have to earn moral authority; meanwhile, what works best is supporting the role of the biological parent. Just as Bowen's approach is influenced by his personal experience, it seems that both Carter and McGoldrick infuse their work as family therapists with their experience as career women and their convictions about the price of inequality.

Family researchers have tested the empirical validity of some of the propositions of Bowen's theory, most prominently the concept of differentiation of self. Three psychometrically sound measures of differentiation of self have been developed. Haber's (1993) Level of Differentiation of Self Scale contains twenty-four items that focus on emotional maturity, such as "I make decisions based on my own set of values and beliefs" and "When I have a problem that upsets me, I am still able to consider different options for solving the problem." This scale significantly correlates (negatively) with chronic anxiety and psychological distress, which is consistent with Bowen theory. Skowron's Differentiation of Self Inventory (DSI) (Skowron & Friedlander, 1998) contains four subscales: Emotional Cutoff ("I need to distance myself when people get too close to me," "I would never consider turning to any of my family members for emotional support."); "I"-Position ("I do not change my behavior simply to please another person"); Emotional Reactivity ("at times my feelings get the best of me and I have trouble thinking clearly"); and Fusion with Others ("it has been said of me that I am still very attached to my parents"). As Bowen theory predicts, the DSI correlates significantly with chronic anxiety, psychological distress, and marital satisfaction. Chabot Emotional Differentiation Scale (CED) was designed to measure the intrapsychic aspect of differentiation—the ability to think rationally in emotionally charged situations (Licht & Chabot, 2006). The CED asks subjects to respond to seventeen questions that assess integration of thinking and feeling in nonstressful periods and periods of prolonged stress, as well as when relationships are going well and when there are difficulties in relationships.

Research has supported Bowen's notion that differentiation is related to trait anxiety (negatively) (Griffin & Apostal, 1993; Haber, 1993; Skowron & Friedlander, 1998; Peleg-Popko, 2002; Peleg & Yitzhak, 2011), psychological and physical health problems (negatively) (Davis & Jones, 1992; Haber, 1993; Bohlander, 1995; Skowron & Friedlander, 1998; Elieson & Rubin, 2001; Bartle-Harlin & Probst, 2004), and marital satisfaction (positively) (Haber, 1984; Richards, 1989; Skowron & Friedlander, 1998; Skowron, 2000). Several studies have shown a significant relationship between triangulation and marital distress (Vuchinich, Emery, & Cassidy, 1988; Wood, Watkins, Boyle, Nogueira, Zimand, & Carroll, 1989; Gehring & Marti,1993; Peleg, 2008) as well as problems in intimate relationships (West, Zarski, & Harvill, 1986; Protinsky & Gilkey, 1996). Finally, consistent with Bowen's belief in the multigenerational transmission of emotional process, researchers have found that parents' and children's beliefs are highly correlated (e.g., Troll & Bengston, 1979) and that violence (e.g., Alexander, Moore, & Alexander, 1991), divorce (e.g., Amato, 1996), marital quality (e.g., Feng, Giarrusso, Bengston, & Fry, 1999), eating disorders (e.g., Whitehouse & Harris, 1998), depression (Whitbeck et al., 1992), and alcoholism (e.g., Sher, Gershuny, Peterson, & Raskin, 1997) are transmitted from one generation to the next.

Additionally, some have proposed therapy models that utilize a Bowenian theoretical framework to address a host of presenting complaints. For instance, Kolbert and colleagues have suggested that Bowenian family therapy could be incorporated into individual therapy with adolescents whose families cannot (and in some cases should not) participate in joint sessions (Kolbert, Crothers, & Field, 2013). Others have similarly proposed models inspired by Bowenian family therapy to treat adults who were abused as children (MacKay, 2012), adolescent runaways (Coco & Courtney, 2003), and the homeless (Hertleing & Killmer, 2004). While these authors provide data from successful case studies, to date there are no controlled outcome studies testing the effectiveness of Bowenian therapy (Johnson & Lebow, 2000; Miller, Johnson, Sandberg, Stringer-Seibold, & Gfeller-Strouts, 2000). This, of course, is not surprising, considering that research is usually conducted by academics, most of whom are more interested in behavioral models than in traditional approaches like psychoanalysis and Bowen systems theory.

Ultimately, the status of extended family systems therapy rests not on empirical research but on the elegance of Murray Bowen's theory, clinical experiences with this approach, and the personal experiences of those who have worked at differentiating themselves in their families of origin. Bowen himself was decidedly cool to empirical research (Bowen, 1976), preferring instead to refine and integrate theory and practice. Like psychoanalysis, Bowen systems theory is probably best judged not as true or false but as useful or not useful. On balance, it seems eminently useful.

Summary

Bowen's conceptual lens was wider than that of most family therapists, but his actual unit of treatment was smaller. His concern was always with the multigenerational family system, even though he usually met with individuals or couples. Since first introducing the **three-generational hypothesis of schizophrenia**, he was aware of how interlocking triangles connect one generation to the next—like threads interwoven in a family tapestry. Although Bowenian therapists are unique in sending patients home to repair their relationships with parents, the idea of intergenerational connections has been very influential in the field.

According to Bowen, the major problem in families is *emotional fusion*; the major goal is *differentiation*. Emotional fusion grows out of an instinctual need for others but is an unhealthy exaggeration of this need. Some people manifest fusion directly as an excessive need for togetherness; others mask it with a façade of independence. In either case, contagious anxiety drives automatic responses in close relationships and limits autonomous functioning.

In addition to extending his analysis of family problems deeper into the anxieties of individuals, Bowen also extended the focus wider, making the triangle the universal unit of analysis—in principle and practice. When people can't settle their differences, the automatic tendency to involve third parties stabilizes relationships but freezes conflict in place. Bowen's recognition that the majority of family

problems have triangular complications was one of the seminal ideas in family therapy.

Bowen discouraged therapists from trying to fix relationships and instead encouraged them to remain neutral while exploring the emotional processes in conflictual relationships with process questions. Bowenian therapists rarely give advice. They just keep asking questions. The goal isn't to solve people's problems but to help them learn to see their own role in how their family system operates. This self-discovery isn't merely a matter of introspection, because understanding is seen as a tool for repairing relationships and enhancing one's own autonomous functioning.

Six techniques are prominent in the practice of Bowen family systems therapy:

◆ **Genogram.** In addition to recording biographic data, the genogram is used to trace relationship conflicts, cutoffs, and triangles. This process of collecting information is sometimes therapeutic in and of itself: Family members often say, "It never occurred to me how all those events fit together." The most comprehensive guide to working with genograms is *Genograms in Family Assessment* (McGoldrick & Gerson, 1985).

◆ **Neutralizing Triangles.** If a therapist can remain free of the emotional reactivity families bring to therapy, clients will be better able to reduce their own emotionality and begin to think more clearly about their problems. The danger is that the same process of emotional triangulation families use to stabilize their conflicts will engulf the therapist. If so, therapy will be stalemated. On the other hand, if the therapist can remain free of reactive emotional entanglements—in other words, stay detriangled—the family system and its members will calm down to the point where they can begin to work out their dilemmas.

◆ **Process Questions.** Each family member is asked a series of questions aimed at toning down emotion and fostering objective reflection. Process questions are also used to help manage and neutralize triangles, including the potential triangle(s) that may develop between the therapist and various family members. The process question is aimed at calming anxiety and gaining access to information on how the family perceives the problem and how the mechanisms driving the problem operate. If process questions decrease anxiety, people will be better able to think clearly. This clarity allows them to discover more potential options for managing their problems.

- **Relationship Experiments.** Relationship experiments are carried out around structural alterations in key triangles. The goal is to help family members become aware of systems processes and learn to recognize their own role in them. Perhaps the best illustrations of such experiments are those developed by Fogarty for use with emotional pursuers and distancers. Pursuers are encouraged to restrain their pursuit, stop making demands, decrease pressure for emotional connection, and see what happens, in themselves and in the relationship. This exercise isn't designed to be a magic cure (as some people hope) but to help clarify the emotional processes involved. Distancers are encouraged to move toward their partners and communicate personal thoughts and feelings—in other words, to find an alternative to avoiding or capitulating to the other person's demands.

- **Coaching.** Coaching is the Bowenian alternative to the more emotionally involved role common to other forms of therapy. By acting as a coach, the Bowenian therapist hopes to avoid taking over for clients or becoming embroiled in family triangles. Coaching doesn't mean telling people what to do. It means asking questions designed to help people figure out family emotional processes and their role in them.

- **The "I"-Position.** An "I"-position is a calm and clear statement of personal opinion. In situations of increased tension, it often has a stabilizing effect for one person to be able to detach from the emotionality and adopt an "I"-position. Taking a personal stance—saying what you feel instead of what others are doing—is one of the most direct ways to break cycles of emotional reactivity. It's the difference between saying "You're lazy" and "I wish you would help me more" or between "You're always spoiling the children" and "I think we should be stricter with them." It's a big difference.

Bowenian therapists not only encourage clients to take "I"-positions, but they also do so themselves. For example, after a family session, the mother pulls the therapist aside and confides that her husband has terminal cancer but she doesn't want the children to know. What to do? Take an "I"-position: Say to the mother, "I believe your children have a right to know about this." What she does, of course, is up to her.

Finally, although students of family therapy are likely to evaluate different approaches according to how much sense they make and how useful they promise to be, Bowen himself considered his most important contribution to be showing the way to make human behavior a science. Far more important than developing methods and techniques of family therapy, Murray Bowen made profound contributions to our understanding of how we function as individuals, how we get along with our families, and how these are related.

Click here to apply your knowledge of chapter concepts.

Click here to test your application and analysis of the content found within this chapter.

With their compelling application of cybernetics and systems theory, strategic approaches once captivated family therapy. Part of their appeal was a pragmatic, problem-solving focus, but there was also a fascination with strategies to outwit and provoke families into changing, with or without their cooperation. It was this manipulativeness that eventually turned people against strategic therapy.

The dominant approaches of the twenty-first century have elevated cognition over behavior and encouraged therapists to be collaborative rather than manipulative. Instead of trying to solve problems and provoke change, therapists began to reinforce solutions and inspire change. As a consequence, the once celebrated voices of strategic therapy—Jay Haley, John Weakland, Mara Selvini Palazzoli—have been virtually forgotten. Too bad, because their strategic approaches introduced two of the most powerful insights in family therapy: that families often perpetuate problems by their own actions, and that directives tailored to the needs of a particular family can sometimes bring about sudden and decisive change.

Sketches of Leading Figures

Strategic therapy grew out of the **communications theory** developed in Bateson's schizophrenia project, which evolved into three distinct models: *MRI's brief therapy, Haley and Madanes's strategic therapy*, and the *Milan systemic model*. The birthplace of all three was the Mental Research Institute (MRI), where strategic therapy was inspired by Gregory Bateson and Milton Erickson, the anthropologist and the alienist.

In 1952, funded by a Rockefeller Foundation grant to study paradox in communication, Bateson invited Jay Haley, John Weakland, and Don Jackson to join him in Palo Alto. Their seminal project, which can

CHAPTER 5

STRATEGIC FAMILY THERAPY

Problem Solving

LEARNING OUTCOMES

- ◆ Describe the evolution of strategic family therapy.
- ◆ Describe the main tenets of the three models of strategic family therapy.
- ◆ Describe healthy and unhealthy family development from the perspective of each of the three basic models of strategic family therapy.
- ◆ Describe the clinical goals and the conditions necessary for meeting those goals from the perspective of each of the three basic models of strategic family therapy.
- ◆ Discuss and demonstrate assessment and intervention techniques of each of the three basic models of strategic family therapy.
- ◆ Discuss research support for the three basic models of strategic family therapy.

be considered the intellectual birthplace of family therapy, led to the conclusion that the exchange of multilayered messages between people defines their relationships.

Given Bateson's disinclination to manipulate people, it's ironic that it was he who introduced project members to Milton Erickson. At a time when therapy was considered a laborious, long-term proposition, Erickson's experience as a hypnotherapist convinced him that people could change suddenly, and he made therapy as brief as possible.

Many of what have been called *paradoxical interventions* came out of Erickson's application of hypnotic principles to turn resistance to advantage (Haley, 1981). For example, to induce trance a hypnotist learns not to point out that a person is fighting going under but instead tells the person to keep his or her eyes open, "until they become unbearably heavy."

Don Jackson founded the Mental Research Institute in 1959 and assembled a creative staff, including Richard Fisch, Jay Haley, John Weakland, and Paul Watzlawick. What emerged was an elegantly brief approach based on interrupting vicious cycles that occur when attempts to solve problems only make them worse. This approach, known as the MRI model, was described by Watzlawick, Weakland, and Fisch (1974) in *Change: Principles of Problem Formation and Problem Resolution* and in a follow-up volume *The Tactics of Change: Doing Therapy Briefly* (Fisch, Weakland, & Segal, 1982), which remains the most comprehensive statement of the MRI model.

Jay Haley was always something of a maverick. He entered the field without clinical credentials and established his reputation as a gadfly and critic. His initial impact came from his writing, in which he infused sarcasm with incisive analysis. In "The Art of Psychoanalysis" (Haley, 1963), Haley redefined psychoanalysis as a game of one-upmanship:

> By placing the patient on a couch, the analyst gives the patient the feeling of having his feet up in the air and the knowledge that the analyst has both feet on the ground. Not only is the patient disconcerted by having to lie down while talking, but he finds himself literally below the analyst and so his one-down position is geographically emphasized. In addition, the analyst seats himself behind the couch where he can watch the patient but the patient cannot watch him. This gives the patient the kind of disconcerted feeling a person has when sparring with an opponent while blindfolded. Unable to see what response his ploys provoke, he is unsure when he is one-up and when one-down. Some patients try to solve this problem by saying something like, "I slept with my sister last night," and then whirling around to see how the analyst is responding. These "shocker" ploys usually fail in their effect. The analyst may twitch, but he has time to recover before the patient can whirl fully around and see him. Most analysts have developed ways of handling the whirling patient. As the patient turns, they are gazing off into space, or doodling with a pencil, or braiding belts, or staring at tropical fish. It is essential that the rare patient who gets an opportunity to observe the analyst see only an impassive demeanor. (pp. 193–194)

In 1967 Haley joined Salvador Minuchin at the Philadelphia Child Guidance Clinic. It was there that he became interested in training and supervision, areas in which he made his greatest contribution (Haley, 1996). In 1976 Haley moved to Washington, D.C., where with Cloe Madanes he founded the Family Therapy Institute. Madanes currently works with motivational speaker and life coach Anthony Robbins. In 1995 Haley moved back to California. He died in 2007.

Haley and Madanes are such towering figures that their names often overshadow those who followed in their footsteps. James Keim in California, who developed an innovative way of working with oppositional children, is ably carrying on the Haley–Madanes

Milton Erickson was the guiding genius behind the strategic approach to therapy.

The Milton H. Erickson Foundation

tradition. Other prominent practitioners of this model include Neil Schiff in Washington, D.C.; Scott Sells at the Savannah Family Institute; and Jerome Price in Michigan.

The MRI model had a major impact on the Milan Associates, Mara Selvini Palazzoli, Luigi Boscolo, Gianfranco Cecchin, and Guiliana Prata. Selvini Palazzoli was a prominent Italian psychoanalyst, specializing in eating disorders, when, out of frustration with the psychoanalytic model (Selvini Palazzoli, 1981), she began to develop her own approach to families. In 1967 she led a group of eight psychiatrists who turned to the ideas of Bateson, Haley, and Watzlawick and formed the Center for the Study of the Family in Milan, where they developed the *Milan systemic model*. The Milan Associates eventually split, with Palazzoli and Prata focusing on invariant prescriptions and eventually incorporating more psychoanalytic concepts into their work, and Boscolo and Cecchin focusing on circular questioning. Both groups currently have training centers in Italy.

Giorgio Nardone is another prominent Italian family therapist who trained at the MRI. A close colleague of Watzlawick, the two have written several books together. Nardone currently operates a large clinic and training program in strategic therapy in Arezzo, Italy.

Theoretical Formulations

In *Pragmatics of Human Communication*, Watzlawick, Beavin, and Jackson (1967) sought to develop a calculus of human communication, which they stated in a series of axioms. The first of these axioms is that *people are always communicating*. Since all behavior is communicative and since one cannot *not* behave, then it follows that one cannot *not* communicate.

Mrs. Rodriguez began by saying, "I don't know what to do with Ramon. He's not doing well in school and he doesn't help out around the house. All he wants to do is hang with those awful friends of his. But the worst thing is that he refuses to communicate with us."

The therapist turned to Ramon and said, "What do you have to say about all of this?" Ramon said nothing. He just sat there slouched in the corner with a sullen look on his face.

Ramon isn't *not* communicating. He's communicating that he's angry and refuses to talk about it. Communication also takes place when it isn't intentional, conscious, or successful— that is, in the absence of mutual understanding.

The second axiom is that all messages have *report* and *command* functions (Ruesch & Bateson, 1951). The report (or content) of a message conveys information, while the command is a statement about the relationship. For example, the message "Mommy, Sandy hit me!" conveys information but also implies a command—*Do something about it*. Notice, however, that the implicit command is ambiguous. The reason for this is that the printed word omits contextual clues. This statement shrieked by a child in tears would have very different implications than if it were uttered by a giggling child.

In families, command messages are patterned as *rules* (Jackson, 1965), which can be deduced from repeated patterns of interaction. Jackson used the term **family rules** as a description of regularity, not regulation. Nobody lays down the rules. In fact, families are generally unaware of them.

The rules, or regularities, of family interaction operate to preserve family stability (Jackson, 1965, 1967). Homeostatic mechanisms bring families back to equilibrium in the face of disruption and thus serve to resist change. Jackson's notion of **family homeostasis** describes the conservative aspect of family systems and is similar to the cybernetic concept of **negative feedback**. According to communications analysis, families operate as goal-directed, rule-governed systems.

CASE STUDY

Sam couldn't understand why Mary was giving him such a frantic look from across the room during their first visit to Mary's family. Sam and Mary were going hiking, and Mary's father was lending them a camera. Frank was explaining what type of batteries to buy for the camera. Sam knew of a better battery

> and was saying so to his future father-in-law. As soon as Sam started explaining, Frank narrowed his eyes, pursed his lips, and interrupted to insist on what he was recommending. The rest of the family went silent and anxiously watched this interaction. Sam missed all of these nonverbal cues and kept insisting that he knew a better kind of battery. He was therefore shocked when Frank stood up, threw the camera on the floor, and stomped out of the room, shouting, "Nobody in this family ever listens to me!"
>
> This is how Sam discovered one of the rules in Mary's family: Never challenge Dad's authority.

Communications theorists didn't look for underlying motives; instead, they assumed circular causality and analyzed patterns of communications linked together in chains of stimulus and response as *feedback loops*. When the response to a family member's problematic behavior exacerbates the problem, that chain is seen as a *positive feedback loop*. The advantage of this formulation is that it focuses on interactions that perpetuate problems, which can be changed, instead of inferring underlying causes, which are often not subject to change.

Strategic therapists made the concept of the positive feedback loop the centerpiece of their model. For the MRI group, this translated into a simple yet powerful principle of problem formation: Families encounter many difficulties over the course of their lives; whether a difficulty becomes a problem depends on how family members respond to it (Watzlawick, Weakland, & Fisch, 1974). That is, families often make misguided attempts to solve their difficulties and, on finding that the problem persists, apply more of the same attempted solutions. This only produces an escalation of the problem, which provokes more of the same and so on—in a vicious cycle.

> If Jamal feels threatened by the arrival of a baby sister, he may become temperamental. If so, his father might think he's being defiant and try to get him to act his age by punishing him. But his father's harshness only confirms Jamal's belief that his parents love his sister more than him,

and so he acts even younger. Father then becomes more punitive, and Jamal becomes more alienated. This is an escalating positive feedback loop: The family system is reacting to a deviation in the behavior of one of its members with feedback designed to dampen that deviation (*negative feedback*), but it has the effect of amplifying the deviation (*positive feedback*).

What's needed is for father to reverse his solution. If he could comfort rather than criticize Jamal, then Jamal might calm down. The system is governed, however, by unspoken rules that allow only one interpretation of Jamal's behavior—as disrespectful. For father to alter his solution, this rule would have to be revised.

In most families, unspoken rules govern all sorts of behavior. Where a rule promotes the kind of rigid attempted solution described previously, it isn't just the behavior but the rule that needs to change. When only a specific behavior within a system changes, this is **first-order change**, as opposed to **second-order change**, which occurs when the rules of the system change (Watzlawick et al., 1974). How does one change the rules? One way is by **reframing**—that is, changing father's interpretation of Jamal's behavior from disrespect to fear of displacement, from bad to sad.

First-Order Change	Second-Order Change
Mother starts using gold stars to reward son for doing his chores.	Mother and father work together as a team to address son's behavior.
Parents try several strategies to get daughter to come home by curfew.	Parents start negotiating rules for daughter in recognition that she is growing up.
Father takes a second job to keep up with growing family expenses.	Mother takes a full-time job, and father assumes a greater share of household duties.

Thus, the MRI approach is elegantly simple: (1) identify feedback loops that maintain problems; (2) determine the rules that support those interactions; and (3) find a way to change the rules in order to interrupt problem-maintaining behavior.

Jay Haley added a functionalist emphasis to the cybernetic interpretation with his interest in the interpersonal payoff of behavior. Later, he incorporated structural concepts developed during the years he spent with Minuchin. For example, Haley might notice that whenever Jamal and father quarrel, Jamal's mother protects him by criticizing father for being so harsh. Haley might also see Jamal becoming more agitated when mother criticizes father, trying to get his parents' attention off their conflicts and onto him.

Haley believed that the rules around the **hierarchical structure** of a family are crucial and found inadequate parental hierarchies lurking behind most problems. Indeed, Haley (1976) suggested that "an individual is more disturbed in direct proportion to the number of malfunctioning hierarchies in which he is embedded" (p. 117).

To counter a problem's payoff, Haley borrowed Erickson's technique of prescribing **ordeals**, so that the price for keeping a symptom outweighed that of giving it up (Haley, 1984). To illustrate, consider Erickson's famous maneuver of prescribing that an insomniac set his alarm every night to wake up and wax the kitchen floor.

Like Haley, Mara Selvini Palazzoli and her associates (1978b) focused on power games in families and on the protective function symptoms served for a family. They explored families' histories over several generations, searching for evidence to confirm their hypotheses about how children's symptoms came to be necessary. These hypotheses often involved elaborate networks of family alliances and coalitions. They frequently concluded that patients developed symptoms to protect one or more family members so as to maintain the delicate network of extended family alliances.

Family Dynamics

Those seeking comprehensive explanations of family development should look elsewhere. Strategic therapists say little more than whatever works is normal, and that what makes families malfunction are solutions that don't work. But if your goals are limited to solving the problems families come in with, maybe that's all the theory you need.

◆ Normal Family Functioning

According to **general systems theory**, normal families, like all living systems, depend on two vital processes (Maruyama, 1968). First, they maintain integrity in the face of environmental challenges through *negative feedback*. No living system can survive without a coherent structure. On the other hand, too rigid a structure leaves a system ill-equipped to adapt to changing circumstances. That's why normal families also have mechanisms of *positive feedback*. Negative feedback resists disruptions; positive feedback amplifies innovations to accommodate to changed circumstances. Recognizing that the channel for feedback is communication makes it possible to state the case more plainly: Healthy families are able to adapt because they communicate clearly and are flexible.

The MRI group resolutely opposed standards of normality: "As therapists, we do not regard any particular way of functioning, relating, or living as a problem if the client is not expressing discontent with it" (Fisch, 1978). Thus, by limiting their task to eliminating problems presented to them, the MRI group avoided taking any position regarding how families *should* behave.

The Milan Associates strove to maintain an attitude of *neutrality* (Selvini Palazzoli, Boscolo, Cecchin, & Prata, 1980). They didn't apply preconceived notions or normative models. Instead, by raising questions that helped families examine themselves and that exposed hidden power games, they trusted families to reorganize on their own.

In contrast to the relativism of these two approaches, Haley's assessments *were* based on assumptions about sound family functioning. His therapy was designed to help families reorganize into more functional structures, with clear boundaries and generational hierarchy (Haley, 1976).

◆ Development of Behavior Disorders

According to communications theory, the essential function of symptoms is to maintain the homeostatic equilibrium of family systems.[1] Symptomatic families

---

[1]The notion of symptoms as functional—implying that families *need* their problems—was to become controversial.

were seen as trapped in dysfunctional, homeostatic patterns of communication (Jackson & Weakland, 1961). These families cling to their rigid ways and respond to signs of change as negative feedback. That is, change is treated not as an opportunity for growth but as a threat, as the following example illustrates.

CASE STUDY

Laban was a quiet boy, the only child of Orthodox Jewish parents from Eastern Europe. His parents left their small farming community to come to the United States where they both found factory work in a large city. Although they were now safe from religious persecution, the couple felt alien and out of synch with their new neighbors. They kept to themselves and took pleasure in raising Laban.

Laban was a frail child with a number of peculiar mannerisms, but to his parents he was perfect. Then he started school. Laban began to make friends with other children and, eager to be accepted, picked up a number of American habits. He chewed gum, watched cartoons, and rode his bicycle all over the neighborhood. His parents were annoyed by the gum chewing and by Laban's fondness for television, but they were genuinely distressed by his eagerness to play with gentile children. They may have come to the United States to escape persecution but not to embrace pluralism, much less assimilation. As far as they were concerned, Laban was rejecting their values—"Something must be wrong with him." By the time they called the child guidance clinic, they were convinced that Laban was disturbed, and they asked for help to "make Laban normal again."

In strategic models there are three explanations of how problems develop. The first is *cybernetic*: Difficulties are turned into chronic problems by misguided solutions, forming positive feedback escalations. The second is *structural*: Problems are the result of incongruous hierarchies. The third is *functional*: Problems result when people try to protect or control one another covertly, so that their symptoms serve a function for the system. The MRI group limited itself to the first explanation, while Haley and the Milan Associates embraced all three.

To clarify these differences, consider the following example: Sixteen-year-old Juwan recently began refusing to leave the house. An MRI therapist might ask his parents how they had tried to get him to venture out. The focus would be on the parents' attempted solution, on the assumption that this was likely to be maintaining Juwan's refusal, and on their explanation, or *frame*, for Juwan's behavior, believing that their framing of the problem might be driving their false solution.

A Haley-style therapist might be interested in the parents' attempted solutions but would also inquire about their marriage, the ways in which Juwan was involved in struggles between them or other family members, and the possible protective nature of Juwan's problem. This therapist would be acting on the assumption that Juwan's behavior might be part of a dysfunctional triangle, fueled by unresolved conflict between the parents. Madanes would also be interested in this triangle but, in addition, would be curious about how Juwan's behavior might be protecting his parents from having to face some threatening issue.

A Milan systemic therapist wouldn't focus so much on attempted solutions but instead would ask about past and present relationships in the family. In so doing, the therapist would be trying to uncover a network of power alliances, often continuing across generations, that constituted the family's "game." Some such game left Juwan in the position of having to use his symptoms to protect other family members. The family might reveal, for example, that if Juwan were to grow up and leave home, his mother would be drawn back into a power struggle between her parents, which she had avoided by having a symptomatic child. Also, by not succeeding in life, Juwan might be protecting his father from the shame of having a child who exceeded him in accomplishment.

Mechanisms of Change

Strategic therapists offer a circumscribed perspective on what to change and how to do it. This perspective—which is focused or limited, depending on your point of view—concentrates their attention to identify and alter problem-maintaining solutions.

◆ Goals of Therapy

The MRI group is proudly minimalistic. Once the presenting problem is resolved, therapy is concluded. If a family doesn't ask for help with other issues, they aren't targeted. Because they view people who have problems as stuck rather than sick, MRI therapists see their job as simply getting them moving again.

MRI therapists help families define clear and reachable goals so that everyone knows when treatment has been successful. They often find that much of the therapy takes place simply in the process of pushing clients to set concrete goals, because in doing so clients are forced to clarify vague dissatisfactions. The primary goal is behavior change.

Haley's approach is also behavioral and, even more than the MRI group, downplays the importance of insight. He was scornful of therapists who helped clients understand why they made mistakes but failed to get them to act differently. Haley's ultimate goal is often a structural reorganization of the family, particularly its hierarchy and generational boundaries. Unlike in structural family therapy, however, these structural goals are always directly related to the presenting problem. For example, to improve the relationship between the polarized parents of a rebellious teenager, a structural therapist might get the parents to talk about their marital problems, where Haley would have them talk only about their difficulty working together to deal with their child.

The original Milan approach (Selvini Palazzoli, Boscolo, Cecchin, & Prata, 1978b) was a direct offshoot of the MRI model. They expanded the network of people involved in maintaining problems but still concentrated on interrupting destructive family games. They differed from other strategic schools in being less problem-focused and more interested in changing family members' beliefs about covert collusions and the motives for strange behavior.

◆ Conditions for Behavior Change

In the early days of family therapy the goal was simply to improve communication. Later the goal was refined to altering specific patterns of communication that maintained problems. A therapist can either point out problematic sequences or simply block them to effect therapeutic change. The first strategy relies on insight and depends on a willingness to change. The second does not; it's an attempt to beat families at their own games.

For the MRI school, the way to resolve problems is to reverse the misguided solutions that have been maintaining them. It's believed that through seeing the results of altering rigid behavioral responses, clients will become more flexible in their problem-solving strategies. When this happens, clients achieve second-order change—a change in the rules governing their response to problems.

For example, Maria argues with her father about her curfew and her father grounds her. She then runs away and stays with a friend. A first-order intervention might be to help Maria's father find a more effective punishment to tame his rebellious child. A second-order strategic intervention might be to direct the father to act disappointed and sad around his daughter, implying that he has given up trying to control her. This shifts Maria from feeling controlled by her father to feeling concerned about him, and she becomes more reasonable. Her father learns that when attempted solutions aren't working, he needs to try something different. This change is second order in that it alters the rules governing the way father and daughter interact.

Haley (1976) believed that telling people what they're doing wrong only mobilizes resistance. He was convinced that changes in behavior alter perceptions, rather than the other way around. The Milan group turned this behaviorism on its head. They were more interested in getting families to see things differently (through a reframing technique called *positive connotation* to be discussed later) than in getting family members to behave differently. This shift from behavior to cognition set the stage for the constructivist and narrative movements (see Chapters 3 and 12).

Therapy

◆ Assessment

The goals of an MRI assessment are to (1) define a resolvable complaint, (2) identify attempted solutions that maintain the complaint, and (3) understand the clients' unique language for describing the problem. The first two goals show where to intervene; the third suggests how.

The first step is to get a very specific, behavioral picture of the complaint, who sees it as a problem, and why it's a problem now. When a therapist asks, "What is the problem that brings you here today," clients are often vague, "We don't communicate," or make attributions, "We think our fourteen-year-old is depressed," "Clarence seems to be hyperactive." The MRI therapist inquires about exactly what these complaints mean. "We don't communicate" might mean "My son argues with everything I say" or "My husband never talks to me." "Depressed" might mean sad and withdrawn or sullen and disagreeable; "hyperactive" might mean disobedient or unable to concentrate. A useful device is to ask, "If we had a videotape of this, what would it look like?"

Once the problem has been defined, the therapist tries to determine who has tried to solve it and how. Sometimes the attempted solution seems to have made things worse. For example, a wife who nags her husband to spend more time with her is likely to succeed only in driving him further away. Likewise parents who punish their son for fighting with his sister might convince him that they favor her. Or a husband who does everything his wife asks in order to keep the peace may become so resentful that he starts to hate her.

The Problem Is the Solution

"I nag because you withdraw."
"I withdraw because you nag."

Typically, the strategic objective will be a 180-degree reversal of what the clients have been doing. Although interventions typically involve prescribing some alternative behavior, the key is to stop the performance of the problem-maintaining solution (Weakland & Fisch, 1992).

Grasping the clients' unique language and ways of seeing their dilemmas is important to framing suggestions in ways they will accept. For example, a devoutly religious wife might be amenable to the suggestion that she pray for her husband to become more involved with the family rather than continue to criticize his failings. In another case, cited by Shoham and Rohrbaugh (2002), a young woman was seen as perpetuating her boyfriend's jealous accusations by trying to reassure him. Unfortunately, these efforts to reason with the boyfriend only ended up in arguments, which were painful enough to threaten the relationship. Because the woman was a devotee of mindfulness meditation, the therapist suggested that the next time the boyfriend asked a jealous question and she felt like defending herself, she should tell him that she was feeling stressed and needed to meditate.

Haley's assessment begins with a careful definition of the problem, expressed from the point of view of every member of the family. But unlike the MRI group, Haley also explores the possibility that structural arrangements in the family may be contributing to their problems—especially pathological triangles, or *cross-generational coalitions*.

In addition to structural problems, Haley and Madanes also consider the interpersonal payoff of problem behavior. According to Haley, the apparent helplessness of a patient often turns out to be a source of power in relation to others whose lives are dominated by the demands and fears of the symptomatic person. A person diagnosed with schizophrenia who refuses to take his medication might, for example, avoid having to go to work. While it isn't necessary to decide what is or isn't a real illness, Haley tended to assume that all symptomatic behavior was voluntary. Sometimes this is a crucial distinction—as, for example, in cases of drug addiction or losing one's temper.

In the Milan model, assessment begins with a preliminary hypothesis, which is confirmed or disconfirmed in the initial session. These hypotheses are generally based on the assumption that the problems of the identified patient serve a protective function for the family. Therefore, assessment of the presenting problem and the family's response to it is based on questions designed to explore the family as a set of interconnected relationships. For example, the reply to a question like "Who has been more worried about this problem, you or your wife?" suggests a hypothesis about the closeness and distance of family members. The ultimate goal of assessment is to achieve a systemic perspective on the problem.

◆ Therapeutic Techniques

Although strategic therapists share a belief in the need for indirect methods to induce change in families, they developed distinctly different techniques for doing so.

The MRI Approach

The MRI model follows a six-step treatment procedure:

1. Introduction to the treatment setup
2. Inquiry and definition of the problem
3. Estimation of the behavior maintaining the problem
4. Setting goals for treatment
5. Selecting and making behavioral interventions
6. Termination

Once the preliminaries have been concluded, the therapist asks for a clear definition of the primary problem. If a problem is stated in vague terms, such as "We just don't seem to get along," or in terms of presumptive causes, such as "Dad's job is making him depressed," the therapist helps translate it into a clear and concrete goal, asking questions like "What will be the first small sign that things are getting better?"

After the problem and goals are defined, MRI therapists inquire about attempted solutions. Solutions that perpetuate problems tend to fall into one of three categories:

1. The solution is to deny that a problem exists; action is necessary but not taken. For instance, parents do nothing despite growing evidence that their teenage son is abusing drugs.
2. The solution is an effort to solve something that isn't really a problem; action is taken when it shouldn't be. For example, parents punish a child for masturbating.
3. The solution is an effort to solve a problem within a framework that makes a solution impossible; action is taken but at the wrong level. For instance, a husband buys gifts for his wife, when what she wants is affection.

Once the therapist conceives a strategy for changing the problem-maintaining sequence, clients must be convinced to follow this strategy. To sell their directives, MRI therapists reframe problems to increase the likelihood of compliance. Thus a therapist might tell an angry teenager that when his father punishes him, it's the only way his father knows how to show his love.

To interrupt problem-maintaining sequences, strategic therapists may try to get family members to do something that runs counter to common sense. Such counterintuitive techniques have been called *paradoxical interventions* (Haley, 1973; Watzlawick, Weakland, & Fisch, 1974).

CASE STUDY

Watzlawick and his colleagues (1974) described a young couple who were bothered by their parents' tendency to treat them like children by doing everything for them. Despite the husband's adequate salary, the parents continued to send money and lavish gifts on them, refused to let them pay even part of a restaurant check, and so on. The strategic team helped the couple solve their difficulty with their doting parents by having them become *less* rather than more competent. Instead of trying to show the parents that they didn't need help, the couple was told to act helpless and dependent, so much so that the parents got annoyed and finally backed off.

The techniques most commonly thought of as paradoxical are *symptom prescriptions* in which a family is told to continue or embellish the behavior they complain about. In some contexts, such a prescription might be made with the hope that the family will try to comply with it and thereby be forced to reverse their attempted solution. If Jorge, who is sad, is told to try to become depressed several times a day and his family is asked to encourage him to be sad, then they will no longer try ineffectively to cheer him up, and he won't feel guilty for not being happy.

At other times, a therapist might prescribe the symptom while secretly hoping the clients will rebel against this directive. The therapist might encourage Jorge to continue to be depressed because, in doing so, he's helping his brother (with whom Jorge is competitive) feel superior.

A favorite MRI technique for responding to cycles in which a person engages in self-destructive behavior in response to feeling anxious or depressed is: As soon as a person starts feeling overwhelmed, he or she is instructed to make a list of all the things he or she might do to sabotage his or her life. Doing so takes the rebellion out of the self-destructive behavior, and thus makes it less attractive—and less likely to be done on impulse.

Sometimes a therapist might prescribe the symptom with the hope that in doing so the network of relationships that maintain the problem will be exposed. The therapist says that Jorge should remain depressed because that way he can continue to occupy his mother's attention, which will keep her from looking to his father for affection, since his father is still overinvolved with his own mother, and so on.

Another example of a paradoxical directive would be asking a couple to deliberately have an argument during the week in order to help the therapist understand how they get involved in such no-win encounters and how they are able to get each other to act unreasonably. This assignment may yield diagnostic information, and it creates an incentive for the partners to resist provocation in order not to appear "unreasonable."

 Watch this video of a strategic therapist working with a couple. Which intervention does he use?

To prevent power struggles, MRI therapists avoid an authoritarian posture. Their *one-down stance* implies humility and helps reduce resistance. Although some strategists adopt a one-down position disingenuously, a modest approach was consistent with the late John Weakland's own unassuming character. While sitting clouded in the smoke of his pipe, Weakland discouraged families from trying to change too fast, warning them to go slow and worrying out loud about the possibility of relapse when improvements did occur. This **restraining** technique reinforced the therapist's one-down position.

Clever or Insincere?

Like many strategic interventions, the restraining technique can be honest or manipulative. The truth is most people don't change; things *are* liable to stay the same. A therapist's telling people to go slow or saying that things may not change can both be sincere *and* designed to motivate them to prove him or her wrong at the same time. Similarly while paradoxical directives can be delivered with clumsy reverse psychology—"Oh, no, don't throw me in the briar patch!" (wink, wink); they can be phrased more artfully—"Perhaps you should continue to wake Ricky up for school; after all, you don't want to push him to be too responsible too soon." Because they seemed clever, paradoxical directives got a lot of attention, especially in workshops. But the essence of the MRI approach wasn't to be deceitful, or clever, or provocative: The main thing was to discover what families were doing to perpetuate their problems and then get them to try something different. Indirection was usually resorted to only after a direct approach met with resistance.

The Haley and Madanes Approach

Haley's approach is harder to describe because it's tailored to address the unique requirements of each case. If *strategic* implies *systematic*, as in the MRI approach, it also implies *artful*, which is especially true of Haley's therapy. As with other strategic approaches, the definitive technique is the use of *directives*. But Haley's directives weren't simply ploys to outwit families or reverse what they were doing. Rather, they were thoughtful suggestions targeted to the specific requirements of each case.

Haley (1976) believed that if therapy is to end well, it must begin properly. Therefore, he devoted a good deal of attention to the opening moves of treatment. Regardless of who is presented as the patient, Haley began by interviewing the entire family. His approach to this initial interview followed four stages: a *social stage*, a *problem stage*, an *interaction stage*, and finally a *goal-setting stage*.

Haley used the initial minutes of a first session to help everyone relax. He made a point of greeting each family member and making sure they were comfortable. Like a good host, he wanted his guests to feel welcome. After the *social stage*, Haley got down to business in the *problem stage*, asking each person for his or her perspective. Because mothers are usually more central than fathers, Haley recommended speaking first to fathers to increase their involvement. This suggestion is typical of Haley's strategic maneuvering.

Haley listened carefully to the way each family member described the problem, making sure that no one interrupted until each had a turn. During this phase, Haley looked for clues about triangles and hierarchy, but he avoided making any comments about these observations because that might make the family defensive.

Once everyone had a chance to speak, Haley encouraged them to discuss their points of view among themselves. In this *interactional stage* a therapist can observe, rather than just hear about, the interchanges that surround the problem. As they talk, Haley looked for *coalitions* between family members against others. How functional is the *hierarchy*? Do the parents work as a team, or do they undercut each other?

Sometimes Haley ended the first session by giving the family a task. In subsequent sessions, directives played a central role. Effective directives don't usually take the form of simple advice, which is rarely helpful because problems usually persist for a reason.

The Use of Directives

Directives aren't given only to bring about change, they are also used to establish a type of relationship: When Kendra's parents failed to follow the simple suggestion that they sit down to discuss how to respond to her missing curfew, the therapist took this as negative feedback—a response to his pushing for unwelcome change. Thereafter, the therapist avoided making direct suggestions and concentrated more on listening to the parents' complaints.

Some directives are straightforward: "Instead of arguing back when Javier complains, try listening to his complaints, drawing him out, and avoid contradicting him. Arguments are like ping pong—it takes two to play."

Some directives are indirect: "Don't do anything different this week, but keep a written record of how often your responses to your wife are critical or supportive."

Indirect directives are usually used when straightforward ones aren't followed: When Mr. and Mrs. Montalvo reported that their efforts to take turns talking and listening hadn't gone well, the therapist suggested that they try again, but this time the person listening should take notes about what made it hard for him or her to listen without interrupting.

The following two tasks are taken from Haley's (1976) *Problem-Solving Therapy.* One couple, who were out of the habit of being affectionate with each other, were told to behave affectionately "to teach their child how to show affection." In another case, a mother who was unable to control her twelve-year-old son had decided to send him away to military school. Haley suggested that since the boy had no idea how tough life would be at military school, it would be a good idea for his mother to help prepare him. They both agreed. Haley directed her to teach the boy how to stand at attention, be polite, and wake up early every morning to make his bed. The two of them followed these instructions as if playing a game, with the mother as sergeant and the son as private. After two weeks the son was behaving so well that his mother no longer felt it necessary to send him away.

One thing unique about Haley's approach was his focus on the interpersonal payoff of psychiatric symptoms. The idea that people get something out of their symptoms has been rejected by most schools of family therapy because it was seen as a version of blaming the victim. Haley's point wasn't that people become anxious or depressed in order to manipulate others, but that such problems, once they develop, may come to play a role in interpersonal struggles in the family. It was this covert function of symptoms that Haley explored.

Although MRI therapists speculate about what may be maintaining symptoms, they emphasize misguided solutions and don't consider the possible interpersonal payoff of the symptoms. The primary goal of hypothesizing in Haley's approach is to understand the heart of the family drama that the symptoms revolve around.

Haley focused on the meaning behind people's problems and therefore believed that problems should have reasonable solutions. The answer is to help families find new ways to solve their problems.

CASE STUDY

In a case treated by Jerome Price, a thirteen-year-old girl was referred to juvenile court because of chronic truancy. She had repeatedly failed to show up at school, and both her parents and school officials had tried a range of threats and punishments—all to no avail. The judge referred the girl to therapy. Price began by asking questions designed to find out why the girl was skipping school. The most obvious question was "Where do you go when you don't go to school?" To the therapist's surprise, the girl said that she went to the home of her ninety-two-year-old grandmother. The girl's parents assumed that she was taking advantage of her grandmother. However, when Price asked, "Why there?" he learned that the grandmother lived alone and was in constant fear of falling. Her children rarely visited and didn't address her concerns directly, so the granddaughter had taken it upon herself to see that her grandmother was safe.

Price's directives addressed both the purpose of the girl's truancy and the hierarchical imbalance that it reflected in the family. He encouraged the parents to visit the grandmother more often, hire a caregiver to be there during the day, and arrange activities at a local senior center. Knowing that her grandmother was safe—and that her parents were now taking charge—the girl returned to school.

Unlike many contemporary family therapists, practitioners in the Haley/Madanes tradition openly address the issue of interpersonal power in families. Early in his career, Haley (1963) recognized that communication affects how family members relate to one another in a way that either increases or decreases their influence. This was not meant as a judgment but merely a description of the way things seem to work. Haley devoted much of his early effort to observing how power was used and misused in families, with the idea that therapists can either ignore power struggles or recognize and help families resolve them.

CASE STUDY

When a man beats a woman, people have no trouble seeing this as an issue of power and its misuse. But when sixteen-year-old Brad (Price, 1996) verbally harassed his mother to get the use of her car, his individual therapist didn't see this as Brad's misuse of power. When Brad proceeded to push his mother to the ground and rip the keys out of her hand, the therapist still insisted on exploring Brad's reasons for being angry at his mother.

When Brad's mother got fed up with this approach and sought treatment from a strategic practitioner, the new therapy focused on how Brad had become so powerful and what it would take for his mother to regain leadership. Most of the sessions included the mother and Brad's uncle, who cared very much about him and was therefore more than willing to help discuss and carry out decisions. When Brad was faced with a united front of two adults, who met with him and a therapist and also held meetings at his school, the reformulation of the power balance began calming him down and simplifying his life to the point where he could return to acting like a sixteen-year-old, rather than an abusive husband.

As is often the case, the underlying dynamics in this family didn't emerge until after the presenting problem improved. Once Brad started behaving respectfully and performing better in school, his mother's depression became more apparent. In a way, Brad had kept his mother emotionally occupied by reenacting her struggles with his father, which made it unnecessary for her to make new friends, date, or move forward in her life. With Brad improving and no crises to deal with, his mother became conscious of what was missing in her life, and the therapist was able to help her address her own future. Haley would see Brad as trying to help his mother by giving her a problem that distracted her from her own. In some cases this "helpfulness" is conscious; in other cases it isn't.

Metaphor is another theme in Haley's approach. In the previous case, Brad's misbehavior, which mimicked that of his parents' previous abusive relationship, could be seen as a metaphor for his mother not having resolved her emotional struggle over past abuse. In this approach, a symptom is often seen as a metaphor for an underlying problem. Thus, a school problem in a child may mirror a work problem of a parent. An underachieving child might be a reflection of an underfunctioning parent. An addicted child may be a clue that someone else in the family is secretly acting in self-destructive ways.

Such was the case in which thirty-seven-year-old Margery asked for help with her three-year-old daughter. Whenever the two entered a store, the little girl would steal something, such as a pack of gum or candy. Upon further exploration, the therapist learned that Margery was having an affair with her best friend's husband. The metaphor of stealing thus proved apt.

Madanes (1981) describes how one relationship may metaphorically replicate another. As was the case with Brad and his mother, parents can fight with their children about things they should be addressing between themselves. Two children can fight with each other in the same way their parents would be fighting if they weren't distracted by the children. One child can struggle with parents in a way that deflects the scrutiny that otherwise might be directed at a sibling. This is often the case when there is a young adult at home who is not working or going to school, and is basically stuck on the launching pad. A younger sibling may become symptomatic and start failing at school in a way that serves as metaphor to force the parents to deal with the issue of needing to be productive.

Madanes (1984) also addresses power imbalances in couples and how they play a role in a wide range of symptoms. She looks at the areas of couples' lives in which power is regulated, including money, education, control of children, in-laws, religion, and sex. It often turns out that the partner with the least power develops the most emotional problems. Symptoms such as depression, headaches, substance abuse, eating disorders, phobias, and so on certainly burden the person who suffers them, but they also burden other family members. Others in the family often try desperately to do something about such symptoms, but the symptomatic person may refuse to accept help, thereby maintaining a perverse sort of power by holding onto troublesome symptoms. Again, this process is typically not conscious, and this way of thinking about it is not offered as some objective truth but rather as one possibly useful clinical hypothesis.

Looking at such struggles in the light of power balancing, a therapist is able to have a more flexible

Courtesy of Cloe Madanes

Cloe Madanes's "pretend techniques" are a clever way to help break control-and-rebel cycles.

view of the drama a couple is embroiled in. Is the abuser someone who actually needs more of a role in his children's lives? Does a partner need an avocation that can help him or her feel more successful?

CASE STUDY

This dynamic was the case with Mark and Brianna. Mark became more and more depressed and refused to seek a job after being laid off. Six months had passed, and he had done little. He spent money as if his income were still coming in, while Brianna stayed home with the children despite being in demand as a registered nurse. Brianna berated Mark about his lack of action, shouting at him at times and generally exacerbating his general sense of failure. *She* was the expert on the children. *She* took them to church. *She* had a master's degree, while he had only two years of college.

As Mark became more depressed and did increasingly less, Brianna was forced to go back to work and give up staying home with the children. By what he didn't do—"because he was depressed"—Mark dominated the family that had previously dominated him. He now took care of the children (albeit not to Brianna's satisfaction) and stayed home while she worked, and no one went to church because Brianna had to work the graveyard shift on Saturday nights. Mark's depression had equalized the power imbalance that developed when he lost his job and began to feel like a failure. Brianna's emotional control over their lives had previously been offset by the fact that Mark was the breadwinner. When he lost that role, the couple went into imbalance and Mark had to find another form of power to replace his income. Ironically, the helplessness of depression provided that power.

The artful commonsense component of Haley's strategic therapy can be understood by looking at high-conflict divorce. Rather than think of a high-conflict couple as pathological, Haley would look at them developmentally and in terms of the family life cycle (Haley, 1973; Haley & Richeport-Haley, 2007). This approach attempts to come up with benevolent hypotheses that describe clients in the best possible light. Rather than see the ex-spouses as personality disordered, a Haley-style therapist would more likely see them as still in need of an emotional divorce (Gaulier, Margerum, Price, & Windell, 2007). Such a conceptualization offers a therapist ideas about what needs to be done to resolve problems.

CASE STUDY

Even after they were divorced, Rob and Melissa continued to argue over every aspect of their seventeen-year-old daughter Marta's existence. When the therapist asked Marta if these arguments looked like the arguments her parents had when they were married, she sighed and said that the arguments "were identical." The therapist asked the parents whether they were willing to let go of each other, once and for all. Both resisted the idea that they were still emotionally married, but the therapist challenged them to prove that they were not.

The therapist asked both parents to collect memorabilia and write accounts of events from their marriage that they would like to leave behind. The therapist led them through a ritual over about a month, in which they brought in the items and accounts, described them to each other and said why they no longer wanted the effects of these things in their lives, and then ritually burned them in the therapist's presence. Rob and Melissa were directed to collect the ashes in a jar and sent on a weekend trip to northern Michigan, where they stopped in a virgin pine forest and ritually buried the ashes. At the therapist's suggestion, they took a boat trip and, at a specific time and in a specific way, threw their wedding rings (which they had kept) into the depths of Lake Superior.

James Keim and Jay Lappin (2002) describe a strategic approach to a case with a nagging wife and withdrawing husband. First they reframe the problem as a "breakdown in the negotiation process." A *negotiation*, the couple is told, is a conversation in which one party makes a request and the other names a price. This reframing allows the wife to make requests without thinking of herself as a nag—and the husband to see himself as having something to gain in negotiations, rather than as a brow-beaten husband who is forced to give in to his wife.

Keim and Lappin recommend introducing couples to the negotiation process as a "fun exercise" designed to get them back on track in reaching agreements. Then the couple is given a handout with elaborate instructions for negotiating in a constructive fashion and asked to progress from negotiating easy issues in the session to doing so at home and then tackling more difficult issues, first in the session and then at home. Finally, the couple is cautioned that even after negotiating some exchanges, they may choose not to accept the **quid pro quo** terms. Sometimes it's preferable to endure certain problems than pay the price of trying to change them.

Madanes used the observation that people will often do something they wouldn't ordinarily do if it's framed as play to develop a range of **pretend techniques**. One such strategy is to ask a symptomatic child to pretend to have the symptom and encourage the parents to pretend to help. The child can give up the actual symptom now that pretending to have it is serving the same family function. The following two cases, summarized from Madanes (1981), illustrate the pretend technique.

CASE STUDY

A mother sought therapy because her ten-year-old son had night terrors. Madanes suspected that the boy was concerned about his mother, who was poor, spoke little English, and had lost two husbands. Since the boy had night terrors, the therapist asked all the members of the family to describe their dreams. Only the mother and the son had nightmares. In the mother's nightmare someone was breaking into the house. In the boy's, he was being attacked by a witch. When Madanes asked what the mother did when the boy had nightmares, she said that she took him into her bed and told him to pray to God. She explained that she thought his nightmares were the work of the devil.

Madanes's conjecture was that the boy's night terrors were both a metaphorical expression of the mother's fears and an attempt to help her. As long as the boy was afraid, his mother had to be strong. Unfortunately, while trying to protect him, she frightened him further by talking about God and the devil. Thus, both mother and child were helping each other in unproductive ways.

The family members were told to pretend that they were home and mother was afraid that someone might break in. The son was asked to protect his mother. In this way the mother had to pretend to need the child's help instead of really needing it. At first the family had difficulty playing the scene because the mother would attack the make-believe thief before the son could help. Thus she communicated that she was capable of taking care of herself and didn't need the son's protection. After the scene was performed correctly, with the son attacking the thief, they all discussed the performance. The mother explained that it was difficult to play her part because she was a competent person who could defend herself.

Madanes sent the family home with the task of repeating this dramatization every evening for a week. If the son started screaming during his sleep, his mother was to wake him up and replay the scene. They were told that this was important to do no matter how late it was or how tired they were. The son's night terrors soon disappeared.

CASE STUDY

A mother sought treatment for her five-year-old because he had uncontrollable temper tantrums. After talking with the family for a few minutes Madanes asked the boy to show her what his tantrums were like by pretending to have one. "Okay," he said, "I'm the Incredible Hulk!" He puffed out his chest, flexed his muscles, made a monster face, and started screaming and kicking the furniture. Madanes asked the mother to do what she usually did in such circumstances. The mother responded by telling her son, in a weak and ineffective way, to calm down. She pretended to send him to another room as she tried to do at home. Next, Madanes

asked the mother if the boy was doing a good job of pretending. She said he was.

Madanes asked the boy to repeat the scene. This time he was Frankenstein's monster and his tantrum was performed with a rigid posture and a grimacing face. Then Madanes talked with the boy about the Incredible Hulk and Frankenstein's monster and congratulated the mother for raising such an imaginative child.

Following this discussion, mother and son were told to pretend that he was having a tantrum while she was walking him to his room. The boy was told to act like the Incredible Hulk and to make lots of noise. Then they were told to pretend to close the door and hug and kiss. Next Madanes instructed the mother to pretend that *she* was having a tantrum, and the boy was to hug and kiss her. Madanes instructed mother and son to perform both scenes every morning before school and every afternoon when the boy came home. After every performance the mother was to give the boy milk and cookies, if he did a good job. Thus the mother was moved from a helpless position to one of authority, in which she was in charge of rewarding her son's make-believe performance. The next week the mother called to say that they didn't need to come for therapy because the boy was behaving very well and his tantrums had ceased.

Haley (1984) returned to his Ericksonian roots in a book called *Ordeal Therapy*, a collection of case studies in which ordeals were prescribed to make symptoms more trouble than they're worth. "If one makes it more difficult for a person to have a symptom than to give it up, the person will give up the symptom" (p. 5). A standard ordeal is for a client to have to get up in the middle of the night and exercise strenuously whenever he or she had symptoms during that day. Another example might be for the client to have to give a present to someone with whom he or she has a poor relationship—for example, a mother-in-law or ex-spouse—each time the symptoms occur.

Haley also used ordeals to restructure families. For example, a sixteen-year-old boy put a variety of items up his behind and then expelled them, leaving his stepmother to clean up the mess. Haley (1984) arranged that after each such episode, the father had to take his son to their backyard and have the boy dig a hole three feet deep and three feet wide, in which he was to bury all the things he was putting up his rear end. After a few weeks of this, Haley reported that the symptom stopped, the father became more involved with his son, and the stepmother became closer to the father.

The current form of Haley/Madanes therapy, called *strategic humanism*, still involves giving directives, but the directives are now more oriented toward increasing family members' abilities to soothe and love than to gain control over one another. This represents a major shift and is in synch with family therapy's movement away from the power aspects of hierarchy and toward finding ways to increase harmony.

An excellent example of strategic humanism's blend of compassion and cleverness is James Keim's work with oppositional children (Keim, 1998). Keim begins by reassuring anxious parents that they aren't to blame for their children's oppositionalism. Next he explains that there are two sides of parental authority—discipline and nurture. To reinforce the parents' authority while avoiding power struggles, Keim encourages them to concentrate on being sympathetic and supportive for a while. The parent who soothes a child with the forgotten language of understanding is every bit as much in charge as one who tries to tell the child what to do. After progress has been made in calming the child down—especially in breaking the pattern by which oppositional children control the mood in the family by arguing with everything their parents say—Keim coaches the parents to post rules and enforce consequences. This strategy puts parents back in charge without the high-intensity melodrama that often attends work with unruly children.

The Milan Model

The original Milan model was highly scripted. Families were treated by male–female cotherapists and observed by other members of the team. The standard format had five parts: *presession, session, intersession, intervention*, and *postsession* discussion. As Boscolo, Cecchin, Hoffman, and Penn (1987) describe:

> During the presession the team came up with an initial hypothesis about the family's presenting problem. . . . During the session itself, the team members would validate, modify, or change the

hypothesis. After about forty minutes, the entire team would meet alone to discuss the hypothesis and arrive at an intervention. The treating therapists would then go back to deliver the intervention to the family, either by positively connoting the problem situation or by a ritual to be done by the family that commented on the problem situation and was designed to introduce change. . . . Finally, the team would meet for a postsession discussion to analyze the family's reactions and to plan for the next session. (p. 4)

As indicated in this description, the primary intervention was either a *ritual* or a *positive connotation*.

The **positive connotation** was the most distinctive innovation to emerge from the Milan model. Derived from the MRI technique of reframing symptoms as serving a protective function—for example, Carlo needs to continue to be depressed to distract his parents from their marital issues—the positive connotation avoided the implication that family members benefited from the patient's symptoms. This implication made for resistance that the Milan team found could be circumvented if the patient's behavior was construed not as protecting specific people but as preserving the family's overall harmony. Indeed, every family member's behavior was often connoted in this system-serving way.

The treatment team would hypothesize about how the patient's symptom fit into the family system and, after a mid-session break, the therapists would deliver this hypothesis to the family, along with the injunction that they should not try to change. Carlo should continue to sacrifice himself by remaining depressed as a way to reassure the family that he will not become an abusive man like his grandfather. Mother should maintain her overinvolvement with Carlo as a way to make him feel valued while he sacrifices himself. Father should continue to criticize mother and Carlo's relationship so that Mother will not be tempted to abandon Carlo and become a wife to her husband.

Positive Connotations

Implying that some members of a family are "good" and others are "bad" makes it difficult to treat the family as a systemic unity. Positive connotations, therefore, must include the entire family system and confirm the behavior of all family members as maintaining the stability and cohesion of the group:

"You two are very generous. Leon, you keep secrets so that Marta won't worry. And, Marta, you question Leon about his comings and goings so that he'll know you care."

"Henry, you keep busy at work so as not to interfere with Candice's handling of the children. Candice, you control the children's activities so that they will not waste their time and Henry will not be bothered to participate. Seth and Paula, you avoid initiating your own activities so that your mother will continue to feel needed."

Rituals were used to engage families in a series of actions that ran counter to or exaggerated rigid family rules and myths. For example, one family that was enmeshed with their large extended family was told to hold family discussions behind locked doors every other night after dinner during which each family member was to speak for fifteen minutes about the family. Meanwhile they were to redouble their courtesy to the other members of the clan. By exaggerating the family's loyalty to the extended family while simultaneously breaking that loyalty's rule by meeting apart from the clan and talking about it, the nuclear family was defining itself as a unit distinct from the clan, permitting, without explicitly saying so, each member to express his or her own thoughts and feelings without being contradicted, and preventing, through the prohibition of discussions outside these ritualized family meetings, the persistence of secret coalitions.

Rituals were also used to dramatize positive connotations. For example, each family member might have to express his or her gratitude each night to the patient for having the problem (Boscolo et al., 1987). The Milan group also devised a set of rituals based on an odd-and-even-days format (Selvini Palazzoli et al., 1978a). For example, a family in which the parents were deadlocked over parental control might be told that on even days of the week Father should be in charge of the patient's behavior and Mother should

act as if she weren't there. On odd days, Mother is in charge and Father is to stay out of the way. Here, again, the family's rigid sequences are interrupted, and family must react differently to each other.

Positive connotations and rituals were powerful and provocative interventions. To keep families engaged while using such methods, the therapeutic relationship is crucial. Unfortunately, the Milan team originally saw therapy as a power struggle between therapists and families. Their main advice to therapists was to remain neutral in the sense of avoiding the appearance of taking sides. This **neutrality** was often manifest as distance, so that therapists delivered their dramatic pronouncements while acting aloof; not surprisingly, families often became angry and didn't return.

In the early 1980s, the original Milan team split around the nature of therapy. Selvini Palazzoli maintained the model's strategic and adversarial bent, although she stopped using paradoxical interventions. Instead she and Guiliana Prata experimented with a specific ritual called the **invariant prescription**, which they assigned to every family they treated.

Selvini Palazzoli (1986) believed that psychotic and anorexic patients are caught up in a "dirty game," a power struggle originally between their parents that these patients are pulled into and ultimately wind up using their symptoms in an attempt to defeat one parent for the sake of the other. In the invariant prescription, parents were to go out together without telling anyone else in the family of their whereabouts and to be mysterious about where they went. The goal was to strengthen the parental alliance and reinforce the boundary between generations.

In the 1990s Selvini Palazzoli reinvented her therapy once more, this time abandoning short-term, strategic therapy (invariant prescription included) for long-term therapy with patients and their families (Selvini Palazzoli, 1993). Thus, she came full circle, beginning with a psychodynamic approach, then focusing on family patterns, and finally returning to a long-term therapy that emphasizes insight and focuses again on the individual. This new therapy revolves around understanding the denial of family secrets and suffering over generations. In this way it is linked conceptually, if not technically, to her former models.

Boscolo and Cecchin also moved away from strategic intervening but toward a collaborative style of therapy. This approach grew from their conclusion that the value in the Milan model wasn't so much in the directives (positive connotations and rituals), which had been the model's centerpiece, but in the interview process itself. Their therapy came to center around **circular questioning**, a clinical translation of Bateson's notion of double description. Circular questions are designed to shift clients from thinking about individuals and linear causality and toward reciprocity and interdependence. For example, a therapist might ask: "Did she start losing weight before or after her sister went off to college?" "How might your father have characterized your mother's relationship with your sister, if he had felt free to speak with you about it?" "If she had not been born, how would your marriage be different today?" "If you were to divorce, which parent would the children live with?" Such questions are structured so that one has to give a relational description in answer.

Circular questions were further refined and cataloged by Penn (1982, 1985) and Tomm (1987a, 1987b). Boscolo (Boscolo & Bertrando, 1992) remains intrigued with their potential. As an example, let's return to Carlo's family and imagine the following conversation (adapted from Hoffman, 1983):

CASE STUDY

Q: Who is most upset by Carlo's depression?

A: Mother.

Q: How does Mother try to help Carlo?

A: She talks to him for hours and tries to do things for him.

Q: Who agrees most with Mother's way of trying to help Carlo?

A: The psychiatrist who prescribes his medication.

Q: Who disagrees?

A: Father. He thinks Carlo shouldn't be allowed to do what he wants.

Q: Who agrees with Father?

A: We all think Carlo is babied too much. And Grandma too. Grandpa would probably agree with Mother but he died.

Q: Did Carlo start to get depressed before or after Grandfather's death?

A: Not long after, I guess.

Q: If Grandfather hadn't died, how would the family be different now?

A: Well, Mother and Grandma probably wouldn't fight so much because Grandma wouldn't be living with us. And Mother wouldn't be so sad all the time.

Q: If Mother and Grandma didn't fight so much and Mother wasn't so sad, how do you think Carlo would be?

A: Well, I guess he might be happier too. But then he'd probably be fighting with Father again.

By asking circular questions, the frame for Carlo's problem gradually shifts from a psychiatric one to being symptomatic of changes in the family structure.

Boscolo and Cecchin became aware that the spirit in which these questions were asked determined their usefulness. If a therapist maintains a strategic mindset—uses the questioning process to strive for a particular outcome—the responses of family members will be constrained by their sense that the therapist is after something. If, on the other hand, the therapist asks circular questions out of genuine curiosity (Cecchin, 1987), as if joining the family in a research expedition regarding their problem, an atmosphere can be created in which the family can arrive at new understandings of their predicament.

Other Contributions

Strategic therapists pioneered the *team approach* to therapy. Originally, the MRI group used teams behind one-way mirrors to help brainstorm strategies, as did the Milan group. Papp (1980) and her colleagues at the Ackerman Institute brought the team directly into the therapy process by turning the observers into a "Greek chorus" who reacted to events in the session. For example, the team might, for strategic purposes, disagree with the therapist. In witnessing the staged debates between the team and their therapist over what a family should do, family members might feel that both sides of their ambivalence were being represented. Having the team interact openly with the therapist or even with the family during sessions paved the way for later approaches in which the team might enter the treatment room and discuss the family while the family watched (Andersen, 1987).

Jim Alexander was a behaviorist who, out of frustration with the limits of his behavioral orientation, incorporated strategic ideas. The result was *functional family therapy* (Alexander & Parsons, 1982), which, as the name implies, is concerned with the function that family behavior is designed to achieve (see also Chapter 10). Functional family therapists assume that most family behaviors are attempts to become more or less intimate and through *relabeling* (another word for *reframing*) help family members see each other's actions in that benign light. They also help family members set up contingency management programs to help them get the kind of intimacy they want. Functional family therapy represents an interesting blend of strategic and behavioral therapies and, unlike other strategic models, retains the behaviorist ethic of basing interventions on sound research.

Evaluating Therapy Theory and Results

Communications family therapy wasn't just an application of psychotherapy to families; it was a radically new conceptualization that altered the very nature of imagination. What was new was a focus on the *process* of communication, rather than it's content. Communication was described as feedback and as a tactic in interpersonal power struggles.

When communication takes place in a closed system—an individual's fantasies or a family's private conversations—there is little opportunity for objective analysis. Only when someone outside the system provides input can correction occur. Because the rules of family functioning are largely unknown to the family, the best way to examine them is to consult an expert in communication. Today, the concepts of communications theory have been absorbed into the mainstream of family therapy, and its symptom-focused interventions have become the basis of the strategic and solution-focused models.

Strategic therapy reached the height of its popularity in the 1980s. It was clever, prescriptive, and expedient—qualities appreciated by therapists who often felt overwhelmed by the emotionality of families in treatment. Then a backlash set in, and people began criticizing strategic therapy's manipulative aspects. Unfortunately, when strategic therapists were confounded by the anxious inflexibility of some families, they may have exaggerated the irrational power of the family system.

In the 1990s the strategic approaches described in this chapter were replaced on family therapy's center stage by more collaborative models. But even as the field moves away from an overreliance on technique and manipulation, we shouldn't lose sight of useful aspects of strategic therapy. These include having clear therapeutic goals, anticipating how families might react to interventions, tracking sequences of interaction, and the creative use of directives.

Historically, most of the research on the effectiveness of strategic therapy hasn't been very rigorous. More than any other model in this book, information about strategic therapy is exchanged through the case report format. Nearly all of the articles and books on strategic therapy include at least one description of a successful treatment outcome. Thus strategic therapy appeared to have a great deal of anecdotal support for its efficacy (although people tend not to write about their failed cases). Recently, researchers have revisited these strategic ideas and have attempted to provide more rigorous empirical support.

Some early studies of the outcome of family therapies based on strategic therapy helped fuel its popularity. In their classic study, Langsley, Machotka, and Flomenhaft (1971) found that family crisis therapy, with similarities to the MRI and Haley models, drastically reduced the need for hospitalization. Alexander and Parsons found their functional family therapy to be more effective in treating a group of delinquents than a client-centered family approach, an eclectic-dynamic approach, or a no-treatment control group (Parsons & Alexander, 1973). Stanton, Todd, and associates (1982) demonstrated the effectiveness of combining structural and strategic family therapies for treating heroin addicts. The results were impressive because family therapy resulted in twice as many days of abstinence from heroin than a methadone maintenance program.

In the early 1980s the Milan Associates offered anecdotal case reports of amazing outcomes with anorexia nervosa, schizophrenia, and delinquency

(Selvini Palazzoli, Boscolo, Cecchin, & Prata, 1978b, 1980). Later, however, members of the original team expressed reservations about the model and implied that it wasn't as effective as they originally suggested (Boscolo, 1983; Selvini Palazzoli, 1986; Selvini Palazzoli & Viaro, 1988).

Although the original Milan model appears to have gone the way of the dinosaurs, there are currently three thriving strategic camps: the MRI group on the West Coast, the Washington School started by Haley and Madanes on the East Coast, and Nardone's Strategic Therapy Center in Italy.

Some followers of the MRI model have focused their attention on accumulating empirical support for the social cybernetic ideas. Several studies of both individual problems (Shoham, Bootzin, Rohrbaugh, & Ury, 1996; Shoham-Salomon, Avner, & Neeman, 1989; Shoham-Salomon & Jancourt, 1985) and couples problems (Goldman & Greenberg, 1992) suggest that strategic interventions are more effective than straightforward affective or skill-oriented interventions when clients are resistant to change. For example, Shoham and Rohrbaugh adapted the MRI model of strategic therapy and developed a couples-focused intervention for change-resistant health problems, including smoking and alcoholism (e.g., Shoham, Rohrbaugh, Stickle, & Jacob, 1998; Shoham, Rohrbaugh, Trost, & Muramoto, 2006). To date, their studies targeting smoking cessation have shown that this approach is, at the very least, as successful as existing smoking-cessation interventions and possibly demonstrates increased effectiveness for certain higher-risk subpopulations (e.g., female smokers and dual-couple smokers) (Shoham et al., 2006). Additionally, in their study of couples with a male alcoholic they found that couples who engaged in high levels of demand-withdraw interactions (a positive feedback loop) were more likely to drop out of the CBT conditions, while the level of demand-withdraw did not affect drop out in their strategic couples-focused interventions (Shoham et al., 1998). This would seem to suggest that characteristics of the couples dynamic might be important when determining what treatment would be the most effective. Strategic therapy, which tends to be less confrontational and less directive, might fit better with couples who engage in these types of demand-withdraw interactions.

A group of researchers in Miami have spent the last several decades developing Brief Strategic Family Therapy (BSFT), an intervention for adolescent substance abuse and behavioral problems. Several of the central tenets of this model borrow from the Haley and Madanes model of strategic therapy. They claim that BSFT is (1) pragmatic (using whatever means necessary to encourage change), (2) problem focused (only targeting interactions associated with the identified problem), and (3) planful. Additionally, in line with Madanes's thinking about the function of the symptom, the developers of BSFT posit that the role of the symptom is to maintain family patterns of interaction and if the symptom is removed, the pattern of interaction is threatened. Over the years, the developers of BSFT have conducted numerous clinical trials and found that their model is successful in engaging and retaining families in treatment (Robbins et al., 2003, 2008; Szapocznik et al., 1988), decreasing adolescent substance abuse and associated problem behaviors, as well as improving family functioning (Robbins et al., 2000, 2012; Santiseban et al., 2003). Interestingly, one study found that reductions in adolescent substance abuse were related to the amount of therapist demand/adolescent withdraw in therapy sessions. Specifically, adolescents from families who exhibited high levels of parent demand/adolescent withdraw before treatment and went on to experience high levels of therapist demand/client withdraw in sessions were more likely to have increased drug use at follow-up compared to low demand/withdraw adolescents (Rynes et al., 2014). These findings highlight the importance of attending to client/therapist interactions that might mirror problematic family interactions involved in maintaining symptomatic behavior.

◆ ◆ ◆

What people came to rebel against was the gimmickry of formulaic techniques. But gimmickry wasn't inherent in the strategic models. For example, the MRI's emphasis on reversing attempted solutions that don't work is a sound idea. People *do* stay stuck in ruts as long as they continue to pursue self-defeating strategies. If, in some hands, blocking more-of-the-same solutions resulted in rote applications of reverse psychology, that's not the fault of the cybernetic metaphor but of the way it was applied.

Strategic therapists are currently integrating new ideas and keeping up with the postmodern spirit of the twenty-first century. Haley published a book in which the evolution of his thinking is apparent (Haley, 1996), and a new book on the influence of the MRI on the field was released (Weakland & Ray, 1995). In addition, some authors have integrated MRI strategic concepts with narrative approaches (Eron & Lund, 1993, 1996). It's good to see that strategic thinking is evolving, because even in this era of the nonexpert therapist, there is still room for thoughtful problem-solving strategies and therapeutic direction.

Summary

Communications therapy was one of the first and most influential forms of family treatment. Its theoretical development was based on general systems theory, and the therapy that emerged was a systems approach *par excellence*. Communication was the detectable input and output therapists used to analyze the black box of interpersonal systems.

Another significant idea of communications therapy was that families are rule-governed systems, maintained by feedback mechanisms. Negative feedback accounts for the stability of normal families—and the inflexibility of dysfunctional ones. Because such families don't have adequate positive feedback mechanisms, they have difficulty adjusting to changing circumstances.

While there were major differences among the therapeutic strategies of Haley, Jackson, Satir, and Watzlawick, they were all committed to altering destructive patterns of communication. They pursued this goal by direct and indirect means. The direct approach, favored by Satir, sought change by coaching clear communication. This approach involved establishing ground rules, or metacommunicational principles, and included such tactics as telling people to speak for themselves and pointing out nonverbal and multilevel channels of communication.

The trouble is, as Haley noted, one of the difficulties of telling patients what to do is that "psychiatric patients are noted for their hesitation about doing what they are told." For this reason, communications therapists began to rely on more indirect strategies, designed to provoke change rather than foster awareness. Telling family members to speak for themselves, for example, may challenge a family rule and therefore meet with resistance. With this realization, communications therapy evolved into a treatment of resistance.

Resistance and symptoms were treated with a variety of paradoxical directives, known loosely as *therapeutic double binds*. Milton Erickson's technique of prescribing resistance was used as a lever to gain control, as, for example, when a therapist tells family members not to reveal everything in the first session. The same ploy was used to prescribe symptoms, an action that made covert rules explicit, implied that such behavior was voluntary, and put the therapist in control.

Strategic therapy, derived from Ericksonian hypnotherapy and Batesonian cybernetics, developed a body of powerful procedures for treating psychological problems. Strategic approaches vary in the specifics of theory and technique but share a problem-centered, pragmatic focus on changing behavioral sequences, in which therapists take responsibility for the outcome of therapy. Insight and understanding are eschewed in favor of directives designed to change the way family members interact.

The MRI model is strictly interactional—observing and intervening into sequences of interaction surrounding a problem rather than speculating about the intentions of the interactants. Haley and Madanes, on the other hand, are interested in motives: Haley mainly in the desire to control others and Madanes in the desire to love and be loved. Unlike the MRI group, Haley and Madanes believe that successful treatment often requires structural change, with an emphasis on improving family hierarchy.

Like Haley, the Milan Associates originally saw power in the motives of family members. They tried to understand the elaborate multigenerational games that surrounded symptoms. They designed powerful

interventions—positive connotation and rituals—
to expose those games and change the meaning of
problems. Later the original group split, with Selvini
Palazzoli going through several transformations until
her current long-term approach based on family secrets. Cecchin and Boscolo moved away from formulaic interventions, became more interested in the
questioning process as a way to help families to new
understandings, and in so doing paved the way for
family therapy's current interest in conversation and
narrative.

Click here to apply your knowledge of chapter
concepts.

Click here to test your application and analysis of
the content found within this chapter.

One of the reasons family therapy can be difficult is that families often appear as collections of individuals who affect each other in powerful but unpredictable ways. Structural family therapy offers a framework that brings order and meaning to those transactions. The consistent patterns of family behavior are what allow us to consider that they have structure, although of course only in a functional sense. The emotional boundaries and coalitions that make up a family's structure are abstractions; nevertheless, the concept of family structure enables therapists to intervene in a systematic and organized way.

Families usually seek help for a specific problem. It might be a child who misbehaves or a couple who doesn't get along. Family therapists look beyond the specifics of those problems to the family's attempts to solve them. This leads to the dynamics of interaction. The misbehaving child might have parents who scold but never reward him. The couple may be caught up in a pursuer–distancer dynamic, or they might be unable to talk without arguing.

What structural family therapy adds to the equation is a recognition of the overall organization that regulates those interactions. The "parents who scold" might turn out to be partners who undermine each other because one is wrapped up in the child while the other is an angry outsider. If so, attempts to encourage effective discipline are likely to fail unless the structural problem is addressed and the parents develop a real partnership. Similarly a couple who don't get along may not be able to improve their relationship until they create a boundary between themselves and intrusive in-laws.

The discovery that families are organized in **subsystems** with **boundaries** regulating the contact family members have with each other

CHAPTER 6

STRUCTURAL FAMILY THERAPY

The Organization of Family Life

LEARNING OUTCOMES

♦ Describe the evolution of structural family therapy.

♦ Describe the main tenets of structural family therapy.

♦ Describe healthy and unhealthy family development from a structural family therapy perspective.

♦ Describe the clinical goals and the conditions necessary for meeting those goals from a structural family therapy perspective.

♦ Discuss and demonstrate the assessment and intervention techniques of structural family therapy.

♦ Discuss research support for structural family therapy.

turned out to be one of the defining insights of family therapy. Perhaps equally important, though, was the introduction of **enactments**, in which family members are encouraged to deal directly with each other in sessions, permitting the therapist to observe and modify their interactions.

Sketches of Leading Figures

When he first burst onto the scene, Salvador Minuchin's galvanizing impact was as a master of technique. His most lasting contribution, however, was a theory of family structure and a set of guidelines to organize therapeutic techniques.

Minuchin was born and raised in Argentina. He served as a physician in the Israeli army and then came to the United States, where he trained in child psychiatry with Nathan Ackerman. After completing his studies Minuchin returned to Israel in 1952 to work with displaced children. He moved back to the United States in 1954 to begin psychoanalytic training at the William Alanson White Institute, where he studied the interpersonal psychiatry of Harry Stack Sullivan. After the White Institute, Minuchin took a job at the Wiltwyck School for delinquent boys, where he suggested to his staff that they start seeing families.

At Wiltwyck, Minuchin and his colleagues—Dick Auerswald, Charlie King, Braulio Montalvo, and Clara Rabinowitz—taught themselves to do family therapy, inventing it as they went along. To do so, they built a one-way mirror and took turns observing each other work. In 1962 Minuchin made a hajj to what was

then the Mecca of family therapy, Palo Alto. There he met Jay Haley and began a friendship that blossomed into an extraordinarily fertile collaboration.

The success of Minuchin's work with families at Wiltwyck led to a groundbreaking book, *Families of the Slums* (1967), which first outlined the structural model. Minuchin's reputation as a virtuoso therapist grew, and he became the director of the Philadelphia Child Guidance Clinic in 1965. The clinic then consisted of fewer than a dozen staff members. From this modest beginning, Minuchin created one of the largest and most prestigious child guidance clinics in the world.

Among Minuchin's colleagues in Philadelphia were Braulio Montalvo, Jay Haley, Bernice Rosman, Harry Aponte, Carter Umbarger, Marianne Walters, Charles Fishman, Cloe Madanes, and Stephen Greenstein, all of whom had a role in shaping structural family therapy. By the 1970s structural family therapy had become the most widely practiced of all systems of family therapy.

After leaving Philadelphia in 1981, Minuchin started his own center in New York, where he continued to practice and teach until 1996, when he retired and moved to Boston. Although he retired (again) and moved to Boca Raton, Florida, in 2005, Minuchin still travels and teaches throughout the world.

Following Minuchin's retirement the center in New York was renamed the Minuchin Center for the Family, and the torch was passed to a new generation. The staff of leading teachers at the Minuchin Center now includes Amy Begel, Cara Brendler, Jorge Colapinto, Patricia Dowds, Ema Genijovich, David Greenan, Richard Holm, Daniel Minuchin, Roni Schnadow, George Simon, and Wai-Yung Lee. Among Minuchin's other prominent students are Charles Fishman, in private practice in Philadelphia; Jay Lappin, who works with child welfare for the state of Delaware; and Michael Nichols, who teaches at the College of William and Mary.

Theoretical Formulations

Beginners often get bogged down in the content of family problems because they don't have a blueprint to help them see the pattern of family dynamics. Structural family therapy offers such a blueprint.

Courtesy of Salvador Minuchin

Salvador Minuchin's structural model is the most influential approach to family therapy throughout the world.

Three constructs define structural theory: *structure*, *subsystems*, and *boundaries*.

It's easy to understand what's meant by the structure of a house: It's the way the components of the house are organized, how many rooms there are, where the rooms are located, how they are connected, and so on. The family that lives in the house is also organized, but their structure is a little harder to characterize.

Family structure refers to the way a family is organized into subsystems whose interactions are regulated by interpersonal boundaries. The *process* of family interactions is like the patterns of conversation at the dinner table. The *structure* of the family is where family members sit in relation to one another. Who sits next to whom makes it easier to interact with some people and less so with others.

To grasp a family's structure, you must look beyond their interactions to the organizational framework within which they occur, and you must keep in mind that what goes on in one part of a family is affected by the organization of the whole system. Now let's see how this organizational structure comes about.

As family transactions are repeated they foster expectations that establish enduring patterns. Once patterns are established, family members use only a fraction of the options available to them. The first time the baby cries or a teenager misses the school bus, it's not clear who will do what. Will the load be shared? Will there be a quarrel? Will one person get stuck with most of the work? Soon, however, patterns are set, roles assigned, and things take on a sameness and predictability. "Who's going to. . . ?" becomes "She'll probably. . ." and then "She always. . . ."

Family structure is reinforced by the expectations that establish rules in a family. For example, a rule such as "family members should always look out for one another" will be manifest in various ways depending on the context and who is involved. If a boy gets into a fight with another boy in the neighborhood, his mother will go to the neighbors to complain. If a teenager has to wake up early for school, her mother wakes her. If a husband is too hung over to go to work in the morning, his wife calls to say he has the flu. If the parents have an argument, their children interrupt. The parents are so preoccupied with the doings of their children that it keeps them from spending time alone together. These sequences are *isomorphic*: They're structured. Modifying any of them may not change the basic structure, but altering the

underlying structure will have ripple effects on all family transactions.

Family structure is shaped partly by universal and partly by idiosyncratic constraints. For example, all families have some kind of hierarchical structure, with adults and children having different amounts of authority. Family members also tend to have reciprocal and complementary functions. Often these become so ingrained that their origin is forgotten and they are presumed necessary rather than optional.

> If a young mother, overwhelmed by the demands of her infant, gets upset and complains to her husband, he can respond in various ways. Perhaps he'll move closer and share the demands of childrearing. This creates a united parental team. If, on the other hand, he decides that his wife is depressed, she may end up in psychotherapy to get the emotional support she needs. This creates a structure where the father remains distant from the mother, and she has to turn outside the family for sympathy.

Whatever the pattern, it tends to be self-perpetuating. Although alternatives are available, family members are unlikely to consider them until changing circumstances produce stress in the system.

Families don't walk in and hand you their structural patterns as if they were bringing an apple to the teacher. What they bring is chaos and confusion. You have to discover the subtext—and you must be careful that it's accurate, not imposed but discovered. Two things are necessary: a theoretical system that explains structure and seeing the family in action. Knowing that a family is a single-parent family or that the parents are having trouble with a middle child doesn't tell you what their structure is. Structure becomes evident only when you observe actual interactions among family members.

> Consider the following. A mother calls to complain of misbehavior in her fifteen-year-old son. She is asked to bring her husband, son, and their three other children to the first session. When they arrive, the mother begins to describe a series of minor ways in which the son is disobedient. He

interrupts to say that she's always on his case; he never gets a break. This spontaneous bickering between mother and son reveals a preoccupation with each other—a preoccupation no less intense simply because it's conflictual. This sequence doesn't tell the whole story, however, because it doesn't include the father or the other children. They must be engaged to observe their role in the family structure.

If the father sides with his wife but seems unconcerned, then it may be that the mother's preoccupation with her son is related to her husband's lack of involvement. If the younger children tend to agree with their mother and describe their brother as bad, then it becomes clear that all the children are close to the mother—close and obedient up to a point, then close and disobedient.

Families are differentiated into *subsystems*—based on generation, gender, and function—which are demarcated by interpersonal *boundaries*, invisible barriers that regulate contact with others. A rule forbidding phone calls at dinnertime establishes a boundary that shields the family from intrusion. If children are permitted to freely interrupt their parents' conversations, the boundary separating the generations is eroded, and the couple's relationship is subverted to parenting. If parents always step in to settle arguments between their children, the children won't learn to fight their own battles.

Interpersonal boundaries vary from rigid to diffuse (Figure 6.1). Rigid boundaries are restrictive and permit little contact with outside subsystems, resulting in *disengagement*. Disengaged subsystems are

FIGURE 6.1 Boundaries

Rigid Boundary
_____
Disengagement

Clear Boundary
- - - - - - - - -
Normal Range

Diffuse Boundary
· · · · · · · ·
Enmeshment

independent but isolated. On the plus side, this fosters autonomy. On the other hand, disengagement limits affection and support. Disengaged families must come under extreme stress before they mobilize assistance. *Enmeshed* subsystems offer closeness, but at the expense of independence. Too much closeness cripples initiative.

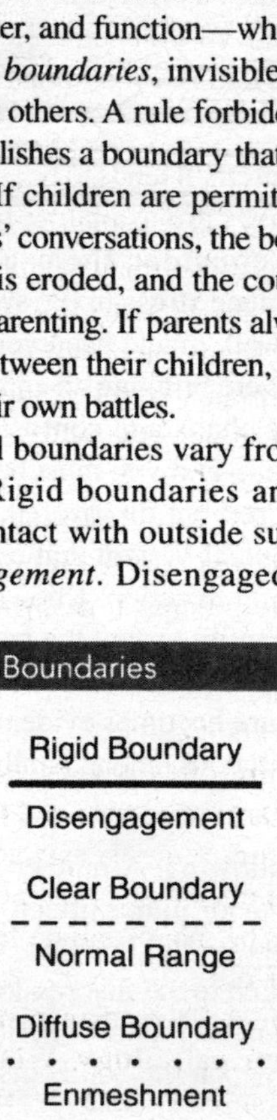

Although *structure* suggests a static condition, like all things human, family structure goes through a process of development (Minuchin, 1974). Families begin when two people in love decide to share their lives together, but a period of often difficult adjustment is required before they complete the transition from courtship to a functional partnership. They must learn to *accommodate* to each other's needs and styles of interaction. He learns to accommodate to her wish to be kissed hello and goodbye. She learns to leave him alone with his morning paper and coffee. These little arrangements, multiplied a thousand times, may be accomplished easily or only after intense struggle.

The couple must also develop complementary patterns of support. Some patterns are transitory. Perhaps, for instance, one works while the other completes school. Other patterns are more lasting. Exaggerated complementary roles can detract from individual growth; moderate complementarity enables couples to divide functions to support and enrich each other. When one has the flu, the other takes over. One's permissiveness may be balanced by the other's strictness. Complementary patterns exist in all couples; they become problematic when they are so rigid that they create a dysfunctional subsystem.

The spouse subsystem must also develop a boundary that separates it from parents, children, and other outsiders. All too often, husbands and wives give up the space they need for supporting each other when children are born.

A clear boundary enables children to interact with their parents but excludes them from the spouse subsystem. Parents and children eat together, play together, and share much of each others' lives; but there are some spouse functions that need not be shared. Husbands and wives are sustained as loving couples and enhanced as parents if they have time to be alone together—to talk, to go out to dinner occasionally, to fight, and to make love. Unhappily, the clamorous demands of children often make parents lose sight of the need to maintain a boundary around their relationship.

In addition to maintaining privacy for a couple, a clear boundary supports a hierarchical structure in which parents occupy a position of leadership. All too often this hierarchy is subverted by a child-centered ethos, which influences helping professionals as well as parents. Parents enmeshed with their children argue with them about who's going to do what and misguidedly share—or shirk—responsibility for making parental decisions.

In *Institutionalizing Madness* (Elizur & Minuchin, 1989), Minuchin makes a compelling case for a systems view of emotional problems that extends beyond the family to encompass the entire community. As Minuchin points out, unless therapists learn to look beyond the limited slice of ecology where they work to the larger social structures within which their work is embedded, their efforts may amount to little more than spinning wheels.

Family Dynamics

By considering the underlying organization of families, structural therapists are able to explain what regulates families and why they behave as they do—how they form and flourish, and sometimes get stuck.

◆ Normal Family Functioning

When two people join to form a couple, the structural requirements for the new union are **accommodation** and **boundary making**. The first priority is mutual accommodation to manage the myriad details of everyday living. Each partner tries to organize the relationship along familiar lines and pressures the other to comply. They must agree on major issues, such as where to live and whether to have children. Less obvious, but equally important, they must coordinate daily rituals, like what to watch on television, what to eat for supper, when to go to bed, and what to do there.

In accommodating to each other, a couple must establish a boundary between them as well as a boundary separating them from the outside. A diffuse boundary

exists between a couple if they call each other at work frequently, if neither has their own friends or independent activities, and if they come to view themselves only as a pair rather than as two separate personalities. On the other hand, they've established a rigid boundary if they spend little time together, have separate bedrooms, take separate vacations, have different checking accounts, and are more invested in careers or outside relationships than in their relationship.

Each partner tends to be more comfortable with the level of proximity that existed in his or her own family. Because these expectations differ, a struggle ensues that may be the most difficult of the new union. He wants to play poker with the boys; she feels deserted. She wants to talk; he wants to watch ESPN. His focus is on his career; hers is on the relationship. Each thinks the other is unreasonable.

Couples must also define a boundary between them and their original families. Rather suddenly, the families they grew up in must take second place to the new marriage. This, too, can be a difficult adjustment, both for newlyweds and for their parents.

The birth of a child transforms the structure of a new family into a *parental subsystem* and a *child subsystem*. A woman's commitment to a unit of three is likely to begin with pregnancy, since the child in her womb is an unavoidable reality. Her husband, on the other hand, may only begin to feel like a father when the child is born. Many men don't accept the role of father until their infants are old enough to respond to them. Thus, even in healthy families, children often bring stress and conflict. A mother's life is usually more radically transformed than a father's. She sacrifices a great deal and now needs more support from her husband. The husband, meanwhile, continues his job, and the new baby is far less of a disruption. Though he may try to support his wife, he's likely to resent some of her demands.

Children require different styles of parenting at different ages. Infants need care and feeding. Children need guidance and control, and adolescents need independence and responsibility. Good parenting for a two-year-old may be inappropriate for a five-year-old or a fourteen-year-old.

Minuchin (1974) warns therapists not to mistake growing pains for pathology. What distinguishes normal families isn't the absence of problems but a functional structure for dealing with them. Normal families experience anxiety and disruption as their members grow and change. Many families seek help at transitional stages, and therapists should keep in mind that they may simply be in the process of modifying their structure to adjust to new circumstances.

◆ Development of Behavior Disorders

Modifications in structure are required when a family or one of its members encounters external pressures (a parent is laid off, the family moves) and when developmental transitions are reached (a child reaches adolescence, parents retire). Healthy families accommodate to changed circumstances; dysfunctional families increase the rigidity of structures that are no longer working.

In disengaged families, boundaries are rigid and the family fails to mobilize support when it's needed. Disengaged parents may be unaware that a child is depressed or experiencing difficulties at school until the problem is advanced.

A single mother recently brought her twelve-year-old son to the clinic after discovering that he had missed two weeks of school. *Two weeks!* thought the therapist; that's a long time not to know your child's been skipping school.

A structural perspective would make two important points. First, the obvious disengagement between this mother and child is no more significant than the disengagement between the mother and school authorities. Second, a structural analysis might help to get past blaming this woman for failing to know what was going on in her son's life. If she's disengaged from her son, what is occupying her elsewhere? Maybe the financial burden of single parenthood is overwhelming. Maybe she's still grief stricken over the death of her husband. The point to remember is that if someone is disengaged in one relationship, he or she is likely to be preoccupied elsewhere.

In enmeshed families, boundaries are diffuse and family members become dependent on one another. Intrusive parents create difficulties by stunting the development of their children and interfering with their ability to solve their own problems.

Although we may refer to families as *enmeshed* or *disengaged*, it's more accurate to describe particular subsystems as being enmeshed or disengaged. In fact, enmeshment and disengagement tend to be reciprocal, so that, for example, a father who's overly involved with his work is likely to neglect his family. A frequently encountered pattern is the enmeshed mother/disengaged father syndrome—"the signature arrangement of the troubled middle-class family" (Minuchin & Nichols, 1993, p. 121).

Feminists have criticized the notion of an enmeshed mother/disengaged father syndrome because they worry about blaming mothers for an arrangement that is culturally sanctioned. This concern is valid. But stereotyping and blaming are due to insensitive application of these ideas, not to the ideas themselves. Skewed relationships, whatever their origin, can be problematic, though no one individual should be expected to do all the changing.

Hierarchies can be rigid and unfair, or weak and ineffective. In the first case, children may find themselves unprotected because of a lack of guidance; in the second, their growth as individuals may be impaired and power struggles may ensue. Just as a functional hierarchy is necessary for a family's stability, flexibility is necessary for it to adapt to change.

One problem often seen by family therapists arises when parents who are unable to resolve conflicts between themselves divert the focus of concern onto a child. Instead of worrying about themselves, they worry about the child (Figure 6.2). Although this reduces the strain on father (F) and mother (M), it victimizes the child (C).

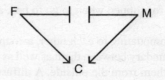

FIGURE 6.2 Scapegoating as a Means of Detouring Conflict

FIGURE 6.3 Cross-Generational Coalition

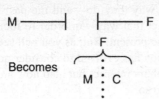

An equally common pattern is for the parents to argue through the children. Father says mother is too permissive; she says he's too strict. He may withdraw, causing her to criticize his lack of concern, which in turn makes him withdraw further. The enmeshed mother responds to children's needs with excessive concern. The disengaged father may not respond at all. Both may be critical of the other's way, but they perpetuate each other's behavior with their own. The result is a **cross-generational coalition** (Figure 6.3).

Some families function well when the children are young but are unable to adjust to an older child's need for discipline. Young children in enmeshed families receive wonderful care: Their parents give them lots of attention. Although such parents may be too tired from caring for the children to have much time for each other, the system may be moderately successful.

If, however, these doting parents don't teach their children to obey rules and respect authority, the children may be unprepared to negotiate their entrance into school. Used to getting their own way, they may be resistant to authority. Several possible consequences may bring the family into treatment. The children may be reluctant to go to school, and their fears may be reinforced by "understanding" parents who permit them to stay home (Figure 6.4). Such a case may be labeled as school phobia and may become entrenched if the parents permit the children to remain at home for more than a few days.

Alternatively, the children of such a family may go to school, but since they haven't learned to accommodate to others, they may be rejected by their schoolmates. Such children often become depressed. In other cases, children enmeshed with their parents become discipline problems at school, in which case school authorities may initiate counseling.

A major upheaval that requires structural realignment occurs when divorced or widowed spouses remarry. Such *blended families* either readjust their boundaries or soon experience transitional conflicts. When a woman divorces, she and her children must learn to adjust to a structure that establishes a clear boundary separating the divorced spouses but still permits contact between father and children; then if she remarries, the family must readjust to a new husband and stepfather (Figure 6.5).

Sometimes it's hard for a mother and children to allow a stepfather to participate in the parental subsystem. Mother and children have long since learned to accommodate to each other. The new parent may be treated as an outsider who's supposed to learn the right way of doing things, rather than as a new partner who will give as well as receive ideas about childrearing (Figure 6.6).

The more the mother and children insist on maintaining their familiar patterns without including the stepfather, the more frustrated he'll become. The result may lead to child abuse or chronic arguing between

FIGURE 6.4 School Phobia

FIGURE 6.5 Divorce and Remarriage

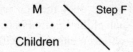

FIGURE 6.6 Failure to Accept a Stepparent

$$M \qquad Step F$$
$$\cdot \quad \cdot \quad \cdot \quad \cdot$$
$$Children$$

the parents. The sooner such families enter treatment, the easier it is to help them adjust to the transition.

An important aspect of structural family problems is that symptoms in one member reflect not only that person's interactions but also other relationships in the family. If Johnny, age sixteen, is depressed, it's helpful to know that he's enmeshed with his mother. Discovering that she demands absolute obedience from him and refuses to accept independent thinking or outside relationships helps to explain his depression (Figure 6.7). But that's only one segment of the family system.

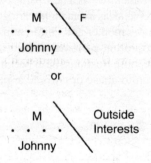

FIGURE 6.7 Johnny's Enmeshment with His Mother and Disengagement with Outside Interests

Why is the mother enmeshed with her son? Perhaps she's disengaged from her husband. Perhaps she's a widow who hasn't made new friends. Helping Johnny resolve his depression may best be accomplished by helping his mother satisfy her need for closeness with other adults in her life.

Mechanisms of Change

Like most of the classic models of family therapy, structural therapy was once a strictly action-oriented approach. Family therapy pioneers differentiated themselves from psychoanalysis by aggressively ignoring emotion and cognition—why family members interact the way they do—and the past—how they learned to act that way—in order to focus on interactions in the present. But, as you will see, structural family therapy has evolved to consider not only how family members interact but also how and why they learned to do so.

Goals of Therapy

Structural treatment is designed to alter the organization of a therapy so that its members can solve their own problems. The goal of therapy is structural change; problem solving is a by-product.

The idea that family problems are embedded in dysfunctional family structures has led to the criticism of structural family therapy as pathologizing. Critics see structural maps of dysfunctional organization as implying a pathological core in client families. This isn't true. Structural problems are viewed as a failure to adjust to changing circumstances. Far from seeing families as inherently flawed, structural therapists see their work as activating latent adaptive patterns that are already in families' repertoires (Simon, 1995).

Although every family is unique, there are common structural goals. Most important is the creation of an effective hierarchy. Parents should be in charge, not relate to their children as equals. With enmeshed families the goal is to differentiate individuals and subsystems by strengthening the boundaries around them. With disengaged families the goal is to increase contact by making boundaries more permeable.

Conditions for Behavior Change

A therapist produces change by **joining** the family, probing for areas of flexibility, and then activating dormant structural alternatives. Joining gets the therapist into the family; *accommodating* to their style gives him or her leverage; and *restructuring* transforms the family structure.

To join, a therapist conveys acceptance of family members and respect for their ways of doing things.

Comstock/Stockbyte/Getty Images

Structural therapists emphasize the need for parents to maintain a clear hierarchical position of authority.

If parents come for help with a child's problems, the therapist doesn't begin by asking for the child's opinion. This would show lack of respect for the parents. Only after successfully joining with a family is it fruitful to attempt restructuring—the often dramatic confrontations that challenge families and encourage them to change.

The first task is to understand the family's view of their problems. This is accomplished by tracking their perspectives in the words they use to explain them and in the behavior with which they demonstrate them.

What makes structural family therapy unique is the use of **enactments** to reveal structural patterns, and later to change them. This is the *sine qua non* of structural family therapy: observing and modifying the structure of family transactions in the immediate context of the session. Structural therapists work with what they see, not what family members describe.

Therapy

◆ Assessment

Structural therapists make assessments by observing how family members respond to their dilemmas. Suppose a young woman complains of having

trouble making decisions. In responding to the therapist's questions during an initial meeting, the young woman becomes indecisive and glances at her father. He speaks up to clarify what she was having trouble explaining. Now the daughter's indecisiveness can be linked to the father's helpfulness, suggesting a pattern of enmeshment. Perhaps when the therapist asks the parents to discuss their daughter's problems, they start to argue and the discussion doesn't last long. This suggests disengagement between the parents, which may be related (as cause and effect) to enmeshment between parent and child.

It's important to note that structural therapists make no assumptions about how families *should be* organized. Single-parent families can be perfectly functional, as can families with two moms or dads or indeed any other family variation. It's the fact that a family seeks therapy for a problem they have been unable to solve that gives a therapist license to assume that something about the way they are organized may not be working for them.

Because problems are a function of the entire family structure, it's important to include the whole group for assessment. But sometimes even the whole family isn't enough, because the family may not be the only relevant context. A mother's depression might be due more to problems at work than at home. A son's difficulties at school might be due more to the situation at school than to the one in the family.

Finally, some problems may be treated as problems of the individual. As Minuchin (1974) has written, "Pathology may be inside the patient, in his social context, or in the feedback between them" (p. 9). Elsewhere Minuchin (Minuchin, Rosman, & Baker, 1978) referred to the danger of "denying the individual while enthroning the system" (p. 91). While interviewing a family to see how the parents deal with their children, a careful clinician may notice that one child has a neurological problem or a learning disability. These problems need to be identified and appropriate referrals made. Usually when a child has trouble in school, there's a problem in the family or school setting. Usually, but not always.

Making an assessment is best done by focusing on the presenting problem and exploring the family's response to it. Consider the case of a thirteen-year-old girl whose parents complain that she lies. The first question might be, "Who is she lying to?" Let's say the answer is both parents. The next question would be, "How good are the parents at detecting when the daughter is lying?" And then, less innocently, "Which parent is better at detecting the daughter's lies?" Perhaps it turns out to be the mother. In fact, let's say the mother is obsessed with discovering the daughter's lies—most of which have to do with seeking independence in ways that raise the mother's anxiety. Thus a worried mother and a disobedient daughter are locked in struggle over growing up that excludes the father.

To carry this assessment further, a structural therapist would explore the relationship between the parents. The assumption would not, however, be that the child's problems are the result of marital problems, but simply that the mother–daughter relationship might be related to the one between the parents. Perhaps the parents got along famously until their child approached adolescence, and then the mother began to worry more than the father. Whatever the case, the assessment would also involve talking with the parents about growing up in their own families in order to explore how their pasts helped shape the way they react to things now.

Minuchin and his colleagues recently described the process of assessment as organized in four steps (Minuchin, Nichols, & Lee, 2007). The first step is to ask questions about the presenting complaint until family members begin to see that the problem goes beyond the symptom bearer to include the entire family. The second step is to help family members see how their interactions may be perpetuating the presenting problem. The third step is a brief exploration of the past, focusing on how the adults in the family came to develop the perspectives that influence their interactions. The fourth step is to explore options that family members might take to interact in more productive ways to create a shift in the family structure and help resolve the presenting complaint.

In a recent study of how experienced therapists implement these four steps, Nichols and Tafuri (2013) offered the following guidelines.

Guidelines for Structural Family Assessments

In step one, the goal is to open up the presenting complaint—to challenge the settled certainty that the problem is some kind of fixed flaw. A therapist's opening questions should give family members a chance to tell their stories and express their feelings. On the other hand, a therapist should not accept at face value a family's description of their problems as residing entirely within one person. To be effective at this stage, a therapist conveys the attitude, "I don't quite understand, but I'm interested in how you see things." A therapist who tries to ingratiate himself or herself by saying, "Oh, yes, I understand!" closes off exploration.

In step one a therapist might point out that the identified patient seems to behave more competently than the presenting complaint would have suggested. For example, when parents sought help for what they described as an out-of-control ten-year-old, the therapist talked with the boy about his interests and friends, which encouraged the boy to respond in an appropriate and respectful manner. This gave the therapist leverage to suggest that since the boy *could* be well behaved, something must be going on in the family that allowed him to misbehave. The point isn't to shift blame, but to open a discussion about how family members' interactions may be influencing each other.

A common technique used in opening up the presenting complaint is asking family members what other family members do to provoke a certain response from them. In one case, when a husband described his intolerance as the primary problem, the therapist asked, "What does your wife do that's hard to tolerate?" This intervention led to the recognition of a pursuer–distancer dynamic in the couple, and to the husband recognizing that his distancing only provoked further pursuit.

Therapists often block third parties from interrupting and ask family members if they want others in the family to behave differently toward them. Thus, in the opening stage, there is a consistent attempt to shift the focus from personalities to patterns of interaction.

The second step in a structural assessment is exploring how family members may be responding in ways that contribute to the presenting problem. This is not to suggest that family problems are typically *caused* by how other people treat the identified patient. By helping family members see how their actions may be perpetuating the problems that plague them, a therapist empowers them to become their own agents of change. A father who realizes that his nagging his son to wake up in the morning allows the boy to avoid taking responsibility for himself can stop acting as his son's alarm clock.

Among the techniques commonly used in the second step, therapists often ask family members if they respond in a certain way to certain behaviors from other family members, ask family members if they play a role in a problematic dynamic, initiate enactments, describe the dynamics of a problematic interaction, or simply tell family members that they must be doing something to perpetuate the presenting problem.

The third step is a brief, focused exploration of the past in order to help family members understand how they came to their present assumptions and ways of responding to each other. One thing that distinguishes therapy from advice giving is trying to uncover *why* people do things that aren't good for them, rather than merely trying to get them to stop. The rationale for exploring family members' past experience is to help make their current behavior intelligible—not to debunk their beliefs, but to put them in a more understandable context. However, it only makes sense to ask family members how they learned a certain way of behaving after they realize that their behavior is in fact counterproductive. In one case, for example, a mother complained that her fourteen-year-old daughter was defiant. Only after almost an hour of careful questioning did

the mother begin to see that her overprotectiveness might be playing a role in the daughter's defiance. Then, and only then, was the mother open to the therapist's question about how she learned to be overprotective.

After developing a clear picture of what's keeping a family stuck and how they got that way, in the fourth step they and the therapist talk about who needs to change what—and who is willing or unwilling to do that. Without this step, which turns the process of assessment from an operation performed *on* families into a collaboration *with* them, therapy often becomes a process of pushing people where they see no reason to go. No wonder they resist.

◆ Therapeutic Techniques

In *Families and Family Therapy*, Minuchin (1974) listed three overlapping stages in structural family therapy. The therapist: (1) joins the family in a position of leadership, (2) maps the family's underlying structure, and (3) intervenes to transform this structure. The program is simple, in the sense that it follows a clear plan, but complicated because of the endless variety of family patterns.

If a therapist's interventions are to be effective, they cannot be formulaic. Good therapists are more than technicians. The strategy of therapy, on the other hand, must be organized. In general, structural family therapy follows these steps:

1. Joining and accommodating
2. Enactment
3. Structural mapping
4. Highlighting and modifying interactions
5. Boundary making
6. Unbalancing
7. Challenging unproductive assumptions

Joining and Accommodating

Individual patients generally enter therapy already predisposed to accept a therapist's authority. By seeking treatment, an individual tacitly acknowledges a need for help and willingness to trust the therapist. Not so with families.

A family therapist is an unwelcome outsider. After all, why did he or she insist on seeing the whole family? Family members expect to be told that they're doing something wrong, and they're prepared to defend themselves.

The therapist must first disarm defenses and ease anxiety. This is done by building an alliance of understanding with each member of the family.

Greet the family and then ask for each person's view of the problem. Listen carefully and acknowledge what you hear: "I see, Mrs. Jones, you think Sally must be depressed about something that happened at school." "So, Mr. Jones, you see some of the same things your wife sees, but you're not convinced that it's a serious problem. Is that right?"

Everyone has a story to tell, and in unhappy families almost everyone feels misunderstood. The first step in breaking the cycle of misunderstanding is to offer the empathy family members may be temporarily unable to provide each other. Hearing and acknowledging each person's account of the family's sorrows provides information—and begins to release family members from the resentment of unheard feelings. *Joining*, as this empathic connection is called, opens the way for family members to begin listening to each other and establishes a bond with the therapist that enables them to accept the challenges to come.

These initial conversations convey respect, not only for the individuals in the family but also for the family's structural organization. A therapist shows respect for parents by honoring their authority. They, not their children, are asked first to describe the problems. If a family elects one person to speak for the others, the therapist notes this but does not initially challenge it.

Children have special concerns and capacities. They should be greeted gently and asked simple questions: "Hi, I'm so-and-so; what's your name? Oh, Keisha, that's a nice name. Where do you go to school, Keisha?" Avoid the usual platitudes ("And what do *you* want to be when you grow up?"). Try something a little fresher ("What do you hate most about school?"). Those who wish to remain silent should be allowed to do so. They will anyway.

"And what's your view of the problem?"
(Grim silence.)
"You don't feel like saying anything right now? That's fine. Perhaps you'll have something to say later."

It's particularly important to join powerful family members as well as angry ones. Special pains must be taken to accept the point of view of the father who thinks therapy is hooey or the embittered teenager who feels like an accused criminal. It's also important to reconnect with such people at frequent intervals, particularly when things begin to heat up.

Enactment

Family structure is manifest in the way family members interact. It can't always be inferred from their descriptions. Families often describe themselves more as they think they should be than as they are.

Getting family members to talk with each other runs counter to their expectations. They expect to present their case to an expert and then be told what to do. If asked to discuss something in the session, they'll say "We've already talked about this," or "It won't do any good, he (or she) doesn't listen," or "But *you're* supposed to be the expert."

If a therapist begins by giving each person a chance to speak, usually one will say something about another that can be a springboard for an enactment. When, for example, one parent says that the other is too strict, the therapist can initiate an enactment by saying, "She says you're too strict; can you answer her?" Picking a specific issue is more effective than vague requests, such as "Why don't you talk this over?"

Working with enactments requires three operations. First, the therapist notices a problematic sequence. Perhaps, for example, when a mother talks to her daughter, they talk as peers, and the little brother is left out. Second, the therapist initiates an enactment. For example, the therapist might say to the mother, "Talk this over with your kids." Third and most important, the therapist guides the family to modify the enactment. If the mother talks to her children in such a way that she doesn't take responsibility for major decisions, the therapist encourages her to do so as the family continues the enactment.

Once an enactment is begun, a therapist can discover many things about a family's structure. How long can two people talk without being interrupted—that is, how clear is the boundary? Does one attack, the other defend? Who is central; who is peripheral? Do parents bring children into their discussions—that is, are they enmeshed?

> ▶ Watch this video of a structural family therapist initiating an enactment. What makes enactments so powerful?

Families demonstrate enmeshment by interrupting, speaking for each other, doing things for children that they can do for themselves, or constantly arguing. In disengaged families one may see a husband sitting impassively while his wife cries, a total absence of conflict, a surprising ignorance of important information about the children, or a lack of concern for each other's interests.

When an enactment breaks down, a therapist intervenes in one of two ways: commenting on what went wrong or pushing them to keep going. For example, if a father responds to the suggestion to talk with his twelve-year-old daughter about how she's feeling by berating her, the therapist could say to the father, "Congratulations." The father then might ask, "What do you mean?" The therapist could respond, "Congratulations. You win; she loses." Or the therapist could simply nudge the transaction by saying to the father, "Good, keep talking, but help her express her feelings. She's still a little girl; she needs your help."

If, as soon as the first session starts, the kids begin running around the room while the parents protest ineffectually, the therapist doesn't need to hear descriptions of what goes on at home to see the executive incompetence. If a mother and daughter rant and rave at each other while the father sits silently in the corner, it isn't necessary to ask how involved he is at home.

Structural Mapping

Preliminary assessments are based on interactions in the first session. In later sessions these formulations are refined or revised. Although there is some danger of bending families to fit categories when they're applied too early, the greater danger is waiting too long. Families quickly *induct* therapists into their culture. A family that initially appears to be chaotic and enmeshed soon comes to be just the familiar Jones family. For this reason, it's important to develop structural hypotheses relatively early in the process.

Suppose that you're about to see a family consisting of a mother, a sixteen-year-old daughter, and a stepfather. The mother called to complain of her daughter's misbehavior. What do you imagine the structure might be, and how would you test your hypothesis? A good guess might be that the mother and daughter are enmeshed, excluding the stepfather. This can be tested by seeing if the mother and daughter talk mostly about each other in the session—whether positively or negatively. The stepfather's disengagement would be confirmed if he and his wife are unable to converse without the daughter's intrusion.

Structural assessments take into account both the problem the family presents and the structural dynamics it displays. And they include all family members. In this instance, knowing that the mother and daughter are enmeshed isn't enough; you also have to know what role the stepfather plays. If he's close with his wife but distant from the daughter, finding mutually enjoyable activities for stepfather and stepdaughter will help increase the girl's independence from her mother. On the other hand, if the mother's proximity to her daughter appears to be a function of her distance from her husband, then the marital pair might be a more productive focus.

Highlighting and Modifying Interactions

Once families begin to interact, problematic transactions emerge. Recognizing their structural implications requires focusing on process, not content.

Perhaps a wife complains, "We have a communication problem. My husband won't talk to me; he never expresses his feelings." The therapist then initiates an enactment to see what actually does happen. "Your wife says you have a communication problem; can you respond to that? Talk with her." If, when they talk, the wife becomes domineering and critical while the husband grows increasingly silent, then the therapist sees what's wrong: The problem isn't that he doesn't talk (which is a linear explanation). Nor is the problem that she nags (also a linear explanation). The problem is that the more she nags, the more he withdraws, and the more he withdraws, the more she nags.

The trick is to modify this pattern. This may require forceful intervening, or what structural therapists call **intensity**.

Structural therapists achieve intensity by selective regulation of affect, repetition, and duration. Tone, volume, pacing, and choice of words can be used to raise the affective intensity of interventions. It helps if you know what you want to say. Here's an example of a limp statement: "People are always concerned with themselves, kind of seeing themselves as the center of attention and just looking for whatever they can get. Wouldn't it be nice, for a change, if everybody started thinking about what they could do for others?" Compare that with "Ask not what your country can do for you—ask what you can do for your country." John Kennedy's words had impact because they were brief and to the point. You don't need to make speeches, but you do occasionally have to speak forcefully to get your point across.

Affective intensity isn't a matter of clever phrasing. You have to know how and when to be provocative.

> ▶ Watch this video of a structural family therapist using intensity to highlight and modify family interactions. What effect did intensity have on the family?

CASE STUDY

Mike Nichols once worked with a family in which a twenty-nine-year-old woman with anorexia nervosa was the identified patient. Although the family maintained a facade of togetherness, it was rigidly structured; the mother and her anorexic daughter were enmeshed, while the father was excluded. In this family, the father was the only one to express anger openly, and this was part of the rationale for why he was excluded. His daughter was afraid of his anger, which she freely admitted. What was less clear, however, was that the mother had covertly taught the daughter to avoid her father, because she herself couldn't deal with him. Consequently,

the daughter grew up afraid of her father, and of men in general.

At one point the father, describing how isolated he felt from his daughter, said he thought it was because she feared his anger. The daughter agreed, "It's his fault, all right." The therapist asked the mother what she thought, and she replied, "It isn't *his* fault."

The therapist said, "You're right."

The mother went on, denying her real feelings to avoid conflict, "It's no one's fault."

The therapist answered in a way that got her attention, "That's not true."

Startled, she asked what he meant.

"It's *your* fault," he said.

This level of intensity was necessary to interrupt a rigid pattern of conflict-avoidance that sustained a destructive **coalition** between mother and daughter. The content—who really is afraid of anger—was less important than the structural goal: freeing the daughter from her overinvolvement with her mother.

Intensity can also be achieved by extending the duration of a sequence beyond the point where homeostasis is reinstated. A common example is the management of tantrums. Temper tantrums are maintained by parents who give in. They *try* not to give in; they just don't try long enough.

CASE STUDY

A four-year-old girl began to scream bloody murder when her sister left the room. She wanted to go with her sister. Her screaming was almost unbearable, and the parents were ready to back down. However, the therapist urged that they not allow themselves to be defeated and suggested that they hold her until she calmed down. She screamed for twenty minutes! Everyone in the room was frazzled. But the little girl finally realized that this time she wasn't going to get her way, and so she calmed down. Subsequently, the parents were able to use the same intensity of duration to break her of this destructive habit.

Sometimes intensity requires repetition of a theme in a variety of contexts. Infantilizing parents may have to be told not to hang up their child's coat, not to speak for her, not to take her to the bathroom, and not to do many other things that she's capable of doing for herself.

What we're calling *intensity* may strike some as overly aggressive. Although there's no denying that Minuchin and his followers tend to be interventionists, the point of intensity isn't to bully people but to push them past the point where they give up on getting through to each other. An alternative strategy is to use **empathy** to help family members get beneath the surface of their defensive wrangling.

If, for example, the parents of a disobedient child are locked in a cycle of unproductive quarreling in which the mother attacks the father for not being involved and he responds with excuses, a therapist could use intensity to push them to come up with a plan for dealing with their child's behavior. Or the therapist could interrupt their squabbling and, using empathy, talk to each of them one at a time about what they're feeling. The wife who shows only anger might be covering up the hurt and longing she feels. The husband who neither gets involved nor fights back when he feels attacked might be too annoyed at his wife's anger to see that she needs him. Once these more genuine emotions are articulated, they can serve as a basis for clients reconnecting with each other in a less defensive manner.

Shaping competence is another method of modifying interactions. Intensity is used to block the stream of interactions. Shaping competence is like altering the direction of the flow. By reinforcing positives, structural therapists help family members use functional alternatives that are already in their repertoire.

Even when people make a lot of mistakes, it's usually possible to pick out something they're doing light. A sense of timing helps.

CASE STUDY

In a large chaotic family the parents were extremely ineffective at controlling their children. At one point the therapist turned to the mother and said, "It's too noisy in here; would you quiet the kids?" Knowing how much difficulty the woman had with discipline, the therapist was poised to comment on any step in the direction of effective management. The mother had to yell "Quiet!" three or four times before the children momentarily stopped what they were doing. Quickly—before the children resumed

their misbehavior—the therapist complimented the mother for "loving her kids enough to be firm with them." Thus the message was "You're a competent person, you know how to be firm." If the therapist had waited until the chaos resumed before telling the mother she should be more firm, the message would be "You're incompetent."

Boundary Making

In enmeshed families, interventions are designed to strengthen boundaries. Family members are urged to speak for themselves, interruptions are blocked, and dyads are helped to finish conversations without intrusion. A therapist who wishes to support the sibling system and protect it from unnecessary parental intrusion might say, "Susie and Sean, talk this over, and everyone else will listen carefully." If children interrupt their parents, a therapist might challenge the parents to strengthen the hierarchical boundary by saying, "Why don't you get them to butt out so that you two grownups can settle this."

Although structural therapy is begun with the whole family, subsequent sessions may be held with individuals or subgroups to strengthen their boundaries. An overprotected teenager is supported as an independent person by participating in some individual sessions. Parents so enmeshed with their children that they never have private conversations may begin to learn how if they meet separately with the therapist.

CASE STUDY

When a forty-year-old woman called the clinic for help with for depression, she was asked to come in with the rest of her family. It soon became apparent that this woman was overburdened by her four children and received little support from her husband.

The therapist's strategy was to strengthen the boundary between the mother and the children and help the parents move closer to each other. This was done in stages. First the therapist joined the oldest child, a sixteen-year-old girl, and supported her competence as a potential helper for her mother. Once this was done, the girl was able to assume a good deal of responsibility for her younger siblings, both in sessions and at home.

Freed from their preoccupation with the children, the parents now had the opportunity to talk more with each other. They had little to say, however. This wasn't the result of hidden conflict but instead reflected a marriage of two relatively nonverbal people. After several sessions of trying to get the pair talking, the therapist realized that although talking may be fun for some people, it might not be for others. So to support the bond between the couple, the therapist asked them to plan a special trip together. They chose a boat ride on a nearby lake.

When they returned for the next session, they were beaming. They had a wonderful time. Subsequently, they decided to spend a little time out together each week.

Disengaged families tend to avoid conflict, and thus minimize interaction. A structural therapist intervenes to challenge conflict avoidance and block detouring in order to help disengaged family members break down the walls between them.

When beginners see disengagement, they tend to think of ways to encourage positive interaction. In fact, disengagement is usually a way of avoiding arguments. Therefore, people isolated from each other usually need to confront their differences before they can become closer.

Most people underestimate the degree to which their own behavior influences the behavior of those around them. This is particularly true in disengaged families. Problems are usually seen as the result of what someone else is doing, and solutions are thought to require that others change. Structural therapists move family discussions from linear to circular perspectives by stressing **complementarity**. The mother who complains that her son is a troublemaker is taught to consider what she's doing to trigger or maintain his behavior. The wife who nags her husband to spend more time with her must learn to make increased involvement more attractive. The husband who complains that his wife never listens to him may have to listen to her more, before she's willing to reciprocate.

Unbalancing

In boundary making, a therapist aims to realign relationships *between* subsystems. In unbalancing, the goal is to change the relationship *within* a subsystem. What often keeps families stuck in stalemate is that members in conflict are balanced in opposition and, as a result, remain frozen in inaction. In unbalancing, the therapist joins and supports one individual or subsystem.

Taking sides—let's call it what it is—seems like a violation of therapy's sacred canon of neutrality. However, a therapist takes sides to unbalance and realign the system, not as an arbiter of right and wrong. Ultimately, balance and fairness are achieved because the therapist sides in turn with various members of the family.

CASE STUDY

When the MacLean family sought help for an "unmanageable" child, a terror who'd been expelled from two schools, Dr. Minuchin uncovered a covert split between the parents, held in balance by not being talked about. The ten-year-old boy's misbehavior was dramatically visible; his father had to drag him kicking and screaming into the consulting room. Meanwhile, his little brother sat quietly, smiling engagingly. The good boy.

To broaden the focus from an "impossible child" to issues of parental control and cooperation, Minuchin asked about the little brother, seven-year-old Kevin, who misbehaved invisibly. He peed on the floor in the bathroom. According to his father, Kevin's peeing on the floor was due to "inattentiveness." The mother laughed when Minuchin said, "Nobody could have such poor aim."

Minuchin talked with the boy about how wolves mark their territory and suggested that he expand his territory by peeing in all four corners of the family room.

Minuchin: Do you have a dog?

Kevin: No.

Minuchin: Oh, so you are the family dog?

In the process of discussing the boy who peed—and his parents' response—Minuchin dramatized how the parents polarized and undercut each other.

Minuchin: Why would he do such a thing?

Father: I don't know if he did it on purpose.

Minuchin: Maybe he was in a trance?

Father: No, I think it was carelessness.

Minuchin: His aim must be terrible.

The father described the boy's behavior as accidental; the mother considered it defiant. One reason parents fall under the control of their young children is that they avoid confronting their differences. Differences are normal, but they become detrimental when one parent undermines the other's handling of the children. (It's cowardly revenge for unaddressed grievances.)

Minuchin's gentle but insistent pressure on the couple to talk about how they respond, without switching to focus on how the children behave, led to their bringing up long-held but seldom-voiced resentments.

Mother: Bob makes excuses for the children's behavior because he doesn't want to get in there and help me find a solution for the problem.

Father: Yes, but when I did try to help, you'd always criticize me. So after a while I gave up.

Like a photographic print in a developing tray, the spouses' conflict had become visible. Minuchin protected the parents from embarrassment (and the children from being burdened) by asking the children to leave the room. Without the preoccupation of parenting, the spouses could face each other, man and woman—and talk about their hurts and grievances. It turned out to be a sad story of lonely disengagement.

Minuchin: Do you two have areas of agreement?

He said yes; she said no. He was a minimizer; she was a critic.

Minuchin: When did you divorce Bob and marry the children?

She turned quiet; he looked off into space. She said, softly, "Probably ten years ago."

What followed was a painful but familiar story of how a marriage can drown in parenting. The conflict was never resolved because it never surfaced. And so the rift never healed.

With Minuchin's help, the couple took turns talking about their pain—and learning to listen. By unbalancing, Minuchin brought enormous pressure to bear to help this couple break through their differences, open up to each other, fight for what they want, and finally begin to come together—as husband and wife, and as parents.

Unbalancing is part of a struggle for change that sometimes takes on the appearance of combat. When a therapist says to a father that he's not doing enough or to a mother that she's excluding her husband, it may seem that the combat is between the therapist and the family—that he or she is attacking them. But the real combat is between them and fear—fear of change.

Challenging Unproductive Assumptions

Although structural family therapy is not primarily a cognitive approach, its practitioners sometimes challenge the way clients see things. Changing the way family members interact offers alternative views of their situation. The converse is also true: Changing the way family members view their situation enables them to change the way they interact.

When six-year-old Cassie's parents complain about her behavior, they say she's "hyper," "sensitive," a "nervous child." Such constructions have tremendous power. Is a child's behavior "misbehavior," or is it a symptom of "nervousness?" Is it "naughty," or is it a "cry for help?" Is the child mad or bad, and who is in charge? What's in a name? Plenty.

Sometimes therapists act as teachers, offering information and advice, often about structural matters. Doing so is likely to be a restructuring maneuver and must be done in a way that minimizes resistance. A therapist does this by delivering a "stroke and a kick." If the therapist were dealing with a family in which the mother speaks for her children, he might say to her, "You are very helpful" (stroke). But to the child, "Mommy takes away your voice. Can you speak for yourself?" (kick). Thus mother is defined as helpful but intrusive (a stroke and a kick).

Effective challenges describe what people are doing and its consequences. However, in order for family members to hear what is being pointed out they must not feel attacked. Saying "that's interesting . . ." before pointing something out makes it an object of curiosity rather than an occasion for defensiveness. Moreover, although it's tempting to tell people what they *should* do, doing so reduces the likelihood of them learning to see what they are doing—and its consequences.

Evaluating Therapy Theory and Results

In *Families and Family Therapy*, Minuchin (1974) taught family therapists to see what they were looking at. Through the lens of structural family theory, previously puzzling interactions suddenly swam into focus. This enormously successful book not only taught us to see *enmeshment* and *disengagement* but also let us hope that changing them was just a matter of *joining*, *enactment*, and *unbalancing*. Minuchin made changing families look easy. It isn't.

Like the field itself, structural therapy has evolved over the years. Today's practitioners still use the patented confrontations ("Who's the sheriff in this family?"), but there is a greater emphasis on helping families understand their organization and less of the combative attitude that sometimes characterized therapists thirty years ago. What's important to keep in mind is that structural family therapy isn't a set of techniques; it's a way of looking at families.

Some of the strongest empirical support for structural family therapy comes from a series of studies with psychosomatic children and young adult drug addicts. Studies demonstrating the effectiveness of therapy with severely ill psychosomatic children are convincing because of the physiological measures employed and dramatic because of the life-threatening nature of the problems. Minuchin, Rosman, and Baker (1978) reported how family conflict can precipitate ketoacidosis crises in diabetic children. As their parents argued, only the psychosomatic children got really upset. Moreover, these children's manifest distress was accompanied by dramatic increases in free fatty acid levels, a measure related to ketoacidosis. This study provided strong confirmation of the clinical observation that psychosomatic children are involved in the regulation of stress between their parents.

Minuchin, Rosman, and Baker (1978) summarized the results of treating fifty-three cases of anorexia nervosa with structural family therapy. After a course of treatment that included hospitalization followed by outpatient family therapy, forty-three anorexic children were "greatly improved," two were "improved," three showed "no change," two were "worse," and three had dropped out. Although ethical considerations precluded a control group with these seriously ill children, the 90 percent improvement rate is impressive, especially compared with the usual 30 percent mortality rate for this disorder. Moreover, the positive results at termination were maintained at follow-up intervals of several years. Several more recent studies have replicated these findings and shown that structural family therapy is effective in the treatment of anorexia nervosa (e.g., Campbell & Patterson, 1995). Others have subsequently adopted some structural components in their treatment of eating disorders (e.g., Lock, Le Grange, Agras, & Dare, 2001; Eisler, Simic, Russell, & Dare, 2007; Lock, Le Grange, Agras, Moye, Bryson, & Jo, 2010). Structural family therapy has also been shown to be effective in treating psychosomatic asthmatics and psychosomatically complicated cases of diabetes (Minuchin, Baker, Rosman, Liebman, Milman, & Todd, 1975). Lastly, building on these successes some have called for the development of structurally informed family-based interventions for pediatric obesity (Jones, Lettenbeger, & Wickel, 2011; Skelton, Buehler, Irby, & Grzywacz, 2012).

Early structural family therapy studies demonstrated effectiveness in treating disruptive behavior and adolescent substance abuse. For example, in *Families of the Slums* Minuchin and his colleagues (1967) described the structural characteristics of low-socioeconomic families and demonstrated the effectiveness of family therapy with this population. Prior to treatment, mothers in patient families were found to be either over- or undercontrolling; either way their children were more disruptive than those in control families. After treatment, mothers used less coercive control yet were clearer about their rules and firmer in enforcing them. Seven of eleven families improved significantly after six months to a year of family therapy. Although no control group was used, the authors compared their results favorably to the usual 50 percent rate of successful treatment at Wiltwyck. Duke Stanton showed that structural family therapy can be effective for drug addicts and their families. In a well-controlled study, Stanton and Todd (1979) compared family therapy with a family placebo condition and individual therapy. Symptom reduction was significant with structural family therapy; the level of positive change was more than double that achieved in the other conditions, and these positive effects persisted at follow-up of six and twelve months.

More recently, studies have shown that structural family therapy can be effective when addressing problem behavior spanning the externalizing spectrum (e.g., disruptive behavior, adolescent substance abuse, conduct disorder, attention-deficit hyperactivity disorder). Structural family therapy has been successful in reducing the likelihood that African American and Latino youth would initiate drug use (Santisteban, Coatsworth, Perez-Vidal, Mitrani, Jean-Gilles, & Szapocznik, 1997), engaging and retaining families in treatment (Robbins et al., 2003, 2008; Szapocznik et al., 1988), decreasing adolescent substance use and associated problem behavior, as well as improving parental and family functioning (e.g., Grief & Dreschler, 1993; Robbins et al., 2000; Santisteban et al., 2003). Other studies indicate that structural family therapy is equal in effectiveness to communication training and behavioral management training in reducing negative communication, conflicts, and expressed anger between adolescents diagnosed with attention-deficit hyperactivity disorder and their parents (Barkley, Guevremont, Anastopoulos, & Fletcher, 1992). Structural family therapy has also been effective for treating adolescent disorders, such as conduct disorders (Chamberlain & Rosicky, 1995; Santisteban et al., 2003; Szapocznik et al., 1989), and anorexia nervosa (Campbell & Patterson, 1995).

In addition to adolescent behavioral problems, therapy models grounded in structural family systems ideas have also shown modest effectiveness in treating adult problems. For instance, Structural Ecosystems Therapy has been shown to improve family functioning, and in turn boost drug abstinence, for women living with HIV or AIDS (Mitrani, McCabe, Burns, & Feaster, 2012). A structural family therapy approach also yielded encouraging results in the alleviation of maternal depressive symptoms and mixed results in terms of child functioning (Weaver, Greeno, Marcus, Fusco, Zimmerman, & Anderson, 2013). Although more investigation is needed, these studies highlight the advantage of family-based approaches that target not only adult functioning but also mitigate the adverse effects on other family members.

Although structural family therapy is so closely identified with Salvador Minuchin that they were once synonymous, it may be a good idea to differentiate the man from the model. When we think of structural family therapy, we tend to remember the approach as described in *Families and Family Therapy*, published in 1974. That book remains a good introduction to structural theory but emphasizes the

techniques Minuchin favored at the time. Minuchin himself has evolved considerably in the last forty years, from an often blunt young therapist, always ready to challenge families, to a more seasoned clinician, still challenging but far gentler in his approach. If some of the examples in this chapter strike you as overly aggressive, you may be right. Some of these vignettes were taken from the 1970s, when family therapists tended to favor a confrontational style. While the confrontational style may have characterized some practitioners of structural family therapy, it was never an essential feature of this approach.

Minuchin has evolved conceptually as well, from an almost exclusive focus on interpersonal interactions to consider the cognitive perspectives guiding those interactions as well as the genesis of those perspectives (Minuchin, Nichols, & Lee, 2007). But the structural approach he created also exists independently of his work, and is embodied in the definitive literature on this model (e.g., Minuchin, 1974; Minuchin & Fishman, 1981; Minuchin & Nichols, 1993) as well as in the ongoing work of his students and colleagues.

The structural model directs clinicians to look beyond the content of problems and even beyond the dynamics of interaction to the underlying family organization that supports and constrains those interactions. Much has changed since 1974, but the structural model still stands, and it continues to be the most widely used way of understanding what goes on in troubled families.

Summary

Minuchin may be best known for the artistry of his clinical technique, yet his structural theory has become the most influential conceptual model in the field. The reason structural theory is so popular is that it's simple, inclusive, and practical. The basic concepts—boundaries, subsystems, alignments, and complementarity—are easily grasped and applied. They take into account the individual, family, and social context, and they provide a clear framework for understanding and treating families.

The most important tenet of this approach is that every family has a structure, and this structure is revealed only when the family is in action. According to this view, therapists who fail to consider the entire family's structure and intervene in only one subsystem are unlikely to effect lasting change. If a mother's overinvolvement with her son is part of a structure that includes distance from her husband, no amount of therapy for the mother and son is likely to bring about basic change in the family.

Subsystems are units of the family based on function. If the leadership of a family is exercised by a mother and daughter, then they, not the husband and wife, are the executive subsystem. Subsystems are regulated by interpersonal boundaries. In healthy families boundaries are clear enough to protect independence and permeable enough to allow mutual support. Enmeshed families have diffuse boundaries; disengaged families have rigid boundaries.

Once they've gained a family's trust, therapists promote family interaction while they assume a decentralized role. From this position they can observe and make a structural assessment, which includes the problem and the organization that supports it. These assessments are framed in terms of boundaries and subsystems, easily conceptualized as two-dimensional maps used to suggest avenues for change.

After they have successfully joined and assessed a family, structural therapists proceed to activate dormant structures using techniques that alter alignments and shift power within and between subsystems. These restructuring techniques are concrete and sometimes forceful. However, their success depends as much on effective joining and assessment as on the power of the techniques themselves.

Click here to apply your knowledge of chapter concepts.

Click here to test your application and analysis of the content found within this chapter.

An experiential branch of family therapy emerged from the humanistic wing of psychology that, like the expressive therapies that inspired it, emphasized immediate, here-and-now experience. Experiential therapy was popular when family therapy was young, when therapists talked about systems but borrowed their techniques from individual and group therapies. From Gestalt therapy and encounter groups came techniques like *role-playing* and *emotional confrontation*, while other expressive methods such as *family sculpting* and *family drawing* bore the influence of the arts and of psychodrama.

In focusing more on emotional experience than on the dynamics of interaction, experiential therapists seemed out of step with the rest of family therapy. Indeed, by emphasizing individuals and their feelings, experiential treatment may never have been as well suited to family therapy as were approaches that dealt with systems and interaction. With the passing of the inspirational leaders of this tradition, Virginia Satir and Carl Whitaker, the methods they popularized began to seem a little dated, more a product of the 1960s than of today's world.

Recently, however, experiential approaches have been enjoying a revival and, as we will see, two of the newer models—Johnson's (2004) emotionally focused couples therapy and the internal family systems model (Schwartz, 1995)—have combined the emotional impact of an experiential focus on the individual with a more sophisticated understanding of family systems.

As the first great cathartic therapist, Sigmund Freud, discovered, getting in touch with painful feelings is not by itself a complete form of psychotherapy. On the other hand, ignoring or rationalizing unhappy emotions may cheat clients out of the opportunity to get to the

CHAPTER 7

EXPERIENTIAL FAMILY THERAPY

Family Therapy as an Emotional Encounter

LEARNING OUTCOMES

♦ Describe the evolution of experiential family therapy.

♦ Describe the main tenets of experiential family therapy.

♦ Describe healthy and unhealthy family development from an experiential perspective.

♦ Describe the clinical goals and the conditions necessary for meeting those goals from an experiential perspective.

♦ Discuss and demonstrate the assessment and intervention techniques of experiential family therapy.

♦ Discuss research support for experiential family therapy.

heart of their problems. Thus the experiential emphasis on emotional expression may be a useful counterweight to the reductionistic emphasis on behavior and cognition in today's problem-solving approaches.

Sketches of Leading Figures

Two giants stand out in the development of experiential family therapy: Carl Whitaker and Virginia Satir. Whitaker was the leading exponent of a freewheeling, intuitive approach aimed at puncturing pretense and liberating family members to be themselves. He was among the first to do psychotherapy with families, and although he was considered a maverick, he eventually became one of the most admired therapists in the field. Iconoclastic, even outrageous at times, Whitaker nevertheless retained the respect of the family therapy establishment. He may have been their Puck, but he was one of them.

Whitaker grew up on a dairy farm in upstate New York. Rural isolation bred a certain shyness but also conditioned him to be less bound by social convention. After medical school and a residency in obstetrics and gynecology, Whitaker went into psychiatry, where he became fascinated by the psychotic mind. Unfortunately—or fortunately—back in the 1940s Whitaker couldn't rely on antipsychotic drugs to blunt the hallucinatory imaginings of his patients; instead, he listened and learned to understand thoughts crazy but human, thoughts most of us usually keep buried.

After working at the University of Louisville College of Medicine and the Oakridge Hospital, Whitaker accepted the chair of Emory University's Department of Psychiatry, where he remained from 1946 to 1955. Then, in the face of mounting pressure to make the department more psychoanalytic, Whitaker and his entire faculty, including Thomas Malone, John Warkentin, and Richard Felder, resigned to establish the Atlanta Psychiatric Clinic. Experiential psychotherapy was born of this union, and the group produced a number of provocative and challenging papers (Whitaker & Malone, 1953). In 1965 Whitaker moved to the University of Wisconsin Medical

School. After his retirement in the late 1980s, he traveled widely to share his wisdom and experience at conventions and workshops. He died in 1995. Among Whitaker's best-known students are Augustus Napier, now in private practice in Atlanta; and David Keith, at the State University of New York in Syracuse.

The other towering figure among experiential family therapists was Virginia Satir. As an early member of the Mental Research Institute (MRI), Satir emphasized communication (see Chapters 1 and 5) as well as emotional experiencing.

Satir began seeing families in private practice in Chicago in 1951. In 1955 she was invited to set up a training program for residents at the Illinois State Psychiatric Institute (where one of her students was Ivan Boszormenyi-Nagy). In 1959 Don Jackson invited her to join him at MRI, where Satir became the first director of training. She remained until 1966, when she left to become the director of the Esalen Institute in Big Sur, California.

Satir was the archetypal nurturing therapist in a field enamored with abstract concepts and strategic maneuvers. Her warmth and genuineness gave her tremendous appeal as she traveled the country giving demonstrations and workshops. Her ability to move audiences made her family therapy's most celebrated humanist. Satir died of pancreatic cancer in 1988.

Among the most recent experiential approaches is emotionally focused couples therapy, which draws on Perls, Satir, Bowlby's attachment theory, and the MRI group (Greenberg & Johnson, 1985, 1986, 2010; Johnson, 2004). Susan Johnson has emerged as this main proponent of the model. Another specialized approach to the emotional life of families is Schwartz's (1995) internal family systems therapy, in which clients' conflicting inner voices are personified as "parts" and then reintegrated using a variety of psychodramatic techniques.

Theoretical Formulations

Experiential family therapy is founded on the premise that the root cause of family problems is emotional suppression. Although children must learn that they can't always do whatever they feel like doing, many parents have an unfortunate tendency to confuse the *instrumental* and *expressive* functions of emotion. They try to regulate their children's actions by controlling their feelings. As a result, children learn to blunt their emotional experience to avoid criticism. Although this process is more or less universal, dysfunctional families tend to be less tolerant of unruly emotions than most. Children in such families often grow up estranged from themselves and feeling only the residues of repressed affect: boredom, apathy, and anxiety.

While systemic therapists see the roots of symptomatic behavior in the dance of family interactions, experientialists view those interactions as the result of family members' shadow dancing with the projections of each other's defenses. From this perspective, attempts to bring about positive change in families are more likely to be successful if family members first get in touch with their real feelings—their hopes and desires as well as their fears and anxieties. Thus, experiential family therapy works from the inside out, helping individuals uncover their honest emotions, and then forging more genuine family ties out of this enhanced authenticity.

The exception to the experiential de-emphasis on theory is emotionally focused couples therapy, which draws on attachment theory (Bowlby, 1969). According to Greenberg and Johnson (2010), emotion organizes attachment responses and serves a communicative function in relationships. When people express their vulnerability directly, they're likely to elicit a compassionate response from their partners. But when an insecurely attached person fears vulnerability and shows anger instead, the response is more likely to be withdrawal. Thus the person most in need of attachment may, by being afraid to expose that need, push away the loved ones he or she longs to get close to. The antidote for this dilemma is what experiential therapy is all about: helping people relax defensive fears so that deeper and more genuine emotions can emerge.

Family Dynamics

In focusing on the importance of honest emotional experience and expression, the experientialists offered a useful corrective to the original family therapists' narrow focus on behavioral interaction. This same corrective influence is relevant today, in the field's narrow emphasis on biology and cognition.

◆ Normal Family Functioning

Experiential therapists share the humanistic faith in the natural wisdom of honest emotion. According to this point of view, if people are allowed to follow their own instincts they tend to flourish. Problems arise because this innate tendency toward *self-actualization* (Rogers, 1951) runs afoul of social pressures. Society enforces repression to tame people's instincts and make them fit for group living. Unhappily, self-control is achieved at the cost of "surplus repression" (Marcuse, 1955). Families add their own controls to achieve peace and quiet, perpetuating **family myths** (Gehrke & Kirschenbaum, 1967) and relying on **mystification** (Laing, 1967) to alienate children from their experience.

In the ideal situation, parental control isn't excessive, and children grow up in an atmosphere of support for their feelings and creative impulses. Parents appreciate their children, accept their feelings, and validate their experience. Children are encouraged to experience life fully and to express the full range of human emotions.

Experiential therapists describe the family as a place of sharing experience (Satir, 1972). Functional families are secure enough to support and encourage a wide range of experiencing; dysfunctional families are frightened and bloodless. Neither problem-solving skills nor particular family structures are considered as important as nurturing spontaneous experiencing. In short, the healthy family offers its members the freedom to be themselves.

◆ Development of Behavior Disorders

From an experiential perspective, denial of impulses and suppression of feeling are the root of family problems. Dysfunctional families are locked into self-protection and avoidance (Kaplan & Kaplan, 1978). In Harry Stack Sullivan's (1953) terms, they seek *security* rather than *satisfaction*. Their presenting complaints are many, but the basic problem is that they smother emotion and desire.

According to Whitaker (Whitaker & Keith, 1981), there's no such thing as a marriage—only two scapegoats sent out by their families to perpetuate themselves. Together they must work out the inherent conflict in this situation. Couples who remain together eventually reach some kind of accommodation. Whether based on compromise or resignation, reconciling themselves to each other lessens the friction. Dysfunctional families, fearful of conflict, adhere rigidly to the rituals that they establish. Having experienced the anxiety of uncertainty, they now cling to their routines.

In her portrayal of troubled families, Satir (1972) emphasized the atmosphere of emotional deadness. Such families are cold; they seem to stay together only out of habit or duty. The adults find their children annoying, and the children learn not to respect themselves or care about their parents. In consequence of the lack of warmth in the family, people avoid each other and preoccupy themselves with work and other distractions.

It's important to notice that the dysfunction Satir described isn't the kind found in diagnostic manuals. Like others in the experiential camp, Satir was as concerned with normal people who lead lives of quiet desperation as with the officially recognized patients families usually focus on. As she (Satir, 1972) put it,

It is a sad experience for me to be with these families. I see the hopelessness, the helplessness, the loneliness. I see the bravery of people trying to cover up—a bravery that can still bellow or nag or whine at each other. Others no longer care. These people go on year after year, enduring misery themselves or in their desperation, inflicting it on others. (p. 12)

Satir stressed the role of destructive communication in smothering feeling and said that there were four dishonest ways people communicate: blaming, placating, being irrelevant, and being super reasonable. What's behind these patterns of inauthentic communication? *Low self-esteem.* If people feel bad about themselves, it's hard to tell the truth about their own feelings—and threatening to hear what others feel.

A healthy relationship, according to Susan Johnson, is a secure attachment bond—that is, one characterized by emotional accessibility and responsiveness (Johnson & Denton, 2002). Secure attachment refers both to having grown up with a sense of being loved and to the confidence that comes from having a dependable intimate relationship. But when attachment security is threatened, people typically respond with anger—a protest that, unfortunately, may drive the other person away rather than evoke the desired responsiveness. Recently, Johnson (2004) has introduced the notion of *attachment injuries*: traumatic occurrences that damage the bond between partners and, if not resolved, maintain negative cycles and attachment insecurities (Johnson, 2004).

Mechanisms of Change

There are two unique aspects of the experiential perspective on change. The first is an emphasis on challenging emotional defenses. In this model, it might be said that the customer is always wrong—in the sense that family members often don't know what they really feel. This leads directly to the second distinguishing characteristic of this approach, which is that experientialists tend to be fairly aggressive in attacking defenses to promote emotional expression.

◆ Goals of Therapy

Experientialists emphasize the feeling side of human nature: creativity, spontaneity, and emotional honesty—and, in therapy, the value of emotional experience for its own sake.

Emotional expression from family members is thought to break down rigid expectancies and unblock awareness—all of which promotes individuation (Kaplan & Kaplan, 1978). Bunny and Fred Duhl (1981) speak of their goals as a heightened sense of competence, well-being, and self-esteem. In emphasizing self-esteem, the Duhls echo Satir (1964), who believed that low self-esteem and the destructive communication responsible for it were the main problems in unhappy families. Whitaker (1976a) thought that families come to treatment because they're unable to be close and therefore unable to individuate. By helping family members recover their own potential for experiencing, he believed that he was also helping them recover their ability to care for one another.

Conditions for Behavior Change

Among the misconceptions of those new to family therapy is that families are fragile and therapists must be careful to avoid breaking them. A little experience teaches the opposite: Effective treatment requires powerful interventions—and for experiential family therapists that power comes from emotional experiencing.

Gus Napier (Napier & Whitaker, 1978) wrote, in *The Family Crucible*, a nice description of what experiential therapists think causes change. Breakthroughs occur when family members risk being "more separate, divergent, even angrier" as well as "when they risk being closer and more intimate." To help clients take those risks, experiential therapists are alternately provocative and warmly supportive. This permits family members to drop their protective defenses and open up to each other.

Existential encounter is believed to be the essential force in the psychotherapeutic process (Kempler, 1973; Whitaker, 1976a). These encounters must be reciprocal; instead of hiding behind a professional role, the therapist must be a genuine person who catalyzes change using his or her personal impact on families. As Kempler (1968) said:

> In this approach the therapist becomes a family member during the interviews, participating as fully as he is able, hopefully available for appreciation and criticism as well as he is able to dispense it. He laughs, cries and rages. He feels and shares his embarrassments, confusions and helplessness. (p. 97)

For Satir, caring and acceptance were the keys to helping people open up to experience, and to each other:

> Some therapists think people come into therapy not wanting to be changed; I don't think that's true. They don't think they *can* change. Going into some new, unfamiliar place is a scary thing.

> When I first begin to work with someone, I am not interested in changing them. I am interested in finding their rhythms, being able to join with them, and helping them go inside to those scary places. Resistance is mainly the fear of going somewhere you have not been. (quoted in Simon, 1989, pp. 38–39)

Therapy

Experiential family therapists share the humanistic belief that people are naturally resourceful and, if left to their own devices, will be creative, loving, and productive (Rogers, 1951). The task of therapy is therefore seen as unblocking defenses and releasing people's innate vitality.

Assessment

Because experientialists are less interested in solving problems than in enhancing family functioning, they pay limited attention to the specifics of the presenting problem. Moreover, because they focus on individuals and their experience, they have little interest in the structure of family organization.

For most experientialists, assessment takes place informally as the therapist gets to know a family. In the process of developing a relationship, the therapist learns what kind of people he or she is dealing with. Whitaker began by asking each family member to describe the family and how it works. In this way, he got a composite picture of individual family members and their perceptions of the family group. This kind of inquiry is about as formal as most experiential therapists get in sizing up families. The majority of what serves as assessment in this approach is an attempt to decode the defenses that emerge in the ongoing course of trying to help family members open up to each other.

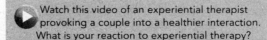
Watch this video of an experiential therapist provoking a couple into a healthier interaction. What is your reaction to experiential therapy?

◆ Therapeutic Techniques

In experiential therapy, according to Kempler (1968), there are no techniques, only people. This epigram neatly summarizes the faith in the curative power of the therapist's personality. It isn't so much what therapists do that matters, but who they are.

However, this point is at least partly rhetorical. Whoever they are, therapists must also do something. Even if what they do isn't planned, it can nevertheless be described. Moreover, experiential therapists tend to do a lot; they're highly active and some (including Kempler) use a number of evocative techniques.

Some use structured devices such as *family sculpting* and *choreography*; others like Satir and Whitaker rely on the spontaneity of just being themselves.

Satir had a remarkable ability to communicate. Like many great therapists, she was a dynamic personality. But she didn't rely merely on personal warmth. Rather, she worked actively to clarify communication, turned people away from complaining toward finding solutions, supported the self-esteem of every member of the family, pointed out positive intentions (long before *positive connotation* became a strategic device), and showed by example how to be affectionate (Satir & Baldwin, 1983). She was a loving but forceful healer.

One of Satir's hallmarks was the use of touch. Hers was the language of tenderness. She often began by making physical contact with children, as evidenced in her case "Of Rocks and Flowers." Bob, a recovering alcoholic, was the father of two boys, Aaron (four) and Robbie (two), whose mother had abused them repeatedly—pushing them down stairs, burning them with cigarettes, and tying them up under the sink. At the time of the interview, the mother was under psychiatric care and didn't see the children. Bob's new wife, Betty, had been abused by her previous husband, also an alcoholic. She was pregnant and afraid that the boys would abuse the baby. The boys had already been expressing the violence they'd been exposed to—slapping and choking other children. Bob and Betty, acting out of frustration and fear, responded roughly to the boys, which only increased their aggressiveness.

Throughout the session, Satir showed the parents how to touch the children tenderly and how to hold them firmly to stop them from misbehaving. When Bob started to tell Aaron something from a distance, Satir insisted on proximity and touch. She sat Aaron down in front of his father and asked Bob to take the little boy's hands and speak directly to him.

The following fragments from the session are taken from Andreas (1991).

Courtesy of the Virginia Satir Global Network

Virginia Satir focused more on helping family members connect than on the psychological and systemic forces that kept them apart.

CASE STUDY

Those little hands know a lot of things; they need to be reeducated. OK. Now, there is a lot of energy in both these youngsters, like there is in both of you. And I am going to talk to your therapist about making some room for you to have some respite (from the children). But use every opportunity you can to get this kind of physical contact. And what I would also recommend that you do is that the two of you are clear about what you expect.

And if you (Bob) could learn from Betty how to pay attention (to the kids) more quickly, I would like you to be able to get your message without a "don't" in it—and that your strength when you pick them up—I don't know if I can illustrate it to you, but let me have your arm for a minute (reaching for Bob's forearm). Let me show you the difference. Pick up my arm like you were going to grab me. (Bob grabs her arm.) All right. Now when you do that, my muscles all start to tighten, and I want to hit back. (Bob nods.) Now pick up my arm like you wanted to protect me. (Bob holds her arm.) All right. I feel your strength now, but I don't feel like I want to pull back like this. (Bob says, "Yeah.")

And what I'd like you to do is *lots* and lots of touching of both of these children. And when things start to get out of hand, then you go over—don't say anything—go over to them and just take them (demonstrating the protective holding on both of Robbie's forearms) but you're not pulling them (Aaron briefly puts his hands on top of Virginia's and Robbie's arms) like this (demonstrating), but you are taking them in a strong way (stroking Bob's arm with both hands), like you saw the difference.

(Virginia turns to Betty and offers her forearm.) OK. Now I'd like to do the same with you. So, take my arm really tight. . . . (Betty grabs Virginia's arm, and Aaron does, too.) Yeah, that's right, like you really wanted to give me "what for." OK. All right. Now give it to me like you want to give me support, but you also want to give me a boundary.

So the next time you see anything coming, what you do is you go and make that contact (Virginia demonstrates by holding Aaron's upper arm.) and then let it go soft. Now, Aaron, I'd like you to come up here so I could demonstrate something to your mother for a minute. (Aaron says, "OK.") Now, let's suppose some moment I'm not thinking and I take you like that (grabbing Betty's arms suddenly with both hands). You see what you want to do? (Betty nods.) All right. Now I am going to do it another way. I am giving you the same message (Virginia holds Betty's arm firmly with both hands, looking directly into her eyes, and starts to stand up.), but I am doing it like this. And I am looking at you, and I'm giving you a straight message. OK. Now your body at that point is not going to respond negatively to me. It is going to feel stopped, but not negative. And then I will take you like this. (Virginia puts one arm around Betty's back and the other under her upper arm.) Just like this (Virginia puts both arms around Betty and draws her close.) and now I will hold you. I will hold you like that for a little bit.

Following this session, Satir commented on her technique:

There had been so many things happening, and the fear was so strong in relation to these children that if you thought of one image it was like they were monsters. So one of the things that I wanted to do was also to see that they had the capacity to respond with a touch, using myself in that regard by having them put their hands on my face—that was a kind of mirror for the

family itself, the people in the family. And then allowing them, and encouraging them to do that with their own parents. See, touch, that comes out of the kind of ambience which was there at the time, says things no words can say.

To encourage empathy and bring family members closer together, Satir often used the following exercise (adapted from Satir & Baldwin, 1983):

1. Think of a difficult situation with your child. Perhaps your child has been doing something that you haven't known how to handle or that drives you up the wall.

2. Run your movie of this situation from your own point of view. Imagine you are going through this situation with your child again. Notice how you feel, what you see, what you hear.

3. Reexperience this situation, but this time as your child. Visualize the entire situation slowly and in detail, as you would imagine seeing it through the eyes of your child. Let yourself feel what your child must be feeling. Do you notice any feelings that you weren't aware your child might be having? Do you notice something that your child might need or want that you hadn't been aware of?

4. Reexperience the same situation, this time as an observer. Watch and listen to what's happening, and allow yourself to observe both your child and yourself. Do you notice anything about the way you and your child respond to each other? What do you see more clearly about yourself and your child?

Because Whitaker favored a personal encounter over a calculated approach, it's not surprising that his style was the same with individuals, couples, and groups (Whitaker, 1958). He assiduously avoided directing real-life decisions, preferring instead to open family members up to their feelings and join them in their uncertainty. This may sound trite, but it's an important point. As long as a therapist (or anyone else for that matter) is anxious to change people, it's hard, very hard, to help them feel understood—and even harder to really empathize with them.

A comparison between Whitaker's early (Whitaker, 1967; Whitaker, Warkentin, & Malone, 1959) and later work (Napier & Whitaker, 1978) shows how he changed over the years. He started out as deliberately outlandish. He might fall asleep in sessions and then report his dreams; he wrestled with patients; he talked about his own sexual fantasies. In later years he was less provocative. This seems to be what happens to therapists as they mature; they have less need to impose themselves and more willingness to listen.

Because Whitaker's treatment was so intense and personal, he believed that two therapists should work together. Having a cotherapist to share the burden keeps therapists from being absorbed in the emotional field of a family. Family therapy tends to activate therapists' own feelings toward certain types of family members. A detached, analytic stance minimizes such feelings; emotional involvement maximizes them.

The trouble with countertransference is that it tends to be unconscious. Therapists are more likely to become aware of such feelings after sessions are over. Easier still is to observe countertransference in others. Consider the example of Dr. Fox, a married man who specializes in individual therapy but occasionally sees married couples. In 75 percent of such cases, Dr. Fox encourages the couple to seek a divorce, and his patients have a high rate of following his advice. Perhaps if Dr. Fox were happier in his own marriage or had the courage to change it, he'd be less impelled to guide his patients where he fears to go.

To minimize countertransference, Whitaker recommended sharing feelings openly with families. If feelings are openly expressed they're less likely to be acted out.

Whitaker's first sessions (Napier & Whitaker, 1978) were fairly structured, and they included taking a family history. For him, the first contacts with families were opening salvos in "the battle for structure" (Whitaker & Keith, 1981). He wanted the family to know that the therapist was in charge.[1] This began with the first telephone call. Whitaker (1976b) insisted that the largest possible number of family members attend; he believed that three generations were necessary to ensure that grandparents would support, not oppose, therapy and that their presence would help correct distortions. If significant family members wouldn't attend, Whitaker generally refused

to see the family. Why begin with the cards stacked against you?

Along with Satir, Whitaker was among the foremost exponents of the therapist's use of self as a catalyst for change. But whereas Satir offered a warm, supportive presence, Whitaker was at times blunt, even confrontational. Actually, the provocative interventions of someone like Whitaker only become acceptable to families after the therapist has proven to be an understanding and caring person. Before challenging people, it is first necessary to win their trust.

Regardless of whether they are provocative or supportive, experiential therapists are usually quite active. Instead of leaving family members to work out their own issues with each other, they say "Tell him (or her) what you feel!" or ask "What are you feeling right now?" Just as the best way to get a school teacher's attention is to misbehave, the best way to get an experiential therapist's attention is to show signs of emotion without actually expressing it.

CASE STUDY

Therapist: I see you looking over at dad whenever you ask mom a question, what's that about?

Kendra: Oh, nothing . . . .

Therapist: It must mean *something.* Come on, what were you feeling?

Kendra: Nothing!

Therapist: You must have been feeling something. What was it?

Kendra: Well, sometimes when mom lets me do something, dad gets mad. But instead of yelling at her, he yells at *me* (crying softly).

Therapist: Tell him.

Kendra: (angrily, to the therapist) Leave me alone!

Therapist: No, it's important. Tell your Dad how you feel.

Kendra: (sobbing hard) You're always picking on me! You never let me do anything!

Experiential therapists use a number of expressive techniques in their work, including family sculpting (Duhl, Kantor, & Duhl, 1973), family puppet interviews (Irwin & Malloy, 1975), family art therapy

---

[1] We might add that there is a big difference between trying to control the structure of sessions and trying to control people's lives.

Experiential therapists encourage emotional expression as a vehicle for change.

(Geddes & Medway, 1977), conjoint family drawings (Bing, 1970), and Gestalt therapy techniques (Kempler, 1973). Among the accoutrements of experiential therapists' offices are toys, dollhouses, clay, teddy bears, drawing pens and paper, and batacca bats.

In **family sculpting**, the therapist asks one member of a family to arrange the others in a tableau. This is a graphic means of portraying each person's perceptions of the family and his or her place in it. This was a favorite device of Satir, who frequently used ropes and blindfolds to dramatize the constricting roles family members trap each other into (Satir & Baldwin, 1983).

The following example of sculpting occurred when a therapist asked Mr. N. to arrange the members of his family into a scene typical of the time when he comes home from work.

CASE STUDY

Mr. N.: When I come home from work, eh? Okay (to his wife) honey, you'd be by the stove, wouldn't you?

Therapist: No, don't talk. Just move people where you want them to be.

Mr. N.: Okay.

He guided his wife to stand at a spot where the kitchen stove might be and placed his children on the kitchen floor, drawing and playing.

Therapist: Fine, now, still without any dialogue, put them into action.

Mr. N. then instructed his wife to pretend to cook but to turn frequently to see what the kids were up to. He told the children to pretend to play for awhile but then to start fighting and complaining to mommy.

Therapist: And what happens, when you come home?

Mr. N.: Nothing. I try to talk to my wife, but the kids keep pestering her, and she gets mad and says to leave her alone.

Therapist: Okay, act it out.

Mrs. N. acted out trying to cook and referee the children's fights. The children, who thought this a great game, pretended to fight and tried to outdo each other getting mommy's attention. When Mr. N. "came home," he reached out for his wife, but the children came between them, until Mrs. N. finally pushed all of them away.

Afterwards, Mrs. N. said that she hadn't realized her husband felt ignored. She just thought of him as coming home, saying hello, and then withdrawing into the den with his newspaper and a bottle of beer.

Family sculpting is also used to illuminate scenes from the past. A typical instruction is, "Remember standing in front of your childhood home. Walk in and describe what typically happened." The idea is to make a tableau portraying one's perceptions of family life. It's a device to focus awareness and heighten sensitivity.

Peggy Papp and her colleagues at the Ackerman Clinic (Papp, Scheinkman, & Malpas, 2013) introduce sculpting by asking couples if they're willing to try a playful way to communicate their feelings about their relationship. If the couple agrees, the therapist asks them to close their eyes and relax. Once they are relaxed, they're told to think about the main problem in their relationship and the feelings that emerge. After they've gotten in touch with their feelings, the therapist asks them to imagine what symbolic forms each of them would take (e.g., David and Goliath, a cop and a criminal, fire and ice) and then imagine what movement between these forms might be as they are trying to deal with the problem between them. "How would they interact?" "Where would this take place? In a meadow, the living room, a circus?"

"What is impasse between the two forms?" "What are the solutions that each of them tries that don't work?" "Do they try anything else?" "What is your greatest fear if the problem is never solved?" "What is your best hope?" "What would be an ideal way for the two forms to interact?"

Then the therapist has the couple open their eyes and each partner in turn directs the pantomime and tells the partner what to do.

CASE STUDY

Papp and her colleagues describe the use of sculpting in a couple who had gone from having sex several times a week to once a month. In the sculpting exercise Jack saw himself as a sponge and Diane as a bottle of water. Try as he might, the sponge could not open the bottle of water. He imagined that if the sponge never got the bottle of water to open up he would dry up and die. Diane's fantasy was that she was a column of ice and Jack, in his eager pursuit of her, was like a blazing fire that frightened her.

Using the couple's own images, the therapist suggested that Jack experiment with other ways of melting the ice other than being a passive sponge or a raging fire. She asked Diane to imagine other forms that water might take, like a sparkling brook,

an elegant fountain, or a splashing waterfall. Imagining these alternative images helped each of the partners consider new ways of approaching and reacting to each other. In imagining a new way to approach Diane, Jack remembered that she always seemed more relaxed when he helped out around the house. Diane acknowledged her resentment of the uneven division of labor and how this resentment had interfered with her sexual desire. Diane's imagining herself as a more active form of water, helped her feel less passive and threatened by Jack's "fire."

Another expressive exercise is *family art therapy*. Kwiatkowska (1967) instructs families to produce a series of drawings, including a "joint family scribble," in which each person makes a quick scribble and then the whole family incorporates the scribble into a unified picture. Bing (1970) describes the conjoint **family drawing** as a means to warm families up and free them to express themselves. In this procedure families are told to "draw a picture as you see yourselves as a family." The resulting portraits may disclose perceptions that haven't previously been discussed, or the task may stimulate the person drawing the picture to realize something that he or she had never thought of before.

CASE STUDY

A father drew a picture of the family that showed him off to one side, while his wife and children stood holding hands. Although he was portraying a fact well-known to his wife and himself, they hadn't spoken openly of it. Once he showed his drawing to the therapist, there was no avoiding discussion.

In another case, when the therapist asked each of the family members to draw the family, the teenage daughter was uncertain what to do. She had never thought much about the family or her role in it. When she started to work, her drawing just seemed to emerge. She was surprised to discover that she'd drawn herself closer to her father and sisters than to her mother. This provoked a lively discussion between her and her mother about their relationship. Although the two of them spent time together, the daughter didn't feel close because she thought her mother treated her like a child, never talking about her own concerns, and showing only superficial interest in the daughter's life. For her part, the mother was surprised, and not at all displeased, that her daughter felt ready to establish a relationship on a more mutual, caring basis.

In *family puppet interviews*, Irwin and Malloy (1975) ask one of the family members to make up a story using puppets. This technique, originally used in play therapy, is designed to highlight conflicts and alliances. Puppets also provide a safe avenue for symbolic communication. For example, a child who has used a specific puppet to symbolize his anger (e.g., a dinosaur) may simply reach for the dinosaur whenever he feels threatened.

Diana Arad recently developed the animal attribution storytelling technique, which requires family members to choose animals to represent all the members of the family and then tell a story about the animal protagonists. The following case study from Arad (2004) illustrates the application of this technique in a family with an aggressive, acting-out nine-year-old.

CASE STUDY

Sara and Jacob Cohen came to therapy with their daughter Dana (four) and son Roy (nine), who was diagnosed with oppositional defiant disorder. Roy was aggressively rebellious, wet his bed, and alternated between depression and angry outbursts in which he said he wished he were dead. He also showed extreme sibling rivalry with his little sister and frequently punched her during arguments.

Roy entered the office for the first session firmly in his father's grasp. He'd been crying and was determined not to cooperate. The therapist assured him that he wasn't going to be forced to do anything and that he didn't have to participate if he didn't want to.

When the therapist introduced the animal storytelling game, she began by asking Dana, the youngest member of the family, to begin (to prevent her from copying other family members' stories). "If your mother were an animal," the therapist asked Dana, "what animal would she be?"

Dana replied that her mother would be a horse, her father a squirrel, her brother a chicken, and herself a wolf. When asked to make up a story about these animal characters, Dana related the following:

> Once upon a time, a horse went to visit his friend the chicken. At the same time, a wolf came to eat the chicken, but the horse saved the chicken. Then the squirrel took the chicken and the horse to visit him under his tree and made the chicken laugh.

What this story revealed was that four-year-old Dana, who was seen as the good child and her brother's victim, saw herself (wolf) as an aggressor to her brother (chicken) and as an outsider to the family interaction (not invited to the fun under the squirrel's tree). Her parents were extremely surprised by this portrayal of the family. When she was asked for an example of acting like a wolf, Dana described how when Roy used the computer, she would watch from the door and then "attack" his mouse-using hand and run to her mother. Roy would chase her, "clucking" like a chicken, but he couldn't retaliate because Dana was protected by mother. Roy usually shouted and raged and then got punished, leaving the computer free for Dana to use.

> Here's Roy's story:
> Once upon a time, when an elephant (dad) went for a walk in the jungle, he stepped on a cockroach (Dana). The cockroach got squished, but the elephant did not notice and went on his way. A cat (Roy) came, found the squished cockroach, and thought it was a Frisbee. He took it to his friend the dog (mom) in order to play with it. They played Frisbee with it until they were fed up and threw it back to where the cat had found it. The elephant came back, took the squished cockroach, and ate it. The cockroach recovered and ran around inside the elephant. This tickled him so that he burst out laughing, expelling the cockroach through his mouth so hard that it landed in the same place where he was stepped on before. Then one day, the elephant went for a walk again and stepped on it again.

Both children's stories portrayed the father as a disengaged figure—a funny squirrel who appears after the danger is gone and a passing elephant who does damage without even noticing. This picture, which did not match the family's official version of the father as loving and involved, was also reflected in the mother's story, in which the father was represented as a mischievous but unapproachable dolphin. The children's stories helped the parents to see Roy in a different light. They agreed that when Roy started raging, cursing, and throwing things, they would consider it "clucking like a chicken," and they would keep their distance. Moreover, the parents took the children's perspectives into account and stopped blaming Roy for all the fights. They decided to enforce equal consequences when the children fought. They were both sent to time out—"just in case the wolf was at it again." Roy thought this was fair, and sibling rivalry decreased considerably.

Courtesy of Susan Johnson

Susan Johnson's focus on emotional longings can be seen as an antidote to the field's current preoccupation with cognition.

Eliana Gil (1994) describes a number of play therapy techniques and explains how they can be used to engage young children in family treatment. In the *typical day interview*, Gil asks children to pick days of the week and select dolls (or puppets) to represent the people in their families. Then the therapist asks the children to use the figures to show where people are and what they do throughout the day. Gil recommends asking specifically about television watching, eating habits, sleeping habits, hygiene, anger, and affection. One ten-year-old who had described everything in his house as fine responded to a question about what he watched on television after school by listing twelve shows, ending with David Letterman. When the therapist asked, "What happens after you watch Letterman?" the boy replied, "I go to sleep." "Who's at home when you go to sleep?" "No one" (Gil, 1994).

Role-playing is another favorite device. Its use is based on the premise that experience, to be real, must be brought to life in the present. Recollection of past events and consideration of hoped-for or feared future developments can be made more immediate by role-playing them in a session. Kempler (1968) encourages parents to fantasize and role-play scenes from childhood. A mother might be asked to role-play what it was like when she was a little girl, or a father might be asked to imagine himself as a boy caught in the same dilemma as his son.

When someone who isn't present is mentioned, therapists may introduce the Gestalt *empty chair technique* (Kempler, 1973). If a child talks about her

grandfather, she might be asked to speak to a chair, which is used to personify grandfather. Whitaker (1975) used a similar role-playing technique, which he called "psychotherapy of the absurd." This consists of augmenting the unreasonable quality of a patient's response to the point of absurdity. It often amounts to calling a person's bluff, as the following example illustrates:

Patient: I can't stand my husband!

Therapist: Why don't you get rid of him, or take up a boyfriend?

At times this takes the form of sarcastic teasing, such as mock fussing in response to a fussy child. The hope is that patients will get objective distance by participating in the therapist's distancing; the danger is that patients will feel hurt at being made fun of.

These techniques have proven useful in individual therapy (Nichols & Zax, 1977) to intensify emotional experiencing by bringing memories into focus and acting out suppressed reactions. Whether such devices are necessary in family therapy is open to question. In individual treatment patients are isolated from the significant figures in their lives, and role-playing may be useful to approximate being with those people. But because family therapy is conducted with significant people present, it seems doubtful that role-playing or other means of fantasy are necessary. If emotional action is wanted, plenty is available simply by opening dialogue between family members.

Two recent experiential approaches to family therapy that represent a more sophisticated understanding of family dynamics are emotionally focused couples therapy and the internal family systems model.

Emotionally Focused Couples Therapy

Emotionally focused couples therapy works on two levels in succession—uncovering the hurt and longing beneath defensive expressions of anger and withdrawal and then helping couples understand how these feelings are played out in their relationship. To begin with, the therapist acknowledges each client's immediate feelings—hurt and anger, say—to make them feel understood (Johnson, 1998).

 Watch this video of Dr. Susan Johnson explain emotionally focused couples therapy. What is your favorite aspect of her approach?

www.youtube.com/watch?v=xQCg-jC25fo

CASE STUDY

"You're getting angrier and angrier. It's upsetting for you to hear Will picture himself as innocent, isn't it?"

By interrupting a couple's quarrel and reflecting what each of them is feeling, the therapist defuses hostility and helps them focus on their experience, rather than on each other's crimes. Then, to explore the perceptions that underlie the partners' emotional responses to each other, the therapist asks for a description of what happens at home.

"Oh, so part of you believes him, but part of you is suspicious?"
"Part of you is watching and expecting that he'll hurt you?"
"Can you tell me about the part that believes he's being honest?"

Next the therapist points out how the couple's emotions are driving them into cycles of escalating polarization.

The cycle was formulated in terms of Will's protecting himself by staying distant and avoiding Nancy's anger, and Nancy's being vigilant and fighting to avoid being betrayed again. As she became more insecure and distrustful, Will felt more helpless and distanced himself further. As he distanced, she felt betrayed and became more enraged. Both were framed as victims of the cycle, which I continually framed as a common problem that the

partners need to help each other with (Johnson, 1998, pp. 457–458).

The couple's growing awareness of how their emotional reactivity frustrates their longings sets the stage for uncovering and expressing the deep emotions that lie beneath their sparring. The resulting cathartic expression makes it possible for the couple to deepen their understanding of their destructive pattern with each other, and this circular process continues to be explored in the process of working through.

Attachment theory helps the emotionally focused couples therapist pinpoint the issues that get stirred up when couples talk about their hurts and longings.

"Maybe you feel like no one really loves you?"
"You feel helpless and alone, don't you?"

The impact of this emotional evocation is enhanced by the fact that the partner is present to be addressed in this new and more compassionate way.

"So, can you tell her that?"

The ultimate aim of this work is to enable the partners to risk being vulnerable with each other by acknowledging and expressing their attachment needs.

"Only you can face your fear and decide to risk depending on Will. He can't do it, can he? The only one who can drop your defenses and risk trusting him is you, isn't it?"
"What's the worst thing that could happen?"

Again, working together with the couple means that once the partners risk expressing their needs and fears, their mates can be encouraged to respond.

"What happens to you, Will, when you hear this?"

The response to this question will of course be very different once the partners let down their guard and begin to talk about what they're afraid of and what they really want from each other.

The therapist frames couples' experiences in terms of deprivation, isolation, and loss of secure connectedness. This perspective, from attachment theory, helps family members focus on their longings rather than on each other's faults and failings.

What attachment theory adds is an understanding of how children whose caregivers were emotionally unresponsive develop an *insecure attachment* (Bowlby, 1988). They come to believe that other people can't be depended on, and when their emotional security is threatened in adult romantic relationships they try to restore emotional comfort by either frantically pulling their partner closer (as is common with *anxious attachment*) or become distant and aloof in an effort to not need their partner and therefore not feel hurt by their rejection (a pattern common to *avoidant attachment*). A common *pursue/withdraw pattern* emerges wherein one partner pursues closeness while the other withdraws emotionally. Even though the underlying motivation for each partner is to establish emotional security, their attachment fears of rejection or abandonment lead them to act in a way that pushes their partner away, thus giving each of them less of what they long for (Johnson, 2004). Their solution has become the problem.

When attachment is threatened, a person initially feels *primary emotions*—"soft" emotions such as sadness, fear, hurt, and longing. The expression of primary emotions tends to evoke compassionate responses from people. But a person who feels unsafe expressing primary emotions, will instead express defensive, *secondary emotions* such as anger, contempt, or coldness. The expression of secondary emotions tends to provoke similarly distancing responses from the partner, which puts in motion a cycle where both people want closeness, but are acting in a way that produces more distance. The challenge for a therapist is to learn to see behind secondary emotions, and to help couples do the same— for example, to see anger as an attempt to modify the other partner's inaccessibility, and to see withdrawal as an attempt to avoid risking rejection (Johnson, 2004).

In short, the purpose of emotionally focused therapy is to help foster secure attachment. This is done by helping partners recognize their primary attachment needs, express those needs to their partner openly and directly, and to recognize and respond to their partner's attachment needs. As this happens, healing interactional cycles form, deep-seated views of the self as unlovable and needs as being shameful shift, and individuals become more secure. For example, say a couple argues over the frequency of sex. The pursuer may want sex to reassure his or her

fears of rejection. The distancer may reject sex, or participate grudgingly, as a means of not getting too close or of being overwhelmed by their fears. Once the frequency of sex no longer symbolizes attachment fears, it is much easier for the couple to agree on the frequency of sex (or whatever their conflict may be).

As the name suggests, emotionally focused therapy is experiential, not analytic or didactic. In contrast to the more free-wheeling experiential approaches of Whitaker and Satir, however, emotionally focused therapy outlines nine steps divided across three broad stages, with interventions associated with each step (Johnson, Bradley, Furrow, Lee, Palmer, Tilley, & Woolley, 2005). The stages and steps are:

Stage 1: Cycle De-escalation
   1. Assessment
   2. Identify negative interactional cycle(s)
   3. Access unacknowledged emotions
   4. Reframe problems in terms of attachment needs

Stage 2: Changing Interactional Positions
   5. Promote identification with disowned needs
   6. Promote acceptance of partner's experience
   7. Facilitate expression of needs and wants

Stage 3: Consolidation and Integration
   8. Emergence of new solutions to old problems
   9. Consolidate new positions and attachment cycles

In all of these steps the therapist moves between helping partners uncover and express their emotional experience and helping them reorganize the pattern of their interactions. For example:

The therapist might, then, first help a withdrawn, guarded spouse formulate his sense of paralyzed helplessness that primes his withdrawal. The therapist will validate this sense of helplessness by placing it within the context of the destructive cycle that has taken over the relationship. The therapist will heighten this experience in the session and then help his partner to hear and accept it, even though it is very different from the way she usually experiences her spouse. Finally, the therapist moves to structuring an interaction around this helplessness, as in, "So can you turn to her and can you tell her, 'I feel so helpless and defeated. I just want to run away and hide.' " This kind of statement, in and of itself, represents a move away from passive withdrawal and is the beginning of active emotional engagement. (Johnson, Hunsley, Greenberg, & Schindler, 1999, p. 70)

Internal Family Systems Therapy

In the internal family systems model (Schwartz, 1995, 2001), conflicting inner voices are personified as subpersonalities or "parts." What makes this device powerful is that when family members are at odds with each other, their conflicts are often based on polarizations of only part of what they feel. The truth is that people in conflict with each other are also often in conflict within themselves.

The adolescent's defiance and her parents' distrust are only one aspect of the complex feelings they have for each other. Or to choose a different example, a couple caught in a pursuer–distancer pattern may be acting out only those parts of them that are terrified of abandonment and engulfment. By dramatizing the elements of their inner conflicts, internal family systems therapy helps family members sort out their feelings and reconnect with each other in less polarized ways.

To help clients begin to distinguish among their conflicting inner voices, Schwartz begins by introducing the language of parts.

CASE STUDY

"So there's a part of you that gets upset and angry when your son gets down on himself. Do you think that if that part didn't get so stirred up, it would be easier for you to help him?"

"It sounds like part of you agrees with your husband about getting stricter with the kids, but there's another part that says he's being too harsh. What is that second part? What does it say to you? What is it afraid of?"

By listening carefully to what clients are feeling and then construing their reactions as coming from a part of them, the therapist initiates a shift in family polarizations. It's easier for people to acknowledge that "a part of them" feels—angry, helpless, or whatever—than that "they" (as in all of them) feel that way. A parent who has trouble admitting that he's angry at his son for not doing well in school may find it easier to acknowledge that a part of him gets angry at his son's failures—and, moreover, that the angry part gets in the way of his sympathetic part.

Once the idea is introduced that various parts of family members are reacting to each other, instead of seeing themselves intrinsically at odds, they can begin to see that parts of one are triggering parts of another. The obvious implication is that if their aggravating emotions are contained in only parts of them, they have other feelings and other possibilities for interaction.

Thus: "So that angry part of your father seems to trigger a sad and helpless part of you, is that right?"

And since many such polarizations become triangles, it might be that the father's angry part also triggers a protective part in his wife.

"So when you see your husband's angry part responding to your son, that triggers a protective part in you? A part of you feels that you need to fight your husband to protect your son?"

So instead of having a son who is a failure, a father who is unsympathetic, and parents who can't agree, the family discovers that each of them is having trouble with some of their parts. The father is transformed from a tyrant to a parent struggling with a frustrated and angry part of him. His wife ceases to be basically at odds with him and instead is seen as having a protective part that gets triggered by his angry part. And instead of being a failure, the son becomes a boy with a part of him that feels helpless in the face of his father's angry part and his parents' conflict.

Like all experiential models, internal family systems therapy is founded on the belief that underneath people's emotionally reactive parts lies a healthy core self. When the therapist notices various parts taking over, he or she asks the person first to visualize them, and then help them to calm down. If, for example, an angry part were seen as a snarling dog, that person might find that she could calm her anger by imagining reassuring the dog and petting it until it felt safe and settled down. Or to use another example (cited by Schwartz, 1998), if a frightened part were conceived as a rag doll, the client might relax her fears by imagining holding and comforting that doll.

Thus, by personifying people's polarizing emotional reactions as parts and then helping them visualize and reassure these reactive parts, internal family systems therapy releases people from the domination of fear and anger, which in turn allows them to work together more effectively to solve personal and family problems.

Evaluating Therapy Theory and Results

Experiential therapy helps family members get beneath the surface of their interactions to explore the feelings that drive them. At its best, this approach helps people drop their defenses and come together with more immediacy and authenticity. Given our contemporary emphasis on behavior and cognition, the effort to help clients uncover the feeling side of their experience is surely a welcome addition.

Regardless of what approach to family therapy one takes, shifting to individuals and their experience is a good way to break through defensive squabbling. When family members argue, they usually lead with their defenses. Instead of saying "*I'm* hurt," they say "*You* make me mad." Instead of admitting they're afraid, they criticize each other. An effective way to interrupt the unproductive escalation of arguments is to explore the feelings of the participants, one at a time. By talking to individuals about what they're feeling—and the roots of such feelings—family members can be helped to get past the defensiveness that keeps them apart and to reconnect on a more genuine level.

However, just as approaches that focus entirely on families and their interactions leave something out, so too does an approach that concentrates too narrowly on individuals and their emotional experience. At the peak of their popularity in the 1970s, experiential therapists approached family therapy

as if it were an encounter group for relatives. They put great faith in the value of emotional experiencing and had limited appreciation of the role family structure plays in regulating that experience. Not surprisingly, therefore, as family therapy focused more on organization, interaction, and narrative in the 1980s and 1990s, the experiential model fell out of favor.

As we have already suggested, a therapy designed primarily to elicit feelings may be more suited to encounter groups than to family therapy. However, the prevailing behavioral and cognitive models of family therapy could do with a little more attention to people's feelings. If "more attention to people's feelings" sounds a little vague, allow us to make it more concrete. Helping family members get in touch with their feelings accomplishes two things: It helps them as individuals discover what they really think and feel—what they want and what they're afraid of—and it helps them as a family begin to relate to each other in a more honest and immediate way.

Two particularly creative approaches to helping individuals get in touch with their inner experience are emotionally focused couples therapy and internal family systems therapy. What sets Johnson and Greenberg's therapy apart is its combination of emotional expressiveness and attention to the dynamics of interaction between couples. Emotionally focused couples therapy begins, as all emotive approaches do, by exploring the feelings clients come in with—even, or especially, if those feelings are defensive. You don't get beneath the surface of what people are feeling by ignoring it.

The combination of uncovering deeper and more vulnerable emotions and teaching couples about the reactive patterns their feelings drive them through creates a meaningful cognitive experience. As Lieberman, Yalom, and Miles (1973) demonstrated with encounter groups, an emotionally intense therapeutic experience only brings lasting value when paired with an intellectual understanding of the significance of those emotions. The only caveat we might offer is that explanations are most useful following an emotionally significant process of uncovering—which is what distinguishes psychotherapy from a conversation with your Aunt Harriet.

Emotionally focused couples therapy maintains that relationship difficulties generally stem from the disowning of attachment needs, creating defensive interactional cycles and ineffective communication patterns. The model identifies these issues and destructive cycles, helps clients acknowledge the feelings underlying these cycles, encourages empathy for the partner's position, and encourages couples to communicate needs and emotions more effectively in the spirit of generating solutions and increasing intimacy.

Schwartz's internal family systems approach helps family members come together with more understanding by helping individuals sort out their own conflicted experience. Personifying unruly emotions as "parts" is a powerful device for helping people achieve a clarifying distance from their conflicts. Unlike emotionally focused therapy, internal family systems therapy does not lean heavily on didactic explanations. In this approach, emotional experiencing is clarified by learning to differentiate among one's own feelings rather than by explanations offered by a therapist.

Emotionally focused couples therapy has received a good deal of empirical support (e.g., Johnson, 2003; Johnson, Maddeaux, & Blouin, 1998; Johnson, Hunsley, Greenberg, & Schindler, 1999; Denton, Burleson, Clark, Rodriguez, & Hobbs, 2000). Specifically, recent studies have suggested that emotionally focused couples therapy helps to alleviate marital distress, as well as promote trust and forgiveness (Greenberg, Warwar, & Malcolm, 2010). Emotionally focused couples therapy is also a promising treatment for couples who are experiencing marital distress and the female partner is suffering from symptoms of major depression (Dessaulles, Johnson, & Denton, 2003). More recently, proponents of emotionally focused therapy have suggested its potential utility for couples facing breast cancer (Tie & Poulsen, 2013) and terminal illness (Adamson, 2013). One controlled randomized trial did show that couples facing end-stage cancer who participated in emotionally focused therapy reported improved marital function and patient perceived caregiver empathy (McLean, Walton, Rodin, Epslen, & Jones, 2013).

Recently, researchers seeking to study the effectiveness of experiential techniques have followed Mahrer's (1982) suggestion to focus on the process, rather than the outcome, of therapy. Because he believed that studies of outcome have little impact on practitioners (who already know that what they do works), Mahrer recommended studying *in-therapy outcomes*—that is, what kinds of interventions produce desired results (emotional expression, more open communication) within sessions. Following Mahrer (1982) and others (Pierce, Nichols, & DuBrin, 1983) who looked at such in-therapy outcomes in individual treatment, Leslie Greenberg and Susan Johnson have found that helping an angry and attacking partner to reveal his or her softer feelings characterizes the best session of successful cases (Johnson & Greenberg, 1988) and that intimate self-disclosure leads to more productive sessions (Greenberg, Ford, Alden, & Johnson, 1993).

Once feeling-expression occupied center stage in psychological therapies; today that place is held by behavior and cognition. Psychotherapists have discovered that people think and act, but that doesn't mean we should ignore the immediate emotional experience that is the main concern of experiential family therapy.

Summary

Experiential therapy works from the inside out—strengthening families by encouraging individual self-expression, reversing the usual direction of effect in family therapy. Experiential family therapy is also distinguished by a commitment to emotional well-being as opposed to problem solving. Personal integrity and self-fulfillment are seen as innate human capacities that will emerge spontaneously once defensiveness is overcome. To challenge the familiar and enhance experiencing, therapists use their own lively personalities as well as a host of expressive techniques.

Although the experiential model lost popularity in the 1980s, it is now enjoying something of a resurgence, especially in the innovative work of emotionally focused couples therapy and the internal family systems approach. Once, the idea that families are systems was novel and controversial; today it is the new orthodoxy. Now that the pendulum has swung so far in the direction of systems thinking, individuals and their private joys and sorrows are rarely mentioned. One of the major contributions of experiential family therapy is to remind us not to lose sight of the self in the system.

Click here to apply your knowledge of chapter concepts.

Click here to test your application and analysis of the content found within this chapter.

Many of the pioneers of family therapy, including Nathan Ackerman, Murray Bowen, Ivan Boszormenyi-Nagy, Carl Whitaker, Don Jackson, and Salvador Minuchin, were psychoanalytically trained. But with the eager enthusiasm of converts they turned away from the old—psychodynamics—and toward the new—systems dynamics. Some, like Jackson and Minuchin, moved far indeed from their psychoanalytic roots. Others, like Bowen and Boszormenyi-Nagy, retained a distinctly analytic influence in their work.

In the 1960s and 1970s family therapy followed Jackson and Minuchin in totally rejecting psychoanalytic thinking. Jackson (1967) went so far as to declare the death of the individual, and Minuchin (1989) proclaimed, "We understood that the decontexted individual was a mythical monster, an illusion created by psychodynamic blinders."

Then in the 1980s a surprising shift occurred: Family therapists took a renewed interest in the psychology of the individual. This revival of interest reflected changes in psychoanalysis—from the individualism of Freudian theory to the more relationship-oriented object relations theories and self psychology—as well as changes in family therapy itself, especially dissatisfaction with the mechanistic elements of the cybernetic model. Among the books calling for a rapprochement with psychoanalysis were *Object Relations: A Dynamic Bridge between Individual and Family Treatment* (Slipp, 1984), *Object Relations Family Therapy* (Scharff & Scharff, 1987), and *The Self in the System* (Nichols, 1987).

The reason these psychodynamic voices found a receptive audience was that while family therapists discovered profound truths about systemic interactions, many believed they were wrong to turn their backs on depth psychology. Anyone who does not flee from self-awareness knows

PSYCHOANALYTIC FAMILY THERAPY

Rediscovering Psychodynamics

LEARNING OUTCOMES

- ♦ Describe the evolution of psychoanalytic family therapy.
- ♦ Describe the main tenets of psychoanalytic family therapy.
- ♦ Describe healthy and unhealthy family development from a psychoanalytic family therapy perspective.
- ♦ Describe the clinical goals and the conditions necessary for meeting those goals from a psychoanalytic family therapy perspective.
- ♦ Discuss and demonstrate the assessment and intervention techniques of psychoanalytic family therapy.
- ♦ Discuss research support for psychoanalytic family therapy.

that the inner life is awash in conflict and confusion, most of it never expressed. While systems therapists focused on the outward expression of this inner life—family interactions—psychoanalytic therapists probed beneath family dialogues to explore individual family members' private fears and longings.

Jill and David Scharff are leading exponents of object relations family therapy.

Sketches of Leading Figures

Freud was interested in the family but saw it as old business—the place where people learned neurotic fears, rather than the current context where such fears were maintained. Faced with a phobic Little Hans, Freud (1909) was more interested in the boy's Oedipus complex than in what was going on in his family.

From the 1930s to the 1950s, psychoanalytic researchers became more interested in the contemporary family. Erik Erikson explored the sociological dimensions of ego psychology. Erich Fromm's observations about the struggle for individuality foreshadowed Bowen's work on differentiation of self. Harry Stack Sullivan's interpersonal theory emphasized the mother's role in transmitting anxiety to her children.

In the 1950s, American psychoanalysis was dominated by ego psychology (which focuses on intrapsychic structures), while object relations theory (which lends itself to interpersonal analysis) flourished an ocean away in Britain. In the 1940s Henry Dicks (1963) established the Family Psychiatric Unit at the Tavistock Clinic in England, where teams of social workers attempted to reconcile couples referred by the divorce courts. By the 1960s Dicks (1967) was applying object relations theory to the understanding and treatment of marital conflict.

Edith Jacobson (1954) and Harry Stack Sullivan (1953) helped bring American psychiatry to an interpersonal point of view. Less well known but more important to the development of family therapy was the work carried out at the National Institute of Mental Health (NIMH). When NIMH opened in 1953, Irving Ryckoff developed a research project on families of schizophrenics under the leadership of Robert Cohen. He was joined by Juliana Day and Lyman Wynne, and

later by Roger Shapiro and John Zinner. This group introduced such concepts as *pseudomutuality* (Wynne, Ryckoff, Day, & Hirsch, 1958), *trading of dissociations* (Wynne, 1965), and *delineations* (Shapiro, 1968). But perhaps their most important contribution was the application of *projective identification* (from Melanie Klein) to family relationships.

In the 1960s Ryckoff and Wynne inaugurated a course in family dynamics at the Washington School of Psychiatry, which led to a family therapy training program. They were joined by Shapiro, Zinner, and Robert Winer. In 1975 they recruited Jill Savege (now Scharff) and David Scharff. By the mid-1980s the Washington School of Psychiatry, under the directorship of David Scharff, had become a leading center of psychoanalytic family therapy. The Scharffs left in 1994 to form their own institute.

Among others who have incorporated psychoanalytic theory into family therapy are Helm Stierlin (1977), Robin Skynner (1976), William Meissner (1978), Arnon Bentovim and Warren Kinston (1991), Fred Sander (1979, 1989), Samuel Slipp (1984, 1988), Michael Nichols (1987), Nathan Epstein, Henry Grunebaum, and Clifford Sager.

Theoretical Formulations

The essence of psychoanalytic treatment is uncovering unconscious impulses and defenses against them. It isn't a question of analyzing individuals instead of family interactions; rather, it's knowing where to look to discover the basic wants and fears that keep those individuals from interacting in a mature way. Consider the case of Carl and Peggy (Nichols, 1987).

CASE STUDY

Whenever Peggy talked to Carl about their relationship, she got upset and started criticizing. Carl, feeling attacked, was cowed into submission. The more Peggy complained, the quieter Carl became. Only after enduring her tirades for several minutes did Carl get mad and start to shout back at her. As a result, Peggy got the opposite of what she was looking for. Instead of understanding her concerns, Carl felt threatened and withdrew. When that didn't work, he lost his temper. At home, he sometimes slapped her.

The therapist concentrated on interrupting this cycle and then helping the couple see the pattern so that they could prevent its recurrence. Unfortunately, while Carl and Peggy learned to relate more effectively in the therapist's office, at home they forgot. Week after week it was the same story. They'd manage to listen to each other in their sessions, but at least once a month they'd lose it at home.

As actors, perhaps we take ourselves too seriously; as observers, we take other selves not seriously enough. As family therapists, we see the actions of our clients as a product of their interactions. Yes, people are connected, but that connectedness should not obscure the fact that the nature of their interactions is partly dictated by psychic organization of unsuspected depth and complexity.

CASE STUDY

Why couldn't (wouldn't) Carl stop hitting his wife? The fact that she provoked him doesn't really explain anything. Not every husband who is provoked hits his wife. Looking back, the therapist remembered how Carl used to say with exaggerated concern, "I *must* control my temper!" She also remembered how dramatically he described his intimidating outbursts and his wife's cowering. And she remembered that when Peggy talked about Carl's brutality, a smile played around the corner of his mouth. These hints of a willful, motivated quality

to Carl's abuse could be described in the jargon of psychodynamics, which, because it is alien, might lead some people to dismiss it as a relic of outmoded thinking. Psychodynamic language might imply that Carl's unconscious was responsible for his abusing his wife; he was helpless in the face of his inner conflicts.

Psychodynamic theory may be useful to understand the self in the system, but it isn't necessary to be highly technical. If we were to write a dramatic narrative about Carl, we could say that he was misrepresenting, even to himself, his feelings and intentions. He fooled his wife, and he fooled himself. Carl, who thinks himself concerned about his temper (his version of nonhuman agency), is actually pleased with his power to intimidate his wife and the manliness it implies. This explanation does not replace the interactional one; it only complicates it. Carl's attacks were triggered by the couple's interactions, but they were propelled by his own unrecognized insecurities. Knowing the motives behind his behavior enables us to help Carl understand that he hits his wife to make up for feeling weak and to help him find some other way to feel powerful. As long as therapists stay at the surface level of interaction, they will make little headway with a certain number of their cases.

Recognizing that people are more complicated than billiard balls means that we sometimes have to delve deeper into their experience. Psychoanalytic theory gets so complex when you get into the specifics that it's easy to get lost. Here are the basics.

◆ Freudian Drive Psychology

At the heart of human nature are the drives—libidinal and aggressive. Mental conflict arises when children learn, and mislearn, that acting on these impulses may lead to punishment. The resulting conflict is signaled by *anxiety*, that is, emotional distress associated with the idea (often unconscious) that one will be punished for acting on a particular impulse—for example, the anger you're tempted to express might make your partner stop loving you. *Depression* is emotional distress plus the idea (often unconscious) that the feared calamity has already happened—for example, your anger at your mother made her stop loving you; in fact, nobody loves you.

Internal conflict can be shifted in one of two ways: by strengthening the defenses against one's impulses or by relaxing defenses to permit some gratification.

◆ Self Psychology

The essence of **self psychology** (Kohut, 1971, 1977) is that every human being longs to be appreciated. If our parents demonstrate their appreciation, we internalize this acceptance in the form of a self-confident personality. But to the extent that our parents are unresponsive or rejecting, then our craving for appreciation is retained in a primitive manner. As adults we alternately suppress the desire for attention and then allow it to break through whenever we're in the presence of a receptive audience.

The child lucky enough to grow up with appreciative parents will be secure, able to stand alone as a center of initiative, and able to love. The unhappy child, cheated out of loving affirmation, will move through life forever craving attention. This is the root of **narcissism**.

◆ Object Relations Theory

Psychoanalysis is the study of individuals; family therapy is the study of relationships. The bridge between them is **object relations theory**. While the details of object relations theory can be complicated, its essence is simple: We relate to others on the basis of expectations formed by early experience. The residue of these formative relationships leaves **internal objects**—mental images of self and others built up from experience and expectation. As adults, we interact with other people as much on the basis of these internal objects as on those people's real characteristics.

The internal world of object relations never corresponds exactly to the actual world of real people. It's an approximation, strongly influenced by the earliest object images, introjections, and identifications. This inner world gradually matures and develops, becoming progressively synthesized and closer to reality. The individual's internal capacity for dealing with conflict and failure is related to the depth and maturity of the internal world of object relations. Trust in one's self and in the goodness of others is based on the confirmation of love from internalized good objects.

A child is developmentally incapable of thinking of his or her caregivers as both good and bad. If a father is generally responsive to his child's needs, the child will prosper. If there is a trauma such as abuse, however, or other pattern of shaming such as being overly harsh or critical, intense anger and so forth, the child is faced with a dilemma: how to maintain a connection with his father while at the same time acknowledging that sometimes his father stirs up feelings of intense fear and anxiety? In other words, in the dichotomous, black and white mind of a child, dad needs to be an *all good object* in order to stay safely connected; and yet dad's behavior at times makes the child feel as dad is an *all bad object*. Holding those two seeming dichotomies proves too much for the child's developing ego, so he engages in *splitting* and introjection (Fairbairn, 1952). Splitting occurs as the child splits off the bad aspects of his father (e.g., intense anger) in order to maintain an image of his dad as safe and dependable.

CASE STUDY

Tim complained about Maria's "anger issues," while Maria countered that Tim was "weak." The therapist taught Maria anger management techniques and helped Tim try to become more assertive, all to little avail.

Curious about the lack of progress, the therapist hypothesized that the problem might lie deeper—perhaps Tim split off his anger, and Maria split off her weakness. When exploring their family histories, it emerged that Tim resented his father's volatile temper, and swore he'd never be like his dad. When asked how he was similar and dissimilar to his dad, Tim said "I'm proud to say I'm not like that guy in any way!" suggesting he viewed his dad as all bad.

Maria's family emigrated from Cuba soon after her birth with pennies in their pockets and went on to establish a highly successful real estate business. In her family's scramble to the top, not standing up for yourself, being passive or needy was viewed as shameful weakness and promptly and severely punished. Consequently Maria split off the more sensitive, gentle parts of herself and projected them onto Tim, whom she loved very much except for his annoying habit of "letting himself get walked all over." A predictable pattern formed where Maria projected her weakness onto Tim by walking all over him; he would feel anger but passive-aggressively project it onto Maria, thus setting her off; wherein Maria would again yell at Tim for being such a wimp; and around and around the cycle would go.

Once the intense anger (or whatever the negative attribute may be) has been split from the parental object, through *introjection* the child represses that attribute in his unconscious and labels that attribute and anyone possessing it as all bad. Left unresolved, the child will unconsciously carry this label into adulthood; all people who exhibit intense anger, himself included, will be considered "all bad," and he will treat them accordingly. Here's the problem—when introjecting a split object, you inevitably become more susceptible to embodying that split object and thus viewing yourself as all bad. In other words, a father's expression of intense anger raises his child's anxiety and triggers avoidance strategies. Consequently, the child never learns how to effectively regulate his own anger and as an adult is thus susceptible to either repeating his father's violent outbursts or keeping his anger bottled up. Either way he loses. Because acting like his father triggers the painful belief that he is all bad, the adult must avoid anger at all costs in order to see himself as good. If you've ever tried to never feel something, you'll understand how difficult that can be. You simply can't choose to never feel something; the more you try to avoid a feeling, the more it consumes you.

Here is where *projective identification* comes into play. Projective identification occurs when a person projects the emotion they have split off onto others by treating them in a way that they embody that emotion. If a person has split off anger, for example, rather than acknowledge feeling angry themselves, they will do something to make their partner angry. Through projective identification each person embodies the parts of their partner that the partner has repressed. The catch is that each person thinks their partner is "bad" for embodying the characteristic they projected onto their partner to begin with. Consciously, they will likely want their partner to not have that

conflicted emotion. Unconsciously, the last thing they want is for their partner to get rid of that projected emotion—otherwise the split person would have to acknowledge that emotion in himself or herself. That is often why behaviorally focused interventions fail when projective identification is in play—because unconsciously, each partner needs the other to not change so each can maintain their damaged sense of self.

Watch this video of object relations therapists Drs. Jill and David Scharff work with a family. What effects did the son's suicide have on family dynamics from an object relations perspective?

CASE STUDY

The therapist knew that in order to improve their relationship, Tim and Maria needed to have a deeper understanding of the emotions they were struggling with. First, the therapist helped each of them understand that feelings, including anger, vulnerability, and fear were value neutral; they are neither good nor bad, nor are the people who have them. Behavior that flows from those feelings, however, can be helpful or hurtful. The more Tim and Maria repressed their feelings, the less they were in control of their behavior in relation to those feelings, and the more ashamed of the behavior they were when it came out. They'd each been avoiding their feelings of anger and weakness in order to avoid feelings of shame. Tim and Maria were encouraged to let themselves feel anger and weakness without thinking of themselves as bad for doing so. This was a new idea for them, and it took a while for them to believe that they could show anger or weakness and still be loved. It was easier for Tim to do this when the therapist helped deepen and expand his understanding of his father (and other people who showed anger) as more complex than all good or all bad. The same was true for Maria and weakness.

Gradually, Tim learned healthy ways to express his anger as did Maria for weakness and vulnerability. A risk was that each would swing like a pendulum from repressed anger to unchecked rage, or fierce independence to inconsolable emoting—opposite sides of the same coin. Tim learned to identify what was upsetting him and then assert himself in a healthy way. Maria learned to identify when she was feeling vulnerable and how to express this.

Tim eventually let himself truly feel the anger that he'd been repressing, and Maria did the same with weakness. They each took the difficult step of letting the dreaded feelings become conscious without acting on them.

Through a combination of redefining identifying and owning their disowned feelings, redefining themselves and others as good people who sometimes get angry or show weakness, experiencing those feelings without acting on them, and asserting himself in a healthy way and letting herself be vulnerable, Tim and Maria were able to stop the painful cycle and form a deep, satisfying marriage.

For a couple to resolve their conflicts, each must acknowledge that it is not primarily their partner's expression of emotion they can't deal with—it is *their own* repressed version of that emotional issue that they can't deal with. Until they acknowledge that, nothing will change. For this to occur, a couple needs new insights into their splitting process. The unconscious needs to be made conscious, felt, and then reprocessed. Current experience needs to be linked to childhood experience. This process is called *integrating split objects*. The main object relations technique for integrating split objects is an *interpretation* offered in a safe *holding environment* (Scharff & Scharff, 1987). In order to avoid a shaming power struggle, interpretations are best offered tentatively, using phrases such as "I wonder if . . .," ". . . am I getting it?" and "It seems to me like . . . ." Here's an example of how that interpretive process could be used with Tim:

> When you feel furious with Maria, you withdraw to avoid acting like your father did with you, and you don't want anyone to feel the way you did back then. However, I wonder if over time you have learned that your withdrawal and passivity also serve to express your anger at Maria?

Interactional cycles can form around any issue on which a couple is split. Common cycles include over/underresponsible, pursue/withdraw, and so forth.

Here's an example of how the process of integrating split objects could be applied to a pursue/withdraw couple:

Therapist: (to pursuer): When your wife is late, how do you feel?

Client: Totally ignored, like I don't exist.

Therapist: When was the first time you remember feeling that way?

Client: When everyone in my family ignored me.

Therapist: What did you do then?

Client: I chewed my nails until they bled so they knew I was feeling neglected.

Therapist: Do you have other ways that you could let your wife know that you would like to be taken care of?

Therapist: When your boyfriend is yelling at you, how do you feel?

Client: Totally worthless, like I don't count for anything.

Therapist: When have you felt that way before?

Client: With my father, when he criticized me.

Therapist: What did you do as a girl when your father was angry at you?

Client: There was nothing to do. I would freeze and withdraw. I felt I could never be good enough so why bother trying.

Therapist: What can you do now that you have other options as a grown woman?

Client: I can tell him that I am angry that he treats me like I am not worthwhile.

Not all interactional cycles, of course, are fueled by projective identification of introjected split objects. Some are simply a product of habit, differing cultural values, or failures of communication. Those couples will often respond well to behavioral interventions, and would probably find object relations theory frustratingly complex. When clients keep sabotaging direct work on their interactions, however, object relations theory may prove extremely useful.

Family Dynamics

Psychoanalysis offers by far the richest and most comprehensive theories on family development and problem formation. The best we can do is to

Psychoanalysts see early childhood experience as the key to later problems in relationships.

summarize them, focusing on those elements that family clinicians find most practically applicable.

◆ Normal Family Functioning

A child doesn't mature in sublime indifference to the interpersonal world. From the start, we need a facilitating environment in order to thrive. This environment doesn't have to be ideal; an *average expectable environment* with *good-enough mothering* (Winnicott, 1965a) is sufficient.

The parents' capacity to provide security for a baby's developing ego depends on whether they themselves feel secure. To begin with, a mother must be secure enough to channel her energy into caring for her infant. She withdraws interest from herself and her marriage and focuses it on the baby. As the baby comes to need less, the mother gradually recovers her self-interest, which allows her to permit the child to become independent (Winnicott, 1965b).

To the very young child, parents are not quite separate individuals; they are, in Kohut's (1971, 1977) term, **selfobjects**, experienced as part of the self. As a self-object, a mother transmits her love by touch, tone of voice, and gentle words, as though they were the child's own feelings. When she whispers, "Mommy loves you," the baby learns that he or she is: (1) a person and (2) lovable.

In self psychology, two things are deemed essential for the development of a secure and cohesive self. The first is **mirroring**—understanding plus acceptance. Attentive parents convey a deep appreciation of how their children feel. Their implicit "I see how you feel" validates the child's inner experience. Parents also offer models for **idealization**. The little child who can believe "My mother (or father) is terrific, and I am part of her (or him)" has a firm base of self-esteem. In the best of circumstances, the child, already basically secure in his or her self, draws additional strength from identifying with the power and strength of the parents.

The most significant recent contribution to the psychoanalytic study of normal family development is the work of Daniel Stern (1985). Stern painstakingly traced the development of the self through detailed observations of infants and young children. The most revolutionary of Stern's findings was that child development is *not* a gradual process of separation and individuation (Mahler, Pine, & Bergman, 1975). Rather, infants differentiate themselves almost from birth and then progress through increasingly complex modes of relatedness. From *attunement* (reading and sharing the child's affective state) to *empathy*, attachment and dependency are needs throughout life.

Some of the most interesting and productive psychoanalytic ideas are contained in descriptions of the psychodynamics of marriage. In the 1950s the marital bond was described as a result of unconscious fantasy (Stein, 1956). We marry a blurry blend of real and hoped-for mates. More recently and more interestingly, psychoanalysts have described the overlapping and interlocking of fantasies and projections (Blum, 1987; Sander, 1989).

Among psychodynamic family therapists, few have made more important contributions than Boszormenyi-Nagy's **contextual therapy**, which emphasizes the ethical dimension of family development. In a field that often seeks refuge in the illusion of neutrality, Nagy reminded us of the importance of decency and fairness (Boszormenyi-Nagy, Grunebaum, & Ulrich, 1991).

◆ Development of Behavior Disorders

According to classical psychoanalytic theory, symptoms are attempts to cope with unconscious conflicts over libido and aggression. As psychoanalytic emphasis shifted from instincts to object relations, infantile dependence and incomplete ego development replaced the oedipal complex and repressed instincts as the core problems in development. Fear-dictated flight from object relations, which begins in early childhood, is now considered the deepest root of psychological problems.

One important reason for relationship problems is that people distort their perceptions by attributing the qualities of one person to someone else. Freud (1905) called this phenomenon **transference** when his patient Dora displaced feelings for her father onto him and terminated treatment abruptly just as it was on the threshold of success. Others have observed similar phenomena and called it *scapegoating* (Vogel & Bell, 1960); *irrational role assignments* (Framo, 1970); *delineations* (Shapiro, 1968); and *family projection process* (Bowen, 1965). Regardless of the name, all are variants of Melanie Klein's (1946) concept of *projective identification*.

Projective identification is a process whereby a subject perceives an object as if it contained unwelcome elements of the subject's personality and evokes responses from the object that conform to those perceptions. Unlike projection, projective identification is interactional. Not only do parents project anxiety-arousing aspects of themselves onto their children, but the children collude by behaving in a way that confirms their parents' fears. By doing so, they may be stigmatized or scapegoated, but they also gratify aggressive impulses (for instance, in delinquent behavior) (Jacobson, 1954), act out their own fantasies, receive subtle reinforcement from their families, and avoid the terrible fear of rejection for not conforming (Zinner & Shapiro, 1976). Meanwhile the parents are able to avoid the anxiety associated with certain impulses, experience vicarious gratification, and still punish the children for expressing these impulses. In this way, intrapsychic conflict becomes externalized, with the parent acting as a superego, punishing the child for acting on the dictates of the parental id. That's one reason parents overreact: They're afraid of their own impulses.

CASE STUDY

The J. family sought help controlling fifteen-year-old Paul's delinquent behavior. Arrested several times for vandalism, Paul seemed neither ashamed of nor able to understand his compulsion to strike out against authority. As therapy progressed, it became clear that Paul's father harbored a deep but unexpressed resentment of the social conditions that made him work long hours for low wages in a factory, while the "fat cats didn't do shit, but still drove around in Cadillacs." Once the therapist became aware of Mr. J.'s suppressed hatred of authority, she also began to notice that he smiled slightly whenever Mrs. J. described Paul's latest exploits.

Parents' failure to accept that their children are separate beings can take extreme forms, leading to the most severe psychopathology. Lidz (Lidz, Cornelison, & Fleck, 1965) described a mother of identical twins who, when she was constipated, would give her two sons an enema.

Poorly differentiated children face a crisis in adolescence, when developmental pressures for independence conflict with infantile attachments.

The outcome may be continued dependence or violent rebellion. But the teenager who rebels as a reaction to unresolved dependency needs is ill-equipped for mature relationships. Behind their facade of proud self-reliance, such individuals harbor deep longings for dependence. When they marry, they may seek constant approval or automatically reject any influence, or both.

CASE STUDY

Mr. and Mrs. B.'s complaints were mirror images. He claimed she was "bossy and demanding"; she said that he "had to have everything his own way." Mr. B. was the youngest in a close-knit family of five. He described his mother as warm and loving but said she tried to smother him and that she discouraged all his efforts to be independent. Subjected to these same pressures, his two older sisters knuckled under and still remain unmarried, living with his parents. Mr. B., however, rebelled against his mother's domination and left home to join the Marines at seventeen. As he related his experience in the Marine Corps and successful business ventures, it was clear that he was fiercely proud of his independence.

Once the story of Mr. B.'s success in breaking away from his domineering mother was brought into the open, both Mr. and Mrs. B. had a clearer understanding of his tendency to overreact to anything he perceived as controlling. Deeper analysis revealed that while Mr. B. staunchly rejected what he called "bossiness," he nevertheless craved approval. He had learned to fear his deep-seated dependency needs and protect himself with a facade of "not needing anything from anybody"; nevertheless, the needs were still there and had in fact been a powerful determinant of his choice of wife.

When it comes to choosing a romantic partner, psychoanalysts tell us, love is blind. Freud (1921) wrote that the overvaluation of the loved object when we fall in love leads us to make poor judgments based on *idealization*. The "fall" of falling in love reflects an overflow of narcissistic libido, so that the object of our love is elevated as a substitute for our own unattained ideals. Our own identity glows in the reflected radiance of an idealized companion.

Further complicating marital choice is that we hide some of our own needs and feelings in order to win approval. Children tend to suppress feelings they fear may lead to rejection. Winnicott (1965a) dubbed this phenomenon the *false self*—children behave as if they were perfect angels, pretending to be what they are not. In its most extreme form, a false self leads to schizoid behavior (Guntrip, 1969); even in less severe manifestations it affects the choice of a mate. During courtship most people present themselves in the best possible light. Powerful dependency needs, narcissism, and unruly impulses may be submerged before marriage, but once married, spouses relax into themselves, warts and all.

Families as well as individuals experience **fixation** and **regression**. Most families function adequately until they're overtaxed, at which time they become stuck in dysfunctional patterns (Barnhill & Longo, 1978). When faced with too much stress, families tend to revert to earlier levels of development. The amount of stress a family can tolerate depends on its level of development and the type of fixations its members have.

♦ ♦ ♦

Psychoanalysts have been criticized (Szasz, 1961) for absolving people of responsibility for their actions. To say that someone "acted-out" "repressed" sexual urges in an extramarital affair is to suggest that he is not accountable. However, Boszormenyi-Nagy stressed the idea of ethical accountability in families. Good family relationships include behaving ethically with other family members and considering each member's welfare and interests. Boszormenyi-Nagy believed that family members owe one another *loyalty* and that they acquire *merit* by supporting each other. To the degree that parents are fair and responsible, they engender loyalty in their children; however, parents create loyalty conflicts when they ask their children to be loyal to one parent at the expense of the other (Boszormenyi-Nagy & Ulrich, 1981).

Pathological reactions may develop from **invisible loyalties**—unconscious commitments children take on to help their families to the detriment of their own well-being. For example, a child may get sick to unite parents in concern. Invisible loyalties are problematic because they're not subject to rational scrutiny.

Mechanisms of Change

Given the richness and complexity of psychoanalytic theory, it may come as a surprise that the psychoanalytic view of how therapy works is relatively straightforward and simple. (But keep in mind, simple isn't the same as easy.)

◆ Goals of Therapy

The goal of psychoanalytic family therapy is to free family members from **unconscious** constraints so that they'll be able to interact with one another as healthy individuals. Plainly, this is an ambitious task.

It's easy to say that the goal of psychoanalytic therapy is personality change, but it is rather more difficult to specify precisely what's meant by that. The most common objective is described as *separation–individuation* (Katz, 1981) or *differentiation* (Skynner, 1981). Both terms emphasize autonomy. (Perhaps one reason for emphasizing separation–individuation is that enmeshed families are more likely to seek treatment than disengaged families.) Individual therapists often think of individuation in terms of physical separation. Thus adolescents and young adults may be treated separately from their families in order to help them become independent. Family therapists believe that personal autonomy is best achieved by working through emotional conflicts within the family. Rather than isolate individuals from their families, psychoanalytic therapists convene families to help them learn to be independent as well as related. The following example illustrates how the goals of psychoanalytic family therapy were implemented with a particular family.

CASE STUDY

Three months after he went away to college, Barry J. had his first psychotic break. A brief hospital stay made it clear that Barry was unable to withstand separation from his family without decompensating; therefore, the hospital staff recommended that he live apart from his parents in order to help him become more independent. Accordingly, he was discharged to a supportive group home for young adults and seen twice weekly in individual psychotherapy. Unfortunately, he suffered a second breakdown and was rehospitalized.

As the time for discharge from this second hospitalization approached, the ward psychiatrist decided to convene the family in order to discuss plans for Barry's posthospital adjustment. During this meeting it became painfully obvious that powerful forces within the family were impeding any chance for genuine separation. Barry's parents were pleasant and effective people who separately were most engaging and helpful. Toward each other, however, they displayed an icy disdain. During the few moments in the interview when they spoke to each other, rather than to Barry, their hostility was palpable. Only their concern for Barry prevented their relationship from becoming a battleground—a battleground on which Barry feared one or both of them might be destroyed.

At the staff conference following this interview, two plans for disposition were advanced. One group recommended that Barry be removed as far as possible from his parents and treated in individual therapy. Others on the staff disagreed, arguing that only by treating them conjointly could the collusive bond between Barry and his parents be resolved. After lengthy discussion the group reached a consensus to try the latter approach.

Most of the early family meetings were dominated by the parents' anxious concern about Barry: about the apartment complex where he lived, his job, his friends, how he was spending his leisure time, his clothes, his grooming—in short, about every detail of his life. Gradually, with the therapist's support, Barry was able to limit how much of his life was open to his parents' scrutiny. As he did so, and as they were less able to preoccupy themselves with him, they began to focus on their own relationship. As Barry became more successful at handling his own affairs, his parents became openly combative with each other.

Following a session during which the parents' relationship was the primary focus, the therapist recommended that the couple come for a few separate sessions. Unable to divert their attention to Barry, the J.'s fought viciously, leaving no doubt that theirs was a seriously destructive relationship. Rather than getting better in treatment, their relationship got worse.

After two months of internecine warfare—during which time Barry continued to improve—Mr. and

Mrs. J. sought a legal separation. Once they were separated, both parents seemed happier, more involved with their friends and careers, and less worried about Barry. As they released their stranglehold on their son, both parents began to develop a warmer and more genuine relationship with him. Even after the parents divorced they continued to attend family sessions with Barry.

Conditions for Behavior Change

Analytic therapists foster insight by looking beyond behavior to the hidden motives below. Naturally, families defend against baring their innermost feelings. After all, it's a great deal to ask of anyone to expose old wounds and deep longings. Psychoanalysts deal with this problem by creating a climate of trust and proceeding slowly. Once an atmosphere of security is established, an analytic therapist can begin to identify projective mechanisms and bring them back into the marital relationship. Once they no longer need to rely on projective identification, partners can integrate previously split-off parts of their own egos.

The therapist helps couples begin to recognize how their present difficulties emerged from unconscious perpetuation of conflicts from their own families. This work is painful and cannot proceed without the security offered by a supportive therapist. Nichols (1987) emphasizes the need for empathy to create a "holding environment" for the whole family.

Therapy

Assessment

Analysts don't postpone treatment until they've made an exhaustive study of their cases; on the contrary, they may not even arrive at a final formulation until the latter stages of treatment. Although analytic clinicians may continue to refine their understanding over the course of treatment, therapy cannot proceed effectively without a preliminary dynamic formulation. Beginning therapists—who lack theory as well

as experience—sometimes proceed on the assumption that if they just sit back and listen, understanding will emerge. This rarely works in family therapy. The following is an abbreviated sketch of an initial psychoanalytic evaluation of a family.

CASE STUDY

After two sessions with the family of Sally G., who was suffering from school phobia, the therapist made a preliminary formulation of the family's dynamics. In addition to the usual descriptions of the family members, the presenting problem, and the family history, the formulation included assessments of the parents' object relations and the collusive, unconscious interaction of their marital relationship.

Mr. G. had been initially attracted to his wife as a libidinal object who would fulfill his sexual fantasies. Counterbalancing this was a tendency to idealize his wife. Thus he was deeply conflicted and intensely ambivalent in sexual relations with her.

At another level, Mr. G. had unconscious expectations that his wife would be the same long-suffering, self-sacrificing kind of person that his mother was. Thus he longed for motherly consolation. However, these dependent longings were threatening to his sense of masculinity, so he acted as though he were self-sufficient and needed no one. That he had a dependent inner object inside himself was shown by his tender solicitude toward his wife and children when they were ill. But they had to be in a position of weakness and vulnerability to enable him to overcome his defenses enough for him to gratify his own infantile dependency needs vicariously.

Mrs. G. expected marriage to provide her with an ideal father. Given this unconscious expectation, the very sexuality that attracted men to her was a threat to her wish to be treated like a little girl. Like her husband, she was highly conflicted about sexual relations. Raised as an only child, she expected to come first. She was even jealous of her husband's warmth toward Sally and attempted to maintain distance between father and daughter by her own intense attachment to Sally.

Thus, at an object-relations level, both spouses felt themselves to be deprived children, each wanting to be taken care of without having to ask. When these magical wishes weren't granted, both seethed with resentment. Eventually, they reacted to trivial provocations with the underlying rage, and horrible quarrels erupted.

When Sally witnessed her parents' violent altercations, she became terrified that her own hostile fantasies might come true. Although her parents hated their own internalized bad-parent figures, they seemed to act them out with each other. Further enmeshing Sally in their conflict was the fact that the ego boundaries between herself and her mother were blurred—almost as though mother and daughter shared one joint personality.

Dynamically, Sally's staying home from school could be seen as an attempt to protect her mother–herself from her father's attacks and to defend both parents against her own, projected, aggressive fantasies.

An excellent model for developing a psychodynamic focus is the work of Arnon Bentovim and Warren Kinston in Great Britain (Bentovim & Kinston, 1991), who offer a five-step strategy for formulating a focal hypothesis:

1. How does the family interact around the symptom, and how does the family interaction affect the symptom?

2. What is the function of the current symptom?

3. What disaster is feared in the family that keeps them from facing their conflicts more squarely?

4. How is the current situation linked to past trauma?

5. How would the therapist summarize the focal conflict in a short, memorable statement?

Among the metaphors used to describe psychoanalytic treatment, *depth* and *uncovering* feature prominently. The truth is, all therapies aim to uncover something. Even behaviorists look to uncover unnoticed contingencies of reinforcement before switching to a directive stance. What sets analytic therapy apart is that the process of discovery is protracted and directed not only at conscious thoughts and feelings, but also at fantasies and dreams.

◆ Therapeutic Techniques

For all the complexity of psychoanalytic theory, psychoanalytic therapy is relatively simple—not easy, but simple. There are four basic techniques: listening, empathy, interpretations, and analytic neutrality. Two of these—listening and analytic neutrality—may not seem that different from what other therapists do, but they are.

Listening is a strenuous but silent activity, rare in our culture. Most of the time we're too busy waiting to get a word in edgewise to listen more than perfunctorily. This is certainly true in family therapy, where therapists feel a tremendous pressure to *do* something to help troubled families.

This is where the importance of *analytic neutrality* comes in. To establish an analytic atmosphere, it's essential to concentrate on understanding without worrying about solving problems. Change may come about as a by-product of understanding, but an analytic therapist suspends anxious involvement with outcomes. It's impossible to overestimate the importance of this frame of mind in establishing a therapeutic climate of exploration.

An analytic therapist resists the temptation to reassure, advise, or confront families in favor of a sustained but silent immersion in their experience. When analytic therapists do intervene, they express *empathy* in order to help family members open up, and they make *interpretations* to illuminate hidden aspects of experience.

Take, for example, a couple who reported having an argument over the breakfast table. A systemic therapist might ask them to talk with each other about what happened, hoping to observe what they do to keep the argument from getting settled. The focus would be on communication and interaction. A psychoanalytic therapist would be more interested in the partners' emotional reactions. Why did they get so angry? What do they want from each other? What did they expect? Where did these feelings come from? Rather than try to resolve the argument, an analytic therapist would explore the fears and longings that lie underneath it.

The signal of intrapsychic conflict is affect. Instead of focusing on who did what to whom, analytic therapists key in on a strong feeling and use it as a starting point for detailed inquiry into its origins.

"What were you feeling?" "When have you felt that way before?" "And before that?" "What do you remember?" Rather than stay on the horizontal plane of family members' current behavior, the therapist looks for openings into the vertical dimension of their internal experience.

To summarize, psychoanalytic therapists organize their explorations along four channels: (1) internal experience, (2) the history of that experience, (3) how family members trigger that experience, and, finally, (4) how the context of the session and therapist's input might contribute to what's going on between family members. Here's a brief example.

· CASE STUDY

Having made great strides in understanding over the course of their first few couples sessions, Andrew and Gwen were all the more upset by their inability to discuss, much less settle, an angry disagreement about buying a new car. It wasn't the car but how to pay for it that set them so infuriatingly at odds. Andrew wanted to take money out of savings for the down payment, to keep the monthly payments low. This made Gwen furious. How could he even consider cutting into their savings! Didn't he understand that their mutual fund paid twice as much interest as they'd have to pay on a car loan?

Unfortunately, they were both too bent on changing the other's mind to make any real effort to understand what was going on inside it. The therapist interrupted their arguing to ask each of them what they were feeling and what they were worried about. He wasn't primarily interested in settling the disagreement—although asking about the feelings underlying an altercation is often an effective opening to understanding and compromise; rather, he felt that the intensity of their reactions indicated that this issue touched key concerns.

Andrew was worried about the burden of monthly expenses. "Don't you see," he implored, "if we don't take out enough to make a substantial down payment, we'll have to worry every month about making the payments?" Gwen was ready to dispute this, but the therapist cut her off. He was more interested in the roots of Andrew's worry than in the couple's trying to convince each other of anything.

It turned out that Andrew had a lifelong fear of not having enough money. Having enough money turned out to mean not a big house or a fancy car but enough to spend on things that might be considered indulgent—nice clothes, going out to dinner, flowers, presents. Andrew connected his urge to reward himself with modest material luxuries to memories of growing up in a spartan household. His parents were children of the Depression who thought that things like going out to dinner and buying clothes except when absolutely necessary were frivolous and wasteful.

At a deeper level, Andrew's memories of austerity were a screen for his never having gotten the attention and affection he craved from his rather reserved mother.[1] And so he'd learned to soothe himself with a new shirt or fancy dinner at times when he was feeling low. One of Gwen's chief attractions was her giving and expressive nature. She was openly affectionate and almost always happy to indulge Andrew's wish to buy something for himself.

Gwen connected her anxiety about having a cushion against the unexpected to memories of her father as an unreliable breadwinner. Unlike Andrew's parents, hers spent freely. They went out to dinner three or four times a week and took expensive vacations, and everyone in the family wore nice clothes. But although her father was a free spender, Gwen remembered him as lacking the discipline and foresight to invest wisely or to expand his business beyond its modest success. Although it had never been part of her conscious memories, it seemed that although her father lavished attention and affection on her, he never really took her seriously as a person. He treated her, in the familiar phrase, like "Daddy's little girl," as adorable—and insubstantial—as a kitten. That's why she was so attracted to what she saw as Andrew's serious and self-disciplined nature—and his high regard for her.

How did these two trigger such virulent reactions in each other? Not only did Gwen's anxious need to have money in the bank conflict with Andrew's need to have money to spend, but they each felt betrayed by the other. Part of Gwen's unconscious bargain with Andrew was that she could count on him to be a secure, steady pillar and to build for the future. Part of his unconscious expectations of her was that she would indulge him. No wonder they were so reactive to each other on this issue.

---

[1] In Kohut's terms, Andrew's mother provided an inadequate *mirroring* selfobject function.

And the therapist's role in all this? On reflection he realized that he'd been a little too anxious to smooth things over with this couple. Out of his own desire to see marital happiness he'd controlled the level of conflict in the sessions, intervening actively as a peacemaker. As a result, the couple's progress had come at a price. Deep longings and resentments had been pushed aside rather than explored and resolved. Perhaps, the therapist thought, he'd picked up the couple's fears of facing their own anger.

What use should a therapist make of such countertransferential reactions? Should he disclose his feelings? To say that **countertransference** may contain useful information isn't to say that it's oracular. Perhaps the most useful thing to do is look to countertransference for hypotheses that need confirming evidence from the patients' side of the experience. In this case the therapist acknowledged his sense that he'd been trying too hard to smooth things over, and he asked Gwen and Andrew whether they, too, were a little afraid to open up their anger.

Like many descriptions of clinical work, this one may seem a little pat. How did we get so quickly from arguing about buying a car to hunger for a mirroring selfobject? Part of the explanation lies in the inevitably condensed account. But it's also important to recognize that one of the things that enables a psychoanalyst to see beneath the surface of things is knowing where to look.

Sessions begin with the therapist inviting family members to discuss their current concerns. In subsequent meetings, the therapist might begin by saying nothing or perhaps "Where would you like to begin today?" The therapist then leans back and lets the family talk. Questions are limited to requests for amplification or clarification. "Could you tell me more about that?" "Have the two of you discussed how you feel about this?"

When initial associations and spontaneous interactions dry up, the therapist probes gently, eliciting history, people's thoughts and feelings, and their ideas about family members' perspectives. "What does your father think about your problems? How would he explain them?" This technique underscores the analytic therapist's interest in assumptions and projections. Particular interest is paid to childhood memories. The

following vignette shows how transitions are made from the present to the past.

CASE STUDY

Among their major disappointments in each other, Mr. and Mrs. S. both complained that the other one "doesn't take care of me when I'm sick, or listen to my complaints at the end of the day." Not only did they share the perception of the other's lack of "mothering," but they both steadfastly maintained that *they* were supportive and understanding. Mrs. S.'s complaint was typical: "Yesterday was a nightmare. The baby was sick and fussy, and I had a cold. Everything was twice as hard, and I had twice as much to do. All day long I was looking forward to John's coming home. But when he finally did, he didn't seem to care about how I felt. He only listened to me for a minute before starting to tell me some dumb story about the office." Mr. S. responded by telling a similar account but with the roles reversed.

At this point the therapist intervened to ask both spouses to describe their relationships with their mothers. What emerged were two very different but revealing histories.

Mr. S.'s mother was a taciturn woman, for whom self-reliance and personal sacrifice were paramount virtues. Though she loved her children, she withheld indulgence and affection, lest they become "spoiled." Nevertheless, Mr. S. craved his mother's attention and constantly sought it. Naturally, he was often rebuffed. A particularly painful memory was of a time he came home in tears after getting beaten up by a bully in the schoolyard. Instead of the consoling him, his mother scolded him for "acting like a baby." Over the years he learned to protect himself from these rebuffs by developing a facade of independence.

With the second significant woman in his life, his wife, Mr. S. maintained his rigid defensiveness. He never talked about his problems, but since he continued to yearn for understanding, he resented his wife for not drawing him out. His failure to risk rejection by asking for support served as a self-fulfilling prophecy, confirming his expectation, "She doesn't care about me."

Mrs. S.'s background was quite different from her husband's. Her parents were indulgent and demonstrative. They doted on their only child, communicating their love by expressing constant, anxious concern for her well-being. When she was a little girl, the slightest bump or bruise was an occasion for lavish expressions of concern. She came to marriage used to talking about herself and her problems. At first Mr. S. was enchanted. "Here is someone who really cares about feelings," he thought. But when he discovered that she didn't ask him to talk about his own concerns, he became resentful and progressively less sympathetic. This convinced her, "He doesn't care about me."

After the roots of current family conflicts have been uncovered, interpretations are made about how family members continue to reenact past and often distorted images from childhood. The data for such interpretations come from transference reactions to the therapist or to other family members, as well as from childhood memories. Psychoanalytic therapists deal less with recollections of the past than with reenactments of the past's influence in the present.

Don Catherall (1992) described a very useful process for interpreting projective identification in couples therapy. It's important to understand that projective identification isn't some mysterious force transmitted from an actor to a recipient, like a ventriloquist and his dummy. Rather, feelings are communicated and provoked by subtle, but usually unnoticed, signals. You may have experienced projective identification yourself if you've ever been around someone who was behaving seductively but then acted shocked when you made an advance.

The first step in working with projective identification in couples therapy is to interrupt repetitive squabbling, which is likely to mask the partners' real feelings. Couples caught up in recurring patterns of conflict and misunderstanding are colluding to avoid feelings of vulnerability. Once a couple's quarreling is blocked, the therapist can explore what the individuals are feeling. Catherall recommends focusing first on what the *recipient* of the projection is feeling. Once that person's feelings are clarified, he or she can be helped to communicate those feelings to the partner. To avoid provoking defensiveness, the recipient describing the formerly disavowed feelings is coached to describe only the feelings themselves,

not what the projecting partner did to provoke them. Meanwhile, the *projecting partner* is told just to listen and not comment. When the recipient has finished, the projector is directed to feed back what he or she understood the partner to be saying. This encourages the projecting partner to assume the recipient's point of view and therefore makes it difficult to block identification with those feelings.

The projecting partner is encouraged to empathize with the recipient. Hopefully, at this point, the couple can stop trading accusations and start trying to understand how each other feels. Ideally, this sharing of feelings will help bring the partners closer—to understanding, and to each other.

CASE STUDY

Catherall cites the example of David and Sheila. The more anxious David was to have sex with Sheila, the more sensitive he was to any hint of rejection. He would respond to her disinterest by withdrawing, and they would remain distant until Sheila reached out. Sheila ended up feeling the same unloved feelings that David had felt when his mother shut him out. Meanwhile David felt powerless with Sheila, just as she had felt with an uncle who had molested her. Each, in other words, was experiencing concordant identifications stimulated through a mutual process of projective identification.

The therapist pursued Sheila's feelings by inquiring what it was like for her when David was so distant. Her initial answer was that it made her angry, but the therapist asked what did it make her angry about and what was she feeling prior to getting angry. Sheila was then able to identify feelings of being unloved, uncared for, and generally lonely. These were the feelings that had been stimulated by David's projective identification, and they were feelings that Sheila would normally disavow by becoming angry and cold.

Then the therapist asked Sheila to talk with David about what it was like for her to feel lonely and unloved. The therapist was careful to keep Sheila focused on herself and what she was feeling, not on David and what he may have done to cause those feelings. Now that he was not being blamed, David was able to empathize and identify with the feelings of loneliness that Sheila was describing. When the therapist asked him if he knew what it was like to feel that way, David was finally able to talk more directly about the painful feelings that he had been warding off by projecting them onto Sheila.

Psychoanalytic family therapists emphasize that much of what is hidden in family dialogues is not consciously withheld but rather repressed into unconsciousness. The approach to this material is guarded by resistance often manifest in the form of transference. The following vignette illustrates the interpretation of resistance.

CASE STUDY

Mr. and Mrs. Z. had endured ten years of a loveless relationship in order to preserve the fragile security that marriage offered them. Mrs. Z.'s unexpected and uncharacteristic affair forced the couple to acknowledge the problems in their relationship, and so they consulted a family therapist.

Although they could no longer deny the existence of conflict, both spouses exhibited major resistance to confronting their problems openly. In the first session, both partners said that married life had been "more or less okay"; that Mrs. Z. had some kind of "midlife crisis"; and that it was she who needed therapy. This request for individual therapy was seen as a resistance to avoid a painful examination of the marriage, and the therapist said so. "It seems, Mr. Z., that you'd rather blame your wife than consider how the two of you might both be contributing to your difficulties. And you, Mrs. Z., seem to prefer accepting all the guilt in order to avoid confronting your husband with your dissatisfaction."

Accepting the therapist's interpretation and agreeing to examine their relationship deprived the couple of one form of resistance, as though an escape hatch had been closed. In the next few sessions both partners attacked each other vituperatively, but they talked only about her affair and his reactions rather than about problems in their relationship. These arguments weren't productive, because whenever Mr. Z. felt anxious he attacked his wife, and whenever she felt angry she became guilty and depressed.

Sensing that their fighting was unproductive, the therapist said, "It's clear that you've put each other through a lot of unhappiness and you're both quite bitter. But unless you get down to talking about specific problems in your marriage, there's little chance that you'll get anywhere."

Thus focused, Mrs. Z. timidly ventured that she'd never enjoyed sex with her husband and wished that he would take more time with foreplay. He snapped back, "Okay, so sex wasn't so great. Is that any reason to throw away ten years of marriage and start whoring around?" At this, Mrs. Z. buried her face in her hands and sobbed uncontrollably. After she regained her composure, the therapist intervened, again confronting the couple with their resistance: "It seems, Mr. Z., that when you get upset, you attack. What makes you so anxious about discussing sex?" Following this the couple was able to talk about their feelings about sex in their marriage until near the end of the session. At this point, Mr. Z. again lashed out at his wife, calling her a whore and a bitch.

Mrs. Z. began the following session by saying that she'd been depressed and upset, crying off and on all week. "I feel so guilty," she sobbed. "You *should* feel guilty!" retorted her husband. Once again, the therapist intervened. "You use your wife's affair as a club. Are you still afraid to discuss problems in your marriage? And you, Mrs. Z., cover your anger with depression. What is it that you're angry about? What was missing in the marriage? What did you want?"

This pattern continued for several more sessions. The spouses who had avoided discussing or even thinking about their problems for ten years used a variety of resistances to veer away from them in therapy. The therapist persisted in pointing out their resistance and urging them to talk about specific complaints.

Psychoanalytic therapists endeavor to foster insight and understanding; they also urge clients to consider what they're going to do about the problems they discuss. This effort—part of the process of *working through* (Greenson, 1967)—is more prominent in family therapy than in individual therapy.

Boszormenyi-Nagy believed that family members should not only be made aware of their motivations but also held accountable for their behavior. In contextual therapy, Boszormenyi-Nagy (1987) pointed out that the therapist must help people face the stifling expectations involved in invisible loyalties, and then help them find more positive ways of making loyalty payments in the family ledger. What this boils down to is developing a balance of fairness.

Evaluating Therapy Theory and Results

Too many family therapists neglect psychology in general and psychoanalytic theory in specific. Regardless of what approach a therapist uses, the writings of psychoanalytically informed clinicians are a rich resource.

Having said this, we also wish to make a cautionary point: Doctrinaire psychoanalytic family therapies are powerful in the hands of trained psychoanalysts. However, some therapists who get discouraged with the usual contentious family dialogues gravitate to psychoanalytic methods as a way to cut through the defensive wrangling. Interrupting a family's arguments to explore the individuals' feelings is an excellent way to cut through arguments. But if therapists make themselves overly central (by directing all conversation through themselves), or overemphasize individuals and neglect family interactions, then the power of family therapy—addressing relationship problems directly—may be lost. Interrupting defensive sparring to get to the hopes and fears that lie beneath is all to the good. But unless these interrogatories are followed by free interchanges among family members themselves, these explorations may produce the illusion of change only as long as the therapist is present to act as detective and referee.

Psychoanalytic therapists have generally resisted empirical attempts to evaluate their work. Because symptom reduction isn't the goal, it can't serve as the measure of success. And since the presence or absence of unconscious conflict isn't apparent to outside observers, whether an analysis is successful depends on subjective judgment. Psychoanalytic clinicians consider the therapist's observations a valid means of evaluating theory and treatment. The following quotation from the Blancks (1972) illustrates

this point. Speaking of Margaret Mahler's ideas, they wrote:

> Clinicians who employ her theories technically question neither the methodology nor the findings, for they can confirm them clinically, a form of validation that meets as closely as possible the experimentalist's insistence upon replication as criterion of the scientific method. (p. 675)

Another example of this point of view was expressed by Robert Langs. "The ultimate test of a therapist's formulation," says Langs (1982), "lies in the use of the therapist's impressions as a basis for intervention" (p. 186). What then determines the validity and effectiveness of these interventions? Langs doesn't hesitate; the patient's reactions, conscious and unconscious, constitute the ultimate litmus test. "True validation involves responses from the patient in both the cognitive and interpersonal spheres."

Is the ultimate test of therapy then the patient's reactions? Yes and no. First, patients' reactions are open to interpretation—especially since validation is sought not only in manifest responses but also in unconsciously encoded derivatives. Moreover, this point of view doesn't take into account the changes in patients' lives that occur outside the consulting room. Occasionally therapists report on the outcome of psychoanalytic family therapy but mostly in uncontrolled case studies. One such report is Dicks's (1967) survey of the outcome of psychoanalytic couples therapy at the Tavistock Clinic, in which he rated as having successfully treated 72.8 percent of a random sample of cases.

More recently, proponents of psychoanalytic family therapy have published case studies aimed at illustrating treatment modalities for various emotional and behavioral problems, including childhood trauma (Mackay, 2002; Paris, 2013), adolescent depression (Christogiorgos et al., 2010), schizophrenia (Morey, 2008), borderline personality disorder (Allen, 2001), and the parent–infant relationship (Cutner, 2014; Diaz Bonino, 2013; Emanuel, 2012; Salomonsson, 2013). These case studies provide clear case conceptualizations based on psychoanalytic theory and outline the course of treatment and eventual outcomes.

A few have gone further and undertaken intervention studies comparing treatments with psychoanalytic components to other treatment modalities (e.g., Dare et al., 2001; Trowell et al., 2007); however, results show little significant differences in outcome.

Summary

Psychoanalytically trained clinicians were among the first to practice family therapy, but when they began treating families most of them traded in depth psychology for systems theory. Since the mid-1980s there's been a resurgence of interest in psychodynamics among family therapists, especially in object relations theory and self psychology. In this chapter we've sketched the main points of these theories and shown how they're relevant to a psychoanalytic family therapy, integrating depth psychology and systems theory. A few practitioners (e.g., Kirschner & Kirschner, 1986; Nichols, 1987; Slipp, 1984) have combined elements of both; some have developed more frankly psychoanalytic approaches (notably Sander, 1989; Scharff & Scharff, 1987); none has achieved a true synthesis.

Freud's theories were never the last word, any more than were Newton's laws of physics. They both offered valuable observations, but they did not account for all natural phenomena and certainly not those at the edge of chaos. Object relations theory and self psychology joined Freudian drive psychology in offering useful explanations of development, each most applicable to various contemporary pathologies. In the twenty-first century, we see the complexity of cultural context on self and family development, the essential unpredictability of life, and the way in which theories, though useful, will never be more than partial explanations of life's infinite mysteries.

In recent years, cognitive and biological perspectives have held center stage in the study of clinical phenomena. Research on attachment theory, theories of affect regulation and neurological development, and trauma theory have added useful insights, but none of them has replaced psychoanalytic theory as the richest source of ideas about people and their problems.

The essential aim of psychoanalytic therapy is to help people understand their deepest desires and resolve conflicts over expressing them. Freudians emphasize libidinal and aggressive impulses, self psychologists focus on the longing for appreciation, and object relations therapists concentrate on the need for secure attachment. But all are united in the belief that couples and families can be helped to get along better if their individual members understand and begin to resolve their own personal conflicts.

Click here to apply your knowledge of chapter concepts.

Click here to test your application and analysis of the content found within this chapter.

When they first began working with families, behavior therapists applied learning theory to train parents in behavior modification and teach communication skills to couples. Although these approaches were effective with simple problems and well-motivated individuals, behaviorists had little appreciation of how misbehavior and poor communication were embedded in family systems. Since then, however, behavioral family therapy has evolved with increasing use of cognitive principles and attention to family dynamics.

CHAPTER 9

COGNITIVE-BEHAVIORAL FAMILY THERAPY

Beyond Stimulus and Response

Sketches of Leading Figures

The early principles of behavior therapy were developed by two key figures: Joseph Wolpe and B. F. Skinner. In 1948 Wolpe introduced *systematic desensitization*, with which he achieved great success in the treatment of phobias. Systematic desensitization deconditions anxiety through *reciprocal inhibition* by pairing responses incompatible with anxiety to previously anxiety-arousing stimuli. Thus, for example, if a woman was afraid of spiders, Wolpe would teach her deep muscle relaxation and then have her imagine approaching a spider in gradual steps. Each time the woman became anxious, she would be told to relax. In this way her anxiety about spiders would be systematically extinguished.

An even greater influence on behavioral therapy was Skinner's **operant conditioning**. While most people look to the past for the cause of problems, *Skinner* taught us that behavior is regulated by its consequences. Responses that are *positively reinforced* will be increased; those that are *punished* or ignored will be *extinguished*.

The operant conditioner carefully observes target behavior and quantifies its frequency and rate. Then, to complete a **functional analysis of behavior**, the consequences of the behavior are noted to determine the *contingencies of reinforcement*. For example, someone interested in a child's temper tantrums

LEARNING OUTCOMES

♦ Describe the evolution of cognitive-behavioral family therapy.

♦ Describe the main tenets of cognitive-behavioral family therapy.

♦ Describe healthy and unhealthy family development from a cognitive-behavioral perspective.

♦ Describe the clinical goals and the conditions necessary for meeting those goals from a cognitive-behavioral family therapy perspective.

♦ Discuss and demonstrate the assessment and intervention techniques of cognitive-behavioral family therapy.

♦ Discuss research support for cognitive-behavioral family therapy.

would begin by observing when they occurred and what the consequences were. A typical finding might be that the child throws a tantrum whenever his parents deny his requests and that the parents give in if the tantrums are prolonged. Thus the parents would be reinforcing the very behavior they objected to.

Operant conditioning is particularly effective with children because parents have control over their rewards and punishment. Gerald Patterson, at the Oregon Social Learning Center, pioneered behavioral parent training. Patterson's treatment was based on the premise that if parents change their contingencies of reinforcement, then their children's behavior will change. An excellent example of Patterson's approach is described in *Case Studies in Couple and Family Therapy* (Forgatch & Patterson, 1998). In this case, the therapist taught a single mother to develop a family management program to encourage her unruly child with prosocial behavior and discourage his misbehavior. The mother learned to do this gradually with skills taught in sequence (*shaping*). She was first helped to define her child's positive and problematic behaviors in terms of specific and readily observable actions. After a week of keeping track of her child's target behaviors, the mother was taught to reinforce prosocial behavior through contingent encouragement with incentive charts. This process also promotes positive relationships between parents and children. Children earn rewards while they learn prosocial skills and, in the process, their self-esteem grows with their success and their parents' positive attention.

Patterson also took the lead in introducing disciplinary techniques, such as time-out, because he discovered that ignoring problem behavior is not always sufficient, especially with aggressive children. Among others prominent in behavioral parent training are Anthony Graziano, Rex Forehand, Daniel and Susan O'Leary, and Roger McAuley.

During the 1970s, behavioral family therapy evolved into three major packages: parent training, behavioral couples therapy, and sex therapy. At present, the leading figures in behavioral couples therapy include Robert Weiss, Richard Stuart, Michael Crowe, Mark Dadds, Ian Falloon, Gayola Margolin, and Matthew Sanders.

While the behavioral approach, with its emphasis on stimulus and response, was initially seen as linear and simplistic by family systems therapists, behaviorists have grown increasingly sophisticated in their understanding of family dynamics. The late Ian Falloon, for example, was a strong proponent of an open systems approach. He considered the physiological status of individuals as well as their cognitive-behavioral and emotional responses, along with the interpersonal transactions that occur within their family, social, vocational, political, and cultural networks (Falloon, 1985).

Cognitive-behavioral therapy refers to those approaches inspired by the work of Albert Ellis (1962) and Aaron Beck (1976) that emphasize the need for attitude change to promote behavior modification. According to the *cognitive mediation model* (Beck, 1976), emotions and actions are mediated by specific cognitions. Understanding these cognitions (beliefs, attributions, and expectancies) makes it possible to identify factors that trigger dysfunctional emotional and behavioral patterns. In practice, this boils down to uncovering hidden assumptions that keep people stuck.

Rational-emotive therapists help family members see how illogical beliefs serve as the foundation for their emotional distress. According to the *A-B-C theory*, family members blame their problems on certain events in the family (A) and are taught to look for irrational beliefs (B), which are then challenged (C). The therapist's role is to teach the family how emotional problems are caused by unrealistic beliefs and that, by revising these self-defeating ideas, they may improve the quality of family life (Ellis, 1978).

The cognitive-behavior method, which balances an emphasis on cognition and behavior, takes a more expansive approach by focusing in greater depth on patterns of family interaction (Epstein, Schlesinger, & Dryden, 1988; Leslie, 1988). Cognitions, emotions, and behavior are seen as exerting mutual influence on one another, so that a cognitive inference can evoke emotion and behavior, and emotion and behavior can influence cognition.

The late 1980s and early 1990s saw the cognitive-behavior approach applied more widely in family therapy. Edited books by Epstein, Schlesinger, and Dryden (1988) and a short text by Huber and Baruth (1989) were among the first works to address the cognitive approach to family therapy. This was elaborated in subsequent articles by Schwebel and Fine (1992), Dattilio (1994, 1997), and Teichman (1992). Dattilio

(1998) produced a major casebook that discusses the integration of cognitive-behavioral strategies with various modalities of couples and family therapy, as well as a comprehensive textbook describing the cognitive-behavioral approach (Dattilio, 2010). Among the leaders in cognitive-behavioral family therapy are Donald Baucom at the University of North Carolina, Norman Epstein at the University of Maryland, and Frank Dattilio at Harvard Medical School and the University of Pennsylvania.

Theoretical Formulations

The basic premise of behaviorism is that behavior is maintained by its consequences. Consequences that increase behavior are *reinforcers*; those that decrease behavior are *punishers*.

Some responses may not be recognized as operants—something done to get something—because people aren't aware of the reinforcing payoffs. For example, whining is often reinforced by attention, although the people doing the reinforcing may not realize it.

As behavior therapists shifted their attention from individuals to family relationships, they came to rely on Thibaut and Kelley's (1959) **theory of social exchange**, according to which people strive to maximize rewards and minimize costs in relationships. In a successful relationship partners work to maximize mutual rewards. In unsuccessful relationships the partners are too busy protecting themselves from getting hurt to consider how to make each other happy.

Despite the mechanistic sound of "maximizing rewards and minimizing costs," behavior therapists have increasingly become aware that people not only act but also think and feel. This recognition has led to efforts to integrate stimulus-response behaviorism (Skinner, 1953) with cognitive theories (Mahoney, 1977). The central tenet of the cognitive approach is that our interpretation of other people's behavior affects the way we respond to them. Among the most troublesome of automatic thoughts are those based on *arbitrary inference*, distorted conclusions, shaped by a person's **schemas**, or core beliefs. What makes

these underlying beliefs problematic is that although they are generally not conscious, they bias how we respond to everything and everyone.

Family Dynamics

By teaching us that behavior is maintained by its consequences, behaviorists have given us a simple but powerful way to understand what makes relationships flourish, or flounder. By pointing out that hidden assumptions have a potent impact on how people perceive and react to each other, cognitive-behaviorists have added depth and richness to the behavioral model.

◆ Normal Family Functioning

According to **behavior exchange theory** (Thibaut & Kelley, 1959), a good relationship is one in which giving and getting are balanced—or, in the model's terms, there is a high ratio of benefits to costs. Examples of "costs" might be a spouse's outbursts of temper or one sibling borrowing another's clothes without asking. In some relationships costs are outweighed by rewards, such as a spouse's affection or siblings' loyalty to each other. Thus it is the balance of costs and rewards that determines family satisfaction.

Weiss and Isaac (1978) found that affection, communication, and child care are the most important elements in marital satisfaction. Earlier, Wills, Weiss, and Patterson (1974) found that unpleasant behavior reduced marital satisfaction more than positive behavior increased it. A good relationship, then, is one in which there is an exchange of positive responses and, even more important, minimal unpleasantness. Another way of putting this is that good relationships are under *positive reinforcement control*.

In time all couples run into conflict and, therefore, a critical skill in maintaining family harmony is conflict resolution (Gottman & Krokoff, 1989). Healthy families aren't problem free, but they have the ability to resolve conflicts when they arise. They focus on issues and keep them in perspective, and they discuss specific behaviors of concern to them. They describe their own feelings and request changes in the behavior of others, rather than just criticizing and complaining. "I've been feeling lonely and I wish you and I could go out more often" is more likely to get a positive response than "You never do anything I want!"

Some people assume that good relationships will evolve naturally if people love each other. Behaviorists emphasize the need to develop relationship skills. Good marriages, they believe, aren't made in heaven but are a product of learning effective coping behavior. The late Neil Jacobson (1981) described a good relationship as one in which the partners work to maintain a high rate of rewards:

> Successful couples . . . expand their reinforcement power by frequently acquiring new domains for positive exchange. Spouses who depend on a limited quantity and variety of reinforcers are bound to suffer the ill effects of satiation. As a result, over time their interaction becomes depleted of its prior reinforcement value. Successful couples cope with this inevitable reinforcement erosion by varying their shared activities, developing new common interests, expanding their sexual repertoires, and developing their communication to the point where they continue to interest one another. (p. 561)

◆ Development of Behavior Disorders

Behaviorists view symptoms as learned responses. They don't look for hidden motives or blame marital conflict for children's problems. Instead they look for specific responses that reinforce problem behavior.

At first glance it might seem puzzling that family members would reinforce undesirable behavior. Why would parents reward temper tantrums? Why would a wife reinforce her husband's distance? The answer lies not in some convoluted motive for suffering but in the simple fact that people often aren't aware that they reinforce those responses that cause them the most distress.

Parents commonly respond to misbehavior by scolding and lecturing. These responses may seem like punishment, but they may in fact be reinforcing, because attention—even from a critical parent—is a powerful *social reinforcer* (Skinner, 1953). The truth

of this is reflected in the axiom, "Ignore it, and it will go away."

The problem is most parents have trouble ignoring misbehavior. Notice, for example, how quickly children learn that certain words get a big reaction.[1] Moreover, even when parents do try to ignore misbehavior, they usually don't do so consistently. This can make things worse, because *intermittent reinforcement* is the most resistant to extinction (Ferster, 1963). That's why compulsive gambling is so difficult to extinguish.

In addition to behavior problems unwittingly maintained by parental attention, others persist because parents don't know how to make effective use of punishment. They make threats they don't follow through on; they punish too long after the fact; they use punishments so mild as to have no effect; or they use punishments so severe as to generate more anxiety than learning.

Learning, moreover, isn't just a one-way street. Consider the behavior of a mother and daughter in the supermarket:

> The little girl asks her mother for a candy bar. The mother says no. The child begins crying and complaining. The mother says, "If you think I'm going to buy you candy when you make such a fuss, you have another thing coming, young lady!" But the child escalates her tantrum, getting louder and louder. Finally, exasperated and embarrassed, the mother gives in: "All right, if you'll quiet down, I'll buy you some cookies."

Obviously, the child has been reinforced for having a tantrum. Not so obvious, but also true, the mother has been reinforced for giving in—by the child's calming down. Thus a spiral of undesirable behavior is maintained by *reciprocal reinforcement*.

The reinforcement of undesirable behavior can take even more complex forms in family dynamics. The following is a typical example: A mother, father, and small child are riding in the car. The father speeds up to make it through a yellow light. His wife insists

[1]Some of these children grow up to become stand-up comedians.

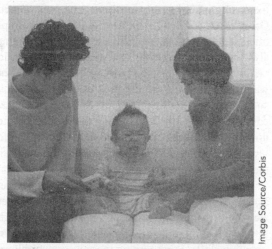

Parents often unintentionally reinforce temper tantrums by giving in or merely by giving the tantruming child extra attention.

that he slow down and drive more carefully. The father, who hates being told what to do, gets angry and starts driving faster. Now his wife yells at him to slow down. The argument escalates until the child, crying, says, "Don't fight, Mommy and Daddy!" Mother turns to the child and says, "It's okay, honey. Don't cry." Father feels guilty and begins to slow down. Consequently, the child learns at a young age the power and control she has in the family.

The use of **aversive control**—crying, nagging, withdrawing—is a major determinant of marital unhappiness (Stuart, 1975). Spouses tend to reciprocate their partners' use of aversive behavior, and a vicious cycle develops (Patterson & Reid, 1970).

People in distressed relationships also show poor *problem-solving skills* (Vincent, Weiss, & Birchler, 1975; Weiss, Hops, & Patterson, 1973). When discussing a problem, they frequently change the subject; they phrase wishes and complaints in vague and critical ways; and they respond to complaints with countercomplaints. The following exchange demonstrates sidetracking, cross-complaining, and name-calling, all typical of distressed marriages:

> "I'd like to talk about all the sweets you've been giving the kids lately."

> "What sweets! Talk about *me*, you're always stuffing your face. And what do you ever do for the kids? You just come home and complain. Why don't you just stay at the office! The kids and I get along better without you."

Most behavioral analyses point to a lack of reinforcement for positive behavior in distressed families. The old adage "The squeaky wheel gets the grease" seems to apply. Depression, headaches, and temper tantrums tend to elicit concern and therefore get more attention than pleasant behavior. Because this process is unwitting, family members are often mystified about their role in reinforcing annoying behavior.

According to cognitive-behaviorists, the schemas that plague relationships are learned in the process of growing up. Some of these dysfunctional beliefs are assumptions about specific family roles, while others are about family life in general. These schemas are the basis of biased assumptions that poison relationships by distorting family members' responses to each other. The following are typical cognitive distortions:

1. Arbitrary inference: Conclusions are drawn in the absence of supporting evidence; for example, a man whose wife arrives home late from work concludes, "She must be having an affair," or parents whose child comes home late assume, "He must be up to no good."

2. Selective abstraction: Certain details are highlighted while other important information is ignored; for example, a woman whose husband fails to answer her greeting first thing in the morning concludes, "He must be angry at me again," or a child who is in a bad mood may be perceived by his or her siblings as ignoring them.

3. Overgeneralization: Isolated incidents are taken as general patterns; for example, after being turned down for a date, a young man decides that "Women don't like me; I'll never get a date"; or a teenager whose parents deny him a night out generalizes to, "They never let me do anything."

4. Magnification and minimization: The significance of events is unrealistically magnified or diminished; for example, a husband considers the two times in one month he shops for groceries as fulfilling his share of the household duties, while his wife thinks, "He never does anything."

5. Personalization: Events are arbitrarily interpreted in reference to oneself; for example, a teenager wants to spend more time with his friends, so his father assumes that his son doesn't enjoy his company.

6. Dichotomous thinking: Experiences are interpreted as all good or all bad; for example, Jack and Diane have some good times and some bad times, but he remembers only the good times, while she remembers only the bad times.

7. Labeling and mislabeling: Behavior is attributed to undesirable personality traits; for example, a woman who avoids talking with her mother about her career because her mother always criticizes is considered "withholding."

8. Mind reading: This is the magical gift of knowing what other people are thinking without the aid of verbal communication; for example, a husband doesn't ask his wife what she wants because he "knows what's going on in her mind"; and children often believe that their parents know what is bothering them without them having to express themselves.

Mechanisms of Change

Although the cognitive aspect of cognitive-behavior therapy gets the lion's share of attention these days, it's well to remember that, in this model, cognitive restructuring is useful to the extent that it leads to changed behavior, which can then be reinforced.

Goals of Therapy

Cognitive-behavior therapists tailor treatment to fit the case, but the general intent is to extinguish undesired behavior and reinforce positive alternatives (Azrin, Naster, & Jones, 1973). Thus, for example, parents of a child with temper tantrums might be taught to ignore the tantrums and reward the child for putting his feelings into words.

Sometimes it may be necessary to redefine a family's goal of decreasing negative behavior in terms of increasing incompatible, positive responses (Umana, Gross, & McConville, 1980). Couples, for example, often state their goals negatively: "I wish he wouldn't always argue with me" or "She nags too much." Most people have difficulty describing behavior that they want their mates to accelerate. To help them do so, some therapists (Azrin, Naster, & Jones, 1973) ask couples to make a list of pleasing things their partners do during the week. Reviewing these lists in the following session provides an opportunity to emphasize the importance of positive feedback.

Cognitive-behavior therapy also has an educational agenda. In addition to applying learning theory to alleviate specific behavioral problems, cognitive-behaviorists also teach communication, problem-solving, and negotiation skills. Furthermore, these therapists not only help clients reexamine distorted beliefs to solve specific complaints, but also make an effort to teach families how to use cognitive strategies to resolve problems in the future.

Conditions for Behavior Change

The basic premise of behavior therapy is that behavior will change when the contingencies of reinforcement are altered. Behavioral family therapy aims to resolve targeted family problems through identifying behavioral goals, learning theory techniques for achieving these goals, and social reinforcers to facilitate this process.

The first task of the therapist is to observe the frequency of problem behavior, as well as the stimulus conditions that precede it and the reinforcement that follows it. In addition to the reinforcing responses that immediately follow a specific behavior, more remote reinforcers also play a part. These may include tacit approval of aggressive behavior, particularly by men in the family, often accompanied by modeling of this behavior. Spanking children for fighting demonstrates by example the violence a parent may wish to discourage. In addition, behavior that is reinforced by peers may be difficult to modify at home—especially if the therapist fails to take this wider context into account.

The primary approach in behavioral parent training is operant conditioning, where the reinforcers

Behavior therapists teach parents to use positive reinforcement rather than aversive control.

employed may be tangible or social. In fact, praise and attention have been found to be as effective as money or candy (Bandura, 1969). Operant techniques may be further divided into *shaping, token economies, contingency contracting, contingency management,* and *time-out.*

Shaping (Schwitzgebel & Kolb, 1964) consists of reinforcing change in small steps. **Token economies** (Baer & Sherman, 1969) use points to reward children for good behavior. **Contingency contracting** (Stuart, 1971) involves agreements by parents to make certain changes following changes made by their children. **Contingency management** (Schwitzgebel, 1967) consists of giving and taking away rewards based on children's behavior. **Time-out** (Rimm & Masters, 1974) is a punishment where children are made to sit in the corner or sent to their rooms.

Barton and Alexander, who call their approach *functional family therapy* (Barton & Alexander, 1981; Morris, Alexander, & Waldron, 1988), point out that members of unhappy families tend to attribute their problems to negative traits in others (laziness, irresponsibility, poor impulse control). Such negative

attributions leave family members with a limited sense of control over their lives. After all, what can one person do to change another person's "laziness," "irresponsibility," or "poor impulse control"?

Because cognitive appraisal plays such a significant role in how family members respond, restructuring distorted beliefs is thought to play a pivotal role in changing dysfunctional behavior. Thus, uncovering and reevaluating schemas, or core beliefs, of family members is thought to be essential in helping them modify emotions and interactions that surround problem behavior.

Therapy

◆ Behavioral Parent Training

Assessment

In common with other forms of behavior therapy, parent training begins with a thorough assessment. While the procedure varies from clinic to clinic, most assessments are based on Kanfer and Phillips's (1970)

SORKC model of behavior: S for stimulus, O for the state of the organism, R for the target response, and KC for the contingency of consequences. For example, in the case of parents who complain that their son pesters them for cookies between meals and throws tantrums if they don't give him any, the tantrums would be considered the target behavior, R. O, the state of the organism, might turn out to be hunger or, more likely, boredom. The stimulus, S, might be the sight of cookies in the cookie jar; and the contingency of consequences, KC, might be that the parents give in by feeding the boy cookies occasionally, especially if he makes enough of a fuss.

In simple cases such as this applying the SORKC model is straightforward, but it quickly becomes more complex with families, in which there are long chains of interrelated behavior. Consider the following.

CASE STUDY

Mr. and Mrs. J. complained that their two small children whine and fuss at the dinner table. A home observation reveals that when Mr. J. yells at the children for misbehaving, they start to whine and stand by their mother's chair.

Given this sequence it's not difficult to apply the SORKC model. Imagine, however, that the above sequence is only part of a more complex picture.

In the morning, Mr. J. makes a sexual overture to his wife, but she, tired from taking care of the children, rolls over and goes back to sleep. Mr. J. is hurt and leaves for work after making some unkind remarks to his wife. She, feeling rejected by her husband, spends the entire day playing with the children for solace.

By the time she has to cook dinner, Mrs. J. is exasperated with the children. Mr. J. comes home after a hard day at the office and tries to make up with his wife by hugging her. She responds but only perfunctorily because she's busy trying to cook. While she's at the stove, the children and Mr. J. vie for her attention, each one wanting to tell her something. Finally, she blows up—at her husband—"Can't you see I'm busy!" He goes into the den and sulks until dinner is ready.

Just as his wife finds it difficult to express her anger at the children and takes it out on him, Mr. J. has trouble directing anger at his wife and so tends to divert it onto the children. At the dinner table he yells at them for the slightest infraction, at which point they whine and turn to their mother. She lets one sit on her lap while she strokes the other's hair.

In this longer, but not atypical sequence, what is stimulus and what is response? Obviously these definitions become circular, and their application depends on the perspective of the observer.

Assessment in behavioral parent training entails observing and recording the frequency of the behavior to be changed, as well as the events that precede it and those that follow. Interviews, usually with the mother, are designed to provide a definition of the problem and a list of potential reinforcers. Observations may be conducted behind a one-way mirror or during home visits. Typically, parents are trained to pinpoint problem behavior, record its occurrence, and note various actions that might serve as stimuli and reinforcers. Checklists and questionnaires provide information that may have been overlooked in interviews.

Therapeutic Techniques

Once the assessment is complete, the therapist decides which behaviors should be increased and which decreased. To accelerate behavior, the **Premack principle** (Premack, 1965) is applied; that is, high-probability behavior (popular activities) is chosen to reinforce behavior with a low probability of occurrence. Where once it was thought that reinforcers must satisfy some basic drive, such as hunger or thirst, it's now known that any behavior chosen more frequently (given a variety of choices) can serve as a reinforcer for those chosen less frequently.

CASE STUDY

Mrs. G. complained that she couldn't get her five-year-old son Adam to clean his room in the morning. She went on to say that she tried rewarding him with candy, money, and toys, but "Nothing works!" A functional analysis of Adam's behavior revealed that, given his choice of things to do, the most probable behaviors were watching television, riding his bicycle, and playing in the mud behind his house. Once these activities were made contingent on tidying his room, he quickly learned to do so.

A variety of material and social reinforcers have been used to accelerate desired behaviors, but as the Premack principle demonstrates, to be effective, reinforcers must be popular with the child. Although money and candy seem like powerful rewards, they may not be as effective for some children as a chance to play in the mud.

Once effective rewards are chosen, parents are taught to *shape* desired behavior by reinforcing successive approximation to their goals. They are taught to raise the criteria for reinforcement gradually and to present reinforcement immediately after the desired behavior.[2] Once a child is regularly performing the desired response, reinforcement becomes intermittent in order to increase the durability of the new behavior.

Disciplinary techniques are usually instituted after progress has been made in reinforcing positive behavior. For preadolescent children, the most widely used punishment is *time-out*. Time-out involves removal to a boring place for five minutes. (Older children are sent to graduate school and required to sit through lectures.) When a child refuses to go to time-out, parents are taught to add additional time, up to a ten-minute maximum. If the child continues to refuse, a privilege is removed. When parents are consistent, children soon learn to go to time-out rather than lose the opportunity to watch TV or use the computer.

Other techniques used to decelerate behavior include verbal reprimand and ignoring. Simply repeating commands to children is the most ineffective way to change their behavior (Forehand, Roberts, Doleys, Hobbs, & Resnick, 1976). Chores are broken down into steps, with points given for each step. Rewards include food treats, special time with a parent, household resources (e.g., computer or TV time), privileges, and toys. Rewards are changed regularly to keep things interesting.

Because of the inconvenience of reinforcing behavior immediately, token systems have been popular with parent trainers. Points are earned for desirable behavior and lost for undesirable behavior (Christophersen, Arnold, Hill, & Quilitch, 1972).

[2]The importance of immediate proximity is what makes time-out such an effective punishment and grounding such an ineffective one.

Design Pics Inc/Alamy

Time-out is a highly effective form of punishment for young children.

CASE STUDY

Mrs. F. is a mother of two small children who came to the clinic complaining of headaches and crying spells. The intake interviewer found her to be mildly depressed and concluded that the depression was primarily a reaction to difficulty coping with her children. Suzie, age five, was a shy child who had frequent temper tantrums. Robert, who was eight, was more sociable but did poorly in school. The children were a handful, and Mrs. F. felt helpless in dealing with them.

A functional analysis of behavior revealed that Suzie's shyness resulted in extra attention from her anxious mother. Whenever Suzie declined an invitation to play with other children, her mother spent a great deal of time doing things to make her feel better. The therapist selected social behavior (not shyness) as the first target response and instructed Mrs. F. to reinforce all efforts at socializing and to ignore Suzie when she avoided social contact. Thereafter, whenever Suzie made any attempt to socialize with other children, Mrs. F. would immediately reinforce her with attention and praise. When Suzie chose to stay home rather than play with other children, her mother ignored her, instead busying herself with her own activities. In three weeks, Mrs. F. reported that Suzie "seemed to have gotten over her shyness."

Following this initial success the therapist felt it was time to help Mrs. F. tackle the more difficult problem of Suzie's tantrums. Since the tantrums were unlikely to occur while the family was at the clinic or during home visits, the therapist instructed Mrs. F. to make observational notes for a week. These notes revealed that Suzie generally had tantrums when her parents denied her requests for a treat or some special indulgence, such as staying up to watch television. Tantrums were especially likely to occur at the end of the day when Suzie (and her parents) was tired. As for how the parents responded to these maddening outbursts, Mrs. F. reported, "We've tried everything. Sometimes we try to ignore her, but that's impossible; she just screams and shrieks until we can't stand it anymore. Then sometimes we spank her—or give her what she wants, just to shut her up. Sometimes after we spank her she cries so much that we let her watch television until she calms down. That usually works."

After listening to this description, the therapist explained how Mr. and Mrs. F. had inadvertently been reinforcing the tantrums and told them what they would have to do to stop them. For the next week, the F.'s were instructed to ignore fits of temper whenever they occurred. If they occurred at bedtime, Suzie was to be put in bed; if she continued to cry and fuss, she was to be left alone until she stopped. Only when she stopped were her parents to talk with her about what was on her mind.

The following week Mrs. F. reported that the tantrums had indeed decreased, except for one night when they took on a new and more troubling form. When Suzie was told that she wouldn't be able to stay up late to watch television she began to yell and cry as usual. Instead of relenting, Mrs. F. put Suzie in her room and told her to get ready for bed. However, realizing that her parents were going to ignore her, as they had earlier in the week, Suzie began to scream and smash things in her room. "It was awful; she was completely out of control. She even smashed the little dog-shaped lamp I bought her. We didn't know what to do, so just that once we let her stay up." Again the therapist described the consequences of such behavior and explained to Mrs. F. how, should Suzie again become destructive, both parents should hold her until the tantrum subsided.

At the next session, Mrs. F. described how Suzie did "get out of control again." This time, however, instead of giving in, the parents held her as they had been told. Mrs. F. was amazed at the fury and duration of the resulting tantrum. "But we remembered what you said—there was no way we were going to

give in!" It took twenty minutes, but Suzie finally calmed down. This, it turned out, was the last time Suzie ever became violent during a temper tantrum. Nevertheless she did continue to have occasional flare-ups during the next few weeks.

According to Mrs. F., the few tantrums that did occur seemed to take place in different settings or under different conditions than the usual episodes at home (which Suzie had now learned would not be reinforced). For example, one episode took place in the supermarket when Suzie was told she couldn't have a candy bar. By this time, however, Mrs. F. was thoroughly convinced of the necessity of not reinforcing the tantrums, and so she didn't. Because she was embarrassed at all the noise her daughter was making in public, she did find it necessary to take Suzie out of the store. But she made Suzie sit in the car and took pains not to let it be a pleasant experience. Very few tantrums followed this one.

Next the therapist turned her attention to Robert's school performance. A careful assessment revealed that Robert usually denied that he had any homework. After checking with Robert's teacher the therapist discovered that the children generally did have homework and that they were expected to work between thirty minutes and an hour a night. Mrs. F. selected a high-probability behavior, watching television, and made it contingent on Robert's having completed his homework. For the first two weeks of this regimen, Mrs. F. found it necessary to call the teacher every night to verify the assignments. But soon this was no longer necessary. Doing homework fairly quickly became a habit for Robert, and his grades increased from D's and C's to B's and A's. At this point, everyone was happier, and Mrs. F. felt the family no longer needed help.

A follow-up session in the fall found things continuing to go well. Suzie was now much more sociable and hadn't had any temper tantrums in months. Robert was doing well in school, although he had begun to neglect some of his more difficult assignments. To address this, the therapist explained to Mrs. F. how to institute a token system, and she was able to use it with excellent results.

With teenagers, contingency contracting (Alexander & Parsons, 1973; Rinn, 1978) is more widely used. Contracting is introduced as a way for everybody in the family to get something by compromising. Parents and teenagers are asked to specify what behavior they'd like each other to change. These requests form the nucleus of an initial contract. In order to help family members arrive at contracts, the therapist encourages: (1) clear communication of wishes and feelings, (2) clear presentation of requests, leading to (3) negotiation, with each person receiving something in exchange for some concession.

◆ Behavioral Couples Therapy

Assessment

As with parent training, behavioral couples therapy begins with a thorough assessment. This process usually includes clinical interviews, ratings of specific target behaviors, and marital satisfaction questionnaires. The most widely used is the Locke–Wallace Marital Adjustment Scale (Locke & Wallace, 1959), a twenty-three-item questionnaire covering various aspects of marital satisfaction, including communication, sex, affection, social activities, and values.

Assessments are designed to reveal strengths and weaknesses of a couple's relationship and the manner in which rewards and punishments are exchanged. Interviews and questionnaires are used to specify and elaborate target behaviors. Jacobson (1981) offers an outline for pretreatment assessment (see Table 9.1).

Therapeutic Techniques

Richard Stuart (1975) lists five strategies that summarize the behavioral approach to troubled marriages:

1. Couples are taught to express themselves in clear, behavioral descriptions, rather than in vague complaints.

2. Couples are taught new behavior exchange procedures, emphasizing positive control in place of aversive control.

3. Couples are helped to improve their communication.

4. Couples are encouraged to establish clear and effective means of sharing power and making decisions.

5. Couples are taught strategies for solving future problems as a means to maintain and extend gains initiated in therapy.

Behavior exchange theory procedures are taught to increase the frequency of desired behavior. A typical device is to ask each partner to list three things he or she would like the other to do more often. While explicitly exchanging "strokes" in this way, couples are implicitly learning ways of influencing each other through positive reinforcement. Stuart (1976) has couples alternate "caring days," where one partner demonstrates caring in as many ways as possible.

The following vignette, taken from a video workshop series, illustrates how Stuart concentrates on helping couples learn to make each other happy, rather than trying to solve the problems that bring them to therapy.

CASE STUDY

Wesley and Adele are a middle-aged, working-class couple. This is her third marriage and his fourth. Wesley feels rejected because Adele frequently works late; at the same time, she feels that he isn't affectionate with her and that he pulls away whenever she makes a sexual overture. Dr. Stuart begins with a brief family history of each spouse and then explores the history of their relationship. In the second half of the interview, Dr. Stuart offers suggestions for improving the couple's relationship by making an effort to act "as if" things were good and they cared for each other.

When Stuart tells the couple that they can *choose* to make their marriage work by acting in loving ways toward each other, they seem a little skeptical. When Adele reveals that she doesn't know if Wesley is committed to staying in the relationship, Dr. Stuart suggests that she needs to feel safe in his commitment and, using the example of his own marriage, tells them again that they can accentuate the positive by making a point of expressing their caring for each other.

Later Stuart suggests that Wesley start acting "as if" he felt close to Adele and reassures him that if he acts affectionately, she will respond in kind. Again, Stuart uses his own marriage as an example of how two people can make themselves happy by making a point of acting lovingly toward each other. In fact, he guarantees Wesley that if he acts affectionately Adele will respond, and Stuart asks Wesley to agree to try doing so as an experiment. Though they still seem a little skeptical, both Wesley and Adele agree to try the idea of acting positively toward each other.

TABLE 9.1   Jacobson's Pretreatment Assessment for Marital Therapy

A. Strengths and skills of the relationship

What are the major strengths of this relationship?

What behaviors on the part of each spouse are highly valued by the other?

What shared activities does the couple currently engage in?

B. Presenting problems

What are the major complaints, and how do these complaints translate into explicit behavioral terms?

What are the reinforcers maintaining these behaviors?

What behaviors occur at less than the desired frequency or fail to occur at appropriate times from the standpoint of each spouse?

What are the consequences of these behaviors currently, when they occur?

C. Sex and affection

Is either spouse currently dissatisfied with rate, quality, or diversity of sex life together?

If sex is currently a problem, was there a time when it was mutually satisfying?

What are the sexual behaviors that seem to be associated with current dissatisfaction?

Are either or both partners dissatisfied with the amount or quality of nonsexual physical affection?

D. Future prospects

Are the partners seeking therapy to improve their relationship, to separate, or to decide whether the relationship is worth working on?

What are each spouse's reasons for continuing the relationship despite current problems?

E. Assessment of social environment

What are each person's alternatives to the present relationship?

How attractive are these alternatives to each person?

Is the environment (parents, relatives, friends, work associates, children) supportive of either continuance or dissolution of present relationship?

F. Individual functioning of each spouse

Does either spouse exhibit emotional or behavioral problems?

Have they been in therapy before, either alone or together? What kind of therapy? Outcome?

What is each spouse's past experience with intimate relationships?

How is the present relationship different?

Source: Adapted from: Jacobson, N. S. 1981. Behavioral marital therapy. In *Handbook of Family Therapy*, A. S. Gurman and D. P. Kniskern, eds. (pp. 565–566). Reproduced by permission of Taylor and Francis Group, LLC, a division of Informa plc.

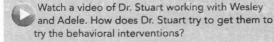
Watch a video of Dr. Stuart working with Wesley and Adele. How does Dr. Stuart try to get them to try the behavioral interventions?

In a carefully designed longitudinal study, Gottman and Krokoff (1989) found that arguments and angry exchanges, which have often been considered destructive to relationships, may not be harmful in the long run. These patterns were correlated with immediate dissatisfaction but were predictive of improved satisfaction after three years. Defensiveness, stubbornness, and withdrawal from conflict, on the other hand, *did* lead to long-term deterioration in marriages. Conflict makes most people uneasy, but it may be an essential prelude to facing and solving problems. The anger that accompanies direct expression of dissatisfaction may be painful, but it may also be healthy. Gottman and Krokoff (1989) conclude, "If the wife must introduce and elaborate disagreements in marriages, our data suggest that, for the sake of long-term improvement in marital satisfaction, she may need to do this by getting her husband to confront areas of disagreement and to openly vent disagreement and anger" (p. 51). In other words, confrontation is effective only if it doesn't make the partner defensive. It isn't just honesty that counts but honesty expressed in a way the partner can tolerate.

Training in communications skills may be done in a group format (Hickman & Baldwin, 1971; Pierce, 1973) or with individual couples. Couples are taught to be specific, phrase requests in positive terms, respond directly to criticism instead of cross-complaining, talk about the present and future rather than the past, listen without interruption, minimize punitive statements, and eliminate questions that sound like declarations.

Once a couple has learned to communicate in ways that are conducive to problem solving, they are introduced to the principles of contingency contracting— agreeing to make changes contingent on the partner making changes. In **quid pro quo** contracts (Knox, 1971), one partner agrees to make a change after a prior change by the other. Each partner specifies desired behavior changes, and with the therapist's help they negotiate agreements. At the end of the session a written list is made and both partners sign it.

An alternative form of contracting is a *good faith contract*, in which partners agree to make changes that aren't contingent on what the other does (Weiss, Hops, & Patterson, 1973). Each partner's independent changes are independently reinforced. For example, a husband who comes home each night by 6:00 p.m. and plays with the children after supper might reward himself by buying a new shirt at the end of the week or be rewarded by his wife with a back rub.

Problem-solving training is used in situations that are too complicated for simple exchange agreements.

Negotiations are preceded by a careful definition of problems. Discussions are limited to one problem at a time. Each person begins by paraphrasing what the other has said, and they are taught to avoid inferences about motivation—especially inferences of malevolent intent. They're encouraged to avoid aversive responses. When defining a problem, it's more effective to begin with a positive statement; instead of saying, "You never . . .," partners are taught to say, "I appreciate the way you . . . and in addition I wish. . . ."

The following guidelines for problem-solving communication are adapted from *The Lost Art of Listening* (Nichols, 2009).

1. Speak for yourself and express your perspective as your own thoughts and feelings, not as absolute truths.

2. Ask for what you want in the form of specific requests, not general complaints.

3. Speak calmly and don't go on and on. Give your partner a chance to respond.

4. Knock to enter: Don't try to talk when your partner is unprepared or is doing something else.

5. Invite your partner to express his or her thoughts and feelings.

6. Listen with the intent to understand, rather than just waiting to respond.

7. Try to understand what the other person is feeling, rather than just reacting to the words.

8. Let your partner know that you understand by acknowledging what he or she has said—and invite him or her to elaborate or correct your impression.

9. When there is major conflict or misunderstanding, devote one entire conversation to drawing out and acknowledging your partner's point of view. Wait until you've demonstrated that you understand him or her before trying to express your side, perhaps in a subsequent conversation.

10. When it comes to discussing solutions, invite your partner's ideas first. Listen to and acknowledge those ideas.

11. When suggesting your own solutions, make sure they address both of your needs.

12. Find a solution that's agreeable to both of you, but plan to implement it on a trial basis, and review the solution at the end of the trial period.

The Cognitive-Behavioral Approach to Family Therapy

Assessment

The goals of a cognitive-behavioral assessment are to (1) identify strengths and problems in individuals, the couple or family, and the environment; (2) place individual and family functioning in the context of developmental stages; and (3) identify cognitive, emotional, and behavioral aspects of family interaction that might be targeted for intervention.

Among the family patterns of interaction therapists look for are the style and degree to which family members express their thoughts and feelings to each other, who interrupts whom, and who speaks for whom. These unstructured observations may be supplemented by structured communication tasks in the initial interview (Epstein & Baucom, 2002). Based on information provided by the clients, a therapist can select an unresolved issue in the family and ask them to spend ten minutes or so discussing it. Family members might be asked just to express their feelings about the topic at hand, or they might be asked to try to resolve the issue in the allotted time. Either way, the therapist has an opportunity to observe how family members think about their problems and how they interact with one another.

Some cognitive-behaviorists use coding systems, such as the Marital Interaction Coding System-IV (Heyman, Eddy, Weiss, & Vivian, 1995), as guidelines for identifying sequences of family members' interactions (e.g., positive physical contact, constructive and counterproductive behavior, and complaints). These results yield hypotheses which then require verification through repeated observations and reports from family members about their interactions at home.

For example, if parents say that they have rules for their teenage son and that they work together to enforce them, a therapist might assume that there is a clear power hierarchy in the family. However, if in a subsequent interview the son says that he can easily bend the rules and usually talk his parents out of

punishments, and later the parents fail to respond when their son repeatedly interrupts them, the therapist might revise the initial hypothesis and conclude that the parents have little authority and are disorganized in their parenting skills.

After collecting sufficient information from interviews, questionnaires, and behavioral observations, the therapist meets with the family and offers a summary of the patterns that have emerged, including the family's strengths, major concerns, stressors, and patterns of interaction that seem to be influencing their present difficulties. At this juncture the therapist and family together set priorities for change, as well as discuss some of the interventions that might be used to alleviate problems.

Therapeutic Techniques

Cognitive-behavioral family therapy assumes that members of a family simultaneously influence and are influenced by each other. The behavior of one family member triggers behavior, cognitions, and emotions in other members, which in turn elicit reactive cognitions, behavior, and emotions in the original member. Epstein and Schlesinger (1996) cite four means by which family members' cognitions, behavior, and emotions may contribute to spirals of conflict:

1. The individual's own cognitions, behavior, and emotions regarding family interaction (e.g., the person who notices himself or herself withdrawing from the rest of the family)

2. The actions of individual family members toward him or her

3. The combined (and not always consistent) reactions several family members have toward him or her

4. The characteristics of the relationships among other family members (e.g., noticing that two other family members usually are supportive of each other's opinions)

Just as individuals maintain schemas, or core beliefs, about themselves, their world, and their future, they also maintain beliefs about their families. Dattilio (2005) suggests that individuals maintain two sets of schemas about family life: (1) schemas related to the parents' experiences growing up in their own families and (2) schemas related to families in general, or personal theories of family life. Both types of schemas influence how individuals react in the family setting. For example, a woman raised with the belief that family members should do things together is likely to feel threatened if her husband wants to do certain things on his own.

Teaching families the principles of cognitive-behaviorism promotes a collaborative relationship and increases their cooperation with treatment. Therapists typically give a brief overview of the model and periodically refer to specific concepts during therapy. In addition to presenting such information, readings are often assigned. Understanding the model keeps family members attuned to the process of treatment and reinforces the importance of taking responsibility for their own thoughts and actions.

Cognitive interventions are designed to increase family members' skills at monitoring the validity of their own cognitions. This is an important point: Cognitive therapy should not be reduced to generic interpretations ("It's a mistake to be dependent on others." "Who says it's disastrous when things go wrong?"), nor should the therapist do all the work. Rather, for cognitive intervention to be effective, specific cognitive distortions must be uncovered, and clients must learn to test their own assumptions. This exploration is carried out in a process of Socratic questioning.

A major goal of the cognitive approach is to help family members learn to identify automatic thoughts that flash through their minds. The importance of identifying such thoughts (*She's crying—she must be mad at me.*) is that they often reflect underlying schemas (*Women usually hold men responsible for their unhappiness.*) which may be inaccurate.

To improve their skill in identifying automatic thoughts, clients are encouraged to keep a diary and jot down situations that provoke automatic thoughts and the resulting emotional responses. The therapist's role then is to ask a series of questions about these assumptions, rather than to challenge them directly. Here's an example.

CASE STUDY

When thirteen-year-old Kylie's parents caught her walking home from school with a boy she was forbidden to see, they responded by saying "We can't

trust you!" and grounded her for a week. Kylie's automatic thought was *They'll never trust me again*, which made her feel, in turn, worried and then angry. This conclusion was followed by the thought *Now I'll never have any freedom. To hell with it, I'm going to do what I want.*

After helping Kylie identify these thoughts, the therapist asked her to test these assumptions and then to consider alternative explanations. "What evidence exists to substantiate this idea?" "Might there be alternative explanations?" "How would you test this assumption?"

Kylie decided that it was too soon to be sure how her parents would treat her in the future. She decided to test the proposition that if she stopped lying to them they would eventually start to trust her again, and that, in this way, she could slowly win back her freedom. Kylie was also asked to examine her defiance and think about the specific connotation it had (anger? emancipation? pride?).

The following questions may be asked to help family members examine their thoughts:

"Based on your past experiences or events in your life, what evidence exists that supports the thoughts you just shared? How could you obtain additional information to better help you assess whether your thought is accurate?"

"Could you consider an alternative explanation that might explain your partner's (or child's or sibling's) behavior?"

"Referring to the list of cognitive distortions, which cognitive distortion, if any, do you view your automatic thoughts applying to?"

The following case (taken from Dattilio, 2005) is an example of how this process plays out in treatment.

CASE STUDY

The family entered treatment because of conflict over the mother's rigid attitudes. Based on her experience with her own fragile and demanding parents, she tended to overreact to any sign of problems in her husband or children. Her anxiety made her intolerant of the children's crying and complaining. The family felt they needed to "walk on eggshells" to avoid making her worry. Thus, the father and children became aligned against the mother, whom they came to regard as a "nut case."

The father's own mother was controlling and overbearing, which led to his developing a schema that women were bossy and unreasonable. His failure to challenge his wife about what he saw as her unreasonableness was thus partly a carryover from his experience with his mother. Instead of confronting his wife, he formed a coalition with his children against her, just as he and his father had joined forces to cope with his own domineering mother.

The therapist used the cognitive technique of the *downward arrow* to identify the mother's core beliefs (see Figure 9.1). This technique was implemented by asking a series of questions to uncover the basic schemas underlying each person's assumptions: "So if that were to occur, what would it mean?"

FIGURE 9.1 Downward Arrow Technique

"There's no room for weakness in life."

↓

"If my family members are weak, they'll give in to the overwhelming forces of life."

↓

"That's when people break down, become immobilized, and become a burden to others and a risk to themselves."

↓

"This outcome could easily result in death or suicide."

↓

"If I'm weak, I'll die."

↓

"Hence, we must avoid any signs of weakness."

The children were afraid to be themselves around their mother. They saw her as unreasonable and attributed her unyielding views to having grown up with a mother who had attempted suicide and blamed her daughter for not being attentive to her concerns. When the therapist attempted to uncover the children's core beliefs about the situation, one daughter said, "I think my mother is probably on the edge, with all of the stress she's been under her entire life. We have to go along with her, or something

bad might happen to her, and we don't need that—although we resent having to live this way—all because of my stupid grandmother's problems." The schema adopted by this child was "Children must be cautious with parents who have problems."

In addressing the schemas in this family, the therapist followed a series of eight steps to uncover and reexamine them:

1. *Identify family schemas and highlight those areas of conflict that are fueled by them* (e.g., "We have to walk on eggshells with mom. If we show any signs of weakness, she flips out."). Schemas are uncovered by probing automatic thoughts through techniques such as the downward arrow. Once schemas have been identified, verification should be made by obtaining agreement from other family members.

2. *Trace the origin of family schemas and how they evolved to become an ingrained mechanism in the family process.* This is done by exploring the parents' backgrounds. Similarities and differences between the parents' upbringings should be highlighted to help them understand areas of agreement and conflict. In this case, the father was brought up to believe that it's okay to show vulnerability to those you love, while the mother was taught that it's dangerous to show any sign of weakness.

3. *Point out the need for change, indicating how the restructuring of schemas may facilitate more adaptive and harmonious family interaction.* The therapist stressed to the mother how she was overburdened by her belief that she was always responsible for everyone else in the family. The therapist emphasized how much her perceptions had been distorted by her experience with her mother and how she was unintentionally placing a similar burden on her own husband and children.

4. *Elicit acknowledgment of the need to change or modify existing dysfunctional schemas.* This step paves the way for collaborative efforts to change. When family members have different goals, the therapist's job is to help them find common ground.

5. *Assess the family's ability to make changes, and plan strategies for facilitating them.* In this case, the mother was asked what evidence supported her idea that signs of weakness were always a problem. She was helped to consider that this

idea might be a distortion based on her own childhood experience. As an experiment, she was asked to see if an occasional display of emotion really was dangerous by allowing herself to cry once in a while in front of her family. The fact that her husband and children seemed relieved to see her show her feelings helped her to think that maybe it's not so terrible to show unhappy emotions at times. "In fact, it felt kind of good," she noted. In a similar process, the husband discovered that if he avoided interfering to protect his wife when she seemed upset, the children were able to be supportive and "nothing terrible happened." The children found out that when they expressed the wish to avoid being put in the middle of their parents' conflicts, they were free to be themselves without worrying about negative consequences.

6. *Implement change.* The therapist encouraged family members to consider modifying some of their beliefs in a collaborative process of brainstorming ideas and weighing their implications. This family considered how they would act with each other if they decided to adopt the belief that "It is important to be tactful in expressing negative feelings to other family members, but family members should have the freedom to share such feelings with each other."

7. *Enact new behaviors.* This step involves trying out changes and seeing how they work. Family members were each asked to select an alternative behavior consistent with the modified schema and to see how acting on it affected the family. Once the children began to see their mother's behavior as her way of expressing love for them in order to protect them from what she went through as a child, they became less defensive and more supportive of her—which, in turn, softened her anxious vigilance.

8. *Solidify changes.* This step involves establishing the new schema and its associated behavior as a permanent pattern in the family. Family members were urged to remain flexible about the possible need for future reevaluations. Although the mother might be seen as the identified patient in this family, the therapist felt it was important for the father and children to recognize their own roles in perpetuating the status quo. They began this process by expressing how they felt, instead of just avoiding the mother. Then, in an effort to challenge their automatic thoughts about the family and see how their own beliefs might be part of the problem, all of the family members were asked to weigh alternative explanations and consider their implications. Dattilio notes that this process is similar to *reframing* but with an important difference: In cognitive-behavior therapy, family members are asked to gather data and weigh the evidence in favor of changing their thinking, rather than merely accept the therapist's alternative explanations.

Imagery and role-playing may be used to help family members remember past incidents that helped them form assumptions. On occasion, family members are coached to switch places in role plays to increase their empathy for each other's feelings (Epstein & Baucom, 2002). An example of this would be having siblings play each other's role in reenacting a recent argument. Focusing on the other person's frame of reference provides new perspective that may help family members soften their views of each other.

Even while cognitive interventions have become increasingly important, cognitive-behavior therapists still use many of the elements of traditional behavioral therapy, including communications training, problem-solving training, and homework assignments. In summarizing some of the problem-solving strategies taught in cognitive-behavioral therapy, Epstein and Baucom (2002) describe helping clients learn to set clear, behavioral goals without attacking other family members' ideas, evaluating the advantages and disadvantages of each proposed solution, and then selecting a solution that appears to be feasible and agreeable to all. A trial period is then proposed to test the implementation of the proposed solution and assessing its effectiveness.

Among the homework assignments commonly used in this approach are practicing communication skills—for example, deliberately engaging in an argument but without attacking or using condescending language; assigned readings, linked to particular issues that emerge in the course of treatment; self-monitoring exercises in which clients are asked to keep track of their thoughts and moods between sessions. In the "Daily Dysfunctional Thought Sheet" (Beck, Rush, Shaw, & Emery, 1979), clients are asked to record their thoughts during arguments and make connections about how their thoughts, moods, and behavior are interrelated.

Frank Dattilio (1999) introduced the "pad-and-pencil" technique to help family members overcome the annoying habit of interrupting each other. Family members are given a pad and pencil and asked to record the automatic thoughts that go through their minds when someone else in the family is talking.

One of the early criticisms of cognitive-behavior therapy was that it neglected the role of emotions. If that was once true, it isn't now. Contemporary cognitive-behaviorists see emotions and cognitions as interrelated in a circular process of mutual influence. Research has shown that dysphoric emotions cloud cognitive processing and lead to a depressing frame of mind that may be consuming, such as in someone who is always looking on the dark side of things (Gottman, 1994). Gottman found that pessimistic moods initiate pessimistic cognitive processing, which then leads to selective attention to negative events. From this selective attention, negative attributions develop and lead to negative expectations for the future. Beck described this as "negative frame" which renders individuals vulnerable to seeing the world in a pessimistic light.

> ▶ Watch this video of Dr. Frank Dattilio dispelling common misconceptions of cognitive-behavioral couples therapy. Does he challenge any assumptions you may have had of cognitive-behavioral couples therapy?
>
> www.youtube.com/watch?v=rbFeMG_Uoxw

Cognitive-behavior therapy offers a host of interventions to improve emotional regulation (Epstein & Baucom, 2002; Dattilio, 2010). Therapists provide guidelines and coaching to help clients learn to express themselves in ways that won't lead to recrimination. This may involve using *downward arrow* questioning to help family members learn to differentiate and articulate their feelings and the cognitions underlying them, coaching clients to notice internal cues to their emotional state, having them learn to express their emotions in understandable terms, refocusing attention on emotional topics when clients attempt to change the subject, and engaging family members in role plays about relationship conflicts in order to elicit emotional responses and learn to express them in productive ways.

Recently, *mindfulness meditation* has been employed as an adjunct to cognitive-behavior therapy. Mindfulness teaches open and receptive attention to the present moment, which in turn promotes a less reactive response to challenging emotions. Recent studies have indicated that improving emotional skills and mindfulness were related to improved marital adjustment (Hayes, 2004). Mindfulness meditation has also proven helpful in teaching couples to improve their level of empathy for each other and greater closeness in their relationships.

◆ Treatment of Sexual Dysfunction

The introduction of *systematic desensitization* (Wolpe, 1958) and *assertiveness training* (Lazarus, 1965) led to major advances in the treatment of sexual dysfunction. While these behavioral remedies were often helpful, the real breakthrough came with the publication of Masters and Johnson's (1970) approach. This was followed by others who applied and extended Masters and Johnson's basic procedure (Kaplan, 1974, 1979; Lobitz & LoPiccolo, 1972). More recently Weekes and Gambescia (2000, 2002) have offered a more comprehensive treatment model, integrating couples therapy, sex therapy, and medical treatment.

Although the details vary, there is a general approach followed by most sex therapists. As with other behavioral methods, the first step is a thorough assessment, including a complete medical examination and extensive interviews to determine the nature of the dysfunction and establish goals for treatment. In the absence of medical problems, cases involving lack of information, poor technique, and poor communication are most amenable to sex therapy.

Therapists following Masters and Johnson tended to lump sexual problems into one category—anxiety that interferes with couples' ability to relax into passion. Helen Singer Kaplan (1979) pointed out that there are three stages of the sexual response and hence three types of problems: disorders of desire, arousal disorders, and orgasm disorders. *Disorders of desire* range from low sex drive to sexual aversion. Treatment focuses on: (1) deconditioning anxiety and (2) helping clients resist negative thoughts. *Arousal disorders* include decreased emotional arousal and difficulty achieving and maintaining an erection or dilating and lubricating. These problems are often helped with a combination of relaxation and teaching couples to focus on the physical sensations of touching and caressing, rather than worrying about what comes next. *Orgasm disorders* include the timing of orgasm (premature or delayed), the quality of the orgasm, or the requirements for orgasm (e.g., some people have orgasms only during masturbation).

Premature ejaculation usually responds well to sex therapy; lack of orgasm in women may respond to sex therapy, usually involving teaching the woman to practice on her own and learning to fantasize (Weekes & Gambescia, 2000, 2002).

Although sex therapy must be tailored to specific problems, most treatments are initiated with *sensate focus*, in which couples are taught how to relax and enjoy touching and being touched. They're told to find a time when they're both reasonably relaxed and free from distraction and get in bed together naked. Then they take turns gently caressing each other. The person being touched is told to relax and concentrate on the feeling of being touched. Later the one being touched will let the partner know which touch is most pleasing and which is less so. At first couples are told not to touch each other in the sensitive breast or genital areas in order to avoid possible anxiety.

After they learn to relax and exchange gentle caressing, couples are encouraged to gradually become more intimate—but to slow down if either should feel anxious. Thus sensate focus is a form of *in vivo desensitization*. Couples who are highly anxious and fearful of having sex (which some people reduce to a hectic few minutes of poking and panting) learn to overcome their fears through a gradual and progressively intimate experience of mutual caressing. As anxiety decreases and desire mounts, they're encouraged to engage in more intimate exchanges. In the process, couples are taught to communicate what they like and don't like. So, for example, instead of enduring something unpleasant until she finally gets so upset that she snaps at her partner

or avoids sex altogether, a woman might be taught how to gently show him "Like this."

Once sensate focus exercises have gone smoothly, the therapist introduces techniques to deal with specific problems. Among women the most common sexual dysfunctions are difficulties with orgasm (Kaplan, 1979). Frequently these problems are rooted in lack of information. The woman and her partner may be expecting her to have orgasms reliably during intercourse without additional clitoral stimulation. In men, the most common problem is premature ejaculation, for which part of the treatment is the *squeeze technique* (Semans, 1956), in which the woman stimulates the man's penis until he feels the urge to ejaculate. At that point, she squeezes the frenulum (at the base of the head) firmly between her thumb and first two fingers until the urge to ejaculate subsides. Stimulation begins again until another squeeze is necessary.

Techniques to deal with erectile failure are designed to reduce performance anxiety and increase sexual arousal. These include desensitization of the man's anxiety; discussions in which the partners describe their expectations; increasing the variety and duration of foreplay; the *teasing technique* (Masters & Johnson, 1970), in which the woman alternately starts and stops stimulating the man; and beginning intercourse with the woman guiding the man's flaccid penis into her vagina.

Successful sex therapy usually ends with the couple's sex life much improved but not as fantastic as frustrated expectations had led them to imagine—expectations that were part of the problem in the first place. As in any form of directive therapy, it's important for sex therapists to gradually fade out their involvement and control. Therapeutic gains are consolidated and extended by reviewing the changes that have occurred, by anticipating future trouble spots, and by planning in advance to deal with problems according to principles learned in treatment.

Evaluating Therapy Theory and Results

The principles of behavioral family therapy are derived from classical and operant conditioning and, increasingly, cognitive theory. Target behavior is carefully defined in operational terms; operant conditioning, classical conditioning, social learning theory, and cognitive strategies are then used to produce change. As behavior therapists have gained experience with family problems, they have begun to address such nonbehavioral concerns as the therapeutic alliance, the need for empathy, and the problem of resistance, as well as communication and problem-solving skills. However, even when dealing with such traditional issues, behaviorists are distinguished by their methodical approach. More than by any technique, behavior therapy is characterized by careful assessment and evaluation.

Behavior therapy was born and bred in a tradition of research, and so it's not surprising that it is the most carefully studied form of family treatment. Two trends emerge from this substantial body of evidence. The first is that both behavioral parent training and behavioral couples therapy have repeatedly been shown to be effective. Among the most well-supported versions of these approaches are Gerald Patterson's parent training therapy (Patterson, Dishion, & Chamberlain, 1993; Patterson & Forgatch, 1995), Neil Jacobson's behavioral couples therapy (Crits-Christoph, Frank, Chambless, Brody, & Karp, 1995), and Fals-Stewart and colleagues' behavioral couples therapy (Fals-Stewart et al., 2000).

The second trend in research on behavioral family therapy is that exponents of this model have begun to see the need to extend their approaches beyond the basic contingency contracting and operant learning procedures of traditional behavior therapy. One form this has taken has been the incorporation of cognitive techniques into traditional stimulus-response behaviorism (Epstein & Baucom, 2002; Dattilio & Padesky, 1990; Dattilio, 2010).

Cognitive-behavior therapy still emphasizes behavior change. There are two general categories of intervention: substituting positive for aversive control and skills training. An example of the former would be, to counteract the negativity that characterizes many distressed couples, a cognitive-behavior therapist might ask each partner to write down one positive thing that the other person did each day, compliment or express appreciation to that individual for this action, and bring the list to therapy for further discussion (Baucom, Epstein, & LaTaillade, 2002).

The cognitive component of cognitive-behavioral therapy comes into play when clients' attitudes and assumptions get in the way of positive behavior changes—when, for example, family members notice only negative things about each other. The cognitive-behavior therapist helps clients explore their assumptions in a process of Socratic questioning. Thus, cognitive-behavior therapy still focuses on behavior; therapists are still active and directive, but there is more attention paid to unhappy emotions and the assumptions underlying them.

Patterson and colleagues' parent management training (PMTO), based on social learning theory, emphasizes the role of the child's social environment in the maintenance of delinquent behavior. PMTO utilizes behavioral analysis and operant conditioning to help parents bring about positive changes in their children. Patterson and his colleagues have done extensive research to identify different parent practices (discipline, positive support, monitoring, problem solving, parent involvement) and how these practices are associated with aggressive behavior in children (Forgatch & DeGarmo, 2002). They have also conducted intervention studies showing that PMTO effectively reduces delinquent behavior in chronically offending adolescents (e.g., Bank, Marlowe, Reid, Patterson, & Weinrott, 1991). A version of PMTO has also been shown to effectively prevent the emergence of delinquent behavior in adolescents at risk for substance abuse (Dishion, Nelson, & Kavanagh, 2003), families in high crime areas (Reid, Eddy, Fetrow, & Stoolmiller, 1999), divorced mothers (Forgatch & DeGarmo, 1999), and stepparent families (Forgatch, DeGarmo, & Beldavs, 2005). Recent studies have also demonstrated that PMTO can successfully be disseminated in other countries, such as Thailand, Mexico, Norway, and Iceland (Arunothong & Waewsawangwong, 2012; Baumann, Rodriques, & Amador, 2014; Forgatch & DeGarmo, 2011; Sigmarsdottir & Gundsdottir, 2013). Lastly, some researchers have begun to explore whether PMTO can be successfully delivered in less traditional therapy settings, such as primary care offices, an initial finding suggests that this may indeed be worthwhile (Gomez et al., 2014; Kjobli & Ogden, 2012).

The late Neil Jacobson, in partnership with Andrew Christensen, went even further in modifying traditional behavioral couples therapy by incorporating elements of experiential therapy. They retained the behavioral change techniques but added strategies to bring about increased emotional acceptance in clients (Jacobson & Christensen, 1996). In other words, before they start working with couples to produce changes in the partners' behavior, they endeavor to help them learn to be more accepting of each other. So different, in fact, is the resulting approach that we will consider it more extensively in our chapter on integrative approaches (Chapter 13).

Fals-Stewart, O'Farrell, and colleagues have amassed substantial support for the use of another variation of behavioral couples therapy in the treatment of substance abuse. This version of behavioral couples therapy emphasizes the therapeutic benefit of partners rewarding abstinence, suggesting that reduction in marital distress can decrease the likelihood of substance abuse and relapse. This model primarily targets substance-related couple interactions in hopes of modifying them to support positive changes in substance-abusing behavior (Ruff, McComb, Coker, & Sprenkle, 2010). In particular, research has shown that BCT can successfully reduce alcohol (Fals-Stewart, Birchler, & Kelley, 2006; Fals-Stewart, Klosterman, Yates, O'Farrell, & Birchler, 2005) and illicit drug abuse (Fals-Stewart et al., 2000, 2001; Kelley & Fals-Stewart, 2007). It has also been shown to improve relationship adjustment (Fals-Stewart, Birchler, & Kelley, 2006; Kelley & Fals-Stewart, 2008) as well as child psychosocial outcomes (Kelley & Fals-Stewart, 2007, 2008). A number of studies have also examined the effect of BCT in reducing intimate partner violence (which often occurs when one member of a couple is abusing substances) (Fals-Stewart, Kashdan, O'Farrell, & Birchler, 2002; Fals-Stewart et al., 2006).[3]

As you are probably aware, cognitive-behavior therapy is one of the most widely taught approaches to psychological treatment. In a survey conducted by the American Association for Marriage and Family Therapy (Northey, 2002) that asked family therapists to describe their primary treatment approach, the most frequent response (named by 27.3 percent of 292 randomly selected therapists) was cognitive-behavior therapy.

One reason for this popularity is that cognitive-behavioral couples therapy has been subjected to more controlled outcome studies than any other therapeutic approach. Baucom and associates' (1998) review of outcome studies indicated that cognitive-behavioral couples therapy is effective in reducing relationship distress, especially as an addition to a program that includes communication training, problem-solving training, and behavioral contracts. While outcome studies have demonstrated the effectiveness of behaviorally oriented family interventions with child conduct disorders (Nichols & Schwartz, 2006), cognitive interventions per se have not been evaluated.

Despite increased public and professional interest in sex therapy, there are few well-controlled studies of its effectiveness. In a careful review, Hogan (1978) found that most of the literature consists of clinical case studies. These reports are little more than "box scores" of successes and failures. Absent are pre- and postmeasures, specification of techniques, points of reference other than the therapist, and follow-up data. Moreover, since most of these reports have come from the same handful of therapists, it's impossible to discern what's being evaluated—the techniques of sex therapy or the skills of these particular therapists. This state of the research hadn't changed much by 1990, according to later summary reports (Crowe, 1988; Falloon & Lillie, 1988).

Sex therapy appears to be an effective approach to some very vexing problems. Most observers (Gurman & Kniskern, 1981) agree that it should be considered the treatment of choice when there is an explicit complaint about a couple's sex life.

Three areas of research in family intervention that seem ready to move to a more advanced stage of development are: conduct disorders in children (Morris, Alexander, & Waldron, 1988; Patterson, 1986), marital conflict (Follette & Jacobson, 1988), and schizophrenia (Falloon, 1985).

Summary

Although behavior therapists have been applying their techniques to family problems for more than forty years, they have done so for the most part within a linear frame of reference. Family symptoms are

---

[3]It should be noted that questions have been raised about the legitimacy of Fals-Stewart's findings (*Business First*, February 16, 2010).

treated as learned responses, involuntarily acquired and reinforced. Treatment is generally time limited and symptom focused.

Initially, the behavioral approach to families was based on social learning theory, according to which behavior is maintained by its consequences and can be modified by altering those consequences. This focus has been broadened considerably by the introduction of cognitive interventions to address unhelpful assumptions and distorted perceptions. An essential adjunct to social learning theory is Thibaut and Kelley's theory of social exchange, according to which people strive to maximize interpersonal rewards while minimizing costs. Hence, the general goals of behavioral family therapy are to increase the rate of rewarding exchanges, decrease aversive exchanges, and teach communication and problem-solving skills.

More contemporary approaches to cognitive-behavioral therapy have expanded this approach to include the examination and restructuring of thoughts and perceptions. So, while specific techniques are applied to target behaviors, families are also taught general principles of behavior management along with methods for reevaluating automatic thoughts with an attempt to identify distortions and address misconceptions.

The behaviorists' focus on modifying the consequences of problem behavior accounts for the strengths and weaknesses of this approach. By concentrating on concrete problems, behaviorists have been able to develop an impressive array of effective techniques. Even such relatively intractable problems as delinquent behavior in children and severe sexual dysfunctions have yielded to behavioral technology. Contemporary cognitive-behavior therapists take the posture, however, that behavior is only part of the human condition, and the problem person is only part of the family. You can't simply teach people to change if unresolved conflict is keeping them stuck.

Unhappiness may center around a behavioral complaint, but resolution of the behavior may not resolve the unhappiness. Treatment may succeed with the symptom but fail the family. Attitudes and feelings *may* change along with changes in behavior but not necessarily. And teaching communication skills may not be sufficient to resolve real conflict. Behavior change alone may not be enough for family members

whose ultimate goal is to feel better. "Yes, he's doing his chores now," a parent may agree. "But I don't think he *feels* like helping out. He still isn't really part of our family." Behavior isn't all that family members in distress are concerned about, and to be responsive to their needs therapists need to deal with cognitive and affective issues as well.

Traditional behaviorists rarely treat whole families. Instead they see only those subsystems they consider central to the targeted behavior. Unfortunately, failure to include—or at least consider—the entire family in therapy may doom treatment to failure. A therapeutic program to reduce a son's aggressiveness toward his mother can hardly succeed if the father wants an aggressive son or if the father's anger toward his wife isn't addressed. Moreover, if the whole family isn't involved in change, new behavior may not be reinforced and maintained.

Despite the earlier shortcomings, cognitive-behavior therapy offers impressive techniques for treating problems with children and troubled marriages. Furthermore, its weaknesses can be corrected by broadening the focus of treatment to include families as systems. Perhaps the greatest strength of behavior therapy is its insistence on observing what happens and then measuring change. Cognitive-behaviorists have developed a wealth of reliable assessment methods and applied them to evaluation, treatment planning, and monitoring progress and outcome. A second important advance has been the gradual movement from eliminating or reinforcing discrete marker behaviors to the teaching of general problem-solving, cognitive, and communicational skills. A third major advance in current behavioral family therapy is modular treatment interventions organized to meet the specific and changing needs of the individual and the family.

Click here to apply your knowledge of chapter concepts.

Click here to test your application and analysis of the content found within this chapter.

Unlike approaches organized around a single model (psychoanalysis, behavior therapy), family therapy was always a diverse enterprise with competing schools and conflicting theories. What they shared was a belief that problems run in families. Beyond that, however, each school was a distinct faction, with its own doctrine and ways of doing therapy.

Today all of that has changed. The field is no longer neatly divided into separate schools, and practitioners no longer share a universal adherence to systems theory. As family therapists have always been fond of metaphors, we might say that the field has grown up. No longer cliquish or cocksure, family therapy has been shaken and transformed by a series of challenges—to the idea that any one approach has all the answers, about the nature of men and women, about the shape of the American family, indeed about the possibility of knowing anything with certainty.

Challenges to Traditional Family Systems Models

◆ Erosion of Boundaries

The boundaries between schools of family therapy gradually blurred in the 1990s to the point where now few therapists would characterize themselves as purely Bowenian or structural or what have you. One reason for this decline in sectarianism was that as they gained experience, practitioners began to borrow each other's techniques. Suppose, for example, that a card-carrying structural therapist were to read White and Epston's little gem of a book *Narrative Means to Therapeutic Ends* and started spending more time exploring the stories clients tell about their lives. Would this therapist still be a structuralist? A narrative therapist? Or perhaps a little of both?

Suppose our hypothetical therapist were to hear Jim Keim describing his strategic approach to families with oppositional children and started using it

CHAPTER 10

FAMILY THERAPY IN THE TWENTY-FIRST CENTURY

The Shape of Family Therapy Today

LEARNING OUTCOMES

◆ Describe the major challenges to traditional family systems models in the twenty-first century.

◆ Describe contemporary sociocultural factors relevant to family therapy.

◆ Describe the unique needs of minority families.

◆ Describe how to tailor treatment to diverse families and contexts.

in her own practice. What would we call this therapist now? Structural-narrative-strategic? Eclectic? Or maybe just a family therapist?

In response to this blurring of boundaries, Blow, Sprenkle, and Davis (2007) urged therapists to study theories of change rather than concentrate on learning a particular model of therapy. They suggest that therapists become familiar with several approaches so that they can apply them selectively to the needs of particular clients. This may be good advice. However, it's not clear that what therapists actually do in therapy is so similar across models (e.g., Davis & Piercy, 2007). While there are common elements in most therapies—empathy, encouragement, questioning assumptions—there are also distinct differences. While Bowenians reason with family members one at a time, structuralists push them to talk to each other; while most schools carefully explore the presenting complaint, solution-focused therapists believe that this only reinforces problem-centered thinking. So, while it's clear that family therapists borrow from each other, there are still distinct conceptual models, each with its own implications for doing therapy.

Another reason for the erosion of orthodoxy was the growing recognition of the need for specialized approaches to deal with specific problems and populations. Once family therapists cherished their models; if a particular family didn't quite fit the paradigm, maybe they just weren't "an appropriate treatment case." Today, one-size-fits-all therapies are no longer seen as sufficient.

◆ Postmodernism

Advances in science at the beginning of the twentieth century gave us a sense that the truth of things could be uncovered through objective observation and measurement. The universe was a mechanism whose laws of operation awaited discovery. Once those laws were known, we could control our environment. This modernist perspective influenced the way family therapy's pioneers approached families— as cybernetic systems to be analyzed and reprogrammed. The therapist was the expert. Structural and strategic blueprints were used to search for flaws that needed repair, regardless of whether families saw things that way themselves.

Postmodernism was a reaction to this hubris. Not only were we losing faith in the validity of scientific, political, and religious truths, but we were also coming to doubt whether absolute truth can ever be known. As Walter Truett Anderson (1990) wrote in *Reality Isn't What It Used to Be*, "Most of the conflicts that tore the now-ending modern era were between different belief systems, each of which professed to have the truth: this faith against that one, capitalism against communism, science against religion. On all sides the assumption was that somebody possessed the real item, a truth fixed and beyond mere human conjecture" (p. 2). In family therapy, it was structural truth versus psychodynamics, Bowen versus Satir.

Einstein's relativity undermined our faith in certainties. Marx challenged the right of one class to dominate another. In the 1960s, we lost trust in the establishment. The feminist movement challenged assumptions about gender that had been considered laws of nature. As the world shrinks and we are increasingly exposed to different cultures, we'll have to reexamine our assumptions about other people's "peculiar" beliefs.

This mounting skepticism became a major force in the 1980s and shook the pillars of every human endeavor. In literature, education, religion, political science, and psychology, accepted practices were **deconstructed**—that is, shown to be social conventions developed by people with agendas. Social philosopher Michel Foucault interpreted the accepted principles in many fields as stories perpetuated to protect power structures and silence alternative voices. The first and perhaps most influential of those voices to be raised in family therapy was the feminist critique.

◆ The Feminist Critique

Feminism prompted family therapy's rudest awakening. In an eye-opening critique heralded by an article of Rachel Hare-Mustin's in 1978, feminist family therapists not only exposed the gender bias inherent in existing models but also advocated a style of therapy that called into question systems theory itself.

The Batesonian version of cybernetics had claimed that personal control in systems was impossible because all elements are continually influencing one another in circular feedback loops. If all parts of a system are equally involved in its problems, no one is to blame. To feminists, the notion of equal responsibility for problems looked suspiciously like a sophisticated version of "blaming the victim and rationalizing the status quo" (Goldner, 1985, p. 33). This criticism was particularly germane in crimes against women, such as battering, incest, and rape, for which psychological theories have long been used to imply that women provoke their own abuse (James & MacKinnon, 1990).

The family constellation most commonly cited as contributing to problems was the peripheral father, overinvolved mother, and symptomatic child. For years, psychoanalysts blamed mothers for their children's symptoms. Family therapy's contribution was to show how a father's lack of involvement contributed to a mother's overinvolvement, and so therapists tried to pry the mother loose by inserting the father in her place. This wasn't the boon for women that it might have seemed, because in too many cases, mothers were viewed no less negatively. Mothers were still "enmeshed," but now a new solution appeared—bringing in good old dad to the rescue.

What feminists contended that therapists failed to see was that "the archetypal 'family case' of the overinvolved mother and peripheral father is best understood not as a clinical problem, but as the product of an historical process two hundred years in the making" (Goldner, 1985, p. 31). Mothers were overinvolved and insecure not because of some personal flaw but because they were in emotionally isolated, economically dependent, overresponsible positions in families, positions that were crazy-making.

Only when we become more gender sensitive will we stop blaming mothers and looking to them to do all of the changing. Only then will we be able to fully counter the unconscious bias toward seeing women as responsible for childrearing and housekeeping, as needing to support their husbands' careers by neglecting their own, and as needing to be married or at least to have a man in their lives (Anderson, 1995). Only then can we stop relying on traditional male traits, such as independence and competitiveness, as the standards of health and stop denigrating or ignoring traits traditionally encouraged in women, like emotionality, nurturance, and relationship focus.

In the following section, we'll see how these principles are translated into action.

◆ Feminist Family Therapy

Traditional family therapists focused on interactions within the family while ignoring the social realities that mold those interactions. Feminist therapists extend

Peggy Papp, Olga Silverstein, Marianne Walters, and Betty Carter, founding members of the Women's Project in Family Therapy.

Sylvia Plachy

the level of analysis beyond the family to the cultural context and are committed to changing values that trap women and men in narrow and unequal roles.

Thus, feminist therapy is deliberately political. The aim is to replace patriarchy with a feminist consciousness. This involves helping clients realize that how they define themselves and relate to others is often distorted by gender-role expectations. But having a political agenda imposes a challenge for therapists. There is a fine line between *clinical neutrality*, not taking a position, and *indoctrination*, imposing one's own position on clients.

Deborah Luepnitz (1988), whose book *The Family Interpreted: Feminist Theory in Clinical Practice* is one of the landmark texts of feminist family therapy, says that the ability to challenge patriarchy in a clinical context has to do with having a feminist *sensibility*, rather than a feminist *agenda*. Therapy is not indoctrination. It has to do with creating space for people to examine their assumptions about what it means to live as women and men and to explore greater flexibility in their lives, as illustrated in the following vignette (Luepnitz, personal communication, September 25, 2006).

CASE STUDY

LeRoy Johnson was an African American adolescent who had been in trouble since kindergarten. At fifteen, he had been expelled from a school for delinquents and was on the road to jail. During the assessment for a thirty-day inpatient stay, his mother would hardly look at the consultant as she explained the one-way mirror. The family had nine bouts of therapy with as many therapists. They saw Ms. Johnson as "ineffectual," "depressed," "narcissistic," "dependent," "disengaged," and "overinvolved." Realizing that the hopelessness the mother was feeling might be something the therapists needed to address, Luepnitz tried, as a feminist therapist, to intervene constructively.

Luepnitz: Ms. Johnson, I want to tell you something that I don't think anyone has told you before.

Ms. Johnson: Go ahead.

Luepnitz: LeRoy's problems are not your fault.

Ms. Johnson (after a long pause): Well, that is news.

For years Ms. Johnson had gotten the message from schools, guidance counselors, judges, and relatives that she had ruined her child's life and that if he was on his way to prison, that too was her doing. She sat, looking thoughtful.

Ms. Johnson: I have done a lot of things wrong.

Luepnitz: How about the things you've done right?

Ms. Johnson: Such as?

Luepnitz: Who has fed and clothed this child all his life? Who has talked to teachers and therapists and worked two or three jobs?

Ms. Johnson: Any mother does those things if she has to.

Luepnitz: Mothers need help. Who helped you?

Ms. Johnson: I'm self-sufficient.

Luepnitz: Self-sufficient people need loving friends. Who has loved you?

Ms. Johnson: Nobody.

Following this interchange Ms. Johnson and the consultant formed a therapeutic alliance, something this mother had never had before with the more problem-solving, patriarchal clinicians she'd seen. From this base, the family was able to work hard and undergo a major transformation. LeRoy was allowed to return home. He went to college and was never in trouble with the law again.

Feminist therapists have also helped women rethink their relationship with their bodies (e.g., Orbach, 1997). By examining the effects of social expectations communicated by the media, women can worry less about their appearance and focus more on being themselves.

To illustrate the difference between *advocacy* and *indoctrination*, consider how a therapist might raise the issue of cultural conditioning with a young woman struggling with an eating disorder. What are the implications of a therapist saying "Our society is obsessed with thinness" versus asking "Do you know where you got the idea that it was important for a woman to be thin?" The first comment suggests that the therapist knows why the client feels pressured to eat the way she does and invites her to join the therapist in seeing her problem as something imposed on her. The second comment invites the client to join in a mutual search for understanding her problem and empowers her to take an active role in that process.

When it comes to the politics of the family, feminists make a point of exploring the income and work potential of husbands and wives and the implications for the balance of power in their relationships. They help couples clarify the rules by which roles are chosen and rewarded in the family. Useful questions include the following:

Who handles the finances?

Who handles emotional matters?

Who makes social arrangements?

Who decides where the couple is going to live and when they will move?

Who buys and wraps birthday presents?

Who cleans the toilets?

What do the couples believe about appropriate gender roles of a wife and a husband?

What gender roles were modeled by their own parents—both positive and negative?

One of the core elements of feminist therapy is *empowerment*. Women are typically brought up to empower others—to foster other people's growth and well-being. If the greatest shame for a man is weakness, then the greatest shame for a woman is selfishness. Underlying the specific conflicts between men and women in families is the cultural programming for men to seek success and for women to nurture and support them, even at the expense of their own development. Feminist therapists aim to redress this imbalance by empowering women to feel competent. Thus, empowerment is in the service of *power to*, not *power over*. *Power to* means being able to perform and produce and having the resources to do so. *Power over* refers to domination and control.

Some men have trouble understanding how women are disempowered, because they don't feel powerful in their relationships with their wives and mothers. But the fact that a man may feel powerless in individual circumstances does not cancel his membership in the dominant class or eliminate the privileges that attend that membership (Goodrich, 1991).

Empowerment need not be a zero-sum game. Both people in a relationship can learn to interact in ways that increase their connection and enhance their own personal power (Miller, 1986; Surrey, 1991). Mutual empowerment means helping women and men differentiate between what they have been taught is socially acceptable and what is actually in their best interest.

In recent years, the standard model of marriage has shifted from *complementary* to *symmetrical*. In an egalitarian marriage, mutuality and reciprocity replace hierarchy and control. But the reproduction of patriarchy still appears in the family—from who gets the kids ready for school to who drives the car, from who pleads for conversation to who has the last word, from minor acts of deference to major decisions. Here's an example of one couple's struggle to achieve mutual empowerment.

CASE STUDY

Raised in a generation that takes gender equality for granted, Olivia and Noah found that actually implementing that ideal was easier said than done. Both of them believed that Noah should be as responsible for housework as Olivia, but he had trouble assuming those responsibilities, and she had trouble letting go of them. Olivia expected to be in charge of looking after things, as her mother had been, and she tended to criticize Noah's efforts when he did make them.

Even when a man expresses willingness to assume more responsibility, both he and his partner need to make concessions. Noah insisted on doing the laundry his own way, even if it meant that stains would set and colors would bleed. He wanted to do the grocery shopping when he got around to it, even though that meant that occasionally there would be nothing to pack for school lunches.

A man who wants to share in the responsibility of being part of a family, rather than just "help out," must submit to suggestions. And his partner must let go some. Asking a husband to explain why it's so hard to accept advice from his wife may be a useful way to clear away some of his resentment. Taking suggestions does involve a loss of freedom. You can't just do things your own way if doing so will cause problems for the other person.

Family therapists are so used to having women as customers and men as reluctant presences that they tend to ask very little of men. This attitude begins with accepting that dad can't attend sessions "because he has to work." A therapist who wants to be part of the solution to sexist family arrangements has to stop accepting the nonparticipation of fathers and start insisting that both partners be actively involved in therapy.

The political agenda in feminist therapy has evolved to include greater equality not only in the institution of the family but also in the world outside the home. For career-oriented women, the challenge has shifted from access to flexibility. Twenty years ago, the gender debate centered on breaking the glass ceiling that kept women out of top management and professional jobs, gaining equal access to the workplace, and securing equal pay for equal work. Today, concerns often revolve around reshaping the climate of the work world to *keep* women involved, including compensating managers for achieving diversity goals and reaching out to women employees with families. Businesses and institutions are beginning to realize that women's needs are often different from those of men, and they are making efforts to accommodate the needs of women with families.

For poor and working-class women, the challenge isn't so much finding a rewarding career as finding someone to watch the kids so they can keep the minimum-wage job they so desperately need. Helping these women out of poverty takes more than talk therapy. What's needed are flexible schedules, affordable child care, and greater availability of part-time work.

◆ Social Constructionism and the Narrative Revolution

Constructivism was the lever that pried family therapy away from its claim to objectivity—the assumption that what one sees in families is what *is* in families. Human experience is fundamentally ambiguous; fragments of experience are understood only through a process that organizes it and assigns meaning. Instead of focusing on patterns of family interaction, constructivism shifted the emphasis to exploring the perspectives that people with problems have about them.

In the 1980s and 1990s, Harlene Anderson and Harry Goolishian translated constructivism into an approach that democratized the therapeutic relationship. Along with Lynn Hoffman and others, these

collaborative therapists united in opposition to the cybernetic model and its mechanistic implications. Their version of postmodernism focused more on caring than curing, and they sought to move the therapist out of the position of authority into a more egalitarian partnership with clients.

Perhaps the most striking example of this democratization was introduced by Norwegian psychiatrist Tom Andersen, who leveled the playing field by hiding nothing from his clients. He and his team openly discuss their reactions to what a family says. This **reflecting team** (Andersen, 1991) has become a widely used device in the collaborative model's therapy by consensus. Observers come out from behind the one-way mirror to discuss their impressions with the therapist and family. This creates an open environment in which the family feels part of a team and the team feels more empathy for the family (Brownlee, Vis, & McKenna, 2009; Sparks, Ariel, Pulleyblank Coffey, & Tabachnik, 2011).

What these collaborative therapists shared was the conviction that too often clients aren't heard because therapists are doing therapy *to* them rather than *with* them. To redress this authoritarian attitude, Harlene Anderson (1993) recommended that therapists adopt a position of "not knowing," which leads to genuine conversations with clients in which "both the therapist's and the client's expertise are engaged to dissolve the problem" (p. 325).

This new perspective was in the tradition of an approach to knowledge that emerged from biblical studies called **hermeneutics**, from the Greek word for *interpretation*. From a hermeneutic perspective, what a therapist knows isn't simply discovered through a process of free association and analysis—or enactment and circular questioning. It's organized, constructed, and fitted together by the therapist alone or collaboratively with the patient or family. Although there's nothing inherently democratic about hermeneutic exegesis, its challenge to essentialism went hand in hand with the challenge to authoritarianism.

Constructivism focused on how individuals create their own realities, but family therapy has always emphasized the power of interaction. As a result, another postmodern psychology called **social constructionism** now influences family therapy.

Social psychologist Kenneth Gergen (1985) emphasized the power of social convention in generating meaning for people. Gergen challenged the notion that we are autonomous individuals holding independent beliefs and argued instead that our beliefs fluctuate with changes in our social context.

This view has several implications. The first is that no one has a corner on the truth: All truths are social constructions. This idea invites therapists to help clients understand the origins of their beliefs, even those they assumed were laws of nature. The second implication is that therapy is a linguistic exercise; if therapists can lead clients to new constructions about their problems, the problems may open up. Third, therapy should be collaborative. Because neither therapist nor client brings truth to the table, new realities emerge through conversations in which both sides share opinions and respect each other's perspective.

Social constructionism was welcomed with open arms by those who were trying to shift the focus of therapy from action to cognition, and it became the basis for an approach that took family therapy by storm in the 1990s, *narrative therapy* (Chapter 12). The question for the narrative therapist isn't one of truth but of which points of view are useful. Problems aren't in persons (as psychoanalysis had it) or in relationships (as systems theory had it); rather, problems are embedded in points of view about individuals and their situations.

◆ Multiculturalism

Family therapy has always billed itself as a treatment of people in context. In the postwar United States of family therapy's birth, this principle was translated into a pragmatic look at the influence of family relationships. As we've become a more diverse country enriched by an influx of immigrants from Asia, Central and South America, Africa, and Eastern Europe, family therapy has shown a willingness to embrace the positiveness of others.

Monica McGoldrick and her colleagues (McGoldrick, Pearce, & Giordano, 1982) dealt the first blow to our ethnocentricity with a book describing the characteristic values and structure of a host of different ethnic groups. Following this and a spate of related works (e.g., Falicov, 1983, 1998;

Boyd-Franklin, 1989; Saba, Karrer, & Hardy, 1989; Mirkin, 1990; Ingoldsby & Smith, 1995; Okun, 1996; McGoldrick, 1998; Fontes, 2008), we are now more sensitive to the need to know something about the ethnic background of our client families, so we don't assume they're wrong just because they're different.

Multiculturalism is certainly an advance over ethnocentrism. Yet in highlighting differences, there is a danger of identity politics. Discrimination, even in the name of ethnic pride, isolates people and breeds prejudice. Perhaps *pluralism* is a better term than *multiculturalism* because it implies a balance between ethnic identity and connection to the larger group.

In the twenty-first century, we have moved beyond stereotyping—the Irish drink, Italians are volatile—and beyond tolerance to a recognition that being open to other cultures enriches our own. As we suggested in Chapter 3, ethnic sensitivity doesn't require becoming an expert—or thinking that you're an expert—on every culture you might conceivably work with. If you don't know how a rural Mexican family feels about their children leaving home or what Korean parents think about their teenage daughter dating American boys, you can always ask.

◆ Race

In the early days of family therapy, African American families received some attention (e.g., Minuchin et al., 1967), but for many years it seemed that the field, like the rest of the country, tried to ignore people of color and the racism they live with every day. Finally, however, African American family therapists such as Nancy Boyd-Franklin (1993) and Ken Hardy (1993) brought race out of the shadows and forced it into the field's consciousness.

White therapists still, of course, have the option to walk away from these issues. People of color don't have that luxury (Hardy, 1993):

To avoid being seen by whites as troublemakers, we suppress the part of ourselves that feels hurt and outraged by the racism around us, instead developing an "institutional self"—an accommodating facade of calm professionalism calculated to be nonthreatening to whites. . . . Familiar only with our institutional selves, white people don't

Nancy Boyd-Franklin's *Black Families in Therapy* was one of the first—and best—books on treating ethnic minority families.

Ken Hardy advises therapists not to overlook the impact of racism on their clients—or in the therapeutic relationship.

appreciate the sense of immediate connection and unspoken loyalty that binds black people together. (pp. 52–53)

Laura Markowitz (1993) quotes a black woman's therapy experience:

I remember being in therapy years ago with a nice white woman who kept focusing me on why I was such an angry person and on my parents as inadequate individuals. . . . Years later, I saw a therapist of color and the first thing out of her mouth was, "Let's look at what was going on for your parents." It was a joyous moment to be able to see my dad not as a terrible person who hated us but as a survivor living under amazingly difficult conditions. (p. 29)

The worst abuses of the Jim Crow era may have been eliminated, but the moral outrage inspired by personal encounters with bigotry remains the most powerful vehicle for conveying the indignities of racial inequality. Even wealthy and successful blacks suffer innumerable slights, insults, and unspoken prejudice that leave them with enduring bitterness. Successful blacks still feel they must work harder than whites to get ahead, and a host of invisible but potent institutionalized impediments block the path of the less fortunate. Consider, for example, the deliberate targeting of minority households by banks peddling subprime mortgages (Cose, 2011) and the tragic consequences of decades of punitive criminal penalties for poor blacks.

The task of therapists working with nonwhite families is to understand their reluctance to engage in treatment (particularly if the therapist is white) in the context of a history of negative interaction with white people, including many of the social service agents they encounter. In addition, the therapist must recognize the family's strengths and draw from their networks or, if the family is isolated, help them create networks of support.

> ▶ Watch this video discussing the African American women and the struggle for equal rights. What can you do as a therapist to be more sensitive to issues of race?

Finally, therapists must look inside and face their own attitudes about race, class, and poverty. Toward this end, several authors recommend curricula that go beyond lectures to personal encounters—that is, confronting our own demons of racism (Pinderhughes, 1989; Boyd-Franklin, 1989; Green, 1998).

◆ Poverty and Social Class

Money and social class are subjects that most people don't like to discuss. The shame of economic disadvantage is related to the ethic of self-reliance—people are responsible for their own success. If you're poor, it must be your own fault.

Despite decreasing fees due to managed care, most therapists are able to maintain a reasonably comfortable lifestyle. They have little appreciation of the obstacles their poor clients face and the psychological impact of those conditions. When poor clients don't show up for appointments or don't comply with directives, some therapists see them as apathetic or irresponsible. This is often the way poor people come to see themselves—and that negative self-image can be an enormous obstacle.

How can we counter this tendency to think that poor people just can't cut it? First, therapists need to educate themselves to the social and political realities of being poor in the United States. Journalist Barbara Ehrenreich (1999) spent a year trying to live like a former welfare recipient coming into the workforce. Living in a trailer park and working as a waitress left her with almost nothing after expenses:

How former welfare recipients and single mothers will (and do) survive in the low-wage workforce, I cannot imagine. Maybe they will figure out how to condense their lives—including child-raising, laundry, romance, and meals— into the couple of hours between full-time jobs. Maybe they will take up residence in their vehicles [as she found several fellow workers had done], if they have one. All I know is that I couldn't hold two jobs and I couldn't make enough money to live on with one. And I had advantages unthinkable to many of the long-term poor—health, stamina, a working car, and no children to care for or support. . . . The thinking behind welfare reform was that even the humblest jobs are morally uplifting and psychologically buoying. In reality these are likely to be fraught with insult and stress. (p. 52)

The fact is, this isn't the land of equal opportunity. The economy has built-in disparities that make it extremely difficult for anyone to climb out of poverty and that keep nearly one in four children living in privation (Walsh, 1998).

> ▶ Watch this video of a client discussing his financial stresses with his therapist. What does the therapist do to help him not feel ashamed about his situation?

These days, it isn't just families of poverty who live with financial insecurity. As mortgages, energy costs, and college tuitions mount up and corporations lay off employees suddenly and ruthlessly, family life at all but the wealthiest levels is increasingly dominated by economic anxiety. Median family income has declined in the past three decades to the point where young families can't hope to do as well as their parents, even with the two incomes needed to support a very modest standard of living.

Therapists can't pay their clients' rent, but they can help them appreciate that the burdens they live with are not all of their own making. Even when clients don't bring it up, a sensitive therapist should be aware of the role financial pressures play in their lives. Asking how they manage to get by not only puts this issue on the table, but it can also lead to a greater appreciation of the effort and ingenuity that it takes to make ends meet these days.

◆ Gay and Lesbian Rights

Few social movements have transformed our culture as rapidly as the fight for gay rights. In 2008 California's Proposition 8, a state constitutional amendment banning same-sex marriage, brought to the forefront a deep cultural divide over the right to equality of gays and lesbians. The increased attention made many people rethink their stance on gays and lesbian issues, and their right to marry in particular. When Proposition 8 was on the ballot, no states allowed gay marriage. Connecticut legalized gay marriage later that year, and over the next seven years rapidly gaining momentum peaked in a 2015 Supreme Court ruling declaring gay marriage legal in all fifty states. Openly gay athletes, politicians, and entertainers have become more commonplace, and gays and lesbians in general enjoy more acceptance today than at any other time in our history.

That said, gay and lesbian individuals, couples and families continue to face unique challenges. A few years of cultural enlightenment doesn't erase generations of homophobia, neither in the internal experience of gays and lesbians nor in the society in which their families live.

Family therapy's consciousness was raised about gay and lesbian rights in the same way it was about race. After a long period of neglect and denial, family therapy in the late 1980s began to face the discrimination that a sizable percentage of the population lives with (Carl, 1990; Krestan, 1988; Laird, 1993; Roth & Murphy, 1986; Sanders, 1993). The release in 1996 of a major clinical handbook (Laird & Green, 1996) and the magazine *In the Family* (edited by Laura Markowitz) meant that gay and lesbian issues were finally out of family therapy's closet.

Despite gains in tolerance in some segments of our society, however, gays and lesbians continue to face humiliation, discrimination, and even violence because of their sexuality. After a childhood of shame and confusion, many gays and lesbians are rejected by their families when they come out. Due to the lack of social support, the bonds in gay and lesbian relationships can be strained by jealousy, stress, and isolation.

Parents often feel guilty, in part because they blame themselves for their children's sexual orientation. Parental reactions range from denial, self-reproach, and fear for their child's future, to hostility, violence, and disowning (LaSala, 2010). Therapists should remember that a gay or lesbian child may have struggled for years to come to grips with his or her identity, and that child's parents may need time to catch up after the initial shock.

When working with gay, lesbian, bisexual, or transgender clients, we recommend that therapists get as much information as they can about the unique issues that these individuals face. Therapists who aren't well informed about gay and lesbian experience should seek supervision from someone who is or refer these clients to a clinician with more experience.

We hope the day will come when gay and lesbian families, bisexual and transgender persons, African Americans, and other marginalized groups are studied by family therapists to learn not only about the problems they face but also about how they survive and thrive against such great odds. For example, gays and lesbians often create "families of choice" out of their friendship networks (Johnson & Keren, 1998). As Joan Laird (1993) suggested, these families have much to teach us "about gender relationships, about parenting, about adaptation to tensions in this society, and especially about strength and resilience" (p. 284). The question is whether we are ready to learn.

New Frontiers

◆ Advances in Neuroscience

Scientists have come a long way from looking at bumps on the skull for clues to brain functioning. Now, instead of phrenology, we have: *fMRI*—functional Magnetic Resonance Imaging, which measures increases in blood flow to the most active regions of the brain; *PET scan*—Positron Emission Tomography, which provides a sectional view of the brain and its activity; *ERP*—Event Related Potentials, which measure brain activity via electrical signals; and *TMS*—Transcranial Magnetic Stimulation, which involves magnetic fields administered to the cortex to induce a virtual lesion or to pre-activate a neural system using single pulses.

These technological advances have produced a growing body of evidence suggesting that people keep doing things they shouldn't, and fail to do things they should, because their brains are programmed to make decisions for them. Studies of the amygdala, hippocampus, and prefrontal cortex show that the brain becomes conditioned to respond automatically to certain cues by activating neural response circuits that propel people into programmed patterns of thinking and acting (LeDoux, 1996; Siegel, 1999).

These conditioned patterns are similar to what cognitive-behavior therapists refer to as *schemata* (see Chapter 9)—cognitive constructions by which we interpret present experiences on the basis of past experience; but the difference is that many of these schemata are encoded in *implicitmemory* and therefore not subject to conscious recall or rational reevaluation.[1]

The evidence from neuroscience is that emotion, not cognition, is the primary organizer of human experience. Thinking counts, but not nearly as much as we have assumed.

There is a good deal of evidence suggesting that the brain gets wired for specific kinds of neural activations at a very young age, and that once these activations are set, they tend to persist throughout a

[1]Implicit memory is a form of memory based on emotional, behavioral, and perceptual priming, rather than conscious awareness.

person's life. The discovery of the brain's neural operating systems helps explain why people persist in self-defeating interactions, even when they know that it would be in their best interests to change. "Emotional responses are, for the most part, generated unconsciously" (LeDoux, 1996, p. 17). It turns out that Freud was right when he described consciousness as the tip of the iceberg.

The amygdala acts like an emotional watchdog, ever alert for signs of threat. If an experience registers as potentially dangerous, the amygdala broadcasts a distress signal to the entire brain, which sets off a surge of physiological responses, from the release of adrenaline and noradrenaline to speeded-up heart rate to rising blood pressure and muscles mobilized for fight or flight. Within milliseconds, we may explode with rage or freeze in fear, well before our conscious minds can assess what's happening, much less persuade us to pause long enough to think about what to do.

The role of this hair-trigger brain mechanism in creating marital misery has been documented by John Gottman at the University of Washington. What Gottman (1999) found was that the brain's atavistic emotional reactions were highly correlated with criticism, contempt, and stonewalling. The emerging portrait of the emotional brain offers an illuminating window on why many clients find it so difficult to contain their reactivity in intimate relationships. It turns out that the trajectory of divorce often originates with frequent, nasty arguments that eventually cause partners to develop a kind of bio-emotional hypersensitivity to each other.

For those who wish people could just learn to get along, the point to remember is that the amygdala often sets off its emotional fireworks before the neocortex ever gets into the act. That's why a therapist can spend hours getting a couple to communicate better only to see the whole thing go up in smoke when one partner says something that feels to the other like an arrow to the heart—or, to put in context, activates a primitive neural circuit.

Exciting as some of these neuroscientific discoveries are, they can lead to unfortunate conclusions. When we describe an individual's actions in human terms—"She flies off the handle," "He doesn't listen," and so on—we tend to hold people responsible. And we believe that therapy can help. But shifting to a biological explanation may seem to rob people of free will. How can you reason with a pre-programmed neural response circuit? The current vogue of biological determinism suggests that people do things *because of* what happens in their brain. But this is false.

Biological events don't *cause* human actions; they occur on a different level of analysis. Understanding that the primitive responses of the amygdala can overwhelm the logical deliberations of the prefrontal cortex sheds light on why it's difficult to avoid reacting emotionally in certain situations; but we can still hold people accountable for their actions.

If a man punches his wife during an argument, the fact that his amygdala triggered the emotional circuits of his brain doesn't excuse his behavior. It may explain what happened in biological terms, but we still expect the man to learn to resist his aggressive impulses—regardless of the level, biological or behavioral, on which we describe that process. In terms of human action, we might say that the man can learn to resist the impulse to hit his wife, even when he gets very upset. In biological terms, affective neuroscientists, such as Richard Davidson (2001, 2003), have found that the prefrontal cortex can moderate emotional reactivity—and that people can learn to activate their prefrontal cortexes and restrain their emotional reactions.

It may be that cognitive intervention only works when clients are calm (Atkinson, 2005)—that is, before their amygdalas have short-circuited the prefrontal cortexes, but isn't this what Murray Bowen taught us fifty years ago: that family members can't reason together until the therapist has helped them reduce the level of their anxiety?

Neural circuits control the creation of meaning, the regulation of bodily states, the modulation of emotion, the organization of memory, and the capacity for interpersonal communication. But since these same functions are also influenced by relationship experiences, we can see that interpersonal experience and the structure of the brain interact in a circular fashion. In other words, the brain shapes experience and experience shapes the structure and function of the brain.

◆ Sex and the Internet

Few things have transformed the landscape of the twenty-first century like electronic technology—e-mail, cell phones, pagers, instant messaging, electronic games, and, of course, the Internet. The Internet facilitates research and communication: It informs, it helps people connect, and it helps people disconnect—to escape from active participation in relationships into a private reverie of solitary pursuits.

Contemporary technologies bring many advantages, but it is important for anyone practicing marriage and family therapy to be aware of at least one area where technology can create problems in family relationships. That area is cybersex.

A recent survey found that the majority of marriage and family therapists are seeing clients presenting with cybersex problems, and the number of such cases is increasing (Goldberg, Peterson, Rosen, & Sara, 2008). Therapists who see families with adolescents may be called on to deal with issues related to adolescent exposure to pornography and the dangers of inappropriate sexual contact. And therapists who work with couples will almost certainly encounter cases with problems associated with compulsive consumption of pornography as well as more active forms of infidelity.

Complicating the clinician's task is the fact that although problems with cybersex are widespread, they are still shameful and therefore not easily talked about. Consequently, it's important to know what kinds of questions to ask.

Although there are other temptations, the World Wide Web is usually the first place teens experiment with online sexual behavior. Social networking sites (MySpace, Facebook, Bebo, Friendster, Orkut, Ecrush, eSpintheBottle, Tagged, LinkedIn), video and photo-sharing technologies (GooglePlus, Webshots, Photobucket, YouTube, YahooPhotos, SmugMug, Flickr), and online gaming (Gunz, Runescape, World of Warcraft, Grand Theft Auto, Dance Dance Revolution, Guitar Hero, Madden NFL, Kongregate, Halo3) all present opportunities for inappropriate sexual activities. These include posting sexually provocative photos and videos, as well as sexual communications via chat rooms, e-mail, or other postings (Gillispie & Gackenbach, 2007).

In addition to understanding the various online venues where teenagers may engage in problematic sexual behavior, it's important to have a grasp of the lingo used online. Two resources that can help educate parents and therapists about online slang are

Netlingo (www.netlingo.com) and Noslang (www.noslang.com). Here are some examples:

Cybering—Engaging in sexual activity with someone online.

POS—Parent over shoulder.

IWSN—I want sex now.

Q2C—Quick to cum.

Lurking—Nonparticipation in a chat room; chat observer.

RUH—Are you horny?

LMIRL—Let's meet in real life.

TDTM—Talk dirty to me.

P911—Parent alert.

8—Oral sex.

CU46—See you for sex.

GNOC—Get naked on camera.

When discussing technology with families, it's important to inquire about all forms of Internet access, because cell phones, smart phones, gaming systems, and iPods all provide access to the Internet and its temptations. It can be hard for parents to supervise their children's computer use because in most families, it is the youngest members who are the most computer savvy. Moreover, the invention of removable storage media (jump drives, USB drives, portable hard drives) allows users to store information from the Internet and other sources onto small devices that can easily be hidden.

Various software programs are designed to screen out sexual content and conversations on a child's computer. But while these programs may be effective with younger children, such programs are easily circumvented by older teens. Although parents may appreciate recommendations about software to prevent problems, these programs should not give a false sense of security about adolescents' Internet use.

Even with the use of blocking software, most teens will be exposed to pornographic pictures, videos, stories, or sexual conversations on the Internet. In fact, 70 percent of all children ages 10–17 admit that they have been exposed to some form of pornography on the Internet. The following are some indicators that online behavior problems may be occurring (Delmonico & Griffin, 2008).

♦ Sacrificing previously enjoyed activities to spend more time on the computer.

♦ Maintaining secrecy about the frequency or types of online activities.

♦ Signs of depression or anxiety, especially noticeable after Internet use or during times when Internet access is unavailable.

♦ Taking increased risks with online activity—using computers for pornography at school, meeting people from the Internet without precautions.

♦ Jeopardizing important activities because of Internet use—missing school or arriving late, losing relationships, and so on.

The dangers to which the Internet exposes children include not only pornography but also cyberbullying and cyberharassment and, more ominously, inappropriate sexual contact with people in the real world.

The friend a teenager meets online in a chat room may turn out to be an adult predator. As many as 19 percent of American teenagers have been the target of unwanted sexual solicitation. Girls, older teens, troubled youth, frequent Internet users, chat room participants, and those who communicate online with strangers are at greatest risk (Mitchell, Finkelhor, & Wolak, 2001). Therapists should be prepared to educate young people about these dangers, including urging them to report such encounters to their parents or other responsible adults.

Here are some suggestions for protecting children from cybersex predators (Weiss & Schneider, 2006).

♦ Limit computer privacy by placing any computer with Internet access where it can be easily monitored.

♦ Monitor the child's Internet use by checking the computer's bookmarks, history of Web sites accessed, and caches. Consider computer software such as Disk Tracy (www.disktracy.com) that provides a list of every online site accessed by the computer on which it is installed.

♦ Install blocking software such as CyberPatrol (www.cyberpatrol.com) which will deny access to sexually inappropriate sites, including instant messaging.

♦ Consider using a "family oriented" Internet service provider that blocks sexually inappropriate material from ever reaching your computer.

♦ Teach children never to reveal to anyone their real name, address, or phone number, or to provide any information (such as the name of their school) that will make it easy to locate them.

♦ Let children know that it is never acceptable to meet in person someone whom they have met online without parental supervision.

♦ Talk with children about their Internet activities. Encourage them to discuss any online experiences that make them feel guilty or uncomfortable.

♦ If you believe a child is being sexually exploited or that someone is attempting to exploit him or her, consider this a sex crime and report it to the FBI.

Finally, although technology may facilitate problematic sexual behavior, it would be a mistake to think that solving such problems is simply a matter of technology. Although parents may want to install protective software on their children's computers, it's probably more important for therapists to encourage dialogue between parents and teenagers regarding Internet use and sexuality. Moreover, therapists may need to help parents understand that when it comes to protecting teenagers from unhealthy sexual experiences, adult supervision and control isn't the only answer. Once children reach a certain age, parental control—especially if it's seen as unfair—may produce as much rebellion as compliance. If the issue is curfews or chores, the rebellion may be obvious and take the form of arguments. But when the issue is something as shame-sensitive as sexuality, rebellion may take the form of "silent arguing" (Nichols, 2009)—that is, apparent compliance but with surreptitious acting out. Thus, it's wise to involve teenagers in discussions about limiting computer use, because they are far more likely to accept decisions to which they have had a chance to contribute.

♦ ♦ ♦

When it comes to adults, it can be argued that pornography and other forms of sexual experience are harmless private activities and that they can even enhance the passion in a couple's relationship. But pornography, online relationships, and sexual behavior can become compulsions and are often characterized by secrecy that's detrimental to the trust and intimacy of relationships (Cooper, 2002). As a result, therapists have been seeing more and more cases involving compulsive viewing of pornography and Internet infidelity (Gonyea, 2004). Among the sexually oriented activities that can become problematic are:

♦ Viewing pornography and masturbating.
♦ Reading and writing sexually oriented stories and letters.
♦ Using e-mail to set up meetings.
♦ Placing ads to meet sexual partners.
♦ Visiting sexually oriented chat rooms.
♦ Interactive affairs (including sharing nudity and sexual behavior via webcams).

With the advent of digital video streaming and the relatively modest cost of webcams, images can be captured and sent, and messages returned, all in real time. As the technology of the Internet has advanced, the experience of cybersex has gone beyond photos and recorded videos to live-action images and on-demand sexual responses, or virtual sex. These developments make the experience more compelling and the sense of betrayal in the partner more profound. Given the growing number of cases presenting with cybersex-related issues, therapists should be sufficiently well versed in the ways of technology to know what questions to ask and how to pose them.

The following questions adapted from Weiss and Schneider (2006) are designed to explore the nature and extent of a client's online sexual activities:

1. Do you find yourself spending increasing amounts of time online looking at porn or engaged in sexual or romantic intrigue?

2. Have you been involved in romantic or sexual affairs online?

3. Does pornography or online sexual activity violate your marital commitments?

4. Have you been unable to cut back on the frequency of your online sexual activity despite thinking that you should?

5. Have you been unable to stay away from sexual material, sites, or interactions that have made you feel guilty or ashamed of yourself?

6. Does your pornography use interfere with home life, work, or school (including making you tired or late for obligations)?

7. Does pornography use intrude on relationships that are important to you?

8. Do you collect pornography?

9. Do you engage in fantasy acts online or view porn depicting illegal or violent sexual acts, such as rape, bestiality, or child porn?

10. Has the time you spend with friends, family, and loved ones decreased because of your porn use or fantasy involvement?

11. Do you lie or keep secrets about the amount of time you spend viewing porn, the type of porn you choose, or the types of activities you engage in online?

12. Do you have sex—either in fantasy online or in person—with someone other than your spouse or partner?

13. Are you hearing complaints from family or friends about the amount of time you spend online using porn or the type of porn you use?

14. Do you get irritable or angry when asked to give up or reduce porn involvement?

15. Has the primary focus of your sexual or romantic life become increasingly related to images found in magazines, videos, or Internet activity?

Three or more positive answers are grounds for concern.

As with the old-fashioned kind of infidelity, it isn't fair to say that Internet infidelity is caused by problems in relationships. However, from the circular perspective of systems theory, it doesn't matter whether problems in a relationship caused problems with sex on the Internet or the other way around. They feed each other. Instead of worrying about which came first, a clinician can address both fronts simultaneously: encouraging an end to compulsive sexual activity and looking at problems in the relationship that may fuel this activity. For example, anger at one's partner, especially unexpressed or at least unresolved anger, leads some people to feel that they are entitled to seek soothing and excitement outside the relationship.

Like drug and alcohol addiction, sexual obsession affects both men and women. Approximately 25 percent of people in sex addiction recovery programs are women (Cooper, 2002). While men are more likely to download pornography, women typically prefer chat rooms and personal ads where there is more of a chance to actually get to know the objects of their interest.

Without outside intervention, most compulsive behavior escalates over time. This is especially true with highly reinforcing activities like drug taking and sexual behavior. Only when the consequences are severe enough do most people caught up in compulsive self-gratification seek help. When it comes to compulsive sexual behavior, these consequences may include relationship problems, job loss, public shaming, sexually transmitted diseases, arrest, and even imprisonment.

While there are obviously many different approaches to therapy and not all therapists see compulsive sexual behavior as a *sex addiction* or adhere to a twelve-step treatment model, it's important to remember that therapists should not attempt to treat problems outside the range of their expertise. If a therapist doesn't understand pornography abuse and compulsive sexual behavior or have experience in treating these problems, he or she should refer the case to someone who does. The Society for the Advancement of Sexual Health maintains a Web site (www.sash.net) that includes a list of professionals knowledgeable about compulsive sexual behavior organized by country and state.

The problems in couples' relationships that are related—as cause and effect—to outside sexual activity involve communication, boundaries, and commitment. In addressing problems in a couple's communication, a therapist should encourage the partners to talk about their needs and how to meet them. The obvious boundary problem with extramarital affairs that originate with Internet pornography is an inadequate boundary that fails to protect the relationship from one or both partners straying. However, like all boundaries, this one is reciprocal. The complement of a diffuse boundary around a relationship is disengagement between the partners. And the thing to remember about disengagement is that it exists for a reason. If a couple is disengaged, one or both partners are probably harboring unresolved resentment.

If one of the partners goes outside of a relationship to find sexual excitement and intimacy, or just plain attention, there is obviously a problem with commitment. The question for a therapist to explore is why?

◆ Spirituality and Religion

Throughout the twentieth century, psychotherapists largely avoided bringing religion into the consulting room. They also tried to stay out of the moralizing business, striving to remain neutral so that clients could make up their own minds about their lives.

In the twenty-first century, however, as increasing numbers of people have found modern life isolating and empty, spirituality and religion emerged as antidotes to a widespread feeling of alienation—both in the popular press and in the family therapy literature (Brothers, 1992; Burton, 1992; Doherty, 1996; Prest & Keller, 1993; Walsh, 1999). The majority of people in the United States say that spirituality is an important part of their life (Gallup, 2007), and pressure for therapists to provide spiritually sensitive therapy is increasing. Nevertheless, the rate of spirituality and religiosity tends to be lower among mental health professionals than the general population (Erickson et al., 2002). Upon graduation, most marriage and family therapists feel unprepared to address spirituality with their clients, and most training programs do an inadequate job of preparing therapists to have these important discussions (Ahn & Miller, 2009). When a client's religion and spirituality is incorporated into therapy, however, clients often report that the work becomes deeper and more meaningful (Hook, Worthington, Davis, & Atkins, 2014).

How can a therapist work effectively with a spiritual or religious client? The same principles of openness, respect, and curiosity that form the basis of culturally sensitive therapy apply (Richards & Bergin, 2005). During the intake, it's important to assess the degree, if any, to which religion or spirituality is a factor in client's life and whether he or she would like to incorporate it into therapy. Some people want to; others don't. You don't need to be an expert on spiritual practices to ask clients what they gain from participation, what about it they might draw on to deal with their current challenges, and so forth. If you are religious, don't assume that you see things the same way as your clients—even if they happen to share your particular faith. If you aren't religious, don't assume that your client's religion is the source of their problems—the real problem may be your lack of understanding. Countertransference is common around religion and spirituality, so be sure to seek supervision if you find yourself reacting emotionally to such a client.

Tailoring Treatment to Populations and Problems

When family therapists came down from the ivory towers of their institutes to grapple with the messy problems of the real world, they found it increasingly necessary to fit their approaches to the needs of their clients, rather than the other way around. The maturing of family therapy is reflected in its literature. Once most of the writing was about the classic models and how they applied to families in general (e.g., Haley, 1976; Minuchin & Fishman, 1981). Beginning in the 1980s, books not tied to any one school began to focus on how to do family therapy with a host of specific problems and family constellations.

Books are now available on working with families of people who abuse drugs (Barth, Pietrzak, & Ramier, 1993; Stanton, Todd, & Associates, 1982), alcohol (Elkin, 1990; Steinglass, Bennett, Wolin, & Reiss, 1987; Treadway, 1989), food (Root, Fallon, & Friedrich, 1986; Schwartz, 1995), and each other (Friedrich, 1990; Madanes, 1990; Trepper & Barrett, 1989).

There are books about treating single-parent families (Morawetz & Walker, 1984), stepparent families (Visher & Visher, 1979, 1988), divorcing families (Ahrons & Rogers, 1989; Emery, 1994; Sprenkle, 1985; Wallerstein & Kelley, 1980), blended families (Hansen, 1982; Sager et al., 1983), and families in transition among these states (Falicov, 1988; Pittman, 1987).

There are also books on treating families with young children (Bailey, 1999; Combrinck-Graham, 1989; Freeman, Epston, & Lobovits, 1997; Gil, 1994; Nichols, 2004; Selekman, 1997; Smith & Nylund, 1997; Wachtel, 1994), with troubled adolescents (Micucci, 1998; Price, 1996; Sells, 1998) and young adults (Haley, 1980), and with problems among siblings (Kahn & Lewis, 1988). There are even books on

normal families (Walsh, 1982, 1993) and successful families (Beavers & Hampson, 1990).

There are books for working with schizophrenic families (Anderson, Reiss, & Hogarty, 1986), families with bipolar disorder (Miklowitz & Goldstein, 1997), and families with AIDS (Boyd-Franklin, Steiner, & Boland, 1995; Walker, 1991); families who have suffered trauma (Figley, 1985) or chronic illness or disability (McDaniel, Hepworth, & Doherty, 1992; Rolland, 1994); families who are grieving a death (Walsh & McGoldrick, 1991), have a child with a disability (Seligman & Darling, 1996), or have an adopted child (Reitz & Watson, 1992); poor families (Minuchin, Colapinto, & Minuchin, 1998); families with aging members (Peluso, Figley, & Kisler, 2013); and families of different ethnicities (Boyd-Franklin, 1989; Falicov, 1998; Lee, 1997; McGoldrick, Pearce, & Giordano, 2007; Okun, 1996). There are also several books about treating gay and lesbian families (Greenan & Tunnell, 2003; Laird & Green, 1996).

In addition to these specialized books, the field has extended systems thinking beyond the family to include the impact of larger systems like other helping agents or social agencies and schools (Elizur & Minuchin, 1989; Imber-Black, 1988; Schwartzman, 1985), the importance of family rituals and their use in therapy (Imber-Black, Roberts, & Whiting, 1988), and the sociopolitical context in which families exist (McGoldrick, 1998; Mirkin, 1990).

There are practical guides to family therapy not connected to any one school (Patterson, Williams, Graul-Grounds, & Chamow, 1998; Taibbi, 2007) and edited books that include contributions from several schools but that are focused on specific problems or cases (Dattilio, 1998; Donovan, 1999). Thus, as opposed to the earlier days of family therapy when followers of a particular model read little outside of what came from that school, the trend toward specialization by context rather than by model has made the field more pluralistic in this postmodern age.

Among the most frequently encountered family constellations with unique challenges are single-parent families, African American families, and gay and lesbian families. The following recommendations are offered as introductions to some of the issues encountered in treating these groups.

Single-Parent Families

The most common structural problem in single-parent families is the same as in most two-parent families: an overburdened mother enmeshed with her children and cut off from adult relationships. From this perspective, the goal of therapy is to strengthen the mother's hierarchical position in relation to her children and help her become more fulfilled in her own life. However, it's important to keep in mind that single parents rarely have the resources to manage much of a social life on top of working all day and then coming home at night to take care of the kids, cook dinner, wash dishes, and do three loads of laundry.[2]

In working with single-parent families, therapists should keep in mind that supporting the parent's care of her children and helping her find more satisfaction in her own life are reciprocal achievements. Effective therapy with a single parent begins with an actively supportive therapeutic relationship. An empathic therapeutic alliance helps shore up a single parent's confidence to make positive changes and later serves as a bridge to help her connect with other people in her environment. To begin with, it's well to recognize that single parents are often angry and disappointed over the loss of a relationship, financial hardship, and trying to cope with the demands of work and children.

Poverty may be the most overwhelming burden on single parents and their children (Duncan & Brooks-Gunn, 1997). Therapists should not underestimate the impact of financial hardship on a mother's depression, self-esteem, and independence—and the decisions she makes about putting up with soul-draining jobs and abusive relationships. Many single-parent families live on the edge of crisis, managing most of the time but always aware that any unexpected emergency can push them over the edge. A supportive therapist recognizes the burdens of financial hardship, makes accommodations to the parent's work schedule, and in some cases helps the single parent consider

options, like going back to school, that might help her to become more financially stable.

Often one of the most readily available sources of support for a single parent is her family. Here the therapeutic task is twofold: facilitating supportive connections and reducing conflicts. Sometimes it's easier to develop dormant sources of support than to resolve contentious ones. The sister who lives twenty miles away may be more willing to look after her nieces and nephews from time to time than a depressed single mother thinks. A single parent's family can provide financial support, a place to stay, and help with the children. However, since most parents have trouble getting over treating their grown children as children—especially when they ask for help—a therapist may have to meet with the grandparents, develop an alliance, and then help them and their adult children negotiate effective working relationships.

Pointing out these potential sources of assistance for single parents should not be taken to suggest that a family therapist's only function should be supportive counseling. Most families, single-parent or otherwise, seek clinical services because they're stuck in conflict—psychological, interpersonal, or both. In working with single parents, a therapist's most important job is to identify and help resolve the impediments holding clients back from taking advantage of their own personal and interpersonal resources.

Sometimes the most significant conflict for single-mother households isn't visible: it's the absence of the children's father, who is not infrequently described as "out of the picture." He may be out of the picture, but in most cases he shouldn't be.

Facilitating the continued involvement of teen fathers deserves special attention because it's so challenging (Lehr & MacMillan, 2001). Since it's relatively easy for teen fathers to abandon their children, it's important to reach out to them, to establish rapport, and to encourage them in becoming responsible parents (Ngu & Florsheim, 2011).

Even invisible fathers may well desire more contact and be willing to take on more responsibility for the sake of their children. The therapist should consider contacting the noncustodial father to assess his potential contribution to his children's emotional and financial support.

[2]Single-parent families come in many varieties (U.S. Census Bureau, 2014). The children may be living with a teenage mother and her parents, a divorced college professor, or a father whose wife died of cancer. In the discussion that follows, we will concentrate on the most common situation encountered clinically: a financially burdened mother with children who is going it alone.

Here, too, triangles can complicate the picture. In an effort to be sympathetic to their mates (and sometimes from unconscious jealousy), new partners often fan the flames of conflict with the noncustodial parent, which only reinforces the cutoff.

CASE STUDY

Elana Santos contacted the clinic because her ten-year-old son, Tony, was depressed. "He's having trouble getting over my divorce," she said "I think he misses his father." After two sessions, the therapist determined that Tony was not depressed and, although he did miss his father, it was his mother who hadn't gotten over the divorce. Tony *had* stopped hanging out with his friends after school; however, it was worrying about his mother, who'd become bitter and withdrawn, rather than depression that was keeping him in the house.

The therapist's formulation was that Mrs. Santos was enmeshed with her son and both were disengaged from contacts outside the family. The therapist told Mrs. Santos that her son was sad because he worried about her. "Do you need your son to be your protector?" the therapist asked.

"No," Mrs. Santos insisted.

"Then I think you need to fire him. Can you convince Tony that he doesn't need to take care of you, that he can spend time with friends and that you'll be all right?"

Mrs. Santos did "fire" her son from the job of being her guardian angel. The therapist then talked about getting Tony more involved in after-school activities where he could meet friends. "Who knows?" the therapist said. "Maybe if Tony starts making friends, you'll have some time to do the same thing."

The only person Mrs. Santos could think of to help look after Tony so that she could have some time for herself was the boy's father, and he was "completely unavailable." Rather than accept this statement at face value, the therapist expressed surprise "that a father would care nothing about his son." When Mrs. Santos insisted that her ex wouldn't be willing to spend any time with Tony, the therapist asked permission to call him herself.

When the therapist told Mr. Santos that she was worried about his son and thought the boy needed his father's involvement in his life, Mr. Santos seemed responsive. But then the therapist heard someone talking in the background, and Mr. Santos started to back off.

What had begun as a problem firmly embedded in one person's head—"It's my son, he's depressed"—turned out to involve not just the interaction between the boy and his mother but also a triangular complication in which the father's girlfriend objected to his involvement because she didn't want "that bitch of an ex-wife of his taking advantage of him." What followed were a series of meetings—with the father and his girlfriend, the father and mother, the father and son, and finally all four of them together—in which the therapist concentrated on helping them clear the air by voicing feelings of resentment that stood in the way of their working cooperatively together.

The father's girlfriend had made the same mistake that a lot of us make when someone we love complains about how someone is treating them. In response to his complaints about his ex-wife's angry phone calls, she had urged him to have nothing to do with her. In response to these feelings and to Mrs. Santo's own anger and resentment, the therapist helped them to understand an important distinction between two subsystems in a divorce. The first (*the couple*) was dead and should be buried; the second (*the parents*) still needed to find a way to cooperate in the best interests of their child. "Burying" the divorced couple's relationship in this case was facilitated by Mrs. Santo's having an opportunity to ventilate her bitterness and anger at having been abandoned by the man she loved, although most of these discussions took place in individual sessions with the therapist.

Live-in partners provide additional sources of support and conflict. Many compete with the children for the mother's attention. Some undermine the mother's authority, while others try to enforce their own rules, setting up a triangle in which the mother is forced to side either with her boyfriend or with her children. Live-in partners' attempts to enforce discipline are frequently rebuffed, especially by adolescents. Their job isn't that of a parent but of a backup for the mother as the primary authority over her children.

Children may benefit from increased social contacts to help balance the intensity of the single-parent-and-child connection. Resources to consider include teachers, coaches, Big Brothers and Big Sisters, activity group leaders, community groups (Parents Without Partners and Mother's Day Out), Boys and Girls Clubs, religious congregations, craft classes, and workplace contacts.

Families take many forms; the single-parent family is one of them. Families don't get broken or destroyed, but they do change shapes. Unfortunately, the transition from being together to being apart is a road without maps. No wonder there is so much pain and confusion.

◆ African American Families

Therapists working with African American families should be prepared to expand the definition of family to include an *extended kinship system*. There may be a number of aunts, uncles, "big mamas," boyfriends, older brothers and sisters, cousins, deacons, preachers, and others who operate in and out of the African American home (White, 1972, p. 45).

However, many families who come to the attention of mental health workers have become isolated from their traditional support network. Part of a therapist's task is to search for persons in the family or kin network who represent islands of strength and enlist their support in helping the family. Asking "Who can you depend on when you need help?" is one way to locate such individuals. These potential connections include an extensive kinship network, made up of both family and friends (Billingsley, 1968; McAdoo, 2002). These extended connections, real and potential, mean that family boundaries and lines of authority can become blurred, as the following example illustrates.

CASE STUDY

When Juanita Williams entered a residential drug treatment program, she was lucky to have her neighbor and friend, Deena, willing to take in her three children. Six months later Juanita was ready to leave rehab and return home. By that time the Williams children had grown accustomed to living with "Aunt Deena" and her two teenagers.

When the children's case worker arranged a meeting with Juanita and her children and "Aunt Deena," Deena praised Juanita for completing the rehab program and preparing to resume the responsibility for her children. "You know I love them, almost like they were my own," she said to Juanita, who nodded. "But now it's time for them to move back with their rightful mother." However, it appeared to the social worker that Deena had effectively taken over the family and Juanita had lost her position of authority. Deena did most of the talking while Juanita sat quietly, looking down. Martin (fourteen), Jesse (twelve), and Coretta (eleven) said nothing.

The social worker concluded that Deena and the Williams children were enmeshed while Juanita was disengaged, and the worker saw her job as helping Juanita and her children reconnect while Deena stepped back into a supportive but less controlling role. Toward this end she said that Juanita was lucky to have such a good friend to act as foster mother to her children, but now it was time for her to reclaim her role as head of the family. She then set up an enactment in which she asked Juanita to talk with her children about her plans for the immediate future.

When Juanita began by telling the children how much she missed them, Deena spoke up to say that the children missed her, too. Deena's intentions were good, but her interruption was a sign of her overly central role. The therapist complimented Deena for being helpful but said that it was time to show her support by letting Juanita speak for herself. Juanita resumed talking to her children, saying, "I know that I can't promise anything, but every day I will try my hardest to be the right kind of mother to you and not to give in to my disease. And," she went on with tears in her eyes, "I know that with God's help we can be the family that we used to be."

Martin looked down, Jesse and Coretta had tears in their eyes. Then Martin turned to the therapist and said, "Can I speak?" "Of course, Martin, you can say whatever you want."

"I love you, Mommy," he said. "And I hope to God that you don't go back to the drugs. But I will never—*never*—live in a house where I have to watch my mother going into the streets again. When I don't know whether we're going to have any supper that night because you're out getting high. You will never put me through that again."

"Martin—" Once again Deena started to interrupt, and once again the social worker blocked her.

Martin went on talking for fifteen minutes about the pain and rage of growing up with a mother who was a drug addict. He held nothing back. Juanita

hard. When Martin finished, there was a
eavy silence.

hen Juanita spoke up. "I know what I put you
hrough, Martin. What I put all my children through.
And I know that I can never, ever make up for that.
But, as God is my witness, I will do everything in my
power never, ever again to let you down or make
you ashamed of me. All I want is another chance."

It was a gut-wrenching exchange. Martin had
spoken straight from the heart, and he and his
mother had gotten through to each other—with no
interference from well-meaning friends or helpful
professionals anxious to put a good face on things.

The prominence of religion and spirituality in African American family life (Hines & Boyd-Franklin, 1982) provides another potential resource. Therapists who work with black families can profit from developing a relationship with ministers in the community, who can often help mobilize support for an isolated single mother, an adolescent who is abusing drugs, or a mentally ill adult who is cut off from support following the death of a caregiver (Boyd-Franklin, 2003).

One reason father-absent households are so common among African Americans is that there are far fewer men than women in the black community. Among the reasons for the absence of African American men are substance abuse, death related to hazardous jobs, delays in seeking health care, military service, homicide, and of course the astonishingly high percentage of young black men in prison (U.S. Bureau of the Census, 2014). Not only are there fewer African American men, but their participation in family life is often undermined by limited job opportunities and a tendency on the part of mental health professionals to overlook men in the extended family system, including a father's kinship network and a mother's male friends, who may be involved in the children's lives.

Too many therapists resign themselves to the nonparticipation of fathers. A father who is regarded as unavailable may agree to attend if contacted directly by the therapist. Even if a father has trouble getting away from work, he may agree to come to one or two sessions if he's convinced that he's really needed. Therapists can also use phone calls and letters to keep

a father involved in his family's treatment. Respecting a father's family role decreases the likelihood of his sabotaging treatment (Hines & Boyd-Franklin, 1996), and even limited participation may lead to a structural shift in the family.

Partly as a consequence of absent fathers, many families in the African American community are three-generational systems, made up of a mother, her children, and a grandmother. Grandmothers who take over may have trouble letting go. They see their young adult children behaving irresponsibly, and they treat them accordingly. Unfortunately, this perpetuates the classic control-and-rebel cycle that so many young people get caught up in with their parents. Therapists can't always remain neutral in this kind of impasse. It may be useful to support a young mother or father in the role of parent, while respecting the grandmother's contribution and availability for advice and support (Minuchin, Nichols, & Lee, 2006).

Even the healthiest families have trouble functioning effectively under the crushing weight of financial hardship. When survival issues—like food, housing, and utilities—are involved, these take precedence over family conflicts. Therapists can act as resources to encourage family members to work with available community and social agents in dealing with housing, job training, employment, and child care (Rojano, 2004).

The combination of racism and poverty has produced a "fierce anger" in many African Americans (Cose, 1993). Service providers must realize that some of this anger may be directed at them. It's important not to get defensive. Nancy Boyd-Franklin (1989) recommends that mental health providers expect a certain amount of distrust and join with their black clients to build trust at the outset of treatment. Communicating respect is key to successfully engaging families.

In working with inner-city African American families, therapists must take into account that they may be enmeshed with a variety of organizations such as schools, hospitals, police courts, juvenile justice systems, welfare, child protective services, and mental health services (Henggeler & Borduin, 1990). Empowering families in this context can be accomplished by: (1) setting up meetings with various agencies involved with the family, (2) writing letters in support of the family, and (3) setting up conferences with

Wavebreakmedia Micro/Fotolia

African American clients may not feel comfortable with therapists who are not African American.

the supervisors of resistant workers (Boyd-Franklin, 2003). The point is to empower families by encouraging them to take charge of these issues themselves. Therapists can help but should not take over.

◆ Gay and Lesbian Families

Gay and lesbian partners struggle with the same sorrows of heartache and longing as any intimate partners. But same-sex couples also face unique challenges, including homophobia; resolving relational ambiguities in the areas of commitment, boundaries, and gender-linked behavior; differences about being "out" professionally or socially; and developing networks of social support (Green & Mitchell, 2002). To work effectively with gay and lesbian clients, it's important neither to ignore nor exaggerate the unique nature of same-sex pairings.

While it may be reassuring for heterosexual therapists to dissociate themselves from the overt homophobia in our culture, it's a little more difficult to deal with internalized homophobia—in themselves and in their clients. Therapists who aren't comfortable with love and sex between two men or two women may have trouble talking frankly with gay couples—or behave with patronizing deference. A therapist who is overly anxious to convey his or her progressive

attitude may find it difficult to push for change or to ask the kinds of tough questions that may be necessary with couples who aren't getting along.

CASE STUDY

Stephen and David sought therapy during a crisis induced by Stephen's wanting to open up their relationship to other partners and David refusing to even discuss this possibility. Their therapist, who was anxious to distance himself from the stereotype that gay men are promiscuous, got caught up in trying to solve the problem of Stephen's inability to commit, rather than exploring the broader problem of the couple's difficulty communicating and making decisions. Had the couple been a man and a wife disagreeing over whether to buy a house or rent an apartment, it's unlikely that the therapist would have so quickly taken sides and reduced therapy to an exercise in problem solving.

In working with same-sex couples, it's important to probe for subtle manifestations of negative images of homosexuality and same-sex relationships. One stereotype that can be particularly destructive is the cultural expectation that same-sex pairings are inherently unstable. Many people, gay as well as straight, believe that enduring love relationships between same-sex partners (especially gay men) are impossible to achieve.

As with many issues, it's probably more useful for therapists to examine their own attitudes than to imagine themselves to be without bias. Identifying your assumptions makes it easier to hold them in check; pretending that you don't have assumptions allows them to act on you unsuspectingly.

Working with gay and lesbian couples requires sensitivity to the internalization of traditional gender norms. Heterosexual partners have typically been socialized for complementary roles. Women and men may no longer expect to be "Leave-It-to-Beaver" parents, but like it or not, women are still taught to be more caring and to have a less distanced sense of self (Jordan et al., 1991), while men are brought up to be in control, to be territorial, to tolerate distance, and to thrive on competition. So what happens when same-sex partners get together? Who picks up the towels from the bathroom floor? Who initiates sex?

Many gay and lesbian couples struggle as much as heterosexual couples over whether and when to have children. But unlike their heterosexual counterparts, gays and lesbians have to resolve the issue of who (if either) will be the biological parent.

CASE STUDY

Rachel and Jan had been together ten years and were considering having a child. Both agreed that they would like to have a biological child. However, both women very much wanted to be the sperm recipient.

Seeing that Rachel and Jan were at an impasse, the therapist suggested that they consider adopting. Worn out and frustrated by their inability to decide which of them would give up the wish to carry their baby, the women jumped at this suggestion. However, their relief turned to anger when they discovered that the state they lived in did not allow gay and lesbian couples to adopt children. Their experience made them lose confidence in their therapist and they dropped out of treatment.

One of the issues in therapy with same-sex couples is likely to be the need to negotiate clear agreements about commitments and boundaries and roles. Among the questions a therapist might usefully ask are these:

"What are the rules in your relationship about monogamy?"
"What are your agreements about finances, pooling of resources, and joint ownership of property?"
"Who does what tasks in the household, and how is this decided?"

Some of the usual expectations that heterosexuals bring to marriage don't necessarily apply to same-sex couples unless they are discussed and agreed to (Green & Mitchell, 2002). Among these expectations are monogamy, pooled finances, caring for each other through serious illness, moving together for each other's career advancement, caring for each other's families in old age, and mutual inheritance, to name just a few. Because there are no familiar models for being a same-sex couple, partners may have discrepancies in their visions about how these issues will be handled. We suggest that therapists be aware of these issues and prepared to help clients discuss them but not introduce topics that clients don't yet seem ready to deal with.

Some therapists might be surprised to learn that many gay men maintain stable relationships that allow outside sexual activity (Bringle, 1995; Bryant & Demian, 1994). In studying this phenomenon, Michael LaSala (2004a) found no differences on the Dyadic Adjustment Scale between monogamous and nonmonogamous gay male couples. However, couples who'd agreed to be monogamous but in which one or both partners engaged in extrarelational sex were less well adjusted. LaSala (2004b) found that men in successful open relationships establish guidelines that safeguard their health and affirmed couple primacy. Obviously, therapists need to respect their clients' preferences and help them decide what type of relationship works best for them.

Heterosexual therapists may underestimate the complexities involved in coming out to family and friends (LaSala, 2010). Here it may be well to remember that therapy isn't about pushing people to go where they're afraid to go but helping them recognize and resolve the fears that hold them back.

Another difficulty that heterosexual therapists may overlook in same-sex relationships is the prevalence of jealousy on the part of one of the partners (Green &

Mitchell, 2002). This jealousy is based on the belief that others are a threat because of lack of respect for the couple's commitment to each other. After all, how can a relationship be real if the partners aren't married?

CASE STUDY

Jim enjoyed the club scene as a way to socialize with his friends in the gay community. His partner, Kyle, preferred to avoid bars and clubs. According to Kyle, his objections weren't so much to Jim's having a good time, but that he believed other men in the clubs had little respect for the fact that Jim was part of a couple. "They don't care about us if they think they can get in your pants." Kyle was also concerned about the prevalence of designer drugs—like ecstasy, cocaine, and crystal meth—that were part of the club atmosphere. Jim insisted that he wasn't interested in other men and didn't do drugs. He just wanted to hang out with his friends.

Although some therapists might see Jim's insistence on going to bars as a failure to accept that he was no longer single, the therapist in this case was aware that in fact not going to bars and clubs can result in a significant disconnect from much of the gay community. And so, rather than accept the Hobson's choice the couple presented—either Jim gave in and stayed home or Kyle gave in and Jim continued to go clubbing—the therapist wondered out loud if there were alternative ways for the couple to socialize within the gay community.

Maybe the best advice for therapists working with gay and lesbian couples is to have them ask themselves, what messages am I communicating to this couple about the value of same-sex relationships? It isn't just negative messages that therapists should be alert to but also the danger of glorifying same-sex relationships. Denigration and idealization have an equal potential for harm.

◆ ◆ ◆

Imagine what it feels like to be a woman trapped in a man's body, or that nature played a cruel trick on you by making you a boy on the inside but a girl on the outside. Or perhaps you don't feel completely male or female but some combination of both? Now imagine you love a person struggling with these contradictions. Such are the challenges facing transgender persons and their families.

All too often, transgender people are sensationalized, pathologized, medicalized, and marginalized. Like gays and lesbians, transgender people face a world intolerant of any deviation from gender norms. A woman who acts like a man or a man who acts like a woman can unnerve some people. Like most people in our society, parents are uncomfortable with cross-gendered behavior, especially in their own children. So it can be extremely difficult for parents to adjust to the news that their children feel as if their psychological gender is at odds with the bodies they were born with. Mallon (1999) and Lev (2006) describe how deeply distressing such a disclosure can be for parents and how children coming out as transgender risk being ejected from their homes. For spouses, the discovery that a husband or wife is transgender can feel like a devastating betrayal (Lev, 2006). When transgender people come to terms with themselves, they desperately need the support of the very people who may have the most difficulty accepting them—their families.

Fortunately, like parents of gay and lesbian individuals, families of transgender people can adjust over time, and the process is made a little easier if they get sound information and guidance. Arlene Istar Lev (2004) developed a stage model of how families react to the discovery that a spouse, son, or daughter is transgender. These stages progress from *discovery* to *turmoil* to *negotiation* and *balance*. In a study of eighteen mothers of female-to-male transgender children, respondents spoke of feelings of loss, the need for support outside the family, and how seeing their children happy helped them adjust (Pearlman, 2006). There are profound challenges faced by families of transgender persons, and much more work in this area is needed. Nevertheless, armed with the right tools and information, family therapists can bring compassion and understanding to help anguished families through the emotional challenges that arise when transgender members come to terms with their true selves. For further guidance, therapists might consult Lev's (2004) seminal text, *Transgender Emergence: Therapeutic Guidelines for Working with Gender-Variant People and their Families*.

◆ Home-Based Services

Like traditional family therapy, home-based services target the family as the primary recipient of mental health care (Friesen & Koroloff, 1990). Unlike conventional models, however, the home-based approach focuses more on expanding the network of a family's resources than on repairing family dysfunction (Henggeler & Borduin, 1990). While home-based services recognize and address problems in the family system, the primary emphasis is on building relationships between the family and community resources.

Home-based services generally include four elements: family support, therapeutic intervention, case management, and crisis intervention (Lindblad-Goldberg, Dore, & Stern, 1998). *Family support* includes respite care as well as assistance with food, clothing, and shelter. *Therapeutic intervention* may include individual, family, or couples treatment. The overriding therapeutic goal is strengthening and stabilizing the family unit. Families are empowered by helping them utilize their own resources for solving problems rather than relying on out-of-home placement of the children. *Case management* involves developing links to community resources, including such things as medical care, welfare, education, job training, and legal services. *Crisis intervention* means making available twenty-four-hour emergency services, either with the home-based agency or by contracting with an outside mental health emergency service.

Visiting a family at home gives a therapist the opportunity to show interest in the things that define their identity, such as children, pets, religious artifacts, mementos, and awards. Looking through photo albums can be a valuable method in joining with a family and learning about their history and their hopes and dreams.

Once a positive relationship has been established—but not before—the therapist can ask the family to reduce such distractions as smoking, loud television playing, or barking dogs. (Barking cats are less often a problem.) Roles and boundaries that are implicit in an office setting may need to be spelled out. Clarifying roles begins with defining what the process of treatment entails, the ground rules for sessions, and what the therapist's and family members' roles will be. The following comments illustrate the process of clarifying roles (adapted from Lindblad-Goldberg, Dore, & Stern, 1998).

CASE STUDY

"Before we start, I want to say that I have no intention of coming here and telling you how to run your lives. My job is to help you figure out how you want to deal with your children. I can't solve your problems. Only you can do that."

"In our meetings, it's important for you to say whatever you think and feel. We need to be honest. Tell me what you expect of me, and I'll tell you what I expect of you. I won't act like I have all the answers, because I don't."

"Will Grandmother be coming tonight? If not, that's okay, but I would like her to attend future sessions, because I'm sure she has valuable ideas to contribute."

"Tonight, I'd like to get to know each of you a little bit. After that, I'd like to hear what concerns each of you have about your family life and what you'd like to change."

While family therapists often refer to their "eco-systemic" orientation, home-based workers really must coordinate their efforts with other service systems (Boyd-Franklin & Bry, 2000). Rather than being critical of school personnel or juvenile justice workers who don't seem to support the family and child, home-based workers must learn to appreciate that these other agencies are equally concerned about the needs of their clients, even though their approaches may differ. A family served by multiple agencies that don't see eye to eye is no different from a child caught in a triangle between parents who don't work together as a team.

Several studies have found the most important element in the success of home-based therapy is the quality of the therapeutic relationship (e.g., Cortes, 2004). Therapists who are warm and nonjudgmental are perceived as most helpful (Thompson, Bender, Lantry, & Flynn, 2007). Clients also want therapists to be real with them. This means, for example, not insinuating that they "understand" what the clients are going through. It also means being willing to share their own personal experiences. But clients want therapists to be more than simply friendly; they want therapists to be direct with them, letting them know how things stand in a kind of "this is how it works" approach (McWey, Humphreys, & Pazdera, 2011).

One of the most damaging things that can happen in any form of psychotherapy is for clients to recreate with their therapists the same unsatisfying kinds of relationships they have with most people. Perhaps the most important thing a therapist can do is to avoid being drawn into the usual pattern. The most dangerous pattern for home-based workers to repeat is moving in too close and then pushing clients to go where they are afraid to go. Rather than start pushing for change right away, it's often more effective to begin by recognizing the obstacles to change.

Beleaguered families fear abandonment; insecure therapists fear not being helpful. The worker who feels a pull to do everything for a client may subsequently feel overwhelmed by the family's needs and back away by setting rigid limits and withholding support. The "rescuer" then becomes another "abandoner." This process reactivates the clients' anxiety and inevitably pushes them away. The lessons for the family are clear: Nothing will ever change—and don't trust anyone.

◆ Psychoeducation and Schizophrenia

The search for a cure for schizophrenia launched the field of family therapy in the 1950s. Ironically, while we now know that schizophrenia is a biological illness, family therapy, or at least the psychoeducational model, is once again considered part of the most effective treatment for this baffling disorder.

The psychoeducational model was born of dissatisfaction with both traditional family therapy and psychiatric approaches to schizophrenia. As Carol Anderson, Douglas Reiss, and Gerald Hogarty (1986) lamented,

> We have blamed each other, the patients themselves, their parents and grandparents, public authorities, and society for the cause and for the too often terrible course of these disorders. When hope and money become exhausted, we

frequently tear schizophrenic patients from their families, consigning them to the existential terror of human warehouses, single room occupancy hotels, and more recently to the streets and alleys of American cities. (p. vii)

In their attempts to get at the function of the schizophrenic's symptoms, family therapists urged family members to express bottled-up feelings and thus created sessions of highly charged emotion, which often did little more than stir up tension. Meanwhile, studies began to show that the patients who fared best after hospitalization were those who returned to the least stressful households. A British group, including George Brown, John Wing, Julian Leff, and Christine Vaughn, focused on what they called *expressed emotion (EE)* in the families of schizophrenics—criticism, hostility, and emotional overinvolvement—and found that patients returning to high EE households had higher rates of relapse (Brown, Birley, & Wing, 1972; Vaughn & Leff, 1976; Vaughn et al., 1984).

Research on expressed emotion suggests that schizophrenia is a thought disorder that renders individuals particularly sensitive to criticism and hostility (Hooley, Gruber, Scott, Hiller, & Yurgelun-Todd, 2005; McFarlane & Cook, 2007). Intense emotional input makes it difficult for patients to cope with the welter of chaotic thoughts that plague them. When recovering patients return to stressful family settings, where EE is high, intrusive overconcern and critical comments lead to increased emotional arousal, and it is this affective overload that triggers relapse.

The benefits of reducing EE in helping families cope with schizophrenia has been repeatedly demonstrated (Atkinson & Coia, 1995). Lowering EE has also been shown to contribute to reduced relapse rates for major depression and bipolar disorder (Muesser & Glynn, 1995).

With this in mind, three different groups in the late 1970s began experimenting with ways to reduce stress in the most common environments for schizophrenic patients: their parents' homes. Michael Goldstein led a group at UCLA (Goldstein et al., 1978) who designed a brief, structured model focused on anticipating the stresses a family was likely to face and reducing conflict around the patient. Following the Goldstein study, groups headed by Ian Falloon at the University of Southern California (whose model is primarily behavioral) and Carol Anderson at the Western Psychiatric Institute in Pittsburgh experimented with psychoeducational models.

Psychoeducators seek to establish a collaborative partnership in which family members feel supported and empowered to deal with the patient. To achieve this kind of partnership, Anderson and her colleagues (1986) find that they must reeducate professionals to give up ideas that the family is somehow responsible for schizophrenia, reinforce family strengths, and share information with the family about this disease. It is this information sharing that constitutes the educational element of psycho *education*. Information about the nature and course of schizophrenia helps family members develop a sense of mastery—a way to understand and anticipate the often chaotic and apparently uncontrollable process.

One of psychoeducation's key interventions is to lower expectations—to reduce pressure on the patient to perform normally. For example, the goals for the first year following an acute episode are primarily the avoidance of a relapse and the gradual taking on of some responsibilities in the home. Family members should view the patient as someone who's had a serious illness and needs to recuperate. Patients may need a great deal of sleep, solitude, and limited activity for some time following an episode; they may also seem restless and have trouble concentrating. By predicting these developments, psychoeducators try to prevent conflict between the patient and the family.

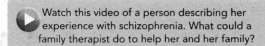
Watch this video of a person describing her experience with schizophrenia. What could a family therapist do to help her and her family?

Anderson's psychoeducational approach looks very much like structural family therapy, except that the family's structural flaws are construed as the *result* of rather than *cause* of the presenting problem. Much of the therapy follows familiar themes: reinforcing generational boundaries, opening up the family to the outside world and developing support

networks, urging parents to reinvest in their marriage, and getting family members to not speak or do for the patient.

Anderson and her colleagues begin with a day-long survival skills workshop in which they teach family members about the prevalence and course of schizophrenia, its biological etiology, current modes of pharmacologic and psychosocial treatment, common medications, and prognosis. The patient's needs and the family needs are discussed and family coping skills are introduced. Research findings on expressed emotion are presented and guidelines are offered for keeping EE in check. Families are encouraged not to pressure recovering patients or to urge them to hurry back to normal functioning. Families are also advised to respect boundaries and to allow the recovering family member to withdraw whenever necessary.

The goal for the patient is symptom reduction rather than cure. Families are encouraged to provide a quiet, stable milieu in which the recovering patient doesn't feel criticized or blamed and told not to expect too much of him or her during recuperation. The goal for the family is to learn coping techniques for the difficult and long-term task of living with a schizophrenic person and preventing or delaying his or her relapse and rehospitalization. Table 10.1 presents a set of typical psychoeducational guidelines for managing rehabilitation following a schizophrenic episode.

Is the psychoeducational model effective? Yes. Consider results of the study by Anderson and colleagues (1986):

Among treatment takers (n = 90), 19% of those receiving family therapy alone experienced a psychotic relapse in the year following hospital discharge. Of those receiving the individual behavioral therapy, 20% relapsed, but *no* patient in the treatment cell that received both family therapy and social skills training experienced a relapse. These relapse rates constitute significant effects for both treatments when contrasted to a 41% relapse rate for those receiving only chemotherapy and support. (p. 24)

Other studies have shown equally impressive results (Falloon et al., 1982; Leff et al., 1982). There seems to be little question that psychoeducation can

TABLE 10.1 Psychoeducational Guidelines for Families and Friends of Schizophrenics

Here is a list of things everyone can do to make things run more smoothly.

1. *Go slow.* Recovery takes time. Rest is important. Things will get better in their own time.
2. *Keep it cool.* Enthusiasm is normal. Tone it down. Disagreement is normal. Tone it down, too.
3. *Give 'em space.* Time out is important for everyone. It's okay to offer. It's okay to refuse.
4. *Set limits.* Everyone needs to know what the rules are. A few good rules keep things calmer.
5. *Ignore what you can't change.* Let some things slide. Don't ignore violence or use of street drugs.
6. *Keep it simple.* Say what you have to say clearly, calmly, and positively.
7. *Follow doctor's orders.* Take medications as they are prescribed. Take only medications that are prescribed.
8. *Carry on business as usual.* Reestablish family routines as quickly as possible. Stay in touch with family and friends.
9. *No street drugs or alcohol.* They make symptoms worse.
10. *Pick up on early signs.* Note changes. Consult with your family physician.
11. *Solve problems step by step.* Make changes gradually. Work on one thing at a time.
12. *Lower expectations, temporarily.* Use a personal yardstick. Compare this month with last month rather than with last year or next year.

Source: Republished with permission of Taylor and Francis Group LLC Books, from McFarlane, W. R. 1991. Family Psychoeducational Treatment. In Handbook of *Family Therapy*, Vol. II, A. S. Gurman and D. P. Kniskern, eds. New York: Brunner/Mazel. P.375; permission conveyed through Copyright Clearance Center, Inc.

delay relapse and readmission to a hospital better than other approaches to schizophrenia.

◆ Medical Family Therapy

Chronic illness has a devastating impact. It can take over a family's life, ravaging health, hope, and peace of mind. As Peter Steinglass says, it can be like a thief in the night "who has appeared on the doorstep, barged inside the home and demanded everything the family has" (quoted in McDaniel et al., 1992, p. 21).

In medical family therapy, the system isn't just the sick person's family; it's the family and the physicians and nurses involved in the sick person's care. The goal, therefore, is to foster communication and support not only within the family but also between the family and medical personnel (Atwood & Gallo, 2010; Wright & Bell, 2009; Schmaling & Sher, 2000). Illness leaves people feeling helpless and confused. Medical family therapy is designed to combat such feelings by fostering communication and a sense of agency.

Medical family therapists work in collaboration with pediatricians, family practitioners, rehabilitation specialists, and nurses. They advocate that near the time of diagnosis, families should receive a routine consultation to explore their resources relative to the demands of the illness or disability. They cite the growing body of research suggesting a strong relationship between family dynamics and the clinical course of medical conditions (Campbell, 1986) and more recent research showing that family therapy has a positive effect on physical health and health care use (Law, Crane, & Russell, 2000).

Psychoeducational and medical family therapy share many elements with the other models in this chapter, which together represent a significant trend: a move toward a collaborative partnership with families. Therapists are now encouraged to look for a family's strengths rather than deficits and to find ways to lift families out of the guilt and blame that often accompany their problems.

◆ Relationship Enrichment Programs

The psychoeducational method has also been applied to couples and families for coping with everyday relationship problems. Some therapists are skeptical that self-help courses can substitute for the individual attention of a professionally trained therapist, yet these programs are enormously popular, not least because participants in *marital enrichment programs* feel little of the stigma that attaches to "being in therapy."

One of the best known of these programs is the Relationship Enhancement system developed by Bernard Guerney, Jr. (1977). Facilitators teach participants to clarify their conflicts and to express what they are feeling, accept each other's feelings, negotiate and work through problems, and learn to achieve satisfaction by becoming emotional partners (Ginsberg, 2000). Both lectures and experiential training take place in each session, and homework assignments are given to practice and extend skills in participants' everyday lives.

Relationship Enhancement programs provide couples with training in three sets of core skills (Ginsberg, 2000):

- The *Expressive (Owning) Skill*—gaining awareness of one's own feelings and taking responsibility for them without projecting them onto others.
- The *Empathic Responding (Receptive) Skill*—learning to listen to the other person's feelings and motives.
- The *Conversive (Discussion-Negotiation/ Engagement) Skill*—learning to acknowledge the meaning of what was heard; partners may switch positions between listener and speaker.

To help couples assess their preparation for marriage, David Olson and his colleagues developed the Premarital Personal and Relationship Inventory (PREPARE). This 165-item questionnaire (Olson, 1996) is designed to help couples understand and discuss their backgrounds, expectations, and areas where they might encounter difficulties. Attitudes and expectations are explored in eleven areas, including marriage expectations, communication, sexual relationship, personality differences, financial management, conflict resolution, childrearing, leisure, family and friends, marital roles, and spiritual beliefs. PREPARE has proven useful for identifying potential conflicts and promoting discussions that may head off problems in the future (Stahmann & Hiebert, 1997).

By far the most popular of the relationship enhancement programs is the *marriage encounter* weekend, first introduced in Barcelona by a Jesuit priest, Father Gabriel Calvo (Chartier, 1986). These weekend retreats, which provide support and enrichment for Catholic couples, were imported into this country in the late 1960s and have since been widely adopted by a variety of church groups (Stahmann & Hiebert, 1997). Thousands of couples have taken advantage of these weekend enrichment programs to work on their

communication, problem-solving skills, sexual intimacy, and spiritual issues. Some denominations even require couples to participate in such a program before they can be married in the church.

A more carefully researched relationship enrichment program is the Prevention and Relationship Enhancement Program (PREP), developed by Floyd, Markham, Kelly, Blumberg, and Stanley (1995) at the University of Denver. This social learning approach, developed in the 1980s, teaches communication and conflict resolution skills and explores attitudes and expectations about marriage. The primary goal is to help couples learn to face and resolve conflicts, and thus avoid incorporating unhealthy defensive patterns in their relationship (Silliman, Stanley, Coffin, Markman, & Jordan, 2002).

Table 10.2 offers some guidelines for making relationships work.

Summary

Family therapists taught us to see past individual personalities to the patterns that make them a family, an organization of interconnected lives governed by strict but unspoken rules. But in the process they created a mechanistic entity—the family system—and then set about doing battle with it. Most of the challenges that have reshaped family therapy have been in reaction to this mechanism. But if the systemic revolution went too far in one direction, the same may be true of some of its critics.

The feminist critique was the first and perhaps most influential of the challenges to family therapy's traditions. In taking a stand against mother bashing, feminists challenged the essence of systems thinking by pointing out that concepts like complementarity and circular causality can imply that subjugated women were as much to blame as their oppressors.

Family therapy's bridge to the twenty-first century was social constructionism. Much as was the case when the pioneers shifted their focus from individuals to families, this recent shift from behavior to cognition and from challenging to collaborating is opening up a new world of possibilities. We'll see just how exciting some of those possibilities are in the next few chapters.

TABLE 10.2 Critical Skills for Effective Functioning as a Couple

A. Structure

1. **Accommodation**

   Learn to accept and adjust to each other's preferences and expectations, compromising on some issues, but not always giving in, so as not to build up resentment.

   She learned to accept his wish to eat supper early, while he agreed to join her for weekly religious services. But she didn't agree to put her career on a part-time basis; and he continued to take his yearly fishing trip with his brothers despite her hating to be left behind.

2. **Boundary Making**

   Create a protective boundary around your relationship that reduces but doesn't eliminate contact with outsiders.

   He stopped going out three nights a week with his buddies; she started asking him if it was okay before agreeing to let her parents come for the weekend.

   Demonstrating your commitment to your partner builds a secure base of attachment as well as confidence in the permanence of your relationship. Make sure your partner knows that you care, and that you are committed.

   He stopped defending himself by saying "If you don't like it, why don't you find someone else," because it only made her insecure and angry. She made a point of telling him who she had lunch with, because she knew his jealousy made him worry.

B. Communication

1. Listen to and acknowledge your partner's point of view.

   She discovered that making a sincere effort to say things like "So you like that one better because . . ." before countering with her own opinion made him feel that she respected his point of view. When it came to the most contentious issues, he discovered that asking first how she felt and then listening at length was essential. In some cases it was a good idea not even to express his side of the matter until a later time.

2. Short-circuit escalation in arguments by learning to back off before negative spirals get nasty. Call a time-out and agree to talk at a specific time later.

   "I'm getting upset; let's stop and talk about this tonight after supper, okay?"

3. Avoid invalidation and put-downs.

   "You're so irresponsible" may be obvious but is no more invalidating than "I think you're overreacting." Don't criticize your partner's personality or deny what he or she is feeling.

C. Problem Solving

1. Make positive requests, such as *"Would you be willing . . . ?"* rather than criticisms, such as *"You never . . . !"*

2. If you ask for something, be prepared to give something in return.

   It was easier to get him to do things with her and the children if she also made a point of suggesting times when he could do some of the things he liked to do by himself. He learned that occasionally volunteering to do the shopping or cook dinner made her feel more like doing things for him—and that volunteering worked better than trying to make deals.

3. Wait until you're not angry before bringing up a problem to be solved. Raise concerns directly but gently.

   She was furious that he took her father's side against her in an argument. But she decided not to say anything until she calmed down. The following night after supper she began by saying "Honey, I want to talk about something I'm feeling but I'm afraid to because it might make you mad." Emphasizing that it was her feelings and saying that she was concerned about how he might react helped put him in a receptive mood.

4. Think of the two of you as a team working against the problem.

   Instead of battling over his "coldness" and her "dependency," they started talking about how they could adjust for their "different comfort levels." As a result they planned their next vacation so that they could play golf and tennis together, and she could visit friends while he took one day off for fishing.

(Continued)

TABLE 10.2 *(Continued)*

5. Be sure you understand your partner's concerns before trying to work on a solution.

He was upset that she wanted to make only a minimal down payment on their new house, because it would result in large mortgage payments. To him it made more sense to put down as much as they could in order to make the monthly payments as low as possible. But instead of continuing to argue he asked her what she was worried about. Her concern turned out to be that without a cushion of savings, they might be wiped out by some unforeseen emergency. Now at least he understood how she felt.

D. Consideration

1. Do pleasing things for your partner and the relationship.

Spontaneous gestures—like compliments, hugs, little presents, calling in the middle of the day to say "I love you"—reassure your partner that you care and help to maintain a positive feeling about the relationship.

E. Fun

1. Make the effort to spend enjoyable time together, and don't use fun activities as a time to discuss difficult issues or conflicts.

He got in the habit of inviting her to join him for a movie, a walk in the park, or a visit to the museum and then supper out on Saturdays. She learned that bringing up problems on these trips tended to spoil the mood.

Source: Adapted from Nichols, M. P. 2009. *The Lost Art of Listening*, 2nd ed. New York: Guilford Press.

The headline story of family therapy's evolution from first- to second-order cybernetics, from MRI to solution-focused therapy, from Milan systemic to Hoffman and Goolishian, and from constructivism to social constructionism and now narrative, is what's been in the forefront of intellectual discussion. While these front-page developments were taking place, family therapists practicing less trendy approaches (behavioral, psychoanalytic, structural, Bowenian, and experiential) have continued their work. So it can be a mistake to think that what's new is the only thing going on in the field.

The collaborative movement raised new questions about the therapist's style of leadership. When Harlene Anderson and Harry Goolishian advocated a collaborative approach, what was being rejected was the medical model—an authoritarian role model in which the clinician plays the expert to whom the patient looks for answers. But being an expert doesn't mean being a bully. Here the advance is challenging the medical model, which ironically was perpetuated in such avant-garde models of family therapy as the strategic and Milan systemic approaches. No longer do we see the therapist as a technocrat of change. But

that doesn't mean therapists shouldn't be experts—leaders in the process of change.

Just as family therapy hasn't stood still in recent years, neither has the family. Today's family is evolving and stressed. We've gone from the complementary model of the family in the 1950s to a symmetrical version—although we haven't come to terms with the new model yet. Perhaps it's time to ask this question: As the American family struggles through this stressful time of transition, what concepts does family therapy offer to help us understand and deal with the protean family forms of the twenty-first century?

Click here to apply your knowledge of chapter concepts.

Click here to test your application and analysis of the content found within this chapter.

M ost therapy is based on the premise that when a client presents a problem—depression, say, or perhaps a misbehaving child—the clinician's job is to figure out what's causing the problem so that he or she will know how to solve it. Solution-focused therapists believe that it isn't necessary to know what causes problems in order to make things better.

Solution-focused practitioners assume that people who come to therapy are capable of behaving effectively but that their effectiveness has been blunted by a negative mindset. Drawing their attention to forgotten capabilities helps release clients from preoccupation with their failures and restores them to their more capable selves. Problems are seen as overwhelming because clients see them as *always* happening. Times when problems aren't happening aren't noticed, or dismissed as trivial. The art of solution-focused therapy becomes a matter of helping clients see that their problems have **exceptions**—times when they don't occur—and that these exceptions are solutions they already have in their repertoires.

Sketches of Leading Figures

Solution-focused therapy grew out of the work of Steve de Shazer, Insoo Berg, and their colleagues at the Brief Family Therapy Center (BFTC) in Milwaukee. This training institute was started in 1979 when some of the staff at a community agency who were drawn to the MRI model became dissatisfied with the agency's constraints and broke off to form the BFTC. The initial group included married partners Steve de Shazer and Insoo Berg, Jim Derks, Elaine Nunnally, Marilyn La Court, and Eve Lipchik. Their students included John Walter, Jane Peller, and Michele Weiner-Davis.

The late Steve de Shazer was the founder of solution-focused therapy, and his writings are among

LEARNING OUTCOMES

♦ Describe the evolution of solution-focused therapy.

♦ Describe the main tenets of solution-focused therapy.

♦ Describe healthy and unhealthy family development from a solution-focused therapy perspective.

♦ Describe the clinical goals and the conditions necessary for meeting those goals from a solution-focused therapy perspective.

♦ Discuss and demonstrate the assessment and intervention techniques of solution-focused therapy.

♦ Discuss research support for solution-focused therapy.

the most inventive in this approach (e.g., de Shazer, 1988, 1991). A scholar as well as a clinician, de Shazer was intrigued by Bateson's theories of communication and Milton Erickson's pragmatic ideas about how to influence change. Early in his career, de Shazer worked in Palo Alto and followed the MRI approach. De Shazer died in Vienna on September 11, 2005.

Insoo Kim Berg was, along with Steve de Shazer, one of the primary architects of the solution-focused approach. She trained therapists all over the world and authored a host of books and articles applying the model to a variety of problems and service settings, including alcoholism (Berg & Miller, 1992), marital therapy (Berg, 1994a), and family-based services to the poor (Berg, 1994b). She died in 2007.

After training with de Shazer, Michele Weiner-Davis converted an agency program in Woodstock, Illinois, to the solution-focused model. Weiner-Davis (1992) applied the model to marital problems in her popular book *Divorce-Busting*.

Although Bill O'Hanlon never formally studied at the BFTC, he was trained in brief problem-solving therapy by Milton Erickson, and so the step toward solution-focused therapy was an easy one. O'Hanlon collaborated with Weiner-Davis to write one of the early books on solution-focused therapy (O'Hanlon & Weiner-Davis, 1989) and was thereafter prominently associated with the approach. He is a popular workshop presenter and has written a number of books and articles on his pragmatic approach, which he calls *possibility therapy* (O'Hanlon, 1998).

As a student of Berg and de Shazer since the mid-1980s, Yvonne Dolan has applied the solution-focused model to the treatment of trauma and abuse (Dolan, 1991) and coauthored an influential volume of case studies (Berg & Dolan, 2001). She has also written about the model's application in agency settings (Pichot & Dolan, 2003) and most recently the state of the art of solution-focused therapy (de Shazer, Dolan, Korman, Trepper, Berg, & McCollum, 2007).

Other well-known solution-focused therapists include Eve Lipchik, Scott Miller, John Walter, and Jane Peller. Lipchik, who worked at the BFTC for eight years until she left in 1988, pioneered the application of the solution-focused model to wife battering (Lipchik & Kubicki, 1996), and published one of the most useful books about how to do solution-focused therapy (Lipchik, 2011). Scott Miller worked at the BFTC for three years, directing the alcohol and drug treatment services, and has written widely about the model. John Walter and Jane Peller practice together in Chicago. They trained at the BFTC and, after writing a book laying out the steps of the approach (Walter & Peller, 1992), became popular presenters on the workshop circuit.

Theoretical Formulations

Like the MRI group, solution-focused therapists believe that people are constrained by narrow views of their problems into perpetuating rigid patterns of false solutions. When you put all your eggs in one basket, you must clutch that basket for dear life. As O'Hanlon and Weiner-Davis (1989) put it:

> So, the meanings people attribute to behavior limit the range of alternatives they will use to deal with a situation. If the methods used do not produce a satisfactory outcome, the original assumption about the meaning of the behavior is generally not questioned. . . . Instead, people often redouble their efforts to solve the problem in an ineffective way, thinking that by doing it more, harder or better (e.g., more punishments, more heart-to-heart talks, and so on) they will finally solve it. (p. 48)

The MRI model was inspired by Milton Erickson's view of people as containing vast reservoirs of untapped creativity. According to this view, people may only need a shift of perspective to release their potential. Part of that shift involves changing the way people talk about their problems.

Courtesy Yvonne Dolan

Yvonne Dolan is a leader in solution-focused therapy.

The language of problems tends to be different from the language of solutions. As Ludwig Wittgenstein (1958) put it, "The world of the happy is quite another than that of the unhappy." Usually, problem talk is negative, focuses on the past, and implies the permanence of problems. The language of solutions is more hopeful and future oriented. Part of a therapist's job is to steer clients from problem talk to solution talk. In the solution-focused model, the future is negotiable.

Family Dynamics

In presenting this model, it's tempting to skip family dynamics, because solution-focused therapists don't have much to say on this subject. But there is a reason for this. The more you emphasize family dynamics, the more you see people embedded in a network of connections that constrain their actions. Solution-focused therapists pay less attention to the forces controlling family members because they see people as relatively fluid and changeable—and they treat them that way in therapy.

◆ Normal Family Development

In the solution-focused model, clients are assumed to be the experts on their own lives. Just as they know what's troubling them, so, too, they know what they need. This philosophy is exemplified by the practice of routinely asking clients "Is there anything else I should have asked you or that you need to tell me?" As described by De Jong and Berg (2002), "If as a practitioner, you wish to put clients into the position of being experts on their own lives, you will have to know how to set aside your own frame of reference as much as possible and explore those of your clients" (p. 20).

Solution-focused therapists assume that people are resourceful. The problems they have are not seen as evidence of failure but rather as normal life-cycle complications. This optimistic perspective needn't be dismissed as Pollyannaish. Rather, it can be seen as a commitment to the belief that families have the ability to construct solutions that can enhance their lives.

Implicit in this model is an asymptomatic perspective on family normality; that is, a normal family is simply one that has been freed of its presenting problems and thus returned to its own unique functional way of living.

Solution-oriented therapists don't believe that there is any single "correct" or "valid" way to live one's life. We have come to understand that what is unacceptable behavior in one family or for one person is desirable behavior in another. Therefore, clients, not therapists, identify the goals to be accomplished in treatment (O'Hanlon & Weiner-Davis, 1989, p. 44).

◆ Development of Behavior Disorders

In the solution-focused world, this subject is closed. The very act of categorizing people suggests that they are a certain way all the time. When we say that a couple is "disengaged," does this mean that there are never times when they are not disengaged? Unfortunately, the act of labeling draws attention away from those other times.

Just as solution-focused therapists steer clients away from speculating about problem formation, they also avoid such conjecture themselves. Their conviction is that solutions are often unrelated to the way problems developed and that exploring etiology is engaging in problem talk—exactly what they seek to avoid. They believe that problem-focused thinking keeps people from discovering effective solutions. Problems persist in the way people define situations and in the misdirected actions they persist in taking.

Mechanisms of Change

Solution-focused therapy works by setting clear goals and building on exceptions to problems. In the following sections we will emphasize these defining characteristics. But keep in mind that good therapy is never a simple matter of implementing a few specific techniques. It is—or should be—a complicated enterprise involving all the elements that make helping relationships work.

Goals of Therapy

The goal of solution-focused therapy is to resolve the presenting complaint as expeditiously as possible. The search for underlying flaws is rejected. As de Shazer (1991) writes, "Structuralist thought points to the idea that symptoms are the result of some underlying problem, a psychic or structural problem such as incongruent hierarchies, covert parental conflicts, low self-esteem, deviant communication, repressed feelings, 'dirty games,' etc." Solution-focused therapists don't believe that it's necessary to delve into these deeper issues in order to help people resolve their problems. The goal is never about how families should be structured but only what they want different in their lives.

The process of goal setting itself is an important intervention in this approach. Walter and Peller (1992) emphasize the importance of assisting clients in creating well-defined goals, framed in positive terms and modest enough to be achievable. Helping people to stop dwelling on their dissatisfactions and envision what they want to be doing instead is seen as the first step in helping them get there. Thus, although clients often come in with complaints stated in negative terms—"I want to be less depressed," "We want Roger to stop smoking pot"—solution-focused therapists help recast these complaints into positive goals by asking "What will you (or he) be doing instead?" If you've ever tried to lose weight, you've probably discovered that it's a lot more effective to take positive steps, like exercising and eating low-fat meals, than it is to concentrate on *not* eating Big Macs and french fries.

Conditions for Behavior Change

Solution-focused therapy works by helping clients amplify *exceptions* to their problems—effective solutions already in their repertoire. From Berg and de Shazer's (1993) point of view, what's needed for change is a shift in the way a problem is "languaged":

> Rather than looking behind and beneath the language that clients and therapists use, we think that the language they use is all that we have to go on. . . . What we talk about and how we talk about it makes a difference, and it is these differences that can be used to make a difference (to the client). . . . [W]e have come to see that the meanings arrived at in a therapeutic conversation are developed through a process more like negotiation than the development of understanding or an uncovering of what it is that is "really" going on. (p. 7)

Thus, changing the way people talk about their problems is all that needs to be accomplished, because "as the client and therapist talk more and more about the solution they want to construct together, they come to believe in the truth or reality of what they are talking about. This is the way language works, naturally" (Berg & de Shazer, 1993, p. 9). This is why solution-focused therapy can be so brief: It's a lot easier to get people to talk differently about their problems than it is to get them to change their behavior. The assumption is that getting them to talk positively will help them think positively—and ultimately to act positively to solve their problems.

Therapy

Assessment

After getting a brief description of the presenting complaint, solution-focused practitioners move directly to asking clients how things will be different in their lives when their problems are solved. Then, instead of formulating some kind of intervention plan, the therapist asks about times in the clients' lives when their problems do not happen or are less severe. The following questions (adapted from Lipchik, 2011) suggest the proactive nature of a solution-focused assessment:

"What do you think the problem is now?"

"How will you know when the problem is solved?"

"How will you know you don't have to come here anymore? What will the signs be?"

"What will have to be different for that to happen in terms of your behavior, thoughts, and feelings?"

"What will you notice that is different about others involved in the situation?"

"What is your wildest fantasy about what you want to happen?"

Because they aren't interested in assessing family dynamics, solution-focused practitioners don't feel the need to convene any particular group of people. Instead, they say that anyone who is concerned about the problem should attend sessions. They also need little intake information because they want to hear clients' constructions of their problems firsthand. Solution-focused therapists ask more about perceptions than about feelings. And they affirm the clients' position. All clients want some indication that their therapist has understood the point of view that guides their actions.

The process of assessment in this model differs radically from problem-solving approaches. The solution-focused therapist doesn't function as an expert in determining what's wrong (enmeshment, triangulation) and planning how to correct it. In this therapy, clients are the experts on what they want to change (Walter & Peller, 1992). Although solution-focused therapists don't play the role of an authority figure who will help clients solve their problems, they do take an active position in moving clients away from worrying about their predicament and toward steps to solution.

The following sorts of questions are asked to lay the groundwork for therapeutic goal development:

"What needs to happen as a result of coming here, so that afterward you will look back and be able to say that it was a good idea?"

"What needs to happen so that this will not have been a waste of your time?"

"Often in our experience, we have found that in between scheduling an appointment and coming in, something happens that contributes to making a problem better. Has anything happened to improve the problem that brought you here today?"

Based on the answers to these questions, the therapist and clients begin to construct a more detailed description of the therapeutic goal. Once this description of the goal has been developed, the therapist asks the clients to assess their current level of progress toward that goal by imagining a scale of 1–10, where 1 represents the problem at its worst, and 10 is the point at which the problem is gone or the clients are coping with it so well that it's no longer problematic.

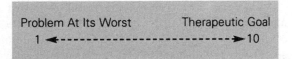

The clients' rating makes it possible to assess how far they are from the goal. Later, the same scale can be used to determine what specific actions will allow the clients to move toward the goal and to evaluate progress. If the clients identify new problems, the therapist makes a new scale to depict desired outcomes and to assess progress toward new solutions.

In an approach as direct as solution-focused therapy, it's important to assess clients' motivation for change. Following de Shazer (1988), practitioners distinguish between *visitors, complainants*, and *customers*.

A **visitor** is someone who's not really in the market for therapy. Visitors are there at someone else's insistence—a judge, a parent, the school principal—but they don't really have a complaint and don't want to be there. Therapists should not offer any suggestions to these clients or seek to convince them that they really need therapy.

With visitors it's important to pay attention to how they were referred and to consider who the real client is—that is, the person who wants something to change. If the people in your office are present only because someone pressured them to be there, a useful strategy is to ask them what they need to do to satisfy the authority that compelled them to seek therapy:

"So, what has to happen to get your mother off your back?"

"What's the minimum we need to accomplish so that you won't have to keep coming for more sessions?"

Complainants do have clear complaints, but they're usually about someone else. Parents often seek therapy because their children are having problems. But while parents of young children may see the need to be involved in the solution, parents of older children often think that it's only the child who has the problem—drugs, depression, shyness—and may not see themselves as part of the solution. Wives seek couples therapy because their "husbands don't communicate," while husbands often show up only to placate their wives.

With complainants, it may be useful to suggest noticing exceptions in the problem behavior of the other family member. The solution-focused therapist accepts the complainant's views, gives compliments, and may suggest observing exceptions to the complaint pattern, as the following example illustrates.

> *Client:* It's my daughter. All she does is hang out with her friends. She never does her homework, and she never helps out around the house.
> *Therapist:* So how can I be of help to you?
> *Client:* Nothing I've ever done seems to make a difference. She just doesn't want to grow up and take responsibility for herself.

With such clients, solution-focused therapists try to shift the conversation from problem talk to solution talk.

> *Therapist:* What do you think needs to happen so that your daughter will be a little easier to live with?
> *Client:* She has to start doing her homework. I keep telling her that she won't get anywhere unless she finishes high school.
> *Therapist:* That seems like a big change. But suppose that did happen—suppose she did start doing her homework. What would your daughter be saying about how you are different with her then?
> *Client:* She hates it when I nag her. So she'd probably say that I wasn't nagging as much anymore.

Notice how the therapist at no point challenges the client's notion that the problem is her daughter. Nevertheless, by talking about a solution, the conversation comes around to how the mother might behave differently as part of the solution. This opens the door to her seeing that nagging less may be part of a more productive approach to her daughter.

Some clients who fit the description of a complainant are less flexible than the mother in this example. We've all seen people who steadfastly maintain that everything is someone else's fault. With such clients you can always ask "How were you hoping I might be useful to you?" Then strategize with them about how they can act differently to influence those recalcitrant others.

Customers have clear complaints and are ready to take action. With a customer, you can move directly to establish goals and look for solutions. It's much easier to work with people who are ready to make changes.

It should be pointed out that these distinctions—visitor, complainant, and customer—aren't qualities of character but qualities of the therapeutic relationship, and therefore fluid. With an apparently unmotivated complainant, a therapist's job is to engage in a solution-focused conversation, compliment the client, and possibly give an assignment to observe exceptions to the problem. By not pushing for change but instead shifting attention away from problems and toward solutions, the relationship may evolve into one in which the client becomes a customer for change.

◆ Therapeutic Techniques

Solution-focused techniques are organized around two fundamental strategies. The first is developing well-focused *goals* within the clients' frame of reference. The second is generating solutions based on *exceptions* (De Jong & Berg, 2002). Therapy is usually brief (three to five sessions), and appointments are made one at a time, on the assumption that one more may be enough.

Problem Description

Therapy begins with a description of the clients' problem: "How were you hoping I could help you?" Solution-focused therapists take pains to work within the clients' frame of reference. They ask for the clients' perceptions and are careful to acknowledge them, using the clients' own language as much as possible.

> *Therapist:* So you were saying that you want to do something about being so disorganized?
>
> *Client:* Yes, I can't keep track of half the things I'm supposed to be doing, and I end up scrambling to turn in assignments at the last minute. I hate myself for that! Sometimes I think maybe I just don't want to be doing this job.
>
> *Therapist:* So you think that maybe being disorganized has something to do with not really liking the work you're doing, and you've been feeling discouraged and down on yourself, is that right?

It's a good idea to ask clients what they've already tried to resolve their difficulties. People usually attempt various strategies to deal with their problems, and these efforts may have been more or less successful. Either way, these previous attempts at solution now play an important part in the clients' perception of what works and doesn't work for them.

Goal Setting

After hearing and acknowledging the clients' description of their problems and what they've tried to do about them, the next step is to establish clear and concrete goals. Solution-focused therapists help translate vague or amorphous goals into specific, behavioral terms by asking questions like:

"Specifically how will you be doing this?"

"How will the two of you know when you have solved your problems? How will things be different?"

"What will be the first sign (or smallest step) that will tell you that you're moving in the right direction? What else?"

The clearer the goal, the easier it is to measure progress. If, for example, a woman says that she would like to get along better with her husband, a therapist might ask: "Can you tell me more specifically what will be happening when you two are getting along better? What will you be doing differently? What will

your husband notice that will tell him that you two are getting along as opposed to not getting along?"

Notice in this example how the therapist asks the woman who wants to have a better relationship "What will you be doing differently?" Part of the process of solution-focused therapy is helping clients think about constructive actions *they* can take, rather than how they can get someone else to change. Useful goals are specific and include positive actions. They are also modest enough to be achievable.

Once when Insoo Berg was interviewing a client whose life seemed out of control, she asked the woman what needed to happen in order for things to be better. She replied that she wasn't sure—she had so many problems. "Maybe only a miracle will help, but I suppose that's too much to expect." Picking up on the client's words, Berg asked, "OK, suppose a miracle happened, and the problem that brought you here is solved. What would be different about your life" (De Jong & Berg, 2002, p. 85).

To Berg's surprise, this woman, who had seemed so overwhelmed and helpless, began to describe a clear and realistic picture of a well-functioning family. Thus was born one of the mainstays of solution-focused therapy: the **miracle question**. Here's how de Shazer (1988) phrases it:

> Now, I want to ask you a strange question. *Suppose* that while you are sleeping tonight and the entire house is quiet, a *miracle* happens. The miracle is that *the problem which brought you here is solved.* However, because you are sleeping, you don't know that the miracle has happened. So, when you wake up tomorrow morning, *what will be different* that will tell you that a miracle has happened and the problem which brought you here is solved? (p. 5)

The miracle question invites clients to envision positive outcomes and begins to activate a problem-solving mindset by giving them a mental picture of their goals—in the same way that visualizing the perfect serve helps a tennis player. The miracle question also helps clients look beyond the problem to see that what they really want might not be the elimination of the problem per se but to be able to do the things that the problem has been obstructing. If the therapist can encourage them to begin doing those things despite the problem, suddenly the problem may not loom as large.

For example, Mary says that if she wasn't bulimic, she'd get closer to people and have more fun. If, with her therapist's encouragement, Mary begins to take interpersonal risks and has more fun, then her bulimia may become less of a problem in her life.

Exploring Exceptions

Probing for exceptions—times when clients didn't have the problem—invites them to recognize that some potential solutions may already be in their grasp. Such probing involves asking **exception questions** like these:

"When in the recent past might the problem have happened but didn't (or was less intense or more manageable)?"

"What's different about those times when the problem doesn't happen?"

"How have you let your partner know when he or she does something that makes a positive difference to you?"

Finding exceptions in the recent past is most useful because clients can remember them in greater detail. Also, and since these exceptions just happened, it's more plausible that they could happen again. By exploring these times and what was different about them, clients find clues to what they can do to expand these exceptions.

For example, Mary, who has bulimia, may remember times the previous week when she had the urge to binge and purge but didn't. She may discover that at those times she was away from her parents and so didn't feel like she was disappointing them. She may decide that it's time to become more independent.

▶ Watch this video of Bill O'Hanlon exploring exceptions with a client. Do you think it is helping the family view the situation differently?

Exploring exceptions allows the therapist and client to build on past successes. Failing that, the therapist can ask why things aren't worse—"How did you manage that?"—and then build on that accomplishment. **Coping questions** can help clients recognize that simply by enduring, they are more resourceful than they realize:

"What keeps you going under such difficult circumstances?"

"How come things aren't worse?"

"What have you done to keep them from getting worse?"

If the client provides answers, the therapist can build on them with questions about how that endurance can be maintained and how more of that effort can be brought to bear.

A solution-focused therapist spends most of the session listening for evidence of previous solutions, exceptions, and goals. When such evidence comes out, the therapist punctuates it with enthusiasm and support. The therapist then works to keep solution talk in the forefront. This requires different skills from those used in traditional problem-focused therapies. Whereas a problem-focused therapist is concerned about missing clues to what caused or is maintaining a problem, a solution-focused therapist is concerned about missing clues to progress and solution. Yvonne Dolan (personal communication) demonstrates this process in the following case study.

CASE STUDY

Mother: She comes home and then just ignores me, acts like I'm not there. Comes home from school, just runs into her room. Who knows what she's doing in there? But I have a feeling it's not good.

Daughter: You say we fight all the time, so I just go in my room so we don't fight.

Mother: See? She admits she just tries to avoid me. I don't know why she can't just come home and talk to me a little about school or something, like she used to.

Therapist: Wait a second, when did she "used to"? Cheryl, when did you come home and tell your mom about school?

Daughter: I did that a lot; last semester I did.

Therapist: Can you give me an example of the last time you did that?

Mother: I can tell you. It was last week, actually. She was all excited about her science project getting chosen.

Therapist: Tell me more, what day was that?

Mother: I think last Wednesday.

Therapist: And she came home . . .?

Mother: She came home all excited.

Therapist: What were you doing?

Mother: I think I was getting dinner ready. And she came in all excited, and I asked her what was up, and she told me her science project was chosen for the display at school.

Therapist: Wow, that's quite an honor.

Mother: It is.

Therapist: So then what happened?

Mother: Well, we talked about it, she told me all about it.

Therapist: Cheryl, do you remember this?

Daughter: Sure, it was only last week. I was pretty happy.

Therapist: And would you say that this was a nice talk, a nice talk between you two?

Daughter: Sure. That's what I mean; I don't always go in my room.

Therapist: Was there anything different about that time, last week, that made it easier to talk to each other?

Mother: Well, she was excited.

Daughter: My mom listened. She wasn't doing anything else.

Therapist: Wow, this is a great example. Thank you. Let me ask this: If it were like that more often, where Cheryl talked to you about things that were interesting and important to her, and where Mom, you listened to her completely without doing other things, is that what you two mean by *"better communication?"*

Daughter: Yeah, exactly.

Mother: Yes.

In this example, the therapist used a variety of solution-focused interventions. First, she listened carefully for an exception to the problem—a time when the problem

could have happened but didn't. Second, she punctuated that exception by getting more details about it and congratulating the clients on it. Third, she connected the exception to their goal by asking how their goal would be reached if this exception were to occur more often.

Scaling Questions

Scaling questions were introduced to help therapists and clients talk about vague topics such as depression and communication, where it's difficult to identify concrete changes. Berg and de Shazer (1993) describe the use of **scaling questions**:

> The therapist asks the depressed client, for example, "On a scale of 1–10, with 1 being how depressed you felt when you called me and 10 being how you feel the day after the miracle, how do you feel right now?"
>
> The client might say 2 and the therapist might say, "So you feel a little better than when you called. How did you achieve this improvement?" Or the therapist might ask, "What do you think you need to do to achieve a 3?" In this way, the therapist and client can recognize and nurture small changes toward the goal rather than being stuck in the "I'm either depressed or I'm not" kind of thinking that typifies such problems.

Scaling questions are also used to get clients to quantify their confidence that they can maintain their resolve: "On a scale of 1–10, how confident are you that you will be able to avoid losing your temper this week?" This device has a kind of "prove-it" implication. The response is followed up by asking clients what they might do to increase the odds of success: "What do you have to do to stick to your guns this time?" Asking scaling questions is a useful way of anticipating and disarming resistance and backsliding and of encouraging commitment to change.

Here's an example of the use of scaling questions from a case of a couple who wanted to improve their communication.

Therapist: What I want to do now is scale the problem and the goal. Let's say 1 is as bad as the problem ever could be—you never talk, only fight, or avoid all the time. And let's say 10 is where you talk all the time, with perfect communication, never have a fight ever.

Susan: That's pretty unrealistic.

Therapist: That would be the ideal. So where would you two say it was for you at its worst? Maybe right before you came in to see me.

Susan: It was pretty bad. . . . I don't know. . . . I'd say a 2 or a 3.

Jim: Yeah, I'd say a 2.

Therapist: Okay (writing) . . . a 2 or 3 for you and a 2 for you. Now tell me what you would be satisfied with when therapy is over and successful?

Jim: I'd be happy with an 8.

Susan: Well, of course I'd like a 10, but that's unrealistic. Yeah, I agree. An 8 would be good.

Therapist: What would you say it is right now?

Susan: I would say it's a little better, because he's coming here with me, and I see that he's trying. I'd say maybe a 4?

Jim: Well, that's nice to hear. I wouldn't have thought she'd put it that high. I would say it's a 5.

Therapist: Okay, a 4 for you and a 5 for you. And you both want it to be an 8 for therapy to be successful, right?

This intervention has two major components. First, it's a solution-focused assessment device. That is, if it's used each session, the therapist and clients have an ongoing measure of progress. Second, it's a powerful intervention by itself, because it allows the therapist to focus on previous solutions and exceptions and to punctuate new changes as they occur. Like the changes made before the first session, one of three things can happen between each session: things can get better; things can stay the same; or things can get worse.

If things get better from one session to the next, the therapist compliments the clients and then gets details about how they were able to make such changes. This not only supports and solidifies the changes, but it also nudges clients to do more of the same. If things stay the same, the clients can be complimented on maintaining their changes or for not letting things get

worse: "How did you keep it from going down?" It's interesting how often that question will lead to a description of changes clients have made, in which case the therapist can again compliment and support and encourage more of that change.

CASE STUDY

Therapist: Susan, last week you were a 4 on the scale of good communications. I'm wondering where you are this week?

Susan (pause): I'd say a 5.

Therapist: A 5! Wow! Really, in just one week?

Susan: Yes, I think we communicated better this week.

Therapist: How did you communicate?

Susan: Well, I think it was Jim. He seemed to try to listen to me more.

Therapist: That's great. Can you give me an example of when he listened to you more?

Susan: Well, yes, yesterday for example. He usually calls me once a day at work, and—

Therapist: Sorry to interrupt, but did you say he calls you once a day?

Susan: Yes.

Therapist: I'm just a little surprised, because not all husbands call their wives every day.

Susan: He's always done that.

Therapist: Is that something you like? That you wouldn't want him to change?

Susan: Yes, for sure.

Therapist: Sorry, go on. You were telling me about yesterday when he called.

Susan: Well, usually it's kind of a quick call. But I told him about some problems I was having, and he listened for a long time, seemed to care, gave me some good ideas. That was nice.

Therapist: So that was an example of how you would like it to be—where you can talk about something, a problem, and he listens and gives good ideas? Support?

Susan: Yes.

Therapist: Jim, did you know that Susan liked your telephoning her at work and listening to her?

Jim: Yeah, I guess so. I've really been trying this week.

Therapist: That's great. What else have you done to try to make the communication better this week?

This example shows how going over the scale with the couple served as a vehicle for tracking their progress. The therapist gathered more and more information about the small changes the clients had made on their own that led to an improvement on the scale. This would naturally lead to suggesting that the couple continue to do the things that are working.

Compliments

Compliments are conveyed with questions that take the form of "How did you do that?" or, to be more accurate, "Wow! How did you do *that*?" Notice that this phrasing calls attention to the fact that the clients have already accomplished something. Rather than ask questions like "Have you ever had a job before" ask "What kinds of jobs have you had before?" Doing so invites clients to describe their successes and thus helps foster self-confidence.

To be effective, **compliments** should point toward what to do more, not what to eliminate. Most clients know what's wrong but have run out of ideas about how to avoid repeating the same old mistakes. Compliments can be used to highlight successful strategies and keep clients focused on those that work.

The following case study from Yvonne Dolan (personal communication) illustrates how compliments can be artfully woven in to support and enhance a client's efforts to make her life better.

CASE STUDY

Session 1

Therapist: What needs to happen as result of coming here in order for you to be able to say when you leave today that it's been useful?

Client: It's my mother. She has Alzheimer's, and she's driving me crazy.

Therapist: That sounds hard.

Client: You have no idea! She forgets to do things like turn the gas burner off, and sometimes she leaves the front door open. She forgets to put her clothes on if I don't remind her. I have to watch her all the time.

Therapist: So you're with her full time?

Client: Well, I have a woman who comes in a couple of times a week. Then I can get to the grocery store and, well, you know, do things like get my hair cut, do errands. Once in a while I get to see a friend. The rest of the time I'm either working or taking care of Mom.

Therapist: Oh, so you work outside the home as well?

Client: Yes. I'm a nail technician. I work part time.

Therapist: I'm impressed that you hold down a job plus being a full-time caregiver. It sounds like an awful lot to do. I can't imagine how you manage it all.

Client: Well, (hesitates) I guess that's why I'm here. It is pretty hard.

Therapist: It sounds like it takes a lot of continuous effort. I think most people would feel overwhelmed.

Client: Well, that's good to hear. But I've got to do something.

Therapist: Well, there is a strange question that sometimes helps in situations like this. I have to warn you, though, that it's a pretty weird question. Is it okay if I ask you this strange question?

Client: Okay.

Therapist: Well, let's suppose that tonight you go home and you eat dinner, perhaps watch some television, things like that—the sorts of things you would normally do. (Client nods.) And eventually it gets dark outside, and you get ready for bed. It gets later, and eventually the house is quiet and your mom is sleeping and eventually you fall asleep, too. And sometime during the night, something really strange happens while you are sleeping: a sort of miracle, but not just any kind of miracle, because in this case, the miracle is that you have found a way to cope with or alter this situation with your mom that really satisfies you. So let's suppose it's now the morning after the miracle, and you wake up and you don't know that the miracle has happened. What would be the first thing that you would notice that would tell you that something is different—that a miracle has happened and things are better?

Client: Gee, I really don't know. (Long pause while client looks down. Then she stares into the distance and begins speaking.) Well, the first thing is I would be glad to wake up. I would be looking forward to the day.

Therapist: How would that show up?

Client: I would get right up, put on some sort of outfit that had some color in it, and well, I would be able to do that because I would have my laundry done.

Therapist: So you would have an outfit ready, and it would be colorful. Then what?

Client: Well, my mom would still be there, I suppose, but I wouldn't be mad at her. I wouldn't resent her for being in my house. I mean, it isn't her fault that she has Alzheimer's. So I would fix coffee for both of us, and I'd let the dogs out, and maybe she and I would go out and have our breakfast out on the back porch.

Therapist: Sounds kind of nice . . .

Client: We have a really pretty view from the back porch.

Therapist: So what else?

Client: Well, then I wouldn't have to go to work because this is a miracle, right? (laughs)

Therapist: What would you do instead?

Client: I guess I would go for a walk, only I couldn't do this with my mom. I guess, well, I don't want to say that she wouldn't be there, but if she wasn't there, maybe I could take a walk.

Therapist: So you would take a walk—that's part of your miracle. What else?

Client: Well, after the walk, I would call my friend. I haven't talked to my friend for almost a month.

Therapist: You'd call your friend. I wonder what you would talk about.

Client: Well, I wouldn't be complaining about my mother, and I wouldn't be complaining about my weight.

Therapist: I wonder what you would be doing instead.

Client: Well, this is a miracle, so I would have lost the weight the doctor told me to lose.

Therapist: So the extra weight would be gone. And what else?

Client: Well, I would be going out at night sometimes, maybe even a date.

Therapist: Dating?

Client: Yes.

Therapist: Anything else?

Client: Not really. I mean, I suppose I would have lots of money, but other than that. . . . I don't know. (Looks down at floor, sighs.) My life is pretty far from that right now I guess.

Therapist: Let's see if I understand. I want you to imagine a scale. (Picks up a pen and draws a line and numbers on piece of paper.) At one end is a 1, and that represents this problem at its worst, and 10 means that you are coping with it and responding to it the best anyone could ever imagine. In fact, you are managing to live as if this miracle really has happened. Where would you say you are now on the scale? (Therapist hands the pen to the client, who draws a dot slightly to the left of the middle of the line.)

Client: I would say that I'm at a 4.

Therapist: A 4. How come a 4 and not a 3 or a 2?

Client: Well, I do have somebody coming in twice a week, and I probably could also get my sister to come over or take Mom to her house one of the weekend nights. I mean she has offered. . . .

Therapist: So that's something you might be able to do? Do you think it would make a difference if you were able to do that?

Client: Well, yeah, probably. I would probably go up on the scale if I knew that I could go out on the weekends even one night. Of course, I would have to find someone to go out with. I mean, so many of my friends have kids, or husbands. . . .

Therapist: Assuming you did, that would be something that would make a difference?

Client: Yeah. I guess that would make me . . . something like a 4½.

Therapist: It would make a difference. Hmm, I'm wondering. I know that 10 would be the ideal—you know, the miracle version. What do you think would be the lowest number that would be tolerable—I mean reasonably satisfactory. Would it be 10, or would it be a bit lower do you think?

Client: Are you kidding? I'd be happy with a 7.

Therapist: Really? Tell me what a 7 would look like.

Client: Well, I would have lost ten pounds, my laundry would be done, I would have plans for the weekend and someone to watch Mom, and I would have a cleaning lady one day a week who would also watch Mom, and I would have some plans in place with my sister for what we need to do if we ever get to the point when Mom starts to deteriorate more mentally.

Therapist: That seems like quite a lot to me. Is that all part of the 7?

Client: Well, I guess it would be an 8.

Therapist: I see . . . I'm going to take a short break to think about everything we talked about, and then I'll come back. But before I do that, is there anything else I should have asked or that you think would be important for me to know?

Client: I don't think so.

Therapist: Okay, I'll be back in ten minutes.

Break

Therapist (re-enters room): Hello again. I spent some time thinking about everything you said. I wrote some things down so I wouldn't forget them.

Client: Really? (Looks curious.)

Therapist: Here's what I came up with. May I read it to you?

Client: Of course.

Therapist: Well, the first thing that came to mind was what a remarkable woman you are: managing to hold down a job, caring for an aging mother with Alzheimer's, and then also with two dogs that you take care of. And the fact that you have friends tells me that other people see something in you, too—perhaps some of the same qualities I see, perhaps different ones. And at the same time, there's something very practical about you. You recognized that things at home are hard, that there's a lot of stress, and you decided to come and see someone to try to work out a way to cope in the best way possible. You decided to take action.

Client: Well, actually, I *am* very practical. My mom was always very practical. She had to be. She raised us alone. And I'm kind of like her a little bit that way, I guess, although when I was

younger, I didn't ever want to think I was like my mom. God no! But I don't think that's what my friends see. I think they probably see a different side of me. Probably they think I'm really strong and I have a good sense of humor.

Therapist: Oh, you do? Well, I can actually, I can imagine that. . . . I bet they would have a lot to say about what you do that makes them think you're strong.

Client: Oh yeah, I suppose. Well, maybe. (She smiles, looking somewhat embarrassed.)

Therapist: Anyway, I was thinking that perhaps if you wanted to, it might be a good idea in the next week to keep track of anything that you do that helps you move even a little bit in the direction of that 8. What do you think?

Client: Okay. I'll give it a try.

Session 2: One Week Later

The client said that she had gotten her sister and brother-in-law to care for her mother the previous Saturday night and gone to a movie by herself, because none of her friends were available. She and her mother had enjoyed breakfast on the back porch on two occasions. She had also contacted the local Weight Watchers organization and was thinking of going. When the therapist asked if she'd found anything additional that was helpful, the client answered that it helped to remember all the things that her mother had done for her when she was a little girl, because remembering this made her feel love rather than resentment toward her mother. She rated herself at a 4½. The therapist complimented her and invited her to continue to do what she was doing.

Session 3: Two Weeks Later

The client had joined Weight Watchers. She was frustrated, saying that she had now given up one of her few pleasures: eating chocolate at night while watching television. Her mother had been difficult and angry on two occasions. Nevertheless, the client again rated herself at 4½. The therapist asked how she was managing to cope to the degree she was and maintain the 4½, and the client said that the fact that she was doing something about her weight helped.

Session 4: Two Weeks Later

The client rated herself at a 5. She had lost three pounds. She was exploring the possibility of adult day care for her mother on the days when the caretaker did not come to the house. She said it had been a "pretty good week." The therapist complimented her on her weight loss and for taking the initiative to find out about adult day-care programs.

Session 5: Three Weeks Later

The client rated herself at a 6½. She ascribed this to losing weight, discussing with her sister long-term care options for her mother, and generally feeling "less alone" with the situation. She was still looking into day-care possibilities. She said she felt less resentful about her situation, although sometimes she did feel sorry for herself. The therapist said that this was a situation most people would find challenging. The therapist wondered aloud what might raise the scale even a little bit. The client said she really had no idea, but she would think about it. She said that she felt that things were going "relatively okay" and decided to come back in a month.

Session 6: Four Weeks Later

The client came in smiling. She was thinner and had a new haircut. She brought a photograph of her mother. Her sister and brother-in-law had cared for her mother the previous weekend, and she had taken a trip to a nearby city with a friend. She rated herself at a 6¾. Her sister had agreed to take her mother one weekend a month so that the client could have some respite, and the client said that while it was still a hard situation, she was feeling better. Also, she was going to the local YMCA and swimming after work one day a week, and she thought that had made some difference, too. She was also going to some social activities as part of her church, to which she was able to bring her mother as well. These things together had contributed to her rating herself at 6¾. She decided that although she had originally set the goal at 7, in fact, 6¾ was good enough and she could terminate therapy for the time being. She said that she would call for a follow-up appointment if she began to slip below 5 on the scale.

Three years later, the therapist ran into the client at a local grocery store. After they exchanged a brief greeting, the client told the therapist that she and her sister had eventually had to put her mother in a nursing home, but she was glad she had been able to take care of her at home as long as possible. Looking back on it, even though it had been really hard at times, it had really meant a lot to her to be

able to give something back to her mother after all her mother had done for her.

The therapist complimented her, saying "I wonder how you got to be such a kind, loving, and generous person?"

The client paused for a moment, and then answered with a smile, "Probably I got that from my mother."

◆ Taking a Break and Giving Feedback

Solution-focused therapy is often practiced in a team approach, with a therapist in the session and colleagues observing behind the mirror. Whether working with a team or alone, the therapist usually takes a ten-minute break near the end of the session. During this time, the therapist (with the team or alone) composes a summary message to the clients.

Building on the solution-focused idea that it is the clients who do the real work, Sharry, Madden, Darmody, and Miller (2001) describe how the session break can be used to promote a collaborative mindset:

> We're nearing the end of the session and I'd like to take a ten-minute break. This is to give you time to think and reflect about what we have discussed; to pick out any important ideas that came up, or to make decisions or plans. You might also like to think about whether this session has been useful and how you would like us to be further involved, if that would be helpful. While you're thinking, I will consult with my team for their thoughts. We will think together about what you said. When we get back together, I'll be interested to hear what stood out for you today. I'll also share the teams' thoughts with you. Together, then, we can put something together that will be helpful. (pp. 71–72)

The summary message begins with a recap of what the therapist heard the clients say during the interview, including the problem, its background, the clients' goals, and presession progress and strengths: "What I heard you tell me today, Mr. and Mrs. X, is that . . ." "Did I hear all of you correctly?" "Is there anything of importance that I omitted or that you want to add?"

This recap is followed by a statement reflecting the therapist's reaction, including an expression of empathy ("I'm not surprised you're so depressed!"), a reflection of the emotional impact on the client ("My sense is that you must really be hurting"), compliments on presession changes or strengths ("I was impressed by how many things you've tried to make things better"), and some comment on the clients' goals.

The therapist then makes suggestions about building on positives: "I would suggest that you notice what Patrick is doing at school that you want him to continue doing." "Patrick, I would suggest that you try to notice what's happening at school with the kids and your teacher that you like and want to continue to have happen."

Among the suggestions used commonly in solution-focused therapy are the following:

1. *The formula first-session task* (de Shazer, 1985). "Between now and next time we meet, I would like you to observe what happens in your family that you want to continue to have happen."

2. *Do more of what works.* "Since you said that you usually can talk together when you go for a walk, maybe you should try that once or twice and see what happens."

3. *Do something different.* "You mentioned that when you rely on Janine to be responsible for her own homework, she often fails to do it. Maybe you should try something different?" The suggestion to do something different can be given as an experiment. This was illustrated by Insoo Berg's example of parents who were exasperated by their son's encopresis. When given the suggestion to try something different, they started filling the boy's potty seat with water and a toy boat and telling him that his job was to sink the boat (Berg & Dolan, 2001). It worked!

4. *Go slow.* This suggestion, taken from the MRI model, is designed to help clients overcome fear of change by asking about possible negative consequences of changing and warning against trying to change too rapidly. "I have what may seem like a strange question: Could there possibly be any advantages to things staying the way they are?"

5. *Do the opposite.* This suggestion is based on the notion that many problems are maintained by attempted solutions. Suggesting that clients try the opposite of what they have been doing is especially useful for problems that exist between just two people (one member of a couple or one parent who's having trouble with a child). If scolding a child for being bad isn't working, parents can be encouraged to start praising him or her for being good. If a husband's attempt to avoid conversations with his wife about "the relationship" isn't working, he could try initiating them himself when he's in the mood.

6. *The prediction task* (de Shazer, 1988). "Before you go to bed tonight, predict whether the problem will be better or the same tomorrow. Tomorrow night rate the day and compare it with your prediction. Think about what may have accounted for the right or wrong prediction. Repeat this every night until we meet again."

As you can see, the compliments and suggestions of the summation message continue the basic thrust of the solution-focused approach, drawing attention to the family's resources and encouraging them to capitalize on their strengths in order to focus on solutions rather than problems.

◆ Later Sessions

Later sessions are devoted to finding, amplifying, and measuring progress. When a family returns for a subsequent session, the solution-focused therapist endeavors to create a cooperative mindset and then inquires about progress, seeking detailed descriptions of any movement toward the family's goal and the clients' role in attaining it. Then the therapist assists the clients in looking forward to how they will plan their next steps toward solution:

"What's better?" or "What happened that you liked?"
"Tell me more. Walk me through how the two of you did that."
"Wow! That sounds great. What part did you especially enjoy?"
"And what else is better? So what do you think the next step might be? On a scale of 1 to 10, you say your progress is now at a 5. What would a 6 look like?"

If there was no discernable progress, coping questions may be asked:

"How did you keep things from getting worse?"
"What's your idea about what might be helpful?"
"What do you think the next step should be?"

"Sure, If You Tell Them We Did Most of the Work." To illustrate the process of solution-focused therapy with couples, we will summarize a case reported by Michael Hoyt (2002).

CASE STUDY

Frank, age twenty-nine, and Regina, thirty, had been living together for seven months. For the last three months, since Regina had been pregnant, all they seemed to do was argue.

The therapist began by saying, "Welcome. The purpose of our meeting is briefly to work together to find a solution to whatever brings you here today. What's up?"

Regina said she was tired of all their arguing. Lately, it seemed as if all she and Frank did was fight.

Frank responded by saying, "Everything's all my fault, huh?"

After a few minutes of bickering, the therapist broke in to say, "Wait a minute! You came here because you want things to be better, don't you?" They nodded. "That's why you're here. You used to get along, so you know *how to.* It seems you came here because you want some help figuring out how to get back to being happy, right?"

They agreed but without much enthusiasm.

The therapist then asked each of them to rate where their relationship was now on a scale from 1 (horrible) to 10 (great). They both gave it a 2.

"Okay," said the therapist. "That gives us some room to work." Then he asked what each of them would have to do to move their level of satisfaction up to a 3 or a 4.

Neither of them had any ideas. So he asked the miracle question: "Suppose tonight, while you're sleeping, a miracle happens . . . and the problems that brought you here are solved. Tomorrow when you wake up, what would be some of the things you'd notice that would tell you that 'Hey, things are better?'"

They both laughed.

Then Regina said, "We'd be getting along, not hassling."

"Yeah," Frank said, "we'd talk, and she wouldn't get so mad at me."

The therapist moved quickly to concretize this goal. "You'd be getting along. What will you be saying and doing?"

In the discussion that followed, the couple described their meeting and courtship, an enjoyable vacation they'd taken, and their hopes for raising a happy child together. When they slipped back into arguing, the therapist redirected them toward their positive experiences. With prompting—"When was the last time you got along okay, even for a few minutes?"—the couple identified some recent moments when things were briefly good between them. The therapist asked numerous questions to expand on those exceptions, and the conversation gradually took on a more optimistic quality.

As the session drew toward a close, the therapist asked whether the meeting had been helpful and, if so, how. The couple agreed that it was helpful to talk without arguing and to be reminded about how they used to get along well. The therapist complimented them for coming in, describing it as an indication of their caring for each other and their desire to make a happy home for their baby. He then asked if they wanted to make another appointment. They did. He offered them a homework assignment to observe whatever they both do to make things better: "It may not be perfect, but try to keep track of whatever positives you or your partner do or attempt to do."

In the second session, Frank and Regina said that they'd had a couple of really good days. The therapist complimented them and asked, "How did you do that?" However, they then described an argument that had ensued one evening when Frank came home late from work. The therapist interrupted and said that he had made a mistake. He went on to say that while some therapists try to figure out what people are doing wrong, his approach was to help them figure out what they're doing right and then help them do more of it.

Frank then said that the day after their fight, Regina had called him at work and apologized. "I know I was wrong for being late, but it really hurt my feelings the way she yelled at me."

"She called and apologized?"

"Yeah. I really appreciated it, too."

"You called?"

Thus, even though Frank and Regina were still upset about their argument, the therapist was able to help them focus on how they'd made a constructive effort to get past it. Having helped them recover more positive feelings about each other, he went on to ask them what they appreciated about each other and how they showed it.

Frank acknowledged that when his feelings got hurt, he withdrew, which only served to make Regina angrier. Here, he was moving from a complainant to a customer.

The therapist then asked the couple for their ideas about how to handle tense situations better, and they discussed these and role-played a couple of examples.

At the end of the session, the therapist complimented Regina and Frank again for their efforts and suggested that they keep track of the things that happen that they wanted to continue to happen. When asked when they would like to return, they said three weeks, which would give them time to practice.

The couple began the third session by describing a series of positive things each of them had been doing. Regina appreciated Frank's increased help around the house, and he beamed at this praise. They each rated the relationship now as between a 5 and a 6.

The couple did, however, have one significant argument when they were buying things for the new baby's room. Regina was annoyed that Frank wasn't more enthusiastic, and he in turn felt that she didn't appreciate all the efforts he was making. Rather than pursue the feelings behind these complaints, the therapist asked for examples of times when the couple had compromised successfully: "What did you do differently during those times you coped constructively with your frustration?" This redirection helped them to think more about how they were able to work together when they didn't let their hurt and anger get the best of them.

The homework assignment this time was to keep track of whatever either of them did that showed they were working together. The therapist also suggested that they each pick a fun outing to do together.

The fourth session occurred three weeks later. The couple said it had been the best three weeks since Regina got pregnant. The therapist offered compliments ("Wow!") and asked for details to help them focus on the constructive things they'd done.

At this point, Regina rated the relationship a 9, and Frank said 10. The therapist congratulated them on their teamwork, and they scheduled a follow-up session three weeks later.

In the fifth session, Regina complained about feeling tired. Frank was also feeling tired from working overtime, but he was able to express sympathy and support for Regina. They agreed that they had continued doing well and had even thought of canceling the session, but they decided to come in to review their progress and talk about how to keep it going. As the couple talked about what they had accomplished, the therapist offered compliments about all the constructive things they reported.

The therapist then asked them how they would remember to work as a team if their problems once again got them down in the future. They replied that they knew they'd have problems in the future but that they'd learned that they can solve their problems. "Now when we start to have an argument, we stop and remember . . . what we've talked about in here—how to use what you called 'solution talk,' how we used to fight, and how we know how to treat each other respectfully, and how to take time out if we need it, and how to listen to each other, and stuff like that."

When the therapist asked whether they wanted to make another appointment, they said not now but that they would call if they needed one.

"I wished them well and asked whether it would be OK for me to write up their story and put it in a book chapter. 'Sure,' they said, 'but only if you promise to tell people that we did most of the work.'"

 Watch this video of Bill O'Hanlon work with a family. Which solution-focused interventions does he use?

◆ Interviewing Children

Peter De Jong and Insoo Berg (2008) offer the following suggestions for interviewing children:

◆ Notice some positive about the child: her colorful sneakers, his team cap.
◆ Use relationship questions: What would your mother tell me is your best subject in school? What else does your mother like about you that

you are too shy to tell me about? What would you mother need to see from you that would tell her you don't need to be here anymore?

♦ Avoid "why" questions: Try asking "how come"; it's less intimidating.

♦ Responding to "I don't know": Acknowledge that it was a hard question, and then say "So suppose you did know, what would you say?" Or "What would your best friend say?"

♦ Assume competence: "I bet you have very good reasons for . . . Can you tell me about your good reasons?"

Evaluating Therapy Theory and Results

Judging by its popularity, solution-focused therapy may be the treatment for our times. Now one of the most widely used psychotherapy approaches in the world (Trepper, Dolan, McCollum, & Nelson, 2006), its promise of quick solutions has endeared it to the managed care industry, and providers have been eager to identify themselves as solution focused. Its applications include couples therapy (Hoyt & Berg, 1998; Hudson & O'Hanlon, 1992; Murray & Murray, 2004); family therapy (Campbell, 1999; McCollum & Trepper, 2001); behavioral problems in children (Conoley, Graham, Neu, Craig, O'Pry et al., 2003; Corcoran, 2002; Lee, 1997); families with suicidal members (Softas-Nall & Francis, 1998); domestic violence (Lipchik & Kubicki, 1996); sexual abuse (Dolan, 1991; Tambling, 2012); alcoholism (Berg & Miller, 1992; de Shazer & Isebaert, 2003); sex therapy (Ford, 2006); families with severely intellectual children (Lloyd & Dallos, 2008; Zhang, Yan, Du, & Liu, 2014); and schizophrenia (Eakes, Walsh, Markowski, Cain, & Swanson, 1997).

In addition, there has been a spate of self-help books written from a solution-focused perspective (Dolan, 1998; O'Hanlon, 1999; Weiner-Davis, 1992). Some have proposed models that incorporate solution-focused techniques (e.g., scaling questions, the miracle question) into other forms of family therapy, most commonly structural family therapy, in the treatment of adolescent substance abuse (Springer & Orsborn,

2002); adoption (Becker, Carson, Seto, &Becker, 2002); and low-conflict divorce (Ramish, McVicker, & Sahin, 2009). The solution-focused model has also been applied outside of traditional therapeutic practice to include interventions in family medicine clinics (Park, 1997); social service agencies (Pichot & Dolan, 2003); nursing care (Tuyn, 1992); educational settings and model schools (Franklin & Streeter, 2004; Rhodes & Ajmal, 1995); and business systems (Berg & Cauffman, 2002).

What besides its remarkably appealing name has made solution-focused therapy so popular? It is brief and pragmatic, but then so are many other approaches to family therapy. Perhaps the two most powerful ingredients in solution-focused therapy are building on what works and helping people identify what they want rather than what they don't want.

Searching for exceptions turns out to be a simple but powerful intervention. People who come for help often think of the times when their problems don't occur as unimportant because these occasions seem accidental or inconsistent. Calling attention to past successes and latent abilities helps clients rediscover their own best coping strategies.

The miracle question, which can sound like just another gimmick when you first read about it, is a powerful tool, tapping as it does that wonderful human capacity not just to see things as they are but to imagine things as they might be. One of the great things about the imagination is that with very limited encouragement, people can see themselves as succeeding rather than fumbling and failing (Singer, 1981). What makes this kind of positive thinking more than empty optimism is that in the solution-focused therapist, clients have a coach and guide to help them work toward this brighter future.

To critics, solution-focused therapy seems simplistic, and its emphasis on solution talk instead of problem talk is seen as manipulative. Like any approach in the early stages of evolution, solution-focused therapy was sometimes presented in a cookbook style, leading some to imagine that treatment can be reduced to a set of formulaic techniques.

Is it true that all you have to do in therapy is ask the miracle question and then talk about times when the problem wasn't a problem? No, of course not. With any new model of therapy, there is a tendency to emphasize what is distinctive—in this case, the miracle question, the search for exceptions, scaling questions, and compliments. The unique features of solution-focused therapy are deceptively easy to describe, but like all therapies, it takes great skill to implement effectively.

A second major criticism of solution-focused therapy is that its insistence on solution talk may cut off clients from empathy and understanding. People want to tell their stories. When they come to therapy, they want someone to understand their problems and be willing to help solve them. Reassuring someone who's worried that there's nothing to worry about isn't very reassuring. It can make you believe that your feelings aren't valid, because you wouldn't have them if you would only look at the bright side of things. Most people aren't very eager to be changed by someone they feel doesn't understand them.

The issue of whether solution-focused therapy is genuinely collaborative has been raised frequently (Efran & Schenker, 1993; Efron & Veendendaal, 1993; Miller, 1994; Nylund & Corsiglia, 1994; O'Hanlon, 1996; Storm, 1991; Wylie, 1990). This approach has even been called "solution-forced therapy" by some because of the perceived tendency for therapists to pressure clients into discussing only positives. As Efran and Schenker (1993) ask, "What assurance is there that clients of solution-focused therapists haven't simply learned to keep their complaints to themselves in the presence of the therapist?"

More recently, solution-focused therapists have stressed the importance of the therapeutic relationship. Eve Lipchik, for example, said, "The speed and success of solution construction depend on the therapist's ability to stay connected with the clients' reality throughout the course of therapy. This is the underpinning for the whole collaborative process, the grease that keeps the axles turning" (Friedman & Lipchik, 1999, p. 329). Like any other therapy, the solution-focused approach won't likely be effective if therapists, in a rush to get to their own agenda, fail to listen to clients and make them feel understood.

Considering the popularity of solution-focused therapy, it's unfortunate that more research hasn't been done to test its effectiveness. Thus far, most of the research has been conducted by solution-focused practitioners themselves. Initial follow-up studies conducted by de Shazer and his colleagues at the Brief Therapy Center in Milwaukee involved surveying clients about their progress and found good success rates (e.g., De Jong & Hopwood, 1996; de Shazer, 1985; de Shazer et al., 1986). More recently, de Shazer and Isebaert (2003) published a follow-up report on male alcoholics who received solution-focused therapy in a hospital setting in Belgium. Of 118 patients contacted by phone four years postdischarge, 84 percent were judged to be improved. When possible, contacts with family members were used to confirm the patients' reports.

In a systematic evaluation of the solution-focused brief therapy literature, Bond and colleagues (2013) reviewed thirty-eight studies. They concluded that while methodological weaknesses existed in most cases, the studies do provide tentative support for the use of solution-focused brief therapy in the treatment of child internalizing and externalizing behaviors. They also concluded that solution-focused therapy may hold more promise as a mode of early intervention when the presenting problem is not as severe.

Summary

Solution-focused therapy takes the elegance of the MRI model and turns it on its head: One aims to help clients do less of what doesn't work; the other promotes more of what does. Both of these pragmatic approaches focus on the presenting complaint and aim to resolve it as quickly as possible. The MRI model does so by looking for failed solutions to eliminate; the solution-focused approach searches for forgotten solutions to rediscover.

An additional difference between these models is that while the MRI approach focuses on behavior, the solution-focused model emphasizes cognition as well as behavior. MRI therapists urge clients to *do* things differently; solution-focused therapists urge them to *view* things differently (Shoham, Rohrbaugh, & Patterson, 1995). Problems are seen as persisting in the way people define situations and in the misdirected actions they persist in taking. The idea is that people often get stuck in their problems because by trying to get to the bottom of them, they overlook solutions that are right under their noses.

This notion has led to the development of a set of techniques for changing *problem talk* into *solution talk*. These techniques include *exception questions* ("Can you think of a time when you didn't have the problem? What were you doing then?"); the *miracle question* ("Suppose you went to sleep and a miracle happened such that when you awoke, your problem was solved. What would be different?"); *scaling questions* ("On a scale from 1 to 10, how do you feel now compared to when you called?"); *coping questions* ("Given how bad that was, how were you able to cope?"); the *formula first-session task* ("After you leave today, observe what happens that you want to continue during the next week."); and *compliments* ("Wow, you must be very smart to have thought of that!"). These techniques are put into practice as soon as possible to keep the work brief and to discourage clients from dwelling on the negative side of their experience.

More recently, therapists have questioned the emphasis on technique and speculated that qualities of the therapist–client relationship may be at the heart of the model's effectiveness. This has led to a call for greater collaboration with clients so that their feelings are acknowledged and validated before solution-focused techniques are introduced.

Solution-focused therapy continues to have enormous appeal in the world of psychotherapy. Some of its popularity can be attributed to therapists' struggle to find ways to feel effective while living with managed care's limited number of sessions. In addition, the techniques of this therapy are relatively easy to learn (the basics can be picked up in a few workshops), and its upbeat nature makes it more enjoyable for many therapists. Yet its easy-to-learn formula leads some therapists to dismiss it as superficial.

Critics question whether therapists are really having a respectful conversation with clients when they only coax optimism. Do such insistently upbeat dialogues have the effect of silencing people's doubts and pain? Can solution-focused therapists find ways to honor client perceptions that don't fit the formula? Can clients trust the feedback of therapists who never challenge or question them? Can clients be honest regarding the outcome of their therapy with therapists who seem to want so much for them to feel better about things?

Other questions highlight the model's strengths. For example, isn't it important for therapists to have clear, concrete guidelines so therapy doesn't become vague and directionless? Isn't it more empowering to help people envision their future goals and focus on their strengths than on their problems and deficits? If people's experience of pain is tied to the way they think or talk about it, then isn't it better to use language that will lead people out of pain rather than dwell on it?

Click here to apply your knowledge of chapter concepts.

Click here to test your application and analysis of the content found within this chapter.

The narrative approach is a perfect expression of the postmodern revolution. When all knowledge is regarded as constructed rather than discovered, it's fitting that a leading approach to family therapy is concerned with the ways people interpret their behavior rather than how they behave.

The underlying premise is that personal experience is fundamentally ambiguous. This doesn't mean that experience isn't real or that it's necessarily opaque. Rather, it means that understanding human experience, including our own, is never simply a matter of observing it. The elements of experience are understood only through a process that organizes those elements, puts them together, assigns meaning, and prioritizes them. To say that experience is ambiguous is to say that its meaning isn't fixed but instead lends itself to multiple interpretations.

Consider the difference between calling the heart-racing tension most people feel before speaking in public "stage fright" or "excitement." The first description makes this agitation a problem, something to overcome. The second suggests that it's a natural response to standing up in front of people whose approval you hope to win.

Whether people experience anxiety or excitement depends on how they interpret their arousal. Strategic therapists give clients *reframes*, or new interpretations, for their experience: "The next time you're speaking, think of yourself as excited rather than frightened." Narrative therapists believe that such interpretations won't take unless they fit people's stories. A man who thinks he has nothing interesting to say will have trouble seeing his trembling as due to excitement, no matter how hard someone tries to convince him. If the same man were helped to construct a new, more positive story of himself, the reframe becomes unnecessary.

CHAPTER 12

NARRATIVE THERAPY
Restorying Lives

LEARNING OUTCOMES

♦ List the main figures in narrative therapy and their contributions.

♦ Describe the main tenets of narrative therapy.

♦ Describe healthy and unhealthy family development from a narrative therapy perspective.

♦ Describe the clinical goals and the conditions necessary for meeting those goals from a narrative therapy perspective.

♦ Discuss and demonstrate the assessment and intervention techniques of narrative therapy.

♦ Discuss research support for narrative therapy.

Once he starts to think well of himself, he will expect people to appreciate what he has to say.

Unlike the cybernetic metaphor, which focused on self-defeating patterns of *behavior*, the narrative metaphor focuses on self-defeating *cognitions*—the stories people tell themselves about their problems. With the cybernetic metaphor, therapy meant blocking maladaptive interactions. The narrative metaphor, on the other hand, focuses on expanding clients' thinking to allow them to consider alternative ways of looking at themselves and their problems.

Sketches of Leading Figures

Michael White, founder of the narrative movement, lived in Adelaide, Australia. He and Cheryl White were based at the Dulwich Centre, out of which came training, clinical work, and publications related to White's approach. In the late 1970s, White was drawn to the work of Gregory Bateson but found himself more interested in what Bateson said about how people construe the world than in the behavioral patterns of systems-based models. Under the influence of Bateson and Michel Foucault, who criticized the dehumanizing aspects of institutions, White developed his novel ideas about how problems affect people—regarding them as something operating on persons, rather than as things people are doing. He set an inspiring example of seeing the best in people even when they'd lost faith in themselves. Sadly, Michael White died in 2008.

David Epston, a family therapist from Auckland, New Zealand, is the second most influential leader of the narrative movement. Through his interest in anthropology, Epston encountered the narrative metaphor and convinced White that it was more useful than cybernetics. He'd long had an interest in literature and for years was known as a storyteller, writing the "Story Corner" for the *Australian and New Zealand Journal of Family Therapy*.

Epston has contributed to most aspects of narrative theory and practice but in particular emphasized that

for clients to maintain their new narratives, they need supportive communities. He fostered the development of self-help "leagues," groups of clients battling similar problems, such as the Anti-Anorexia/Anti-Bulimia League of New Zealand. He also advocates writing letters to clients, pointing out that long after the influence of the therapist's presence has faded, clients can reread letters that bolster their new stories and resolve.

Jill Freedman and Gene Combs direct a training center in Evanston, Illinois. Before joining the narrative camp, they were strategic therapists and social activists, drawn to White's approach in large part by its political emphasis. This combination—strategic therapy and political activism—characterizes the backgrounds of many prominent narrative therapists. Freedman and Combs's (1996) book *Narrative Therapy* is an excellent guide to narrative therapy.

Jeffrey Zimmerman and Vicki Dickerson were cofounders of the Bay Area Family Therapy Training Associates and together with John Neal taught narrative therapy at the Mental Research Institute in Palo Alto. These two creative therapists pioneered the use of narrative therapy with difficult adolescents and with couples (Dickerson & Zimmerman, 1992; Zimmerman & Dickerson, 1993) and also contributed *If Problems Talked: Narrative Therapy in Action* (Zimmerman & Dickerson, 1996) to the narrative therapy literature.

Stephan Madigan (1994; Madigan & Epston, 1995) in Vancouver, Canada, has also contributed greatly to narrative theory and is the founder of the Vancouver Anti-Anorexia/Anti-Bulimia League, a grassroots organization that provides support and encouragement to resist media images that promote "body guilt." Other prominent narrative therapists include Kaethe Weingarten, Sallyann Roth, and Bill Madsen at the Family Institute of Cambridge and Janet Adams-Wescott in Tulsa, Oklahoma.

Theoretical Formulations

The narrative approach first found its way into psychotherapy in the **hermeneutic** tradition of psychoanalysis. Following Freud, classical analysts believed there was one correct way to interpret experience. Patients might not understand their dreams or symptoms because their motives were unconscious, but an analyst possessed of the truth of psychoanalytic theory could discover unconscious meaning, much like an archeologist uncovers the buried remains of the past.

Then in the 1980s, revisionists such as Donald Spence, Roy Schafer, and Paul Ricoeur began to argue against this positivistic conception of psychoanalytic reality. The truth of experience, they said, isn't discovered; it's created. The goal of therapy shifted from historical truth to narrative intelligibility. The challenge was to construct truths in the service of self-coherence, not to resurrect a true picture of the past. The therapist became more of a novelist than an archeologist.

Family therapists found this narrative metaphor extremely useful. As they began to ask clients about their stories, therapists came to recognize how much narrative accounts affected people's perceptions. Stories don't just mirror life; they shape it. That's why people have the interesting habit of becoming the stories they tell about their experience.

CASE STUDY

According to Tim, Kayla was never satisfied. All she did was complain. Their apartment, the furniture, her clothes—nothing was ever good enough. No matter what they had, she wanted more.

Kayla had no idea what Tim was talking about. She was perfectly content. Well, except for one thing. Every time she'd see a picture in a magazine of a beautiful sofa or a pretty dress, she'd point it out to Tim. "Wow, look at that," she'd say. "Maybe we should get one of those." She was just dreaming out loud. But to Tim, who was brought up never to ask for anything, Kayla's fantasies felt like complaints. Notice, however, that it wasn't so much what Kayla said that hurt Tim, but how he interpreted it.

Looking deeper, it turned out that Tim was never satisfied with his own accomplishments. Growing up with a mother who wasn't given much to praise, Tim dreamt of someday doing great things. Unfortunately, his own very real achievements never lived up to his fantasies. Sure, other people praised him, but he still secretly dreamed the grand and glorious dreams of childhood.

Until he could begin to accept himself, it was hard for Tim to believe that anyone else could truly appreciate him. Trying to get such a man to change his behavior without addressing his controlling life story would be futile, because no matter how many successes he had, he'd still find ways to dismiss them and continue to dwell on his failures—and his partner's (presumed) dissatisfaction.

Narrative therapists oppose the functionalist elements in family systems and psychoanalytic models, which imply that problems are inherent in individuals (as psychoanalysis would have it) or families (as family systems would have it). Instead, they believe that problems arise when people are indoctrinated into narrow and self-defeating views of themselves (White, 2007).

To counter the way society convinces people that they are their problems, narrative therapists **externalize** problems. Instead of *having* a problem or *being* a problem, clients are encouraged to think of themselves as *struggling against* their problems. Neither the patient nor the family is the problem; the *problem* is the problem. Accordingly, narrative therapists aren't interested in problem-maintaining interactions or structural flaws. They aren't interested in the family's impact on the problem but rather in the problem's impact on the family.

As narrative therapists shifted their attention from families as the source of problems and toward cultural beliefs and practices, they turned to the writings of Michel Foucault (1965, 1980), a French social philosopher who devoted his life to exposing how social discourses objectified and dehumanized marginalized groups. Foucault believed not only that those constructing the dominant narratives in a society (those deemed to have expert knowledge) had the power to subjugate but that the narratives themselves became internalized truths, such that people judged their bodies, achievements, and personalities on the basis of standards set by society's judges (doctors, educators, clergy, psychotherapists, politicians, celebrities). Thus, Foucault influenced White to take the **social constructionism** axiom that there are no absolute truths in a political direction, toward deconstructing (reexamining) established truths that oppress people's lives.

Family Dynamics

Narrative therapists have little to say about family dynamics because they reject the idea that families are responsible for the problems of family members. Rather than looking for failings in their client families, narrative therapists are far more likely to locate responsibility in the mindless programming of the cultural world.

◆ Normal Family Development

Narrative therapists not only avoid judgments about what is normal but also reject the very idea of categorizing people. Recall how Foucault criticized the way theories of normality were used to perpetuate patterns of privilege and oppression. Too often in human history, the judgments made by people in power regarding normality and abnormality have been used to subjugate those with no voice in the matter.

 Watch this video of narrative therapist Dr. Steve Madigan explore societal influences on a family's problem. Which influences does he emphasize?

While it's easy to see the dangers of reducing people to DSM-V diagnoses, family therapists may have trouble seeing their own concepts—such as *rigid boundaries, cross-generational coalitions*, and *enmeshment*—as dehumanizing. But becoming a postmodern therapist means giving up all such categories. Narrative therapists avoid pigeonholing people as normal or abnormal and reject general principles about what causes problems or resolves them. They try not to stand over people in judgment—in any way—but instead strive to help them make sense of their own experience.

In the spirit of collaboration, narrative therapists endeavor to *situate* themselves with clients; that is, to disclose the beliefs that inform their therapy so that clients can know what they're getting into. Clients are also encouraged to educate therapists regarding their cultural predicaments and to correct them when they make assumptions that don't fit the clients' experience (Freedman & Combs, 1996).

Although narrative therapists try not to make judgments, it may be impossible not to have some opinions about people and what makes them flourish. From the ideas described in the previous section, we can distill certain basic assumptions narrative therapists make about normal families. People (1) have good intentions (they don't need or want problems); (2) are profoundly influenced by the discourses around them; (3) are not their problems; and (4) can develop alternative, empowering stories once separated from their problems and the cultural myths they have internalized.

◆ Development of Behavior Disorders

When the stories people take on lead them to construe their experience in unhelpful ways, they tend to get bogged down with problems. Such problems are likely to persist as long as these unhelpful stories remain fixed, obscuring other, more hopeful versions of events.

A single mother struggles to be everything she can be as a parent of her teenage daughter, believing that as a single mother she can never do enough. Thus, when her daughter violates her curfew, she tends to react furiously. The cultural narrative about being a perfect parent makes the mother notice all the times her daughter stays out late or leaves cigarette butts on the porch and not notice the times when she gets her homework done or volunteers to wash the dishes. Each of the daughter's transgressions confirms the mother's story line that she isn't doing a good job.

The daughter, in turn, dwells on how often her mother criticizes her friends or explodes over small mistakes but doesn't remember the times her mother showed respect for her opinions or praised her achievements. The daughter gradually develops a narrative around never being able to satisfy people and becomes increasingly controlled by "rebelliousness." This makes her not care what her mother thinks and instead prompts her to indulge in whatever makes her feel better, like partying late into the night.

In short, both sides remain stuck, not simply in a pattern of control and rebellion but more specifically of noticing only incidents of control and rebellion.

This analysis might not sound all that different from one that other schools of family therapy might make of an escalating cycle of antagonism between a mother and daughter. The difference is that the narrative approach doesn't focus on their behavior. Narrative therapists reject the cybernetic notion that the mother and daughter are stuck in a dysfunctional feedback loop—acting and reacting to each other in unhelpful ways. Instead, they concentrate on the way the mother and daughter narrate their exchange. It's their *stories* (needing to be a perfect mother, being picked on by a parent) that affect not only what they notice (lateness, scolding) but also how they interpret it.

Narrative therapists refer to these patterns of tunnel vision as **problem-saturated stories**, which, once they take hold, encourage people to respond to each other in ways that perpetuate the problem story. As long as parents focus on their children's misbehavior, they will concentrate on criticizing and controlling them. As long as children think of their parents as unfair, they will remain reactive and rebellious. Their responses to each other become invitations to more of the same and lead to further hardening of problem stories.

Such closed and rigid narratives make people vulnerable to being overtaken by destructive emotional states that narrative therapists portray as alien invaders. These therapists don't really see problematic feelings or beliefs as external entities, but they do believe that such emotional responses *are* external in the sense that they are socially constructed. Externalizing problems cuts down on guilt and blame. The daughter isn't the problem, "rebelliousness" is. The mother isn't the problem, "oversensitivity" is. Mother and daughter can unite to combat rebelliousness and oversensitivity rather than each other.

Mechanisms of Change

Unlike most clinicians, narrative therapists do not strive for clinical neutrality. On the contrary, they are active advocates who take sides with their clients and encourage them to see themselves as courageous warriors against the forces that try to trap them in pessimistic mindsets.

◆ Goals of Therapy

Narrative therapists aren't problem solvers. Instead, they help people separate themselves from problem-saturated stories (and destructive cultural assumptions) to open space for new and more constructive views of themselves. Narrative therapy transforms identities from flawed to preferred, not by getting family members to confront their conflicts but by separating persons from problems and then uniting the family to fight a common enemy. This is facilitated by combing the family's history for **unique outcomes**, or "sparkling events"—times when they resisted the problem or behaved in ways that contradicted the problem story.

Thus, narrative therapists see their work as a political enterprise—freeing people from unthinking indoctrination in the prejudices of our times and empowering them to become active authors of their own lives. Once liberated from problem-saturated stories, family members can unite with one another and with communities of support to deal with their problems with more optimism and persistence.

If Alice sees herself as codependent because of the way she relates to men, a narrative therapist wouldn't explore the reasons for this condition, nor would he give Alice suggestions for altering this pattern. Instead, the therapist would ask questions about what codependency means to Alice and come up with a name for the negative effects of these ideas on her.

If, for example, Alice says that her codependency gets her to blame herself, the therapist might ask about the effect of *Self-blame* on her life, ask family

Family arguments are fueled by negative story lines about other family members.

members to help her defeat *Self-blame*, and highlight times in Alice's life when she related to men in ways she prefers. The therapist might also invite Alice to consider how our society's view of women contributed to *Self-blame*'s grip on her life.

◆ Conditions for Behavior Change

Narrative therapists help clients *deconstruct* unproductive stories in order to *reconstruct* new and more productive ones. **Deconstruction**, a term borrowed from literary criticism, entails questioning assumptions.

Reconstruction involves creating new and more optimistic accounts of experience. Narrative therapists use externalizing conversations to help separate persons from problems. This is one way to deconstruct disempowering assumptions. Rather than talk of "Sally's laziness," for example, they'll inquire about times when "*Procrastination* takes hold of her." Once a problem has been externalized and redefined in more experience-near terms, a person can begin to resist it. By viewing the problem as an external entity, narrative therapists free families to challenge its influence on their lives.

In externalizing conversations, therapists ask *effects questions*—for instance, How does the problem affect you? Your attitudes? Your ideas about yourself? Your relationships? Through this process, the problem's field of influence is broadened so that clients can begin to notice areas of their lives where the problem has been less powerful. It is in these areas that clients can notice *unique outcomes*—experiences that would not be predicted by a telling of the problem story, times when they resisted the problem's influence. Identifying unique outcomes creates room for counterplots, new and more empowering ways of construing events.

A man who identifies himself as depressed sees life through a glass darkly. Depression becomes a career, a lifestyle. But if the man begins to think of, say, "*Self-doubt* getting the best of him," then he may be able to remember times when he didn't let *Self-doubt* get him down. These newly recognized times of effectiveness provide openings around which to weave a new and more optimistic story.

Just as narrative therapists use externalizing conversations to shift clients' perceptions of themselves, they also endeavor to shift family members' perceptions of each other from *totalizing views*, which reduce them to one set of frustrating responses. Thus, parents who see their teenagers as "irresponsible," as though that were the sum total of their being, are likely to be seen in return as "unfair." Likewise,

Nancy Ney/Photodisc/Getty Images

parents who totalize their children as "lazy" may be seen as "bossy" or "demanding." As long as both sides remain fixed in polarized perspectives, they may be too busy to think about their own preferences. In unhappy families, people are often so busy *not being* what others expect that they have no time to figure out what they want for themselves.

Therapy

 ## Assessment

A narrative assessment begins with getting the family's story, including not only their experience with their problems but also their assumptions about those problems. Getting a family's story isn't just information gathering; it's a deconstructive inquiry, designed to move clients from passivity and defeatism toward realizing that they already have some power over the problems that plague them.

Once problems have been personified as alien entities, the therapist first *maps the influence of the problem* on the family and then *maps the influence of the family* on the problem. In mapping the influence of the problem on the family, the therapist explores the distressing impact of the problem on their lives. Clients' responses to this line of inquiry usually highlight their own sense of inadequacy.

> ▶ Watch this video of narrative therapist Dr. Steve Madigan asking questions to help deconstruct the nature of the problem and its influence. Which techniques do you see him use?

CASE STUDY

Alesha Jackson, a single mother of four with a live-in boyfriend, sought therapy because her four-year-old was getting into trouble at preschool. Two or three times a week Jermaine got into arguments that resulted in his hitting and biting other children. Jermaine was also a problem at home. Although he got along reasonably well with his brothers and sisters, he frequently threw tantrums when his mother tried to make him do something. Alesha sheepishly admitted that she was probably too easy on Jermaine, but she had gotten to the point where she felt helpless.

"I don't know what to do," she said. "I've tried everything. Nothing I do makes any difference. Luke, that's my boyfriend, he can make Jermaine behave, but he can get mean about it. He thinks I spoil Jermaine. Lately, Luke's been getting mad and going out after supper by himself, which leaves me all alone with the kids."

The therapist listens not just to get Alesha's story of the problem but also to explore the conclusions she's drawn from her experience. The therapist asks questions like these:

"What conclusions about yourself as a mother have you drawn because of your problems with Jermaine?"

"What conclusions have you drawn about your relationship with Luke because of this problem?" (Note that it is the problem affecting the relationship, rather than the relationship causing the problem.)

This line of questioning allows Alesha to tell her unhappy story but also tries to make her aware that the problem is burdening her. She begins to realize that it's not that she and her family are somehow dysfunctional; rather, they're struggling against an enemy.

In mapping family members' influence on the problem, the therapist explores the extent to which they have been able to stand up to the problem's oppression. To supply this information, family members are encouraged to recognize their own competence. Questions of the following sort are asked:

"How have you been able to avoid making mistakes that most people with similar problems usually make?"

"Were there times in the recent past when this problem may have tried to get the better of you, and you didn't let it?"

"How did you do that?"

This mapping process not only creates a sense of empathy and understanding between the therapist and family, but it is also an empowering experience for the family.

We tend to think of memory as a recorder or a camera, where the past is filed and can be called up at will. But memory is neither of these things. Memory is a storyteller. It creates shape and meaning by emphasizing some things and leaving others out. A narrative therapist's assessment explores two sides of the clients' memory—beginning with the problem narrative, a story of affliction (not pathology). These problem stories are understood not as personal failings but as stories of domination, alienation, and frustration. Then the therapist helps clients search their memories for the other side of the story—the side that honors their courage and persistence, the side that offers hope.

◆ Therapeutic Techniques

Narrative interventions are phrased as questions. These therapists almost never make interpretations. They just ask question after question, following the clients' lead, often repeating the answers and writing them down.

In the first session, the therapist begins by finding out how clients spend their time. This gives the therapist a chance to appreciate how clients see themselves without getting into a lengthy history and the attributions of blame that so frequently accompany such histories. The therapist pays special attention to talents and competencies. As a further means of establishing a collaborative atmosphere, Zimmerman and Dickerson (1996) encourage clients to ask any questions they might have about the therapist: "Okay. Is there anything you would like to know about me, either professionally or as a person?"

The therapist can also invite clients to read his or her notes if they wish. Therapists often take notes as each person talks; doing so helps them retain important points and gives clients the sense that their points of view are being respected.

Externalizing Conversations

Narrative therapists begin by asking clients to tell their problem-saturated story and listen long enough to convey their appreciation for what the family has been going through. By using externalizing language, the therapist separates the client from the problem, making its destructive effects apparent and establishing a sense of partnership with the client.

Each person is asked for his or her own perspective on the problem. The therapist asks about the problem's effects rather than its causes (causative questions usually lead to attributions of blame), mapping the influence of the problem:

"How does *Guilt* affect you?"
"What other effects does it have?"
"What does *Guilt* 'tell' you?"

The therapist's questions about the identified problem imply that it isn't possessed by the clients but instead is trying to possess them. For example, in a case where parents describe the problem as a lack of trust in their daughter because of her sneakiness, the therapist doesn't reflect back "So your daughter's sneakiness bothers you." Instead, the therapist might say, "So *Sneakiness* made your daughter act in ways that brought discord between you. Is that right?"

Sometimes patterns of interaction are externalized. For example, in a case in which a teenager's parents were responding to her sneakiness with increasing control, Vicki Dickerson chose to highlight the rift that was encouraging this pattern. One thing they could all agree on was that they didn't like the breach that was splitting them apart. Thus, instead of identifying the daughter's sneakiness or the parents' distrust as the problem, the *Rift* became the enemy. The *Rift* told the parents that their daughter couldn't be trusted; the *Rift* made the daughter more secretive and told her to pull away from her parents. The *Rift* was something they could join forces against (Zimmerman & Dickerson, 1996).

Problems are almost always personified—portrayed as unwelcome invaders that try to dominate people's lives. For example, while discussing her eating problems, a woman is asked how *Anorexia* convinces her to starve herself. A phobic child is asked how often *Fear* is able to make him do what it wants and how often he is able to stand up to it. A guilt-ridden mother is asked how *Self-hate* is making her feel bad about her parenting.

This line of questioning can be disconcerting, unaccustomed as most people are to talking about imaginary entities in their households. Therapists who treat externalization as a gimmick may lack the conviction necessary to overcome the initial awkwardness of talking this way. On the other hand, therapists will find that externalizing questions flow naturally if they actually learn to think of problems as enemies that feed on polarization and misunderstanding. One way to get more comfortable with this way of thinking is to start using externalization as a way to think about problems in your own life. (It isn't just clients who can benefit from a little more compassion.)

While externalization may initially be a difficult concept to embrace, it can be profoundly helpful in reducing self-blame. For example, a woman who thinks of herself as *being insecure* or *having insecurity* has internalized the problem and come to see it as who she is. Over time, people become identified with their problems. They believe that the problem's existence is proof of their flawed character.

This way of thinking poisons confidence. When a problem is externalized, it's as if the person can peek out from behind it, and family members can see the healthier person that the problem has been hiding from them. Helping an "insecure woman" shift to seeing herself as *struggling with* Self-Criticismfrees her from identifying with this problem and encourages her to discover her ability to do something about it.

Externalizing helps clinicians develop a more sympathetic view of clients who engage in "inappropriate behavior." For example, thinking of a woman as being captured by emotions such as fear of abandonment or rage, rather than as being histrionic or ill-tempered or a borderline personality, makes it easier to empathize with her. You can dislike the emotional reaction rather than the client. From there, you can look for times when she was able to avoid being captured by those emotions or was able to respond differently, despite the emotion's pressure.

CASE STUDY

William Madsen (2007) describes how a young woman who came to therapy complaining of depression began to talk about Self-Doubt. As she examined her experience with Self-Doubt, "Marie" described her fear of not living up to expectations: "I'm not thin enough, I'm not attractive enough, I'm not making enough money to suit my middle-class parents, and I'm not satisfying my boyfriend sexually."

Madsen's inquiring about the *Expectations* that encouraged self-doubt helped Marie consider the pernicious effects of gender stereotypes. When asked where her life would be headed if *Expectations* were to set the direction, Marie said that *Expectations* would encourage her to "starve myself, get plastic surgery, get a job I hated to satisfy my parents, and become a sexual slave to my boyfriend." From there, she began to consider what direction she would prefer to set for her own life.

Placing *Expectations* in a larger cultural context only helped Marie escape the burden of self-loathing but also to develop a more sympathetic view of her parents and boyfriend as also falling under the influence of *Expectations*. As Marie put it, "They're just caught up in that middle-class success thing, and he's just worried that he's not gonna be a real man without some Barbie doll on his arm."

Sallyann Roth and David Epston (1996) developed an exercise to help therapists grasp what it's like to think of problems as external. They have a group of trainees take turns being a problem—such as *Self-hatred*—while others interview them. The interviewers might ask the person playing *Self-hatred* such questions as "Under what circumstances do you manage to get into X's world?" and "How are you intervening in the lives of X's family and friends?"

Who's in Charge, the Person or the Problem?

Over many sessions, therapists ask a multitude of questions that explore how a problem has managed to disrupt or dominate a family versus how much they have been able to control it. These are called **relative influence questions**. By including all family members in the discussion, it usually becomes clear that the problem has succeeded in disturbing their relationships with each other, dividing and conquering them:

> "How much has the *Bulimia* that's taken over Jenny kept you from being the way you want to be with her?"

> "When *Depression* gets the better of Dad, how does that affect family life?"

> "When *Tantrums* convince Joey to yell and scream, do you think your response gives *Tantrums* more or less fuel?"

The following vignette, showing how John Neal explores the relative influence of a problem, is adapted from a case study in James Donovan's *Short-Term Couple Therapy* (Neal, Zimmerman, & Dickerson, 1999).

CASE STUDY

John: So what's the problem you would like some help with?

Larry: Well, we have more than one problem. Let's see, certainly money is a problem, and that aggravates other problems. Communication is a problem. Sex is a problem.

John: So money is a problem, and it aggravates communication and sex?

Larry: Yes.

John: I'll want to come back and ask you more about this, but if it's okay, first I'm going to ask Elizabeth the same question. Okay? (He nods.) Elizabeth, what's your experience?

Elizabeth: All that's true. We went through some counseling before, and we made some progress. The anger got less, and we started talking. Then we just slid back into our old ways.

John: So there was a time when you were experiencing the anger as decreasing and felt some

progress. Then it slid back into the way it was before?

Elizabeth: We had been given some things to focus our energy on. Given the opportunity to not focus on each other, we don't. We just get distant.

John: So together these things create distance between the two of you?

Elizabeth: Yes.

John: And when you notice that distance, how do you find it affects you?

Elizabeth: I think it's sad, and I'm not quite sure what to do. And if I know that we have to go to counseling, then I put it on the back burner and wait to bring it up here. We don't really talk to each other, unless we're going to counseling.

John: So the distance makes you sad and not sure what to do about it, and it gets you to put things on the back burner? Do you mean you put communication on the back burner?

Elizabeth: I put the relationship on the back burner. We can do the day-to-day stuff in a habitual way, but I don't want our relationship to be like that. It's bad, but it's better than not getting along. (She starts to cry.)

John: When the distance or the arguing take over, do they encourage you to see Larry in a certain way?

Elizabeth: Yes, I get real judgmental. He finds it insulting, but that's not what I'm trying to do. I feel real judgmental and critical. I'm wanting more from him, and I'm not getting it.

John: So you find yourself wanting more, and these feelings encourage you to see Larry in judgmental and critical ways. Do these feelings also get you to view the relationship in certain ways?

The therapist returns to the husband and continues posing "effects" questions for several more minutes. Finally, after diligently exploring the effects of the couple's problems, Neal is able to summarize their experience using externalizing language.

John: Okay, let me summarize my understanding to make sure I've got it right. Certain things are difficult to talk about that create trouble between the two of you, money being the most difficult. And the way it works is that the trouble about this creates distance—that this distance gets Larry to withdraw rather than bring things up, to kind of "check out," as Elizabeth says. And the distance puts Elizabeth in the position of not being able to bring things up, of putting the relationship on the "back burner" out of concern that if she does bring it up, she will say the wrong thing. In spite of the ways this trouble has created distance, there have been some times when the two of you have found ways to talk. Elizabeth, in spite of this, has found a way over the past few years to open up about how dealing with money is difficult. And Elizabeth, you noticed that Larry is more present at those times, right? (Both partners nod their agreement.)

Reading between the Lines of the Problem Story

While asking relative influence questions, the therapist listens for sparkling events or unique outcomes—times when clients were able to avoid the problem's effects—and then asks for elaboration on how that was done:

"Can you remember a time when *Anger* tried to take you over, but you didn't let it? How did you do that?"

"Have there been times when your daughter didn't believe the lies *Anorexia* tells her about her body?"

"When Jenny has withstood the tremendous pressure she feels from *Alcoholism*, have you appreciated the magnitude of that accomplishment?"

These unique outcomes become the building blocks of new, more preferred stories.

CASE STUDY

In *Collaborative Therapy with Multi-Stressed Families*, Bill Madsen (2007) describes his work with a secretary referred by her employee assistance plan after a run-in with her boss in which she became distraught and angry. Fran described herself as depressed, disorganized, and intimidated by her boss. She had trouble sleeping and couldn't focus at work.

In the first session, Fran said that she felt worthless and unlikable, an accusation supported by an abusive father and a painful history of being teased at school. Depression's hold on Fran was strong, and

the few exceptions to its influence that she noticed were quickly dismissed by her as inconsequential.

In the second session, Fran came in looking tired after attending a science fiction movie marathon. She was an avid fan who read voraciously and was familiar with almost every science fiction movie made. Even though she was exhausted, there was a sparkle in her eyes, which contrasted sharply with how she looked in the first session. In that session, when Fran described coping with the teasing she experienced as a child by watching endless hours of science fiction movies on TV, Madsen had thought of this as an escape from painful reality. Now he began to wonder what science fiction might be an entry into rather than an escape from.

When Fran spoke enthusiastically about an upcoming science fiction conference, Madsen asked her to describe the Fran one would see at this conference.

"A big kid," she replied, "a nut who has fun, wears outrageous costumes, and enjoys herself; a girl who is confident and not afraid of people, someone who is friendly and open." They agreed that the conference was like a depression-free zone, and the following conversation ensued.

Fran: You know, it's like I live in a sea of depression and there are these islands of sanctuary where it can't get me. Some, like the conference, are bigger islands and some are very small. Some aren't even islands. They're like coral reefs where I can just keep my head above water.

Bill: What is it that you like about the islands?

Fran: I'll drown out in the sea. The seas will kill me. The islands sustain me.

They talked further about Fran's struggle with teasing and taunting in grade school and then eventually returned to her metaphor of islands and coral reefs.

Bill: You talked about wanting to get more solid places to stand like islands. What do you think would need to happen to build some of those coral reefs into islands?

Fran: I need to do what always happens to coral reefs: add sediment. The sediment is the people around me who will help me remember who I am and not get washed away by depression.

In the sessions that followed, Fran and her therapist fleshed out what she felt was the solid foundation in her life and the people who made her happy and brought out the best in her. In looking back on this successful treatment, Madsen observed:

> All too often in our work as therapists, we focus on the sea of problems, rather than the islands of client abilities, skills, and know-how. It is an ironic and tragic paradox that our attempts to help often result in therapists and clients learning more about problems' influence and less about clients' resistance and coping. Again, it is important to not ignore the influence of problems but to juxtapose the dominant tragic story of the problem's influence with a heroic counter-story of client agency.

Reauthoring

Evidence of competence relative to the problem, gathered from sifting through the clients' history, can serve as the start of new narratives regarding what kind of people they are. To make this connection, the therapist begins by asking what past victories over the problem say about the client:

"What does it say about you as a person that you were able to defeat *Depression* on those occasions?"

"What qualities of character must your son possess to be able to do that?"

The therapist can also expand the historical purview beyond episodes relating to the problem to find more evidence to bolster the new self-narrative:

"What else can you tell me about your past that helps me understand how you were able to handle *Anger* so well?"

"Who knew you as a child who wouldn't be surprised that you have been able to stand up to *Fear* on these occasions?"

As the new self-narrative begins to take shape, the therapist can shift the focus to the future, inviting clients to envision upcoming changes that will fit the new story:

"Now that you've discovered these things about yourself, how do you think these discoveries will affect your relationship with *Self-hate*?"

The self-story now has a past, present, and future. It's a complete narrative.

Here's how John Neal moved into the reauthoring process with the couple whose trouble communicating resulted in distancing from each other.

CASE STUDY

John: So (turning to Larry), feelings of inadequacy and (turning to Elizabeth) overresponsibility have been interfering in your relationship. But you (Elizabeth) said sometimes you've been feeling it's not you?

Elizabeth: Yes, the two times I thought about it I didn't feel defensive . . . and I didn't feel angry. And things have been better in general.

John: During those two times, you were feeling better about yourself?

Elizabeth: Yes, I could understand that Larry was struggling and let him know I understood. So we've been communicating better.

John: Did this cause problems for the distance?

Elizabeth: (laughing) Yes, you could say that.

Larry: (also laughing) I would agree.

John: (to Elizabeth) In the moments when you felt better about yourself—can you tell me a little more about that?

Elizabeth: Well, maybe because I wasn't defensive, he was more like he used to be, really listening to me.

John: And how did that affect you?

Elizabeth: Well, it was really great (smiling). That's what gave distance the trouble.

John: So (later turning to Larry) you noticed a difference between the two of you also? What was your experience?

Larry: Things have been better, and I've been feeling better, too.

John: When you were aware of that, what was going on?

Larry: Elizabeth has been different, and I thought about what you said, that the feelings of inadequacy are there for everybody. It's not true that I'm inadequate. I've always known that's true, but I've never really thought about it in terms of feeling badly about myself.

John: And that helped give distance a run for it?

Larry: (again laughing) Sometimes.

John: Are you surprised that Elizabeth is seeing you differently at these times?

Larry: Not really. I think I have been different.

And then because preferred developments usually have a history, even if it is often forgotten in the face of current problems, the therapist invited the couple to reflect back on the strengths that drew them to each other in the first place.

John: Is this closeness something that used to be much more a part of the relationship?

Larry: Yes, things used to be like this a lot more.

John: If you think back to that time, was that before the kids?

Larry: Yes.

John: If back then, you could have looked into the future and seen the last few weeks, would either you or Elizabeth have been surprised that the two of you have been giving distance a run for it?

Larry: No, not at all.

John: So it speaks to something that was true of you back then?

Larry: Yes. I've always felt, or I used to feel, that we wanted to understand each other. She made the effort to understand me, and I think I was good at being present for her.

Elizabeth: That's definitely true. It was one of the things that attracted me to Larry. I felt respected, and we were real partners.

Reinforcing the New Story

Because narrative therapists believe that the self is constituted in social interaction, they make a point of helping clients find audiences to support their progress in constructing new stories for themselves. Clients might be asked to contact people from their past who can authenticate their new story—who can confirm and add to examples of their acting capably. Clients are also encouraged to recruit people in their lives who can serve as supportive witnesses, or "allies" (Dickerson, 2004a) to their new story. Sometimes "leagues" are formed, support groups of people with similar problems, to reinforce one another's efforts to resist the problem. For example, the Vancouver Anti-Anorexia/Anti-Bulimia League (Madigan, 1994) has a newsletter and monitors the media, writing letters to company presidents, newspapers, and magazines that portray an emaciated ideal for women and encourage them to diet.

> Watch this video of Dr. Steve Madigan helping a family find a community of concern to support the client's changes. What impact do you think Dr. Madigan's concern had on this family?

David Epston has pioneered the use of letter writing to extend the therapeutic conversation beyond the session. These letters often convey a deep appreciation of what the client endured, the outline of a new story, and the therapist's confidence in the client's ability to continue to progress. The advantage of this technique is that the words in a letter don't vanish the way words do after a conversation. Clients have reported that they reread letters Epston sent them years earlier to remind themselves what they went through and how far they have come (Epston, 1994).

Guidelines for Therapeutic Letters

- Use the clients' language as much as possible.
- Acknowledge the unhappiness that's taken hold of the clients' lives.
- Use questions to open up possibilities instead of closing them.
- Express optimism and enthusiasm in separating the person from the problem.
- Make it clear that you are the client's side against the difficulties that have been making a mess of their lives.
- Opinions and suggestions should be offered as tentative, and should invite the client to consider what he or she thinks.
- Highlight clients' strengths and competencies.
- Emphasize what you are learning from the family and what you are learning from your work with them.

The following are examples of the kinds of letters a narrative therapist might write.

"Dear Mr. Williams,

I'm sorry we didn't get to meet last Thursday. I gather you were pretty busy at work.

I heard from your wife that fighting was driving a rift between your boys and making life difficult for the two of you. If I understood her correctly, she thought that "sibling rivalry" was to be expected but that things had gotten out of hand. I've been thinking about the problems I heard about, and I might come up with some suggestions, but I wouldn't want to propose any course of action that you might not favor. If there is any way you can share your ideas with me, I'd find that most useful. Do you think that if you shared your thoughts with your wife, that she'd be able to do a good job of communicating your ideas to me?"

"Dear Marion and Raymond,

I'm sure you've had the experience of thinking of something important after an encounter. So it will come as no surprise to you that I thought of some questions I should have asked after our session.

Raymond, how did you avoid the temptation to lash out in anger at Marion? And how do you think your leaving the house might have come across to her?

Marion, how did you manage to avoid letting your disappointment make you give up on Raymond? And do you think another way of letting him know how you feel might have a better chance of getting through to him?"

I look forward to getting your thoughts on these things. By the way, what ideas occurred to you after our meeting?

"Dear Carla and Max,

We really enjoyed catching up to you, and thought you might like to hear some of our thoughts about the meeting.

Carla it was clear that you have progressed a long way since the previous meeting, even though you hadn't fully realized the extent of this. You'd taken some giant steps in your escape from the early training you were given in being a person. Instead, you've been investigating new ways of being your own person.

You've been taking a stand against keeping your feelings hidden and resisting everyone else telling you what to do. You've been finding your own voice in which to express your own opinions.

Max, we were impressed by some of the realizations that you've been having about the danger of accepting invitations to know Carla's mind, and impressed with the speed at which your were able to identify possibilities for declining such invitations in the future. In so doing, it was clear that you are supporting Carla in her project of becoming her own person.

We're proud of both of you for this growth in your lives and in your relationship."

All of these efforts—recruiting authenticators and audiences, forming teams and leagues, writing letters—are in keeping with the social constructionist emphasis on interaction in creating and maintaining change. For people to solidify a new identity, they need communities that confirm and reinforce revisioned narratives and that counter cultural and family messages to the contrary. What happens in a session is just a beginning, because the goal isn't just to solve a problem; it's to change the whole way of performing one's life.

At the end of each session, narrative therapists summarize what happened, being sure to use externalizing language and emphasizing any unique outcomes that were mentioned. These summaries are what Epston often puts into his letters. The effect of these reviews is to convey to clients that the therapist is with them and celebrates their blossoming new identity. This sense of being cheered on by the therapist can be extremely encouraging.

Deconstructing Destructive Cultural Assumptions

At times, narrative therapists make the connection to cultural narratives more explicit. For example, an anorexic woman might be asked how she was recruited into the belief that her worth depended on her appearance. This would lead to other questions regarding the position of women in society. Similarly, a violent man might be asked how he came to believe that men should never be weak or tender, and a deconstructing of the messages men receive would ensue.

To clarify what this deconstructing of cultural attitudes might look like, we will present one of White's cases, as described by Mary Sikes Wylie (1994):

> John . . . came to see White because, says White, "he was a man who never cried"—he had never been able to express his emotions—and he felt isolated and cut off from his own family. As a child, John had been taught, both at home and at his Australian grammar school, that any show of gentleness or "softness" was unmanly and would be met with harsh punishment and brutal public humiliation. White asks John a series of questions that are at once political and personal, eliciting information about the man's "private" psychological suffering and linking it to the "public" cultural practices, rigidly sexist and aggressively macho, that dominated his youth. "How were you recruited into these thoughts and habits [of feeling inadequate, not sufficiently masculine, etc.]? What was the training ground for these feelings? Do you think the rituals of humiliation [public caning by school authorities, ridicule by teachers and students for not being good at sports or sufficiently hard and tough] alienated you from your own life? Were they disqualifications of you? Did these practices help or hinder you in recognizing a different way of being a male?" (p. 43)

After deconstructing the masculine image in this way, White helped John to remember times when he resisted it and to recognize the nobility of his efforts to remain gentle and loving in spite of his socialization.

A Case of Sneaky Poo

White's therapy comes to life in his case descriptions, as in the following excerpt from his description of a family with an encopretic child (White, 1989).

When mapping the influence of family members in the life of what we came to call "Sneaky Poo," we discovered that:

1. Although Sneaky Poo always tried to trick Nick into being his playmate, Nick could recall a number of occasions during which he had not allowed Sneaky Poo to "outsmart" him. These were occasions during which Nick could have cooperated by "smearing," "streaking," or "plastering," but he declined to do so. He had not allowed himself to be tricked into this.

2. There was a recent occasion during which Sneaky Poo could have driven Sue into a heightened sense of misery, but she resisted and turned on the stereo instead. Also, on this occasion, she refused to question her competence as a parent and as a person.

3. Ron could not recall an occasion during which he had not allowed the embarrassment caused by Sneaky Poo to isolate him from others. However, after Sneaky Poo's requirements of him were identified, he did seem interested in the idea of defying these requirements. . . .

4. It was established that there was an aspect to Sue's relationship with Nick that she thought she could still enjoy, that Ron was still making some attempts to persevere in his relationship with Nick, and that Nick had an idea that Sneaky Poo had not destroyed all of the love in his relationship with his parents.

After identifying Nick's, Sue's, and Ron's influence in the life of Sneaky Poo, I introduced questions that encouraged them to perform meaning in relation to these examples, so that they might "re-author" their lives and relationships.

How had they managed to be effective against the problem in this way? How did this reflect on them as people and on their relationships? . . . Did this success give them any ideas about further steps that they might take to reclaim their lives from the problem? . . . In response to these questions, Nick thought that he was ready to stop Sneaky Poo from outsmarting him so much, and decided that he would not be tricked into being its playmate anymore. (pp. 10–11)

Two weeks later, White found that Nick had fought Sneaky Poo valiantly, having only one minor episode, and he seemed happier and stronger. Sue and Ron had also done their parts in the battle. In her effort not to cooperate with Sneaky Poo's requirements for her to feel guilty, Sue had begun to "treat herself" when Sneaky Poo was getting her down, and Ron had fought Sneaky Poo's attempts to keep him isolated by talking to friends about the problem. As White explains:

> I encouraged the family to reflect on and to speculate about what this success said about the qualities that they possessed as people and about the attributes of their relationships. I also encouraged them to review what these facts suggested about their current relationship with Sneaky Poo. In this discussion, family members identified further measures that they could take to decline Sneaky Poo's invitations to them to support it. (p. 11)

White reports that the family expanded these efforts in the interim, and by the third session they felt confident that Sneaky Poo had been defeated. At a six-month follow-up, they were still doing well.

Evaluating Therapy Theory and Results

By externalizing problems, deconstructing pessimistic life stories, and conveying unwavering confidence in their clients, narrative therapists have constructed a powerful recipe for change. Packaging interventions in the form of questions makes their input less like advice to be resisted and fosters a sense of partnership with clients.

The two most powerful ingredients in narrative therapy are the narrative metaphor itself and the technique of externalizing problems. Both the strength and the weakness of this approach is its cognitive focus. In rejecting the cybernetic model (families stuck in dysfunctional feedback loops), narrative therapists repudiated the idea that families with problems have something wrong with them. Unfortunately, at least early on, narrative therapists also turned their backs on the three defining innovations of family therapy: (1) recognizing that psychological symptoms are often related to family conflict; (2) thinking about human problems as interactional, which means thinking in terms of twos (complementarity, reciprocity) and threes (triangles); and (3) treating the family as a unit.

Viewing problems as stories to be deconstructed overlooks the fact that some families have real conflicts that don't disappear because they join together temporarily to fight an externalized problem. For example, parents whose lives are empty may have trouble letting their children grow up. Does that emptiness evaporate after they help their children battle *Rebelliousness*?

In the process of helping people restory their experience, narrative therapists often subscribe to a view of unhappy emotions (anger, fear, anxiety, depression) as annoyances to avoid rather than explore. They ask how anger or fear "defeats" clients but rarely why clients are angry or what they are afraid of.

Early versions of family therapy *did* cast families in a bad light and blamed them for their problems. The narrative movement helped shift the field toward a more collaborative stance. In the process of rejecting the patronizing consciousness of that earlier age, however, narrative therapists have often neglected systems thinking (Phipps & Vorster, 2009), emphasizing its mechanistic elements while ignoring its more humanistic aspects. One of family therapy's greatest contributions was to bring a contextual understanding of people and their problems into the consulting room. Nonsystemic therapists, influenced by the disease model, had encouraged people to fight problems (with medication, support groups, education) rather than explore the network of relationships in which their problems were embedded. Although opposed to the disease model, narrative therapists return to a similarly acontextual view of problems as things to be fought, and they eschew efforts to understand their interpersonal roots.

Most narrative therapists would agree with Vicki Dickerson's statement that narrative therapy is "primarily about situating problems in their cultural context" (Freedman, 1996). That is, helping clients identify and challenge the ubiquitous but commonly unexamined prejudices that permeate society and make self-worth and harmonious relating difficult. But how does one do that without imposing one's own political biases?

Although some therapists still make a case for strict therapeutic neutrality, many now agree that it's sometimes necessary to question cultural assumptions. It's true that popular culture promotes many unhealthy values. The question is "What is the best way to help people free themselves from those influences without imposing one's own values?" This is a complex problem, and narrative therapy answers it one way. We hope their example inspires all family therapists to grapple with this issue.

◆ ◆ ◆

The narrative model captured the imagination of the field in the 1990s, only to suffer the inevitable backlash to new ideas. The approach was too convoluted or too simplistic, it was just another form of cognitive therapy, or it was just about stories.

The fallout from the backlash was twofold. The first had to do with a watering down of the political aspect of the model, attending to the story aspect only and reducing externalizing to a linguistic sleight of hand. Some incorporated narrative techniques into other models (e.g., Eron & Lund, 1996); others found much to criticize from a family systems perspective (Minuchin, 1998). Little has been written that successfully distinguishes between a narrative metaphor and a systems approach, although Levy (2006) recently addressed this issue. What adherents of this approach maintain is that the narrative metaphor is applicable to either an intrapsychic *or* a systemic approach (Dickerson, 2007).

The second effect of the backlash was a rejection of social constructionism. This was the "too convoluted" argument. Also, because evidence-based therapies, along with more multidimensional approaches, are being promoted in the twenty-first century, theorists have moved away from conversations about ways of knowing.

Finally, as with all models, the narrative approach continues to evolve. Kaethe Weingarten (2003), for example, in her book *Common Shock: Witnessing Violence Every Day*, offers a framework for understanding human psychology and behavior that is social constructionist in spirit but goes beyond a narrative therapy approach. Bill Madsen (2007), in the second edition of *Collaborative Therapy with Multi-Stressed Families*, applies a narrative approach to community work in difficult circumstances. Helen Gremillion (2003), who teaches gender studies at Indiana University, looks at the connections between contemporary anthropology and a narrative approach to young women with eating disorders in her ethnography *Feeding Anorexia*. Vicki Dickerson (2004b) extends narrative thinking to show that you sometimes have to break the rules to get what you want in life in a self-help book for young women called *Who Cares What You're Supposed to Do?* Art Fisher, from Nova Scotia, travels extensively showing how he has adapted narrative ideas to his approach for working with men who are violent.

While little empirical support currently exists, clinicians and researchers alike have begun to propose interventions that utilize narrative techniques for a variety of presenting problems and some are in the beginning stages of testing their effectiveness. For instance, some have suggested using narrative therapy to address issues in blended families (Shalay & Brownlee, 2007), couples struggling with the immigration experience (D'Urso, Reynaga, & Patterson, 2009), as well as situations in which adolescents coming out as gay, lesbian, or bisexual to their parents (Saltzburg, 2007). Others have advocated the use of narrative therapy in a group format to strengthen family identity in the face of homelessness (Fraenkel, Hameline, & Shannon, 2009) and facilitate discussions between depressed individuals and their families (Lemmons, Eisler, Migerode, Heireman, & Demyttenaere, 2007). More recently, case studies have shown the potential utility of narrative therapy approaches with families struggling with childhood cancer (Hedtke, 2014), brain injury (Butera-Prinzi, Charles, & Story, 2014), and other chronic illnesses (Abdalla & Novis, 2014). Finally, other proposals integrate attachment theory and narrative therapy in the treatment of eating disorders (Dallos, 2001, 2004); couples therapy for problems associated with infidelity (Duba, Kindsvatter, & Lara, 2008); and early childhood maltreatment (May, 2005).

Summary

The narrative approach is built around two organizing metaphors: personal narrative and social construction. When memory speaks, it tells a narrative truth, which comes to have more influence than historical truth. The "facts" presented to a therapist are partly historical and partly constructions. The constructions that make up the shared reality of a family represent mutual understandings and shared prejudices—some of which are useful, some of which are not.

Narrative therapists seek to break the grip of unhelpful stories by *externalizing* problems. By challenging pessimistic versions of events, therapists make room for hope. Uncovering *unique outcomes* provides an opening for more optimistic stories. Finally, clients are helped to create audiences of support to encourage their progress in restorying their lives along preferred lines.

The strategies of narrative therapy fall into three stages: (1) recasting the problem as an affliction (externalizing) by focusing on its effects rather than its causes; (2) finding exceptions, or partial triumphs, over the problem and instances of effective action; and (3) recruiting support. Encouraging some kind of public ritual to reinforce new and preferred interpretations moves cognitive constructions past private insight into socially supported action.

Putting these strategies into practice involves an elaborate series of questions:

♦ *Deconstruction questions:* To externalize the problem. "What does Depression whisper in your ear?" "What conclusions about your relationship have you drawn because of this problem?"
♦ *Opening space questions:* To discover unique outcomes. "Has there ever been a time when Arguing could have taken control of your relationship but didn't?"
♦ *Preference questions:* To make sure unique outcomes represent preferred experiences. "Was this way of handling things better or worse?" "Was that a positive or a negative development?"

♦ *Story development questions:* To develop a new story from the seeds of (preferred) unique outcomes. "How is this different from what you would have done before?" "Who played a part in this way of doing things?" "Who will be the first to notice these positive changes in you?"
♦ *Meaning questions:* To challenge negative images of self and emphasize positive agency. "What does it say about you that you were able to do that?"
♦ *Questions to extend the story into the future:* To support changes and reinforce positive developments. "What do you predict for the coming year?"

The social constructionist foundation of narrative therapy gives the approach its political cast and deemphasizes family dynamics and conflict. Instead of looking within families for dysfunctional interactions, narrative therapists look outside for destructive influences of cultural values and institutions. These therapists invite family members to pull together to oppose these values and practices. Instead of neutrality, narrative therapists offer advocacy.

Click here to apply your knowledge of chapter concepts.

Click here to test your application and analysis of the content found within this chapter.

T he explosive growth of family therapy crowded the field with competing models and produced a rich and varied literature, bearing witness to the vitality of the profession, while at the same time creating a confusing array of concepts and methods. See Table 13.1 for a summary of these models. Each school proclaims a set of truths, yet despite some overlap there are notable conflicts among these truths.

Theoretical Formulations

Theories organize our awareness and help us make sense of what families are doing. Instead of a "blooming, buzzing confusion," we begin to see patterns of pursuit and distance, enmeshment and disengagement, and problem-saturated stories. Once you begin to see ineffectual attempts to settle arguments between children as enmeshment, your goal shifts from intervening more effectively to backing off and letting the children settle their own disputes. Here we evaluate theories in terms of their pragmatic function: understanding families in order to help them.

◆ Families as Systems

Communications therapists introduced the idea that families are systems. More than the sum of their parts, **systems** are the parts *plus* the way they function together.

Once, not accepting systems theory was like not believing in apple pie and motherhood. Now the postmodern movement has challenged systems thinking as just another modernist framework, a metaphor taken too literally, and has shifted emphasis from behavior to cognition and from the organization of the family to the thinking of its members.

It's easy to say that a good therapist takes into account both the self—thoughts and feelings—*and* the system—interactions and organization. In practice, however, deciding when to delve into individual experience or focus on interactional patterns presents a host of hard choices.

LEARNING OUTCOMES

◆ Describe how different models view various basic concepts of family therapy.

◆ Compare and contrast the views of different models in regards to healthy and unhealthy family development.

◆ Compare and contrast the assessment procedures and interventions used by different models.

◆ Describe three different types of integrative models.

◆ Describe community mental health family therapy.

TABLE 13.1 Models of Family Therapy

	Bowenian	Strategic	Structural
Founder(s)	Murray Bowen	Don Jackson Jay Haley	Salvador Minuchin
Key theoretical constructs	Differentiation of self	Homeostasis Feedback loops	Subsystems Boundaries
Core problem dynamic	Triangles Emotional reactivity	More-of-the-same solutions	Enmeshment/ Disengagement
Key techniques	Genogram Process questions	Reframing Directives	Enactments Boundary making
	Experiential	**Psychodynamic**	**Cognitive-behavioral**
Founder(s)	Virginia Satir Carl Whitaker	Nathan Ackerman Henry Dicks Ivan Boszormenyi–Nagy	Gerald Patterson Robert Liberman Richard Stuart
Key theoretical constructs	Authenticity Self-actualization	Drives Selfobjects Internal objects	Reinforcement Extinction Schemas
Core problem dynamic	Emotional suppression Mystification	Conflict Projective identification Fixation and regression	Inadvertent reinforcement Aversive control
Key techniques	Confrontation Structured exercises	Silence Neutrality Interpretation	Functional analysis Teaching positive control
	Solution-focused	**Narrative**	
Founder(s)	Steve de Shazer Insoo Kim Berg	Michael White David Epston	
Key theoretical constructs	Language creates reality	Narrative theory Social constructionism	
Core problem dynamic	Problem talk	Problem-saturated stories	
Key techniques	Focusing on solutions Identifying exceptions	Externalization Identifying unique outcomes Creating audiences of support	

◆ Stability and Change

Communications theorists described families as rule-governed systems with a tendency toward stability or homeostasis (Jackson, 1965). But in order to adjust to changing circumstances, families must also be capable of revising their rules and modifying their structure.

The dual nature of families—*homeostatic* and *changing*—is best appreciated by the communications, structural, and strategic models. They don't presume that symptomatic families are inherently dysfunctional but rather that they have failed to adapt to changing circumstances.

Anyone who ignores this developmental principle runs the risk of placing undue emphasis on pathology. A therapist who sees a family having trouble but fails to consider that they may be stuck at a transitional impasse is apt to think they need an overhaul when a tune-up might do. Therapies that emphasize long-range goals are all susceptible to this therapeutic overkill. Psychoanalytic, experiential, and Bowenian practitioners are inclined to assume that families need fundamental reorganization. Because they have the equipment for major surgery—long-term therapy—they tend to see their clients as needing it.

The pioneers of family therapy (with the notable exception of Virginia Satir) tended to overestimate homeostatic forces in families and underestimate their resourcefulness. This perspective encouraged therapists to act as critics. The corollary of the family trapped by systemic forces they can't understand was the clever therapist who would do the understanding for them.

Many of the newer approaches are designed to elicit families' resources rather than attack their deficiencies. These models encourage therapists to collaborate with families to work out solutions rather than assume they won't change unless provoked. But when some of these "collaborative" approaches—like solution-focused therapy, for example—presume that change is easy, that seems as much naive as optimistic.

◆ Process/Content

Most schools of family therapy emphasize the **process** of family interaction. Psychoanalysts and experientialists try to reduce defensiveness and foster open expression of thoughts and feelings; communications therapists increase the flow of interactions and help family members reduce the incongruence between levels of communication; Bowenians block triangulation and encourage self-focus; strategic therapists counter problem-maintaining interactions; behaviorists teach parents to use positive control and couples to reduce coercive communication; structural therapists realign boundaries and strengthen parental authority.

Despite their commitment to process, however, therapists often get caught up in **content**. Psychoanalysts lose sight of process when they concentrate on individual family members and their memories of the past. Experientialists often become overly central while trying to help individuals overcome emotional defensiveness. The danger is that by so doing, a therapist will neglect interactional processes that affect individual expression.

Behaviorists neglect process in favor of content when they isolate behavior from its context and

ignore the interactional patterns surrounding it. They often interfere with the process of family interaction by assuming a didactic role. (As long as a teacher stands in front of the class lecturing, there's little opportunity to find out what the students can do on their own.)

Process concepts are so central to Bowen systems therapy that there's little danger of forgetting them. Only naive misunderstanding of Bowen's theory would lead someone to think of reestablishing family ties without also being aware of processes of triangulation, fusion, and differentiation. The same is true of structural family therapy; process issues are always center stage.

The newer models, with their de-emphasis on systems thinking, have moved away from process. Narrative constructivists are less interested in interactional patterns than in how family members understand their problems. They're less interested in influencing processes of interaction than in expanding stories. Similarly, because solution-focused therapists have no interest in how problems got started, they ignore the family processes that surround them. The only processes they attend to are interactions that constitute "exceptions"—times when the problem wasn't a problem.

◆ Monadic, Dyadic, and Triadic Models

Some therapists (e.g., psychoeducational) continue to focus on the individual patient and include the rest of the family only as an adjunct to that person's treatment. Keep in mind that psychoeducational therapists work primarily with serious mental illness (schizophrenia, bipolar disorder), where the family's influence is probably less than in the majority of cases treated by family therapists.

The same cannot be said for narrative therapists, whose focus on cognition leads them to concentrate on individuals and largely ignore the defining characteristics of family therapy: (1) recognizing that psychological symptoms are often the result of family conflict; (2) thinking about human problems as interactional, which means thinking in twos and threes (complementarity, triangles); and (3) treating the family as a unit. Although narrative therapists disregard family conflict in their formulations, their efforts to redefine problems as alien invaders have the effect of uniting families to overcome the problem's influence. It would be interesting to speculate on whether ignoring family conflict but rallying family members to unite in concern would be more effective in cases like anorexia, where problems take on a life of their own, than in others, like school refusal or misbehavior, where the problem is more likely to indicate family conflicts.

Psychoanalysts think about personality dynamics, whether they meet with individuals or families. They see family life as a product of internalized relationships from the past, and they're often more concerned with these mental ghosts than with the flesh-and-blood families of the present. Behaviorists use a **monadic model** when they accept a family's definition of a symptomatic child as the problem and set about teaching parents to modify the child's behavior. Experientialists focus on individuals to help them uncover and express their feelings.

Actually, no living thing can adequately be understood with a monadic model. A bird's egg may be the closest thing in nature to a self-contained unit: The fetus is locked inside its shell with all the nutrients it needs to survive. Even this view is incomplete, however, for there is an exchange of heat between the egg and the surrounding environment. Without its mother's warmth, a baby bird will die.

Dyadic concepts are necessary to explain how people act in relation to one another. Even a psychoanalytic patient, free-associating on the couch, filters memories and dreams through reactions to the analyst. Most of the time family therapists operate with dyadic concepts. Even with a large family in treatment, the focus is usually on various pairs or units of the family.

Helping two people learn to relate better doesn't always mean that the therapist thinks in dyadic terms. Behavior therapists work with couples but treat them as individuals, each deficient in the art of communicating. A true **dyadic model** is based on the recognition that two people in a relationship aren't independent agents interacting with each other; each defines the other. Using this model, a wife's agoraphobia would be understood as, in part, a reaction to her husband and a means of influencing him. Likewise, his decision to send her for behavior modification might reflect his reluctance to accept more of a role in her life.

Family therapists of all schools use dyadic concepts: *unconscious need complementarity, expressive/instrumental, projective identification, symbiosis, intimacy, quid pro quo, double bind, symmetrical/complementary, pursuer/distancer*, and *behavioral contract*. Some terms are based on dyadic thinking even though they may involve more than two people: *compliant* (referring to a family's relationship to a therapist) and *defiant*. Some seem to involve only one person: *countertransference, dominant*, and *supercompetent*. Still other concepts are capable of encompassing units of three or more but are often used to refer to units of two: *boundary, coalition, fusion*, and *disengagement*.

The advantage of the **triadic model** is that it permits a more complete understanding of behavior in context. If a child misbehaves when his or her mother doesn't use effective discipline, teaching her to be stricter won't work if her behavior reflects her relationship with her husband. Perhaps she allows her child to misbehave as a way of undermining her husband's authority, or she and her husband may have worked out a relationship where her ineffectiveness reassures him that he's the strong one.

Murray Bowen said that human behavior is always a function of triangles. Structural therapists have consistently emphasized that enmeshment or disengagement between two people is a function of reciprocal relationships with third parties. Communications therapists wrote about triadic relationships but tended to think in units of two. The same is true of most strategic therapists, although Haley and Selvini Palazzoli were consistently aware of triangles.

The fact that triadic thinking permits a more complete understanding doesn't mean that family therapists must always include all parties in treatment. The issue isn't how many people are in the consulting room but whether the therapist considers problems in their full context.

◆ Boundaries

The most useful concepts of interpersonal boundaries are found in the works of Murray Bowen and Salvador Minuchin. Bowen is best at describing the boundary between the self and others; Minuchin is better at identifying boundaries among various family subsystems. In Bowen's terms, individuals vary on a continuum from **fusion** to differentiation, while Minuchin describes boundaries as ranging from diffuse to rigid, with resultant **enmeshment** or **disengagement**.

Bowen's thinking reflects the psychoanalytic emphasis on *separation* and *individuation* (Mahler, Pine, & Bergman, 1975), with special attention to the resolution of oedipal attachments and leaving home. In this model, we become ourselves by learning to stand alone. Bowen paid less attention to the emotional isolation stemming from rigid boundaries, treating it as an artifact—a defense against a lack of psychological separateness. Bowen used a variety of terms—*togetherness, fusion, undifferentiation, emotional reactivity*—all referring to the danger of people losing themselves in relationships.

Minuchin offers a more balanced view, describing problems that result when **boundaries** are either too weak or too strong. *Diffuse boundaries* allow too much interference into the functioning of a subsystem; *rigid boundaries* allow too little support. Bowen focused on one boundary problem—fusion—and one goal—differentiation. Minuchin speaks of two possibilities—enmeshment or disengagement—and his therapy is designed to fit the specific case.

Bowen's *fusion* and Minuchin's *enmeshment* both deal with blurred boundaries, but they aren't synonymous. *Fusion* is a psychological quality of individuals, the opposite of individuation. The dynamics of fusion have an impact on relationships (especially in the form of reactivity and triangulation), but fusion is *within* a person. Enmeshment is *between* people.

These conceptual differences also lead to differences in treatment. Bowenian therapists encourage relationships but emphasize autonomy. Success is measured by *differentiation of self*. Structuralists encourage authenticity but strive to restructure family relationships by either strengthening *or* weakening boundaries. Success is measured by the harmonious functioning of the whole family.

Family Dynamics

◆ Normal Family Development

Family therapists interested in the past, especially members of Bowenian and psychoanalytic schools, have had the most to say about normal development.

Although most schools of family therapy aren't concerned with how families get started, Bowenians and psychoanalysts have a great deal to say about marital choice. Bowen talked about *differentiation, fusion*, and *triangles*, while psychoanalytic writers speak of *unconscious need complementarity, projective identification*, and *idealization*. However, they seem to be using different terms to describe similar phenomena. Psychoanalysts speak of marital choice as an object of *transference* from the family of origin and of people choosing partners to match their own level of maturity; Bowen said that people pick partners who replicate familiar patterns of family interaction and select mates at similar levels of differentiation.

These are descriptions of ways in which people marry their own alter egos. Both schools discuss how people choose mates who appear to be different, at least on the surface, in ways that are exciting and seem to make up for deficiencies in the self. Obsessive individuals tend to marry histrionic individuals, and according to Bowen, togetherness-oriented people often marry distancers. This brings up another way in which the Bowenian and psychodynamic schools are similar to each other and different from others. Both recognize that personalities have layers. Both think that the success of a relationship depends not only on shared interests and values but also on the nature of the partners' internal object images.

Even if they don't emphasize the past, most of the other schools of family therapy have concepts for describing normal family development. Communications therapists speak of *quid pro quos* (Jackson, 1965) exchanged in normal marriages, while behaviorists describe the same phenomenon in terms of *social exchange theory* (Thibaut & Kelley, 1959). Virginia Satir described normal families as those in which communication is direct and honest, where differences are faced rather than hidden, and where emotions are openly expressed. Under these conditions, she believed, people develop healthy *self-esteem*, which enables them to take the risks necessary for authentic relationships.

According to Minuchin (1974), clinicians should have some appreciation of the facts of ordinary family life in order to distinguish functional from dysfunctional structures, as well as pathological structures from structures that are simply transitional.

Ciaran Griffin/Stockbyte/Getty Images

It is impossible to understand relationships without taking into account the social and cultural forces impinging on the partners.

by implication, what's functional must be just the opposite.

Development of Behavior Disorders

In the early days of family therapy, patients were seen as victims—"scapegoats"—whose symptoms maintained family stability. Much of the literature was about dysfunctional ways of keeping the peace: *scapegoating, pseudomutuality, family projection process, double bind, mystification,* and so on. These malignant mechanisms may have torn young people apart, but they kept families together. It was a simple and satisfying tale of malevolence. No one exactly blamed the parents—their coercions weren't really deliberate—but these explanations did rest on parental faults and failings and as such had mythic force. The idea that schizophrenia was a sacrifice children made for their families was absolutely riveting—and absolutely untrue.

Today, family therapists think less about what causes problems than how families unwittingly perpetuate them.

Inflexible Systems

Early observers of schizophrenic families emphasized their inflexibility. Wynne coined the term **rubber fence** to dramatize how psychotic families resist outside influence and **pseudomutuality** to describe their facade of harmony. R. D. Laing showed how parents, unable to tolerate their children's individuality, used mystification to deny their experience. Communication theorists thought that the most striking disturbance in schizophrenic families was that they lacked mechanisms for changing their rules.

This tradition of viewing families of mentally ill patients as rigidly homeostatic was taken into the 1980s by Selvini Palazzoli in her concept of "dirty games." Carol Anderson and Michael White countered this negative perspective by suggesting that family rigidity might be the result rather than the cause of living with serious problems.

Explaining family problems in terms of homeostatic inflexibility was one of the cornerstones of the strategic school. Dysfunctional families respond to problems with a limited range of solutions. Even

Because structural therapy begins by assessing the adequacy of a family's organization, it sometimes appears to impose a standard. In fact, however, normality is defined in terms of functionality, and structural therapists recognize that diverse family forms may be equally functional. The clarity of subsystem boundaries is more important than the composition of the subsystem. For example, a parental subsystem made up of a single parent and oldest child can function effectively if the lines of authority are clearly drawn. Patterns of enmeshment and disengagement are viewed as preferred styles, not necessarily as indications of abnormality.

Therapists in most of the other models don't think in terms of remaking families and therefore believe they have little need for a model of what families should be like. Instead, they intervene around specific problems—problem-maintaining interactions, problem-saturated stories, forgotten solutions—conceptualized in terms of function, not structure. The patterns they observe are dysfunctional; therefore, when the solutions don't work, these families stubbornly keep trying. Behaviorists use a similar idea when they explain symptoms as resulting from faulty efforts to control behavior. Parents who think they're punishing misbehavior are often actually reinforcing it with attention.

According to psychoanalytic and experiential theories, intrapsychic rigidities, in the form of *conflict, developmental arrest*, and *emotional suppression*, are the individual's contribution to family inflexibility. Psychoanalysts see unhealthy families as **closed systems** that resist change. When stressed, inflexible families regress to earlier levels of development, where unresolved conflicts left them fixated.

Experientialists describe dysfunctional families as emotionally stagnant. If it's true that you sometimes have to try something different just to know you're alive, families afraid of rocking the boat become timid and lifeless. The symptom bearer is a victim of the family's opposition to the life force.

Structural therapists locate the inflexibility of families in the boundaries between subsystems. Even normal families may develop problems if they are unable to modify a previously functional structure to cope with a crisis.

Solution-focused and narrative therapists avoid implicating families in the development of their problems. Both camps prefer to focus on the strengths of individuals in the family and on times when they used their resources to triumph over their troubles. What these models identify as problematic are rigid habits of thought that lead people to consider themselves defeated. Solution-focused therapists leave it at that; they don't speculate about the origins of defeatist thinking. Narrative therapists point to what they consider toxic ideas in the culture that are internalized by family members. It's society, not the family, that's inflexible.

◆ Pathologic Triangles

Pathologic triangles are at the heart of several family therapy explanations of behavior disorder. Among these, Bowen's is the most elegant. Bowen explained how when two people are in conflict, the one who experiences the most anxiety will triangle in a third person. This model not only provides an explanation of systems pathology but also serves as

a warning: As long as a therapist remains allied with one party in an emotional conflict, he or she is part of the problem.

In psychoanalytic theory, oedipal conflicts are seen as the root of neurosis. Here the triangle originates in family interactions but becomes lodged in the individual psyche. A mother's tenderness may be seductive and a father's jealousy threatening, but the wish to do away with the father and possess the mother is a product of fantasy. Pathological fixation of this conflict may be caused by developments in the outer space of the family, but the conflict lives in the inner space of a child's mind.

Structural family theory is based on triangular configurations in which a dysfunctional boundary between two subsystems is the reciprocal of a boundary with a third. A father and son's enmeshment reflects the father and mother's disengagement; a single mother's disengagement from her children is the counterpart of her overinvolvement outside the family. Structural theory also uses the concept of pathological triangles to explain *conflict-detouring triads*, whereby parents divert their conflict onto a child. Minuchin, Rosman, and Baker (1978) have even demonstrated that physiological changes occur when parents in conflict transmit their stress to psychosomatic children.

Strategic therapists typically work with a dyadic model, in which one person's symptoms are maintained by others' efforts to resolve them. Haley and Selvini Palazzoli, however, used a triangular model in the form of **cross-generational coalitions**. These "perverse triangles," as Haley (1977) called them, occur when a parent and child collude in covert opposition to the other parent.

Triangular functioning is less central to the newer models because they're not concerned with *how* families develop problems. It might even be argued that ignoring family dynamics is one of the strengths of narrative and solution-focused approaches, if doing so helps these therapists zero in on the constricting habits of thought they're interested in. It might also be said, however, that ignoring family dynamics is one of the weaknesses of these approaches, especially in cases where family conflict isn't just going to disappear because family members work together to solve a common problem.

Therapy

◆ Assessment

Behaviorists place the greatest emphasis on assessment and use the most formal procedures. The advantage of the behavioral emphasis on assessment is that it provides baseline data, clear goals, and a reliable way to measure therapeutic success. The disadvantage is that by using structured interviews and questionnaires, you don't see families in action. By looking at only part of a family (mother and child, or marital couple), you miss the total context; by relying on questionnaires, you learn only what a family reports.

Structural therapists also emphasize assessment, but their evaluations are based on observation. Enactments give a therapist a chance to observe enmeshment and disengagement. The strengths of this school's assessment procedure are that it actually observes a family's patterns of interaction, it includes the entire family, and it's organized in terms that point directly to desired changes (Minuchin, Nichols, & Lee, 2007).

The Bowenian school also does an excellent job of considering the whole family. Unlike structuralists, however, Bowenians rely on what they're told, and they're interested in the past as well as the present.

The breadth of psychoanalytic theory enables practitioners to speculate well ahead of their data; a little information suggests a great deal. The advantage is that the theory provides inroads to hidden meanings. The danger is that the theory may lead therapists to see only what they expect to see. Experientialists have neither these advantages nor disadvantages. Their evaluations are guided by a simple notion about how feelings are suppressed; they may not uncover much that's hidden but they tend not to see things that aren't there.

Two of the newer schools, narrative and solution-focused, eschew assessment. Solution-focused therapists believe that dwelling on problems undermines the positive thinking they hope to generate. They also think that solutions aren't necessarily related to the ways problems arise. Narrative therapists believe that looking within families for problems perpetuates the judgmental stance they want to get away from. By personifying problems and talking about their effects rather than their causes, they circumvent the finger pointing that often accompanies discussions of how problems got started. The danger is that by disregarding how problems arise, they may overlook real conflicts. And conflict, as you may have noticed, doesn't necessarily go away when you ignore it.

◆ Decisive Interventions

Family therapists use a vast array of techniques—some dictated by their model, others by the therapist's personality and experience. Even if we limited our attention to the techniques specific to each of the schools, the list would be long and confusing. Some techniques are used by virtually everyone—asking questions, reflecting feelings, clarifying communication—and this list has been growing as the field has become more integrated. Each school, however, relies on one or two techniques that are unique and decisive.

In psychoanalytic therapy there are two definitive techniques. The first of these, *interpretation*, is well known but not well understood. Properly used, interpretation refers to elucidating unconscious meaning. It doesn't mean statements of opinion ("You need to express your feelings before you can really be close"); advice ("As long as you continue writing to him, the affair isn't over"); theory ("Some of the reasons you were attracted to him were based on unconscious needs"); or confrontations ("You said you didn't care, but you were really angry"). Interpretations are statements of unconscious meaning: "You've been complaining about your son's arguing with you all the time. Based on what you've said previously, I think that some of your anger is deflected from your husband. He does the same thing, but you're afraid to tell him so, and that's why you get so mad at your son."

The second decisive technique in analytic treatment is *silence*. A therapist's silence permits him or her to discover what's on a patient's mind and to test a family's resources; it also lends force to the eventual interpretations. When a therapist is silent, family members talk, following their own thoughts rather than responding to the therapist. When they learn that the therapist won't interrupt, they respond to each other. This produces a wealth of information that might not otherwise emerge. If a father begins by saying "The problem is my depression," and the therapist immediately asks "How long have you been depressed?" he or she may not discover what thoughts are associated in the man's mind with his depression or how the man's wife responds to his complaint.

The decisive technique in experiential therapy is *confrontation*. Confrontations are designed to provoke emotional reactions and are often blunt. It isn't unusual for experiential therapists to tell clients to shut up or to mock them for being insincere. Confrontations are often combined with *personal disclosure*, the second signature technique of this school. Experientialists use themselves as emotionally expressive models. Finally, most experiential therapists also use *structured exercises*. These include role-playing, psychodrama, sculpting, and family drawings. The rationale for these techniques is that they stimulate emotional experiencing; the drawback is that they're artificial. Family members may get something off their chests in a structured exercise but may not transfer this to their interactions at home.

Most people associate reinforcement with behavior therapy, but reinforcement isn't a technique used in cognitive-behavioral family therapy; *observation* and *teaching* are the vehicles of this approach. Behavioralists begin by observing the contingencies of reinforcement. Their aim is to discover the antecedents and consequences of problem behavior. Once they've completed a *functional analysis of behavior*, they become instructors, teaching families how they inadvertently reinforce undesirable behavior. As teachers, their most useful lesson is the use of positive control. They teach parents that it's more effective to reward good behavior than to punish bad behavior; they teach married couples to substitute being nice to each other for their usual bickering.

Positive control—rewarding desirable behavior—is one of the most useful principles in psychotherapy. It's a valuable lesson for families and for therapists. Therapists, like parents, tend to chide their charges for mistakes; unfortunately, if you're told that you're suppressing your feelings, spoiling your children, or using coercive control, you're apt to feel picked on and put down. Although it may be necessary to point

out some mistakes, it's more effective to concentrate on praising the positive aspects of clients' behavior.

As behavior therapists have paid increasing attention to cognition, they have endeavored to uncover and challenge assumptions that underlie unproductive behavior. That is, they do when they're using the cognitive-behavioral model effectively. We have observed a significant difference between some practitioners of this approach who attribute clichéd assumptions to clients—assuming, for example, that anyone who is depressed must be pessimistic about themselves, the world, and the future—and those practitioners who don't make assumptions and don't preach. These cognitive-behaviorists use Socratic questioning to find out what their clients actually believe and then help them test the validity of those assumptions for themselves.

Bowen systems therapists are also teachers, but they follow a different curriculum. They *teach people to be responsible for themselves* and how by doing so they can transform their entire families. Being responsible for yourself means getting clear about what you think and feel—not what your mother says or what you read in the *New York Times* but what you really believe—and then being true to your beliefs in dealings with other people. You don't take responsibility by changing others or wishing they were different; you do so by speaking for yourself and maintaining your own values. The power of this position is tremendous. If a client can accept who he or she is and that other people are different from himself or herself, then he or she no longer has to approach relationships with the idea that someone has to change. This enables the client to be in contact with people without becoming unduly upset or emotionally reactive.

In addition to teaching differentiation, Bowenian therapists promote two corollary lessons: *avoiding triangulation* and *reopening cut-off family relationships*. Taken together, these three lessons enable one person to transform the whole network of his or her family system. Even if her spouse nags, if his children are disobedient, if her mother never comes to visit, the *client* can create a change. Other schools of therapy gain leverage by including the entire family in treatment. Bowenians teach individuals to be themselves, to make contact with others, and to deal directly with the people they have conflicts with. This gives a person a tool for change that's portable and lasting.

Communications family clinicians contributed so much to the theoretical base of family therapy that it's difficult to single out particular interventions. Perhaps their greatest achievement was pointing out that communication is multilayered and that often the most important things being said are said covertly. Therapy was designed to make the covert overt. Initially this was done by *clarifying communication* and pointing out hidden messages. When this approach met with resistance, therapists began using directives to make the rules of family functioning explicit and to provoke changes in the rules.

Strategic therapy is an offshoot of communications theory, and the techniques used by strategists are refinements of those used by communicationists. Principal among these are *reframing, directives,* and *positive connotation.* Strategic practitioners begin by getting concrete descriptions of problems and then attempting to solve them. In the process, they pay particular attention to a family's language and expectations. They try to grasp the family's point of view and acknowledge it—in a positive connotation; then they use reframing to shift the family's point of view and directives to interrupt problem-maintaining behavior.

Directives are designed to interrupt homeostatic patterns, and they are often paradoxical. Although strategic therapists emphasize fitting treatment to the patient, they often assume that indirect interventions are necessary to outwit resistance. This is sometimes but not always true. It's not so much that some families are resistant and others aren't. Rather, it's that resistance isn't a property of families; it's a quality of interaction between therapist and family. A therapist who proceeds on the assumption that families are unable or unwilling to follow advice is likely to encounter the expected resistance.

Structural family therapy is also a therapy of action, but in this approach the action occurs in the session. The decisive techniques are *enactments* and *boundary making.* Rigid boundaries are softened when a therapist gets people to talk with each other and blocks attempts to interrupt them. Diffuse boundaries are strengthened when a therapist supports the autonomy of individuals and subsystems.

Several promising techniques emerged in the 1980s around which whole models of therapy were built. Steve de Shazer and his colleagues expanded the technique of focusing on successful *solutions* that family members had tried but abandoned. The result was solution-focused therapy. Michael White did the same with *externalization*—personifying problems and attributing oppressive intentions to them, which is a powerful device for getting family members to unite against a common enemy.

Actually, externalization is a concept, not a technique. The decisive technique of narrative therapy is a persistent series of *questions*—whereby the therapist begins by trying to understand the clients' experiences of suffering but then switches from understanding to prodding the clients to think about their problems as malevolent agents. Narrative therapists use a relentless series of questions to challenge negative ideas and convince clients that they have reason to be proud of themselves and that their fates are in their own hands.

Conclusions

Family therapy is ultimately a clinical enterprise, its worth measured in results. In what follows, we offer some very subjective comments about a few of the concepts and methods that have proven most valuable in family therapy.

Theories of family functioning have both a scientific and a practical purpose. The most useful theories treat families as systems; have concepts to describe forces of stability and change; notice the process underlying the content of family discussions; recognize the triadic nature of human relationships; remember to consider the context of the nuclear family rather than viewing it as a closed system; and appreciate the function of boundaries in protecting the cohesiveness of individuals, subgroups, and families.

Although clinicians are more concerned with pathology and change than with normality, it's useful to have some ideas about normal family functioning—both to generate treatment goals and to distinguish what's problematic and needs changing from what's normal and doesn't. Some of the most useful concepts of normal family functioning include the structural model of families as open systems in transformation; the communications model of direct and honest communication, with rules firm enough to ensure stability and flexible enough to allow change; the behavioral model of positive control instead of coercion; the strategic model of systemic flexibility, which accommodates to changing circumstances and seeks new solutions when old ones don't work; and the Bowenian model of how differentiation of self enables people to be both independent and intimate.

Most family therapy concepts of behavior disorder focus on systems and interactions, but the psychoanalytic, Bowenian, narrative, and experiential models add psychological depth to the interactional view, bridging the gap between inner experience and outward behavior. The fact that many divorced people repeat the mistakes of their first marriages supports the idea that some of what goes on in families is a product of character. Some of the most valuable concepts of personal dysfunction in families are Bowen's concept of fusion; the experiential concepts of repressed affect and fear of taking risks; and the psychoanalytic concepts of developmental arrest, internal object relations, instinctual conflict, and hunger for appreciation.

These concepts of individual dynamics are useful adjuncts, but the major ideas in the field explain behavior disorder in terms of systems theory. The most influential of these are about inflexible systems, too rigid to accommodate individual strivings or adjust to changing circumstances; symptomatic family members promoting cohesion by stabilizing the family; inadequate hierarchical structure; families too tightly or too loosely structured; and pathologic triangles.

We've looked at some of the major methodological issues and tried to separate out the decisive techniques of the different schools. As is always the case when a number of variables are involved in a final result, it's not easy to know how much each variable contributes to that result or how important each one is. Furthermore, the more we talk about techniques, the greater the danger of seeing family therapy as a purely technical enterprise. Studying families is like solving a riddle; the art of treating them is to relieve suffering and anguish. The job of the theoretician is to decode and decipher, which requires theory and ingenuity. The job of the therapist is healing, which requires theory but also conviction, perseverance, and caring. Treating families isn't just a matter of theory and technique, it's also an act of love.

Integrative Models

The obvious argument for incorporating elements from more than one approach is that human beings are complicated creatures—thinking, feeling, and acting—who exist in a complex system of biological, psychological, and social influences. No therapy can succeed without having an impact on all of these dimensions. There is, however, an equally valid argument that eclecticism can rob therapy of the intensity made possible by focusing on one or two elements of experience. There may be many ways to skin a cat, but it might not be advisable to try all of them at once.

As we see in the following sections, *integration* refers to three very different kinds of approaches. First there is *eclecticism*, which draws from a variety of models and methods. Second is *selective borrowing*, in which relative purists use a few techniques from other approaches. Third are *specially designed integrative models*.

Eclecticism

What do you do in the first session? Make sure that everyone shows up, greet each of them, and try to make them comfortable. Ask about the presenting problem, of course. But then what?

Suppose a mother says that her fourteen-year-old has become disrespectful. Do you focus on her feelings? Ask what her husband thinks? Set up an enactment in which she talks to her teenager? Inquire about exceptions? Any of these options might be useful. But trying to do-all of them may lead to a lack of focus.

Effective integration requires more than taking a little of this and a little of that from various models. In creating a workable integration, there are two things to avoid. The first is sampling techniques from diverse approaches without conceptual focus. The problem here isn't so much inelegance as inconsistency.

A student who was being supervised in a psychodynamic approach asked to present at a case conference when, after some initial progress, the therapy bogged down. Most of the people at the case conference weren't familiar with the psychodynamic model, and they were impressed by what the student had accomplished. But when it came time for discussion, several of those present suggested that the way to get the case moving again might be to try a different approach—cognitive-behavioral, structural, narrative, or what have you, depending on who was doing the suggesting.

The second thing to avoid is switching horses in midstream. Almost every treatment runs into difficulty at some point. When this happens, beginners may be tempted to shift to a different model. If a structural approach isn't working, maybe a narrative one will. The problem here is that almost any strategy will work for a while—and then stall. Getting stuck isn't a reason to change models; rather, it may mean that you and your clients may be getting to the heart of their problems. This is the time to sharpen your tools, not discard them.

Selective Borrowing

To borrow selectively, you need a foundation in one paradigm. Therapists who eventually manage to combine approaches or successfully master more than one usually don't try to learn them all at once. Using techniques from here and there without a unifying conceptual framework produces a muddled form of eclecticism. Effective borrowing doesn't mean a hodgepodge of techniques, and it doesn't mean switching from one approach to another whenever therapy reaches an impasse. Borrowing techniques from other approaches is more likely to be effective if you do so in a way that fits the basic paradigm within which you are operating.

Consider, for example, a structural therapist treating a mother and daughter who are locked in a battle in which the mother constantly criticizes the daughter for being irresponsible, and the daughter continues to act irresponsibly. If the mother would back off and stop criticizing, the girl might feel less browbeaten and begin to take more responsibility for herself—or if the daughter would start to take more responsibility, maybe the mother would back off. But as long as each of them remains preoccupied the awful things the other one is doing, neither is likely to break this cycle.

Suppose the therapist were to try the narrative technique of externalizing the problem. Instead of "nagging" and "irresponsibility" polarizing the mother and daughter, perhaps they could be convinced to start thinking in terms of a *Breach* that's come between them. This shift in thinking might open space for them to establish a more cooperative way of relating. But if the mother and daughter's quarreling was a product of enmeshment, attempting to bring them together in a more harmonious way might not solve the problem.

In fact, the case we've just described isn't hypothetical. Here's how the therapist actually did introduce the technique of externalizing in this situation.

CASE STUDY

Because he saw the mother and daughter's quarreling as a result of enmeshment, the therapist concentrated first on helping the mother address with her husband some of the conflicts that were keeping them apart. As they started to get closer, the mother began to spend less time worrying about what her daughter was doing.

Then in separate sessions with the daughter, the therapist found a useful way to introduce the externalizing technique. As a result of her mother's nagging, the daughter had gotten into the habit of actively shirking responsibility, and consequently her school performance had deteriorated. It was as though when she had a homework assignment, she felt the same kind of oppression she felt from her mother's nagging.

The therapist pointed this out but found that the girl had begun to internalize her mother's harsh characterizations. "I guess I'm just lazy," she'd say, in what had become a self-fulfilling prophecy. The therapist responded by asking her about times when *Procrastination* got the better of her, and times when *It* didn't. This device proved effective in helping the girl separate herself from the negative introject she'd adopted, and, thus energized, she was able to start getting back on track with her schoolwork.

Specially Designed Integrative Models

While most practitioners eventually become selective borrowers, grafting ideas and practices onto their basic model, some therapists create a new synthesis out of complementary aspects of different models. Some of these integrative efforts are comprehensive systems that include a whole range of approaches under one umbrella, while others simply combine elements of one approach with another, forming a hybrid model.

◆ Integrative Problem-Centered Metaframeworks (IPCM) Therapy

IPCM Therapy was developed by Douglas Breunlin, William Pinsof, William Russell, Jay Lebow, and their colleagues at The Family Institute at Northwestern University. Consistent with General Systems Theory (von Bertalanffy, 1968), IPCM views human problems as nested within hierarchies of subsystems, including person, relationship, family, community, and society (Breunlin, Pinsof, Russell, & Lebow, 2011). This approach begins by focusing on the presenting problem and then addressing the most relevant level to find the constraints keeping a family from solving its problems (Breunlin, Schwartz, & Mac Kune-Karrer, 1992).

In an age when therapists often fall back on formulaic techniques, the metaframeworks model challenges clinicians to consider a wide range of possibilities. Consistent with today's cost-conscious health care climate, IPCM begins with the least expensive, most direct, and least complex interventions, and moves to more complex and more expensive interventions only as needed (Pinsof, Breunlin, Russell, & Lebow, 2011). While some problems may be deep-seated, many are not. Some families will respond to behavioral interventions while others may need more in-depth focus.

For example, a depressed woman might be constrained on many fronts simultaneously. At the level of internal process, she may be burdened by guilt over wanting a little time for herself or because her children complain that they have no friends. At the level of family organization, she may be stuck in a stale second marriage to a man obsessed with his career while she's left to run the house and raise the kids. In addition, she may be preoccupied with her hyperactive son and polarized with her mother over how to deal with him. This pattern may be part of a sequence in which her son's behavior gets worse after monthly visits with her ex-husband. Finally, the woman's situation may be part of a transgenerational pattern maintained by the belief that women should be devoted to their families and never be selfish.

To illustrate the IPCM approach, consider a couple in their sixties who have been caught up in picky but intense fights for the past year. They relate the fighting to the husband's impotence. In exploring the meaning each attaches to these events, the therapist finds that the wife sees her husband's lack of sexual response as a reflection of her diminished attractiveness, while he considers it a sign of waning virility. These conclusions are painful to each of them, and so they avoid talking about it.

The therapist forms an alliance with each of them so they feel safe enough to disclose their private pain and clear up their misconceptions about the other's feelings. If at that point they respond well—fewer fights and more satisfactory sex—therapy can stop. If not, the therapist would explore possible physiological causes of the impotence—fatigue, depression, incipient diabetes. If improvements don't follow the exploration at that level, the therapist might discuss with each partner the unexamined assumptions that they have about the aging process. If the problem still remains unsolved, the focus would shift to intrapsychic blocks, and either or both of them might be referred for individual therapy.

◆ The Narrative Solutions Approach

Among the reasons strategic therapy fell into disfavor were its mechanistic assumptions and manipulative techniques. Families were seen as stubborn and not to be reasoned with. Family history was dismissed as irrelevant. The meretriciousness of this kind of thinking, however, wasn't essential to the insight that families often get stuck applying solutions that don't work.

Joseph Eron and Thomas Lund of the Catskill Family Institute in New York began collaborating in the early 1980s as brief strategic therapists. Although they were attracted to the narrative model, there were aspects of the strategic approach they didn't want to give up. So they combined the two. The resulting narrative solutions approach revolves around the concept of the **preferred view**:

◆ Preferred views include the qualities people would like to possess and have noticed by others; for example, "determined," "caring," and "responsible."
◆ Preferred views shape the attributions people make about behavior. "I did that (got into that fight) because I am cool, independent, and able to manage my own affairs."
◆ Preferred views include people's intentions. "I want to be different from my mother who was a self-sacrificing martyr."

Problems arise when people aren't living according to their preferred views. To address this discrepancy, Eron and Lund use a combination of *reframing* from the MRI model and *restorying* from the narrative approach. Conflict, according to this model, is driven by disjunctions between individuals' preferred views of themselves and how they perceive others as responding to them.

Courtesy Catskill Family Institute

Joseph Eron (left) and Thomas Lund (right) developed narrative solutions therapy.

In *Narrative Solutions in Brief Therapy*, Eron and Lund (1996) offer the example of Al, who became depressed in the wake of retirement and the onset of emphysema.

CASE STUDY

Al liked to think of himself as productive and useful. Yet he worried that he might not be able to remain as active as in the past and that his family would no longer view him as someone to rely on.

When Al was asked when he had felt like the person he wanted to be, he recalled several stories that revealed a man who felt close to this family and liked being helpful. When Al recounted these occasions on which he had acted in line with his preferred attributes (being helpful, connected with family members), he became more hopeful.

When the therapist asked Al to envision a future without his problems, he pictured being less depressed and more involved with his family. He imagined himself coping with his emphysema while remaining useful to others and not following in the footsteps of his father who deteriorated with retirement and illness.

The narrative solutions therapist asks **mystery questions**—for example, how did a person with *X* preferred attributes (hard-working, productive) wind up in *Y* situation (acting listless, feeling depressed) and being seen by people in *Z* ways (uncaring, lazy)? Mystery questions inspire reflection in a nonthreatening way. Clients begin to rethink their predicaments,

how they came to act out of line with their preferred views, and what they can do about the situation.

CASE STUDY

Al was asked how it was that someone who had always been there for his family would find himself so withdrawn. How could someone who had faced previous challenges by taking control wind up acting out of character in the wake of emphysema?

Al seemed curious to find an explanation, and he asked the therapist to meet with his family to explore how his behavior had affected them. Al also felt empowered to talk to his doctor about his illness after he was able to recall preferred experiences indicating that he was a take-charge kind of guy. He also began reframing the motives of family members away from the belief that they saw him as useless to viewing them as bewildered, not knowing how to help him. Al's depression lifted after he met with his family and told them what was and wasn't helpful.

◆ Integrative Couples Therapy

Neil Jacobson of the University of Washington, one of the preeminent behavioral family therapists, teamed with Andrew Christensen of UCLA to figure out how to improve the limited success rates they were finding with traditional behavioral couples therapy. They discovered that their results improved when they added a humanistic element to the standard behavioral mix of communication training and problem solving. The approach they developed is called *integrative couples therapy* (Jacobson & Christensen, 1996).

Traditional behavioral couples therapy is based on the behavior exchange model. After a *functional analysis* showing how partners in a relationship influence one another, they're taught to reinforce changes they wish to bring about in each other.

Anyone who's been married for a long time can tell you what's missing from this approach. Therapy may be about change, but a successful relationship involves acceptance of differences. Some things in an unhappy marriage may need to change, but some things are part of the package, and couples who survive the break-in period learn to accept these things.

It's this element, *acceptance*, that Jacobson and Christensen added to their approach.

In contrast to the teaching and preaching of traditional behavioral therapy, integrative couples therapy emphasizes support and empathy, the same qualities that therapists want couples to show each other. To create a conducive atmosphere, therapy begins with a *formulation*, which is aimed at helping couples let go of blaming and open themselves to acceptance and personal change. The formulation consists of three components: a *theme* that defines the primary conflict; a *polarization process* that describes the destructive pattern of interaction; and the *mutual trap*, which is the impasse that prevents the couple from breaking the polarization cycle once it's triggered.

Common themes in couples' problems include conflicts about closeness and distance, a desire for control but unwillingness to take responsibility, and disagreements about sex. Whereas partners view these differences as problems to be solved, Jacobson and Christensen encourage couples to see that some differences are inevitable. This realization can break the cycle of each one constantly trying to change the other. As the formulation phase continues, the partners begin to see that they aren't victims of each other but of a *pattern* they're both trapped in. The couple can then unite to fight a mutual enemy, the pattern. For example, when Jacobson asked a couple to describe their pattern,

> The husband replied, "We fight over whether or not to be close. When she is not as close to me as she wants to be, she pressures me into being close, and I withdraw, which leads to more pressure. Of course, sometimes I withdraw before she has a chance to pressure me. In fact, that's how it usually starts." (Jacobson & Christensen, 1996, p. 100)

Notice how this formulation helps this couple describe their fight as a pattern to which they both contribute, rather than in the accusatory language typical of distressed couples.

Strategies to produce change include the two basic ingredients of behavioral couples therapy: behavior exchange and communication skills training. Behavior exchange interventions involve *quid pro quo* and *good faith* contracts, by which couples learn to exchange favors or to initiate pleasing behavior in the hope of getting the same in return. For example, each partner might be asked to generate a list of things he or she could do that would lead to greater satisfaction for the other. After each compiles a list, he or she is instructed to start doing some of the things that will please the partner—and to observe the effect of this benevolence on the relationship.

The second ingredient—communication training—involves teaching couples to express themselves in direct but nonblaming ways. Learning to use *active listening* and to make *I-statements* is taught by assigned reading, instruction, and practice. As they learn to communicate less defensively, couples not only are better able to resolve conflicts, but they are also more accepting of each other.

In emphasizing acceptance and compassion, integrative couples therapy joins other family therapies of the twenty-first century—from solution-focused to strategic to narrative—in recognizing the importance of nurturing relationships. Carl Rogers would be proud.

◆ Dialectical Behaviorism

Dialectical behavior therapy (DBT) is a psychoeducational approach developed by Marsha Linehan (1993) for the treatment of suicidal people with borderline personality disorder and subsequently extended to people with multiple disorders who are often in crisis. DBT combines cognitive-behavioral techniques for emotion regulation and reality testing with concepts of distress tolerance, acceptance, and mindfulness awareness. In dialectics, every position implies its opposite—or, in this context, that people are always ambivalent. So people usually simultaneously hold two opposing ideas. DBT therapists use this notion as a way of persuading clients not to act on the destructive half of their ambivalence—for example, by committing suicide. DBT was designed for working with individuals, but it can be applied to work with families (Fruzzetti, Santiseban, & Hoffman, 2007).

 Watch this video of Dr. Marsha Linehan discuss dialectical behavior therapy. Which disorders are best suited for dialectical behavior therapy?

www.youtube.com/watch?v=7KiihIE0d0c

Mindfulness meditation, from the Buddhist tradition, involves maintaining a calm awareness of one's bodily sensations, thoughts, and perceptions. As such, mindfulness is a useful antidote to the anxious flight from painful emotional experience typical of people with obsessive-compulsive disorder, borderline personalities, anxiety disorders, eating disorders, and drug and alcohol addiction. Mindfulness is a foundation for the other skills taught in DBT because it helps clients tolerate the powerful emotions they may feel when challenging their habits or exposing themselves to upsetting situations.

"Relationship mindfulness" involves developing awareness of oneself (especially emotions and desires) and awareness of one's partner, child, or other family member. Special attention is given to letting go of judgments and getting underneath anger to the sadness and disappointment below. Families are encouraged to practice focusing attention on everyday activities with loved ones—learning to be together when they are together.

Interpersonal response patterns taught in DBT skills training are similar to those taught in assertiveness and interpersonal problem-solving classes. They include strategies for asking for what one needs, saying no, and coping with interpersonal conflict (Linehan, 1997). Consistent with the psychoeducational nature of this approach, family members are encouraged to maintain nonjudgmental attention and active listening, understand and reflect back the other person's feelings, and try to be tolerant of problem behavior (Fruzzetti, 2006).

DBT parenting skills include: (1) attending to child safety, (2) education about healthy child development, (3) relationship mindfulness, (4) reducing negative reactivity, (5) validation skills, (6) synthesizing parenting polarities, (7) building positive parent–child relationship, (8) setting effective limits, (9) transforming conflict into understanding and validation, and (10) facilitating child competencies (Hoffman & Fruzzetti, 2005). These skills are often taught in multifamily groups with six to eight families. Sessions may be conducted weekly and extend from between twelve weeks to six months (Linehan, 1993).

◆ Other Integrative Models

Although we've singled out some of the most innovative examples, there are in fact so many integrative approaches that it's impossible to list them all. While many of these are new, some of them have been around so long they don't always get the attention they deserve.

Carol Anderson and Susan Stewart wrote one of the most useful integrative guides to family therapy back in 1983. Two other integrative approaches that have been around for a while are those designed by Larry Feldman (1990) and William Nichols (1995). The tradition of offering practical advice that transcends schools of family therapy is upheld in a splendid book by Robert Taibbi (2007) called *Doing Family Therapy*. Others have attempted to integrate structural and strategic therapies (Liddle, 1984; Stanton, 1981), strategic and behavioral (Alexander & Parsons, 1982), psychodynamic and systems theory (Kirschner & Kirschner, 1986; Nichols, 1987; Sander, 1979; Scharff, 1989; Slipp, 1988), and experiential and systems theory (Duhl & Duhl, 1981; Greenberg & Johnson, 1988).

Other integrative approaches haven't received as much attention in mainstream family therapy as they have by federal funding agencies. These include Scott Henggeler's *multisystemic model* (Henggeler & Borduin, 1990) and Howard Liddle's *multidimensional family therapy* (Liddle, Dakoff, & Diamond, 1991). These approaches evolved out of research projects with difficult adolescents, a population that challenges theorists to expand their views beyond the limits of one school of therapy or one level of system.

Liddle developed his integrative approach while working with drug-abusing, inner-city adolescents. His multidimensional family therapy brings together the risk factor models of drug and problem behavior, developmental psychopathology, family systems theory, social support theory, peer cluster theory, and social learning theory. In practice, the model applies a combination of structural family therapy, parent training, skills training for adolescents, and cognitive-behavioral techniques.

One of the most useful aspects of Liddle's approach is the way he integrates individual and systems interventions. While he makes liberal use of the structural technique of enactment, he frequently meets with individual family members to coach them to participate more effectively in these family dialogues. Liddle also uses these individual sessions to focus on teenagers' experiences outside the home. Here, sensitive subjects like drug use and sexual behavior can be explored more safely in private. The need to meet with teenagers to focus on their lives outside the family reflects a growing recognition of the limited influence families have in comparison to peers and culture.

Scott Henggeler of the University of South Carolina and a number of research-oriented colleagues who work with difficult-to-treat children tried to improve on their systems-oriented family therapy by: (1) more actively considering and intervening into the extrafamilial systems in which families are embedded, in particular their school and peer contexts; (2) including individual developmental issues in assessments; and (3) incorporating cognitive-behavioral interventions (Henggeler & Borduin, 1990). This multisystemic model has shown promising results in several well-designed outcome studies of juvenile offenders and families referred for abuse or neglect. For that reason, it is highly regarded among governmental funding agencies, and Henggeler has received a number of large grants.

◆ Community Family Therapy

Many therapists start out working in agencies with poor families, but as they realize how powerless therapy is to deal with many of the problems impoverished families face, they get discouraged and opt for private practice with middle-class clients. Recognizing therapy's limits had the opposite effect on Ramon Rojano.

According to Rojano, the greatest obstacle poor people face is a sense of powerlessness that comes with being controlled by dehumanizing bureaucracies. Rojano uses his personal connections in the helping system to make clients feel reconnected to their communities and empowered to advocate for what they need. Not only does he help families find the resources to survive—child care, jobs, food stamps, housing—which is the essence of traditional casework, but he also begins encouraging aspirations beyond mere survival.

Laura Markowitz (1997) describes Rojano's work this way.

Ramon Rojano is a professional nudge. Let's say you're a single mother on welfare who goes to him because your teenage son is skipping school and on the verge of being expelled. Leaning forward in his chair, the stocky, energetic Rojano will start prodding and poking with his questions in his Spanish accent, zeroing in on your son like he's herding a stray lamb back into the fold. After some minutes of this interrogation, you actually hear your boy admit what's going on with him and promise in a small, sincere voice you haven't heard come out of him in a long time, that he will go to school regularly if he can graduate. As your mouth opens in surprise, Rojano won't even pause. Now he'll urge the fifteen-year-old boy to apply for an after-school job he just heard about from someone who runs a program. . . . Rojano will write the phone number down and put it directly into the boy's hand, look him in the eye and use his name a few times to make sure he knows Rojano actually cares whether or not this kid ends up on the streets or in a gang. . . . You think the session is over, right? Not quite. He has plans for you too. Be prepared—he might ask you something outrageous, like whether you've thought about owning your own house. You may be a single mother barely getting by, but as he leans toward you it's like the force of his confidence in you pulls you in, and now he's pressing a piece of paper into your hand with the number of a woman he knows who runs a program that helps people with no money buy a home of their own. (pp. 25–26)

Rojano asks clients about things that they, in their state of hopelessness and disconnection, never considered—running for the school board, going to college, or starting a business—in such a way that these things seem possible. This is partly because Rojano can see strengths that disheartened clients have forgotten and partly because he has the connections to get the ball rolling.

Rojano also recognizes that community empowerment isn't enough. Without ongoing family therapy, it wouldn't be long before the single parent in the previous scenario might start being late for work because of renewed conflicts with her son, and that dream of a house would evaporate.

Once again we see that integration requires a new way of thinking. Rojano had to step out of the mind-set that said therapy takes place in an office, even though clients are often constrained by forces untouched in the office. Why not take it to the street so the whole system is addressed? It seems like an obvious question—but maybe not so obvious when you're trapped in your circumstances.

Summary

In the founding decades of family therapy, a number of distinct models were developed, and most therapists became disciples of one of these approaches. Each of the major schools focused on a particular aspect of family life. Experientialists opened people up to feeling, behaviorists helped them reinforce more functional behavior, and Bowenians taught them to think for themselves. By focusing their attention this way, practitioners of the classic models concentrated their power for change. If in the process they got a little parochial and competitive, what was the harm?

The harm was that by ignoring the insights of other approaches, disciples of the various schools limited their impact and applicability. Maybe this parochialism should be understood from a developmental perspective—as a necessary stage in the consolidation of the insights of the founding models. Perhaps it was useful for the schools to pursue the truth as they saw it in order to mine the full potential of their ideas. If so, that time has passed.

A successful synthesis must strike a balance between breadth and focus. Breadth may be particularly important when it comes to conceptualization. Contemporary family therapists are wisely adopting a broad, biopsychosocial perspective in which biological, psychological, relational, community, and even societal processes are seen as relevant to understanding people's problems. When it comes to interventions, on the other hand, the most effective approaches don't overload therapists with too many techniques.

Finally, an effective integration must have clear direction. The trouble with being too flexible is that families have a way of inducting therapists into their habits of avoidance. Good family therapy creates an environment where conversations that should happen at home, but don't, can take place. These dialogues won't happen, however, if therapists abruptly shift from one type of intervention to another in the face of resistance.

Click here to apply your knowledge of chapter concepts.

Click here to test your application and analysis of the content found within this chapter.

CHAPTER 14

RESEARCH ON FAMILY INTERVENTION

The Science of Clinical Practice

Florencia Lebensohn-Chialvo
University of Arizona

As family therapy has matured, so too have attempts to study its effectiveness. There is now a substantial body of research demonstrating family therapy's effectiveness in treating a wide variety of clinical problems. Unfortunately, this research has had little impact on the practice of family therapy. In this chapter, we will examine the vast gulf between research and practice in family therapy, discuss research methodology, review family therapy outcome and process studies, and suggest strategies for bridging the gap between science and practice.

Research and Practice: Worlds Apart

Proponents of family therapy made early attempts to provide empirical support for their various models (e.g., Minuchin, Montalvo, Guerney, Rosman, & Schumer, 1967). While the methodologies they used weren't very sophisticated, these studies were influential enough to stimulate interest from the academic community.

One distinct advantage to the field of family therapy continues to be the richness of its theory-based practice. Most of the classic models of family therapy have well-developed and testable theories about (1) how families interact to maintain problems, and probably more importantly, (2) what family therapists can do to help families alleviate their problems. However, the flourishing of theoretical writings and development of therapeutic techniques hasn't been sufficiently coupled with rigorous empirical investigation of these proposed mechanisms of change, as was the case with other up-and-coming therapy models (e.g., cognitive-behavioral therapy [CBT] for anxiety and depression). While family therapy continued to gain ground among mental health practitioners concerned with family functioning, researchers and graduate training instructors gravitated to CBT and other empirically supported treatments. Thus, while enormously popular among clinicians, family therapy lost a certain amount of traction in academic circles.

LEARNING OUTCOMES

♦ Describe reasons for the research/ practice divide in family therapy.

♦ Describe methodological issues in studying family therapy.

♦ Describe the effectiveness of family therapy for treating various common presenting problems.

♦ Describe the purpose of process research and key process research findings.

♦ Describe some of the future directions recommended to reduce the research/ practice divide in family therapy.

Clearly, the field of family therapy (like much of mental health) remains divided. There is a strong base of clinical practitioners who have been trained in various models of family therapy, and gained expertise through experience. These practitioners, working alone or in collegial groups—sometimes across continents—have accumulated practice-based support for many of their clinical approaches. There are also researchers who have dedicated themselves to the empirical investigation of not only how families work but also how to best help them by testing the effectiveness of various therapeutic interventions. Unfortunately, considering the well-documented allegiance of therapy researchers to their own models, some question the objectivity of this research.

A number of researchers have conducted qualitative studies to explore the reasons for the lack of influence of research on clinical practice—not only why practitioners tend to ignore research findings but also why they have reservations about participating in studies and collaborating with researchers.

It's not surprising that some clinicians believe that clinical research isn't relevant to their own clinical practice (Lebow, 1988; Robinson, 1994). This may be especially true of clinicians who have been practicing for many years and find that what they do works well for their clients. Others consider clinical research inaccessible or incomprehensible (Beutler, Williams, & Wakefield, 1993; Sprenkle, 2003).

Some clinicians don't have the background in research design to be able to adequately interpret empirical articles (Sandberg, Johnson, Robila, & Miller, 2002). Regardless of the reasons for the research–practice divide, many people have pointed out that its existence handicaps both family researchers and family therapists (e.g., Sprenkle, 2003).

In order to tackle the problems that result from the gap between clinical practice and scientific research, it's important to have a basic understanding of the methods family researchers use to empirically test their ideas.

Watch this video of Dr. Jonathan Sandberg discuss how research informs his clinical work as an emotionally focused therapist and vice-versa. What are ways to incorporate research into your clinical practice?

www.youtube.com/watch?v=r5g6-NVADzQ&list=UUM9 AhFoYkgeO4ZRmJFwx1eA&index=39

Methodological Issues in Studying the Effectiveness of Family Therapy

The scientific study of therapeutic effectiveness has evolved over the past few decades, driven by several factors. Clinical medicine was the first discipline to develop the *randomized clinical trial* as a way to test the effectiveness of medical treatments. The utility of these methods eventually spread to psychiatrists' examination of drug therapies for emotional and behavioral disorders. Around the same time, clinical psychologists began to apply experimental psychology methods to evaluate the effectiveness of behavioral treatments. This period also saw the development of *program evaluation research* to evaluate the effectiveness of treatment and prevention programs like those implemented in larger social institutions such as schools, clinics, and community agencies. Finally, with the growth of managed care for the treatment of psychiatric disorders, insurers began to look for ways to contain costs by identifying the most effective and efficient practices. This stimulated interest in developing scientific evidence to support the use of specific treatment methods. *Evidence-based practice* and *empirically supported therapy* are terms that reflect the growing emphasis on the use of scientific methods to test intervention effectiveness. More recently, researchers have focused on investigating treatment fidelity to evaluate therapists' adherence to their treatment models and the most effective ingredients in those models (Perepletchikova et al., 2007).

While anyone conducting empirical research must control a number of variables in order to isolate the effects of interest, family therapy researchers are faced with a unique set of challenges due to the complexity of family interactions and the treatments designed to influence them.

In order to study any particular family intervention, it's important to ensure that the intervention is being faithfully applied. For example, it would be difficult to evaluate the effects of structural family therapy if some of the therapists in the study did not address structural problems or use enactments. Calling something "structural family therapy" or "strategic therapy" doesn't mean that what's being studied actually represents how these therapies are practiced in clinical settings. To ensure that interventions are faithful to the treatment models under investigation, researchers have developed *program manuals* to provide guidelines for how the interventions should be applied, and they use *fidelity checks* to evaluate whether therapists are following these guidelines.

When randomized clinical trials are conducted to test the effects of a new medical treatment on a specific condition, researchers usually try to screen out patients with medical problems other than the one they wish to study. For example, if investigators were studying the effectiveness of a new hypertension medication, they would screen out participants with co-occurring medical conditions, such as obesity, that might skew the findings. While some family therapy researchers have selected participants based on the presence of a condition diagnosed in only one family member, this approach can be overly restrictive because many conditions, such as depression, are often comorbid with other disorders and may cluster in families. Therefore, family researchers may use the presence of a single disorder as the criterion for including families but not eliminate families based on the presence of other disorders in the identified patient or other family members.

Some of the early attempts to demonstrate the effectiveness of various models of family therapy involved a series of *case studies*, in which a number of families were followed to see whether changes occurred following treatment. However, as Campbell and Stanley (1963) pointed out, case studies can't rule out that improvements might have occurred even if the family hadn't participated in treatment. For example, a recent study demonstrated that nearly two-thirds of unhappily married couples who were contacted again five years later reported being happy with their marriages (Waite & Luo, 2002). Maybe happy marriages aren't made in heaven; maybe they take a little work—but not necessarily in a therapist's office.

To control for the possibility of such changes over time, family researchers use *comparison groups*, who don't participate in the program being tested. If families in the test condition do better than the comparison group, these differences are not likely due to spontaneous resolution. When other forms of treatment have

already been found to be effective, it's not ethical to have no treatment for the comparison group. In such cases, the comparison group can be a *treatment-as-usual* condition, and the new program compared to the usual types of interventions that families are likely to receive.

In evaluating the outcome of family therapy interventions, researchers distinguish between *efficacy* studies—whether the treatment works under carefully controlled conditions—and *effectiveness* studies—whether the treatment works in actual clinical settings. Outcome measures usually include aspects of individual functioning, such as psychiatric symptoms or problem behavior, as well as features of family functioning, such as marital conflict or parental communication with children. While family interventions can be very brief, lasting only a few weeks, *long-term follow-ups* are needed to study whether treatment effects last over time. Such studies have highlighted that interventions can have *sleeper effects* that emerge months or years later, even when initial improvement was marginal. Finally, as government agencies and insurance companies have become increasingly concerned with health-care costs, researchers have begun to conduct *cost–benefit analyses*, which compare the financial cost of treatment to the benefits to families and the community.

Along with more traditional outcome studies, researchers have also begun to investigate the specific mechanisms responsible for therapeutic effects by developing special techniques for studying the process of family intervention. This allows for more understanding about the particular intervention activities, styles, and procedures that are the most effective in creating positive change.

Studies may also include measures of factors not considered primary outcomes, because these factors may be in areas of family functioning that will be changed by the intervention and will, in turn, lead to changes in the primary outcomes. Such factors are called *mediating variables*. Some early studies of family therapy only assessed individual outcomes such as substance abuse, even though the proposed mechanism for reducing substance abuse involved changes in family interaction. By including measures of both, investigators can test whether the program brought about change in the primary outcome through changing other important targets using *mediation analysis*.

Some studies attempt to determine for whom a particular intervention works best. These studies include measurement of potential *moderator variables*: variables that influence the relationship between assignment to an intervention and outcome at the end of treatment. Moderators can be any characteristic of the participants, such as age, gender, family composition, or ethnicity. For example, a particular treatment may work well for families with young adolescents but not so well for families of older adolescents. In this case, age would be considered a moderating variable. Identification of such variables can help clinicians better understand what type of intervention would work best for a particular family, allowing them modify their treatment plans to maximize positive outcomes and avoid dropout.

It's important to keep in mind that findings from one study are not enough to make conclusive statements about whether an intervention works or not. That's why researchers need to replicate their results and even wait for other independent researchers to do the same before the scientific community will accept their findings as convincing. Researchers accumulate findings from multiple studies in the form of *box score reviews*, based on a simple count of how many studies report significant effects; *narrative reviews*, which discuss the results from a set of studies; and *meta-analyses*, the gold standard which use sophisticated statistical methods to combine results across studies to reach conclusions about intervention effects. Meta-analyses create a common metric for determining the size of the effect attributable to treatment and use statistical methods to combine treatment effects from all studies to form an overall estimate of *treatment effect size*.

Research Findings on the Effectiveness of Family-Focused Interventions

There is now extensive evidence of the effectiveness of family-focused interventions for a host of individual, couple, and family problems. Here is a brief overview of the most pertinent research on interventions for (1) childhood disorders, (2) adult disorders, and (3) relationship problems.

Family Interventions for Childhood Problems

Externalizing Disorders

Family therapy has been shown to be effective in the treatment of a number of externalizing disorders, ranging from conduct disorder to attention deficit/hyperactivity disorder (ADHD). In a number of meta-analyses, family interventions outperformed comparison treatments in treating a host of externalizing problems (e.g., aggression, delinquency) (Chamberlain & Rosicky, 1995; Kazdin & Weisz, 1998). More specifically, McCart and colleagues recently conducted a meta-analysis and found that behavioral parenting training (see Chapter 9) was significantly more effective than individual therapy in reducing childhood problem behaviors (McCart, Priester, Davies, & Azen, 2006).

Conduct Disorder

A number of meta-analyses (e.g., Baldwin, Christian, Berkeljon, Shadish, & Bean, 2012; Woolfenden, Williams, & Peat, 2002; Curtis, Ronan, & Borduin, 2004) have found that functional family therapy (FFT), multisystemic therapy (MST), and multidimensional family therapy (MDFT) were more effective than treatment as usual in reducing behaviors associated with conduct disorder (e.g., jail time, risk of re-arrest). While the majority of the empirical studies of FFT have addressed adolescents with substance abuse problems, some studies have focused on adolescents with behavioral and conduct-related problems. For example, FFT has been shown to be more effective than comparison treatments at reducing recidivism rates (Gordon, Arbuthnot, Gustafson, & McGreen, 1988; Sexton & Turner, 2010). Additionally, MST has been shown to improve family relations (Henggeler et al., 1986; Henggeler, Melton, & Smith, 1992; Borduin et al., 1995; Timmons-Mitchell et al., 2006); decrease behavior problems and psychiatric symptomatology (Henggeler et al., 1986; Borduin et al., 1995; Henggeler et al., 1997); improve pro-social peer relations (Henggeler et al.,

1986; Henggeler, Melton, & Smith, 1992); and lower rates of recidivism (Henggeler et al., 1991; Borduin et al., 1995; Henggeler et al., 1997; Timmons-Mitchell et al., 2006). A number of international dissemination studies of MST for conduct-related behaviors have also shown promise (e.g., Ogden & Halliday-Boykins, 2004; Ogden & Hagen, 2006).

Substance Abuse

Several family therapy approaches have been found effective in the treatment of adolescent substance abuse. Studies have demonstrated that not only does the family system play an important role in the development and maintenance of adolescent substance abuse (e.g., Muck et al., 2001), but that family therapy is more effective than individual therapy, therapeutic communities, outward bound programs, and twelve-step programs (Williams & Chang, 2000). More specifically, a number of recent meta-analyses concluded that family-based interventions—specifically FFT, BSFT, and MDFT—not only help address often related conduct problems but are also more effective than individual or group treatment modalities for the treatment of adolescent substance abuse (Baldwin et al., 2010; Becker & Curry, 2008; Tanner-Smith, Jo Wilson, & Lipsey, 2013; Waldron & Turner, 2008). Now that these treatments are well-established, researchers have turned their attention to identifying for whom these treatments work best. In a recent study of MDFT, results showed that younger adolescents (thirteen to sixteen years) and those with comorbid disorders fared better in MDFT, as compared with CBT (Hendriks, van der Schee, & Blanken, 2012).

Attention Deficit/Hyperactivity Disorder

While pharmacotherapy remains the most frequently used treatment for ADHD, family therapy has been seen as a promising complementary intervention that can address problem-maintaining relationship patterns. Two recent meta-analyses suggest that behavioral parent training is a viable treatment option, particularly with preschool children (Lee, Niew, Yang, Chen, & Lin, 2012; Rajwan, Chacko, & Moeller, 2012). Additional systematic reviews of the literature have concluded that treatments that involve both medication management and family-based behavioral interventions also yield better outcomes (e.g.,

Anastopoulos, Shelton & Barkley, 2005; DuPaul, Eckert, & Vilardo, 2012). Interestingly, family-based approaches have also been proposed for comorbid anxiety and ADHD. In a recent study, families who participated in combined parent management training and family-based cognitive-behavioral treatment showed alleviation of the child's ADHD and anxiety symptoms post-treatment and at the six-month follow-up (Jarrett & Ollendick, 2012). Considering the high comorbidity of ADHD with other externalizing and internalizing behaviors, these findings highlight the possible utility of family-based interventions that simultaneously address a variety of problem-maintaining familial processes.

Internalizing Disorders

Compared to the research on externalizing disorders, empirical support for family-focused interventions in the treatment of internalizing disorders is mixed. There appears to be more support for family therapy in the treatment of childhood depression and anorexia nervosa, while more work is needed to determine its effectiveness in the treatment of childhood anxiety disorders.

Childhood Depression

A recent review suggests that a number of treatments with varying levels of parental involvement are as effective as individual cognitive-behavioral interventions of childhood depression (Stark, Banneyer, Wang, & Arora, 2012). For example, attachment-based family therapy approaches seem to be effective in reducing depressive symptoms, including suicidal ideation (Diamond et al., 2002; Diamond et al., 2010). Other investigators have shown promising results with family group cognitive-behavioral therapy for the prevention of adolescent depression when the parental figures have a history of mood disturbances (e.g., Compas et al., 2011). Although these study findings are encouraging, more research is needed to determine whether treatments that involve parental figures actually result in improvement above and beyond that achieved through individual CBT.

Childhood Anxiety

Family interventions for anxiety disorders have generated mixed findings. A recent study attempted to integrate individual cognitive-behavioral therapy with family therapy and aimed to restructure parent–child interactions, targeting excessive parental control, conflict, and overprotection (Siqueland, Rynn, & Diamond, 2005). Unfortunately, these researchers found no difference between families who were assigned to the combined condition versus the CBT-only condition in reducing adolescent anxiety. Other studies seem to suggest that while family interventions may not outperform CBT in reducing anxiety symptoms, they may be more effective in those cases where a child's parental figures also struggle with anxiety symptoms and may produce more improvements in family functioning (Barmish & Kendall, 2005; Barrett & Shortt, 2003; Diamond & Josephson, 2005; Kaslow, Broth, Smith, & Collins, 2012; Reynolds, Wilson, Austin, & Hooper, 2012). There is also growing empirical support for the benefit of parental involvement in the treatment of separation anxiety (e.g., Pina, Zerr, Gonzales, & Ortiz, 2009) and childhood obsessive–compulsive disorder (e.g., Watson & Rees, 2008). However, more study is needed to conclusively demonstrate that such interventions increase effectiveness over that already achieved by individual psychotherapy or medication management.

Eating Disorders

Family-based approaches in the treatment of anorexia nervosa began with the work of Salvador Minuchin and his colleagues (Minuchin, Rosman, & Baker, 1978). Since then a number of researchers have also developed family-focused interventions, most notably family-based treatment (FBT), also known as the Maudsley method. While this treatment approach does not have a strong theoretical basis, it currently has the strongest empirical support.

A number of studies have demonstrated the effectiveness of FBT. A recent study compared FBT to an adolescent-focused treatment (AFT) and found that adolescents in the FBT intervention showed greater improvements in mean percentile body mass index (BMI) scores and greater changes in eating-related psychopathology; however, these differences were not significant at one-year follow-up. Additionally, FBT showed lower rates of remission and hospitalization than AFT at one-year follow-up (Lock, Le Grange, Agras, Moye, Bryson, & Jo, 2010). Two

long-term studies demonstrated that adolescents who were successfully treated with FBT continued to show improvements four or five years later (Couturier & Lock, 2006; Eisler, Dare, Russell, Szmukler, le Grange, & Dodge, 1997). Additional dissemination studies appear to suggest that FBT can be successfully implemented in diverse environments, both domestically and internationally (Couturier, Isserlan, & Lock, 2006; Loeb, Walsh, Lock, le Grange, Marcus, Weaver, & Dobrow, 2007). Proponents of FBT have also started to examine this model's effectiveness in the treatment of bulimia nervosa (le Grange, Crosby, Rathouz, & Leventhal, 2007); however, further research is needed.

Summary

There is substantial empirical support for the use of family therapy in the treatment of various child externalizing disorders. In the case of adolescent substance abuse and conduct disorder, family-based interventions outperform other approaches and are quickly becoming the standard of care for these conditions. For other problems, including ADHD, more research is needed to determine how family characteristics influence the effectiveness of family treatments in order to identify the subset of children who would most benefit from these types of programs.

Research findings on the effectiveness of family-based interventions for internalizing disorders are less robust. There is only moderate evidence that family-focused depression and anxiety interventions add to the effectiveness of individual cognitive-behavioral forms of intervention. There is, however, growing support for the value of family therapy in the treatment of eating-related disorders.

◆ Family Interventions for Adult Disorders

Researchers have examined the effectiveness of family interventions in the treatment of the following disorders in adulthood: depression, substance abuse, schizophrenia, and bipolar disorder. In all four cases, substantial research has demonstrated associations between family or marital conflict and increased expression of individual distress. Family-focused interventions for these types of presenting complaints appear to be most useful when they target specific aspects of family functioning associated with onset or maintenance of the disorder, or when they help family members support independent functioning of the person experiencing the disorder.

Depression

A number of studies have demonstrated a reciprocal relationship between depressive symptoms and marital discord (Beach, Katz, Kim, & Brody, 2003; O'Leary, Christian, & Mendell, 1994; Whisman, Uebelacker, & Weinstock, 2004), so it's not surprising that researchers have focused on couples therapy as an alternative to individual therapy for adult depression. Recent reviews and meta-analyses have concluded that couple therapies (ranging from systemic to cognitive-behaviorally oriented therapies) are as successful as individual therapies in reducing depressive symptoms (Barbato & D'Avanzo, 2008; Whisman, Johnson, Be, & Li, 2012). Not surprisingly, these therapies are also more effective than individual therapies in reducing marital distress, which is both a risk factor for the initial onset of depressive symptoms and for relapse or worsening of symptoms at the end of treatment (Gilliam & Cottone, 2005; Whisman, 2001). Despite the amount of research in this area, there are no current studies that have directly compared couples treatment to individual treatment to determine which is more effective in alleviating depressive symptoms.

Substance Abuse

Different modalities of couples therapy have also been used in the treatment of substance abuse (see Chapter 10). In summary of the empirical literature in this area, spouse involvement in the treatment of substance abuse is integral to both treatment engagement and short-term abstinence (Fals-Stewart, Birchler, & Kelley, 2006; Fals-Stewart, Klosterman, Yates, O'Farrell, & Birchler, 2005); however, the findings are less clear about how these treatments fare in the long term. More recently, there has been growing interest in developing couples-based treatments for post-traumatic stress disorder (PTSD) based in part on the research on couples therapy for substance abuse. This is especially salient considering the high rates of comorbidity between PTSD and substance abuse. To date, a

handful of studies have shown promising results with both couples cognitive-behavioral therapy (Monson et al., 2012; Rotunda, O'Farrell, Murphy, & Babey, 2008) and emotionally focused therapy for couples alleviation of trauma symptoms and reduction of marital distress (Dalton, Greenman, Classen, & Johnson, 2013). The research that has been done is promising, but not yet well developed (Rotunda, Oesarrell, Murphy, & Babey, 2008; Sautter, Glynn, Thompson, Franklin, & Han, 2009).

Serious Mental Illness

Some of the earliest applications of family therapy were designed for the treatment of Schizophrenia (see Chapter 1). In the years since those early days of family therapy, a substantial body of research has established the genetic and neurobiological vulnerabilities associated with schizophrenia and bipolar disorder, and the primary mode of treatment has subsequently been pharmacological. Although no one can deny the general effectiveness of drug therapies for such disorders, they have been shown to have less of an impact on the negative symptoms of schizophrenia. Researchers have identified the emotional climate of families with schizophrenic members as an important factor in relapse. High levels of *expressed emotion*—critical, hostile, and overinvolved—have been shown to increase the probability of relapse and have a negative impact on the general functioning of the family member with schizophrenia (Miklowitz, 2004). With these findings in mind, researchers have developed *psychoeducational* family programs that can be administered in conjunction with drug treatments for patients with schizophrenia and their families. Similar programs have also been adapted for the treatment of bipolar disorder.

These programs are designed to facilitate the recovery of individuals with mental illness, while simultaneously supporting family members in their attempts to help their loved ones. The educational component of these programs includes a description of what expressed emotion is, how it can trigger symptoms, and what family members can do to reduce the likelihood of relapse. These programs also include techniques borrowed from cognitive-behavioral and supportive therapy models.

A recent series of meta-analyses have demonstrated that psychoeducational family therapy is a highly effective treatment supplement for schizophrenia and bipolar disorder (Loabban et al., 2013; Pfammatter, Junghan, & Brenner, 2006; Pharoah, Mari, Rashbone, & Wong, 2006; Pilling et al., 2002; Pitschel-Walz, Leucht, Bauml, Kissling, & Engel, 2001). The findings suggest that family psychoeducation in combination with antipsychotic medication is associated with fewer relapses and hospitalizations, as compared to medication alone. These programs appear to have the added benefit of increasing adherence to medication regimens, which can often be a struggle. Additionally, family psychoeducation interventions also increase family members' understanding of the disorder, reduce expressed emotion, and improve social adjustment (Pfammatter et al., 2006).

Family Interventions for Relationship Difficulties

Disorders of Attachment

A number of programs have been developed to treat children with insecure attachment by directly involving parents and caregivers. Some controversial attachment therapies have been proposed that use coercive strategies, such as holding and rebirthing, and a number of professional organizations have warned against using them (AACAP, 2005; Chaffin et al., 2006).

However, there is a substantial body of empirically sound studies on child attachment and a number of recent meta-analyses that have examined the effectiveness of various interventions. Bakermans-Kranenburg, van Ijzendoorn, and Juffer (2003) reviewed studies that explored the impact of early preventive interventions targeting maternal sensitivity toward their children in hopes of improving the children's attachment security. They concluded that interventions that educated mothers on how to hold their infants and how to respond to infant signals to minimize distress were effective in improving both parental sensitivity and child attachment. The most efficacious interventions used sixteen or fewer sessions and had a behavioral focus. In another recent meta-analysis, the same researchers demonstrated that the most effective interventions for children with disorganized attachment began after they were more than six months old, focused on parental sensitivity rather than on support or parents' mental representations of their children,

and targeted at-risk children rather than at-risk parents (Bakermans-Kranenburg, van Ijzendoorn, & Juffer, 2005). The most recent meta-analysis from this group of investigators concluded that interventions are particularly effective for families in which both the mother and child initially exhibit more highly reactive and insecure attachment (Klein Velderman, Bakermans-Kranenburg, Juffer, & van Ijzendoorn, 2006). While there is a growing literature on interventions for childhood attachment, more studies are needed to identify the most beneficial types of programs for children with disorganized attachment.

Child Maltreatment

Child maltreatment presents a number of challenges when attempting to design and provide effective interventions (Cicchetti & Toth, 2005). Most definitions of child maltreatment represent legal criteria and there are no clear standards of acceptable discipline and parenting. Even more difficult to navigate in a multicultural society are varying social conventions about childrearing and what is considered appropriate.

Nevertheless, researchers have conducted many studies examining a variety of programs used to treat victims of child maltreatment. These family-based programs often include dyadic therapy with parents and children, home visitation, school-based programs, and parent education. The best programs involve the family, are structured, and last at least six months. They touch on parenting skills, family support, and the child's post-traumatic adjustment (Lundahl, Nimer, & Parsons, 2006; MacLeod & Nelson, 2000; Skowron & Reinemann, 2005).

There is growing empirical support for a handful of family-based treatments; namely, Parent–Child Interaction Therapy (PCIT) (Chaffin et al., 2004; Timmer, Urquiza, Zebell, & McGarth, 2005), MST (Schaeffer, Swenson, Tuerk, & Henggeler, 2013; Swenson, Schaeffer, Henggeler, Faldowski, & Mayhew, 2010), and Cognitive Behavioral Family Therapy (Kolko & Swenson, 2002; Rynyon & Deblinger, 2013). For instance, in a randomized controlled trial mothers with a history or at high risk of maltreating their children who were assigned to PCIT showed a reduction in the number of child welfare notifications, child abuse potential, and increased observed sensitivity (Thomas & Zimmer-Gembeck, 2011). An MST adaptation targeting co-occurring parental substance abuse and child maltreatment also yielded favorable results with participating families when compared to community treatments. Families in the MST condition showed reductions in parental alcohol and drug use, substantiated incidents of maltreatment, and fewer days in out-of-home placements for children (Schaeffer et al., 2013).

Not surprisingly, researchers have given increased urgency to developing and testing interventions for sexual abuse. Corcoran and Pillai, in their recent meta-analysis found that treatments which involve the nonoffending parent were more effective than child-only treatments in reducing internalizing and externalizing behaviors, and more specifically, sexualized behaviors and post-traumatic stress symptoms in children (Corcoran & Pillai, 2008).

Family Therapy Process Research

Outcome studies are designed to find out whether treatment approaches are effective. Such studies evaluate the extent to which families change as a result of therapy. But outcome studies offer limited information about how therapy works. Questions about *why* certain therapies are effective, *how* families change, *what* specific interventions are most productive, and *which* combinations of therapist and client variables are most productive cannot be addressed in outcomes studies. These questions can only be answered by looking inside therapy sessions to discover which therapeutic factors lead to desired effects.

Process research has the potential to improve how therapy is practiced and to help bridge the gap between science and practice by increasing the relevance of empirical findings to practitioners (Pinsof & Wynne, 2000). Practitioners aren't particularly interested in outcome studies—they're already convinced that what they do works. But they may be interested in process studies that help tease out how to make their interventions more effective. As we summarize some of the family therapy process research in the following section, consider the implications of these findings for practicing clinicians.

Researchers often rely on behavioral observation of therapy sessions to evaluate both therapist- and client-related processes. Observational rating systems have been developed to capture a variety of specific family therapy techniques, such as enactments (Allen-Eckert, Fong, Nichols, Watson, & Liddle, 2001), and general therapist styles, such as supportiveness and defensiveness (Waldron, Turner, Barton, Alexander, & Cline, 1997). Recently, researchers have begun quantifying the extent to which therapists adhere to specific *manualized therapies* for family interventions, and their effects on therapy outcomes. For example, Hogue and associates (Hogue et al., 2008) developed the Therapist Behavior Rating Scale-Competence (TBRS-C) to measure therapist adherence to evidence-based practices for adolescent substance abuse treatment. Similarly, Robbins and his colleagues (Robbins, Feaster, Horigian, Puccinelli, Henderson, & Szapocznik, 2011) examined the association between therapist adherence and treatment retention and engagement in the context of a randomized controlled trial for brief strategic family therapy for adolescent substance abuse. Findings showed that observational ratings of therapist adherence (specifically in the therapist's ability to reframe and restructure family interactions) were associated with increased adolescent engagement in treatment.

A less explored area of process research involves experimental single case studies. Traditional case studies have a long history of facilitating the development of therapy techniques, generating ideas and hypothesis that were later tested with a more systematic experimental methodology. These anecdotal case studies have their share of limitations, specifically a lack of controlled conditions and objective measures, the existence of alternative explanations, and limited generalizability to other cases (Kazdin, 2011). Experimental single case designs address these shortcomings, allowing for more systematic evaluation of behavior change in the context of a particular therapeutic intervention. The main components of these types of single case studies include assessment, an experimental design, and data evaluation. Researchers utilizing this methodology must first clearly define the target behavior the intervention is designed to change, as well as outline clearly stated goals. They must also identify measurement instruments that are sensitive enough to detect small changes in the target behavior and administer them frequently, in some cases several times a week.

While experimental case studies have not become common practice, due in part to the superiority of randomized clinical trials, they are an untapped resource when it comes to a more detailed examination of therapeutic processes. For example, a researcher or clinician might choose to conduct a single case study to identify some of the relevant processes that facilitate behavior change in a family-based intervention for adolescent substance abuse. During the course of an intake or initial therapy session, the investigator would want to establish collaborative goals with the family, and then translate those goals into concrete, measurable outcomes. The investigator would also need to employ measurement instruments sensitive enough to pick up on any subtle changes in both the adolescent's problem behavior and possibly relevant family interactions. Then, during the course of therapy, the family would complete these measures daily or weekly, and subsequent analyses could examine how the activities of therapy might covary both with the adolescent and family behavior, as well as the subsequent outcomes.

Common Factors

Process research is especially well suited for the study of *common factors* of effective family therapy. Comparative efficacy studies have consistently found that therapy is effective but that no one theoretical model is more effective than another. Since the model alone isn't the critical ingredient, what makes therapy work? What commonalities exist across models? Are there certain types of therapists who produce better results than others? If so, what makes these therapists more effective? How much of therapy is due to the client, the therapist, or the approach? Research on the common factors of effective therapy is still relatively new, but promises to be one of the most interesting new directions for family therapy research (Sprenkle, Davis, & Lebow, 2009).

Common factors research has yielded several important findings. For example, in spite of how much weight therapists—especially beginning therapists—put on themselves to ensure that therapy works, client attributes such as having an internal locus of control are likely to have as much to do with successful outcomes as anything the therapist does (Tallman & Bohart, 1999). The more resourceful the clients, the more they're likely to work hard and benefit from therapy. On the therapist's side, whether a therapist believes in his or her approach enough to have confidence in success seems to be more important than the approach itself (Blow, Sprenkle, & Davis, 2007). Whether a therapist is warm, caring, an empathic listener, and so forth is likely more important than how well he or she mastered a certain approach.

Watch this video of Dr. Sean Davis discuss common factors in marriage and family therapy. What do you think of the common factors paradigm?

www.youtube.com/watch?v=YSS_1oWFXiA

The Therapeutic Alliance

The quality of the therapeutic relationship may be the single most important contributor to successful outcomes in individual psychotherapy (Orlinsky & Howard, 1986). While a host of studies of individual therapy have explored therapists' empathy and clients' perceptions of a collaborative relationship, there are few comparable studies of family therapy. One reason for this is that family therapists have usually emphasized their techniques more than the quality of the therapeutic relationship. Another reason is that the process of alliance building is more complex in family therapy: Not only are there more people involved, but empathizing with one family member may make it harder to form alliances with other family members.

In a review of the past forty years of family research, Friedlander, Escudero, and Heatherington (2006) concluded that a substantial body of both large-sample quantitative studies and intensive qualitative studies support the importance of therapeutic alliance in leading to both therapy continuation and positive outcomes. A number of self-report and behavioral observation measures have been designed specifically for assessing therapeutic alliance in the context of couple and family interventions. The most widely used are the Couple Therapy Alliance Scale

(CTAS; Pinsof & Catherall, 1986) and the Family Therapy Alliance Scale (FTAS), along with their shorter versions, the CTAS-r and FTAS-r (Pinsof, Zinbarg, & Knobloch-Fedders, 2008). The Vanderbilt Therapeutic Alliance Scale (Shelef & Diamond, 2008) and the System for Observing Family Therapy Alliances (Friedlander et al., 2006; Friedlander, Escudero et al., 2006) are both observational measures that can be used to assess various alliance dimensions.

Several studies have examined the role that the therapeutic alliance plays in couple and family interventions and its association with retention of clients in treatment, as well as various measures of positive outcome. Recent meta-analysis of twenty-four couple and family therapy therapeutic alliance studies, Friedlander, Escudero, Heatherington, and Diamond (2011), found a small to medium effect for the significance of the relationship between therapeutic alliance and retention and outcome measures. The authors noted that the strength of the effect was similar to those findings with individual therapy (Horvath, Del Re, Flückiger, & Symonds, 2011). While the majority of these studies established only a correlational relationship between measures of therapeutic alliance and retention and outcome measures, a number of more recent studies have attempted to demonstrate a causal link between therapeutic alliance and treatment retention and positive therapeutic outcomes.

Couple-specific therapy studies have shown that gender moderates the association between therapeutic alliance and marital adjustment (Bourgeois, Sabourin, & Wright, 1990; Symonds & Horvath, 2004). In the case of family-specific therapy studies, some researchers have pointed out that the relationship between therapeutic alliance and treatment retention is moderated by family role. In other words, the strength of certain family member–therapist alliances and the extent to which they are unbalanced can be more predictive of retention than the overall family–therapist alliance. For instance, Shelef and Diamond (2008) found that in cases with adolescents who have externalizing problems, the parents', but not the adolescents', alliances with the therapist predicted completion. Similar patterns have been found in family-based treatments for anorexia nervosa (Pereira, Lock, & Oggins, 2006). Robbins, Turner, Alexander, and Perez (2003), in a study of functional

family therapy for adolescent substance abusers, found that dropout cases had significantly higher levels of unbalanced alliances—characterized by discrepancies between adolescent and parent alliances with the therapists—than did cases in which families completed treatment. In a similar study, Robbins and his colleagues (2006) found that families were less likely to drop out of therapy if therapists were able to establish strong alliances with both adolescents and their mothers by the second session of multidimensional family therapy. Finally, Robbins et al. (2008), in a study of brief strategic family therapy for adolescent substance abuse, demonstrated that higher levels of therapist alliance were associated with treatment completion. These findings suggest that both the strength of the individual alliance and the relative balance of alliances within the family are important predictors of treatment engagement.

Cultural and ethnic factors also affect the therapeutic alliance. For instance, Jackson-Gilfort, Liddle, Tejeda, and Dakof (2001) found that raising culturally relevant themes (e.g., anger, alienation, the meaning of manhood) in early therapy sessions was particularly important for African American youth with substance abuse problems. Discussion of these themes was associated with enhanced treatment engagement and decreased negativity from adolescents in subsequent sessions. Additionally, Flicker and colleagues (2008) found that unbalanced alliances functioned differently for Hispanic versus Anglo families and that more unbalanced alliances during the first session were associated with dropout, but only in the case of Hispanic families. The authors argue that *familialism*, or making the family a higher priority than personal self-interest, could explain the findings.

Clearly this body of empirical findings suggests the importance of the therapeutic alliance in the context of family therapy. However, more work is needed to examine the causal pathways between therapeutic alliance and outcomes.

◆ Critical Change Events in Family Therapy

Some researchers have examined the effectiveness of specific *techniques* in facilitating therapeutic change, while others have focused on *focal events* during therapy that appear to facilitate significant changes in family interaction or resolution of problems. For example, Robbins and his colleagues, using observational ratings, demonstrated that therapists' attempts at reframing (i.e., making noncritical statements that normalize adolescents' behavior) decreased the probability that adolescents would respond negatively to subsequent therapist statements (Robbins, Alexander, Newell, & Turner, 1996). Butler and his colleagues (2011) explored the role of in-session enactments and found that enactment-based couples sessions, when compared to therapist-centered couples sessions, produced the greatest improvements in attachment security between romantic partners. Similarly, Butler and Wampler (1999) studied the effects of therapist strategies described as "couples-responsible," including enactments and use of accommodation, when compared to strategies labeled "therapist-responsible," where the therapist provided direct instruction or interpretations. Couples' ratings indicated lower conflict and higher perceived responsibility when therapists used more "couple-responsible" strategies. These results suggest that enactments conducted in the context of couples therapy are more beneficial than those where the therapist is more central.

In regard to focal events, a number of more focused qualitative studies have yielded clinically relevant findings. For example, in a qualitative study of structural family therapy cases in which the family was at an impasse, Friedlander, Heatherington, Johnson, and Skowron (1994) identified that specific therapist behaviors helped families move beyond the conflict. Specifically, active solicitation by the therapist of each family member's thoughts and feelings, discussion of the benefits of reengagement, and strategies that facilitated acknowledgement of different points of view were particularly effective. Diamond and Liddle (1996, 1999) identified a number of therapist strategies that were successful in resolving family impasses involving emotional disengagement, negative exchanges, and ineffective problem solving in MDFT sessions. They found that if therapists were able to successfully address and work through negative affect through the use of reframes while facilitating communication, families were more likely to move beyond impasses.

Michael Nichols and his students have studied highly experienced family therapists (Nichols &

Fellenberg, 2000), focusing on the use of enactments. Their findings indicate that breaking through family conflict and helping families shift their relational stance is a complex process that requires active, directive facilitation by the therapist. Essential ingredients of successful enactments include preparing the family prior to the enactment, specifying the agenda and explaining the need for dialogue, giving directions about how the discussion should go, avoiding unnecessary interruptions, pushing family members to work harder during the enactment, and closing by providing clients with clear direction on how to communicate with each other.

Additional studies by this group have shown that the most effective sessions of family therapy appear to be those in which therapists establish clear and focused systemic goals (e.g., reducing enmeshment or disengagement, rather than problem solving) while intensely pushing for change to occur within sessions (Favero, 2002; Fellenberg, 2003; Miles, 2004). However, Hammond and Nichols (2008) found that an empathic therapeutic alliance was a prerequisite to making these forceful interventions effective; that is, focused and forceful intervening seems to be important in producing change in family therapy, but family members appear more willing to accept such challenges when the therapist has established an empathic bond with them.

Some of the most difficult types of studies are those that attempt to identify the mediators or mechanisms responsible for therapeutic improvement. Compas and associates (2010) conducted a randomized clinical trial of a family group cognitive-behavioral prevention program for adolescents' internalizing and externalizing symptoms. The sample consisted of families with parents who had a history of major depressive disorder. Results showed that changes in adolescents' secondary control coping and positive parenting mediated the effects of the intervention on depressive, internalizing, and externalizing symptoms. In a study of MDFT for adolescent substance abuse, Henderson and associates (2009) showed that parental monitoring mediated the relationship between treatment and outcome—suggesting that improvements in parental monitoring were responsible for adolescents abstaining from drug use at the various follow-ups. Due to the methodology used by these researchers, we can be more confident that the therapeutic component they isolated was the active ingredient of the intervention resulting in positive outcomes.

A handful of researchers have begun to conduct exploratory analyses to identify potential mediators or mechanisms of change in therapeutic outcomes that might warrant further investigation. For instance, Lock and his colleagues (2008) examined potential mediators of family-based therapy for bulimia nervosa (FBT-BN). Findings suggest that changes in cognitions associated with bulimia-related behaviors mediate outcome for adolescents assigned to FBT-BN. Finally, Shanley and Niec (2010) explored in vivo feedback in the form of parental coaching as a possible mechanism of change in behavioral parent training. In both cases, the researchers acknowledge the limitations of their current studies and the need for more systematic investigation of these proposed mechanisms of therapeutic improvement.

Future Directions

This chapter highlights some of the advances family researchers have made in developing and implementing effective family-focused intervention and prevention programs for a wide range of behavioral and emotional problems. The development of new scientific methodologies for testing treatment effects and examining therapeutic processes has facilitated the continued advancement of these interventions. However, there are several areas that still require systematic empirical investigation, including identification of the best methods for dissemination and adoption of empirically supported treatments in clinical settings. These challenges only highlight the unfortunate consequences of the continued divide between clinical science and clinical practice.

Some family researchers have offered suggestions about how to go about shrinking the gap between science and practice (e.g., Black & Lebow, 2013; Dattilio, Piercy, & Davis, 2014; Jacobs, Kissil, Scott, & Davey, 2010). Williams, Patterson, and Miller (2006) suggest that marriage and family therapists should become more effective consumers of clinical research and emphasize the importance of individual

clinicians appreciating the value of research as it applies to their own practice, in hopes that that will fuel their curiosity. Similarly, Karam and Sprenkle (2010) propose changes in the way marriage and family therapists are trained, encouraging a "research-informed" approach in place of the "scientist–practitioner" model. Although clinical practitioners may not need to know how to conduct original research, they should be informed consumers of clinical science. Some of Karam and Sprenkle's suggestions for MFT training programs are for professors to encourage students to (1) appreciate the contribution of empirical work in the development of clinical practice; (2) learn how to understand and evaluate empirical studies; (3) think critically about the debate surrounding empirically supported treatments; and (4) learn to appreciate the contributions of common factors and specific mechanisms of change in various models of intervention. Dattilio, Piercy, and Davis (2014) recommend that researchers make their findings more palatable to clinicians by doing qualitative or mixed-methods research, process research, and involving clinicians on research teams. They also recommend studying naturalistic, uncontrolled settings such as clients on a practicing therapist's caseload, and by presenting their findings using nontraditional, appealing methods such as stories or videos.

It's ironic that while family therapy has become a more collaborative enterprise, with therapists treating clients with respect for their privileged insight into their own lives, family researchers have been slow to invite practicing clinicians to advise them about their studies and clinicians have been reluctant to incorporate research findings into their practice.

Some experts have, however, encouraged exploration of ways that researchers and clinicians can work toward a more collaborative relationship, with clinicians becoming more involved in research studies (e.g., Westen, Novotny, & Thompson-Brenner, 2004). For instance, these authors have suggested clinician–researcher partnerships in the utilization of naturalistic study designs for studying real world efficacy of evidence-based practice. While these suggestions were meant for clinical science as a field, they can easily be adapted and applied to family-focused programs. Additionally, innovations in statistical analysis and methodologies for studying both outcomes and therapeutic processes lend themselves to clinician–researcher collaborations. As discussed earlier, ideographic research designs allow for more nuanced single case analyses and provide relevant information for both clinicians and researchers. For researchers, these quantitative single case analyses provide insight into mechanisms of change and findings that can be applied to future, more traditional effectiveness studies. For clinicians, these quantitative case studies provide information similar to the traditional qualitative case studies familiar to therapists, but also provide more research-informed practice.

In summary, despite all the advances in both clinical science and practice, without a significant cultural shift, these two seemingly opposing worlds will continue to resemble bickering spouses rather than a cooperative partnership.

Click here to apply your knowledge of chapter concepts.

Click here to test your application and analysis of the content found within this chapter.

APPENDIX A
Chapter-by-Chapter Recommended Readings

INTRODUCTION

Minuchin, S. 1974. *Families and Family Therapy.* Cambridge, MA: Harvard University Press.

Nichols, M. P. 1987. *The Self in the System.* New York: Brunner/Mazel.

Nichols, M. P. 2008. *Inside Family Therapy*, 2nd ed. Boston: Allyn & Bacon.

CHAPTER 1

Ackerman, N. W. 1958. *The Psychodynamics of Family Life.* New York: Basic Books.

Bell, J. E. 1961. *Family Group Therapy.* Public Health Monograph No. 64. Washington, DC: U.S. Government Printing Office.

Bowen, M. 1960. A Family Concept of Schizophrenia. In *The Etiology of Schizophrenia*, D. D. Jackson, ed. New York: Basic Books.

Greenberg, G. S. 1977. The Family Interactional Perspective: A Study and Examination of the Work of Don D. Jackson. *Family Process* 16:385–412.

Haley, J. 1963. *Strategies of Psychotherapy.* New York: Grune & Stratton.

Jackson, D. D. 1957. The Question of Family Homeostasis. *The Psychiatric Quarterly Supplement* 31:79–90.

Jackson, D. D. 1965. Family Rules: Marital Quid Pro Quo. *Archives of General Psychiatry* 12:589–94.

Lederer, W., and D. D. Jackson. 1968. *Mirages of Marriage.* New York: Norton.

Satir, V. 1964. *Conjoint Family Therapy.* Palo Alto, CA: Science and Behavior Books.

Vogel, E. F., and N. W. Bell. 1960. The Emotionally Disturbed Child as the Family Scapegoat. In *The Family*, N. W. Bell and E. F. Vogel, eds. Glencoe, IL: Free Press.

Watzlawick, P., J. H. Beavin, and D. D. Jackson. 1967. *Pragmatics of Human Communication.* New York: Norton.

Weakland, J. H. 1960. The "Double-Bind" Hypothesis of Schizophrenia and Three-Party Interaction. In *The Etiology of Schizophrenia*, D. D. Jackson, ed. New York: Basic Books.

CHAPTER 2

Anderson, C., and S. Stewart. 1983. *Mastering Resistance: A Practical Guide to Family Therapy.* New York: Guilford Press.

Madsen, W. C. 2007. *Collaborative Therapy with Multi-Stressed Families*, 2nd ed. New York: Guilford Press.

Minuchin, S., and H. C. Fishman. 1981. *Family Therapy Techniques.* Cambridge, MA: Harvard University Press.

Minuchin, S., M. P. Nichols, and W.Y. Lee. 2007. *Assessing Families and Couples: From Symptom to System.* Boston, MA: Allyn & Bacon.

Patterson, J. E., L. Williams, C. Grauf-Grounds, and L. Chamow. 1998. *Essential Skills in Family Therapy.* New York: Guilford Press.

Sheinberg, M., F. True, and P. Fraenkel. 1994. Treating the Sexually Abused Child: A Recursive, Multimodel Program. *Family Process* 33:263–76.

Taibbi, R. 1996. *Doing Family Therapy: Craft and Creativity in Clinical Practice.* New York: Guilford Press.

Trepper, T. S., and M. J. Barrett. 1989. *Systemic Treatment of Incest: A Therapeutic Handbook.* New York: Brunner/Mazel.

Walsh, F. 1998. *Strengthening Family Resilience.* New York: Guilford Press.

CHAPTER 3

Bateson, G. 1971. *Steps to an Ecology of Mind.* New York: Ballantine.

Bateson, G. 1979. *Mind and Nature.* New York: Dutton.

Bertalanffy, L. von. 1950. An Outline of General System Theory. *British Journal of the Philosophy of Science* 1:134–65.

Bertalanffy, L. von. 1967. *Robots, Men and Minds*. New York: Braziller.

Bowlby, J. 1988. *A Secure Base: Clinical Application of Attachment Theory*. London: Routledge.

Carter, E., and M. McGoldrick, eds. 1999. *The Expanded Family Life Cycle: A Framework for Family Therapy*, 3rd ed. Boston, MA: Allyn & Bacon.

Davidson, M. 1983. *Uncommon Sense: The Life and Thought of Ludwig von Bertalanffy*. Los Angeles, CA: Tarcher.

Dell, P. F. 1985. Understanding Bateson and Maturana: Toward a Biological Foundation for the Social Sciences. *Journal of Marital and Family Therapy* 11:1–20.

Haley, J. 1985. Conversations with Erickson. *Family Therapy Networker* 9 (2):30–43.

Hoffman, L. 1981. *Foundations of Family Therapy*. New York: Basic Books.

Meadows, D. H. *Thinking in Systems: A Primer*. White River Junction, VT: Chelsea Green.

Wiener, N. 1948. *Cybernetics or Control and Communication in the Animal and the Machine*. Cambridge, MA: Technology Press.

CHAPTER 4

Anonymous. 1972. Differentiation of Self in One's Family. In *Family Interaction*, J. Framo, ed. New York: Springer.

Bowen, M. 1978. *Family Therapy in Clinical Practice*. New York: Jason Aronson.

Carter, E., and M. M. Orfanidis. 1976. Family Therapy with One Person and the Family Therapist's Own Family. In *Family Therapy: Theory and Practice*, P. J. Guerin, ed. New York: Gardner Press.

Fogarty, T. F. 1976a. Systems Concepts and Dimensions of Self. In *Family Therapy: Theory and Practice*, P. J. Guerin, ed. New York: Gardner Press.

Fogarty, T. F. 1976b. Marital Crisis. In *Family Therapy: Theory and Practice*, P. J. Guerin, ed. New York: Gardner Press.

Guerin, P. J., L. Fay, S. Burden, and J. Kautto. 1987. *The Evaluation and Treatment of Marital Conflict: A Four-Stage Approach*. New York: Basic Books.

Guerin, P. J., T. F. Fogarty, L. F. Fay, and J. G. Kautto. 1996. *Working with Relationship Triangles: The One-Two-Three of Psychotherapy*. New York: Guilford Press.

Guerin, P. J., and E. G. Pendagast. 1976. Evaluation of Family System and Geogram. In *Family Therapy:*

Theory and Practice, P. J. Guerin, ed. New York: Gardner Press.

Kerr, M. E., and M. Bowen. 1988. *Family Evaluation*. New York: Norton.

CHAPTER 5

Cecchin, G. 1987. Hypothesizing, Circularity and Neutrality Revisited: An Invitation to Curiosity. *Family Process* 26:405–13.

Fisch, R., J. H. Weakland, and L. Segal. 1982. *The Tactics of Change: Doing Therapy Briefly*. San Francisco, CA: Jossey-Bass.

Haley, J. 1976. *Problem-Solving Therapy*. San Francisco, CA: Jossey-Bass.

Haley, J. 1980. *Leaving Home*. New York: McGraw-Hill.

Haley, J., and M. Richeport-Haley. 2007. *Directive Family Therapy*. New York: Haworth Press.

Jackson, D. D. 1961. Interactional Psychotherapy. In *Contemporary Psychotherapies*, M. T. Stein, ed. New York: Free Press of Glencoe.

Jackson, D. D. 1967. *Therapy, Communication and Change*. Palo Alto, CA: Science and Behavior Books.

Keim, J. 1998. Strategic Therapy. In *Case Studies in Couple and Family Therapy*, F. Dattilio, ed. New York: Guilford Press.

Lederer, W., and D. D. Jackson. 1968. *Mirages of Marriage*. New York: Norton.

Madanes, C. 1981. *Strategic Family Therapy*. San Francisco, CA: Jossey-Bass.

Madanes, C. 1984. *Behind the One-Way Mirror*. San Francisco, CA: Jossey-Bass.

Price, J. 1996. *Power and Compassion: Working with Difficult Adolescents and Abused Parents*. New York: Guilford Press.

Rabkin, R. 1972. *Strategic Psychotherapy*. New York: Basic Books.

Selvini Palazzoli, M., L. Boscolo, G. Cecchin, and G. Prata. 1978. *Paradox and Counterparadox*. New York: Jason Aronson.

Tomm, K. 1987. Interventive Interviewing: Part 1. Strategizing as a Fourth Guideline for the Therapists. *Family Process* 26:3–14.

Watzlawick, P., J. H. Beavin, and D. D. Jackson. 1967. *Pragmatics of Human Communication*. New York: Norton.

Watzlawick, P., J. Weakland, and R. Fisch. 1974. *Change: Principles of Problem Formation and Problem Resolution*. New York: Norton.

CHAPTER 6

Colapinto, J. 1991. Structural Family Therapy. In *Handbook of Family Therapy*, Vol. II, A. S. Gurman and D. P. Kniskern, eds. New York: Brunner/Mazel.

Minuchin, S. 1974. *Families and Family Therapy*. Cambridge, MA: Harvard University Press.

Minuchin, S., and H. C. Fishman. 1981. *Family Therapy Techniques*. Cambridge, MA: Harvard University Press.

Minuchin, S., and M. P. Nichols. 1993. *Family Healing: Tales of Hope and Renewal from Family Therapy*. New York: Free Press.

Minuchin, S., M. P. Nichols, and W.-Y. Lee. 2007. *Assessing Families and Couples: From Symptom to Psyche*. Boston, MA: Allyn & Bacon.

Nichols, M. P. 1999. *Inside Family Therapy*. Boston, MA: Allyn & Bacon.

Nichols, M. P., and S. Minuchin. 1999. Short-Term Structural Family Therapy with Couples. In *Short-Term Couple Therapy*, J. M. Donovad, ed. New York: Guilford Press.

CHAPTER 7

Duhl, F. J., D. Kantor, and B. S. Duhl. 1973. Learning, Space and Action in Family Therapy: A Primer of Sculpture. In *Techniques in Family Therapy*, D. A. Bloch, ed. New York: Grune & Stratton.

Gil, E. 1994. *Play in Family Therapy*. New York: Guilford Press.

Greenberg, L. S., and S. M. Johnson. 1988. *Emotionally Focused Therapy for Couples*. New York: Guilford Press.

Keith, D. V., and C. A. Whitaker. 1977. The Divorce Labyrinth. In *Family Therapy: Full-Length Case Studies*, P. Papp, ed. New York: Gardner Press.

Napier, A. Y., and C. A. Whitaker. 1978. *The Family Crucible*. New York: Harper & Row.

Neill, J. R., and D. P. Kniskern, eds. 1982. *From Psyche to System: The Evolving Therapy of Carl Whitaker*. New York: Guilford Press.

Satir, V. M., and M. Baldwin. 1984. *Satir Step by Step: A Guide to Creating Change in Families*. Palo Alto, CA: Science and Behavior Books.

Schwartz, R. C. 1995. *Internal Family Systems Therapy*. New York: Guilford Press.

Whitaker, C. A., and D. V. Keith. 1981. Symbolic-Experiential Family Therapy. In *Handbook of Family Therapy*, A. S. Gurman and D. P. Kniskern, eds. New York: Brunner/Mazel.

CHAPTER 8

Ackerman, N. W. 1966. *Treating the Troubled Family*. New York: Basic Books.

Boszormenyi-Nagy, I. 1972. Loyalty Implications of the Transference Model in Psychotherapy. *Archives of General Psychiatry* 27:374–80.

Boszormenyi-Nagy, I. 1987. *Foundations of Contextual Therapy*. New York: Brunner/Mazel.

Dicks, H. V. 1967. *Marital Tensions*. New York: Basic Books.

Meissner, W. W. 1978. The Conceptualization of Marriage and Family Dynamics from a Psychoanalytic Perspective. In *Marriage and Marital Therapy*, T. J. Paolino and B. S. McCrady, eds. New York: Brunner/Mazel.

Middleberg, C. V. 2001. Projective Identification in Common Couples Dances. *Journal of Marital and Family Therapy* 27:341–52.

Mitchell, S. A. 1988. *Relational Concepts in Psychoanalysis*. Cambridge, MA: Harvard University Press.

Nadelson, C. C. 1978. Marital Therapy from a Psychoanalytic Perspective. In *Marriage and Marital Therapy*, T. J. Paolino and B. S. McCrady, eds. New York: Brunner/Mazel.

Nichols, M. P. 1987. *The Self in the System*. New York: Brunner/Mazel.

Sander, F. M. 1989. Marital Conflict and Psychoanalytic Theory in the Middle Years. In *The Middle Years: New Psychoanalytic Perspectives*, J. Oldham and R. Liebert, eds. New Haven, CT: Yale University Press.

Scharff, D., and J. S. Scharff. 1987. *Object Relations Family Therapy*. New York: Jason Aronson.

Stern, M. 1985. *The Interpersonal World of the Infant*. New York: Basic Books.

Zinner, J., and R. Shapiro. 1976. Projective Identification as a Mode of Perception of Behavior in Families of Adolescents. *International Journal of Psychoanalysts* 53:523–30.

CHAPTER 9

Barton, C., and J. F. Alexander. 1981. Functional Family Therapy. In *Handbook of Family Therapy*, A. S. Gurman and D. P. Kniskern, eds. New York: Brunner/Mazel.

Dattilio, F. M. 1998. *Case Studies in Couple and Family Therapy: Systemic and Cognitive Perspectives*. New York: Guilford Press.

Dattilio, F. M. 2010. *Cognitive-Behavioral Therapy with Couples and Families*. New York: Guilford Press.

Epstein, N., S. E. Schlesinger, and W. Dryden. 1988. *Cognitive-Behavioral Therapy with Families*. New York: Brunner/Mazel.

Falloon, I. R. H. 1988. *Handbook of Behavioral Family Therapy*. New York: Guilford Press.

Gordon, S. B., and N. Davidson. 1981. Behavioral Parent Training. In *Handbook of Family Therapy*, A. S. Gurman and D. P. Kniskern, eds. New York: Brunner/Mazel.

Jacobson, N. S., and G. Margolin. 1979. *Marital Therapy: Strategies Based on Social Learning and Behavior Exchange Principles*. New York: Brunner/Mazel.

Kaplan, H. S. 1979. *The New Sex Therapy: Active Treatment of Sexual Dysfunctions*. New York: Brunner/Mazel.

Masters, W. H., and V. E. Johnson. 1970. *Human Sexual Inadequacy*. Boston: Little, Brown.

Patterson, G. R. 1971. *Families: Application of Social Learning Theory to Family Life*. Champaign, IL: Research Press.

Stuart, R. B. 1980. *Helping Couples Change: A Social Learning Approach to Marital Therapy*. New York: Guilford Press.

Weiss, R. L. 1978. The Conceptualization of Marriage from a Behavioral Perspective. In *Marriage and Marital Therapy*, T. J. Paolino and B. S. McCrady, eds. New York: Brunner/Mazel.

CHAPTER 10

Andersen, T. 1991. *The Reflecting Team*. New York: Norton.

Anderson, C. M., D. Reiss, and B. Hogarty. 1986. *Schizophrenia and the Family: A Practitioner's Guide to Psycho Education and Management*. New York: Guilford Press.

Avis, J. M. 1992. Where Are All the Family Therapists? Abuse and Violence within Families and Family Therapy's Response. *Journal of Marital and Family Therapy* 18:225–32.

Fontes, L. A. 2008. *Interviewing Clients across Cultures*. New York: Guilford Press.

Fowers, B., and F. Richardson. 1996. Why is Multiculturalism Good? *American Psychologist* 51:609–21.

Gergen, K. 1985. The Social Constructionist Movement in Modern Psychology. *American Psychologist* 40:266–75.

Goldner, V. 1985. Feminism and Family Therapy. *Family Process* 24:31–47.

Goodrich, T. J., ed. 1991. *Women and Power: Perspectives for Family Therapy*. New York: Norton.

Greenan, D. E., and G. Tunnell. 2002. *Couples Therapy with Gay Men: A Family Systems Model for Healing Relationships*. New York: Guilford Press.

Hare-Mustin, R. T., and J. Marecek. 1988. The Meaning of Difference: Gender Theory, Postmodernism and Psychology. *American Psychologist* 43:455–64.

Held, B. S. 1995. *Back to Reality: A Critique of Postmodern Theory in Psychotherapy*. New York: Norton.

Kellner, D. 1991. *Postmodern Theory*. New York: Guilford Press.

Krestan, J., and C. Bepko. 1980. The Problem of Fusion in the Lesbian Relationship. *Family Process* 19:277–89.

Laird, J., and R. J. Green. 1996. *Lesbians and Gays in Couples and Families: A Handbook for Therapists*. San Francisco, CA: Jossey-Bass.

Luepnitz, D. 1988. *The Family Interpreted: Feminist Theory in Clinical Practice*. New York: Basic Books.

McDaniel, S., J. Hepworth, and W. Doherty. 1992. *Medical Family Therapy*. New York: Basic Books.

McGoldrick, M., J. Pearce, and J. Giordano. 2007. *Ethnicity and Family Therapy*, 3rd ed. New York: Guilford Press.

Rolland, J. 1994. *Helping Families with Chronic and Life-Threatening Disorders*. New York: Basic Books.

Walsh, F., ed. 1993. *Normal Family Processes*, 2nd ed. New York: Guilford Press.

CHAPTER 11

de Shazer, S. 1988. *Clues: Investigating Solutions in Brief Therapy*. New York: Norton.

de Shazer, S. 1991. *Putting Difference to Work*. New York: Norton.

de Shazer, S., Y. Dolan, H. Korman, T. Trepper, I. K. Berg, and E. McCollum. 2007. *More than Miracles: The State of the Art of Solution-Focused Brief Therapy*. Binghamton, NY: Haworth Press.

Dolan, Y. 1991. *Resolving Sexual Abuse: Solution-Focused Therapy and Ericksonian Hypnosis for Adult Survivors*. New York: Norton.

Lipchik, E. 2011. *Beyond Technique in Solution-Focused Therapy*. New York: Guilford Press.

Miller, S., M. Hubble, and B. Duncan. 1996. *Handbook of Solution-Focused Brief Therapy*. San Francisco, CA: Jossey-Bass.

Walter, J., and J. Peller. 1992. *Becoming Solution-Focused in Brief Therapy*. New York: Brunner/Mazel.

CHAPTER 12

Bruner, J. S. 1986. *Actual Minds, Possible Worlds*. Cambridge, MA: Harvard University Press.

Diamond, J. 2000. *Narrative Means to Sober Ends: Treating Addiction and its Aftermath*. New York: Guilford Press.

Dickerson, V. C., and J. Zimmerman. 1992. Families with Adolescents: Escaping Problem Lifestyles. *Family Process* 31:341–53.

Eron, J., and T. Lund. 1996. *Narrative Solutions in Brief Therapy*. New York: Guilford Press.

Freedman, J., and G. Combs. 1996. *Narrative Therapy: The Social Construction of Preferred Realities*. New York: Norton.

Gilligan, S., and R. Price. 1993. *Therapeutic Conversations*. New York: Norton.

Minuchin, S. 1998. Where is the Family in Narrative Family Therapy? *Journal of Marital and Family Therapy* 24:397–403.

Phipps, W. D., and C. Vorster. 2009. Narrative Therapy: A Return to the Intrapsychic Perspective? *South African Journal of Psychology* 39:32–45.

White, M. 1989. *Selected Papers*. Adelaide, Australia: Dulwich Centre Publications.

White, M. 1995. *Re-Authoring Lives: Interviews and Essays*. Adelaide, Australia: Dulwich Centre Publications.

White, M., and D. Epston. 1990. *Narrative Means to Therapeutic Ends*. New York: Norton.

Zimmerman, J., and V. Dickerson. 1996. *If Problems Talked: Narrative Therapy in Action*. New York: Guilford Press.

CHAPTER 13

Anderson, C., and S. Stewart. 1983. *Mastering Resistance: A Practical Guide to Family Therapy*. New York: Guilford Press.

Dattilio, F. M. 1998. *Case Studies in Couple and Family Therapy: Systemic and Cognitive Perspectives*. New York: Guilford Press.

Eron, J., and T. Lund. 1996. *Narrative Solutions in Brief Therapy*. New York: Guilford Press.

Goldner, V. 1998. The Treatment of Violence and Victimization in Intimate Relationships. *Family Process* 37:263–86.

Jacobson, N. S., and A. Christensen. 1996. *Integrative Couple Therapy*. New York: Norton.

Sluzki, C. E. 1983. Process, Structure and World Views: Toward an Integrated View of Systemic Models in Family Therapy. *Family Process* 22:469–76.

Taibbi, R. 2007. *Doing Family Therapy*, 2nd ed. New York: Guilford Press.

CHAPTER 14

Alexander, J. F., A. Holtzworth-Munroe, and P. B. Jameson. 1994. Research on the Process and Outcome of Marriage and Family Therapy. In *Handbook of Psychotherapy and Behavior Change*, 4th ed., A. E. Bergin and S. L. Garfield, eds. New York: John Wiley and Sons.

Barbato, A., and B. D'Avanzo. 2008. Efficacy of Couples Therapy as a Treatment for Depression: A Meta-Analysis. *Psychiatric Quarterly* 79 (2):121–32.

Blanchard, V. L., A. J. Hawkins, S. A. Baldwin, and E. B. Fawcett. 2009. Investigating the Effects of Marriage and Relationship Education on Couples' Communication Skills: A Meta-Analytic Study. *Journal of Family Psychology* 23 (2):203–14.

Blow, A. J., D. H. Sprenkle, and S. D. Davis. 2007. Is Who Delivers the Treatment More Important than the Treatment Itself? The Role of the Therapist in Common Factors. *Journal of Marital and Family Therapy* 33:298–317.

Carr, A. 2009a. The Effectiveness of Family Therapy and Systemic Interventions for Child-Focused Problems. *Journal of Family Therapy* 31:3–45.

Carr, A. 2009b. The Effectiveness of Family Therapy and Systemic Interventions for Adult-Focused Problems. *Journal of Family Therapy* 31:46–74.

The Cochrane Collaboration. 2011. *Cochrane Reviews*. Retrieved from http://www.cochrane.org/index.htm

Friedlander, M. L., V. Escudero, and L. Heatherington. 2006. *Therapeutic Alliances in Couple and Family Therapy: An Empirically Informed Guide to Practice*. Washington, DC: American Psychological Association.

O'Farrell, T. J., and W. Fals-Stewart. 1999. Treatment Models and Methods: Family Models. In *Addictions: A Comprehensive Guidebook*, B. S. McCrady and E. E. Epstein, eds., pp. 287–305. New York: Oxford University Press.

Pinsof, W. M., and J. L. Lebow, eds. 2005. *Family Psychology: The Art of the Science*. New York: Oxford University Press.

Pitschel-Walz, G., S. Leucht, J. Bäuml, W. Kissling, and R. Engel. 2001. The Effect of Family Interventions on Relapse and Rehospitalization in Schizophrenia: A Meta-Analysis. *Schizophrenia Bulletin* 27:73–92.

Sexton, T. L., J. C. Kinser, and C. W. Hanes. 2008. Beyond a Single Standard: Levels of Evidence Approach for Evaluating Marriage and Family Therapy Research and Practice. *Journal of Family Therapy* 30:386–98.

Sprenkle, D. H., S. D. Davis, and J. L. Lebow. 2009. *Common Factors in Couple and Family Therapy: The Overlooked Foundation of Effective Practice*. New York: Guilford.

Stith, S., and K. Rosen. 2003. Effectiveness of Couples Treatment for Spouse Abuse. *Journal of Marital and Family Therapy* 29 (3):407–26.

APPENDIX B
Selected Readings in Family Therapy

GENERAL PRINCIPLES OF FAMILY SYSTEMS

Carter, E., and M. McGoldrick, eds. 1999. *The Expanded Family Life Cycle: A Framework for Family Therapy*, 3rd ed. Boston, MA: Allyn & Bacon.

Guerin, P. J., T. F. Fogarty, L. F. Fay, and J. G. Kautto. 1996. *Working with Relationship Triangles: The One-Two-Three of Psychotherapy*. New York: Guilford Press.

Hoffman, L. 1981. *Foundations of Family Therapy*. New York: Basic Books.

Kerr, M. E., and M. Bowen. 1988. *Family Evaluation*. New York: Norton.

Minuchin, S. 1974. *Families and Family Therapy*. Cambridge, MA: Harvard University Press.

Nichols, M. P. 2008. *Inside Family Therapy*, 2nd ed. Boston, MA: Allyn & Bacon.

Paolino, T. J., and B. S. McCrady, eds. 1978. *Marriage and Marital Therapy*. New York: Brunner/Mazel.

Watzlawick, P., J. H. Beavin, and D. D. Jackson. 1967. *Pragmatics of Human Communication*. New York: Norton.

CULTURE AND FAMILY THERAPY

Boyd-Franklin, N. 1989. *Black Families in Therapy: A Multisystems Approach*. New York: Guilford Press.

Davis, L., and E. Proctor. 1989. *Race, Gender, and Class: Guidelines for Practice with Individuals, Families and Groups*. Upper Saddle River, NJ: Prentice Hall.

Fontes, L. A. 2008. *Interviewing Clients across Cultures*. New York: Guilford Press.

Pedersen, p. 1987. The Frequent Assumptions of Cultural Bias in Counseling. *Journal of Multicultural Counseling and Development* 15:16–24.

Pinderhughes, E. 1989. *Understanding Race, Ethnicity, Power: The Key to Efficacy in Clinical Practice*. New York: Free Press.

Sue, D. W., and D. Sue. 1990. *Counseling the Culturally Different: Theory and Practice*, 2nd ed. New York: Wiley.

Walsh, F. 1998. *Re-Visioning Family Therapy*. New York: Guilford Press.

MARRIAGE

Dicks, H. V. 1967. *Marital Tensions*. New York: Basic Books.

Guerin, P. J., L. Fay, S. Burden, and J. Kautto. 1987. *The Evaluation and Treatment of Marital Conflict: A Four-Stage Approach*. New York: Basic Books.

Lederer, W., and D. D. Jackson. 1968. *Mirages of Marriage*. New York: Norton.

Lerner, H. G. 1985. *The Dance of Anger: A Woman's Guide to Changing Patterns of Intimate Relationships*. New York: Harper & Row.

Scarf, M. 1987. *Intimate Partners: Patterns in Love and Marriage*. New York: Random House.

Solot, D., and M. Miller. 2002. *Unmarried to Each Other*. New York: Marlowe & Company.

IN-LAWS AND THE EXTENDED FAMILY

Guerin, P. J., ed. 1976. *Family Therapy: Theory and Practice*. New York: Gardner Press.

Lerner, H. G. 1989. *The Dance of Intimacy: A Woman's Guide to Courageous Acts of Change in Key Relationships*. New York: Harper & Row.

McGoldrick, M., and R. Gerson. 1985. *Genograms in Family Assessment*. New York: Norton.

FAMILIES WITH BABIES AND SMALL CHILDREN

Brazelton, T. B. 1983. *Infants and Mothers: Differences in Development*, rev. ed. New York: Dell.

Combrinck-Graham, L., ed. 1988. *Children in Family Contexts: Perspectives on Treatment*. New York: Guilford Press.

Faber, A., and E. Mazlish. 1974. *Liberated Parents, Liberated Children*. New York: Grosset & Dunlap.

Ginott, H. 1969. *Between Parent and Child*. New York: Macmillan.

Nichols, M. P. 2004. *Stop Arguing with Your Kids*. New York: Guilford Press.

Patterson, G. 1975. *Families: Application of Social Learning Theory to Family Life*. Champaign, IL: Research Press.

FAMILIES WITH OLDER CHILDREN

Bank, S., and M. Kahn. 1982. *The Sibling Bond*. New York: Basic Books.

Blos, p. 1979. *The Adolescent Passage: Developmental Issues*. New York: International Universities Press.

Faber, A., and E. Mazlish. 1987. *Siblings without Rivalry*. New York: Norton.

Fishel, E. 1979. *Sisters: Love and Rivalry inside the Family and Beyond*. New York: Quill/William Morrow.

Micucci, J. 1998. *The Adolescent in Family Therapy*. New York: Guilford Press.

Schlaadt, R., and P. Shannon. 1986. *Drugs of Choice*, 2nd ed. Upper Saddle River, NJ: Prentice Hall.

Sells, S. 1998. *Treating the Tough Adolescent*. New York: Guilford Press.

DIVORCE, REMARRIAGE, AND STEPPARENTING

Ahrons, C., and R. Rodgers. 1987. *Divorced Families: A Multidisciplinary Developmental View*. New York: Norton.

Isaacs, M. B., B. Montalvo, and D. Abelsohn. 1986. *The Difficult Divorce*. New York: Basic Books.

Vaughan, D. 1986. *Uncoupling: Turning Points in Intimate Relationships*. New York: Oxford University Press.

Visher, E., and J. Visher. 1988. *Old Loyalties, New Ties: Therapeutic Strategies with Stepfamilies*. New York: Brunner/Mazel.

LEAVING HOME AND THE POSTCHILDREARING YEARS

Levinson, D. 1978. *The Seasons of a Man's Life*. New York: Ballantine.

Nichols, M. P. 1987. *Turning Forty in the Eighties*. New York: Fireside/Simon & Schuster.

Viorst, J. 1986. *Necessary Losses*. New York: Simon & Schuster.

FAMILY THERAPY TECHNIQUE

Anderson, C., and S. Stewart. 1983. *Mastering Resistance: A Practical Guide to Family Therapy*. New York: Guilford Press.

Dattilio, F. M. 1998. *Case Studies in Couple and Family Therapy: Systemic and Cognitive Perspectives*. New York: Guilford Press.

Donovan, J. M. 1999. *Short-Term Couple Therapy*. New York: Guilford Press.

Fisch, R., J. H. Weakland, and L. Segal. 1982. *The Tactics of Change: Doing Therapy Briefly*. San Francisco, CA: Jossey-Bass.

Gerson, M.-J. 1996. *The Embedded Self: A Psychoanalytic Guide to Family Therapy*. New York: Analytic Press.

Guerin, P. J., L. Fay, S. Burden, and J. Kautto. 1987. *The Evaluation and Treatment of Marital Conflict: A Four-Stage Approach*. New York: Basic Books.

Minuchin, S., and H. C. Fishman. 1981. *Family Therapy Techniques*. Cambridge, MA: Harvard University Press.

Minuchin, S., and M. P. Nichols. 1993. *Family Healing: Tales of Hope and Renewal from Family Therapy*. New York: Free Press.

Minuchin, S., M. P. Nichols, and W.-Y. Lee. 2006. *Assessing Families and Couples: From Symptom to System*. Boston: Allyn & Bacon.

Taibbi, R. 2007. *Doing Family Therapy*, 2nd ed. New York: Guilford Press.

White, M., and D. Epston. 1990. *Narrative Means to Therapeutic Ends*. New York: Norton.

APPENDIX C
Glossary

accommodation   Elements of a system automatically adjust to coordinate their functioning; people may have to work at it.

attachment   The innate tendency to seek out closeness to caretakers in the face of stress.

aversive control   Using punishment and criticism to eliminate undesirable responses; commonly used in dysfunctional families.

basic assumption theory   Bion's concept that group members become diverted from the group task to pursue unconscious patterns of fight–flight, dependency, or pairing.

behavior exchange theory   Explanation of behavior in relationships as maintained by a ratio of costs to benefits.

black box concept   The idea that because the mind is so complex, it's better to study people's input and output (behavior, communication) than to speculate about what goes on in their minds.

blended families   Separate families united by marriage; stepfamilies.

boundary   Emotional and physical barriers that protect and enhance the integrity of individuals, subsystems, and families.

boundary making   Negotiating the boundaries between members of a relationship and between the relationship and the outside world.

circular causality   The idea that actions are related through a series of recursive loops or repeating cycles.

circular questioning   A method of interviewing developed by the Milan Associates in which questions are asked that highlight differences among family members.

classical conditioning   A form of respondent learning in which an unconditioned stimulus (UCS), such as food, which leads to an unconditioned response (UCR), such as salivation, is paired with a conditioned

stimulus (CS), such as a bell, the result of which is that the CS begins to evoke the same response; used in the behavioral treatment of anxiety disorders.

closed system   A functionally related group of elements regarded as forming a collective entity that does not interact with the surrounding environment.

coalition   An alliance between two persons or social units against a third.

cognitive-behavioral therapy   Treatment that emphasizes attitude change as well as reinforcement of behavior.

collaborative model   A more egalitarian view of the therapist's role; advocated by critics of what is viewed as authoritarianism in traditional approaches to family therapy.

communications theory   The study of relationships in terms of the exchange of verbal and nonverbal messages.

complainant   De Shazer's term for a relationship with a client who describes a complaint but is at present unwilling to work on solving it.

complementarity   The reciprocity that is the defining feature of every relationship.

complementary relationship   Based on differences that fit together, where qualities of one make up for lacks in the other; one is one-up while the other is one-down.

compliments   Used in solution-focused therapy to convey support and encouragement.

concurrent therapy   Treatment of two or more persons, seen separately, usually by different therapists.

conjoint therapy   Treatment of two or more persons in sessions together.

constructivism   A relativistic point of view that emphasizes the subjective construction of reality. Implies that what we see in families may be based as much on our preconceptions as on what's actually going on.

content What families talk about.

context In family therapy, the interpersonal context, including the family but also other social influences.

contextual therapy Boszormenyi-Nagy's model that includes relational ethics.

contingency contracting A behavior therapy technique whereby agreements are made between family members to exchange rewards for desired behavior.

contingency management Shaping behavior by giving and taking away rewards.

coping questions Used in solution-focused therapy to help clients realize that they have been managing difficult circumstances.

countertransference Emotional reactivity on the part of the therapist.

cross-generational coalition An inappropriate alliance between a parent and child, who side together against a third member of the family.

culture Shared patterns of behavior and experience derived from settings in which people live.

cultural competence Familiarity with and, more important, sensitivity to other peoples' ways of doing things.

customer De Shazer's term for a client who not only complains about a problem ("complainant") but is motivated to resolve it.

cybernetics The science of feedback; how information, especially positive and negative feedback loops, can help self-regulate a system.

deconstruction A postmodern approach to exploring meaning by taking apart and examining taken-for-granted categories and assumptions, making possible newer and sounder constructions of meaning.

detriangulation The process by which individuals remove themselves from the emotional field of two others.

differentiation of self Bowen's term for psychological separation of intellect and emotions and independence of self from others; opposite of fusion.

directives Homework assignments designed to help families interrupt homeostatic patterns of problem-maintaining behavior.

disengagement Psychological isolation that results from overly rigid boundaries around individuals and subsystems in a family.

double bind A conflict created when a person receives contradictory messages on different levels of abstraction in an important relationship and cannot leave or comment.

dyadic model Explanations based on the interactions between two persons or objects: Johnny shoplifts to get his mother's attention.

emotional cutoff Bowen's term for flight from an unresolved emotional attachment.

emotional reactivity The tendency to respond in a knee-jerk emotional fashion, rather than calmly and objectively.

emotionally focused couples therapy A model of therapy based on attachment theory, in which the emotional longings beneath a couple's defensive reactions are uncovered as they are taught to see the reactive nature of their struggles with each other, developed by Leslie Greenberg and Susan Johnson.

empathy Understanding someone else's beliefs and feelings.

enactment An interaction stimulated in structural family therapy in order to observe and then change transactions that make up family structure.

enmeshment Loss of autonomy due to a blurring of psychological boundaries.

entitlement Boszormenyi-Nagy's term for the amount of merit a person accrues for behaving in an ethical manner toward others.

epistemology The branch of philosophy concerned with the study of knowledge. Used by Bateson to mean worldview or belief system.

equifinality The ability of complex systems to reach a given final goal in a variety of different ways.

ethnicity The common ancestry through which groups of people have evolved shared values and customs.

exception De Shazer's term for times when clients are temporarily free of their problems. Solution-focused therapists focus on exceptions to help clients build on successful problem-solving skills.

exception question Used in solution-focused therapy to help clients remember times when they haven't been defeated by their problems.

expressive leader Serving social and emotional functions; in traditional families, the wife's role.

extended family The network of kin relationships across several generations.

externalization Michael White's technique of personifying problems as external to persons.

extinction Eliminating behavior by not reinforcing it.

family drawing An experiential therapy technique in which family members are asked to draw their ideas about how the family is organized.

family group therapy Family treatment based on the group therapy model.

family homeostasis Tendency of families to resist change in order to maintain a steady state.

family life cycle Stages of family life from separation from one's parents to marriage, having children, growing older, retirement, and finally death.

family myths A set of beliefs based on a distortion of historical reality and shared by all family members that help shape the rules governing family functioning.

family of origin A person's parents and siblings; usually refers to the original nuclear family of an adult.

family projection process In Bowenian theory, the mechanism by which parental conflicts are projected onto the children or a spouse.

family ritual Technique used by Selvini Palazzoli and her Milan Associates that prescribes a specific act for family members to perform, which is designed to change the family system's rules.

family rules A descriptive term for redundant behavioral patterns.

family sculpting A nonverbal experiential technique in which family members position themselves in a tableau that reveals significant aspects of their perceptions and feelings.

family structure The functional organization of families that determines how family members interact.

family system The family conceived as a collective whole entity made up of individual parts plus the way they function together.

feedback loop The return of a portion of the output of a system, especially when used to maintain the output within predetermined limits (negative feedback), or to signal a need to modify the system (positive feedback).

first-order change Temporary or superficial changes within a system that do not alter the basic organization of the system itself.

first-order cybernetics The idea that an outside observer can study and make changes in a system while remaining separate and independent of that system.

fixation Partial arrest of attachment or mode of behavior from an early stage of development.

formula first-session task Solution-focused therapists routinely ask clients at the end of the first session to think about what they do not want to change as a result of therapy. This focuses them on strengths in their lives and begins the solution-generating process.

function of the symptom The idea that symptoms are often ways to distract or otherwise protect family members from threatening conflicts.

functional analysis of behavior In operant behavior therapy, a study of a particular behavior, what elicits it, and what reinforces it.

fusion A blurring of psychological boundaries between self and others and a contamination of emotional and intellectual functioning; opposite of differentiation.

general systems theory A biological model of living systems as whole entities that maintain themselves through continuous input and output from the environment; developed by Ludwig von Bertalanffy.

genogram A schematic diagram of the family system, using squares to represent males, circles to indicate females, horizontal lines for marriages, and vertical lines to indicate children.

group dynamics Interactions among group members that emerge as a result of properties of the group rather than merely their individual personalities.

hermeneutics The art of analyzing literary texts or human experience, understood as fundamentally ambiguous, by interpreting levels of meaning.

hierarchical structure Family functioning based on clear generational boundaries, where the parents maintain control and authority.

homeostasis A balanced steady state of equilibrium.

idealization A tendency to exaggerate the virtues of someone, part of the normal developmental process in children's relationships to their parents and in intimate partnerships.

identification From psychoanalytic theory, not merely imitation, but appropriation of traits of an admired other.

identified patient (IP) The symptom-bearer or official patient as identified by the family.

instrumental leader Decision-making and task functions; in traditional families, the husband's role.

intensity Minuchin's term for changing maladaptive transactions by using strong affect, repeated intervention, or prolonged pressure.

internal family systems model   A model of the mind that uses systemic principles and techniques to understand and change intrapsychic processes, developed by Richard Schwartz.

internal objects   Mental images and fantasies of oneself and others, formed by early interactions with caregivers.

introjection   A primitive form of identification; taking in aspects of other people, which then become part of the self-image.

invariant prescription   A technique developed by Mara Selvini Palazzoli in which parents are directed to mysteriously sneak away together.

invisible loyalties   Boszormenyi-Nagy's term for unconscious commitments that children take on to help their families.

joining   A structural family therapy term for accepting and accommodating to families to win their confidence and circumvent resistance.

linear causality   The idea that one event is the cause and another is the effect; in behavior, the idea that one behavior is a stimulus, the other a response.

live supervision   Technique of teaching therapy whereby the supervisor observes sessions in progress and contacts the therapist to suggest different strategies and techniques.

managed care   A system in which third-party companies manage insurance costs by regulating the terms of treatment. Managed care companies select providers, set fees, and control who receives treatment and how many sessions they are entitled to.

marital schism   Lidz's term for pathological overt marital conflict.

marital skew   Lidz's term for a pathological marriage in which one spouse dominates the other.

medical family therapy   A form of psychoeducational family therapy involving collaboration with physicians and other health care professionals in the treatment of people with medical problems.

metacommunication   Every message has two levels: report and command; metacommunication is the implied command or qualifying message.

miracle question   Asking clients to imagine how things would be if they woke up tomorrow and their problem was solved. Solution-focused therapists use the miracle question to help clients identify goals and potential solutions.

mirroring   Expression of understanding and acceptance of another's feelings.

modeling   Observational learning.

monadic model   Explanations based on properties of a single person or object: Johnny shoplifts because he is rebellious.

morphogenesis   The process by which a system changes its structure to adapt to new contexts.

multigenerational transmission process   Bowen's concept for the process, occurring over several generations, in which poorly differentiated persons marry equally immature partners, ultimately resulting in children suffering from severe psychological problems.

multiple family group therapy   Treatment of several families at once in a group therapy format; pioneered by Peter Laqueur and Murray Bowen.

multiple impact therapy   An intensive, crisis-oriented form of family therapy developed by Robert MacGregor in which family members are treated in various subgroups by a team of therapists.

mystery questions   Questions designed to get clients wondering how their problems got the best of them, which helps to externalize the problems.

mystification   Laing's concept that many families distort their children's experience by denying or relabeling it.

narcissism   Self-regard. The exaggerated self-regard most people equate with narcissism is pathological narcissism.

narrative therapy   An approach to treatment that emphasizes the role of the stories people construct about their experience.

negative feedback   Information that signals a system to correct a deviation and restore the status quo.

network therapy   A treatment devised by Ross Speck in which a large number of family and friends are assembled to help resolve a patient's problems.

neutrality   Selvini Palazzoli's term for balanced acceptance of family members.

nuclear family   Parents and their children.

object relations   Internalized images of self and others based on early parent–child interactions that determine a person's mode of relationship to other people.

object relations theory   Psychoanalytic theory derived from Melanie Klein and developed by the

British School (Bion, Fairbairn, Guntrip, Winnicott) that emphasizes relationships and attachment, rather than libidinal and aggressive drives, as the key issues of human concern.

open system   A set of interrelated elements that exchange information, energy, and material with the surrounding environment.

operant conditioning   A form of learning whereby a person or animal is rewarded for performing certain behaviors; the major approach in most forms of behavior therapy.

ordeals   A type of paradoxical intervention in which the client is directed to do something that is more of a hardship than the symptom.

paradox   A self-contradictory statement based on a valid deduction from acceptable premises.

paradoxical injunction   A technique used in strategic therapy whereby the therapist directs family members to continue their symptomatic behavior. If they conform, they admit control and expose secondary gain; if they rebel, they give up their symptoms.

parental child   A child who has been allocated power to take care of younger siblings; adaptive when done deliberately in large or single-parent families, maladaptive when it results from unplanned abdication of parental responsibility.

positive connotation   Selvini Palazzoli's technique of ascribing positive motives to family behavior in order to promote family cohesion and avoid resistance to therapy.

positive feedback   Information that confirms and reinforces the direction a system is taking.

postmodernism   Contemporary antipositivism, viewing knowledge as relative and context-dependent; questions assumptions of objectivity that characterize modern science. In family therapy, challenging the idea of scientific certainty and linked to the method of deconstruction.

preferred view   Eron and Lund's term for the way people would like to think of themselves and be seen by others.

Premack principle   Using high-probability behavior (preferred activities) to reinforce low-probability behavior (nonpreferred activities).

prescribing the symptom   A paradoxical technique that forces a patient to either give up a symptom or admit that it is under voluntary control.

pretend techniques   Madanes's playful paradoxical intervention in which family members are asked to pretend to engage in symptomatic behavior. The paradox is if they are pretending to have a symptom, the symptom cannot be real.

problem-saturated stories   The usual pessimistic and blaming accounts that clients bring to therapy, which are seen as helping keep them stuck.

process   How members of a family or group relate.

process research   Research that looks within sessions to determine how therapists and clients affect each other.

projective identification   A defense mechanism that operates unconsciously, whereby unwanted aspects of the self are attributed to another person and that person is induced to behave in accordance with these projected attitudes and feelings.

pseudohostility   Wynne's term for superficial bickering that masks pathological alignments in schizophrenic families.

pseudomutuality   Wynne's term for the facade of family harmony that characterizes many schizophrenic families.

psychoeducational family therapy   A type of therapy developed in work with schizophrenics, which emphasizes educating family members to help them understand and cope with a seriously disturbed family member.

quid pro quo   Literally, "something for something," an equal exchange or substitution.

reconstruction   Reweaving narrative accounts into more palatable and coherent histories.

reflecting team   Tom Andersen's technique of having the observing team share their reactions with the family following a session.

reframing   Relabeling a family's description of behavior to make it more amenable to therapeutic change; for example, describing someone as "lazy" rather than "depressed."

regression   Return to a less-mature level of functioning in the face of stress.

reinforcement   An event, behavior, or object that increases the rate of a particular response. A positive reinforcer is an event whose contingent presentation increases the rate of responding; a negative reinforcer is an event whose contingent withdrawal increases the rate of responding.

reinforcement reciprocity   Exchanging rewarding behaviors between family members.

relative influence questions   Questions designed to explore the extent to which the problem has dominated the client versus how much he or she has been able to control it.

resistance   Anything that patients or families do to oppose or retard the progress of therapy.

restraining   A strategic technique for overcoming resistance by suggesting that a family not change.

rituals   In strategic therapy, a set of prescribed actions designed to change a family system's rules.

role-playing   Acting out the parts of important characters to dramatize feelings and practice new ways of relating.

role rehearsal   Role-playing desired ways of behaving, especially in couples therapy.

rubber fence   Wynne's term for the rigid boundary surrounding many schizophrenic families, which allows only minimal contact with the surrounding community.

runaway   Unchecked positive feedback that causes a family or system to get out of control.

scaling questions   Solution-focused clients are asked to rate on a 10-point scale how much they want to resolve their problems, how bad the problem is, how much better it is than the last time, and so on. Designed to break change up into small steps.

scapegoat   A member of the family, usually the identified patient, who is the object of displaced conflict or criticism.

schemas   Underlying core beliefs that an individual has developed about the world and how it functions.

schizophrenogenic mother   Frieda Fromm Reichmann's term for aggressive, domineering mothers thought to precipitate schizophrenia in their offspring.

second-order change   Basic change in the structure and functioning of a system.

second-order cybernetics   The idea that anyone attempting to observe and change a system is therefore part of that system.

self object   Kohut's term for a person related to not as a separate individual, but as an extension of the self rather than sex and aggression.

self psychology   Heinz Kohut's version of psychoanalysis that emphasizes the need for attachment and appreciation.

separation–individuation   Process whereby the infant begins, at about two months, to draw apart from the symbiotic bond with mother and develop his or her autonomous functioning.

shaping   Reinforcing change in small steps.

shaping competence   encouraging and reinforcing productive behavior rather than criticizing dysfunctional behavior.

social constructionism   Like constructivism, challenges the notion of an objective basis for knowledge. Knowledge and meaning are shaped by culturally shared assumptions.

social learning theory   Understanding and treating behavior using principles from social and developmental psychology as well as from learning theory.

solution-focused therapy   Steve de Shazer's term for a style of therapy that emphasizes the solutions that families have already developed for their problems.

strategic therapy problem   centered pragmatic strategies for altering problem-maintaining sequences of interaction.

structure   Recurrent patterns of interaction that define and stabilize the shape of relationships.

subsystem   Smaller units in families, determined by generation, sex, or function.

symmetrical relationship   In relationships, equality or parallel form.

system   A group of interrelated elements plus the way they function together.

systems theory   A generic term for studying a group of related elements that interact as a whole entity; encompasses general systems theory and cybernetics.

theory of social exchange   Thibaut and Kelley's theory according to which people strive to maximize rewards and minimize costs in a relationship.

three-generational hypothesis of schizophrenia   Bowen's concept that schizophrenia is the end result of low levels of differentiation passed on and amplified across three succeeding generations.

time-out   A behavioral technique for extinguishing undesirable behavior by removing the reinforcing consequences of that behavior; typically, making the child sit in a corner or go to his or her room.

token economy   A system of rewards using points, which can be accumulated and exchanged for reinforcing items or behaviors.

transference Distorted emotional reactions to present relationships based on unresolved, early family relations.

triadic model Explanations based on the interactions among three people or objects: Johnny shoplifts because his father covertly encourages him to defy his mother.

triangle A three-person system; according to Bowen, the smallest stable unit of human relations.

triangulation Detouring conflict between two people by involving a third person, stabilizing the relationship between the original pair.

unconscious Memories, feelings, and impulses of which a person is unaware. Often used as a noun, but more appropriately limited to use as an adjective.

undifferentiated family ego mass Bowen's early term for emotional "stuck-togetherness" or fusion in the family, especially prominent in schizophrenic families.

unique outcome Michael White's term for times when clients acted free of their problems, even if they were unaware of doing so. Narrative therapists identify unique outcomes as a way to help clients challenge negative views of themselves.

visitor De Shazer's term for a client who does not wish to be part of therapy, does not have a complaint, and does not wish to work on anything.

REFERENCES

FRONT MATTER

Einstein, Albert. On the Method of Theoretical Physics, Oxford University Press, 1933.

INTRODUCTION

Anna Karénina, Translated by Nathan Haskell Dole (Thomas Y. Crowell & Co., New York, 1887).

CHAPTER 1

Bateson, G., D. D. Jackson, J. Haley, and J. Weakland. 1956. Toward a Theory of Schizophrenia. *Behavioral Sciences* 1:251–64.

Bell, J. E. 1961. *Family Group Therapy*. Public Health Monograph No. 64. Washington, DC: U.S. Government Printing Office.

Bell, J. E. 1962. Recent Advances in Family Group Therapy. *Journal of Child Psychology and Psychiatry* 3:1–15.

Bell, J. E. 1975. *Family Group Therapy*. New York: Jason Aronson.

Bion, W. R. 1948. Experience in Groups. *Human Relations* 1:314–29.

Boszormenyi-Nagy, I., and G. L. Spark. 1973. *Invisible Loyalties: Reciprocity in Intergenerational Family Therapy*. New York: Harper & Row.

Bowen, M. 1961. Family Psychotherapy. *American Journal of Orthopsychiatry* 31:40–60.

Bowlby, J. P. 1949. The Study and Reduction of Group Tensions in the Family. *Human Relations* 2:123–38.

Broderick, C. B., and S. S. Schrader. 1981. The History of Professional Marriage and Family Therapy. In *Handbook of Family Therapy*, A. S. Gurman and D. P. Kniskern, eds. New York: Brunner/Mazel.

Dicks, H. V. 1964. Concepts of Marital Diagnosis and Therapy as Developed at the Tavistock Family Psychiatric Clinic, London, England. In *Marriage Counseling in Medical Practice*, E. M. Nash, L. Jessner, and D. W. Abse, eds. Chapel Hill: University of North Carolina Press.

Epstein, N. B., D. S. Bishop, and L. M. Baldarin. 1981. McMaster Model of Family Functioning. In *Normal Family Problems*, F. Walsh, ed. New York: Guilford Press.

Fromm-Reichmann, F. 1948. Notes on the Development of Treatment of Schizophrenics by Psychoanalytic Psychotherapy. *Psychiatry* 11:263–74.

Gritzer, P. H., and H. S. Okum. 1983. Multiple Family Group Therapy: A Model for All Families. In *Handbook of Family and Marital Therapy*, B. B. Wolman and G. Stricker, eds. New York: Plenum Press.

Guerin, P. J. 1976. Family Therapy: The First Twenty-Five Years. In *Family Therapy: Theory and Practice*, P. J. Guerin, ed. New York: Gardner Press.

Gurman, A. S. 2008. *Clinical Handbook of Couple Therapy*, 4th ed. New York: Guilford Press.

Gurman, A. S. 2011. Couple Therapy Research and the Practice of Couple Therapy: Can We Talk? *Family Process* 50:280–92.

Haley, J. 1962. Whither Family Therapy? *Family Process* 1:69–100.

Haley, J. 1963. *Strategies of Psychotherapy*. New York: Grune & Stratton.

Hoffman, L. 1981. *Foundations of Family Therapy*. New York: Basic Books.

Howells, J. G. 1971. *Theory and Practice of Family Psychiatry*. New York: Brunner/Mazel.

Jackson, D. D. 1954. Suicide. *Scientific American* 191:88–96.

Jackson, D. D. 1965. Family Rules: Marital Quid Pro Quo. *Archives of General Psychiatry* 12:589–94.

Jackson, D. D., and J. H. Weakland. 1959. Schizophrenic Symptoms and Family Interaction. *Archives of General Psychiatry* 1:618–21.

Jackson, D. D., and J. H. Weakland. 1961. Conjoint Family Therapy, Some Considerations on Theory, Technique, and Results. *Psychiatry* 24:30–45.

Kaslow, F. W. 1980. History of Family Therapy in the United States: A Kaleidoscopic Overview. *Marriage and Family Review* 3:77–111.

Laing, R. D. 1960. *The Divided Self*. London: Tavistock.

Laing, R. D. 1965. Mystification, Confusion and Conflict. In *Intensive Family Therapy*, I. Boszormenyi-Nagy and J. L. Framo, eds. New York: Harper & Row.

Laqueur, H. P. 1966. General Systems Theory and Multiple Family Therapy. In *Handbook of Psychiatric Therapies*, J. Masserman, ed. New York: Grune & Stratton.

Laqueur, H. P. 1976. Multiple Family Therapy. In *Family Therapy: Theory and Practice*, P. J. Guerin, ed. New York: Gardner Press.

Lebow, J. Whither Family Therapy: Alive and Flowering Amidst the Changes. *Family Process* 53:365–70.

Levy, D. 1943. *Maternal Overprotection*. New York: Columbia University Press.

Lewin, K. 1951. *Field Theory in Social Science*. New York: Harper.

Lidz, T., A. Cornelison, S. Fleck, and D. Terry. 1957a. Intrafamilial Environment of the Schizophrenic Patient. I: The Father. *Psychiatry* 20:329–42.

Lidz, T., A. Cornelison, S. Fleck, and D. Terry. 1957b. Intrafamilial Environment of the Schizophrenic Patient. II: Marital Schism and Marital Skew. *Psychiatry* 114:241–8.

MacGregor, R. 1967. Progress in Multiple Impact Theory. In *Expanding Theory and Practice in Family Therapy*, N. W. Ackerman, F. L. Bateman, and S. N. Sherman, eds. New York: Family Services Association.

MacGregor, R. 1972. Multiple Impact Psychotherapy with Families. In *Family Therapy: An Introduction to Theory and Technique*, G. D. Erickson and T. P. Hogan, eds. Monterey, CA: Brooks/Cole.

Madanes, C. 1981. *Strategic Family Therapy*. San Francisco, CA: Jossey-Bass.

McFarlane, W. R. 1982. Multiple-Family Therapy in the Psychiatric Hospital. In *The Psychiatric Hospital and the Family*, H. T. Harbin, ed. New York: Spectrum.

Minuchin, S. 1974. *Families and Family Therapy*. Cambridge, MA: Harvard University Press.

Minuchin, S., B. Montalvo, B. G. Guerney, B. L. Rosman, and F. Schumer. 1967. *Families of the Slums*. New York: Basic Books.

Minuchin, S., and M. P. Nichols. 1993. *Family Healing*. New York: Free Press.

Minuchin, S., M. D. Reiter, and C. Borda. 2014. *The Craft of Family Therapy: Challenging Certainties*. New York: Routledge.

Mittleman, B. 1948. The Concurrent Analysis of Married Couples. *Psychoanalytic Quarterly* 17:182–97.

Nichols, M. P., and S. Tafuri. 2013. Techniques of Structural Family Assessment: A Qualitative Analysis of How Experts Promote a Systemic Perspective. *Family Process* 52:207–15.

Ruevini, U. 1975. Network Intervention with a Family in Crisis. *Family Process* 14:193–203.

Selvini Palazzoli, M., L. Boscolo, G. Cecchin, and G. Prata. 1978. *Paradox and Counterparadox*. New York: Jason Aronson.

Sexton, T., and C. Datachi. 2014. The Development and Evolution of Family Therapy Research. *Journal of Family Therapy* 37:259–61.

Skynner, A. C. R. 1976. *Systems of Family and Marital Psychotherapy*. New York: Brunner/Mazel.

Speck, R. V., and C. A. Attneave. 1973. *Family Networks*. New York: Pantheon.

Stierlin, H. 1972. *Separating Parents and Adolescents*. New York: Quadrangle/New York Times Books.

Watzlawick, P. A., J. H. Beavin, and D. D. Jackson. 1967. *Pragmatics of Human Communication*. New York: Norton.

Whitaker, C. A. 1958. Psychotherapy with Couples. *American Journal of Psychotherapy* 12:18–23.

Whitaker, C. A. 1975. Psychotherapy of the Absurd: With a Special Emphasis on the Psychotherapy of Aggression. *Family Process* 14:1–16.

Whitaker, C. A. 1976. A Family Is a Four-Dimensional Relationship. In *Family Therapy: Theory and Practice*, P. J. Guerin, ed. New York: Gardner Press.

Whitaker, C. A., and T. P. Malone. 1953. *The Roots of Psychotherapy*. New York: Balkiston.

Wynne, L. C. 1961. The Study of Intrafamilial Alignments and Splits in Exploratory Family Therapy. In *Exploring the Base for Family Therapy*, N. W.

Ackerman, F. L. Beatman, and S. N. Sherman, eds. New York: Family Services Association.

Wynne, L. C., I. Ryckoff, J. Day, and S. I. Hirsch. 1958. Pseudomutuality in the Family Relationships of Schizophrenics. *Psychiatry* 21:205–20.

CHAPTER 2

AAMFT. 2011. *Code of Ethical Principles*. Washington, DC: American Association for Marriage and Family Therapy.

ACA. 2014. *ACA Code of Ethics*. Alexandria, VA: American Counseling Association.

Avis, J. M. 1992. Where Are All the Family Therapists? Abuse and Violence within Families and Family Therapy's Response. *Journal of Marital and Family Therapy* 18:223–33.

Bentovim, A., A. Elton, J. Hildebrand, M. Tranter, and E. Vizard, eds. 1988. *Child Sexual Abuse within the Family*. London: Wright.

Bograd, M. 1984. Family Systems Approaches to Wife Battering: A Feminist Critique. *American Journal of Orthopsychiatry* 54:558–68.

Bograd, M. 1992. Values in Conflict: Challenges to Family Therapists' Thinking. *Journal of Marital and Family Therapy* 18:243–57.

Boszormenyi-Nagy, I., and G. Spark. 1973. *Invisible Loyalties: Reciprocity in Intergenerational Family Therapy*. New York: Harper & Row.

Brown, P. D., and K. D. O'Leary. 1995. *Marital Treatment for Wife Abuse: A Review and Evaluation*. Paper presented at the Fourth International Family Violence Research Conference, Durham, NC July.

Campbell, K. A., L. J. Cook, B. J. LaFleur, and H. T. Keenan. 2010. Household, Family, and Child Risk Factors after an Investigation for Suspected Child Maltreatment: A Missed Opportunity for Prevention. *Archives of Pediatric Adolescent Medicine* 164:943–9.

Doherty, W. 1991. Family Therapy Goes Postmodern. *Family Therapy Networker* 15 (5):36–42.

Edelson, E., and R. Tolman. 1992. *Intervention for Men Who Batter*. Newbury Park, CA: Sage.

Edwards, D. L., and E. Gill. 1986. *Breaking the Cycle: Assessment and Treatment of Child Abuse and Neglect*. Los Angeles, CA: Association for Advanced Training in Behavioral Science.

Feldman, C. M., and C. A. Ridley. 1995. The Etiology and Treatment of Domestic Violence Between Adult Partners. *Clinical Psychology: Science and Practice* 2:317–48.

Furniss, T. 1991. *The Multiprofessional Handbook of Child Sexual Abuse: Integrated Management, Therapy, and Legal Intervention*. London: Routledge.

Goldner, V. 1992. Making Room for Both/And. *The Family Therapy Networker* 16 (2):55–61.

Goldner, V. 1998. The Treatment of Violence and Victimization in Intimate Relationships. *Family Process* 37:263–86.

Gondolf, E. W. 1995. Gains and Process in State Batterer Programs and Standards. *Family Violence and Sexual Assault Bulletin* 11:27–8.

Hansen, M. 1993. Feminism and Family Therapy: A Review of Feminist Critiques of Approaches to Family Violence. In *Battering and Family Therapy: A Feminist Perspective*, M. Hansen and M. Harway, eds. Newbury Park, CA: Sage.

Herman, J. L. 1992. *Trauma and Recovery*. New York: Basic Books.

Holtzworth-Munroe, A., J. C. Meehan, U. Rehman, and A. D. Marshall. 2002. Intimate Partner Violence: An Introduction for Couple Therapists. In *Clinical Handbook of Couple Therapy*, 3rd ed., A. Gurman and N. Jacobson, eds. New York: Guilford Press.

Jacobson, N. S., and A. Christensen. 1996. *Integrative Couple Therapy*. New York: Guilford Press.

Johnson, M. P. 1995. Patriarchal Terrorism and Common Couple Violence: Two Forms of Violence against Women. *Journal of Marriage and the Family* 57:283–94.

Kitchens, J. M. 1994. Does This Patient Have an Alcohol Problem? *Journal of the American Medical Association* 272:1782–7.

McGoldrick, M., J. Pearce, and J. Giordano. 2005. *Ethnicity and Family Therapy*, 3rd ed. New York: Guilford Press.

Minuchin, S., and M. P. Nichols. 1993. *Family Healing: Tales of Hope and Renewal from Family Therapy*. New York: Free Press.

Nichols, M. P. 2009. *The Lost Art of Listening*, 2nd ed. New York: Guilford Press.

Patterson, J. E., L. Williams, L. Grauf-Grounds, and L. Chamow. 1998. *Essential Skills in Family*

Therapy: From the First Interview to Termination. New York: Guilford Press.

Ramchandani, P., and P. H. Jones. 2003. Treating Psychological Systems in Sexually Abused Children. *The British Journal of Psychiatry* 183:484–90.

Rasmussen, B. 2013. The Basics of Healthcare Reform. *Family Therapy* 12:10–15.

Schwartz, R. C. 1995. *Internal Family Systems Therapy.* New York: Guilford Press.

Scott, K., and M. Straus. 2007. Denial, Minimization, Partner Blaming and Intimate Aggression in Dating Partners. *Journal of Interpersonal Violence* 22:851–71.

Sheinberg, M., F. True, and P. Fraenkel. 1994. Treating the Sexually Abused Child: A Recursive, Multi-Modal Program. *Family Process* 33:263–76.

Smith, S., K. Rosen, E. McCollum, and C. Thomsen. 2004. Treating Intimate Partner Violence within Intact Couple Relationships: Outcome of Multi-Couple versus Individual Couple Therapy. *Journal of Marital and Family Therapy* 30:305–18.

Trepper, T. S., and M. J. Barrett. 1989. *Systemic Treatment of Incest: A Therapeutic Handbook.* New York: Brunner/Mazel.

Walsh, F. 1998. *Strengthening Family Resilience.* New York: Guilford Press.

CHAPTER 3

Ainsworth, M. D. S. 1967. *Infancy in Uganda: Infant Care and the Growth of Attachment.* Baltimore, MD: Johns Hopkins University Press.

Bateson, G. 1956. *Naven.* Stanford, CA: Stanford University Press.

Bateson, G. 1979. *Mind and Nature.* New York: Dutton.

Bibb, A., and G. J. Casimir. 1996. Hatian Families. In *Ethnicity and Family Therapy*, M. McGoldrick, J. Giordano, and J. K. Pearce, eds. New York: Guilford Press.

Bowen, M. 1978. *Family Therapy in Clinical Practice.* New York: Jason Aronson.

Bowlby, J. 1958. The Nature of the Child's Tie to His Mother. *International Journal of Psycho-Analysis* 41:350–73.

Bowlby, J. 1973. *Attachment and Loss: Vol. 2. Separation.* New York: Basic Books.

Bowlby, J. 1988. A Secure Base: Clinical Applications of Attachment Theory. London: Routledge.

Boyd-Franklin, N. 1989. *Black Families in Therapy: A Multisystems Approach.* New York: Guilford Press.

Buckley, W. 1968. Society as a Complex Adaptive System. In *Modern Systems Research for the Behavioral Scientist: A Sourcebook*, W. Buckley, ed. Chicago, IL: Aldine.

Burlingham, D., and A. Freud. 1944. *Infants without Families.* London: Allen & Unwin.

Carter, E., and M. McGoldrick, eds. 1980. *The Family Life Cycle: A Framework for Family Therapy.* New York: Gardner Press.

Carter, E., and M. McGoldrick. 1999. *The Expanded Family Life Cycle*, 3rd ed. Boston, MA: Allyn & Bacon.

Chodorow, N. 1978. *The Reproduction of Mothering.* Berkeley: University of California Press.

Conway, F., and J. Siegelman. 2005. Dark Hero of the Information Age: In Search of Norbert Wiener, the Father of Cybernetics. New York: Basic Books.

Davidson, M. 1983. *Uncommon Sense*, p. 104. Los Angeles, CA: Tarcher.

Duvall, E. 1957. *Family Development.* Philadelphia, PA: Lippincott.

Easterbrook, M. A., and M. E. Lamb. 1979. The Relationship between Quality of Infant–Mother Attachment and Infant Competence in Initial Encounters with Peers. *Child Development* 50:380–7.

Falicov, C. J. 1998. *Latino Families in Therapy.* New York: Guilford Press.

Feeney, J. A. 1995. Adult Attachment and Emotional Control. *Personal Relationships* 2:143–59.

Foerster, H. von. 1981. *Observing Systems.* Seaside, CA: Intersystems.

Haley, J. 1976. *Problem-Solving Therapy.* San Francisco, CA: Jossey-Bass.

Harlow, H. 1958. The Nature of Love. *American Psychologist* 13:673–85.

Hazan, C., and P. R. Shaver. 1987. Romantic Love Conceptualized as an Attachment Process. *Journal of Personality and Social Psychology* 52:511–24.

Heims, S. 1991. *The Cybernetics Group.* Cambridge, MA: MIT Press.

Hill, R., and R. Rodgers. 1964. The Developmental Approach. In *Handbook of Marriage and the Family*, H. T. Christiansen, ed. Chicago, IL: Rand McNally.

Jackson, D. D. 1957. The Question of Family Homeostasis. *Psychiatric Quarterly Supplement* 31:79–90.

Jackson, D. D. 1959. Family Interaction, Family Homeostasis, and Some Implications for Conjoint Family Therapy. In *Individual and Family Dynamics*, J. Masserman, ed. New York: Grune & Stratton.

Johnson, S. 2002. *Emotionally Focused Couple Therapy with Trauma Survivors: Strengthening Attachment Bonds*. New York: Guilford Press.

Kelly, G. A. 1955. *The Psychology of Personal Constructs*. New York: Norton.

Lee, E. 1996. Asian American Families: An Overview. In *Ethnicity and Family Therapy*, M. McGoldrick, J. Giordano, and J. K. Pearce, eds. New York: Guilford Press.

Lieberman, A. F. 1977. Preschoolers' Competence with a Peer: Relations with Attachment and Peer Experience. *Child Development* 48:1277–87.

Lock, A., and T. Strong. *Social Constructionism: Sources and Stirrings in Theory and Practice*. London: Cambridge University Press.

Lorenz, K. E. 1935. Der Kumpan in der Umvelt des Vogels. In *Instinctive Behavior*, C. H. Schiller, ed. New York: International Universities Press.

Luepnitz, D. A. 1988. *The Family Interpreted: Feminist Theory in Clinical Practice*. New York: Basic Books.

Mahler, M., F. Pine, and A. Bergman. 1975. *The Psychological Birth of the Human Infant*. New York: Basic Books.

Main, M. 1977. Sicherheit und wissen. In *Entwicklung der Lernfahigkeit in der sozialen umwelt*, K. E. Grossman, ed. Munich: Kinder Verlag.

Main, M., and D. Weston. 1981. The Quality of the Toddler's Relationships to Mother and Father: Related to Conflict Behavior and Readiness to Establish New Relationships. *Child Development* 52:932–40.

Matas, L., R. Arend, and L. A. Sroufe. 1978. Continuity of Adaptation in the Second Year: The Relationship between Quality of Attachment and Later Competence. *Child Development* 49:547–56.

Maturana, H. R., and F. J. Varela, eds. 1980. *Autopoiesis and Cognition: The Realization of the Living*. Boston, MA: Reidel.

Meyrowitz, J. 1985. *No Sense of Place*. New York: Oxford University Press.

Minuchin, P., J. Colapinto, and S. Minuchin. 2007. *Working with Families of the Poor*, 2nd ed. New York: Guilford Press.

Minuchin, S. 1974. *Families and Family Therapy*. Cambridge, MA: Harvard University Press.

Minuchin, S. 1991. The Seductions of Constructivism. *Family Therapy Networker* 15 (5):47–50.

Minuchin, S., and M. P. Nichols. 1993. *Family Healing: Tales of Hope and Renewal from Family Therapy*. New York: Free Press.

Minuchin, S., W.-Y. Lee, and G. M. Simon. 1996. *Mastering Family Therapy: Journeys of Growth and Transformation*. New York: Wiley.

Robertson, J. 1953. *A Two-Year Old Goes to the Hospital* [Film]. London: Tavistock Child Development Research Unit.

Sroufe, L. A. 1979. The Coherence of Individual Development: Early Care, Attachment and Subsequent Developmental Issues. *American Psychologist* 34:834–41.

Walters, M., B. Carter, P. Papp, and O. Silverstein. 1988. *The Invisible Web: Gender Patterns in Family Relationships*. New York: Guilford Press.

Waters, E. 1978. The Reliability and Stability of Individual Differences in Infant–Mother Attachment. *Child Development* 49:483–94.

Waters, E., J. Wippman, and L. A. Sroufe. 1979. Attachment, Positive Affect and Competence in the Peer Group: Two Studies of Construct Validation. *Child Development* 51:208–16.

Watzlawick, P., eds. 1984. *The Invented Reality*. New York: Norton.

Watzlawick, P., J. H. Beavin, and D. D. Jackson. 1967. *Pragmatics of Human Communication*. New York: Norton.

White, M., and D. Epston. 1990. *Narrative Means to Therapeutic Ends*. New York: Norton.

Wiener, N. 1948. *Cybernetics or Control and Communication in the Animal and the Machine*. Cambridge, MA: MIT Press.

CHAPTER 4

Alexander, P. C., S. Moore, and E. R. Alexander. 1991. Intergenerational Transmission of Violence. *Journal of Marriage and the Family* 53:657–67.

Amato, P. R. 1996. Explaining the Intergenerational Transmission of Divorce. *Journal of Marriage and the Family* 58:628–40.

Anonymous. 1972. Differentiation of Self in One's Family. In *Family Interaction*, J. Framo, ed. New York: Springer.

Bartle-Haring, S., and D. Probst. 2004. A Test of Bowen Theory: Emotional Reactivity and Psychological Distress in a Clinical Sample. *The American Journal of Family Therapy* 32:419–35.

Bohlander, J. R. 1995. *Differentiation of Self, Need-Fulfillment, and Psychological Well-Being in Married Women*. Unpublished doctoral dissertation, New York University.

Bowen, M. 1966. The Use of Family Theory in Clinical Practice. *Comprehensive Psychiatry* 7:345–74.

Bowen, M. 1971. Family Therapy and Family Group Therapy. In *Comprehensive Group Psychotherapy*, H. Kaplan and B. Sadock, eds. Baltimore, MD: Williams & Wilkins.

Bowen, M. 1974. Toward the Differentiation of Self in One's Family of Origin. In *Georgetown Family Symposium*, Vol. 1, F. Andres and J. Lorio, eds. Washington, DC: Department of Psychiatry, Georgetown University Medical Center.

Bowen, M. 1976. Theory in the Practice of Psychotherapy. In *Family Therapy: Theory and Practice*, P. J. Guerin, ed. New York: Gardner Press.

Carter, B., and M. McGoldrick. 1999. *The Expanded Family Life Cycle*, 3rd ed. Boston, MA: Allyn & Bacon.

Carter, E., and M. M. Orfanidis. 1976. Family Therapy with One Person and the Family Therapist's Own Family. In *Family Therapy: Theory and Practice*, P. J. Guerin, ed. New York: Gardner Press.

Coco, E. L, and L. J. Courtney. 2003. A Family Systems Approach for Preventing Adolescent Runaway Behavior. *Family Therapy* 30:39–50.

Davis, B., and L. C. Jones. 1992. Differentiation of Self and Attachment among Adult Daughters. *Issues in Mental Health Nursing* 13:321–31.

Elieson, M. V., and L. J. Rubin. 2001. Differentiation of Self and Major Depressive Disorders: A Test of Bowen Theory among Clinical, Tradition, and Internet Groups. *Family Therapy* 29:125–42.

Feng, D., R. Giarrusso, V. L. Bengston, and N. Frye. 1999. Intergenerational Transmission of Marital Quality and Marital Instability. *Journal of Marriage and the Family* 61:451–63.

Fogarty, T. F. 1976b. Marital Crisis. In *Family Therapy: Theory and Practice*, P. J. Guerin, ed. New York: Gardner Press.

Gehring, T. M., and D. Marti. 1993. The Family System Test: Differences in Perception of Family Structures between Nonclinical and Clinical Children. *Journal of Child Psychology and Psychiatry* 34:363–77.

Griffin, J. M., and R. A. Apostal. 1993. The Influence of Relationship Enhancement Training on Differentiation of Self. *Journal of Marital and Family Therapy* 19:267–72.

Guerin, P. G., L. Fay, S. Burden, and J. Kautto. 1987. *The Evaluation and Treatment of Marital Conflict: A Four-Stage Approach*. New York: Basic Books.

Guerin, P. J. 1971. A Family Affair. In *Georgetown Family Symposium*, Vol. 1. Washington, DC.

Guerin, P. J., and T. F. Fogarty. 1972. Study Your Own Family. In *The Book of Family Therapy*, A. Ferber, M. Mendelsohn, and A. Napier, eds. New York: Science House.

Guerin, P. J., T. F. Fogarty, L. F. Fay, and J. G. Kautto. 1996. *Working with Relationship Triangles: The One-Two-Three of Psychotherapy*. New York: Guilford Press.

Haber, J. E. 1984. An Investigation of the Relationship between Differentiation of Self, Complementary Psychological Need Patterns, and Marital Conflict. Unpublished doctoral dissertation, New York University.

Haber, J. E. 1993. A Construct Validity Study of a Differentiation of Self Scale. *Scholarly Inquiry for Nursing Practice* 7:165–78.

Hertlein, K. M., and J. M. Killmer. 2004. Toward Differentiated Decision-Making: Family Systems Theory with the Homeless Clinical Population. *American Journal of Family Therapy* 32:255–70.

Herz, F., ed. 1991. *Reweaving the Family Tapestry*. New York: Norton.

Johnson, S., and J. Lebow. 2000. The "Coming of Age" of Couple Therapy: A Decade Review. *Journal of Marital and Family Therapy* 26:23–38.

Kerr, M. 1971. The Importance of the Extended Family. In *Georgetown Family Symposium*, Vol. 1. Washington, DC.

Kerr, M., and M. Bowen. 1988. *Family Evaluation*. New York: Norton.

Kolbert, J. B., L. M. Crothers, and J. E. Field. 2013. Clinical Interventions with Adolescents Using a Family Systems Approach. *The Family Journal* 21:87–94.

Lerner, H. G. 1985. *The Dance of Anger: A Woman's Guide to Changing Patterns of Intimate Relationships*. New York: Harper & Row.

Lerner, H. G. 1989. *The Dance of Intimacy: A Woman's Guide to Courageous Acts of Change in Key Relationships*. New York: Harper & Row.

Licht, C., and D. Chabot. 2006. The Chabot Emotional Differentiation Scale: A Theoretically and Psychometrically Sound Instrument for Measuring Bowen's Intrapsychic Aspect of Differentiation. *Journal of Marital and Family Therapy* 32:167–80.

MacKay, L. 2012. Trauma and Bowen Family Systems Theory: Working with Adults Who Were Abused as Children. *Australian and New Zealand Journal of Family Therapy* 33:232–41.

McGoldrick, M., and R. Gerson. 1985. *Genograms in Family Assessment*. New York: Norton.

McGoldrick, M., J. Pearce, and J. Giordano. 1982. *Ethnicity in Family Therapy*. New York: Guilford Press.

Miller, R. B., L. N. Johnson, J. G. Sandberg, T. A. Stringer-Seibold, and L. Gfeller-Strouts. 2000. An Addendum to the 1997 Outcome Research Chart. *American Journal of Family Therapy* 28:347–54.

Nichols, M. P. 1986. *Turning Forty in the Eighties*. New York: Norton.

Nichols, M. P. 1987. *The Self in the System*. New York: Brunner/Mazel.

Peleg, O. 2008. The Relation between Differentiation of Self and Marital Satisfaction: What Can Be Learned from Married People over the Course of Life? *The American Journal of Family Therapy* 36:388–401.

Peleg, O., and M. Yitzhak. 2011. Differentiation of Self and Separation Anxiety: Is There a Similarity between Spouses? *Contemporary Family Therapy: An International Journal* 33:25–36.

Peleg-Popko, O. 2002. Bowen Theory: A Study of Differentiation of Self, Social Anxiety and Physiological Symptoms. *Contemporary Family Therapy* 25:355–69.

Protinsky, H., and J. K. Gilkey. 1996. An Empirical Investigation of the Construct of Personality Authority in Late Adolescent Women and Their Level of College Adjustment. *Adolescence* 31:291–6.

Richards, E. R. 1989. Self Reports of Differentiation of Self and Marital Compatibility as Related to Family Functioning in the Third and Fourth Stages of the Family Life Cycle. *Scholarly Inquiry for Nursing Practice* 3:163–75.

Sher, K. J., B. S. Gershuny, L. Peterson, and G. Raskin. 1979. The Role of Childhood Stressors in the Intergenerational Transmission of Alcohol Use Disorders. *Journal of Studies on Alcohol* 58:414–27.

Skowron, E. A. 2000. The Role of Differentiation of Self in Marital Adjustment. *Journal of Counseling Psychology* 47:229–37.

Skowron, E. A., and M. L. Friedlander. 1998. The Differentiation of Self Inventory: Development and Initial Validation. *Journal of Counseling Psychology* 45:235–46.

Troll, L., and V. L. Bengston. 1979. Generations in the Family. In *Contemporary Theories about the Family*, Vol. 1, W. R. Burr, R. Hill, F. I. Nye, and I. L. Reiss, eds. New York: Free Press.

U.S. Bureau of the Census. 2014. *Statistical Abstract of the United States*, 133rd ed. Washington, DC: U.S. Government Printing Office.

Vuchinich, S., R. E. Emery, and J. Cassidy. 1988. Family Members as Third Parties in Dyadic Family Conflict: Strategies, Alliances, and Outcomes. *Child Development* 59:1296–302.

West, J. D., J. J. Zarski, and R. Harvill. 1986. The Influence of the Family Triangle on Intimacy. *American Mental Health Counselors Association Journal* 8:166–74.

Whitbeck, L., D. Hoyt, R. Simons, R. Conger, G. Elder, F. Lorenz, and S. Huck. 1992. Intergenerational Continuity of Parental Rejection and Depressed Affect. *Journal of Personality and Social Psychology* 63:1036–45.

Whitehouse, P. J., and G. Harris. 1998. The Intergenerational Transmission of Eating Disorders. *European Eating Disorders Review* 6:238–54.

Wood, B., J. B. Watkins, J. T. Boyle, J. Nogueira, E. Zimand, and L. Carroll. 1989. The "Psychosomatic Family" Model: An Empirical and Theoretical Analysis. *Family Process* 28:399–417.

CHAPTER 5

Alexander, J., and B. Parsons. 1982. *Functional Family Therapy*. Monterey, CA: Brooks Cole.

Andersen, T. 1987. The Reflecting Team: Dialogue and Meta-Dialogue in Clinical Work. *Family Process* 26:415–7.

Boscolo, L. 1983. Final Discussion. In *Psychosocial Intervention in Schizophrenia: An International View*, H. Stierlin, L. Wynne, and M. Wirsching, eds. Berlin: Springer-Verlag.

Boscolo, L., and P. Bertrando. 1992. The Reflexive Loop of Past, Present, and Future in Systemic Therapy and Consultation. *Family Process* 31:119–33.

Boscolo, L., G. Cecchin, L. Hoffman, and P. Penn. 1987. *Milan Systemic Family Therapy*, p. 4. New York: Basic Books.

Cecchin, G. 1987. Hypothesizing, Circularity and Neutrality Revisited: An Invitation to Curiosity. *Family Process* 26:405–13.

Eron, J., and T. Lund. 1993. An Approach to How Problems Evolve and Dissolve: Integrating Narrative and Strategic Concepts. *Family Process* 32:291–309.

Eron, J., and T. Lund. 1996. *Narrative Solutions in Brief Therapy*. New York: Guilford Press.

Fisch, R. 1978. Review of Problem-Solving Therapy, by Jay Haley. *Family Process* 17:107–10.

Fisch, R., J. Weakland, and L. Segal. 1982. *The Tactics of Change*. San Francisco, CA: Jossey-Bass.

Gaulier, B., J. Margerum, J. A. Price, and J. Windell. 2007. *Defusing the High-Conflict Divorce: A Treatment Guide for Working with Angry Couples*. Atascadero, CA: Impact.

Goldman, A., and L. Greenberg. 1992. Comparison of Integrated Systemic and Emotionally Focused Approaches to Couples Therapy. *Journal of Consulting and Clinical Psychology* 60:962–9.

Haley, J. 1963. *Strategies of Psychotherapy*, pp. 193–194. New York: Grune & Stratton.

Haley, J. 1973. *Uncommon Therapy*. New York: Norton.

Haley, J. 1976. *Problem-Solving Therapy*, p. 117. San Francisco, CA: Jossey-Bass.

Haley, J. 1981. *Reflections on Therapy*. Chevy Chase, MD: Family Therapy Institute of Washington, DC.

Haley, J. 1984. *Ordeal Therapy*, p. 5. San Francisco, CA: Jossey-Bass.

Haley, J. 1996. *Learning and Teaching Therapy*. New York: Guilford Press.

Haley, J., and M. Richeport-Haley. 2007. *Directive Family Therapy*. New York: Haworth Press.

Hoffman, L. 1983. A Co-Evolutionary Framework for Systemic Family Therapy. In *Diagnosis and Assessment in Family Therapy*, J. Hansen and B. Keeney, eds. Rockville, MD: Aspen Systems. (Adapted from)

Jackson, D. D. 1965. Family Rules: The Marital Quid Pro Quo. *Archives of General Psychiatry* 12:589–94.

Jackson, D. D. 1967. Aspects of Conjoint Family Therapy. In *Family Therapy and Disturbed Families*, G. H. Zuk and I. Boszormenyi-Nagy, eds. Palo Alto, CA: Science and Behavior Books.

Jackson, D. D., and J. H. Weakland. 1961. Conjoint Family Therapy: Some Consideration on Theory, Technique, and Results. *Psychiatry* 24:30–45.

Keim, J. 1998. Strategic Family Therapy. In *Case Studies in Couple and Family Therapy*, F. Dattilio, ed. New York: Guilford Press.

Keim, J., and J. Lappin. 2002. Structural-Strategic Marital Therapy. In *Clinical Handbook of Couple Therapy*, A. S. Gurman and N. S. Jacobson, eds. New York: Guilford Press.

Langsley, D., P. Machotka, and K. Flomenhaft. 1971. Avoiding Mental Hospital Admission: A Follow-Up Study. *American Journal of Psychiatry* 127:1391–4.

Madanes, C. 1981. *Strategic Family Therapy*. San Francisco, CA: Jossey-Bass.

Madanes, C. 1984. *Behind the One-Way Mirror*. San Francisco, CA: Jossey-Bass.

Marayuma, M. 1968. The Second Cybernetics: Deviation-Amplifying Mutual Causal Processes. In *Modern Systems Research for the Behavioral Scientist*, W. Buckley, ed. Chicago, IL: Aldine.

Papp, P. 1980. The Greek Chorus and Other Techniques of Paradoxical Therapy. *Family Process* 19:45–57.

Parsons, B., and J. Alexander. 1973. Short-Term Family Intervention: A Therapy Outcome Study. *Journal of Consulting and Clinical Psychology* 41:195–201.

Penn, P. 1982. Circular Questioning. *Family Process* 21:267–80.

Penn, P. 1985. Feed-Forward: Further Questioning, Future Maps. *Family Process* 24:299–310.

Price, J. 1996. *Power and Compassion: Working with Difficult Adolescents and Abused Parents*. New York: Guilford Press.

Robbins, M. S., J. F. Alexander, and C. W. Turner. 2000. Disrupting Defensive Family Interactions in Family Therapy with Delinquent Adolescents. *Journal of Family Psychology* 14:688–701.

Robbins, M. S., D. J. Feaster, V. E. Horigian, M. J. Rohrbaugh, V. Shoham, K. Bachrach, and J. Szapocznik. 2012. Brief Strategic Family Therapy versus Treatment as Usual: Results of a Multisite Randomized Trial for Substance Using Adolescents. *Journal of Consulting and Clinical Psychology* 79:713–27.

Robbins, M. S., C. C. Mayorga, W. B. Mitrani, J. Szapocznik, C. W. Turner, and J. F. Alexander. 2008. Adolescent and Parent Alliances with Therapists in Brief Strategic Family Therapy with Drug-Abusing Hispanic Adolescents. *Journal Marital and Family Therapy* 34:316–28.

Robbins, M. S., C. W. Turner, J. F. Alexander, and G. A. Perez. 2003. Alliance and Dropout in Family Therapy for Adolescents with Behavior Problems: Individual and Systemic Effects. *Journal Family Psychology* 17:534–44.

Ruesch, J., and G. Bateson. 1951. *Communication: The Social Matrix of Psychiatry*. New York: Norton.

Rynes, K. N., M. J. Rohrbaugh, F. Lebensohn-Chialvo, and V. Shoham. 2014. Parallel Demand/ Withdraw Processes in Family Therapy for Adolescent Drug Use. *Psychology of Addictive Behaviors* 28:420–30.

Santisteban, D. A., J. D. Coatsworth, A. Perez-Vidal, W. M. Kurtines, S. J. Schwartz, A. LaPerrier, and J. Szapocznik. 2003. Efficacy of Brief Strategic Family Therapy in Modifying Hispanic Adolescent Behavior Problems and Substance Use. *Journal of Family Psychology* 17:121–33.

Selvini Palazzoli, M. 1993. *Major Mental Disorders, Distorted Reality and Family Secrets*. Unpublished manuscript.

Selvini Palazzoli, M. 1981. *Self-Starvation: From the Intrapsychic to the Transpersonal Approach to Anorexia Nervosa*. New York: Jason Aronson.

Selvini Palazzoli, M. 1986. Towards a General Model of Psychotic Games. *Journal of Marital and Family Therapy* 12:339–49.

Selvini Palazzoli, M., L. Boscolo, G. Cecchin, and G. Prata. 1978a. *Paradox and Counterparadox*. New York: Jason Aronson.

Selvini Palazzoli, M., L. Boscolo, G. Cecchin, and G. Prata. 1978b. A Ritualized Prescription in Family Therapy: Odd Days and Even Days. *Journal of Marriage and Family Counseling* 4:3–9.

Selvini Palazzoli, M., L. Boscolo, G. Cecchin, and G. Prata. 1980. Hypothesizing—Circularity—Neutrality: Three Guidelines for the Conductor of the Session. *Family Process* 19:3–12.

Selvini Palazzoli, M., and M. Viaro. 1988. The Anorectic Process in the Family: A Six-Stage Model as a Guide for Individual Therapy. *Family Process* 27:129–48.

Shoham, V., R. R. Bootzin, M. R. Rohrbaugh, and H. Urry. 1996. Paradoxical versus Relaxation Treatment for Insomnia: The Moderating Role of Reactance. *Sleep Research* 24a:365.

Shoham, V., and M. J. Rohrbaugh. 2002. Brief Strategic Couple Therapy. In *Clinical Handbook of Couple Therapy*, A. S. Gurman and N. S. Jacobson, eds. New York: Guilford Press.

Shoham, V., M. J. Rohrbaugh, T. R. Stickle, and T. Jacob. 1998. Demand-Withdraw Couple Interaction Moderates Retention in Cognitive-Behavioral versus Family-Systems Treatments for Alcoholism. *Journal of Family Psychology* 12:557–77.

Shoham, V., M. J. Rohrbaugh, S. E. Trost, and M. Muramoto. 2006. A Family Consultation Intervention for Health-Compromised Smokers. *Journal of Substance Abuse Treatment* 31:395–402.

Shoham-Salomon, V., R. Avner, and R. Neeman. 1989. You're Changed If You Do and Changed If You Don't: Mechanisms Underlying Paradoxical Interventions. *Journal of Consulting and Clinical Psychology* 57:590–8.

Shoham-Salomon, V., and A. Jancourt. 1985. Differential Effectiveness of Paradoxical Interventions for More versus Less Stress-Prone Individuals. *Journal of Counseling Psychology* 32:449–53.

Stanton, D., T. Todd, et al. 1982. *The Family Therapy of Drug Abuse and Addiction.* New York: Guilford Press.

Szapocznik, J., A. Perez-Vidal, A. L. Brickman, F. H. Foote, O. Heris, and W. M. Kurtines. 1988. Engaging Adolescent Drug Abusers and Their Families in Treatment: A Strategic Structural Systems Approach. *Journal of Consulting and Clinical Psychology* 56:552–7.

Tomm, K. 1987a. Interventive Interviewing: Part I. Strategizing as a Fourth Guideline for the Therapist. *Family Process* 26:3–13.

Tomm, K. 1987b. Interventive Interviewing: Part II. Reflexive Questioning as a Means to Enable Self-Healing. *Family Process* 26:167–84.

Watzlawick, P., J. Beavin, and D. Jackson. 1967. *Pragmatics of Human Communication.* New York: Norton.

Watzlawick, P., J. Weakland, and R. Fisch. 1974. *Change: Principles of Problem Formation and Problem Resolution.* New York: Norton.

Weakland, J., and R. Fisch. 1992. Brief Therapy— MRI Style. In *The First Session in Brief Therapy,* S. H. Budman, N. F. Hoyt, and S. Friedman, eds. New York: Guilford Press.

Weakland, J., and W. Ray, eds. 1995. *Propagations: Thirty Years of Influence from the Mental Research Institute.* Binghamton, NY: Haworth Press.

CHAPTER 6

Barkley, R., D. Guevremont, A. Anastopoulos, and K. Fletcher. 1992. A Comparison of Three Family Therapy Programs for Treating Family Conflicts in Adolescents with Attention-Deficit Hyperactivity Disorder. *Journal of Consulting and Clinical Psychology* 60:450–63.

Campbell, T., and J. Patterson. 1995. The Effectiveness of Family Interventions in the Treatment of Physical Illness. *Journal of Marital and Family Therapy* 21:545–84.

Chamberlain, P., and J. Rosicky. 1995. The Effectiveness of Family Therapy in the Treatment of Adolescents with Conduct Disorders and Delinquency. *Journal of Marital and Family Therapy* 21:441–59.

Eisler, I., M. Simic, G. F. Russell, and C. Dare. 2007. A Randomized Controlled Treatment Trial of Two Forms of Family Therapy in Adolescent Anorexia Nervosa: A Five-Year Follow-Up. *Journal of Child Psychology and Psychiatry* 6:552–60.

Elizur, J., and S. Minuchin. 1989. *Institutionalizing Madness: Families, Therapy, and Society.* New York: Basic Books.

Grief, G., and L. Dreschler. 1993. Common Issues for Parents in a Methadone Maintenance Group. *Journal of Substance Abuse Treatment* 10:335–9.

Jones, K. E., C. L. Lettenberger, and K. Wickel 2011. A Structural/Strategic Lens in the Treatment of Children with Obesity. *The Family Journal* 14:340–6.

Lock, J., D. LeGrange, W. Agras, and C. Dare. 2001. *Treatment Manual for Anorexia Nervosa: A Family-Based Approach.* New York: Guilford Press.

Lock, J., D. LeGrange, W. Agras, A. Moye, S. W. Bryson, and B. Jo. 2010. Randomized Clinical Trial Comparing Family-Based Treatment with Adolescent-Focused Individual Therapy for Adolescents with Anorexia Nervosa. *Archives of General Psychiatry* 10:1025–32.

Minuchin, S. 1974. *Families and Family Therapy,* p. 9. Cambridge, MA: Harvard University Press.

Minuchin, S., L. Baker, B. Rosman, R. Liebman, L. Milman, and T. C. Todd. 1975. A Conceptual Model of Psychosomatic Illness in Children. *Archives of General Psychiatry* 32:1031–8.

Minuchin, S., and H. C. Fishman. 1981. *Family Therapy Techniques.* Cambridge, MA: Harvard University Press.

Minuchin, S., B. Montalvo, B. Guerney, B. Rosman, and F. Schumer. 1967. *Families of the Slums.* New York: Basic Books.

Minuchin, S., and M. P. Nichols. 1993. *Family Healing: Tales of Hope and Renewal from Family Therapy,* p. 121. New York: Free Press.

Minuchin, S., M. P. Nichols, and W.-Y. Lee. 2007. *A Four-Step Model for Assessing Families and Couples: From Symptom to Psyche.* Boston, MA: Allyn & Bacon.

Minuchin, S., B. Rosman, and L. Baker. 1978. *Psychosomatic Families: Anorexia Nervosa in Context,* p. 91. Cambridge, MA: Harvard University Press.

Mitrani, V. B., B. E. McCabe, M. J. Burns, and D. J. Feaster. 2012. Family Mechanisms of Structural Ecosystems Therapy for HIV-Positive Women in Drug Recovery. *Health Psychology* 31:591–600.

Nichols, M. P., and S. Tafuri. 2013. Techniques of Structural Family Assessment: A Qualitative Analysis of How Experts Promote a Systemic Perspective. *Family Process* 52:207–15.

Robbins, M. S., J. F. Alexander, and C. W. Turner. 2000. Disrupting Defensive Family Interactions in Family Therapy with Delinquent Adolescents. *Journal of Family Psychology* 14:688–701.

Robbins, M. S., C. Mayorga, V. Mitrani, J. Szapocznik, C. Turner, and J. Alexander. 2008. Parent Alliances with Therapists in Brief Adolescents. *Journal of Marital and Family Therapy* 34:316–28.

Robbins, M. S., C. W. Turner, J. F. Alexander, and G. A. Perez. 2003. Alliance and Dropout in Family Therapy for Adolescents with Behavior Problems: Individual and Systemic Effects. *Journal Family Psychology* 17:534–44.

Santisteban, D., J. Coatsworth, A. Perez-Vidal, W. Kurtines, S. Schwartz, A. LaPerriere, and J. Szapocznik. 2003. The Efficacy of Brief Strategic Family Therapy in Modifying Hispanic Adolescent Behavior Problems and Substance Use. *Journal of Family Psychology* 17 (1):121–33.

Santisteban, D., J. Coatsworth, A. Perez-Vidal, V. Mitrani, M. Jean-Gilles, and J. Szapocznik. 1997. Brief Structural/Strategic Family Therapy with African American and Hispanic High-Risk Youth. *Journal of Community Psychology* 25:453–71.

Simon, G. M. 1995. A Revisionist Rendering of Structural Family Therapy. *Journal of Marital and Family Therapy* 21:17–26.

Skelton, J. A., C. Buehler, M. B. Irby, and J. G. Grzywacz. 2012. Where are Family Theories in Family-Based Obesity Treatment? *International Journal of Obesity* 36:891–900.

Stanton, M. D., and T. C. Todd. 1979. Structural Family Therapy with Drug Addicts. In *The Family Therapy of Drug and Alcohol Abuse*, E. Kaufman and P. Kaufmann, eds. New York: Gardner Press.

Szapocznik, J., A. Perez-Vidal, A. L. Brickman, F. H. Foote, O. Heris, and W. M. Kurtines. 1988. Engaging Adolescent Drug Abusers and Their Families in Treatment: A Strategic Structural Systems Approach.

Journal of Consulting and Clinical Psychology 56:552–7.

Szapocznik, J., A. Rio, E. Murray, R. Cohen, M. Scopetta, A. Rivas-Vazquez, et al. 1989. Structural Family versus Psychodynamic Child Therapy for Problematic Hispanic Boys. *Journal of Consulting and Clinical Psychology* 57:571–8.

Weaver, A., C. G. Greeno, S. C. Marcus, R. A. Fusco, T. Zimmerman, and C. Anderson. 2013. Effects of Structural Family Therapy on Child and Maternal Mental Health Symptomatology. *Research on Social Work Practice* 23:294–303.

CHAPTER 7

Adamson, N. J. 2013. Emotionally Focused Therapy with Couples Facing Breast Cancer: A Theoretical Foundation and Descriptive Case Study. *Journal of Psychosocial Oncology* 31:712–26.

Andreas, S. 1991. *Virginia Satir: The Patterns of Her Magic*. Palo Alto, CA: Science and Behavior Books.

Arad, D. 2004. If Your Mother Were an Animal, What Animal Would She Be? Creating Play Stories in Family Therapy: The Animal Attribution Story-Telling Technique (AASTT). *Family Process* 43:249–63.

Bing, E. 1970. The Conjoint Family Drawing. *Family Process* 9:173–94.

Bowlby, J. 1969. *Attachment and Loss: Vol. 1. Attachment*. New York: Basic Books.

Bowlby, J. 1988. *A Secure Base*. New York: Basic Books.

Denton, W. H., B. R. Burleson, T. E. Clark, C. P. Rodriguez, and B. V. Hobbs. 2000. A Randomized Trail of Emotion-Focused Therapy for Couples in a Training Clinic. *Journal of Marital and Family Therapy* 26:65–78.

Dessaulles, A., S. M. Johnson, and W. H. Denton. 2003. Emotion-Focused Therapy for Couples in the Treatment of Depression: A Pilot Study. *The American Journal of Family Therapy* 31:245–53.

Duhl, B. S., and F. J. Duhl. 1981. Integrative Family Therapy. In *Handbook of Family Therapy*, A. S. Gurman and D. P. Kniskern, eds. New York: Brunner/Mazel.

Duhl, F. J., D. Kantor, and B. S. Duhl. 1973. Learning, Space and Action in Family Therapy: A Primer of Sculpture. In *Techniques of Family Psycho-therapy*, D. A. Bloch, ed. New York: Grune & Stratton.

Geddes, M., and J. Medway. 1977. The Symbolic Drawing of Family Life Space. *Family Process* 16:219–28.

Gehrke, S., and M. Kirschenbaum. 1967. Survival Patterns in Conjoint Family Therapy. *Family Process* 6:67–80.

Gil, E. 1994. *Play in Family Therapy*. New York: Guilford Press.

Greenberg, L. S., C. L. Ford, L. Alden, and S. M. Johnson. 1993. In-Session Change in Emotionally Focused Therapy. *Journal of Consulting and Clinical Psychology* 61:78–84.

Greenberg, L. S., and S. M. Johnson. 1985. Emotionally Focused Couple Therapy: An Affective Systemic Approach. In *Handbook of Family and Marital Therapy*, N. S. Jacobson and A. S. Gurman, eds. New York: Guilford Press.

Greenberg, L. S., and S. M. Johnson. 1986. Affect in Marital Therapy. *Journal of Marital and Family Therapy* 12:1–10.

Greenberg, L. S., and S. M. Johnson. 1988. *Emotionally Focused Therapy for Couples*. New York: Guilford Press.

Greenberg, L. S., and S. M. Johnson. 2010. *Emotionally Focused Therapy for Couples*. New York: Guilford Press.

Greenberg, L. S., S. Warwar, and W. Malcolm. 2010. Emotion-Focused Couples Therapy and the Facilitation of Forgiveness. *Journal of Marital and Family Therapy* 36:28–42.

Irwin, E., and E. Malloy. 1975. Family Puppet Interview. *Family Process* 14:179–91.

Johnson, S. M. 1998. Emotionally Focused Couple Therapy. In *Case Studies in Couple and Family Therapy*, F. M. Dattilio, ed. New York: Guilford Press.

Johnson, S. M. 2003. The Revolution in Couple Therapy: A Practitioner–Scientist Perspective. *Journal of Marital and Family Therapy* 29:365–84.

Johnson, S. M. 2004. The Practice of Emotionally Focused Couple Therapy: Creating Connection, 2nd ed. New York: Brunner-Routledge.

Johnson, S., B. Bradley, J. Furrow, A. Lee, G. Palmer, D. Tilley, and S. Woolley. 2005. *Becoming an Emotionally Focused Therapist: The Workbook*. New York: Brunner/Routledge.

Johnson, S. M., and W. Denton. 2002. Emotionally Focused Couple Therapy: Creating Secure Connections. In *Clinical Handbook of Couple Therapy*, 3rd ed., A. S. Gurman and N. S. Jacobson, eds. New York: Guilford Press.

Johnson, S. M., and L. S. Greenberg. 1985. Emotionally Focused Couples Therapy: An Outcome Study. *Journal of Marital and Family Therapy* 11:313–7.

Johnson, S. M., and L. S. Greenberg. 1988. Relating Process to Outcome in Marital Therapy. *Journal of Marital and Family Therapy* 14:175–83.

Johnson, S. M., J. Hunsley, L. Greenberg, and D. Schindler. 1999. Emotionally Focused Couples Therapy: Status and Challenges. *Clinical Psychology: Science and Practice* 6:67–79, p. 70.

Johnson, S. M., C. Maddeaux, and J. Blouin. 1998. Emotionally Focused Therapy for Bulimia: Changing Attachment Patterns. *Psychotherapy* 35:238–47.

Kaplan, M. L., and N. R. Kaplan. 1978. Individual and Family Growth: A Gestalt Approach. *Family Process* 17:195–205.

Kempler, W. 1968. Experiential Psychotherapy with Families. *Family Process* 7:88–89, p. 97.

Kempler, W. 1973. *Principles of Gestalt Family Therapy*. Oslo: Nordahls.

Kempler, W. 1981. *Experiential Psychotherapy with Families*. New York: Brunner/Mazel.

Kwiatkowska, H. Y. 1967. Family Art Therapy. *Family Process* 6:37–55.

Laing, R. D. 1967. *The Politics of Experience*. New York: Ballantine.

Lieberman, M. A., I. D. Yalom, and M. B. Miles. 1973. *Encounter Groups: First Facts*. New York: Basic Books.

Mahrer, A. R. 1982. *Experiential Psychotherapy: Basic Practices*. New York: Brunner/Mazel.

Marcuse, H. 1955. *Eros and Civilization*. New York: Beacon Press.

McLean, L. M., T. Walton, G. Rodin, M. Epslen, and J. M. Jones. 2013. A Couple-Based Intervention for Patients and Caregivers Facing End-Stage Cancer: Outcomes of a Randomized Controlled Trial. *Psycho-Oncology* 2:28–38.

Napier, A. Y., and C. A. Whitaker. 1978. *The Family Crucible*. New York: Harper & Row.

Nichols, M. P., and M. Zax. 1977. *Catharsis in Psychotherapy*. New York: Gardner Press.

Papp, P., M. Scheinkman, and J. Malpas. 2013. Breaking the Mold: Sculpting Impasses in Couples Therapy. *Family Process* 52:33–45.

Pierce, R., M. P. Nichols, and J. DuBrin. 1983. *Emotional Expression in Psychotherapy*. New York: Gardner Press.

Rogers, C. R. 1951. *Client-Centered Therapy*. Boston, MA: Houghton Mifflin.

Satir, V. M. 1964. *Conjoint Family Therapy*. Palo Alto, CA: Science and Behavior Books.

Satir, V. M. 1972. *Peoplemaking*, p. 12. Palo Alto, CA: Science and Behavior Books.

Satir, V. M., and M. Baldwin. 1983. *Satir Step by Step: A Guide to Creating Change in Families*. Palo Alto, CA: Science and Behavior Books. (Adapted from)

Schwartz, R. C. 1995. *Internal Family Systems Therapy*. New York: Guilford Press.

Schwartz, R. C. 1998. Internal Family Systems Therapy. In *Case Studies in Couple and Family Therapy*, F. M. Dattilio, ed. New York: Guilford Press.

Schwartz, R. C. 2001. *Introduction to the Internal Family Systems Model*. Oak Park, IL: Trailheads Publications.

Simon, R. 1989. Reaching Out to Life: An Interview with Virginia Satir. *The Family Therapy Networker* 13 (1):36–43, pp. 38–39. (Quoted in).

Sullivan, H. S. 1953. *The Interpersonal Theory of Psychiatry*. New York: Norton.

Tie, S., and S. Poulsen. 2013. Emotionally Focused Couple Therapy with Couples Facing Terminal Illness. *Contemporary Family Therapy: An International Journal* 35:557–67.

Whitaker, C. A. 1958. Psychotherapy with Couples. *American Journal of Psychotherapy* 12:18–23.

Whitaker, C. A. 1967. The Growing Edge. In *Techniques of Family Therapy*, J. Haley and L. Hoffman, eds. New York: Basic Books.

Whitaker, C. A. 1975. Psychotherapy of the Absurd: With a Special Emphasis on the Psychotherapy of Aggression. *Family Process* 14:1–16.

Whitaker, C. A. 1976a. The Hindrance of Theory in Clinical Work. In *Family Therapy: Theory and Practice*, P. J. Guerin, ed. New York: Gardner Press.

Whitaker, C. A. 1976b. A Family Is a Four-Dimensional Relationship. In *Family Therapy: Theory and Practice*, P. J. Guerin, ed. New York: Gardner Press.

Whitaker, C. A., and D. V. Keith. 1981. Symbolic-Experiential Family Therapy. In *Handbook of Family Therapy*, A. S. Gurman and D. P. Kniskern, eds. New York: Brunner/Mazel.

Whitaker, C. A., and T. P. Malone. 1953. *The Roots of Psychotherapy*. New York: Blakiston.

Whitaker, C. A., J. Warkentin, and T. P. Malone. 1959. The Involvement of the Professional Therapist. In *Case Studies in Counseling and Psychotherapy*, A. Burton, ed. Englewood Cliffs, NJ: Prentice Hall.

CHAPTER 8

Ackerman, N. W. 1958. *The Psychodynamics of Family Life*. New York: Basic Books.

Ackerman, N. W. 1966. *Treating the Troubled Family*. New York: Basic Books.

Allen, D. M. 2001. Integrating Individual and Family Systems Psychotherapy to Treat Borderline Personality Disorder. *Journal of Psychotherapy Integration* 11:313–31.

Barnhill, L. R., and D. Longo. 1978. Fixation and Regression in the Family Life Cycle. *Family Process* 17:469–78.

Bentovim, A., and W. Kinston. 1991. Focal Family Therapy. In *Handbook of Family Therapy*, Vol. II, A. S. Gurman and D. P. Kniskern, eds. New York: Brunner/Mazel.

Blanck, G., and R. Blanck. 1972. Toward a Psychoanalytic Developmental Psychology. *Journal of the American Psychoanalytic Association* 20:668–710.

Blum, H. P. 1987. Shared Fantasy and Reciprocal Identification: General Considerations and Gender Disorder. In *Unconscious Fantasy: Myth and Reality*, H. P. Blum et al., eds. New York: International Universities Press.

Boszormenyi-Nagy, I. 1987. *Foundations of Contextual Therapy*. New York: Brunner/Mazel.

Boszormenyi-Nagy, I., J. Grunebaum, and D. Ulrich. 1991. Contextual Therapy. In *Handbook of Family*

Therapy, Vol. II, A. S. Gurman and D. P. Kniskern, eds. New York: Brunner/Mazel.

Boszormenyi-Nagy, I., and D. N. Ulrich. 1981. Contextual Family Therapy. In *Handbook of Family Therapy*, A. S. Gurman and D. P. Kniskern, eds. New York: Brunner/Mazel.

Bowen, M. 1965. Family Psychotherapy with Schizophrenia in the Hospital and in Private Practice. In *Intensive Family Therapy*, I. Boszormenyi-Nagy and J. L. Framo, eds. New York: Harper & Row.

Catherall, D. R. 1992. Working with Projective Identification in Couples. *Family Process* 31:355–67.

Christogiorgos, S., E. Stavrou, M. A. Widdershoven-Zervaki, and J. Tsiantis. 2010. Brief Psychodynamic Psychotherarpy in Adolescent Depression: Two Case Studies. *Psychoanalytic Psychotherapy* 24:262–78.

Cutner, N. 2014. The Impact of Insecure Attachment on Mothering: A New Mother's Story. *Journal of Infant, Child & Adolescent Psychiatry* 13:37–50.

Dare, C., I. Eisler, G. Russell, J. Treasure, and L. Dodge. 2001. Psychological Therapies for Adults with Anorexia Nervosa: Randomised Controlled Trial of Outpatient Treatments. *The British Journal of Psychiatry* 178:216–21.

Diaz Bonino, S. 2013. From Torment to Hope: Countertransference in Parent-Infant Psychoanalytic Psychotherapy. *Infant Observation* 16:59–75.

Dicks, H. V. 1963. Object Relations Theory and Marital Studies. *British Journal of Medical Psychology* 36:125–9.

Dicks, H. V. 1967. *Marital Tensions*. New York: Basic Books.

Emanuel, L. 2012. Holding On; Being Held; Letting Go: The Relevance of Bion's Thinking for Psychoanalytic Work with Parents, Infants and Children under Five. *Journal of Child Psychotherapy* 38:268–83.

Fairbairn, W. D. 1952. *An Object-Relations Theory of the Personality*. New York: Basic Books.

Framo, J. L. 1970. Symptoms from a Family Transactional Viewpoint. In *Family Therapy in Transition*, N. W. Ackerman, ed. Boston: Little, Brown.

Freud, S. 1905. Fragment of an Analysis of a Case of Hysteria. In *Collected Papers*. New York: Basic Books.

Freud, S. 1909. Analysis of a Phobia in a Five-Year-Old Boy. In *Collected Papers*, Vol. III. New York: Basic Books.

Freud, S. 1921. Group Psychology and the Analysis of the Ego. In *Standard*, vol. 17, ed. London: Hogarth Press.

Greenson, R. R. 1967. *The Theory and Technique of Psychoanalysis*. New York: International Universities Press.

Guntrip, H. 1969. *Schizoid Phenomena, Object Relations Theory and the Self*. New York: International Universities Press.

Jackson, D. D. 1967. The Individual and the Larger Context. *Family Process* 6:139–47.

Jacobson, E. 1954. *The Self and the Object World*. New York: International Universities Press.

Katz, B. 1981. Separation–Individuation and Marital Therapy. *Psychotherapy: Theory, Research and Practice* 18:195–203.

Kirschner, D., and S. Kirschner. 1986. *Comprehensive Family Therapy: An Integration of Systemic and Psychodynamic Treatment Models*. New York: Brunner/Mazel.

Klein, M. 1946. Notes on Some Schizoid Mechanisms. *International Journal of Psycho-Analysis* 27:99–110.

Kohut, H. 1971. *The Analysis of the Self*. New York: International Universities Press.

Kohut, H. 1977. *The Restoration of the Self*. New York: International Universities Press.

Langs, R. 1982. *Psychotherapy: A Basic Text*. New York: Jason Aronson.

Lidz, T., A. Cornelison, and S. Fleck. 1965. *Schizophrenia and the Family*. New York: International Universities Press.

Mackay, J. L. 2002. A Psychodynamic Understanding of Trauma and Adolescence: A Case Study. *Southern African Journal of Child and Adolescent Mental Health* 14:24–36.

Mahler, M. S., F. Pine, and A. Bergman. 1975. *The Psychological Birth of the Human Infant*. New York: Basic Books.

Meissner, W. W. 1978. The Conceptualization of Marriage and Family Dynamics from a Psychoanalytic Perspective. In *Marriage and Marital Therapy*, T. J. Paolino and B. S. McCrady, eds. New York: Brunner/Mazel.

Minuchin, S. 1989. Personal Communication. In *Institutionalizing Madness*, J. Elizur and S. Minuchin, eds. New York: Basic Books.

Morey, C. M. 2008. Impaired Agency in Schizophrenia: Family Therapy with a Young Adult Patient. *Journal of Family Psychotherapy* 19:345–57.

Nichols, M. P. 1987. *The Self in the System*. New York: Brunner/Mazel.

Oberndorf, C. P. 1938. Psychoanalysis of Married Couples. *Psychoanalytic Review* 25:453–75.

Paris, E. 2013. Interrupting Trauma and Advancing Development: Considering Parent Education in Contemporary Psychoanalytic Treatment. *Clinical Social Work Journal* 41:84–92.

Salomonsson, B. 2013. Transference in Parent-Infant Psychoanalytic Treatments. *The International Journal of Psychoanalysis* 94:767–92.

Sander, F. M. 1979. *Individual and Family Therapy: Toward an Integration*. New York: Jason Aronson.

Sander, F. M. 1989. Marital Conflict and Psychoanalytic Therapy in the Middle Years. In *The Middle Years: New Psychoanalytic Perspectives*, J. Oldham and R. Liebert, eds. New Haven, CT: Yale University Press.

Scharff, D., and J. Scharff. 1987. *Object Relations Family Therapy*. New York: Jason Aronson.

Segal, H. 1964. *Introduction to the Work of Melanie Klein*. New York: Basic Books.

Shapiro, R. L. 1968. Action and Family Interaction in Adolescence. In *Modern Psychoanalysis*, J. Marmor, ed. New York: Basic Books.

Skynner, A. C. R. 1976. *Systems of Family and Marital Psychotherapy*. New York: Brunner/Mazel.

Skynner, A. C. R. 1981. An Open-Systems, Group Analytic Approach to Family Therapy. In *Handbook of Family Therapy*, A. S. Gurman and D. P. Kniskern, eds. New York: Brunner/Mazel.

Slipp, S. 1984. *Object Relations: A Dynamic Bridge between Individual and Family Treatment*. New York: Jason Aronson.

Slipp, S. 1988. *Technique and Practice of Object Relations Family Therapy*. New York: Jason Aronson.

Stein, M. 1956. The Marriage Bond. *Psychoanalytic Quarterly* 25:238–59.

Stern, D. 1985. *The Interpersonal World of the Infant*. New York: Basic Books.

Stierlin, H. 1977. *Psychoanalysis and Family Therapy*. New York: Jason Aronson.

Sullivan, H. S. 1953. *The Interpersonal Theory of Psychiatry*. New York: Norton.

Szasz, T. S. 1961. *The Myth of Mental Illness*. New York: Hoeber-Harper.

Trowell, J., I. Joffe, J. Campbell, C. Clemente, F. Almqvist, M. Soininem, et al. 2007. Childhood Depression: A Place for Psychotherapy. An Outcome Study Comparing Individual Psychodynamic Psychotherapy and Family Therapy. *European Journal of Child and Adolescent Psychiatry* 16:157–67.

Vogel, E. F., and N. W. Bell. 1960. The Emotionally Disturbed as the Family Scapegoat. In *The Family*, N. W. Bell and E. F. Vogel, eds. Glencoe, IL: Free Press.

Winnicott, D. W. 1965a. *The Maturational Process and the Facilitating Environment: Studies in the Theory of Emotional Development*. New York: International Universities Press.

Winnicott, D. W. 1965b. The Maturational Process and the Facilitating Environment: Studies in the Theory of Emotional Development. New York: International Universities Press.

Wynne, L. C. 1965. Some Indications and Contradictions for Exploratory Family Therapy. In *Intensive Family Therapy*, I. Boszormenyi-Nagy and J. L. Framo, eds. New York: Harper & Row.

Wynne, L., I. Ryckoff, J. Day, and S. Hirsch. 1958. Pseudomutuality in the Family Relations of Schizophrenics. *Psychiatry* 21:205–20.

Zinner, J., and R. Shapiro. 1976. Projective Identification as a Mode of Perception and Behavior in Families of Adolescents. *International Journal of Psychoanalysis* 53:523–30.

CHAPTER 9

Alexander, J. F., and B. V. Parsons. 1973. Short-Term Behavioral Intervention with Delinquent Families: Impact on Family Process and Recidivism. *Journal of Abnormal Psychology* 51:219–25.

Alexander, J., and B. V. Parsons. 1982. *Functional Family Therapy*. Pacific Grove, CA: Brooks/Cole.

Arunothong, W., and S. Waewsawangwong. 2012. An Evaluation Study of Parent Management Training (PMT) in Northern Thailand. *ASEAN Journal of Psychiatry* 13:31–48.

Azrin, N. H., J. B. Naster, and R. Jones. 1973. Reciprocity Counseling: A Rapid Learning-Based Procedure for Marital Counseling. *Behavior Research and Therapy* 11:365–83.

Baer, D. M., and J. A. Sherman. 1969. Reinforcement Control of Generalized Imitation in Young Children. *Journal of Experimental Child Psychology* 1:37–49.

Bandura, A. 1969. *Principles of Behavior Modification.* New York: Holt, Rinehart & Winston.

Bank, L., J. H. Marlowe, J. B. Reid, G. R. Patterson, and M. R. Weinrott. 1991. A Comparative Evaluation of Parent Training for Families of Chronic Delinquents. *Journal of Abnormal Child Psychology* 19:15–33.

Barton, C., and J. F. Alexander. 1981. Functional Family Therapy. In *Handbook of Family Therapy*, A. S. Gurman and D. P. Kniskern, eds. New York: Brunner/Mazel.

Baucom, D. H., N. B. Epstein, and J. LaTaillade. 2002. Cognitive-Behavioral Couple Therapy. In *Clinical Handbook of Couple Therapy*, 3rd ed., A. S. Gurman and N. S. Jacobson, eds. New York: Guilford Press.

Baucom, D. H., V. Shoham, K. T. Mueser, A. D. Daiuto, and T. R. Stickle. 1998. Empirically Supported Couples and Family Therapies for Adult Problems. *Journal of Consulting and Clinical Psychology* 66:53–88.

Baumann, A. A., M. M. Rodriguez, and N. G. Amador. 2014. Parent Management Training-Oregon Model in Mexico City: Integrating Cultural Adaptation Activities in an Implementation Model. *Clinical Psychology: Science and Practice* 21:32–47.

Beck, A. T. 1976. *Cognitive Therapy and the Emotional Disorders.* New York: International Universities Press.

Beck, A. T., A. J. Rush, B. F. Shaw, and G. Emery. 1979. *Cognitive Therapy of Depression.* New York: Guilford Press.

Christophersen, E. R., C. M. Arnold, D. W. Hill, and H. R. Quilitch. 1972. The Home Point System: Token Reinforcement Procedures for Application by Parents of Children with Behavioral Problems. *Journal of Applied Behavioral Analysis* 5:485–97.

Crits-Christoph, P., E. Frank, D. L. Chambless, F. Brody, and J. F. Karp. 1995. Training in Empirically Validated Treatments: What Are Clinical Psychology Students Learning? *Professional Psychology: Research and Practice* 26:514–22.

Crowe, M. 1988. Indications for Family, Marital, and Sexual Therapy. In *Handbook of Behavioral Family Therapy*, I. R. H. Falloon, ed. New York: Guilford Press.

Dattilio, F. M. 1994. Families in Crisis. In *Cognitive-Behavioral Strategies in Crisis Interventions*, F. M. Dattilio and A. Freeman, eds. New York: Guilford Press.

Dattilio, F. M. 1997. Family Therapy. In *Casebook of Cognitive Therapy*, R. Leahy, ed. Northvale, NJ: Jason Aronson.

Dattilio, F. M. 1998. Case Studies in Couples and Family Therapy: Systemic and Cognitive Perspectives. New York: Guilford Press.

Dattilio, F. M. 1999. The Pad and Pencil Technique. *Journal of Family Psychotherapy* 10 (1):75–78.

Dattilio, F. M. 2005. The Restructuring of Family Schemas: A Cognitive-Behavioral Perspective. *Journal of Marital and Family Therapy* 31:15–30, by the American Association for Marriage and Family Therapy. Reproduced with permission of the American Association for Marriage and Family Therapy in the format, republish in a book, via Copyright Clearance Center.

Dattilio, F. M. 2010. *Cognitive-Behavioral Therapy with Couples and Families.* New York: Guilford Press.

Dattilio, F. M., and C. A. Padesky. 1990. *Cognitive Therapy with Couples.* Sarasota, FL: Professional Resource Exchange.

Dishion, T. J., S. E. Nelson, and K. Kavanagh. 2003. The Family Check-Up with High-Risk Young Adolescents: Preventing Early-Onset Substance Use by Parent-Monitoring. *Behavior Therapy* 34:553–71.

Ellis, A. 1962. *Reason and Emotion in Psychotherapy.* New York: Lyle Stuart.

Ellis, A. 1978. Family Therapy: A Phenomenological and Active-Directive Approach. *Journal of Marriage and Family Counseling* 4:43–50.

Epstein, N. B., and D. H. Baucom. 2002. *Enhanced Cognitive-Behavior Therapy for Couples: A Contextual Approach.* Washington, DC: American Psychological Association.

Epstein, N., and S. E. Schlesinger. 1996. Cognitive-Behavioral Treatment of Family Problems. In *Casebook of Cognitive-Behavior Therapy with Children and Adolescents*, M. Reinecke, F. M. Dattilio, and A. Freeman, eds. New York: Guilford Press.

Epstein, N., S. E. Schlesinger., and W. Dryden, eds. 1988. *Cognitive-Behavioral Therapy with Families*. New York: Brunner/Mazel.

Falloon, I. R. H. 1985. *Family Management of Schizophrenia: A Study of the Clinical, Social, Family and Economic Benefits*. Baltimore: Johns Hopkins University Press.

Falloon, I. R. H., and F. J. Lillie. 1988. Behavioral Family Therapy: An Overview. In *Handbook of Behavioral Family Therapy*, I. R. H. Falloon, ed. New York: Guilford Press.

Fals-Stewart, W., G. R. Birchler, and M. L. Kelley. 2006. Learning Sobriety Together: A Randomized Clinical Trial Examining Behavioral Couples Therapy with Alcoholic Female Patients. *Journal of Consulting and Clinical Psychology* 74:579–91.

Fals-Stewart, W., T. B. Kashdan, T. J. O'Farrell, and G. R. Birchler. 2002. Behavioral Couples Therapy for Drug-Abusing Patients: Effects on Partner Violence. *Journal of Substance Abuse Treatment* 22:87–96.

Fals-Stewart, W., K. Klosterman, B. T. Yates, T. J. O'Farrell, and G. R. Birchler. 2005. Brief Relationship Therapy for Alcoholism: A Randomized Clinical Trial Examining Clinical Efficacy and Cost-Effectiveness. *Psychology of Addictive Behaviors* 19:363–71.

Fals-Stewart, W., T. J. O'Farrell, and G. R. Birchler. 2001. Behavioral Couples Therapy for Male Methadone Maintenance Patients: Effects on Drug-Abusing Behavior and Relational Adjustment. *Behavior Therapy* 32:391–411.

Fals-Stewart, W., T. J. O'Farrell, M. Feehan, G. R. Birchler, S. Tiller, and S. K. McFarlin. 2000. Behavioral Couples Therapy versus Individual-Based Treatment for Male Substance-Abusing Patients: An Evaluation of Significant Individual Change and Comparison of Improvement Rates. *Journal of Substance Abuse Treatment* 18:249–54.

Ferster, C. B. 1963. Essentials of a Science of Behavior. In *An Introduction to the Science of Human Behavior*, J. I. Nurnberger, C. B. Ferster, and J. P. Brady, eds. New York: Appleton-Century-Crofts.

Follette, W. C., and N. S. Jacobson. 1988. Behavioral Marital Therapy in the Treatment of Depressive Disorders. In *Handbook of Behavioral Family Therapy*, I. R. H. Falloon, ed. New York: Guilford Press.

Forehand, R., M. W. Roberts, D. M. Doleys, S. A. Hobbs, and P. A. Resnick. 1976. An Examination of Disciplinary Procedures with Children. *Journal of Experimental Child Psychology* 21:109–20.

Forgatch, M. S., and D. S. DeGarmo. 1999. Parenting Through Change: An Effective Prevention Program for Single Mothers. *Journal of Consulting and Clinical Psychology* 67:711–24.

Forgatch, M. S., and D. S. DeGarmo. 2002. Extending and Testing the Social Interaction Learning Model with Divorce Samples. In *Antisocial Behavior in Children and Adolescents: A Developmental Analysis and Model for Intervention*, J. B. Reid, G. R. Patterson, and J. Snyder, eds. Washington, DC: American Psychological Association.

Forgatch, M. S., and D. S. DeGarmo. 2011. Sustaining Fidelity in Following the Nationwide PMTO Implementation in Norway. *Prevention Science* 12:235–46.

Forgatch, M. S., D. S. DeGarmo, and Z. G. Beldavs. 2005. An Efficacious Theory-Based Intervention for Stepfamilies. *Behavior Therapy* 36:357–65.

Forgatch, M. S., and G. R. Patterson. 1998. Behavioral Family Therapy. In *Case Studies in Couple and Family Therapy*, F. M. Datillio, ed. New York: Guilford Press.

Gomez, D., A. J. Bridges, A. R. Andrews, T. A. Cavell, F. A. Pastrana, S. J. Gregus, and C. A. Ojeda. 2014. Delivering Parent Management Training in an Integrated Primary Care Setting: Description and Preliminary Outcome Data. *Cognitive and Behavioral Practice* 21:296–309.

Gottman, J. M. 1994. *What Predicts Divorce?* Hillsdale, NJ: Erlbaum.

Gottman, J., and L. Krokoff. 1989. Marital Interaction and Satisfaction: A Longitudinal View. *Journal of Consulting and Clinical Psychology* 57:47–52.

Gurman, A. S., and D. P. Kniskern. 1981. Family Therapy Outcome Research: Knowns and Unknowns. In *Handbook of Family Therapy*, A. S. Gurman and D. P. Kniskern, eds. New York: Brunner/Mazel.

Hayes, S. C. 2004. Acceptance and Commitment Therapy and the New Behavior Therapies: Mindfulness, Acceptance and Relationship.

In *Mindfulness and Acceptance: Expanding the Cognitive-Behavioral Tradition*, S. C. Hayes, V. M. Folette, and M. M. Linehan, eds. New York: Guilford Press.

Heyman, R. E., J. M. Eddy, R. L. Weiss, and D. Vivan. 1995. Factor Analysis of the Marital Interaction Coding System (MICS). *Journal of Family Psychology* 9:209–15.

Hickman, M. E., and B. A. Baldwin. 1971. Use of Programmed Instruction to Improve Communication in Marriage. *The Family Coordinator* 20:121–5.

Hogan, D. R. 1978. The Effectiveness of Sex Therapy: A Review of the Literature. In *Handbook of Sex Therapy*, J. LoPiccolo and L. LoPiccolo, eds. New York: Plenum Press.

Huber, C. H., and L. G. Baruth. 1989. *Rational-Emotive Family Therapy: A Systems Perspective*. New York: Springer.

Jacobson, N. S. 1981. Behavioral Marital Therapy. In *Handbook of Family Therapy*, A. S. Gurman and D. P. Kniskern, eds. New York: Brunner/Mazel.

Jacobson, N. S., and A. Christensen. 1996. *Integrative Couple Therapy: Promoting Acceptance and Change*. New York: Norton Books.

Kanfer, F. H., and J. S. Phillips. 1970. *Learning Foundations of Behavior Therapy*. New York: Wiley.

Kaplan, H. S. 1974. *The New Sex Therapy: Active Treatment of Sexual Dysfunctions*. New York: Brunner/Mazel.

Kaplan, H. S. 1979. *Disorders of Sexual Desire and Other New Concepts and Techniques in Sex Therapy*. New York: Brunner/Mazel.

Kelley, M. L., and W. Fals-Stewart. 2007. Treating Paternal Drug Abuse with Learning Sobriety Together: Effects on Adolescents versus Children. *Drug and Alcohol Dependence* 92:228–38.

Kelley, M. L., and W. Fals-Stewart. 2008. Treating Paternal Alcoholism with Learning Sobriety Together: Effects on Adolescents versus Preadolescents. *Journal of Family Psychology* 21:435–44.

Kjobli, J., and T. Ogden. 2012. A Randomized Effectiveness Trial of Brief Parent Training in Primary Care Settings. *Prevention Science* 13:616–26.

Knox, D. 1971. *Marriage Happiness: A Behavioral Approach to Counseling*. Champaign, IL: Research Press.

Lazarus, A. A. 1965. The Treatment of a Sexually Inadequate Male. In *Case Studies in Behavior Modification*, L. P. Ullmann and L. Krasner, eds. New York: Holt, Rinehart & Winston.

Leslie, L. A. 1988. Cognitive-Behavioral and Systems Models of Family Therapy: How Compatible Are They? In *Cognitive-Behavioral Therapy with Families*, N. Epstein, S. E. Schlesinger, and W. Dryden, eds. New York: Brunner/Mazel.

Lobitz, N. C., and J. LoPiccolo. 1972. New Methods in the Behavioral Treatment of Sexual Dysfunction. *Journal of Behavior Therapy and Experimental Psychiatry* 3:265–71.

Locke, H. J., and K. M. Wallace. 1959. Short-Term Marital Adjustment and Prediction Tests: Their Reliability and Validity. *Journal of Marriage and Family Living* 21:251–5.

Mahoney, M. J. 1977. Reflections on the Cognitive Learning Trend in Psychotherapy. *American Psychologist* 32:5–13.

Masters, W. H., and V. E. Johnson. 1970. *Human Sexual Inadequacy*. Boston: Little, Brown.

Morris, S. B., J. F. Alexander, and H. Waldron. 1988. Functional Family Therapy. In *Handbook of Behavioral Family Therapy*, I. R. H. Falloon, ed. New York: Guilford Press.

Nichols, M. P. 2009. *The Lost Art of Listening*, 2nd ed. New York: Guilford Press.

Nichols, M. P., and R. C. Schwartz. 2006. *Family Therapy: Concepts and Methods*, 6th ed. Boston: Allyn & Bacon.

Northey, W. F. 2002. Characteristics and Clinical Practices of Marriage and Family Therapists: A National Survey. *Journal of Marital and Family Therapy* 28:487–94.

Patterson, G. R. 1986. The Contribution of Siblings to Training for Fighting: A Microsocial Analysis. In *Development of Antisocial and Prosocial Behavior: Research, Theories, and Issues*, D. Olweus, J. Block, and M. Radke-Yarrow, eds. Orlando, FL: Academic Press.

Patterson, G. R., T. J. Dishion, and P. Chamberlain. 1993. Outcomes and Methodological Issues Relating to Treatment of Anti-Social Children. In *Effective*

Psychotherapy: A Handbook of Comparative Research, T. R. Giles, ed. New York: Plenum Press.

Patterson, G. R., and M. S. Forgatch. 1995. Predicting Future Clinical Adjustment from Treatment Outcomes and Process Variables. *Psychological Assessment* 7:275–85.

Patterson, G. R., and J. Reid. 1970. Reciprocity and Coercion; Two Facets of Social Systems. In *Behavior Modification in Clinical Psychology*, C. Neuringer and J. Michael, eds. New York: Appleton-Century-Crofts.

Pierce, R. M. 1973. Training in Interpersonal Communication Skills with the Partners of Deteriorated Marriages. *The Family Coordinator* 22:223–7.

Premack, D. 1965. Reinforcement Theory. In *Nebraska Symposium on Motivation*, D. Levine, ed. Lincoln: University of Nebraska Press.

Reid, J. B., J. M. Eddy, R. A. Fetrow, and M. Stoolmiller. 1999. Description and Immediate Impacts of a Preventive Intervention for Conduct Problems. *American Journal of Community Psychology* 27:483–517.

Rimm, D. C., and J. C. Masters. 1974. *Behavior Therapy: Techniques and Empirical Findings*. New York: Wiley.

Rinn, R. C. 1978. Children with Behavior Disorders. In *Behavior Therapy in the Psychiatric Setting*, M. Hersen and A. S. Bellack, eds. Baltimore, MD: Williams & Wilkins.

Ruff, S., J. L. McComb, C. J. Coker, and D. H. Sprenkle. 2010. Behavioral Couples Therapy for the Treatment of Substance Abuse: A Substantive and Methodological Review of O'Farrell, Fals-Stewart, and Colleagues' Program of Research. *Family Process* 49:439–56.

Schwebel, A. I., and M. A. Fine. 1992. Cognitive-Behavioral Family Therapy. *Journal of Family Psychotherapy* 3:73–91.

Schwitzgebel, R. 1967. Short-Term Operant Conditioning of Adolescent Offenders on Socially Relevant Variables. *Journal of Abnormal Psychology* 72:134–42.

Schwitzgebel, R., and D. A. Kolb. 1964. Inducing Behavior Change in Adolescent Delinquents. *Behaviour Research and Therapy* 9:233–8.

Semans, J. H. 1956. Premature Ejaculation: A New Approach. *Southern Medical Journal* 49:353–7.

Sigmarsdottir, M., and E. V. Gudmundsdottir. 2013. Implementation of Parent Management Training-Oregon Model (PMTOTM) in Iceland: Building Sustained Fidelity. *Family Process* 52:216–27.

Skinner, B. F. 1953. *Science and Human Behavior*. New York: Macmillan.

Stuart, R. B. 1971. Behavioral Contracting within the Families of Delinquents. *Journal of Behavior Therapy and Experimental Psychiatry* 2:1–11.

Stuart, R. B. 1975. Behavioral Remedies for Marital Ills: A Guide to the Use of Operant-Interpersonal Techniques. In *International Symposium on Behavior Modification*, T. Thompson and W. Docken, eds. New York: Appleton.

Stuart, R. B. 1976. An Operant Interpersonal Program for Couples. In *Treating Relationships*, D. H. Olson, ed. Lake Mills, IA: Graphic Publishing.

Teichman, Y. 1992. Family Treatment with an Acting-Out Adolescent. In *Comprehensive Casebook of Cognitive Therapy*, A. Freeman and F. M. Dattilio, eds. New York: Plenum.

Thibaut, J., and H. H. Kelley. 1959. *The Social Psychology of Groups*. New York: Wiley.

Umana, R. F., S. J. Gross, and M. T. McConville. 1980. *Crisis in the Family: Three Approaches*. New York: Gardner Press.

Vincent, J. P., R. L. Weiss, and G. R. Birchler. 1975. A Behavioral Analysis of Problem Solving in Distressed and Nondistressed Married and Stranger Dyads. *Behavior Therapy* 6:475–87.

Weekes, G. R., and N. Gambescia. 2000. *Erectile Dysfunction: Integrating Couple Therapy, Sex Therapy and Medical Treatment*. New York: Norton.

Weekes, G. R., and N. Gambescia. 2002. *Hypoactive Sexual Desire: Integrating Sex and Couple Therapy*. New York: Norton.

Weiss, R. L., H. Hops, and G. R. Patterson. 1973. A Framework for Conceptualizing Marital Conflict, a Technology for Altering It, Some Data for Evaluating It. In *Behavior Change: Methodology, Concepts and Practice*, L. A. Hamerlynch, L. C. Handy, and E. J. Marsh, eds. Champaign, IL: Research Press.

Wills, T. A., R. L. Weiss, and J. Issac. 1978. *Behavior vs. Cognitive Measures as Predictors of Marital*

Satisfaction. Paper presented at the Western Psychological Association meeting, Los Angeles.

Wills, T. A., R. L. Weiss, and G. R. Patterson. 1974. A Behavioral Analysis of the Determinants of Marital Satisfaction. *Journal of Consulting and Clinical Psychology* 42:802–11.

Wolpe, J. 1958. *Psychotherapy by Reciprocal Inhibition*. Stanford, CA: Stanford University Press.

AG Charges Ex-UB Researcher in Fraud. 2010. *Business First* February 16. Retrieved from http://www.bizjournals.com/buffalo/stories/2010/02/15/daily10.html

CHAPTER 10

Ahn, Y. J., and M. M. Miller. 2009. Can MFTs Address Spirituality with Clients in Publically Funded Agencies? *Contemporary Family Therapy* 32:102–16.

Ahrons, C., and R. Rogers. 1989. *Divorced Families: Meeting the Challenges of Divorce and Remarriage*. New York: Norton.

Andersen, T. 1991. *The Reflecting Team*. New York: Norton.

Anderson, C. M. 1995. *Flying Solo*. New York: Norton.

Anderson, C. M., D. Reiss, and G. E. Hogarty. 1986. *Schizophrenia and the Family: A Practitioner's Guide to Psychoeducation and Management*. New York: Guilford Press.

Anderson, H. 1993. On a Roller Coaster: A Collaborative Language Systems Approach to Therapy. In *The New Language of Change*, S. Friedman, ed. New York: Guilford Press.

Anderson, W. T. 1990. *Reality Isn't What It Used to Be*. San Francisco: Harper & Row.

Atkinson, B. J. 2005. *Emotional Intelligence in Couples Therapy: Advances from Neurobiology and the Science of Intimate Relationships*. New York: Norton.

Atkinson, J. M., and D. A. Coia. 1995. *Families Coping with Schizophrenia: A Practitioner's Guide to Family Groups*. New York: Wiley.

Atwood, J., and C. Gallo. 2010. *Family Therapy and Chronic Illness*. New Brunswick, NJ: Aldine/Transaction.

Bailey, E. 1999. *Children in Therapy: Using the Family as a Resource*. New York: Norton.

Barth, R., J. Pietrzak, and M. Ramier. 1993. *Families Living with Drugs and HIV*. New York: Guilford Press.

Beavers, W., and R. Hampson. 1990. *Successful Families: Assessment and Intervention*. New York: Norton.

Billingsley, A. 1968. *Black Families in White America*. Englewood Cliffs, NJ: Prentice-Hall.

Blow, A. J., D. H. Sprenkle, and S. D. Davis. 2007. Is Who Delivers the Treatment More Important Than the Treatment Itself? The Role of the Therapist in Common Factors. *Journal of Marital and Family Therapy* 33:298–317.

Boyd-Franklin, N. 1989. *Black Families in Therapy: A Multisystems Approach*. New York: Guilford Press.

Boyd-Franklin, N. 1993. Race, Class, and Poverty. In *Normal Family Processes*, F. Walsh, ed. New York: Guilford Press.

Boyd-Franklin, N. 2003. Race, Class, and Poverty. In *Normal Family Processes: Growing Diversity and Complexity*, 3rd ed., F. Walsh, ed. New York: Guilford Press.

Boyd-Franklin, N., and B. H. Bry. 2000. *Reaching Out in Family Therapy: Home-Based, School, and Community Interventions*. New York: Guilford Press.

Boyd-Franklin, N., G. Steiner, and M. Boland. 1995. *Children, Families, and HIV/AIDS*. New York: Guilford Press.

Bringle, R. 1995. Sexual Jealousy in the Relationships of Homosexual and Heterosexual Men: 1980 and 1994. *Personal Relationships* 2:313–25.

Brothers, B. J., ed. 1992. *Spirituality and Couples: Heart and Soul in the Therapy Process*. New York: Haworth Press.

Brown, G. W., J. L. T. Birley, and J. K. Wing. 1972. The Influence of Family Life on the Course of Schizophrenic Disorders: A Replication. *British Journal of Psychology* 121:241–58.

Brownlee, K., J. Vis, and A. McKenna. 2009. Review of the Reflecting Team Process: Strengths, Challenges, and Clinical Implications. *The Family Journal* 17:139–45.

Bryant, A. S., and S. Demian. 1994. Relationship Characteristics of American Gays and Lesbians:

Findings from a National Survey. *Journal of Gay & Lesbian Social Services* 1:101–17.

Burton, L. A., ed. 1992. *Religion and the Family*. New York: Haworth Press.

Campbell, T. 1986. Family's Impact on Health: A Critical Review and Annotated Bibliography. *Family Systems Medicine* 4:135–48.

Carl, D. 1990. *Counseling Same-Sex Couples*. New York: Norton.

Chartier, M. R. 1986. Marriage Enrichment. In *Psychoeducational Approaches to Family Therapy and Counseling*, R. F. Levant, ed. New York: Springer.

Combrinck-Graham, L. 1989. *Children in Family Contexts*. New York: Guilford Press.

Cooper, A. 2002. *Sex and the Internet: A Guide for Clinicians*. New York: Brunner-Routledge.

Cortes, L. 2004. Home-Based Family Therapy: A Misunderstanding of the Role and a New Challenge for Therapists. *The Family Journal* 12:184–8.

Cose, E. 1993. *The Rage of the Privileged Class*. New York: HarperCollins.

Cose, E. 2011. *The End of Anger*. New York: Ecco/HarperCollins.

Dattilio, F., ed. 1998. *Case Studies in Couple and Family Therapy*. New York: Guilford Press.

Davidson, R. J. 2001. The Neural Circuitry of Emotion and Affective Style: Prefrontal Cortex and Amygdala Contributions. *Social Science Information* 40 (1):11–37.

Davidson, R. J. 2003. Seven Sins in the Study of Emotion: Correctives from Affective Neuroscience. *Brain and Cognition* 52:129–32.

Davis, S. D., and F. P. Piercy. 2007. What Clients of Couple Therapy Model Developers and Their Former Students Say about Change, Part II: Model-Independent Common Factors and Integrative Framework. *Journal of Marital and Family Therapy* 33:344–63.

Delmonico, D., and E. Griffin. 2008. Cybersex and the E-Teen: What Marriage and Family Therapists Should Know. *Journal of Marital and Family Therapy* 34:431–44.

Doherty, W. 1996. *The Intentional Family*. Reading, MA: Addison-Wesley.

Donovan, J. M., ed. 1999. *Short-Term Couple Therapy*. New York: Guilford Press.

Duncan, G. J., and J. Brooks-Gunn. 1997. *Consequences of Growing Up Poor*. New York: Russell Sage Foundation.

Ehrenreich, B. 1999. Nickel-and-dimed: On (Not) Getting by in America. *Harpers* January:37–52.

Elizur, J., and S. Minuchin. 1989. *Institutionalizing Madness: Families, Therapy and Society*. New York: Basic Books.

Elkin, M. 1990. *Families under the Influence*. New York: Norton.

Emery, R. 1994. *Renegotiating Family Relationships: Divorce, Child Custody, and Mediation*. New York: Guilford Press.

Erickson, M. J., L. Hecker, and D. Kirkpatrick. 2002. Clients' Perceptions of Marriage and Family Therapists Addressing the Religious and Spiritual Aspects of Clients' Lives. *Journal of Family Psychotherapy*. Taylor & Francis online.

Falicov, C. 1983. *Cultural Perspectives in Family Therapy*. Rockville, MD: Aspen Systems.

Falicov, C. 1988. *Family Transitions: Continuity and Change over the Life Cycle*. New York: Guilford Press.

Falicov, C. 1998. *Latino Families in Therapy*. New York: Guilford Press.

Falloon, I. J. R., J. L. Boyd, C. W. McGill, J. Razani, H. B. Moss, and A. M. Gilderman. 1982. Family Management in the Prevention of Exacerbations of Schizophrenia. *New England Journal of Medicine* 306:1437–40.

Figley, C. 1985. *Trauma and Its Wake: The Study and Treatment of Post-Traumatic Stress Disorder*. New York: Brunner/Mazel.

Floyd, F. J., H. Markham, S. Kelly, S. L. Blumberg, and S. M. Stanley. 1995. Preventive Intervention and Relationships Enhancement. In *Clinical handbook of couples therapy*, N. S. Jacobson and A. S. Gurman, eds. New York: Guilford Press.

Fontes, L. A. 2008. *Interviewing Clients across Cultures*. New York: Guilford Press.

Freeman, J., D. Epston, and D. Lobovits. 1997. *Playful Approaches to Serious Problems*. New York: Norton.

Friedrich, W. 1990. *Psychotherapy of Sexually Abused Children and Their Families*. New York: Norton.

Friesen, B. J., and N. M. Koroloff. 1990. Family-Centered Services: Implications for Mental Health Administration and Research. *Journal of Mental Health Administration* 17 (1):13–25.

Gallup. 2007. Gallup poll on religion is American life. Gallup online.

Gergen, K. 1985. The Social Constructionist Movement in Modern Psychology. *American Psychologist* 40:266–75.

Gil, E. 1994. *Play in Family Therapy*. New York: Guilford Press.

Gillispie, J., and J. Gackenbach. 2007. *Cyber Rules: What You Really Need to Know about the Internet.* New York: Norton.

Ginsberg, B. G. 2000. Relationship Enhancement Couples Therapy. In *Comparative Treatments of Relationship Disorders*, F. M. Dattilio and L. J. Bevilacqua, eds. New York: Springer.

Goldberg, P., B. Peterson, K. Rosen, and M. Sara. 2008. Cybersex: The Impact of a Contemporary Problem on the Practices of Marriage and Family Therapists. *Journal of Marital and Family Therapy* 34:469–80.

Goldner, V. 1985. Feminism and Family Therapy. *Family Process* 24:31–47.

Goldstein, M. J., E. H. Rodnick, J. R. Evans, P. R. May, and M. Steinberg. 1978. Drug and Family Therapy in the Aftercare Treatment of Acute Schizophrenia. *Archives of General Psychiatry* 35:1169–77.

Gonyea, J. 2004. Internet Sexuality: Clinical Implications for Couples. *American Journal of Family Therapy* 32:375–90.

Goodrich, T. J. 1991. Women, Power, and Family Therapy: What's Wrong with This Picture. In *Women and Power: Perspectives for Family Therapy*, T. J. Goodrich, ed. New York: Norton.

Gottman, J. M. 1999. *The Marriage Clinic: A Scientifically Based Marital Therapy*. New York: Norton.

Green, R. J. 1998. Training Programs: Guidelines for Multicultural Transformations. In *Re-Visioning Family Therapy*, M. McGoldrick, ed. New York: Guilford Press.

Green, R. J., and V. Mitchell. 2002. Gay and Lesbian Couples in Therapy: Homophobia, Relational Ambiguity, and Social Support. In *Clinical Handbook of Couple Therapy*, 3rd ed., A. S. Gurman and N. S. Jacobson, eds. New York: Guilford Press.

Greenan, D., and G. Tunnell. 2003. *Couple Therapy with Gay Men*. New York: Guilford Press.

Guerney, B. G., Jr., ed. 1977. *Relationship Enhancement: Skills Training for Therapy Problem Prevention and Enrichment*. San Francisco, CA: Jossey-Bass.

Haley, J. 1976. *Problem-Solving Therapy*. San Francisco, CA: Jossey-Bass.

Haley, J. 1980. *Leaving Home*. New York: McGraw-Hill.

Hansen, J. C. 1982. *Therapy with Remarried Families*. Rockville, MD: Aspen Systems.

Hardy, K. 1993. War of the Worlds. *Family Therapy Networker* 17:50–57.

Hare-Mustin, R. 1987. The Problem of Gender in Family Therapy Theory. *Family Process* 26:15–27.

Henggeler, S. W., and C. M. Borduin., eds. 1990. *Family Therapy and Beyond: A Multisystemic Approach to Treating the Behavior Problems of Children and Adolescents*. Pacific Grove, CA: Brooks/Cole.

Hines, P. M., and N. Boyd-Franklin. 1982. Black Families. In *Ethnicity and Family Therapy*, M. McGoldrick, J. K. Pierce, and J. Giordano, eds. New York: Guilford Press.

Hines, P. M., and N. Boyd-Franklin. 1996. African American Families. In *Ethnicity and Family Therapy*, 2nd ed., M. McGoldrick, J. K. Pierce, and J. Giordano, eds. New York: Guilford Press.

Hook, J. N., E. L. Worthington, D. E. Davis, and D. C. Atkins. 2014. Religion and Couple Therapy. *Psychology of Religion and Spitituality* 6:94–101.

Hooley, J. M., S. A. Gruber, L. A. Scott, J. B. Hiller, and D. A. Yurgelun-Todd. 2005. Activation in Dorsolateral Prefrontal Cortex in Response to Maternal Criticism and Praise in Recovered Depressed and Healthy Control Participants. *Biological Psychiatry* 57:807–12.

Imber-Black, E. 1988. *Families and Larger Systems: A Family Therapist's Guide Through the Labyrinth*. New York: Guilford Press.

Imber-Black, E., J. Roberts, and R. Whiting. 1988. *Rituals in Families and Family Therapy*. New York: Norton.

Ingoldsby, B., and S. Smith. 1995. *Families in Multicultural Perspective*. New York: Guilford Press.

James, K., and L. MacKinnon. 1990. The "Incestuous Family" Revisited: A Critical Analysis of Family Therapy Myths. *Journal of Marital and Family Therapy* 16:71–88.

Johnson, T., and M. Keren. 1998. The Families of Lesbian Women and Gay Men. In *Re-Visioning Family Therapy*, M. McGoldrick, ed. New York: Guilford Press.

Jordan, J., A. Kaplan, J. Miller, I. Stiver, and J. Surrey, eds. 1991. *Women's Growth in Connection: Writings from the Stone Center*. New York: Guilford Press.

Kahn, M., and K. G. Lewis. 1988. *Siblings in Therapy*. New York: Norton.

Krestan, J. 1988. Lesbian Daughters and Lesbian Mothers: The Crisis of Disclosure from a Family Systems Perspective. *Journal of Psychotherapy and the Family* 3:113–30.

Laird, J. 1993. Lesbian and Gay Families. In *Normal Family Processes*, 2nd ed., F. Walsh, ed. New York: Guilford Press.

Laird, J., and R. J. Green. 1996. *Lesbians and Gays in Couples and Families: A Handbook for Therapists*. San Francisco, CA: Jossey-Bass.

LaSala, M. 2004a. Extradyadic Sex and Gay Male Couples: Comparing Monogamous and Non-monogamus Relationships. *Families in Society: The Journal of Contemporary Social Services* 85 (3):405–11.

LaSala, M. 2004b. Monogamy of the Heart: Extradyadic Sex and Gay Male Couples. *Journal of Gay & Lesbian Social Services* 17 (3):1–24.

LaSala, M. 2010. *Coming Out, Coming Home: Helping Families Adjust to a Gay or Lesbian Child*. New York: Columbia University Press.

Law, D., D. Crane, and D. Russell. 2000. The Influence of Marital and Family Therapy on Health Care Utilization in a Health-Maintenance Organization. *Journal of Marital and Family Therapy* 26:281–91.

LeDoux, J. 1996. *The Emotional Brain*. New York: Simon & Schuster.

Lee, E. 1997. *Working with Asian Americans*. New York: Guilford Press.

Leff, J., L. Kuipers, R. Berkowitz, R. Eberlein-Vries, and D. Sturgeon. 1982. A Controlled Trial of Social Intervention in the Families of Schizophrenic Patients. *British Journal of Psychiatry* 141:121–34.

Lehr, R., and P. MacMillan. 2001. The Psychological and Emotional Impact of Divorce: The Noncustodial Fathers' Perspective. *Families in Society* 82:373–82.

Lev, A. I. 2004. *Transgender Emergence: Therapeutic Guidelines for Working with Gender-Variant People and Their Families*. New York: Hayworth.

Lev, A. I. 2006. Transgender Emergence within Families. In *Sexual Orientation and Gender Expression in Social Work Practice: Working with Gay, Lesbian, Bisexual, and Transgender People*, D. F. Morrow and L. Messinger, eds. New York: Columbia University Press.

Lindblad-Goldberg, M., M. M. Dore, and L. Stern. 1998. *Creating Competence from Chaos*. New York: Norton.

Luepnitz, D. 1988. *The Family Interpreted: Feminist Theory in Clinical Practice*. New York: Basic Books.

Madanes, C. 1990. *Sex, Love and Violence*. New York: Norton.

Mallon, G. P. 1999. Practice with Transgendered Children. In *Social Services with Transgendered Youth*, G. P. Mallon, ed. New York: Harrington Park Press.

Markowitz, L. 1993. Walking the Walk. *Family Therapy Networker* 17:19–31.

McAdoo, H., ed. 2002. *Black Children: Social, Educational and Parental Environments*, 2nd ed. Thousand Oaks, CA: Sage.

McDaniel, S., J. Hepworth, and W. Doherty. 1992. *Medical Family Therapy*, p. 21. New York: Basic Books.

McFarlane, W. R. 1991. Family Psychoeducational Treatment. In *Handbook of Family Therapy*, Vol. II, A. S. Gurman and D. P. Kniskern, eds. New York: Brunner/Mazel.

McFarlane, W. R., and W. L. Cook. 2007. Family Expressed Emotion prior to the Onset of Schizophrenia. *Family Process* 46:185–97.

McGoldrick, M., ed. 1998. *Re-Visioning Family Therapy*. New York: Guilford Press.

McGoldrick, M., J. Pearce, and J. Giordano. 1982. *Ethnicity and Family Therapy*. New York: Guilford Press.

McGoldrick, M., J. Pearce, and J. Giordano. 2007. *Ethnicity and Family Therapy*, 3rd ed. New York: Guilford Press.

McWey, L., J. Humphreys, and A. Pazdera. 2011. Action-Oriented Evaluation of an In-Home Family Therapy Program for Families at Risk for Foster Placement. *Journal of Marital and Family Therapy* 37:137–52.

Micucci, J. 1998. *The Adolescent in Family Therapy*. New York: Guilford Press.

Miklowitz, D. J., and M. Goldstein. 1997. *Bipolar Disorder: A Family-Focused Treatment Approach*. New York: Guilford Press.

Miller, J. B. 1986. *Toward a New Psychology of Women*, 2nd ed. Boston: Beacon.

Minuchin, P., J. Colapinto, and S. Minuchin. 1998. *Working with Families of the Poor*. New York: Guilford Press.

Minuchin, S., and H. C. Fishman. 1981. *Techniques of Family Therapy*. Cambridge, MA: Harvard University Press.

Minuchin, S., B. Montalvo, B. Guerney, B. Rosman, and F. Schumer. 1967. *Families of the Slums*. New York: Basic Books.

Minuchin, S., M. P. Nichols, and W. Y. Lee. 2006. *Assessing Families and Couples: From Symptom to System*. Boston: Allyn & Bacon.

Mirkin, M. P. 1990. *The Social and Political Contexts of Family Therapy*. Boston: Allyn & Bacon.

Mitchell, K., D. Finkelhor, and J. Wolak. 2001. Risk Factors for and Impact of Online Sexual Solicitation of Youth. *Journal of the American Medical Association* 285:3011–4.

Morawetz, A., and G. Walker. 1984. *Brief Therapy with Single-Parent Families*. New York: Brunner/Mazel.

Muesser, K. T., and S. M. Glynn. 1995. *Behavioral Family Therapy for Psychiatric Disorders*. Boston: Allyn & Bacon.

Ngu, L., and P. Florsheim. 2011. The Development of Relational Competence among Young High-Risk Fathers across the Transition to Parenthood. *Family Process* 50:184–202.

Nichols, M. P. 2004. *Stop Arguing with Your Kids*. New York: Guilford Press.

Nichols, M. P. 2009. *The lost art of listening*, 2nd ed. New York: Guilford Press.

Okun, B. 1996. *Understanding Diverse Families*. New York: Guilford Press.

Olson, D. H. 1996. *PREPARE/ENRICH Counselor's Manual*. Minneapolis, MN: Life Innovations.

Orbach, S. 1997. *Fat Is a Feminist Issue*. Edison, NJ: BBS.

Patterson, J., L. Williams, C. Graul-Grounds, and L. Chamow. 1998. *Essential Skills in Family Therapy*. New York: Guilford Press.

Pearlman, S. F. 2006. Terms of Connection: Mother-Talk about Female-To-Male Transgender Children. In *Interventions with Families of Gay, Lesbian, Bisexual, and Transgender People from Inside Out*, J. J. Bigner and A. R. Gottlieb, eds. Binghamton, NY: Harrington Park Press.

Peluso, P. R., C. R. Figley, and L. J. Kisler. 2013. Changing Aging, Changing Family Therapy: Practicing with 21st Century Realities. In *Helping traumatized families*, 2nd ed., P. R. Peluso, R. E. Watts, and M. Parsons, eds. New York: Routledge.

Pinderhughes, E. 1989. *Understanding Race, Ethnicity and Power: The Key to Efficacy in Clinical Practice*. New York: Free Press.

Pittman, F. 1987. *Turning Points: Treating Families in Transition and Crisis*. New York: Norton.

Prest, L., and J. Keller. 1993. Spirituality in Family Therapy. *Journal of Marital and Family Therapy* 19:137–48.

Price, J. 1996. *Power and Compassion: Working with Difficult Adolescents and Abused Parents*. New York: Guilford Press.

Reitz, M., and K. Watson. 1992. *Adoption and the Family System*. New York: Guilford Press.

Richards, P. S., and A. E. Bergin 2005. *A Spiritual Strategy for Counseling and Psychotherapy*, 2nd ed. Washington, DC: American Psychological Association.

Rojano, R. 2004. The Practice of Community Family Therapy. *Family Process* 43:59–77.

Rolland, J. 1994. *Helping Families with Chronic and Life-Threatening Disorders*. New York: Basic Books.

Root, M., P. Fallon, and W. Friedrich. 1986. *Bulimia: A Systems Approach to Treatment*. New York: Norton.

Roth, S., and B. Murphy. 1986. Therapeutic Work with Lesbian Clients: A Systemic Therapy View. In *Women and Family Therapy*, M. Ault-Riche and J. Hansen, eds. Rockville, MD: Aspen Systems.

Saba, G., B. Karrer, and K. Hardy. 1989. *Minorities and Family Therapy*. New York: Haworth Press.

Sager, C., H. S. Brown, H. Crohn, T. Engel, E. Rodstein, and L. Walker. 1983. *Treating the Remarried Family*. New York: Brunner/Mazel.

Sanders, G. 1993. The Love that Dares Not Speak Its Name: From Secrecy to Openness in Gay and Lesbian Affiliations. In *Secrets in Families and Family Therapy*, E. Imber-Black, ed. New York: Norton.

Schmaling, K. B., and T. C. Sher. 2000. *The Psychology of Couples and Illness: Theory, Research, and Practice*. Washington, DC: American Psychological Association.

Schwartz, R. C. 1995. *Internal Family Systems Therapy*. New York: Guilford Press.

Schwartzman, J. 1985. *Families and Other Systems: The Macrosystemic Context of Family Therapy*. New York: Guilford Press.

Selekman, M. 1997. *Solution-Focused Therapy with Children*. New York: Guilford Press.

Seligman, M., and R. B. Darling. 1996. *Ordinary Families, Special Children: A Systems Approach to Childhood Disability*, 2nd ed. New York: Guilford Press.

Sells, S. 1998. *Treating the Tough Adolescent*. New York: Guilford Press.

Siegel, D. J. 1999. *The Developing Mind: How Relationships and the Brain Interact to Shape Who We Are*. New York: Guilford Press.

Silliman, B., S. M. Stanley, W. Coffin, H. J. Markman, and P. L. Jordan. 2002. Preventive Intervention for Couples. In *Family Psychology: Science-Based Interventions*, H. A. Liddle, D. A. Santisban, R. F. Levant, and J. H. Bray, eds. Washington, DC: American Psychological Association.

Smith, C., and D. Nylund. 1997. *Narrative Therapies with Children and Adolescents*. New York: Guilford Press.

Sparks, J., J. Ariel, E. Pulleyblank Coffey, and S. Tabachnik. 2011. A Fugue in Four Voices: Sounding Themes and Variations on the Reflecting Team. *Family Process* 50:115–28.

Sprenkle, D. 1985. *Divorce Therapy*. New York: Haworth Press.

Stahmann, R. F., and W. J. Hiebert. 1997. *Premarital and Remarital Counseling: The Professional's Handbook*. San Francisco, CA: Jossey-Bass.

Stanton, M. D., T. Todd, et al. 1982. *The Family Therapy of Drug Abuse and Addiction*. New York: Guilford Press.

Steinglass, P., L. Bennett, S. J. Wolin, and D. Reiss. 1987. *The Alcoholic Family*. New York: Basic Books.

Surrey, J. L. 1991. The "Self-in-Relation": A New Theory of Women's Development. In *Women's Growth in Connection*, J. V. Jordan, A. G. Kaplan, J. B. Miller, I. P. Stiver, and J. L. Surrey, eds. New York: Guilford Press.

Taibbi, R. 2007. *Doing Family Therapy*, 2nd ed. New York: Guilford Press.

Thompson, S. J., K. Bender, J. Lantry, and P. M. Flynn. 2007. Treatment Engagement: Building Therapeutic Alliance in Home-Based Treatment with Adolescents and Their Families. *Contemporary Family Therapy* 29:39–55.

Treadway, D. 1989. *Before It's Too Late: Working with Substance Abuse in the Family*. New York: Norton.

Trepper, T. S., and M. J. Barrett. 1989. *Systemic Treatment of Incest: A Therapeutic Handbook*. New York: Brunner/Mazel.

U.S. Bureau of the Census. 2014. *ProQuest Statistical Abstract of the United States*. Lanham, MD: Bernan Press.

Vaughn, C., and J. Leff. 1976. The Measurement of Expressed Emotion in the Families of Psychiatric Patients. *British Journal of Psychology* 15:157–65.

Vaughn, C. E., K. S. Snyder, S. Jones, W. B. Freeman, and I. R. H. Falloon. 1984. Family Factors in Schizophrenic Relapse: Replication in California of British Research on Expressed Emotion. *Archives of General Psychiatry* 41:1169–77.

Visher, E., and J. Visher. 1979. *Stepfamilies: A Guide to Working with Stepparents and Stepchildren*. New York: Brunner/Mazel.

Visher, E., and J. Visher. 1988. *Old Loyalties, New Ties: Therapeutic Strategies with Stepfamilies*. New York: Brunner/Mazel.

Wachtel, E. 1994. *Treating Troubled Children and Their Families*. New York: Guilford Press.

Walker, G. 1991. *In the Midst of Winter: Systemic Therapy with Families, Couples, and Individuals with AIDS Infection*. New York: Norton.

Wallerstein, J., and J. Kelly. 1980. *Surviving the Breakup: How Children and Parents Cope with Divorce*. New York: Basic Books.

Walsh, F. 1982. *Normal Family Processes*. New York: Guilford Press.

Walsh, F. 1993. *Normal Family Processes*, 2nd ed. New York: Guilford Press.

Walsh, F. 1998. *Strengthening Family Resistance*. New York: Guilford Press.

Walsh, F., ed. 1999. *Spiritual Resources in Family Therapy*. New York: Guilford Press.

Walsh, F., and M. McGoldrick., eds. 1991. *Living Beyond Loss: Death in the Family*. New York: Norton.

Weiss, R., and J. Schneider. 2006. *Untangling the Web: Sex, Porn, and Fantasy Obsession in the Internet Age*. New York: Alyson Books.

White, J. 1972. Towards a Black Psychology. In *Black Psychology*, R. Jones, ed. New York: Harper & Row.

Wright, L. M., and J. M. Bell. 2009. *Beliefs and Illness: A Model for Healing*. Calgary, Canada: 4th Floor Press.

CHAPTER 11

Becker, K. W., D. K. Carson, A. Seto, and C. A. Becker. 2002. Negotiating the Dance: Consulting with Adoptive Systems. *The Family Journal* 10:80–86.

Berg, I. K. 1994a. *Family-Based Services: A Solution-Focused Approach*. New York: Norton.

Berg, I. K. 1994b. A Wolf in Disguise Is Not a Grandmother. *Journal of Systemic Therapies* 13:13–14.

Berg, I. K., and L. Cauffman. 2002. Solution Focused Corporate Coaching. *Lernende Organisation* January/February:1–5.

Berg, I. K., and S. De Shazer. 1993. Making Numbers Talk: Language in Therapy. In *The New Language of Change*, S. Friedman, ed, p. 9. New York: Guilford Press.

Berg, I. K., and Y. Dolan. 2001. *Tales of Solutions: A Collection of Hope-Inspiring Stories*. New York: Norton.

Berg, I. K., and S. Miller. 1992. *Working with the Problem Drinker: A Solution-Focused Approach*. New York: Norton.

Bond, C., K. Woods, N. Humphrey, W. Symes, and L. Green. 2013. Practitioner Review: The Effectiveness of Solution-Focused Brief Therapy with Children and Families: A Systematic and Critical Evaluation of the Literature from 1990–2010. *Journal of Child Psychology and Psychiatry* 54:707–23.

Campbell, J. 1999. Creating the "Tap on the Shoulder": A Compliment Template for Solution-Focused Therapy. *American Journal of Family Therapy* 27:35–47.

Conoley, C. W., J. M. Graham, T. Neu, M. C. Craig, A. O'Pry, S. A. Cardin, et al. 2003. A Solution-Focused Family Therapy with Three Aggressive and Oppositional-Acting Children: An N=1 Empirical Study. *Family Process* 42:361–74.

Corcoran, J. 2002. Developmental Adaptations of Solution-Focused Family Therapy. *Brief Treatment and Crisis Intervention* 2:301–13.

De Jong, P., and I. K. Berg. 2002. *Interviewing for Solutions*, 2nd ed. Pacific Grove, CA: Brooks/Cole.

De Jong, P., and I. K. Berg. 2008. *Interviewing for Solutions*, 3rd ed. Pacific Grove, CA: Brooks/Cole.

De Jong, P., and L. E. Hopwood. 1996. Outcome Research on Treatment Conducted at the Brief Family Therapy Center. In *Handbook of Solution-Focused Brief Therapy*, S. D. Miller, M. A. Hubble, and B. L. Duncan, eds. San Francisco, CA: Jossey-Bass.

de Shazer, S. 1985. *Keys to Solutions in Brief Therapy*. New York: Norton.

de Shazer, S. 1988. *Clues: Investigating Solutions in Brief Therapy*. New York: Norton.

de Shazer, S. 1991. *Putting Difference to Work*. New York: Norton.

de Shazer, S., and I. K. Berg. 1993. Constructing Solutions. *Family Therapy Networker* 12:42–43.

de Shazer, S., I. K. Berg, E. Lipchik, E. Nunnally, A. Molnar, W. Gingerich, et al. 1986. Brief Therapy: Focused Solution Development. *Family Process* 25:207–21.

de Shazer, S., Y. Dolan, H. Korman, T. Trepper, I. K. Berg, and E. McCollum. 2007. *More than Miracles: The State of the Art of Solution-Focused Brief Therapy*. Binghamton, NY: Haworth Press.

de Shazer, S., and L. Isebaert. 2003. The Bruges Model: A Solution-Focused Approach to Problem Drinking. *Journal of Family Psychotherapy* 14:43–52.

Dolan, Y. 1991. *Resolving Sexual Abuse: Solution-Focused Therapy and Ericksonian Hypnosis for Survivors*. New York: Norton.

Dolan, Y. 1998. *One Small Step: Moving beyond Trauma and Therapy to a Life of Joy*. Watsonville, CA: Papier-Mache Press.

Eakes, G., S. Walsh, M. Markowski, H. Cain, and M. Swanson. 1997. Family-Centered Brief Solution-Focused Therapy with Chronic Schizophrenics: A Pilot Study. *Journal of Family Therapy* 19:145–58.

Efran, J., and M. Schenker. 1993. A Potpourri of Solutions: How New and Different Is Solution-Focused Therapy? *Family Therapy Networker* 17 (3):71–74.

Efron, D., and K. Veenendaal. 1993. Suppose a Miracle Doesn't Happen: The Non-Miracle Option. *Journal of Systemic Therapies* 12:11–18.

Ford, J. J. 2006. Solution-Focused Sex Therapy for Erectile Dysfunction. *Journal of Couple and Relationship Therapy* 5:65–79.

Franklin, C., and C. L. Streeter. 2004. *Solution-Focused Alternatives for Education: An Outcome Evaluation of Gaza High School*. Retrieved from http://www.utexas.edue/ssw/faculty/franklin

Friedman, S., and E. Lipchik. 1999. A Time-Effective, Solution-Focused Approach to Couple Therapy. In *Short-Term Couple Therapy*, J. M. Donovan, ed. New York: Guilford Press.

Hoyt, M. F. 2002. Solution-Focused Couple Therapy. In *Clinical Handbook of Couple Therapy*, 3rd ed., A. S. Gurman and N. S. Jacobson, eds. New York: Guilford Press.

Hoyt, M. F., and I. K. Berg. 1998. Solution-Focused Couple Therapy: Helping Clients Construct Self-Fulfilling Realities. In *Case Studies in Couple and Family Therapy: Systemic and Cognitive Perspectives*, F. M. Dattilio, ed. New York: Guilford Press.

Hudson, P., and W. H. O'Hanlon. 1992. *Rewriting Love Stories: Brief Marital Therapy*. New York: Norton.

Lee, M. Y. 1997. A Study of Solution-Focused Brief Family Therapy: Outcomes and Issues. *The American Journal of Family Therapy* 25:3–17.

Lipchik, E. 2011. *Beyond Technique in Solution-Focused Therapy*. New York: Guilford Press. (Adapted from)

Lipchik, E., and A. Kubicki. 1996. Solution-Focused Domestic Violence Views: Bridges toward a New Reality in Couples Therapy. In *Handbook of Solution-Focused Brief Therapy*, S. Miller, M. Hubble, and B. Duncan, eds. San Francisco, CA: Jossey-Bass.

Lloyd, H., and R. Dallos. 2008. First Session Solution-Focused Brief Therapy with Families Who Have a Child with Severe Intellectual Disabilities: Mothers' Experiences and Views. *Journal of Family Therapy* 30:5–28.

McCollum, E. E., and T. S. Trepper. 2001. *Creating Family Solutions for Substance Abuse*. New York: Haworth Press.

Miller, S. 1994. The Solution-Conspiracy: A Mystery in Three Installments. *Journal of Systemic Therapies* 13:18–37.

Murray, C. E., and T. L. Murray. 2004. Solution-Focused Premarital Counseling: Helping Couples Build a Vision for Their Marriage. *Journal of Marital and Family Therapy* 30:349–58.

Nylund, D., and V. Corsiglia. 1994. Becoming Solution-Focused in Brief Therapy: Remembering Something Important We Already Knew. *Journal of Systemic Therapies* 13:5–12.

O'Hanlon, W. 1996. Case Commentary. *Family Therapy Networker* January/February:84–85.

O'Hanlon, W. 1998. Possibility Therapy: An Inclusive, Collaborative, Solution-Based Model of Psychotherapy. In *The Handbook of Constructive Therapies*, M. H. Hoyt, ed. San Francisco, CA: Jossey-Bass.

O'Hanlon, W. 1999. *Do One Thing Different: And Other Uncommonly Sensible Solutions to Life's Persistent Problems*. New York: Morrow.

O'Hanlon, W., and M. Weiner-Davis. 1989. *Search of Solutions: A New Direction in Psychotherapy*. New York: Norton.

Park, E. S. 1997. An Application of Brief Therapy to Family Medicine. *Contemporary Family Therapy* 19:81–88.

Pichot, T., and Y. Dolan. 2003. *Solution-Focused Brief Therapy: Its Effective Use in Agency Settings.* New York: Haworth Press.

Ramish, J. L., M. McVicker, and Z. S. Sahin. 2009. Helping Low-Conflict Divorced Parents Establish Appropriate Boundaries Using a Variation of the Miracle Question: An Integration of Solution-Focused Therapy and Structural Family Therapy. *Journal of Divorce and Remarriage* 14:481–95.

Rhodes, J., and Y. Ajmal. 1995. *Solution-Focused Thinking in Schools.* London: BT Press.

Sharry, J., B. Madden, M. Darmody, and S. D. Miller. 2001. Giving Our Clients the Break: Applications of Client-Directed, Outcome-Informed Clinical Work. *Journal of Systemic Therapies* 20:68–76.

Shoham, V., M. Rohrbaugh, and J. Patterson. 1995. Problem- and Solution-Focused Couple Therapies: The MRI and Milwaukee Models. In *Clinical Handbook of Couple Therapy*, N. S. Jacobson and A. S. Gurman, eds. New York: Guilford Press.

Singer, J. L. 1981. *Daydreaming and Fantasy.* Oxford: Oxford University Press.

Softas-Nall, B. C., and P. C. Francis. 1998. A Solution-Focused Approach to Suicide Assessment and Intervention with Families. *The Family Journal: Counseling and Therapy for Couples and Families* 6:64–66.

Springer, D. W., and S. H. Orsbon. 2002. Families Helping Families: Implementing a Multifamily Therapy Group with Substance-Abusing Adolescents. *Health and Social Work* 27:204–7.

Storm, C. 1991. The Remaining Thread: Matching Change and Stability Signals. *Journal of Strategic and Systemic Therapies* 10:114–7.

Tambling, R. B. 2012. Solution-Oriented Therapy for Survivors of Sexual Assault and their Partners. *Contemporary Family Therapy* 34:391–401.

Trepper, T. S., Y. Dolan, E. E. McCollum, and T. Nelson. 2006. Steve de Shazer and the Future of Solution-Focused Therapy. *Journal of Marital and Family Therapy* 32:133–9.

Tuyn, L. K. 1992. Solution-Oriented Therapy and Rogerian Nursing Science: An Integrated Approach. *Archives of Psychiatric Nursing* 6:83–89.

Walter, J., and J. Peller. 1992. *Becoming Solution-Focused in Brief Therapy.* New York: Brunner/Mazel.

Weiner-Davis, M. 1992. *Divorce-Busting.* New York: Summit Books.

Wittgenstein, L. 1958. *The Blue and Brown Books.* New York: Harper & Row.

Wylie, M. S. 1990. Brief Therapy on the Couch. *Family Therapy Networker* 14:26–34, 66.

Zhang, W., T. Yan, Y. Du, and X. Liu. 2014. Effects of Solution-Focused Brief Therapy Group Work on Promoting Post-Traumatic Growth of Mothers Who Have a Child with ASD. *Journal of Autism and Developmental Disorders* 44:2052–6.

CHAPTER 12

Abdalla, L. H., and A. L. Novis. 2014. Uh oh! I Have Received an Unexpected Visitor: The Visitor's Name is Chronic Disease. A Brazilian Family Therapy Approach. *Australian and New Zealand Journal of Family Therapy* 35:100–4.

Butera-Prinzi, F., N. Charles, and K. Story. 2014. Narrative Family Therapy and Group Work for Families Living with Acquired Brain Injury. *Australian and New Zealand Journal of Family Therapy* 35:81–99.

Dallos, R. 2001. ANT-Attachment Narrative Therapy. *Journal of Family Psychotherapy* 12:43–72.

Dallos, R. 2004. Attachment Narrative Therapy: Integrating Ideas from Narrative and Attachment Theory in Systemic Family Therapy with Eating Disorders. *Journal of Family Therapy* 26:40–65.

Dickerson, V. 2004a. Allies against Self-Doubt. *Journal of Brief Therapy* (Special Edition):83–95.

Dickerson, V. 2004b. *Who Cares What You're Supposed to Do? Breaking the Rules to Get What You Want in Love, Life, and Work.* New York: Perigee.

Dickerson, V. 2007. Remembering the Future: Situating Oneself in a Constantly Evolving Field. *Journal of Systemic Therapy* 26:23–37.

Dickerson, V., and J. Zimmerman. 1992. Families with Adolescents: Escaping Problem Lifestyles. *Family Process* 31:341–53.

Duba, J. D., A. Kindsvatter, and T. Lara. 2008. Treating Infidelity: Considering Narratives of Attachment. *The Family Journal* 16:293–9.

D'Urso, S., S. Reynaga, and J. E. Patterson. 2009. The Emotional Experience of Immigration for

Couples. In *Multicultural Couple Therapy*, M. Rastogi and T. Volker, eds. Thousand Oaks, CA: Sage Publications.

Epston, D. 1994. Extending the Conversation. *Family Therapy Networker* 18:30–37, 62.

Eron, J., and T. Lund. 1996. *Narrative Solutions in Brief Therapy*. New York: Guilford Press.

Foucault, M. 1965. *Madness and Civilization: A History of Insanity in the Age of Reason*. New York: Random House.

Foucault, M. 1980. *Power/Knowledge: Selected Interviews and Other Writings*. New York: Pantheon.

Fraenkel, P., T. Hameline, and M. Shannon. 2009. Narrative and Collaborative Practices in Work with Families that Are Homeless. *Journal of Marital and Family Therapy* 35:325–42.

Freedman, J. 1996. AFTA Voices on the Annual Meeting. *American Family Therapy Academy Newsletter* Fall:30–32.

Freedman, J., and G. Combs. 1996. *Narrative Therapy: The Social Construction of Preferred Realities*. New York: Norton.

Gremillion, H. 2003. *Feeding Anorexia*. Chapel Hill, NC: Duke University Press.

Hedtke, L. 2014. Creating Stories of Hope: A Narrative Approach to Illness, Death and Grief. *Australian and New Zealand Journal of Family Therapy* 35:4–19.

Lemmons, G. M., I. Eisler, L. Migerode, M. Heireman, and K. Demyttenaere. 2007. Family Discussion Group Therapy for Major Depression: A Brief Systemic Multi-Family Group Intervention for Hospitalized Patients and Their Family Members. *Journal of Family Therapy* 29:49–68.

Levy, J. 2006. Using a Metaperspective to Clarify the Structural-Narrative Debate in Family Therapy. *Family Process* 45:55–74.

Madigan, S. 1994. Body Politics. *Family Therapy Networker* 18:27.

Madigan, S., and D. Epston. 1995. From "Spy-Chiatric Gaze" to Communities of Concern: From Professional Monologue to Dialogue. In *The Reflecting Team in Action*, S. Friedman, ed. New York: Guilford Press.

Madsen, W. C. 2007. *Collaborative Therapy with Multistressed Families*, 2nd ed. New York: Guilford Press.

May, J. C. 2005. Family Attachment Narrative Therapy: Healing the Experience of Early Childhood Maltreatment. *Journal of Marital and Family Therapy* 31:221–37.

Minuchin, S. 1998. Where Is the Family in Narrative Family Therapy? *Journal of Marital and Family Therapy* 24:397–403.

Neal, J., J. Zimmerman, and V. Dickerson. 1999. Couples, Culture and Discourse. In *Short-Term Couple Therapy*, J. Donovan, ed. New York: Guilford Press.

Phipps, W. D., and C. Vorster. 2009. Narrative Therapy: A Return to the Intrapsychic Perspective. *South African Journal of Psychology* 39:32–45.

Roth, S. A., and D. Epston. 1996. Developing Externalizing Conversations: An Introductory Exercise. *Journal of Systemic Therapies* 15:5–12.

Saltzburg, S. 2007. Narrative Therapy Pathways for Re-Authoring with Parents of Adolescents Coming Out as Gay, Lesbian, and Bisexual. *Contemporary Family Therapy* 29:57–69.

Shalay, N., and K. Brownlee. 2007. Narrative Family Therapy with Blended Families. *Journal of Family Psychotherapy* 18:17–30.

Weingarten, K. 2003. *Common Shock: Witnessing Violence Every Day*. New York: Dutton.

White, M. 1989. *Selected Papers*. Adelaide, South Australia: Dulwich Centre Publications.

White, M. 2007. *Maps of Narrative Practice*. New York: Norton.

Wylie, M. S. 1994. Panning for Gold. *Family Therapy Networker* 18:40–48.

Zimmerman, J., and V. Dickerson. 1993. Bringing Forth the Restraining Influence of Pattern in Couples Therapy. In *Therapeutic Conversations*, S. Gilligan and R. Price, eds. New York: Norton.

Zimmerman, J., and V. Dickerson. 1996. *If Problems Talked: Narrative Therapy in Action*. New York: Guilford Press.

CHAPTER 13

Alexander, J., and B. Parsons. 1982. *Functional Family Therapy*. Pacific Grove, CA: Brooks/Cole.

Anderson, C., and S. Stewart. 1983. *Mastering Resistance: A Practical Guide to Family Therapy*. New York: Guilford Press.

Breunlin, D., W. Pinsof, W. P. Russell, and J. Lebow. 2011. Integrative Problem-Centered Metaframeworks Therapy I: Core Concepts and Hypothesizing. *Family Process* 50:293–313.

Breunlin, D., R. Schwartz, and B. Mac Kune-Karrer. 1992. *Metaframeworks: Transcending the Models of Family Therapy*. San Francisco, CA: Jossey-Bass.

Duhl, B., and F. Duhl. 1981. Integrative Family Therapy. In *Handbook of Family Therapy*, A. Gurman and D. Kniskern, eds. New York: Brunner/Mazel.

Eron, J., and T. Lund. 1996. *Narrative Solutions in Brief Therapy*. New York: Guilford Press.

Feldman, L. 1990. *Multi-Dimensional Family Therapy*. New York: Guilford Press.

Fruzzetti, A. E. 2006. *The High Conflict Couple: A Dialectical Behavior Therapy Guide to Finding Peace, Intimacy, and Validation*. Oakland, CA: New Harbinger.

Fruzzetti, A., D. Santiseban, and P. Hoffman. 2007. Dialectical Behavior Therapy with Families. In *Dialectical Behavior Therapy in Clinical Practice*, L. Dimeff and K. Koerner, eds. New York: Guilford Press.

Greenberg, L. S., and S. M. Johnson. 1988. *Emotionally Focused Therapy for Couples*. New York: Guilford Press.

Haley, J. 1977. Toward a Theory of Pathological Systems. In *The Interactional View*, P. Watzlawick and J. Weakland, eds. New York: Norton.

Henggeler, S., and C. Borduin. 1990. *Family Therapy and Beyond: A Multisystemic Approach to Treating the Behavior Problems of Children and Adolescents*. Pacific Grove, CA: Brooks/Cole.

Hoffman, P. D., and A. E. Fruzzetti. 2005. Psychoeducation. In *Textbook of Personality Disorders*, J. M. Oldham, A. Skodal, and D. Bender, eds. Washington, DC: American Psychological Association.

Jackson, D. D. 1965. Family Rules: The Marital Quid Pro Quo. *Archives of General Psychiatry* 12:589–94.

Jacobson, N., and A. Christensen. 1996. *Integrative Couple Therapy*. New York: Norton.

Kirschner, D., and S. Kirschner. 1986. *Comprehensive Family Therapy*. New York: Brunner/Mazel.

Liddle, H. A. 1984. Toward a Dialectical-Contextual-Coevolutionary Translation of Structural-Strategic Family Therapy. *Journal of Strategic and Systemic Family Therapies* 3:66–79.

Liddle, H. A., G. A. Dakoff, and G. Diamond. 1991. Adolescent Substance Abuse: Multidimensional Family Therapy in Action. In *Family Therapy with Drug and Alcohol Abuse*, 2nd ed., E. Kaufman and P. Kaufman, eds. Boston: Allyn & Bacon.

Linehan, M. 1993. *Cognitive-Behavioral Treatment of Borderline Personality Disorder*. New York: Guilford Press.

Linehan, M. 1997. Validation and Psychotherapy. In *Empathy and Psychotherapy*, A. Bohart and L. S. Greenberg, eds. Washington, DC: American Psychological Association.

Mahler, M. S., F. Pine, and A. Bergman. 1975. *The Psychological Birth of the Human Infant*. New York: Basic Books.

Markowitz, L. 1997. Ramon Rojano Won't Take No for an Answer. *Family Therapy Networker* 21:24–35.

Minuchin, S. 1974. *Families and Family Therapy*. Cambridge, MA: Harvard University Press.

Minuchin, S., M. P. Nichols, and W.-Y. Lee. 2007. *Assessing Couples and Families: From Symptom to System*. Boston: Allyn & Bacon.

Minuchin, S., B. Rosman, and L. Baker. 1978. *Psychosomatic Families: Anorexia Nervosa in Context*. Cambridge, MA: Harvard University Press.

Nichols, M. P. 1987. *The Self in the System*. New York: Brunner/Mazel.

Nichols, W. C. 1995. *Treating People in Families: An Integrative Framework*. New York: Guilford Press.

Pinsof, W., D. Breunlin, W. P. Russell, and J. Lebow. 2011. Integrative Problem-Centered Metaframeworks Therapy II: Planning, Conversing, and Reading Feedback. *Family Process* 50:314–36.

Sander, F. M. 1979. *Individual and Family Therapy: Toward an Integration*. New York: Jason Aronson.

Scharff, J., ed. 1989. *The Foundations of Object Relations Family Therapy*. New York: Jason Aronson.

Slipp, S. 1988. *Technique and Practice of Object Relations Family Therapy*. New York: Jason Aronson.

Stanton, M. D. 1981. An Integrated Structural/Strategic Approach to Family and Marital Therapy. *Journal of Marital and Family Therapy* 7:427–40.

Taibbi, R. 2007. *Doing Family Therapy*, 2nd ed. New York: Guilford Press.

Thibaut, J. W., and H. H. Kelley. 1959. *The Social Psychology of Groups*. New York: Wiley.

Von Bertalanffy, L. 1968. *General Systems Theory: Foundations, Development, Applications*. New York: Braziller.

CHAPTER 14

AACAP. 2005. Practice Parameters for the Assessment and Treatment of Children and Adolescents with Reactive Attachment Disorder of Infancy and Early Childhood. *Journal of the American Academy of Child and Adolescent Psychiatry* 44 (11):1206–19.

Allen-Eckert, H., E. Fong, M. P. Nichols, N. Watson, and H. A. Liddle. 2001. Development of the Family Therapy Enactment Scale. *Family Process* 40 (4):469–78.

Anastopoulos, A., T. Shelton, and R. Barkley. 2005. Family-Based Psychosocial Treatments for Children and Adolescents with Attention-Deficit/Hyperactivity Disorder. In *Psychosocial Treatments for Child and Adolescent Disorders. Emprically Based Strategies for Clinical Practice*, 2nd ed., E. Hibbs and P. Jensen, eds. Washington, DC: American Psychological Association.

Bakermans-Kranenburg, M. J., M. H. Van Ijzendoorn, and F. Juffer. 2003. Less Is More: Meta-Analyses of Sensitivity and Attachment Interventions in Early Childhood. *Psychological Bulletin* 129:195–215.

Bakermans-Kranenburg, M. J., M. H. Van Ijzendoorn, and F. Juffer. 2005. Disorganized Infant Attachment and Preventive Interventions: A Review and Meta-Analysis. *Infant Mental Health Journal* 26:191–216.

Baldwin, S. A., S. Christian, A. Berkeljon, W. R. Shadish, and R. Bean. 2012. The Effects of Family Therapies for Adolescent Delinquency and Substanced Abuse: A Meta-Analysis. *Journal of Marital and Family Therapy* 38:281–304.

Barbato, A., and B. D'Avanzo. 2008. Efficacy of Couples Therapy as a Treatment for Depression: A Meta-Analysis. *Psychiatric Quarterly* 79 (2):121–32.

Barmish, A. J., and P. C. Kendall. 2005. Should Parents Be Co-Clients in Cognitive-Behavioral Therapy for Anxious Youth? *Journal of Clinical Child and Adolescent Psychology* 34 (3):569–81.

Barrett, P. M., and A. L. Shortt. 2003. Parental Involvement in the Treatment of Anxious Children. In *Evidence-Based Psychotherapies for Children and Adolescents*, A. E. Kazdin and J. R. Weisz, eds. New York: Guilford Press.

Beach, S. R. H., J. Katz, S. Kim, and G. H. Brody. 2003. Prospective Effects of Marital Satisfaction on Depressive Symptoms in Established Marriages: A Dyadic Model. *Journal of Social and Personal Relationships* 20:355–71.

Becker, S. J., and J. F. Curry. 2008. Outpatient Interventions for Adolescent Substance Abuse: A Quality of Evidence Review. *Journal of Consulting and Clinical Psychology* 76 (4):531–43.

Beutler, L. E., R. E. Williams, and P. J. Wakefield. 1993. Obstacles to Disseminating Applied Psychological Science. *Applied and Preventive Psychology* 2:53–58.

Black, D. A., and J. Lebow. 2012. Systemic Research Controversies and Challenges. In *Family Psychology*, J. H. Bray and M. Stanton, eds. Malden: Wiley-Blackwell.

Blow, A. J., D. S. Sprenkle, and S. D. Davis. 2007. Is Who Delivers the Treatment More Important than the Treatment Itself?: The Role of the Therapist in Common Cactors. *Journal of Marital and Family Therapy* 33:298–317.

Borduin, C. M., B. J. Mann, L. T. Cone, S. W. Henggeler, B. R. Fucci, D. M. Blaske, et al. 1995. Multisystemic Treatment of Serious Juvenile Offenders: Long-Term Prevention of Criminality and Violence. *Journal of Consulting and Clinical Psychology* 63:569–78.

Bourgeois, L., S. Sabourin, and J. Wright. 1990. Predictive Validity of Therapeutic Alliance in Group Marital Therapy. *Journal of Consulting and Clinical Psychology* 58 (5):608–13.

Butler, M. H., J. M. Harper, and M. S. Mitchell. 2011. A Comparison of Attachment Outcomes in Enactment-Based versus Therapist-Centered Therapy Process Modalities in Couple Therapy. *Family Process* 50:203–20.

Butler, M. H., and K. S. Wampler. 1999. Couple-Responsible Therapy Process: Positive Proximal Outcomes. *Family Process* 38 (1):27–54.

Campbell, D. T., and J. C. Stanley. 1963. *Experimental and Quasi-Experimental Designs for Research*. Chicago: Rand McNally.

Chaffin, M., R. Hanson, B. E. Saunders, T. Nichols, D. Barnett, C. Zeanah, et al. 2006. Report of the APSAC Task Force on Attachment Therapy, Reactive Attachment Disorder, and Attachment Problems. *Child Maltreatment* 11:76–89.

Chaffin, M., J. F. Silovsky, B. Funderburk, L. A. Valle, E. V. Brestan, and T. Balachova. 2004. Parent-Child Interaction Therapy with Physically Abusive Parents: Efficacy for Reducing Future Abuse Reports. *Journal of Consulting and Clinical Psychology* 72:500–10.

Chamberlain, P., and J. G. Rosicky. 1995. The Effectiveness of Family Therapy in the Treatment of Adolescents with Conduct Disorders and Delinquency. *Journal of Marital and Family Therapy* 21 (4):441–59.

Cicchetti, D., and S. L. Toth. 2005. Child Maltreatment. *Annual Review of Clinical Psychology* 1 (1):409–38.

Compas, B. E., J. E. Champion, R. Forehand, D. A. Cole, K. L. Reeslund, J. Fear, et al. 2010. Coping and Parenting: Mediators of 12-Month Outcomes of a Family Group Cognitive-Behavioral Preventive Intervention with Families of Depressed Parents. *Journal of Consulting and Clinical Psychology* 78 (8):623–34.

Compas, B. E., R. Forehand, J. C. Thigpen, G. Keller, E. J. Hardcastle, D. A. Cole, et al. 2011. Family Group Cognitive-Behavioral Preventive Intervention for Families of Depressed Parents: 18- and 24-Month Outcomes. *Journal of Consulting and Clinical Psychology* 79 (4):488–99.

Corcoran, J., and V. Pillai. 2008. A Meta-Analysis for Parent-Involved Treatment for Child Sexual Abuse. *Research on Social Work Practice* 18 (5):453–64.

Couturier, J., L. Isserlan, and J. Lock. 2006. Family-Based Treatment for Adolescents with Anorexia Nervosa: A Dissemination Study. *International Journal of Eating Disorder* 18:199–209.

Couturier, J., and J. Lock. 2006. What Is Remission in Adolescent Anorexia Nervosa? A Review of Various Conceptualizations and a Quantitative Analysis. *International Journal of Eating Disorder* 39:175–83.

Curtis, N., K. Ronan, and C. Borduin. 2004. Multisystemic Treatment: A Meta-Analysis of Outcome Studies. *Journal of Family Psychology* 18 (3):411–9.

Dalton, J., P. Greenman, C. Classen, and S. M. Johnson. 2013. Nurturing Connections in the Aftermath of Childhood Trauma: A Randomized Controlled Trial of Emotionally Focused Couple Therapy (EFT) for Female Survivors of Childhood Abuse. *Couple and Family Psychology: Research and Practice* 2:209–21.

Dattilio, F. M., F. P. Piercy, and S. D. Davis. 2014. The Divide between "Evidence-Based" Approaches and Practitioners of Traditional Theories of Family Therapy. *Journal of Marital and Family Therapy* 40:5–16.

Diamond, G. S., and A. Josephson. 2005. Family-Based Treatment Research: A 10-Year Update. *Journal of the American Academy of Child and Adolescent Psychiatry* 44 (9):872–87.

Diamond, G., and H. A. Liddle. 1996. Resolving a Therapeutic Impasse between Parents and Adolescents in Multidimensional Family Therapy. *Journal of Consulting and Clinical Psychology* 64 (3):481–8.

Diamond, G., and H. A. Liddle. 1999. Transforming Negative Parent–Adolescent Interactions: From Impasse to Dialogue. *Family Process* 38 (1):5–26.

Diamond, G. S., B. F. Reis, G. M. Diamond, L. Siqueland, and L. Issacs. 2002. Attachment-Based Family Therapy for Depressed Adolescents: A Treatment Development Study. *Journal of American Academy Child Adolescent Psychiatry* 41 (10):1190–6.

Diamond, G. S., M. B. Wintersteen, G. K. Brown, G. M. Diamond, R. Gallop, K. Shelef, et al. 2010. Attachment-Based Family Therapy for Adolescents with Suicidal Ideation: A Randomized Controlled Trial. *Journal of American Academy of Child and Adolescent Psychiatry* 49 (2):122–31.

DuPaul, G., T. Eckert, and B. Vilardo. 2012. The Effects of School-Based Interventions for Attention Deficit Hyperactivity Disorder: A Meta-Analysis 1996–2010. *School Psychology Review* 41:387–412.

Eisler, I., C. Dare, G. F. Russell, G. Szmukler, D. Le Grange, and E. Dodge. 1997. Family and

Individual Therapy in Anorexia Nervosa: A Five-Year Follow-Up. *Archives of General Psychiatry* 54:1025–30.

Fals-Stewart, W., G. R. Birchler, and M. L. Kelley. 2006. Learning Sobriety Together: A Randomized Clinical Trial Examining Behavioral Couples Therapy with Alcoholic Female Patients. *Journal of Consulting and Clinical Psychology* 74:579–91.

Fals-Stewart, W., K. Klosterman, B. T. Yates, T. J. O'Farrell, and G. R. Birchler. 2005. Brief Relationship Therapy for Alcoholism: A Randomized Clinical Trial Examining Clinical Efficacy and Cost-Effectiveness. *Psychology of Addictive Behaviors* 19:363–71.

Favero, D. 2002. *Structural Enactments as Methods of Change in Family Therapy*. Unpublished doctoral dissertation, Virginia Consortium Program in Clinical Psychology, Virginia Beach.

Fellenberg, S. 2003. *The Contribution of Enactments to Structural Family Therapy: A Process Study*. Unpublished doctoral dissertation, The Virginia Consortium Program in Clinical Psychology, Virginia Beach.

Flicker, S. M., C. W. Turner, H. B. Waldron, J. L. Brody, and T. J. Ozechowski. 2008. Ethnic Background, Therapeutic Alliance, and Treatment Retention in Functional Family Therapy with Adolescents Who Abuse Substances. *Journal of Family Psychology* 22 (1):167–70.

Friedlander, M. L., V. Escudero, and L. Heatherington. 2006. *Therapeutic Alliances in Couple and Family Therapy: An Empirically Informed Guide to Practice*. Washington, DC: American Psychological Association.

Friedlander, M. L., V. Escudero, L. Heatherington, and G. M. Diamond. 2011. Alliance in Couple and Family Therapy. *Psychotherapy* 48:25–33.

Friedlander, M. L., V. Escudero, A. Horvath, L. Heatherington, A. Cabero, and M. Martens. 2006. System for Observing Family Therapy Alliances: A Tool for Research and Practice. *Journal of Counseling Psychology* 53:214–25.

Friedlander, M. L., L. Heatherington, B. Johnson, and E. A. Skowron. 1994. Sustaining Engagement: A Change Event in Family Therapy. *Journal of Counseling Psychology* 41 (4):438–48.

Gilliam, C. M., and R. Cottone. 2005. Couple or Individual Therapy for the Treatment of Depression: An Update of the Empirical Literature. *American Journal of Family Therapy* 33:265–72.

Gordon, D. A., J. Arbuthnot, K. E. Gustafson, and P. McGreen. 1988. Home-Based Behavioral-Systems Family Therapy with Disadvantaged Juvenile Delinquents. *The American Journal of Family Therapy* 16 (3):243–55.

Hammond, R., and M. P. Nichols. 2008. How Collaborative Is Structural Family Therapy? *The Family Journal: Counseling and Therapy for Couples and Family* 16 (2):118–24.

Henderson, C. E., C. L. Rowe, G. A. Dakof, S. W. Hawes, and H. A. Liddle. 2009. Parenting Practices as Mediators of Treatment Effects in an Early-Intervention Trial of Multidimensional Family Therapy. *The American Journal of Drug and Alcohol Abuse* 35:220–6.

Hendriks, W., E. van der Schee, and V. Blanken. 2012. Matching Adolescents with a Cannabis Use Disorder to Multidimensional Family Therapy or Cognitive Behavioral Therapy: Treatment Effect Moderators in a Randomized Controlled Trial. *Drug and Alcohol Dependence* 125:119–26.

Henggeler, S. W., C. M. Borduin, G. B. Melton, B. J. Mann, L. Smith, J. A. Hall, et al. 1991. Effects of Multisystemic Therapy on Drug Use and Abuse in Serious Juvenile Offenders: A Progress Report from Two Outcome Studies. *Family Dynamics of Addition Quarterly* 1:40–51.

Henggeler, S. W., G. B. Melton, M. J. Brondino, D. G. Scherer, and J. H. Hanley. 1997. Multisystemic Therapy with Violent and Chronic Juvenile Offenders and Their Families: The Role of Treatment Fidelity in Successful Dissemination. *Journal of Consulting and Clinical Psychology* 60:821–33.

Henggeler, S. W., G. B. Melton, and L. A. Smith. 1992. Family Preservation Using Multisystemic Therapy: An Effective Alternative to Incarcerating Serious Juvenile Offenders. *Journal of Consulting and Clinical Psychology* 60 (6):953–61.

Henggeler, S. W., D. J. Rodick, C. M. Borduin, C. L. Hanson, S. M. Watson, and J. R. Urey. 1986. Multisystemic Treatment of Juvenile Offenders: Effects on Adolescent Behavior and Family Interaction. *Developmental Psychology* 22 (1):132–41.

Hogue, A., S. Dauber, P. Chinchilla, A. Fried, C. Henderson, J. Inclan, et al. 2008. Assessing Fidelity in Individual and Family Therapy for Adolescent Substance Abuse. *Journal of Substance Abuse Treatment* 35 (2):137–47.

Horvath, A. O., A. C. Del Re, C. Flückiger, and D. Symonds. 2011. Alliance in Individual Psychotherapy. *Psychotherapy* 48 (1):9–16.

Jackson-Gilfort, A., H. A. Liddle, M. J. Tejeda, and G. A. Dakof. 2001. Facilitating Engagement of African American Male Adolescents in Family Therapy: A Cultural Theme Process Study. *Journal of Black Psychology* 27 (3):321–40.

Jacobs, S., K. Kissil, D. Scott, and M. Davey. 2010. Creating Synergy in Practice: Promoting Complementarity between Evidence-Based and Postmodern Approaches. *Journal of Marital and Family Therapy* 36:185–96.

Jarrett, M. A., and T. H. Ollendick. 2012. Treatemnt of Comorbid Attention-Deficit/Hyperactivity Disorder and Anxiety in Children: A Multiple Baseline Design Analysis. *Journal of Consulting and Clinical Psychology* 80:239–44.

Karam, E. A., and D. H. Sprenkle. 2010. The Research-Informed Clinician: A Guide to Training the Next-Generation MFT. *Journal of Marital and Family Therapy* 36:307–19.

Kazdin, A. E. 2011. *Single-Case Research Designs: Methods for Clinical and Applied Settings*. New York: Oxford University Press.

Kazdin, A. E., and J. R. Weisz. 1998. Identifying and Developing Empirically Supported Child and Adolescent Treatments. *Journal of Consulting and Clinical Psychology* 66 (1):19.

Klein Velderman, M., M. J. Bakermans-Kranenburg, F. Juffer, and M. H. Van IJzendoorn. 2006. Effects of Attachment-Based Interventions on Maternal Sensitivity and Infant Attachment: Differential Susceptibility of Highly Reactive Infants. *Journal of Family Psychology* 20 (2):266–74.

Kolko, D. J., and C. C. Swenson. 2002. *Assessing and Treating Physically Abused Children and Their Families: A Cognitive Behavioral Approach*. Thousand Oaks, CA: Sage Publications.

Lebow, J. 1988. Research into Practice/Practice into Research. *Journal of Family Psychology* 1:337–51.

Lee, P., W. Niew, H. Yang, V. C. Chen, and K. Lin. 2012. A Meta-Analysis of Behavioural Parent Training for Children with Attention-Deficit Hyperactivity Disorder. *Research in Developmental Disabilities* 33:2040–9.

Le Grange, D., R. D. Crosby, P. J. Rathouz, and B. L. Leventhal. 2007. A Randomized Controlled Comparison of Family-Based Treatment and Supportive Psychotherapy for Adolescent Bulimia Nervosa. *Archive of General Psychiatry* 64 (9):1049–56.

Lobban, F., A. Postlethwaite, D. Glenworth, V. Pinfold, L. Wainwright, G. Dunn, and G. Haddock. 2013. A Systematic Review of Randomized Controlled Trials of Interventions Reporting Outcomes for Relatives of People with Psychosis. *Clinical Psychology Review* 33:372–82,

Lock, J., D. Le Grange, W. S. Agras, A. Moye, S. W. Bryson, and B. Jo. 2010. A Randomized Clinical Trial Comparing Family Based Treatment to Adolescent Focused Individual Therapy for Adolescents with Anorexia Nervosa. *Archive of General Psychiatry* 67:1025–32.

Lock, J., D. Le Grange, and R. Crosby. 2008. Exploring Possible Mechanisms of Change in Family-Based Treatment for Adolescent Bulimia Nervosa. *Journal of Family Therapy* 30:260–71.

Loeb, K. L., T. B. Walsh, J. Lock, D. Le Grange, S. Marcus, J. Weaver, et al. 2007. Open Trial of Family-Based Treatment for Adolescent Anorexia Nervosa: Evidence of Successful Dissemination. *Journal of the American Academy of Child and Adolescent Psychiatry* 46:792–800.

Lundahl, B. W., J. Nimer, and B. Parsons. 2006. Preventing Child Abuse: A Meta-Analysis of Parent Training Programs. *Research on Social Work Practice* 16 (3):251–62.

Macleod, J., and G. Nelson. 2000. Programs for the Promotion of Family Wellness and the Prevention of Child Maltreatment: A Meta-Analytic Review. *Child Abuse and Neglect* 24 (9):1127–49.

McCart, M., P. Priester, W. Davies, and R. Azen. 2006. Differential Effectiveness of Cognitive-Behavioral Therapy and Behavioral Parent-Training for Antisocial Youth: A Meta-Analysis. *Journal of Abnormal Child Psychology* 34:527–43.

Miklowitz, D. J. 2004. The Role of Family Systems in Severe and Recurrent Psychiatric Disorders:

A Developmental Psychopathology View. *Development and Psychopathology* 16 (3):667–88.

Miles, D. 2004. *The Effectiveness of Therapist Interventions in Structural Family Therapy: A Process Study*. Unpublished doctoral dissertation, Virginia Consortium Program in Clinical Psychology, Virginia Beach.

Miller, S. D., and M. A. Hubble. 2004. Further Archeological and Ethnological Findings on the Obscure, Late 20th Century, Quasi-Religious Group Known as "The Therapists" (A Fantasy about the Future of Psychotherapy). *Journal of Psychotherapy Integration* 14:38–65.

Minuchin, S., B. Montalvo, B. Guerney, B. Rosman, and F. Schumer. 1967. *Families of the Slums*. New York: Basic Books.

Minuchin, S., B. L. Rosman, and L. Baker. 1978. *Psychosomatic Families: Anorexia Nervosa in Context*. Cambridge, MA: Harvard University Press.

Monson, C., S. Fredman, A. MacDonald, N. Pukay-Martin, P. A. Resnick, and P. Schnurr. 2012. Effect of Cognitive-Behavioral Couple Therapy for PTSD: A Randomized Controlled Trial. *JAMA* 308:700–9.

Muck, R., K. A. Zempolich, J. C. Titus, M. Fishman, M. D. Godley, and R. Schwebel. 2001. An Overview of the Effectiveness of Adolescent Substance Abuse Treatment Models. *Youth and Society* 33:143–68.

Nichols, M. P., and S. Fellenberg. 2000. The Effective Use of Enactments in Family Therapy: A Discovery-Oriented Process Study. *Journal of Marital and Family Therapy* 26 (2):143–52.

Ogden, T., and K. A. Hagen. 2006. Virker MST? Kommentarer Til En Systematisk Forskingsomversikt og Meta-Analyse av MST [Does MST Work: Comments on a Systemic Review and Meta-Analysis of MST]. *Nordish Sosialt Arbeid* 26:222–33.

Ogden, T., and C. A. Halliday-Boykins. 2004. Multisystemic Treatment of Antisocial Adolescents in Norway: Replication of Clinical Outcomes Outside of the US. *Child and Adolescent Mental Health* 9 (2):77–83.

O'Leary, K. D., J. L. Christian, and N. R. Mendell. 1994. A Closer Look at the Link between Marital Discord and Depressive Symptomatology. *Journal of Social and Clinical Psychology* 13 (1):33–41.

Orlinsky, D. E., and K. I. Howard. 1986. Process and Outcome in Psychotherapy. In *Handbook of Psychotherapy and Behavior Change*, 3rd ed., S. Garfield and A. Bergin, eds. New York: Wiley.

Pereira, T., J. Lock, and J. Oggins. 2006. Role of Therapeutic Alliance in Family Therapy for Adolescent Anorexia Nervosa. *The International Journal of Eating Disorders* 39 (8):677–84.

Perepletchikova, F., T. A. Treat, and A. E. Kazdin. 2007. Treatment Integrity in Psychotherapy Research: Analysis of the Studies and Examination of the Associated Factors. *Journal of Consulting and Clinical Psychology* 75:829–41.

Pfammatter, M., U. Junghan, and H. Brenner. 2006. Efficacy of Psychological Therapy in Schizophrenia: Conclusions from Meta-Analysis. *Schizophrenia Bulletin* 32 (Suppl. 1):S64–80.

Pharoah, F., J. Mari, J. Rathbone, and W. Wong. 2006. Family Intervention for Schizophrenia. *Cochrane Database of Sytematic Reviews* (2):CD000088. DOI: 10. 1002/14651858. CD000088, pub. 2.

Pilling, S., P. Beddington, E. Kuipers, P. Farety, J. Geddes, G. Orbach, et al. 2002. Psychological Treatments in Schizophrenia: I. Meta-Analysis of Family Intervention and Cognitive Behavior Therapy. *Psychological Medicine* 32:763–82.

Pina, A., A. Zerr, N. Gonzales, and C. Ortiz. 2009. Psychosocial Interventions for School Refusal Behavior in Children and Adolescents. *Child Development Perspectives* 3:11–20.

Pinsof, W. B., and D. R. Catherall. 1986. The Integrative Psychotherapy Alliance: Family, Couple and Individual Therapy Scales. *Journal of Marital and Family Therapy* 12:137–51.

Pinsof, W. M., and L. Wynne. 2000. Toward Progress Research: Closing the Gap between Family Therapy Practice and Research. *Journal of Marital and Family Therapy* 26:1–8.

Pinsof, W. M., R. Zinbarg, and L. M. Knobloch-Fedders. 2008. Factorial and Construct Validity of the Revised Short Form Integrative Psychotherapy Alliance Scales for Family, Couple, and Individual Therapy. *Family Process* 47 (3):281–301.

Pitschel-Walz, G., S. Leucht, J. Bauml, W. Kissling, and R. Engel. 2001. The Effect of Family Interventions on Relapse and Rehospitalization in

Schizophrenia: A Meta-Analysis. *Schizophrenia Bulletin* 27:73–92.

Rajwan, E., A. Chacko, and M. Moeller. 2012. Nonpharmacological Intervention for Preschool ADHD: State of the Evidence and Implications for Practice. *Professional Psychology: Research and Practice* 43:520–6.

Reynolds, S., C. Wilson, J. Austin, and L. Hooper. 2012. Effects of Psychotherapy for Anxiety in Children and Adolescents: A Meta-Analysis Review. *Clinical Psychology Review* 32:251–62.

Robbins, M. S., J. F. Alexander, R. M. Newell, and C. W. Turner. 1996. The Immediate Effect of Reframing on Client Attitude in Family Therapy. *Journal of Family Psychology* 10 (1):28–34.

Robbins, M. S., D. J. Feaster, V. E. Horigian, M. J. Puccinelli, C. Henderson, and J. Szapocznik. 2011. Therapist Adherence in Brief Strategic Family Therapy for Adolescent Drug Abusers. *Journal of Consulting and Clinical Psychology* 79 (1):43–53.

Robbins, M. S., H. A. Liddle, C. W. Turner, G. A. Dakof, J. F. Alexander, and S. M. Kogan. 2006. Adolescent and Parent Therapeutic Alliances as Predictors of Dropout in Multidimensional Family Therapy. *Journal of Family Psychology* 20 (1):108–16.

Robbins, M. S., C. C. Mayorga, V. B. Mitrani, J. Szapocznik, C. W. Turner, and J. F. Alexander. 2008. Adolescent and Parent Alliances with Therapists in Brief Strategic Family Therapy with Drug-Using Hispanic Adolescents. *Journal of Marital and Family Therapy* 34 (3):316–28.

Robbins, M. S., C. W. Turner, J. F. Alexander, and G. A. Perez. 2003. Alliance and Dropout in Family Therapy for Adolescents with Behavior Problems: Individual and Systemic Effects. *Journal of Family Psychology* 17 (4):534–44.

Robinson, E. H. 1994. Critical Issues in Counselor Education: Mentors, Models, and Money. *Counselor Education and Supervision* 33:339–43.

Rotunda, R., T. O'Farrell, M. Murphy, and S. Babey. 2008. Behavioral Couples Therapy for Comorbid Substance Use Disorders and Combat-Related Posttraumatic Stress Disorder among Male Veterans: An Initial Evaluation. *Addictive Behaviors* 33:180–7.

Rynyon, M., and E. Deblinger. 2013. *Combined Parent-Child Cognitive Behavioral Therapy. An Approach to Empower Families At-Risk for Child Physical Abuse.* New York: Oxford University Press.

Sandberg, J. G., L. N. Johnson, M. Robia, and R. B. Miller. 2002. Clinician Identified Barriers to Clinical Research. *Journal of Marital and Family Therapy* 28:61–67.

Schaeffer, C. M., C. C. Swenson, E. H. Tuerk, and S. W. Henggeler. 2013. Comprehensive Treatment of Co-Occurring Child Maltreatment and Parental Substance Abuse: Outcomes from a 24-month Pilot Study of the MST-Building Stronger Families program. *Child Abuse & Neglect* 37:596–607.

Sautter, F. J., S. M. Glynn, K. E. Thompson, L. Franklin, and X. Han. 2009. A Couple-Based Approach to the Reduction of PTSD Avoidance Symptoms: Preliminary Findings. *Journal of Marital and Family Therapy* 35 (3):343–9.

Sexton, T., and C. W. Turner. 2010. The Effectiveness of Functional Family Therapy for Youth with Behavioral Problems in a Community Practice Setting. *Journal of Family Psychology* 24 (3):339–48.

Shanley, J. R., and L. N. Niec. 2010. Coaching Parents to Change: The Impact of in Vivo Feedback on Parents' Acquisition of Skills. *Journal of Clinical Child and Adolescent Psychology* 39 (2):282–7.

Shelef, K., and G. M. Diamond. 2008. Short Form of the Revised Vanderbilt Therapeutic Alliance Scale: Development, Reliability, and Validity. *Psychotherapy Research* 18 (4):433–43.

Siqueland, L., M. Rynn, and G. S. Diamond. 2005. Cognitive Behavioral and Attachment Based Family Therapy for Anxious Adolescents: Phase I and II Studies. *Journal of Anxiety Disorders* 19 (4):361–81.

Skowron, E., and D. Reinemann. 2005. Effectiveness of Psychological Interventions for Child Maltreatment: A Meta-Analysis. *Psychotherapy: Theory, Research, Practice, Training* 42 (1):52–71.

Sprenkle, D. H. 2003. Effectiveness Research in Marriage and Family Therapy: Introduction. *Journal of Marital and Family Therapy* 29:85–96.

Sprenkle, D. H., S. D. Davis, and J. L. Lebow. 2009. Common Factors in Couple and Family Therapy:

The Overlooked Foundation of Effective Practice. New York: Guilford Press.

Stark, K. D., K. N. Banneyer, L. A. Wang, and P. Arora. 2012. Child and Adolescent Deflession in the Family. *Couple and Family Psychology: Research and Practice* 1:161–89.

Swenson, C. C., C. M. Schaeffer, S. W. Henggeler, R. Faldowski, and A. M. Mayhew. 2010. Multisystemic Therapy for Child Abuse and Neglect: A Randomized Effectiveness Trial. *Journal of Family Psychology* 24 (4):497–507.

Symonds, D., and A. O. Horvath. 2004. Optimizing the Alliance in Couple Therapy. *Family Process* 43 (4):443–55.

Tallman, K., and A. C. Bohart. 1999. The Client as Common Factor: Clients as Self Healers. In *The Heart and Soul of Change: What Works in Therapy*, M. A. Hubble, B. L. Duncan, and S. D. Miller, eds. Washington, DC: APA Press.

Tanner-Smith, E. E., S. Jo Wilson, and M. W. Lipsey. 2013. The Comparative Effectiveness of Outpatient Treatment for Adolescent Substance Abuse: A Meta-Analysis. *Journal of Substance Abuse Treatment* 44:145–58.

Thomas, R., and M. J. Zimmer-Gembeck. 2011. Accumulating Evidence for Parent-Child Interaction Therapy in the Prevention of Child Maltreatment. *Child Development* 82:177–92.

Timmer, S., A. Urquiza, N. Zebell, and J. McGarth. 2005. Parent Child Interaction Therapy. Application to Physically Abusive Parent-Child Dyads. *Child Abuse and Neglect* 29:825–42.

Timmons-Mitchell, J., M. B. Bender, M. A. Kishna, and C. C. Mitchell. 2006. An Independent Effectiveness Trial of Multisystemic Therapy with Juvenile Justice Youth. *Journal of Clinical Child and Adolescent Psychology* 35:227–36.

Waite, L. J., and Y. Luo. 2002. *Marital Quality and Marital Stability: Consequences for Psychological Well-Being.* Paper presented at the meetings of the American Sociological Association, Chicago, IL, August.

Waldron, H. B., and C. W. Turner. 2008. Evidence-Based Psychosocial Treatments for Adolescent Substance Abuse. *Journal of Clinical Child and Adolescent Psychology* 37 (1):238–61.

Waldron, H. B., C. W. Turner, C. Barton, J. F. Alexander, and V. B. Cline. 1997. Therapist Defensiveness and Marital Therapy Process and Outcome. *American Journal of Family Therapy* 25 (3):233–43.

Watson, H. J., and C. S. Rees. 2008. Meta-Analysis of Randomized, Controlled Treatment Trials for Pediatric Obsessive-Compulsive Disorder. *Journal of Child Psychology and Psychiatry* 49:489–98.

Westen, D., C. M. Novotny, and H. Thompson-Brenner. 2004. The Empirical Status of Empirically Supported Psychotherapies: Assumptions, Findings, and Reporting in Controlled Clinical Trials. *Psychological Bulletin* 130 (4):631–63.

Whisman, M. A. 2001. The Association between Depression and Marital Dissatisfaction. In *Marital and Family Processes in Depression*, S. R. H. Beach, ed. Washington, DC: American Psychological Association.

Whisman, M. A., D. P. Johnson, D. Be, and A. Li. 2012. Couple-Based Interventions for Depression. *Couple and Family Psychology: Research and Practice* 1:185–98.

Whisman, M. A., L. A. Uebelacker, and L. M. Weinstock. 2004. Psychopathology and Marital Satisfaction: The Importance of Evaluating Both Partners. *Journal of Consulting and Clinical Psychology* 72:830–8.

Williams, R., and S. Chang. 2000. A Comprehensive and Comparative Review of Adolescent Substance Abuse Treatment Outcome. *Clinical Psychology: Science and Practice* 7:138–66.

Williams, L. M., J. E. Patterson, and R. B. Miller. 2006. Panning for Gold: A Clinician's Guide to Using Research. *Journal of Marital and Family Therapy* 32 (2):17–32.

Woolfenden, S., K. Williams, and J. Peat. 2002. Family and Parenting Interventions for Conduct Disorder and Delinquency a Meta-Analysis of Randomized Controlled Trials. *Archives of Diseases in Childhood* 86 (4):251–6.

INDEX